# SEQUINS, SCANDALS & SALCHOWS

# FIGURE SKATING IN THE 1980S

Every reasonable effort has been made to ensure that the information in this book was accurate and credit all source material included. If errors or omissions have occurred, they will be corrected in future editions provided written notification and supporting documentation has been received by the author.

Copyright © 2024 by Ryan Stevens
Independently published
Cover art by Stefan Prodanovic
Photo credits and licensing listed by page and in Acknowledgments
All rights reserved

**Library and Archives Canada - Canadian Cataloguing in Publication**
Title: Sequins, Scandals & Salchows: Figure Skating in the 1980s / Ryan Stevens
Names: Stevens, Ryan, 1982- author.
ISBN: 9781738198238
Subjects: BISAC SPO023000 SPORTS & RECREATION / Winter Sports / Ice & Figure Skating, SPO058000 SPORTS & RECREATION / Olympics & Paralympics, SPO019000 SPORTS & RECREATION / History, HIS037070 HISTORY / Modern / 20th Century / General, HIS066000 HISTORY / LGBTQ+

This book was written using Canadian English spelling and syntax.

# CONTENTS

| | |
|---|---|
| Introduction | 1 |
| Glossary | 2 |
| | |
| 1979-1980 Season | 4 |
| 1980-1981 Season | 29 |
| 1981-1982 Season | 49 |
| 1982-1983 Season | 68 |
| 1983-1984 Season | 87 |
| 1984-1985 Season | 110 |
| 1985-1986 Season | 131 |
| 1986-1987 Season | 156 |
| 1987-1988 Season | 178 |
| 1988-1989 Season | 208 |
| 1989-1990 Season | 238 |
| | |
| Epilogue | 267 |
| | |
| Sources | 269 |
| Acknowledgments | 275 |
| | |
| Author's Note | 277 |
| Books By This Author | 278 |

# INTRODUCTION

*Sequins, Scandals and Salchows: Figure Skating In The 1980s* is a book intended for people who *love* figure skating, *know* figure skating and maybe – just maybe – *care* a little bit about the sport's history. If that sounds like you, I think you're going to have a blast nerding out about the "Sk80s" with me.

If you're looking for an instructional book that explains the difference between a three-turn and a triple Salchow, this book isn't it. If the idea of reading about who did which jumps and received what scores at competitions bores you to tears, then I'm sorry... but that's kind of the point. Simply put, this is a *skating book* that was lovingly put together specifically for *skating people*.

If you were part of the figure skating community back then, this is going to be a trip down memory lane. If you weren't lucky enough to be, you have no doubt already watched a lot of YouTube videos and flipped through some coffee table books. You know about Bolero, The Battle of The Brians and The Battle of The Carmens. This book will fill in the blanks between the lovely videos and pictures you have seen, providing a greater understanding of what skating in the 80s was all about.

If you picked this book up because of the word *Sequins* on the cover, you will find the sections on skating fashions interesting. If you yearn for salacious *Scandals*, there is certainly enough judging drama to satisfy your appetite. If *Salchows* are more your thing, you're going to love the competition recaps in each chapter.

This book isn't just about *Sequins, Scandals and Salchows* though. We are also going to explore how real-world events like The AIDS Epidemic, The Cold War and The Fall of The Berlin Wall affected the skating world.

Whether you were an exceptional skater in the 1980s or an average one, or if you were involved as a coach, judge, or a devoted fan, your experiences would have been diverse. The perspective on the sport of a professional skater from the United States is going to be completely different from that of a judge from France, a coach from Australia or a fan from South Africa.

This book provides a perspective on figure skating during the 1980s, which may not align with your own experiences. As a Canadian, a member of the LGBTQ+ community and someone who is passionate about studying and preserving the sport's history, this is the perspective I bring to the table. I sincerely hope that you will appreciate it for the spirit in which it was written. There may be individuals who feel that the book neglects certain topics or focuses on others they may not consider newsworthy. Please know that many omissions were due to space limitations rather than intentional oversight.

There is always more to learn about figure skating and I hope you, like me, learn something new as we explore an extraordinary decade of figure skating history.

# GLOSSARY

ABC - American Broadcasting Company (television network)
ACTRA - Alliance of Canadian Cinema, Television and Radio Artists
AIDS - Acquired immunodeficiency syndrome
ARD - "Arbeitsgemeinschaft - der öffentlich-rechtlichen Rundfunkanstalten - der Bundesrepublik Deutschland (television network)
ASW - American Skating World (periodical)
AZT - Azidothymidine
B and B – Natalia Bestemianova and Andrei Bukin
BBC - British Broadcasting Corporation (television network)
BETA - Betamax (video tape format)
CAC - Coaching Association of Canada
CBC - Canadian Broadcasting Corporation (television network)
CBS - Columbia Broadcasting System (television network
CFSA - Canadian Figure Skating Association
CFTO - Canada's Foremost, Toronto's Own (television network)
CH - Calgary Herald (newspaper)
CHMS - Chronicle Herald/Mail-Star (newspapers)
COA - Canadian Olympic Association
CP – Competition Program
CT - Chicago Tribune (newspaper)
CTV - CTV (television network)
CNN - Cable News Network (television network)
CS - Canadian Skater (periodical)
DC - District of Columbia
DELV - Deutsche Eislauf-Verband
DEV - Deutscher Eislauf-Verband
DS - Der Spiegel (newspaper)
DTSB - Deutscher Turn- und Sportbund
EJ - Edmonton Journal (newspaper)
FDA - U.S. Food and Drug Administration
FFSG - Fédération Française des Sports de Glace
G and G - Ekaterina Gordeeva and Sergei Grinkov
GDR - German Democratic Republic (East Germany)
GM - The Globe and Mail (newspaper)
HBO - Home Box Office (television network)
HIV - Human Immunodeficiency Virus
HR - Historical Results and Records , Event Protocols (ISU, CFSA, USFSA etc.)
IOC - International Olympic Committee
IRS – Ice & Roller Skate (periodical)
ISAA - Ice Skating Association of Australia
ISIA - Ice Skating Institute of America
ISU - International Skating Union
ITV - ITV/Independent Television (television network)
LAT - Los Angeles Times (newspaper)
MG - Montreal Gazette (newspaper)
NBC - National Broadcasting Company (television network)
NSA - National Skating Association of Great Britain
NZISA - New Zealand Ice Skating Association
NYT - New York Times (newspaper)
OC - OC (newspaper)
OSP - Original Set Pattern Dance
PBS - Public Broadcasting Service (television network)
PPE - Personal Protective Equipment
PSGA - Professional Skaters Guild of America
SAISA - South African Ice Skating Association
SASK - Stockholm Allmänna Skridskoklubb
SI – Sports Illustrated (periodical)
SK - Skating (periodical)
SP – Show or Tour Program

STASI - Staatssicherheit (Ministry for State Security)
TR - Tracings (periodical)
TS - Toronto Star (newspaper)
TP - The Province (newspaper)
UK - United Kingdom
US/USA - United States of America
USFSA - United States Figure Skating Association
USOC - United States Olympic Committee
USSR - Union of Soviet Socialist Republics (Soviet Union)
VF - Video Footage
VS - Vancouver Sun (newspaper)
V and V - Elena Valova and Oleg Vasiliev
VHS - Video Home System (video tape format)
WCFE – WCFE-TV (television network)
WEV - Wiener Eislauf Verein
WGBH - WGBH (television network)
WP - Washington Post (newspaper)
WS – Windsor Star (newspaper)

# 1979-1980 SEASON

Hit Songs: "Call Me" by Blondie, "Another Brick In The Wall" by Pink Floyd, "Do That To Me One More Time" by Captain & Tennille, "The Rose" by Bette Midler, "Funkytown" by Lipps Inc.
Hit Movies: The Empire Strikes Back, 9 to 5, Airplane!, Private Benjamin, The Blue Lagoon, The Blues Brothers
Hit TV: Three's Company, Alice, M*A*S*H, sctv, Archie Bunker's Place
News: Summer Olympics boycott, Terry Fox's Marathon of Hope, Eruption of Mount St. Helens, Former Canadian Prime Minister Pierre Trudeau re-elected, Miracle of Hope hockey game

## PEOPLE

After giving birth to son Sasha and being off the ice for an entire year, two-time Olympic Gold Medallist Irina Rodnina staged an incredible comeback. Her training regimen, developed with coach Tatiana Tarasova and husband and partner Alexander Zaitsev, included a great deal of cross-country running. In an interview with the Novosti Press Agency, Rodnina said, "With the birth of my son, life for me became more exciting. When I think of him, I feel an upsurge of strength and energy. During workouts, I anticipate with joy the moment I am back home with Alexander Zaitsev Jr."

Janet Thompson and Warren Maxwell, silver medallists at the 1977 World Championships in Tokyo, announced their retirement in the summer due to Thompson's recurring back and leg injuries. The dazzling duo were long-time students of Miss Gladys Hogg. Thompson intended to pursue a career in sales; Maxwell expressed an interest in becoming a skating judge.

Two-time Olympic Gold Medallists Ludmila and Oleg Protopopovs defection became international news in late September. While on an exhibition tour of Switzerland, they disappeared on the very day they were to have flown back to the Soviet Union. They hid under police protection in Bern while awaiting a decision from the Swiss government, then took up residence in Thalwil with Martin Sochor, a Czechoslovakian skater who defected and won the Swiss men's title in 1976. The Protopopovs continued training in Zug. They made trips to America in early 1980 to appear as special guests in the *Ice Capades* and visit the U.S. Figure Skating Museum. Not long after defecting, Oleg Protopopov remarked, "It is not possible to leave the motherland because we are still Russians. We stay Russians to the end of our life but I know our art belongs not only to our country. It belongs to the whole world because it is understandable for everybody."

Two-time World Champions Irina Moiseeva and Andrei Minenkov began working with 1976 Olympic Gold Medallist Lyudmila Pakhomova, who felt their programs the previous season did not reflect their ability. Their goal for the Olympic season was to "follow the untrodden path" and deliver performances geared more towards the audience than the judges.

In October, esteemed coach Freddy Mésot passed away at the age of 74. Mésot made history in 1924 as the first singles skater to represent Belgium at the Winter Olympic Games and had coached at clubs in both Canada and the United States for decades.

Legendary Swiss coach Arnold Gerschwiler celebrated 45 years of coaching. Interviewed while coaching at Richmond Ice Rink in Surrey, 'Gersch' was not shy about his opinions about the judging of school (compulsory) figures: "Professionals throughout the world are giving too little attention to figures, which is wrong. What a shocking example we had in [Vladimir] Kovalev, that [he] could win the figures in a World Championship with the body positions he produced and no running edge. He violated every rule in the book... Whatever the tracings are like, from the ankle up he was awful, and I can't see how that would not be reflected in the tracings, because body position is a strong influence on the tracings." He went on to call Kovalev a "butcher" of skating technique and say, "For me [he] just doesn't exist as a skater."

Morris D. Chalfen passed away at the age of 72 following a heart attack in November. With Emery Gilbert, Chalfen founded *Holiday on Ice* in 1945 and brought the revolutionary tour to Central and South America, Europe, Africa, the Middle East, Asia and the Soviet Union in the decades that followed. He also partnered with Tom Collins to present the 1975 World Tour on behalf of the USFSA and the 1978 World Tour on behalf of the CFSA. Though Chalfen made remarkable contributions to the skating world, his personal life was marred by tragedy. His wife and three young children were all tragically killed in 1960 in a tragic plane crash southwest of Kentucky.

To broaden the horizons of his students, Soviet coach Stanislav Zhuk took his students to see the Moiseyev Dance Company's performances in Moscow. Zhuk explained, "We learn artistic logic, sense of style and artistic boldness from the Moiseyev dancers. That trend in choreography is particularly close to me because I also build the routines of my trainees on folk melodies." Nina Domanovskaya, a former Moiseyev Company soloist, was brought in to work with Zhuk's students.

Fritz Greiger, the President of the Organizing Committee for the 1980 World Championships in Dortmund, died of a sudden heart attack in February, just four days before he was to leave to serve as the lead delegate of the West German team at the 1980 Olympics in Lake Placid. Greiger had served as Chairman of the West German federation and played an instrumental role in the organization of the 1974 World Championships in Munich.

In Vermont in March, Dorothy Glazier Dodson and Stephen Tanner staged a remarkable comeback. The 1940 U.S. Junior Pairs Champions celebrated the fortieth anniversary of their win by recreating their old program, lifts and all, for the annual Burlington carnival.

A future star made his international debut at the Big Sky '80 Championships in Great Falls, Montana in April. A wee Kurt Browning of Rocky Mountain House, Alberta won the intermediate men's event and finished third in the novice compulsory dance with Michelle Pollitt.

The newest inductees to the World Figure Skating Hall of Fame were Olympic Medallists and World Champions Cecilia Colledge, Barbara Wagner and Bob Paul. Colledge won the Olympic silver medal in 1936 and three European titles and went on to be a successful coach in the United States. Wagner and Paul captured the gold at the 1960 Olympics and won 'the triple crown' of gold medals at the Canadian, North American and World Championships.

# AROUND THE WORLD

**Australia.** By 1980, there were no less than five ice rinks in New South Wales alone. The open-air covered rink in Prince Alfred Park in Sydney faced numerous difficulties, including record-high summer temperatures, wind storms and even birds coming into the rink to drink water from the ice. One of the biggest challenges Australian skaters faced was the fact the distances skaters had to travel to compete or train were high, making travel quite expensive.

**Japan.** The National Skating Union of Japan celebrated its 50th anniversary by organizing the NHK Trophy, the first major international skating event in the country since the 1977 World Championships. 53 skaters from 13 countries participated, including athletes from four Asian countries: Japan, China, North Korea and South Korea. It was the first time Chinese skaters participated in a figure skating competition in Japan.

**North Korea.** In April, construction began on the Democratic People's Republic of Korea's first indoor skating facilities. The Ice Rink in Pyongyang opened its doors two years later, with two ice rinks, eight lounges and seating for 6000 people. The Skating Association of the Democratic People's Republic of Korea joined the ISU in 1957, when skaters were limited to practice when ice conditions were suitable outdoors, and set its first skater to the World Championships in 1979.

**Soviet Union.** At a May meeting of the USSR Skating Federation, the sole topic of discussion among the coaches, judges and officials in attendance was how the country could gain the leading positions in international figure skating competitions. They agreed the path forward was the organization of training programs at sports schools. By 1983, there were 800 coaches in the country.

**United States.** In October, Cecilie Mendelssohn-Bartholdy, the widow of three-time Olympic Gold Medallist Gillis Grafström, cut the ribbon at the dedication ceremony of the USFSA's new National Headquarters in Colorado Springs. The Headquarters became the new home of the Association's offices and the U.S. Figure Skating Museum and Hall of Fame, as well as "Skating", which was produced in Massachusetts for nearly six decades. At the USFSA's Governing Council Meeting in San Diego in May, Colorado Springs pharmacist and skating judge Oscar T. Iobst Jr. was elected as the Association's New President. Iobst was previously the Vice-President of the USFSA's Eastern Section and Chairman of the Membership Committee. At the Professional Skaters Guild of America's convention in Colorado Springs in May, USFSA Museum and Hall of Fame Curator Jerry McGaha gave a speech on the history of figure skating and a fashion show of skating costumes past and present was presented. JoJo Starbuck Bradshaw was the guest of honour at the closing banquet.

# MUSIC

By the late 70s and early 80s, cassettes were on the road to completely replacing reel-to-reel tapes and vinyl records. Cassettes made it much easier for coaches to 'cut' their student's music. The CFSA adapted to this shift by releasing its ice dance music on both records and cassettes.

# BEHIND THE SCENES

A hot topic of discussion was the 'Flea and Gorilla' trend of (mostly Eastern Bloc) pairs teams with extreme height differences performing tricks galore but little in between. Former World Champion Hans-Jürgen Bäumler complained that the discipline had devolved into "children's long-distance throwing." Pairs skaters suffered more injuries as the number of triple jumps increased and as a result, there were decreasing numbers in the pairs field at international competitions. In an attempt to curb these problems, the ISU's Figure Skating Committee released Communication No. 536: "The ISU has become increasingly concerned with the trend of recent years not to observe the general principles of pair skating. As a result, there has been a deterioration of the essential aspects of this sport, which has traditionally emphasized artistry and unison in addition to athletic ability... Too great an emphasis has been placed upon purely athletic and solo elements." Referees were instructed to ensure judges appropriately deduct marks if any of the following were observed: "Excessive number of overhead lifts, including repetitions of the same lift, or variations of the same lift. Sustained or carried lifts. Excessive repetition of twist lifts. Excessive number of solo jumps and spins. Excessive shadow or solo skating. Too little footwork; not enough varied, difficult or original step sequences. Lack of primarily pair elements. Use of music unsuitable for pair skating."

At the World Championships in Dortmund, ISU President Jacques Favart made the statement, "The compulsory figures must die. They are a waste of time and prevent skaters from being more creative." Favart's statement sparked considerable controversy, leading the CFSA to poll Canada's top skaters, coaches, judges and past champions on the issue. Donald Jackson, Karen Magnussen, Brian Pockar and Gary Beacom were among those who penned impassioned essays for the Canadian Skater, succinctly explaining why figures should never be eliminated from the sport. Barbara Ann Scott beautifully stated, "The very name of the sport is FIGURE SKATING - not free skating; not exhibition skating. It is a competitive sport. The basic foundation of figure skating is a strong grounding in school figures. Ballet has barre work... pianists have finger exercises... figure skating has school figures. My feeling is that youngsters today are not willing to spend the hours necessary to perfect school figures. The years of practice spent on figures teaches a young person the discipline that is so sadly lacking these days. It not only gives one a solid grounding for good free skating but also helps one to learn concentration and the ability to work hard at something that is not always fun but demands the sacrifice of practice and patience. This discipline carries over into everyday life and teaches the importance of work before play. Unfortunately, TV does not show this important part of skating competitions because figures are not of interest to the general public. But this notwithstanding, the important question is - Are figure skating competitions commercial ventures, entertainment or serious forums for top athletes to compete against each other? There are other opportunities for purely creative endeavours. A real skating competition is not an ice show, exhibition or television special... As one who truly loves the sport of figure skating, I hope and pray that the tradition will never be compromised or abolished." The CFSA proposed that instead of eliminating figures, the number could be reduced from 41 to 23 and the ISU could draw the figures for Championship events at its Congress in June so that skaters wouldn't have to waste time practicing figures that weren't drawn.

# Fall Internationals

**1979 COUPES DES ALPES (Saint Gervais, France and Oberstdorf, West Germany, August 24-26 and August 29-September 2, 1979)**

Grand Prix de St. Gervais Winners:

Rudi Cerne (FRG) - men
Lynn Smith (USA) - women
Kitty and Peter Carruthers (USA) - pairs
Gina Aucoin and Hans-Peter Ponikau (CAN) - ice dance

Nebelhorn Trophy (Oberstdorf) Winners:

Gordon Forbes (CAN) - men
Lynn Smith (USA) - women
Kitty and Peter Carruthers (USA) - pairs
Gina Aucoin and Hans-Peter Ponikau (CAN) - ice dance

**1979 GRAND PRIZE SNP (Banská Bystrica, Czechoslovakia)**

Winners:

Ralf Lewandowski (GDR) - men
Barbora Knotková (CZE) - women
Ingrid Ženatá and René Novotný (CZE) - pairs
Julia Romanova and Juri Gaichenkov (SOV) - ice dance

**1979 ASKÖ CUP OF VIENNA (Vienna, Austria)**

Men:

1. Brian Orser (CAN)
2. Christopher Howarth (GRB)
3. Vladimir Rastschiotnov (SOV)

Women:

1. Marina Ignatova (SOV)
2. Sonja Stanek (AUT)
3. Tracey Wainman (CAN)

**1979 NORTON SKATE/FLAMING LEAVES INTERNATIONAL (Lake Placid, NY, September 20-23, 1979)**

Men:

1. Scott Hamilton (USA)
2. Scott Cramer (USA)
3. Jan Hoffmann (GDR)

Women:

1. Lisa-Marie Allen (USA)
2. Susanna Driano (ITA)
3. Sandy Lenz (USA)

Pairs:

1. Sabine Baeß and Tassilo Thierbach (GDR)
2. Kitty and Peter Carruthers (USA)
3. Vicki Heasley and Robert Wagenhoffer (USA)

Ice Dance:

1. Krisztina Regőczy and András Sallay (HUN)
2. Natalia Bestemianova and Andrei Bukin (SOV)
3. Lorna Wighton and John Dowding (CAN)

**1979 ROTARY WATCHES INTERNATIONAL (London, England, October 9-11, 1979)**

Men:

1. Robin Cousins (GRB)
2. Igor Bobrin (SOV)
3. Brian Pockar (CAN)

Women:

1. Emi Watanabe (JPN)
2. Dagmar Lurz (FRG)
3. Karena Richardson (GRB)

Pairs:

1. Nelli Cherkvotina and Victor Teslia (SOV)
2. Christina Reigel and Andreas Nischwitz (FRG)
3. Susan Garland and Robert Daw (GRB)

Ice Dance:

1. Krisztina Regőczy and András Sallay (HUN)
2. Jayne Torvill and Christopher Dean (GRB)
3. Natalia Karamysheva and Rostislav Sinitsyn (SOV)

**1979 NHK TROPHY (Tokyo, Japan, October 26-28, 1979)**

Men:

1. Robin Cousins (GRB)
2. Fumio Igarashi (JPN)
3. David Santee (USA)

Women:

1. Emi Watanabe (JPN)
2. Lisa-Marie Allen (USA)
3. Sandy Lenz (USA)

Pairs:

1. Irina Vorobieva and Igor Lisovsky (SOV)
2. Vicki Heasley and Robert Wagenhoffer (USA)
3. Sheryl Franks and Michael Botticelli (USA)

Ice Dance:

1. Irina Moiseeva and Andrei Minenkov (SOV)
2. Jayne Torvill and Christopher Dean (GRB)
3. Natalia Karamysheva and Rostislav Sinitsyn (SOV)

**1979 RICHMOND TROPHY (London, England, November 4-5, 1979)**

Women:

1. Alicia Risberg (USA)
2. Carola Weißenberg (GDR)
3. Simone Grigorescu (USA)

# Fall Internationals

**1979 ENNIA CHALLENGE CUP INTERNATIONAL FREE SKATING COMPETITION (The Hague, Netherlands, November 13-18, 1979)**

Men:

1. Robin Cousins (GRB)
2. Gordon Forbes (CAN)
3. Robert Wagenhoffer (USA)

Women:

1. Renata Baierová (CZE)
2. Elaine Zayak (USA)
3. Heather Kemkaran (CAN)

Pairs:

1. Irina Vorobieva and Igor Lisovsky (SOV)
2. Veronika Pershina and Marat Akbarov (SOV)
3. Christina Riegel and Andreas Nischwitz (FRG)

Ice Dance:

1. Liliana Řeháková and Stanislav Drastich (CZE)
2. Elena Garanina and Igor Zavozin (SOV)
3. Susi and Peter Handschmann (AUT)

**1979 POKAL DER BLAUEN SCHWERTER (East Berlin, East Germany, November 14-17, 1979)**

Men:

1. Jan Hoffmann (GDR)
2. Mario Liebers (GDR)
3. Norbert Schramm (FRG)

Women:

1. Anett Pötzsch (GDR)
2. Katarina Witt (GDR)
3. Carola Weißenberg (GDR)

Pairs:

1. Sabine Baeß and Tassilo Thierbach (GDR)
2. Kerstin Stolfig and Veit Kempe (GDR)
3. Cornelia Hauffe and Kersten Bellmann (GDR)

**1979 GOLDEN SPIN OF ZAGREB (Zagreb, Yugoslavia, November 21-25, 1979)**

Pairs:

1. Cornelia Haufer and Kersten Beumann (GDR)
2. Anna Nalgina and Sergej Corovin (SOV)
3. Kathia Dubec and Xavier Dovillard (FRA)

**1979 PRAGUE SKATE (Prague, Czechoslovakia, November 1979)**

Men:

1. Gordon Forbes (CAN)
2. Allen Schramm (USA)
3. Jozef Sabovčík (CZE)

Women:

1. Elaine Zayak (USA)
2. Renata Baierová (CZE)
3. Myriam Oberwiler (SUI)

Pairs:

1. Nelli Chervotkina and Viktor Teslia (SOV)
2. Ingrid Spieglová and Alan Spiegl (CZE)
3. Birgit Lorenz and Knut Schubert (GDR)

Ice Dance:

1. Liliana Řeháková and Stanislav Drastich (CZE)
2. Judy Blumberg and Michael Seibert (USA)
3. Anna Pisanská and Jiří Musil (CZE)

**1979 PRIZE OF MOSCOW NEWS (Moscow, Soviet Union, November 28-December 1, 1979)**

Men:

1. Igor Bobrin (SOV)
2. Vladimir Kotin (SOV)
3. Vladimir Rashetnov (SOV)

Women:

1. Kira Ivanova (SOV)
2. Natalia Strelkova (SOV)
3. Renata Baierová (CZE)

Pairs:

1. Irina Vorobieva and Igor Lisovsky (SOV)
2. Veronika Pershina and Marat Akbarov (SOV)
3. Zhanna Ilina and Aleksandr Vlasov (SOV)

Ice Dance:

1. Natalia Linichuk and Gennadi Karponosov (SOV)
2. Natalia Bestemianova and Andrei Bukin (SOV)
3. Natalia Karamysheva and Rostislav Sinitsyn (SOV)

*Krisztina Regőczy and András Sallay. Photo by Fred & Joan Dean, courtesy Paul Dean, "Ice & Roller Skate" magazine archive.*

## BEHIND THE SCENES

Skating magazines weren't the only thing showing up in skater's mailboxes. You could order just about anything your heart desired by mail. Mail-order businesses popped up selling skates, scribes for patch, tracksuit-style Spandex training outfits, skating stationary and ice dance music. Devoe Sports Systems from Carlstadt, New Jersey, even sold custom home ice rinks! In late 1979, one Sun Valley coach started a mail-order business called 'Choreograflicks'. Skaters completed a form talking about themselves, their skating level and music preferences and sent a cheque off in the mail. Four weeks later, they received a cassette with their program music, a written description of their program with diagrams and a videotape of their coach skating the program. The Professional Skaters Guild of America produced a mail-order BETA and VHS tape collection called *Champion Series.* The instructional tapes featured lessons in both figures and free skating with coaches Peter Burrows and Barbara Roles, demonstrated by their students Elaine Zayak and Lisa-Marie Allen.

Dick Button's production company Candid Productions filed suit against the ISU for "failure on the part of the ISU to negotiate in good faith". The gist of the lawsuit was that ABC only wanted to broadcast figure skating events, while CBS was willing to accept a package to broadcast both figure and speed skating. Candid Productions had partnered with ABC to broadcast the World Championships since 1962. After two years of litigation, a New York judge ultimately ruled in favour of the ISU.

At the ISU's spring Congress in Davos, the first official course for international Referees was approved by the Council. The number of elements in the pairs short program was increased from six to seven, with a spin combination added. The length of the pairs short program was increased to two minutes and fifteen seconds, while the duration of free skating programs for men and pairs was reduced from five minutes to four and a half. Another rule passed was that both the main rink for all Olympics and ISU Championships had to be "closed and covered" (indoor).

## FASHION

The U.S. Figure Skating Museum and Hall of Fame presented an exhibition called *Skating Fashions in the Twentieth Century* featuring costumes worn by Gillis Grafström, Barbara Ann Scott, Carol Heiss, Hayes Alan Jenkins and Dick Button. The famous Chartreuse dress Peggy Fleming wore at the 1968 Olympics in Grenoble was the star of the show.

## ART AND HISTORY

The Skating Club of New York sponsored a four-day exhibit at the Sky Rink's lounge called *Skating Art and Photography*. The club's skaters performed exhibitions each day before wine and cheese receptions and John Curry's book with illustrations by Keith Money was on sale at a discount. The exhibition featured an 18-karat gold sculpture of a skater performing a layback spin by Will Osborne and watercolors of Toller Cranston and Dorothy Hamill by Cecile Johnson.

# SHOWS AND TOURS

The always lavish *Ice Capades* continued to be a huge draw with audiences. Dorothy Hamill and Ludmila and Oleg Protopopov were special guest stars in the "family-friendly" skating tour's New York City show. Tai Babilonia and Randy Gardner made their professional debut in April at the East Company's show at the Los Angeles Sports Arena. Other *Ice Capades* stars in 1980 included Sarah Kawahara, Wendy Burge and Richard Ewell.

Just before the 1979-1980 season, Ringling Bros. and Barnum & Bailey Combined Shows took ownership of both Shipstad & Johnson's *Ice Follies* and the American unit of the *Holiday on Ice* tour. Both had previously been owned by the company founded by Arthur M. Wirtz, who produced Sonja Henie's Hollywood Ice Revue decades prior. The International *Holiday on Ice* tour, which was owned by Madison Square Garden and Chalfen-Holiday Inc. had five different units which played in Europe, South America and Asia. A big draw in the European shows were the performances of World Champions Marika Kilius and Hans-Jürgen Bäumler.

Olympic Medallists Toller Cranston and Donald Jackson starred in *The Vickie*, a benefit ice show for the Ontario Federation for Visually Impaired Children in Toronto in October. The event, produced by Andra McLaughlin Kelly, became an annual event throughout the 80s, featuring special performances by visually impaired American skater Stash Serafin. Hundreds of skaters from The Granite Club and Toronto Cricket Skating and Curling Club participated over the years.

The sixth annual *Superskates* show was held at Madison Square Garden in New York City in November as a benefit to help cover the costs of sending athletes to the 1980 Winter Olympic Games in Lake Placid. Performers included John Curry, Tai Babilonia and Randy Gardner and Charlie Tickner.

The St. Moritz Ice Skating Club in California raised over 2000 dollars for the Indochinese Refugee Resettlement Program of the International Institute of the East Bay, a United Way Agency in Oakland, through its annual carnival. Over 150 refugees attended the show and none of them had ever seen skating before... or snow for that matter! The carnival starred a 16-year-old whose name will come up once or twice in the chapters to come... Brian Boitano.

*The 1980 Olympic Figure Skating Tour*, presented by Tom Collins, visited twelve American cities in April and May. Though Charlie Tickner was the only Olympic Medallist to participate, the tour featured an impressive line-up of stars including Scott Hamilton, Kitty and Peter Carruthers, Brian Pockar and Lorna Wighton and John Dowding.

Queen's Ice Rink in Bayswater, London celebrated its fiftieth anniversary in May with the *Martini International Ice Gala*, starring John Curry and Robin Cousins. It was the first time two Olympic Gold Medallists in men's figure skating from the UK had performed in the same show on British soil.

## BOOKS AND MAGAZINES

1979 saw the publication of an altogether remarkable book by Dennis L. Bird called *Our Skating Heritage: A Centenary History of the National Skating Association 1879-1979*. Painstakingly researched through careful study of primary sources, Bird's book chronicled the history of skating in the UK from the Victorian era to modern times.

Robert Sheffield and Richard Woodward's *The Ice Skating Book* was released by Universe Books in New York City. Promoted as an "informal survey of today's skaters & the skaters of the past", the book was particularly notable for its outstanding collection of historical skating art and photography.

Choreographer Ricky Harris released her popular book *Choreography & Style for Ice Skaters*. Harris taught ballet and jazz and was a member of the support staff at the Squaw Valley Olympic Training Centre. Coach Ron Ludington said, "It's about time for a book like this and Ricky's the one to do it."

Muriel Kay's new book *Origins of Ice Dance Music* offered a historical background of the music used for ice dance programs, providing coaches, choreographers and ice dancers a greater understanding of the history of the Waltz, Polka, Blues, Argentine Tango, Foxtrot, March, Paso Doble and Rhumba. Skaters around the world gained access to the knowledge of expert coaches in a series of excellent educational books. *Figure Skating with Carlo Fassi* featured lessons in both figures and free skating and extensive illustrations, while Lorna Dyer's *Ice Dancing Illustrated* provided a wealth of information on compulsory dances based on Dyer's own experience as a student of World Champion Jean Westwood

## FILMS AND TELEVISION

Toller Cranston's 1978 television special *Dream Weaver* won the Golden Rose of Montreux Award for Best Variety Program at the Montreux Television Festival in Switzerland. It was also one of only four CBC shows to be nominated for an Emmy Award in 1979. Cranston's skating was also featured in the concert film for Joni Mitchell's "Shadows and Light" album.

BBC featured a special figure skating performance by John Curry, Lorna Brown and Catherine Foulkes as part of its Christmas Day programming, filmed at Queen's Ice Rink in Bayswater, London.

In February, CBS aired the first Peanuts special of the 1980s - *She's a Good Skate, Charlie Brown*. The animations for the now classic television special were created using a technique called rotoscoping, with creator Charles M. Schulz's daughter Amy acting as one of the skating models. The same month, skating was also the subject of the ABC after-school special *The Heartbreak Winner: One Girl's Struggle For Olympic Gold*. Actress Melissa Sherman starred as a teenage skater whose Olympic dreams were cut short by rheumatoid arthritis, who was inspired to return to the ice after meeting an inspiring young paraplegic who was determined to regain his ability to walk.

Lynn-Holly Johnson, who received a Golden Globe nomination for her role in the 1978 skating film *Ice Castles*, was cast in a starring role in Disney's supernatural horror film *The Watcher in The Woods*, alongside legendary actress Bette Davis. Johnson was a former competitive skater, winning the silver medal in the novice women's event at the 1974 U.S. Championships.

Peggy Fleming, Dorothy Hamill, Linda Fratianne, John Curry and Toller Cranston all performed on a short-lived NBC variety television series hosted by Dick Clark called *The Big Show* in the spring of 1980. The big-budget production, filmed on a huge set that boasted an ice rink and swimming pool, flopped miserably and was cancelled after only eleven episodes.

In May, *Bob Hope's All-Star Comedy Birthday Party at the Air Force Academy: A USO Salute* aired on television. Filmed at the Air Force Academy in Colorado Springs, the star-studded special featured Tai Babilonia and Randy Gardner, in one of their first television appearances since their tragic withdrawal at the 1980 Winter Olympics.

## COMPETITIONS

**1980 NORDISKA MÄSTERSKAPEN (Trondheim, Norway)**

Men:

1. Antti Kontiola (FIN)
2. Peter Söderholm (SWE)
3. Matthias Eidmann (SWE)

Women:

1. Pia Snellman (FIN)
2. Päivi Nieminen (FIN)
3. Catarina Lindgren (SWE)

**1980 TRI-STATE INTERNATIONAL PRECISION TEAM COMPETITION (Kalamazoo, MI, February 9, 1980)**

Team:

1. The Royal Precisionettes (CAN)
2. London Supremes (CAN)
3. Fraserettes (USA)

Other Winners:

Karen's Kolleens (CAN) - junior
Flamettes (CAN) - novice

**1980 MORZINE INTERNATIONAL TROPHY (Morzine, France, May 1980)**

Ice Dance:

1. Natalia Karamysheva and Rostislav Sinitsyn (SOV)
2. Carol Fox and Richard Dalley
3. Olga Volozhinskaya and Alexandr Svinin (SOV)

*Tai Babilonia and Randy Gardner. Photo by Fred & Joan Dean, courtesy Paul Dean, "Ice & Roller Skate" magazine archive.*

# Professional Competitions

**1980 CANADIAN PROFESSIONAL CHAMPIONSHIPS (Scarborough, Ontario, January 26-27, 1980)**

Men:

1. Kenneth Polk
2. Raymond Naismith
3. Jack Frizelle

Women:

1. Carol Farmer-Wright
2. Elizabeth Purtle
3. Sherri Diane Hunt

Pairs:

1. Sandra and Val Bezic

Ice Dance:

1. Judie Jeffcott and Keith Swindlehurst
2. Shelley MacLeod and John Rait

**1980 CAMPEONATOS DEL MUNDO DE PATINAJE ARTÍSTICO PROFESSIONAL SOBRE HIELO (Jaca, Spain, April 3-6, 1980)**

Men:

1. Scott Cramer (USA)
2. Minoru Sano (JPN)
3. Billy Schober (AUS)

Women:

1. Young Soon Choo (KOR)
2. Sherri Diane Hunt (CAN)
3. Amy Brown (USA)

Pairs:

1. Sandra and Val Bezic (CAN)
2. Kyoko Hagiwara and Hisao Ozaki (JPN)
3. Tania Buhlman and Edgar Pfaner (SUI)

Ice Dance:

1. Shelley MacLeod and John Rait (CAN)
2. Judie Jeffcott and Keith Swindlehurst (CAN)
3. Kathryn Winter and Kim Spreyer (GRB)

*Robin Cousins with his parents. Photo by Fred & Joan Dean, courtesy Paul Dean, "Ice & Roller Skate" magazine archive.*

# NATIONAL CHAMPIONS BY COUNTRY

**Men**

AUS - Michael Pasfield
AUT - Helmut Kristofics-Binder
BUL - Boyko Aleksiev
CZE - Jozef Sabovčík
FIN - Antti Kontiola
FRA - Jean-Christophe Simond
FRG - Rudi Cerne
GDR - Jan Hoffmann
GRB - Robin Cousins
HOL - Gerard van Hattem
HUN - István Simon
JPN - Fumio Igarashi
NZL - John Walkingshaw
POL - Grzegorz Głowania
SAF - Rick Simons
SOV - Igor Bobrin
SUI - Oliver Höner
SWE - Thomas Öberg

**Women**

AUS - Vicki Holland
AUT - Claudia Kristofics-Binder
BUL - Margarita Dimitrova
CZE - Renata Baierová
DEN - Heidi Bartelsen
FIN - Pia Snellman
FRA - Anne-Sophie de Kristoffy
FRG - Dagmar Lurz
GDR - Anett Pötzsch
GRB - Karena Richardson
HOL - Astrid Jansen in de Wal
HUN - Ildikó Segesdi
ITA - Susanna Driano
JPN - Emi Watanabe
KOR - Hea-sook Shin
NOR - Anne Tomasgaard
NZL - Denyse Adam
POL - Helena Chwila
SAF - Irene Anderson
SOV - Elena Vodorezova
SUI - Denise Biellmann
SWE - Bodil Olsson

**Pairs**

AUS - Danielle and Stephen Carr
AUT - Ingrid and Walter Fuchs
CZE - Ingrid Spieglová and Alan Spiegl
FRA - Hélène Glabek and Xavier Videau
FRG - Christina Riegel and Andreas Nischwitz
GDR - Sabine Baeß and Tassilo Thierbach
GRB - Susan Garland and Robert Daw
JPN – Yukiko Okabe and Takashi Mura
POL - Maria Ježak and Lech Matuszewski
SAF – Barbara-Anne Hawkes and Grant Walker
SOV - Marina Pestova and Stanislav Leonovich
SUI - Danielle Rieder and Paul Huber

**Ice Dance**

AUS - Brennice Coates and Leslie Boroczky
AUT - Susi and Peter Handschmann
BUL - Hristina Boyanova and Yavor Ivanov
CZE - Liliana Řeháková and Stanislav Drastich
FRA - Nathalie Hervé and Pierre Béchu
FRG - Henriette Fröschl and Christian Steiner
GRB - Jayne Torvill and Christopher Dean
HUN - Krisztina Regőczy and András Sallay
JPN - Noriko Sato and Tadayuki Takahashi
NZL - Ann (Brennock) Tranter and Alan Tranter
POL - Jolanta Wesołowska and Andrzej Alberciak
SAF - Carol Brown and Robert Du Plessis
SOV - Natalia Karamysheva and Rostislav Sinitsyn
SUI - Regula Lattmann and Hanspeter Müller

*Judy Blumberg and Michael Seibert. Photo by Fred & Joan Dean, courtesy Fred Dean, "Ice & Roller Skate" magazine archive.*

# MAJOR COMPETITIONS

**World Junior Championships.** Talented young skaters from all around the world arrived in The French Alps in January to compete for top honours at the World Junior Championships. There were only six couples entered in the pairs event. Since half of them were from the Soviet Union, they were all scheduled in one practice group. It didn't go unnoticed that all three Soviet pairs did nothing but stroking and footwork for the first 20 minutes of each practice. With zero movement in the standings from the short program to the long, Soviets Larisa Selezneva and Oleg Makarov came out on top. Elena Batanova, who had finished second in the ice dance event the year prior with a different partner, won the dance title with her new partner Alexei Soloviev. Canada's only entry Karen Taylor and Robert Burk finished a strong fifth. Alexandr Fadeev took the top spot in both the short program and free skate on his way to winning the men's event. Both Fadeev and his teammate Vitali Egorov, who placed second, landed triple Lutzes. The bronze went to East Germany's Falko Kirsten. 14-year-old Grzegorz Filipowski of Poland finished third in the free skate, completing a historic triple toe-loop/triple toe-loop combination. Canada's sole entry, 15-year-old Neil Paterson of North Vancouver finished second ahead of Kirsten, Filipowski and Egorov in the short program but dropped to sixth overall. Switzerland's Oliver Höner won the figures but placed only ninth overall after finishing outside of the top ten in both the short and long programs. In a close contest, 15-year-old Rosalynn Sumners of Edmonds, Washington became the fourth American woman in a row to claim the World Junior women's title. Another 15-year-old, Kay Thomson of Toronto, claimed the silver. Sumners won the figures and free skating; Thomson the short program. Outside of the top three, there was considerable movement in the standings, with Carola Paul of East Germany moving up from ninth after the figures to win the bronze medal. Sumners' success in Megève was particularly remarkable in that the American team had arrived late and the U.S. women missed all the practice patches before the figures.

**1980 WORLD JUNIOR CHAMPIONSHIPS**
(Megève, France, January 16-19, 1980)

Men:

1. Alexandr Fadeev (SOV)
2. Vitali Egorov (SOV)
3. Falko Kirsten (GDR)
4. Grzegorz Filipowski (POL)
5. Scott Williams (USA)
6. Neil Paterson (CAN)
7. Laurent Depouilly (FRA)
8. Alexei Sidorov (SOV)
9. Oliver Höner (SUI)
10. Jack O'Brien (USA)

Women:

1. Rosalynn Sumners (USA)
2. Kay Thomson (CAN)
3. Carola Paul (GDR)
4. Manuela Ruben (FRG)
5. Daniela Massanneck (FRG)
6. Marina Serova (SOV)
7. Béatrice Farinacci (FRA)
8. Daniela Zuccoli (ITA)
9. Bunny Blake (USA)
10. Andrea Rohm (AUT)

Pairs:

1. Larisa Selezneva and Oleg Makarov (SOV)
2. Marina Nikitiuk and Rashid Kadyrkaev (SOV)
3. Kathia Dubec and Xavier Douillard (FRA)
4. Kelly Abolt and Kevin Peeks (USA)
5. Elena Kravchenko and Vladimir Starostin (SOV)
6. Gaby and Jörg Galambos (SUI)

Ice Dance:

1. Elena Batanova and Andrei Antonov (SOV)
2. Judit Péterfy and Csaba Bálint (HUN)
3. Renée Roca and Andrew Ouellette (USA)
4. Oksana Gusakova and Genrikh Sretenski (SOV)
5. Karen Taylor and Robert Burk (CAN)
6. Petra Born and Rainer Schönborn (FRG)
7. Sophie Schmidt and Eric Desplats (FRA)
8. Maria Kniffer and Manfred Hübler (AUT)
9. Iwona Bielas and Jacek Jasiaczek (POL)
10. Karan Giles and Russell Green (GRB)

**U.S. Championships.** In January, The Omni in Atlanta played host to the first U.S. Championships ever held in Southeastern America. The Championships drew near-capacity crowds, as an elite figure skating competition was something of a novelty to locals. In the ice dance event, defending Champions Stacey Smith and John Summers narrowly defeated Judy Blumberg and Michael Seibert in a four-three split to take their third consecutive national title. Smith and Summers trained at the Wilmington Skating Club in Delaware and were students of Ron Ludington and Blumberg and Seibert represented the Ice Skating Club of Indianapolis. Carol Fox and Richard Dalley, runners-up at Nationals the previous two years, skated extremely well but slipped to third. World Champions Tai Babilonia and Randy Gardner were heavy favourites in the pairs event, but they did not skate up to their full potential. In the short program, Babilonia overrated her solo double flip and Gardner stumbled on the entrance to their pair spin. Their woes continued in the free skate with a botched landing on their opening throw double Axel. Despite Babilonia and Gardner's bobbles, the overall quality of their skating was still miles ahead in the competition. They earned first-place ordinals from every judge on the way to defending their national title. Kitty and Peter Carruthers claimed their first senior medal at the Nationals, a silver, and Sheryl Franks and Michael Botticelli took the bronze ahead of the previous year's silver medallists, Vicki Heasley and Robert Wagenhoffer. Wagenhoffer did 'double duty' competing in both singles and pairs, as did Paul Wylie who medalled in both junior men's and pairs. Charlie Tickner dominated the senior men's event from start to finish, winning all three phases in the competition. His short program was flawless, but he stumbled on a triple Salchow and double Axel in the free. He earned marks of 5.9 for Composition and Style from all but one of the seven judges in the free skate. David Santee and Scott Hamilton were unanimously second and third, both making mistakes early in their programs but rebounding to finish strongly. The previous year's silver medallist, Scott Cramer, had one of the cleanest skates of the night in the free and the audience booed his marks, which left him in fourth overall and off the Olympic team. Representing the Figure Skating Club of Rockford, deaf skater David Michalowski finished dead last, but the broadcast of his performance on ABC's *Wide World of Sports* served as an inspiration to many. Like Babilonia and Gardner in the pairs, World Champion Linda Fratianne did not have the competition she likely wanted. After decisively winning the figures, Fratianne fell twice in the short program. She only two-footed one jump in the free, but still lost both of the free skating events to Lisa-Marie Allen, who was in excellent form. Fratianne's coach Frank Carroll later revealed that he had considered withdrawing her from the competition because was still quite weak after having the flu the week prior. Though she didn't place in the top three in any phase of the competition, Sandy Lenz of Rockford, Illinois earned four third-place ordinals overall, which was enough for the bronze. The star of the women's event was 14-year-old Elaine Zayak, the talented young student of Peter Burrows who had won the U.S. and World Junior title the previous season. Though kept off the podium with a seventh-place showing in the figures, Zayak landed an incredible eight triple jumps in her free skating program - an average of two a minute. Zayak's technical prowess caught the attention of USFSA officials, who named her as the third member of the World team and the Olympic alternate instead of Lenz. California's Joan Campbell made history as the first woman of colour to win a national novice title. Debi Thomas won the free skate and the silver, making it the first time in history that two African American women were on the podium together at any level at the U.S. Nationals. Another remarkable story from the event was that of 17-year-old Susan Guild of Lansing, Michigan, who placed fourth in the junior women's event. In June of 1978, Guild was diagnosed with acute lymphocytic leukemia and she continued training despite undergoing chemotherapy, spinal taps and bone marrow tests. At the post-competition exhibition, Dick Button had the audience in stitches when he narrated a 'how-to' lesson on skating technique geared to poke fun at all the champions.

**1980 U.S. CHAMPIONSHIPS (Atlanta, GA, January 15-20, 1980)**

Men:

1. Charlie Tickner
2. David Santee
3. Scott Hamilton
4. Scott Cramer
5. Brian Boitano
6. Robert Wagenhoffer
7. Reggie Raiford
8. Mark Cockerell
9. Jimmie Santee
10. Allen Schramm

Women:

1. Linda Fratianne
2. Lisa-Marie Allen
3. Sandy Lenz
4. Elaine Zayak
5. Simone Grigorescu
6. Priscilla Hill
7. Alicia Risberg
8. Jacki Farrell
9. Cindy Moyers
10. Aimee Kravette

Pairs:

1. Tai Babilonia and Randy Gardner
2. Kitty and Peter Carruthers
3. Sheryl Franks and Michael Botticelli
4. Vicki Heasley and Robert Wagenhoffer
5. Lyndy and Hal Marron
6. Tracy and Scott Prussack
7. Maria Di Domenico and Burt Lancon
8. Lea Ann Miller and Bill Fauver
9. Lynne and Jay Freeman
10. Tricia Burton and Larry Schrier

Ice Dance:

1. Stacey Smith and John Summers
2. Judy Blumberg and Michael Seibert
3. Carol Fox and Richard Dalley
4. Kim Krohn and Barry Hagan
5. Ellen Pulver and Donald Adair
6. Elisa Spitz and Scott Gregory
7. Susan Dymecki and Anthony Bardin
8. Hae Sue Park and Robert Yobabaskas
9. Cathleen Marron and Jay Pinkerton
10. Nancy Berghoff and Jim Bowser

Junior Winners:

Tom Dickson (men)
Vikki de Vries (women)
Dana Graham and Paul Wylie (pairs)
Terri Slater and David Lipowitz (ice dance)

Novice Winners:

James Cygan (men)
Joan Campbell (women)

**Canadian Championships.** Kitchener-Waterloo played host to the Canadian Championships at its new Rink in the Park. There were several notable firsts at the event. It was the first time a digital marking display was used at Canadians, making it easier for audiences to follow along. A Honeywell computer system, used for the first time at Canadians the year prior, was used to calculate results in the senior and junior events. Novice results were still tabulated the old-fashioned way. Doping control tests were introduced for the first time, with a random draw determining which skaters would be tested. Another first was the introduction of scientific tests during the actual competition, organized by the University of Waterloo and coach Kerry Leitch. Skaters were monitored via wireless devices which measured their heart rates before, during and after the competition. Lorri Baier and Lloyd Eisler wore special belts that operated ECG's to monitor their heart rates during stress periods. The unusual logo for the event featured a bird, the Distelfink, which was considered by locals to be a good luck symbol. The Canadian Olympic Committee had stringent requirements that only two skaters, Lorna Wighton and John Dowding, met before the competition. As such, they were named to the Olympic team before the competition even began. In the senior men's event, different skaters won each phase of the competition. Gary Beacom led Brian Pockar, Gordon Forbes and Brian Orser in the figures. Gordon Forbes won the short program, executing a difficult triple Lutz combination in his entertaining performance to Boney M's "Rasputin". Both Pockar and Forbes skated well in the free skate, while Beacom struggled with several jumps in his quirky self-choreographed program set to music from The Missouri Breaks, Electric Light Orchestra and the film *Jaws*. Pockar ultimately skated well enough to defend his title. Wighton and Dowding dominated the dance event from start to finish. History was made when two teams from Nova Scotia, Marie McNeil and Rob McCall of Halifax and Gina Aucoin and Hans-Peter Ponikau of Glace Bay, stood on the senior dance podium for the first time. It was the first time any Maritime province had two senior medallists in any discipline at Canadians. In pairs, Barbara Underhill and Paul Martini did the Granite Club proud, defeating Baier and Eisler and Kerry Leitch's other Preston duo, Becky Gough and Mark Rowsom. Spectators were pleased to see six pairs entered. In 1977, there had only been two. Though Heather Kemkaran led the women's field from start to finish and regained her title, defeating the defending Champion Janet Morrissey of Ottawa, it was 12-year-old Tracey Wainman who was the talk of the women's competition. A student of Toller Cranston's coach Ellen Burka, Wainman was something of a child prodigy and the fact she included a triple Salchow in her program at her age did not go unnoticed. Due to the COA's strict requirements, skaters had all been informed by CFSA President Charles Dover at the opening banquet that the Olympic and World teams would not be announced at the conclusion of the event, as was customary. CFSA officials ended up having to bring videos in the competition to a meeting with the COA's Board of Directors. It was speculated that when pleading their case, the CFSA would sacrifice sending a woman to Lake Placid to be allowed to send a man and a pair. All four senior champions were ultimately named to the team, but not without controversy. Kemkaran's letter of invitation made it clear that her "objective should be to place in the top ten" at the Games. This letter also informed her that Wainman was selected for the only spot on the World team. Janet Morrissey, who beat Wainman in the figures and combined free skating, told reporters that she "heard Tracey Wainman would be sent to one of the competitions last summer", which the CFSA dismissed as "idle skater talk and speculation". The Olympic and World selections caused considerable media hoopla, overshadowing what was otherwise a very well-skated competition.

**1980 CANADIAN CHAMPIONSHIPS**
(Kitchener-Waterloo, ON, January 16-20, 1980)

Men:

1. Brian Pockar
2. Gordon Forbes
3. Gary Beacom
4. Brian Orser
5. Daniel Béland
6. Kevin Hicks
7. Kevin Parker
8. Dennis Coi
9. Henri April

Women:

1. Heather Kemkaran
2. Janet Morrissey
3. Tracey Wainman
4. Debbie Albright
5. Sandra Mattiussi
6. Kathryn Osterberg
7. Jamie Lynn Kitching
8. Susan Smith
9. Sandra Leighton
10. Glenna Howley

Pairs:

1. Barbara Underhill and Paul Martini
2. Lorri Baier and Lloyd Eisler
3. Becky Gough and Mark Rowsom
4. Mary Jo Fedy and Tim Mills
5. Katherina Matousek and Eric Thomsen
6. Andrea Derby and Jim Sorochan

Ice Dance:

1. Lorna Wighton and John Dowding
2. Marie McNeil and Rob McCall
3. Gina Aucoin and Hans Peter Ponikau
4. Kelly Johnson and Kris Barber
5. Joanne French and John Thomas
6. Lillian Heming and Murray Carey
7. Martine Vigouret and Alan Atkins
8. Darlene Wendt and Wayne Hussey

Junior Winners:

Neil Giroday (men)
Kerry Smith (women)
Becky Gough and Mark Rowsom (pairs)
Tracy Wilson and Mark Stokes (ice dance)

Novice Winners:

Lloyd Eisler (men)
Diane Mae Ogibowski (women)
Julie Brault and Richard Gauthier (pairs)
Karyn and Rod Garossino (ice dance)

**European Championships.** 100 skaters from 19 countries participated in the European Championships at the Scandinavium arena in Gothenburg. In the pairs event, Soviet pairs swept the podium for the first time since 1977. In a stunning comeback, Irina Rodnina and Alexander Zaitsev claimed their seventh European title - her 11th! It was Rodnina's first international victory as a mother. The previous year's winners, Marina Cherkasova and Sergei Shakhrai, finished second and Marina Pestova and Stanislav Leonovich third. Manuela Mager and Uwe Bewersdorff of East Germany finished off the podium in fifth but made history as the first pair to successfully execute a throw triple Salchow at the European Championships. Natalia Linichuk and Gennadi Karponosov defended their ice dance title, but it was not a cakewalk. The second and third-place teams were so close that ordinal placings had to be calculated to determine who won the silver and bronze. Hungarians Krisztina Regőczy and András Sallay came out on top over Soviets Irina Moiseeva and Andrei Minenkov, with Britain's Jayne Torvill and Christopher Dean finishing just off the podium in fourth but gaining considerable attention with their dynamic style. Interestingly, Regőczy and Sallay and Moiseeva and Minenkov tied in places and Moiseeva and Minenkov had more points. Three-time defending champion Anett Pötzsch of East Germany took a decisive lead in the figures, but the short program was full of surprises. Pötzsch botched both jumps in her combination and finished a shocking ninth, while Denise Biellmann (regarded by many as the world's best free skater) fell on both a triple toe-loop and in her step sequence. Sitting in an unlucky 13th place overall heading into the free skate, Biellmann withdrew, citing a strained hip. The short program was won by West Germany's Dagmar Lurz, who took heat back at home that year for swearing under her breath at a photographer from *Der Spiegel*. Pötzsch rebounded with three triples in the free skate to defend her title, her closest competition in that phase of the competition coming from Yugoslavia's Sanda Dubravčić. Lurz took the silver; Susanna Driano of Italy the bronze. In the men's event, Vladimir Kovalev won the figures, Jan Hoffmann the short program and Robin Cousins the free skate. Kovalev and Hoffmann both attempted four triple jumps in the free skate to Cousins' three but their performances in the final phase of the competition paled in comparison to Cousins' stunning effort, which earned him three perfect 6.0s for artistic impression - including one from the Soviet judge. Cousins' coach Carlo Fassi was delighted with his performance, telling reporters, "I'm proud of him. I'm pleased with the way he skated under pressure." Cousins was only the third British man to claim the European men's crown. Graham Sharp was the first in 1939; John Curry the second in 1976.

**1980 EUROPEAN CHAMPIONSHIPS**
(Gothenburg, Sweden, January 22-27, 1980)

Men:

1. Robin Cousins (GRB)
2. Jan Hoffmann (GDR)
3. Vladimir Kovalev (SOV)
4. Igor Bobrin (SOV)
5. Hermann Schulz (GDR)
6. Jean-Christophe Simond (FRA)
7. Mario Liebers (GDR)
8. Konstantin Kokora (SOV)
9. Jozef Sabovčík (CZE)
10. Thomas Öberg (SWE)

Women:

1. Anett Pötzsch (GDR)
2. Dagmar Lurz (FRG)
3. Susanna Driano (ITA)
4. Kristiina Wegelius (FIN)
5. Sanda Dubravčić (YUG)
6. Debbie Cottrill (GRB)
7. Carola Weißenberg (GDR)
8. Danielle Rieder (SUI)
9. Karin Riediger (FRG)
10. Renata Baierová (CZE)

Pairs:

1. Irina Rodnina and Aleksandr Zaitsev (SOV)
2. Marina Cherkasova and Sergei Shakhrai (SOV)
3. Marina Pestova and Stanislav Leonovich (SOV)
4. Sabine Baeß and Tassilo Thierbach (GDR)
5. Manuela Mager and Uwe Bewersdorf (GDR)
6. Christina Riegel and Andreas Nischwitz (FRG)
7. Kerstin Stolfig and Veit Kempe (GDR)
8. Ingrid Spieglová and Alan Spiegl (CZE)
9. Gabrielle Beck and Jochen Stahl (FRG)
10. Maria Ježak and Lech Matuszewski (POL)

Ice Dance:

1. Natalia Linichuk and Gennadi Karponosov (SOV)
2. Krisztina Regőczy and András Sallay (HUN)
3. Irina Moiseeva and Andrei Minenkov (SOV)
4. Jayne Torvill and Christopher Dean (GRB)
5. Liliana Řeháková and Stanislav Drastich (CZE)
6. Natalia Bestemianova and Andrei Bukin (SOV)
7. Henriette Fröschl and Christian Steiner (FRG)
8. Karen Barber and Nicky Slater (GRB)
9. Susi and Peter Handschmann (SUI)
10. Anna Pisánská and Jiří Musil (CZE)

**Olympic Games.** In February, Lake Placid played host to the first Winter Olympics on American soil since 1960. Over 1000 athletes from 37 nations participated in the Games and several countries were represented in the figure skating events for the first time. Henriette Fröschl and Christian Steiner and Susi and Peter Handschmann were the first West German and Austrian ice dance teams at the Olympics. Sanda Dubravčić and Gloria Mas-Gil were the first women to represent Yugoslavia and Spain in singles. China had its very first representatives in Xu Zhaoxiao and Zhenghua Bao. The official mascot was a skating raccoon called Roni, a shortened version of the Mohawk name for raccoon - ati:ron. There was a minor controversy when organizers accidentally distributed a 'dummy list' of officials and skaters, which listed Lois Lane and Clark Kent as representatives of Yugoslavia in the pairs event. An East German journalist quipped, "The only true amateurs here are the organizers." The facilities used for athlete's quarters in the Olympic Village were anything but luxurious. They were set to be used as a prison after the Games. There were steel bars on the windows, tamper-proof electrical outlets and the doors had an inch and a half thick metal frames. There was no bathroom – only a sink - and skaters had to shower in shared facilities down the hall. Despite the grim accommodations, the world's best figure skaters flourished in the New York resort town. In the Opening Ceremony, Scott Hamilton, Jan Hoffmann and András Sallay carried the flags of the United States, East Germany and Hungary. Though the reigning European and World Champions Natalia Linichuk and Gennadi Karponosov led the ice dance competition from start to finish, their classical style did not resonate with American audiences as much as runners-up Krisztina Regőczy and András Sallay. The Hungarians got standing ovations for both their Foxtrot OSP and free dance and won the latter phase of the competition. Only one ordinal separated the top two teams. Irina Moiseeva and Andrei Minenkov took the bronze, making history as the first ice dance team to win medals in consecutive Olympic Games. Canadian Champions Lorna Wighton and John Dowding placed a strong sixth. Wighton and Dowding's coach Marijane Stong didn't shy away from pointing out the fact that Linichuk and Karponosov made several errors that were not reflected in their marks in the free dance. Wighton and Dowding told reporters they felt they should have been fourth, ahead of the Czechoslovakian team of Liliana Řeháková and Stanislav Drastich and Torvill and Dean. The pairs event was marketed as a classic East .vs. West showdown between defending Olympic Gold Medallists Irina Rodnina and Alexander Zaitsev and defending World Champions Tai Babilonia and Randy Gardner. The world watched on in shock when an injured Gardner fell twice in the warm-up attempting double flip jumps. The team was forced to withdraw moments before their music was played. Gardner had suffered a serious groin injury two weeks prior and had re-injured himself during a practice session at the Games. Babilonia and Gardner received thousands of telegrams wishing them well and a phone call from President Jimmy Carter. Their coach John Nicks told reporters, "There was no option. He wanted to go on, but I withdrew them. He had problems with the lifts and that would have been dangerous to her." Though Babilonia and Gardner's withdrawal overshadowed the event, Rodnina and Zaitsev put on quite a show. They dominated the event from start to finish, completing a difficult split triple twist and side-by-side double Axels in the winning free skate. The Soviets were the first pair to successfully defend an Olympic title since the Protopopovs in the 60s. Rodnina made history as the first pair skater to win three consecutive Olympic gold medals. The only other skater in history to win three Olympic golds was Sonja Henie, in the women's event. Marina Cherkasova and Sergei Shakhrai took the silver and East Germany's Manuela Mager and Uwe Bewersdorff the bronze. Canada's only entry, Barbara Underhill and Paul Martini placed a disappointing ninth.

**1980 WINTER OLYMPIC GAMES** (Lake Placid, NY, February 16-23, 1980)

Men:

1. Robin Cousins (GRB)
2. Jan Hoffmann (GDR)
3. Charlie Tickner (USA)
4. David Santee (USA)
5. Scott Hamilton (USA)
6. Igor Bobrin (SOV)
7. Jean-Christophe Simond (FRA)
8. Mitsuru Matsumura (JPN)
9. Fumio Igarashi (JPN)
10. Konstantin Kokora (SOV)

Women:

1. Anett Pötzsch (GDR)
2. Linda Fratianne (USA)
3. Dagmar Lurz (FRG)
4. Denise Biellmann (SUI)
5. Lisa-Marie Allen (USA)
6. Emi Watanabe (JPN)
7. Claudia Kristofics-Binder (AUT)
8. Susanna Driano (ITA)
9. Sandy Lenz (USA)
10. Kristiina Wegelius (FIN)

Pairs:

1. Irina Rodnina and Alexander Zaitsev (SOV)
2. Marina Cherkasova and Sergei Shakhrai (SOV)
3. Manuela Mager and Uwe Bewersdorff (GDR)
4. Marina Pestova and Stanislav Leonovich (SOV)
5. Kitty and Peter Carruthers (USA)
6. Sabine Baeß and Tassilo Thierbach (GDR)
7. Sheryl Franks and Michael Botticelli (USA)
8. Christina Riegel and Andreas Nischwitz (FRG)
9. Barbara Underhill and Paul Martini (CAN)
10. Susan Garland and Robert Daw (GRB)

Ice Dance:

1. Natalia Linichuk and Gennadi Karponosov (SOV)
2. Krisztina Regőczy and András Sallay (HUN)
3. Irina Moiseeva and Andrei Minenkov (SOV)
4. Liliana Řeháková and Stanislav Drastich (CZE)
5. Jayne Torvill and Christopher Dean (GRB)
6. Lorna Wighton and John Dowding (CAN)
7. Judy Blumberg and Michael Seibert (USA)
8. Natalia Bestemianova and Andrei Bukin (SOV)
9. Stacey Smith and John Summers (USA)
10. Henriette Fröschl and Christian Steiner (FRG)

Jan Hoffmann of East Germany won the men's figures, ahead of Americans Charlie Tickner and David Santee and Great Britain's Robin Cousins. Vladimir Kovalev placed a disappointing fifth and subsequently withdrew. Soviet officials cited a severe flu as the reason for his withdrawal but the North American press speculated that his reputation for being a partier may have been the real reason. Cousins rebounded with an remarkable short program set to Johnny Douglas' score from *The Railway Children*. He received the only perfect mark in the competition, a 6.0 for Presentation from Canadian judge Alice Pinos. First to skate in the final group in the free skate, Cousins attempted four triple jumps, missing only the triple loop. Jan Hoffmann's program was jam-packed with five triple jumps, but it wasn't enough to overcome Cousins, who became the second British man in history to claim the Olympic men's title. Charlie Tickner took the bronze with a dynamic program that featured three triple jumps. Much attention was placed on Tickner's age at the time of his medal win, though John Curry and Toller Cranston had also been 26 when they won medals at the Olympics just four years prior. Canadian Champion Brian Pockar had a disappointing outing, missing his combination in the short program and drawing first to skate in the free. He finished 12th overall. In the women's event, Anett Pötzsch, Dagmar Lurz and Linda Fratianne took the top three spots in the figures. In the short program, Fratianne was flawless to take the win. Pötzsch completed only a double/double combination instead of a triple but still hung onto the overall lead entering the free skate. Both Pötzsch and Fratianne delivered outstanding free skates, with Fratianne finishing second in that phase of the competition and Pötzsch third. The winner of the free skate was Switzerland's Denise Biellmann. Had figures not been a part of the competition, Biellmann would have won the gold medal, but a 12th place finish in the figures kept her off the podium in fourth. Pötzsch claimed the gold and Fratianne the silver. Lurz, who placed fifth and sixth in the short and free, took the bronze. Canada's Heather Kemkaran was 15th – five spots lower than the "goal" the COA had set for her. To this day, strong opinions and conspiracy theories abound surrounding the results of the men's, women's and ice dance events in Lake Placid, with some skating aficionados believing that there was some wheeling and dealing going on. At the time of the events, Mary-Lucile Ager aptly noted, "This seems to be the year of controversial winners of major championships. Today's audiences get very involved and vocal which is good for the sport. Perhaps part of the problem is having so many good skaters in top positions that only a small mistake makes the difference between winning and losing."

*Below: Anett Pötzsch, Jutta Müller and Jan Hoffmann. Contributor: dpa picture alliance / Alamy Stock Photo.*

*Above: Irina Rodnina and Aleksandr Zaitsev. Photo by Fred & Joan Dean, courtesy Paul Dean, "Ice & Roller Skate" magazine archive.*

**World Championships.** In many Olympic years, it is common for a handful of top contenders to skip the World Championships that follow. That was not the case at the Westfalenhallen in Dortmund in 1980, where Irina Rodnina and Alexander Zaitsev were the only Olympic Medallists not to compete due to Rodnina's strained left shoulder. 119 skaters from 23 nations participated, with Wang Zhili, Liu Zhiying, Luan Bo and Yao Bin making history as the first Chinese skaters to compete at the World Championships. Skaters jockeyed for positions in the men's figures, with David Santee taking an early lead but dropping to second overall behind Jan Hoffmann. Charlie Tickner, Jean-Christophe Simond and Robin Cousins rounded out the top five. Cousins slipped during the straight line step sequence in the short program but skated otherwise brilliantly, earning seven marks of 5.9 for Presentation and winning that phase of the competition. Jan Hoffmann had the skate of his life in the free skate, landing six triples. Cousins executed five and skated even better than he did at the Olympics, earning three perfect marks, including 6.0s for both Technical Merit and Artistic Impression from the Soviet judge. They were the only 6.0s awarded during the Championships. Cousins' result in the figures narrowly kept him behind Hoffmann overall, to the delight of Hoffmann's coach Jutta Müller. Frau Müller had coached Christine Errath, Anett Pötzsch and her daughter Gaby Seyfert to the top of the podium at the World Championships, but Hoffmann was her first male student to win the crown. Tickner skated better than he did in Lake Placid to secure the bronze, ahead of Santee, Scott Hamilton and Japan's Mitsuru Matsumura. Canada's only entry, Brian Pockar, bettered his Olympic effort with a top-ten finish. Grzegorz Filipowski of Poland landed an incredible nine triple jumps, including the first triple toe-loop/triple toe-loop combination in a senior ISU Championship. The judges placed him 15th. 1964 Olympic Gold Medallist Manfred Schnelldorfer told reporters Filipowski should have received 5.8s and 5.9s - not 5.2s. With reigning Olympic Gold Medallists Rodnina and Zaitsev and World Champions Tai Babilonia and Randy Gardner not in attendance, the pairs title was very much up for grabs. Stanislav Zhuk's students Marina Cherkasova and Sergei Shakhrai rose to the occasion, decisively winning over three other Eastern Bloc pairs: Manuela Mager and Uwe Bewersdorf, Marina Pestova and Stanislav Leonovich and Sabine Baeß and Tassilo Thierbach. Of the four top pairs, Mager and Bewersdorf were the crowd favourites. It was a highly disappointing event for Canada's Barbara Underhill and Paul Martini, who finished 11th for the second year in a row at the Worlds. A fourth-place finish in the figures behind Anett Pötzsch, Dagmar Lurz and Claudia Kristofics-Binder crushed Linda Fratianne's dream of defending her World title before the free skating events even started. Switzerland's Denise Biellmann, only tenth in figures, won the short program, with Emi Watanabe of Japan second and Fratianne third. The short program continued to be the nemesis of Anett Pötzsch, who placed only sixth. Fratianne won the free skate, landing two different triples and earning two marks of 5.9, but it wasn't enough for her to make up the deficit. Pötzsch and Lurz took the top two spots on the podium despite delivering performances that weren't as strong as those they gave in Lake Placid. Denise Biellmann fell on an exceedingly rare triple Lutz attempt and finished sixth overall. In her debut at the World Championships, Tracey Wainman of Canada climbed from 21st after the figures to 14th overall. Wainman landed a triple Salchow in the free skate and even found time to wave to her mother. This endeared Wainman to the West German audience, who gave her a rousing ovation. Upsets were rare in ice dance but history was made in Dortmund when Krisztina Regőczy and András Sallay came from behind to win gold over Natalia Linichuk and Gennadi Karponosov. It was the first time a Hungarian ice dance team won a World title and the first time an Olympic gold medal-winning ice dance team was dethroned at the Worlds. Ironically, Linichuk and Karponosov had managed to dethrone the reigning World Champions Irina Moiseeva and Andrei Minenkov at the Worlds just two years prior in Ottawa. 'Min and Mo' finished third in Dortmund.

**1980 WORLD CHAMPIONSHIPS**
(Dortmund, West Germany, March 11-16, 1980)

Men:

1. Jan Hoffmann (GDR)
2. Robin Cousins (GRB)
3. Charlie Tickner (USA)
4. David Santee (USA)
5. Scott Hamilton (USA)
6. Mitsuru Matsumura (JPN)
7. Igor Bobrin (SOV)
8. Fumio Igarashi (JPN)
9. Brian Pockar (CAN)
10. Hermann Schulz (GDR)

Women:

1. Anett Pötzsch (GDR)
2. Dagmar Lurz (FRG)
3. Linda Fratianne (USA)
4. Emi Watanabe (JPN)
5. Claudia Kristofics-Binder (AUT)
6. Denise Biellmann (SUI)
7. Lisa-Marie Allen (USA)
8. Kristiina Wegelius (FIN)
9. Debbie Cottrill (GRB)
10. Katarina Witt (GDR)

Pairs:

1. Marina Cherkasova and Sergei Shakhrai (SOV)
2. Manuela Mager and Uwe Bewersdorf (GDR)
3. Marina Pestova and Stanislav Leonovich (SOV)
4. Sabine Baeß and Tassilo Thierbach (GDR)
5. Christina Riegel and Andreas Nischwitz (FRG)
6. Veronika Pershina and Marat Akbarov (SOV)
7. Kitty and Peter Carruthers (USA)
8. Ingrid Spieglová and Alan Spiegl (CZE)
9. Cornelia Haufe and Kersten Bellmann (GDR)
10. Sheryl Franks and Michael Botticelli (USA)

Ice Dance:

1. Krisztina Regőczy and András Sallay (HUN)
2. Natalia Linichuk and Gennadi Karponosov (SOV)
3. Irina Moiseeva and Andrei Minenkov (SOV)
4. Jayne Torvill and Christopher Dean (GRB)
5. Lorna Wighton and John Dowding (CAN)
6. Judy Blumberg and Michael Seibert (USA)
7. Natalia Karamysheva and Rostislav Sinitsyn (SOV)
8. Stacey Smith and John Summers (USA)
9. Henriette Fröschl and Christian Steiner (FRG)
10. Karen Barber and Nicky Slater (GRB)

Crowd favourites Jayne Torvill and Christopher Dean finished just off the podium in fourth, with Canadian duos Lorna Wighton and John Dowding and Marie McNeil and Rob McCall placing fifth and 13th. McNeil and McCall were the first skaters from Atlantic Canada to compete at the World Championships in any discipline.

## PERSONALITIES

### JAN HOFFMANN

Date of Birth: October 26, 1955
Place of Birth: Dresden, East Germany
Coach: Jutta Müller
Choreographer: Rudi Suchy
Home Club: SC Einheit Dresden

### ROBIN COUSINS

Date of Birth: August 17, 1957
Place of Birth: Bristol, England
Coach: Carlo and Christa Fassi
Choreographer: Christa Fassi, Robin Cousins
Home Club: Queen's Ice Club London

### CHARLIE TICKNER

Date of Birth: November 13, 1953
Place of Birth: Layafette, CA
Coach: Norma Sahlin
Choreographer: Norma Sahlin
Home Club: Denver FSC

### ANETT PÖTZSCH

Date of Birth: September 3, 1960
Place of Birth: Karl-Marx-Stadt, East Germany
Coach: Jutta Müller
Choreographer: Rudi Suchy
Home Club: SC Karl-Marx-Stadt

### LINDA FRATIANNE

Date of Birth: August 2, 1960
Place of Birth: Northridge, CA
Coach: Frank Carroll
Choreographer: Bob Paul, Ricky Harris
Home Club: Los Angeles FSC

### DAGMAR LURZ

Date of Birth: January 18, 1959
Place of Birth: Dortmund, West Germany
Coach: Erich Zeller, Carlo Fassii
Home Club: ERC Westphalia

### EMI WATANABE

Date of Birth: August 27, 1959
Place of Birth: Tokyo, Japan
Coach: Carlo and Christa Fassi
Choreographer: Christa Fassi
Home Club: Senshu

### SUSANNA DRIANO

Date of Birth: May 28, 1957
Place of Birth: Seattle, WA
Coach: Carlo and Christa Fassi
Choreographer: John Curry, Christa Fassi
Home Club: Associazione Sportivi Ghiaccio Ambrosiana

### HEATHER KEMKARAN

Date of Birth: August 2, 1958
Place of Birth: Winnipeg, MB
Coach: Ellen Burka
Choreographer: Brian Foley
Home Club: Toronto Cricket, Skating and Curling Club

### IRINA RODNINA AND ALEKSANDR ZAITSEV

Date of Birth: September 12, 1949/June 16, 1952
Place of Birth: Moscow, Soviet Union/Leningrad, Soviet Union
Coach: Tatiana Tarasova
Choreographer: Valeria Kokhanovskaya, Tatyana Matrosova
Home Club: CSKA Moscow

### TAI BABILONIA AND RANDY GARDNER

Date of Birth: September 22, 1959/December 2, 1958
Place of Birth: Los Angeles, CA
Coach: John Nicks
Choreographer: Ricky Harris
Home Club: Los Angeles FSC/Santa Monica FSC

### MARINA CHERKASOVA AND SERGEI SHAKHRAI

Date of Birth: November 17, 1964/June 28, 1958
Place of Birth: Moscow, Soviet Union
Coach: Stanislav Zhuk
Choreographer: Nina Domanovskaya
Home Club: CSKA Moscow

### MANUELA MAGER AND UWE BEWERSDORFF

Date of Birth: July 11, 1962
Place of Birth: Dresden, East Germany/Freital, East Germany
Coach: Uta Hohenhaus
Home Club: SC Einheit Dresden

### MARINA PESTOVA AND STANISLAV LEONOVICH

Date of Birth: December 20, 1963/August 2, 1958
Place of Birth: Sverdlovsk, Soviet Union
Coach: Stanislav Zhuk
Home Club: CSKA Moscow

### BIRGIT LORENZ AND KNUT SCHUBERT

Date of Birth: August 20, 1963/September 9, 1958
Place of Birth: East Berlin, East Germany/Bautzen, East Germany
Coach: Heidemarie Walther-Steiner
Home Club: SC Dynamo Berlin

### SABINE BAEß AND TASSILO THIERBACH

Date of Birth: March 15, 1961/May 21, 1956
Place of Birth: Dresden, East Germany/Karl Marx-Stadt, East Germany
Coach: Irene Salzmann
Home Club: SC Karl-Marx-Stadt

### CHRISTINA RIEGEL AND ANDREAS NISCHWITZ

Date of Birth: August 25, 1965/April 1, 1957
Place of Birth: Stuttgart, West Germany/Leinfelden, West Germany
Coach: Karel Fajfr
Home Club: TuS Stuttgart

### KITTY AND PETER CARRUTHERS

Date of Birth: May 30, 1961/July 22, 1959
Place of Birth: Boston, MA
Coach: Ron Ludington
Choreographer: Ricky Harris
Home Club: SC of Wilmington

### IRINA MOISEEVA AND ANDREI MINENKOV

Date of Birth: July 5, 1955/December 6, 1954
Place of Birth: Moscow, Soviet Union
Coach: Lyudmila Pakhomova, Natalia Dubova
Choreographer: Valeria Kokhanovskaya, Elena Matveeva
Home Club: Lokomotiv

### NATALIA LINICHUK AND GENNADI KARPONOSOV

Date of Birth: February 6, 1956/November 21, 1950
Place of Birth: Moscow, Soviet Union
Coach: Elena Tchaikovskaya
Choreographer: Valeria Kokhanovskaya
Home Club: Dynamo Moscow

### KRISZTINA REGŐCZY AND ANDRÁS SALLAY

Date of Birth: April 19, 1955/December 15, 1953
Place of Birth: Budapest, Hungary
Coach: Betty and Roy Callaway

### LORNA WIGHTON AND JOHN DOWDING

Date of Birth: June 2, 1958/April 23, 1956
Place of Birth: Toronto, ON/Oakville, ON
Coach: Marijane Stong, Bernie Ford
Choreographer: André Denis
Home Club: Granite Club

### STACEY SMITH AND JOHN SUMMERS

Date of Birth: April 3, 1954/April 4, 1957
Place of Birth: Delaware, OH/Bethesda, MD
Coach: Ron Ludington
Choreographer: Diane Agle, Ron Ludington
Home Club: SC of Wilmington

*Robin Cousins. Contributor: PA Images / Alamy Stock Photo.*

## THE SOUNDTRACK OF SKATING

*BRIAN POCKAR*

SP: "The Great Air Race" from *Those Magnificent Men in Their Flying Machines*
FS: "Yugoslav Wedding" from *Summer Holiday*

*HEATHER KEMKARAN*

SP: Rumanian Folk Song
FS: "Carmen" by Bizet/"Le Beau Danube" Ballet by Strauss

*TRACEY WAINMAN*

SP: "Klipp-Klapp Galop" by Strauss
FS: "Gayene" by Khachaturian

*BARBARA UNDERHILL AND PAUL MARTINI*

SP: "Pas de deux du Corsaire" by Drigo
FS: "Jewels of the Madonna - Festa Populaire" by Wolf-Ferrari/"Pagliacci-Intermezzo" by Leoncavallo/"Jewels of the Madonna - Danza Napolitana" by Drigo

*LORNA WIGHTON AND JOHN DOWDING*

OSP: "Music Makers" by Don Raye
FD: "Overture", "Tiger Rag", Theme from *Ben*, "Chopsticks" by Liberace

*MARIE MCNEIL AND ROB MCCALL*

OSP: "Cataline Bounce" by Paul Weirick and Jan Garber
FD: "Rock Around The Clock" by Max Freedman and Jimmy de Knight/"Montoona Clipper" by Wes Hensel/"Le Piano Sur la Vogue" by Paul Mauriat/"12th St. Rag" by Euday L. Bowman and James S. Sumner

# Share your favourite 80s skating photos, memories and stories on social media using the hashtag #TheSk80s

*Jayne Torvill and Christopher Dean. Photo by Fred & Joan Dean, courtesy Fred Dean, "Ice & Roller Skate" magazine archive.*

# 1980-1981 SEASON

Hit Songs: "Bette Davis Eyes" by Kim Carnes, "Lady" by Kenny Rogers, "Jessie's Girl" by Rick Springfield, "9 to 5" by Dolly Parton", "Morning Train (Nine To Five)" by Sheena Easton
Hit Movies: Raiders Of The Lost Ark, Chariots Of Fire, On Golden Pond, Arthur, History of the World (Part 1)
Hit TV: Dallas, The Dukes of Hazzard, The Love Boat, The Jeffersons, Little House on the Prairie
News: Murder of John Lennon, Iran-Iraq War, Inauguration of U.S. President Ronald Reagan, Assassination Attempt of Pope John Paul II, Toronto Bathhouse Raids

## PEOPLE

As is always the case following an Olympic season, several skaters turned professional or retired. Robin Cousins accepted an offer from *Holiday on Ice* and was featured on the famous ITV series *This Is Your Life*. Krisztina Regőczy and András Sallay joined the cast of the *Ice Follies*. Irina Rodnina and Alexander Zaitsev announced their retirement. Rodnina took up coaching, working with young Soviet pairs Veronika Pershina and Marat Akbarov and Inna Bekker and Sergei Lichanski. Zaitsev became the General Secretary of the Figure Skating Section of the USSR Federation. Linda Fratianne signed with the William Morris Agency and formed her own production company in association with Burt Sugarman, a Hollywood producer who worked at the Billboard Music Awards. She appeared in The Big Show and as a headliner for *Holiday on Ice*'s show at Aladdin Hotel in Las Vegas. Charlie Tickner and Lorna Wighton and John Dowding signed contracts with the *Ice Capades*. Jan Hoffmann and Dagmar Lurz both hung up their skates to study medicine. Also leaving the amateur ranks were Manuela Mager and Uwe Bewersdorff, Emi Watanabe, Heather Kemkaran, Liliana Řeháková and Stanislav Drastich and Stacey Smith and John Summers.

In July, a baby was born in Torrance, California to Chinese immigrants from Hong Kong. Little did Michelle Kwan's parents know that their daughter would become one of the most decorated figure skaters in the world in the 90s.

The 1980-1981 season marked the debut of Jamesville Jake and Delwood Loop - The Loop Brothers. David and Jimmie Santee, skating's answer to the Blues Brothers, made their debut in Sun Valley in the summer.

At a ceremony in August, Sheldon Galbraith made history as the first figure skating coach to be inducted into Canada's Sports Hall of Fame. Galbraith had coached a who's who of Canadian figure skating over the years, including Barbara Ann Scott, Frances Dafoe and Norris Bowden, Barbara Wagner and Bob Paul and Donald Jackson. Inductees were selected by an esteemed national selection committee chaired by Ontario Athletes Commissioner James Vipond.

Mr. and Mrs. F. Ritter Shumway celebrated their fiftieth wedding anniversary in September. An institution in American figure skating, F. Ritter Shumway was a former USFSA President, founder of the Memorial Fund and a national dance judge.

The figure skating community said goodbye to many well-known figures during the 1980-1981 season. John Nicks' sister and pairs partner Jennifer suffered a fatal heart attack at the age of 48 in August. The Nicks siblings represented the UK at two Olympic Games, winning both the European and World pairs title in 1953. The following month in Le Chesnay, France, ISU President Jacques Favart of France passed away after suffering from a heart attack after major surgery. At the time of Favart's death in 1980, John R. Shoemaker remarked, "He was intelligent, fair, honest, forceful, innovative, gifted with a marvellous sense of humour, and in every way a person eminently fitted to lead our sport." László Szollás passed away at the age of 73 in Budapest in early October. A physician by profession, Szollás won two Olympic medals and four World titles in the 30s with partner Emília Rotter and later served as President of the Hungarian Skating Association and an international judge. Joachim 'Joe' Geisler passed away the day after Szollás in Quebec. A Canadian Champion during World War II, Geisler served on the Board of Directors of the CFSA and as President of Patinage Quebec. He was a strong advocate for Quebec skaters in CFSA matters and was the Chairman of the first Canada Winter Games. Former USFSA President and international judge H. Kendall Kelley passed away at the age of 83 just two days before Hallowe'en, proving bad things indeed do happen in three's. Olympic Silver Medallist and Canadian Champion Guy Revell tragically committed suicide in Vancouver in March, having struggled to move on when his professional skating career with the *Ice Capades* came to an end. In June, Elna Montgomery, the first woman to win a gold medal at the Swedish Championships and represent her country at the Olympics during the Edwardian era, passed away at the age of 95. A remarkable woman and skating pioneer, Montgomery was so enamoured with the sport that she staged a comeback to competition when she was 38 years old.

A well-timed grant from the Nottingham City Council allowed Jayne Torvill and Christopher Dean the opportunity to take their skating to the next level and train with coach Betty Callaway in Oberstdorf, West Germany, where they could get more ice time. Torvill left her job with an insurance company; Dean quit the Nottingham Police Force. Dean told reporter Frank Taylor, "John Curry and Robin Cousins proved you have to concentrate absolutely on skating and travel abroad for training and competition to become a champion. That's what we have been forced to do. Only time will prove whether it is a wise decision or not."

John Curry traded in his skates for soliloquies in October, making his tage debut in Zev Buffman and The Shubert Organization's adaptation of *Brigadoon* on Broadway, opposite Martin Vidnovic and Meg Bussert. Theater critic Frank Rich mused, "Although Mr. Curry's acting doesn't redeem the evening's villain, his execution of Miss de Mille's famous sword dance is a fine display of delicate physical agility."

Canadian figure skating pioneer Louis Rubenstein was posthumously inducted into the International Jewish Sports Hall of Fame in December in New York. Rubenstein served as President of the CFSA's precursor, the Figure Skating Department of the Amateur Skating Association of Canada and won a gold medal for compulsory figures at an international figure skating competition in St. Petersburg in February of 1890 which marked the 25th anniversary of the historic Neva Skating Association.

History was made just before Christmas when Peggy Fleming became the first figure skater to perform at the White House. Her performance on the South Lawn for President Jimmy Carter, First Lady Rosalynn Carter and hundreds of aides and Secret Service personnel was aired in a segment on World of People in February.

Following in the footsteps of Belita and John Curry, Robin Cousins became the third figure skating 'castaway' featured on the popular BBC Radio program *Desert Island Discs* in January. Each guest was asked to name their favourite piece of music, book and a luxury item. Cousins chose Bizet's "Carmen", James Clavell's *Shogun* and Marzipan.

Richard Dwyer left the *Ice Follies* after a starring role as Mr. Debonair that spanned decades. He later joined the cast of the *Ice Capades* and skated in a series of shows at the Hyatt Regency Hotel in Dubai. Dwyer later recalled, "It was 120 degrees outside but nice and cool inside and the kids were phenomenal."

Around the time of the World Championships in March, an East Berlin newspaper announced the retirement of Anett Pötzsch. The paper alleged that the reason for her retirement wasn't an injury, as previously reported, but instead her involvement "in a dispute with the sports authorities... which led to her suspension." Natalia Linichuk and Gennadi Karponosov also retired from competition, after losing the European title. Linichuk accepted Karponosov's marriage proposal and the Olympic Gold Medallists tied the knot the summer after the 1980-1981 season ended.

In May, Carlo Fassi presented the first Coaches' Clinic at the Broadmoor Skating Club. The two-day educational event featured sessions conducted by the Fassi's, Barbara Roles, Christine Haigler Krall, Pieter Kollen, Carol Heiss and Hayes and David Jenkins. Heiss was the new associate skating pro at the Cleveland Skating Club, having previously worked as a commentator for both ABC and CBS.

Olympic Silver Medallist and two-time World Champion Norris Bowden was the proud recipient of the Professional Engineers Association of Canada's Citizenship Award. A life insurance underwriter and figure skating judge, Bowden was also the founding President of the Centennial Nursery School in Toronto, which served children with intellectual disabilities.

There were four inductees to figure skating's Halls of Fame in 1981. Madge Syers, the first woman to hold both the Olympic and World title, was posthumously elected to the World Figure Skating Hall of Fame, as was Willie Frick, the German-born coach of a who's who of American figure skating, including Maribel Vinson Owen, Tenley Albright, Gretchen van Zandt Merrill and Theresa Weld Blanchard and Nathaniel Niles. William O. Hickok IV, a high-ranking USFSA and ISU official who played an instrumental role in ice dancing's inclusion in the World Championships, was posthumously inducted into both the U.S. and American Halls of Fame. Harold Hartshorne, a prominent international judge and U.S. Champion in ice dancing who tragically perished in the 1961 Sabena Crash, was inducted into the U.S. Hall of Fame.

# AROUND THE WORLD

**Canada.** The CFSA had over 160 000 members. For the first time, two athletes (Robin Cowan and Debbie Albright) were appointed to the Board of Directors, giving a voice to competitive skaters in the Association's affairs. The official announcement in June that Ottawa would play host to the 1984 World Championships caused great excitement.

**China.** After making their debut at the Olympics and World Championships the season prior, China sent its first team to the World Junior Championships during the 1980-1981 season. The country's skating program had several interruptions since it formally started in 1956, and little outside influence aside from an exchange program from Czechoslovakia that was cancelled in the 60s. Skaters received full government support from state-sponsored sports schools and the cost of their costumes, skates and instruction was all fully covered but there were less than half a dozen indoor rinks in the country and only 300 registered skaters in the country. Coach Wang Junxiang told reporters, "We still have a long way to go in training methods."

**South Africa.** Barred from participating in the Olympics and ISU Championships due to the country's policy of apartheid in 1977, South African figure skating became quite insular during the 80s. The country continued to hold annual National Championships which, since television's debut in the country in 1975, helped grow interest in the sport. However, no efforts were made to revive the Skate Safari international competitions of the 70s which saw entries from Austria, Great Britain, South Africa the U.S. and West Germany. As individual federations and not the ISU were responsible for the rosters at international competitions, a handful of skaters did compete abroad on a limited basis. A small contingent, consisting of skaters Rick Simons and Irene Anderson, judge Larry Sanders and coach Basil Michael travelled from Johannesburg to compete in Tours, France in the early 80s. In 1982, Simons won the South African Police's Sportsman of the Year Award. The South African Ice Skating Association regularly published a periodical in the 80s called *The Outside Edge*. An article penned during the decade by Rev. Kevin Reynolds outlined SAISA's efforts to be reinstated to the ISU throughout the 80s, which included sending delegates to every ISU Congress to petition for the country's reinstatement. Many in the South African skating community were opposed to the National Party's apartheid ideals and were frustrated with the role both national and international politicians played in thwarting the country's return to the international figure skating scene. Rev. Reynolds wrote, "It must be honestly admitted that for a long time now (and likely for many years to come) the South African sporting fraternity has been forced to pay the bitter and costly price of being part of the world's pariah... Yet, despite such political adversity, SAISA's members and activities have only continued to flourish... [with] the most brilliant ray of hope... that one day its skaters will return to international competition."

**United States.** In a move towards inclusivity, the USFSA's solo requirement for all dance tests was removed for all legally blind or deaf candidates. The Las Vegas Figure Skating Club sponsored a skating outing for visually impaired skaters, working with a teacher at the Las Vegas School for the Blind. 20 sighted skaters were paired with blind and partially sighted skaters. The USFSA's Squaw Valley training center closed due to the high cost of operations, while the training center in Colorado Springs expanded. Paul Wylie acknowledged that many skaters "took it for granted that the training centers... would always exist... Other countries have them, and it is one of our best chances to get ahead of them. The training centers are a great asset to our future international, World and Olympic teams." When "one door closes another opens"... one of the world's most unusual rinks opened near Milford, Michigan. No one was allowed to skate at the rink at the General Motors Proving Grounds' all-weather test facility. The rink, which had its own Zamboni, was used exclusively to test how vehicles would perform in icy conditions.

## BEHIND THE SCENES

ISU President Jacques Favart was re-elected at the ISU's 1980 Congress and no one in the sport's governing body could have predicted his sudden death. Per the Union's Constitution, ISU Vice-President Olaf Poulsen was promoted to President.

The extensive boycott of the 1980 Summer Olympics in Moscow reverberated into the figure skating world during the 1980-1981 season. In the 80s, fall international competitions like Skate Canada and the NHK Trophy were all invitational events organized by skating associations, not events sanctioned by the ISU. After "a lengthy philosophical debate", the CFSA made a decision not to invite Soviet skaters to Skate Canada and boycott the Prize of Moscow News competition in solidarity with the COA's Boycott of the 1980 Summer Games. In turn, the East German federation declined the CFSA's invitation to send skaters to the event. As the World Junior Championships in London, Ontario were an ISU Championship, the CFSA had no choice but to allow the Soviets to compete.

As new competitions like the U.S. and World Professional Championships cropped up, the ISU tightened its rules surrounding amateurism, restricting professional skaters to 20 percent of the total cast in any kind of sanctioned exhibition, film or television production.

A new scoring system was adopted by the ISU which allowed each part of a competition to be judged separately, factored and totaled for placement. In an article in *Skating*, British sportswriter Howard Bass explained how the system worked thusly: "Instead of the outcome being determined by the overall placings of the judges in the competition as a whole, their placings in each in the competition's three sections will be factored thus: The position a skater is placed in the figures will be multiplied by 0.6. His position in the short free skating will be multiplied by 0.4. His position in the long will not be factorized. By this means a skater coming fourth in the figures (4 X 0.6), second in the short free (2 X 0.4) and second in the long free (2 X 1) would end up with a total placement of 5.2. The lowest placement of any skater thus calculated would be the winner..."

If it had been used during the past four years, Robin Cousins would have been World Champion twice, in 1978 (instead of Charlie Tickner) and in 1979 (instead of Vladimir Kovalev) but he would not have won the Olympic gold medal in 1980. By the same token, Linda Fratianne would have been the World Champion for the past four years and Anett Pötzsch would have been denied the title she gained in 1978 and 1980. Thus it could be argued that the ISU is really implying that the wrong people sometimes won in recent seasons. For this reason if for no other, one wonders if there is enough justification for altering the system in the way that it has been."

## BOOKS AND MAGAZINES

Conceived in the fall of 1980, *American Skating World* published its first issue in April of 1981. The newspaper took pride in being independent from any skating association and this freedom allowed them to cover the sport and skaters quite openly. Unlike *Skating* and the *Canadian Skater*, which largely covered the amateur side of the sport, *American Skating World* provided extensive coverage of the professional skating world. Skating officials called the newspaper the *National Enquirer of Skating*.

Mental health was a taboo topic in figure skating circles in the early 80s and sports psychology was also viewed with a certain amount of skepticism by some coaches. Bill Haggett, an off-ice professional from Tufts University's Athletic Department, took a risk by releasing a sports psychology book marketed to figure skaters called *In Time to be a Champion*. Haggett's techniques were endorsed by Dr. Tenley Albright.

## MUSIC

Just two years after the invention of the Sony Walkman, a company in Novato, California invented the Skatetape - a custom vest that contained a 'micro-recorder unit', allowing skaters to listen to their program music without relying on their rink's PA system. The Skatetape never caught on, largely because it wasn't exactly cheap at 130 dollars American a pop.

## FASHION

The always fashion-forward JoJo Starbuck was featured in a print ad campaign for Lycra Freedom-in-Motion leotards.

Polar Sport Ltd. had a hit with 'Le Suit', a unisex double-knit polyester bodysuit designed specifically for skaters. The pants had full-length zippers so that skaters could drop their drawers without taking off their skates. Designer Anya Robertson purposefully trimmed 'Le Suit' with vertical lines to make skaters look taller.

# Fall Internationals

**1980 COUPES DES ALPES (Saint Gervais, France and Oberstdorf, West Germany, August 23-26 and August 31-September 2, 1980)**

Grand Prix de St. Gervais Winners:

Brian Orser (CAN) - men
Vikki de Vries (USA) - women
Nelli Chervotkina and Viktor Teslia (SOV) - pairs
Olga Volozhinskaya and Alexandr Svinin (SOV) - ice dance

Nebelhorn Trophy (Oberstdorf) Winners:

Tom Dickson (USA) - men
Vikki de Vries (USA) - women
Susan Garland and Robert Daw (GRB) - pairs
Wendy Sessions and Stephen Williams (GRB) - ice dance

**1980 GRAND PRIZE SNP (Banská Bystrica, Czechoslovakia)**

Winners:

Petr Barna (CZE) - men
Nadia Romaniuk (GDR) - women
Katarina Barta and Tobias Schröter (GDR) - pairs
Elena Batanova and Alexei Soloviev (SOV) - ice dance

**1980 ASKÖ CUP OF VIENNA (Vienna, Austria)**

Men:

1. Falko Kirsten (GDR)
2. Leonid Kaznakov (SOV)
3. Neil Paterson (CAN)

Women:

1. Katarina Witt (GDR)
2. Andrea Rohm (AUT)
3. Cornelia Tesch (FRG)

**1980 ST. IVEL ICE INTERNATIONAL (London, England, September 29-October 2, 1980)**

Men:

1. Brian Pockar (CAN)
2. Scott Hamilton (USA)
3. Fumio Igarashi (JPN)

Women:

1. Sandy Lenz (USA)
2. Tracey Wainman (CAN)
3. Sanda Dubravčić (YUG)

Pairs:

1. Barbara Underhill and Paul Martini (CAN)
2. Inna Volanskaia and Valeriy Spiridonov (SOV)
3. Susan Garland and Robert Daw (GRB)

Ice Dance:

1. Jayne Torvill and Christopher Dean (GRB)
2. Elena Garanina and Igor Zavozin (SOV)
3. Karen Barber and Nicky Slater (GRB)

**1980 SKATE CANADA (Calgary, AB, October 30-November 1, 1980)**

Men:

1. Scott Hamilton (USA)
2. Brian Pockar (CAN)
3. David Santee (USA)

Women:

1. Elaine Zayak (USA)
2. Tracey Wainman (CAN)
3. Claudia Kristofics-Binder (AUT)

Ice Dance:

1. Judy Blumberg and Michael Seibert (USA)
2. Karen Barber and Nicky Slater (GRB)
3. Marie McNeil and Rob McCall (CAN)

**1980 RICHMOND TROPHY (London, England, November 2-3, 1980)**

Women:

1. Karen Wood (GRB)
2. Janina Wirth (GDR)
3. Carola Paul (GDR)

**1980 PRAGUE SKATE (Prague, Czechoslovakia, November 1980)**

Men:

1. Jozef Sabovčík (CZE)
2. Daniel Béland (CAN)
3. Grzegorz Głowania (POL)

Women:

1. Carola Paul (GDR)
2. Anna Kondrashova (SOV)
3. Megumi Yanagihara (JPN)

Pairs:

1. Birgit Lorenz and Knut Schubert (GDR)
2. Becky Hough and Mark Rowsom (CAN)
3. Ingrid Zenata and René Novotný (CZE)

Ice Dance:

1. Elena Garanina and Igor Zavozin (SOV)
2. Jana Beránková and Jan Barták (CZE)
3. Gina Aucoin and Hans-Peter Ponikau (CAN)

# Fall Internationals

**1980 ENNIA CHALLENGE CUP INTERNATIONAL FREE SKATING COMPETITION** (The Hague, Netherlands, November 11-16, 1980)

Men:

1. Jean-Christophe Simond (FRA)
2. Mark Cockerell (USA)
3. Daniel Béland (CAN)

Women:

1. Jacki Farrell (USA)
2. Katarina Witt (GDR)
3. Megumi Yanagihara (JPN)

Pairs:

1. Christina Riegel and Andreas Nischwitz (FRG)
2. Kitty and Peter Carruthers (USA)
3. Susan Garland and Robert Daw (GRB)

Ice Dance:

1. Natalia Bestemianova and Andrei Bukin (SOV)
2. Natalia Karymysheva and Rostislav Sinitsyn (SOV)
3. Wendy Sessions and Stephen Williams (GRB)

**1980 POKAL DER BLAUEN SCHWERTER** (Karl-Marx-Stadt, East Germany, November 13-15, 1980)

Men:

1. Grzegorz Głowania (POL)
2. Didier Monge (FRA)
3. Falko Kirsten (GDR)

Women:

1. Anett Pötzsch (GDR)
2. Svetlana Frantsuzova (SOV)
3. Janina Wirth (GDR)

Pairs:

1. Inna Volyanskaya and Valery Spiridonov (SOV)
2. Birgit Lorenz and Knut Schubert (GDR)
3. Cornelia Hauffe and Kersten Bellmann (GDR)

**1980 GOLDEN SPIN OF ZAGREB** (Zagreb, Yugoslavia, November 19-23, 1980)

Men:

1. Jimmie Santee (USA)
2. Ralf Lewandoswki (GDR)
3. Hervé Pornet (FRA)

Women:

1. Sanda Dubravčić (YUG)
2. Priscilla Hill (USA)
3. Janina Wirth (GDR)

*Rob McCall. Courtesy of the Dalhousie University Photographic Collection, PC 1, Box 36, Folder 24, Item 7.*

**1980 NHK TROPHY** (Sapporo, Japan, November 27-30, 1980)

Men:

1. Fumio Igarashi (JPN)
2. Robert Wagenhoffer (USA)
3. Allen Schramm (USA)

Women:

1. Denise Biellmann (SUI)
2. Katarina Witt (GDR)
3. Melissa Thomas (USA)

Pairs:

1. Barbara Underhill and Paul Martini (CAN)
2. Maria Di Domenico and Burt Lancon (USA)
3. Toshimi Ito and Takashi Mura (JPN)

Ice Dance:

1. Carol Fox and Richard Dalley (USA)
2. Karen Barber and Nicky Slater (GRB)
3. Lillian Heming and Murray Carey (CAN)

**1980 PRIZE OF MOSCOW NEWS** (Moscow, Soviet Union, December 10-14, 1980)

Men:

1. Igor Bobrin (SOV)
2. Konstantin Kokora (SOV)
3. Vladimir Kotin (SOV)

Women:

1. Svetlana Frantsuzova (SOV)
2. Janina Wirth (GDR)
3. Anna Kondrashova (SOV)

Pairs:

1. Irina Vorobieva and Igor Lisovsky (SOV)
2. Nelli Chervotkina and Viktor Teslia (SOV)
3. Elena Valova and Oleg Vasiliev (SOV)

# SHOWS AND TOURS

In the summer, Californians were treated to a most unusual ice show, presented at the Kabuki Theatre in San Francisco and the Center for the Performing Arts in San Jose. *War of the Worlds: A Multi-Media Visual Experience on Ice* was based on Jeff Wayne's 1978 album based on the famous H.G. Wells science fiction novel of the same name. The show starred Angela Greenhow and Paul Heath (both medallists at the World Professional Championships in Jaca, Spain in the 70s) and Lisa Carey and Chris Harrison, stars of the *Ice Follies*.

The seventh edition of the annual *Superskates* fundraiser show for the USOC was held at Madison Square Garden in November. Two months before the show, Dick Button received the first annual Superskates Award for his contributions to amateur figure skating at a luncheon at the Sherry Netherland Hotel in New York. The award was presented by Ed Mosler, founder of Superskates and National Finance Chairman of the USOC. Performers in the 1980 show included Peggy Fleming, John Curry, Judy Blumberg and Michael Seibert, David Santee, Lisa-Marie Allen and Scott Hamilton.

In a historic first, a star-studded cast of American figure skaters travelled to China for a week in November to film a television special for ABC's Wide World of Sports. Over 7000 spectators showed up for the show's dress rehearsals and 18 000 people came to both shows. Spectators were told not to applaud, but they did anyway. Tickets to the shows were 25 cents - a minuscule amount to North Americans but a hefty sum in China where 30 dollars was considered a good salary for a month. Don Laws accompanied the group and organized seminars for Chinese skaters. The American skaters in attendance noted that Chinese skaters understood what seniors were doing and could do advanced jumps and spins, but were seriously deficient in the fundamentals of skating like stroking. In between performances, skaters visited The Summer Palace in Beijing and The Great Wall, where Elaine Zayak tried to roller-skate on the cobblestones.

A dinner theater in Atami presented a Las Vegas-style show called *American Circus on Ice*. The show was presented twice a night and skaters only got one day off a month.

In February, Robin Cousins, Emi Watanabe, Karena Richardson and Judy Blumberg and Michael Seibert starred in *Showtime on Ice*, a skating special filmed for public television at the Colorado Skating Club.

Tom Collins' *1981 World Figure Skating Tour* had an international cast of skating stars from Canada, the United States, the Soviet Union United Kingdom, East Germany, Japan and Switzerland. For the first time since 1978, the tour visited Canada, with stops in Montreal, Ottawa, Toronto, Winnipeg and Edmonton. One skater missing on the tour was Brian Pockar. Tom Collins and Associates extended an invitation for him to participate before he lost the Canadian title in Halifax, then rescinded it in favour of Brian Orser. Pockar's mother was not a happy camper, as she had spent over 20 hours sewing a costume for him to wear on the tour.

In England, Bournemouth's Westover Ice Rink and the Ice Drome at Blackpool Pleasure Beach both played host to summer ice revues. Following in the footsteps of Tom Arnold's famous ice pantomimes at Wembley, Gerald Palmer staged several ice revues at the Brighton Centre in the 80s, including *Humpty Dumpty* and *Europe on Ice*. The Hull New Theatre presented its first ice show in eighteen years – *Melody on Ice*. Ice shows were a popular attraction on the Continent in the early 80s as well, with the *Moscow Circus on Ice* and *Cirque Jean Richard* presenting successful ice shows in Paris. The *Circo Sul Ghiaccio*, directed by Moira Orfei, staged ice shows in Italy and Turkey. Angel Cristo staged a circus ice show in Spain as well.

## FILMS AND TELEVISION

The CFSA sanctioned a seven-video mail-order series by Don Jackson's Skating Products and Rogers Cable TV Newmarket. *The World of Figure Skating* had segments on everything from figure skating history to figure and free skating technique, choreography, costuming and off-ice exercises. Donald Jackson hosted the series with Shelley MacLeod. Special guests included Doug Leigh, Uschi Keszler, Brian Orser, Gary Beacom and Kelly Johnson and John Thomas.

Peggy Fleming appeared in Columbia Pictures Television's fantasy/drama series *Fantasy Island*, which starred Ricardo Montalban and Hervé Villechaize. In *The Skater's Edge*, Fleming portrayed a woman whose fantasy was to become a prima ballerina of ice skating. Fleming also appeared in *The Osmond Family Christmas Special* which aired in December of 1980.

U.S. Champion Elaine Zayak was featured on an episode of the long-running game show *To Tell The Truth*. Panelists Peggy Cass, Pat Collins, Henry Morgan and Soupy Sales had to discern which of the three guests was the real Elaine Zayak. Only half of the panel guessed correctly.

## ART AND HISTORY

Peggy Fleming, Carol Heiss, Hayes Alan Jenkins and Tenley Albright attended a reception at the White House hosted by President Ronald Reagan in recognition of the travelling exhibition *Champions of American Sport*. Figure skating was represented in this exhibition by a pair of antique skates from the Jackson Haines era.

In conjunction with the U.S. Championships in California, there was a display in the Broadway department store in San Diego's Fashion Valley of the extensive private skating collection of Victor and Irene Vilchek of Del Mar. The display included oil paintings of Peggy Fleming and Janet Lynn, a 300-year-old Flemish painting of a skating scene and an original pen-and-ink drawing by Winslow Homer. Most remarkable was a French vase, depicting Louis XVI skating, dating back to 1752.

# Professional Competitions

**1981 U.S. PROFESSIONAL CHAMPIONSHIPS (Philadelphia, PA, February 21-22, 1981)**

Men:

1. Scott Cramer
2. Michael Tokar
3. Tim Murphy

Women:

1. Amy Brown
2. Teresa Romano
3. Bernae Peterson

Pairs:

1. Lisa Carey and Chris Harrison
2. Emily Benenson and Jack Courtney
3. Sheryl Franks and Michael Botticelli

Ice Dance:

1. Stacey Smith and John Summers
2. Jennifer and David Young
3. Cathy Macri and Lee Cobb

**1981 CANADIAN PROFESSIONAL CHAMPIONSHIPS (Toronto, ON, March 14, 1981)**

Men:

1. Vern Taylor
2. Ron Shaver
3. Henri April

Women:

1. Lynn Nightingale
2. Sherri Diane Hunt
3. Jamie Lynn Kitching

Pairs:

1. Leslie Casper and Ted Barton
2. Christine McBeth and Dennis Johnson

Ice Dance:

1. Judie Jeffcott and Keith Swindlehurst
2. Diana Flynn and Bob Knapp

**1981 CAMPEONATOS DEL MUNDO DE PATINAJE ARTÍSTICO PROFESSIONAL SOBRE HIELO (Jaca, Spain, April 16-19, 1981)**

Men:

1. Ron Shaver (CAN)
2. Michael Tokar (USA)
3. Vern Taylor (CAN)

Women:

1. Danielle Rieder (SUI)
2. Jamie Lynn Kitching (CAN)
3. Teresa Romano (USA)

Pairs:

1. Tania Buhlman and Edgar Pfaner (SUI)
2. Lisa Carey and Chris Harrison (USA)
3. Emily Benenson and Jack Courtney (USA)

Ice Dance:

1. Stacey Smith and John Summers (USA)
2. Judie Jeffcott and Keith Swindlehurst (CAN)
3. Susi and Peter Handschmann (AUT)

*Angela Greenhow leading the British team at the World Professional Championships in Jaca, Spain. Photo by Fred & Joan Dean, courtesy Paul Dean, "Ice & Roller Skate" magazine archive.*

# National Championships and Other Competitions

## SENIOR NATIONAL CHAMPIONS BY COUNTRY

### Men

AUS - Michael Pasfield
AUT - Helmut Kristofics-Binder
BUL - Boyko Aleksiev
CZE - Jozef Sabovčík
DEN - Fini Ravn
FIN - Antti Kontiola
FRA - Jean-Christophe Simond
FRG - Norbert Schramm
GDR - Hermann Schulz
GRB - Christopher Howarth
HOL - Gerard van Hattem
HUN - István Simon
ITA - Bruno Delmaestro
JPN - Fumio Igarashi
NZL - John Walkingshaw*
POL - Grzegorz Filipowski
SAF - Rick Simons
SOV - Igor Bobrin
SUI - Richard Furrer
SWE - Lars Åkesson

*Australia's Robin Smedley won the men's event but the title was awarded to the top New Zealand finisher, John Walkingshaw.

### Women

AUS - Vicki Holland
AUT - Claudia Kristofics-Binder
BUL - Tatiana Yordanova
CZE - Renata Baierová
DEN - Heidi Bartelsen
FIN - Kristiina Wegelius
FRA - Cécile Antonelli
FRG - Karin Riediger
GDR - Katarina Witt
GRB - Karen Wood
HOL - Rudina Pasveer
HUN - Éva Demény
ITA - Karin Telser
JPN - Reiko Kobayashi
KOR - Hye-kyung Lim
NOR - Tine Mai Krian
NZL - Denyse Adam
POL - Helena Chwila
SOV - Kira Ivanova
SUI - Denise Biellmann
SWE - Catarina Lindgren

### Pairs

AUS - Danielle and Stephen Carr
FRA - Nathalie Tortel and Xavier Videau
FRG - Christina Riegel and Andreas Nischwitz
GDR - Sabine Baeß and Tassilo Thierbach
GRB - Susan Garland and Robert Daw
JPN - Toshimi Ito and Takashi Mura
POL - Maria Ježak and Lech Matuszewski
SOV - Veronika Pershina and Marat Akbarov
SUI - Gaby and Jörg Galambos

### Ice Dance

AUS - P. Leedham and Leslie Boroczky
CZE - Jana Beránková and Jan Barták
FIN - Saila Saarinen and Kim Jacobson
FRA - Nathalie Hervé and Pierre Béchu
FRG - Birgit Goller and Peter Klisch
GRB - Jayne Torvill and Christopher Dean
HUN - Gabriella Remport and Sándor Nagy
ITA - Elisabetta Parisi and Roberto Pelizzola
JPN - Noriko Sato and Tadayuki Takahashi
POL - Iwona Bielas and Jacek Jasiaczek
SOV - Natalia Linichuk and Gennadi Karponosov
SUI - Regula Lattmann and Hanspeter Müller

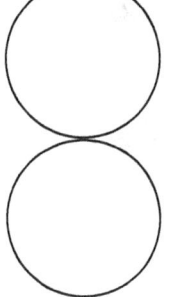

## 1981 NORDISKA MÄSTERSKAPEN (Aarhus, Denmark)

Men:

1. Antti Kontiola (FIN)
2. Todd Sand (DEN)
3. Peter Söderholm (SWE)

Women:

1. Christina Svensson (SWE)
2. Hanne Gamborg (DEN)
3. Lotta Isaksson (FIN)

## 1981 WORLD UNIVERSITY GAMES (Jaca, Spain, February 23-March 4, 1981)

Men:

1. Konstantin Kokora (SOV)
2. Shinji Someya (JPN)
3. Oleg Vasiliev (SOV)

Women:

1. Natalia Strelkova (SOV)
2. Svetlana Frantsuzova (SOV)
3. Lori Benton (USA)

Ice Dance:

1. Elena Garanina and Igor Zavozin (SOV)
2. Natalia Karamysheva and Rostislav Sinitsyn (SOV)
3. Jindra Holá and Karol Foltán (CZE)

## 1981 MORZINE INTERNATIONAL TROPHY (Morzine, France, April 9-10, 1981)

Ice Dance:

1. Karen Barber and Nicky Slater (GRB)
2. Nathalie Hervé and Pierre Béchu (FRA)
3. Kim Krohn and Barry Hagan (USA)

## 1981 MERANO SPRING TROPHY (Merano, Italy, April 1981)

Women:

1. Leslie Sikes (USA)
2. Kelly Webster (USA)
3. Ingrid Karl (FRG)

JoJo Starbuck and John Curry. Photo by Fred & Joan Dean, courtesy Fred Dean, "Ice & Roller Skate" magazine archive.

# MAJOR COMPETITIONS

**World Junior Championships.** In December, the J. Gordon Thompson Complex on the University Of Western Ontario's campus in London, Ontario played host to the first World Junior Championships held on North American soil. 20 nations were represented and more than 10 000 spectators showed up to see the competition unfold. In the pairs event, Kerry Leitch's students Lorri Baier and Lloyd Eisler produced back-to-back throw double Axels in the free skate, but it was only enough for second behind defending Champions Larisa Selezneva and Oleg Makarov of the Soviet Union. The bronze went to another Soviet pair, Marina Nikituk and Rashid Kadyrkaev. Ice dancer Elena Batanova arrived from Moscow with the wrong suitcase, which carried nothing but men's shirts and slacks. The compulsory dances were delayed by 35 minutes due to a blinding snowstorm. Poor road conditions delayed shuttles from the host hotel and many skaters arrived late. Despite the mishaps, Batanova and her partner Soloviev managed to squeak out a win, but it was not awarded without a minor controversy. In the compulsories, the Soviet judge gave them a 5.3; all other marks were in the 4's. The silver went to their teammates Natalia Annenko and Vadim Karkachev and the bronze to Alberta siblings Karyn and Rod Garossino, who were coached by Michael Jiranek and Roy Bradshaw. 14-year-old Oliver Höner of Switzerland, the winner of the school figures in the previous season's World Junior Championships in Megève, France, again won the figures but dropped to eighth overall in the men's event. The gold went to Carlo Fassi's student Paul Wylie, who finished second in the figures but won both the short program and free skate, earning a standing ovation in the latter phase of the competition. Yuri Bureiko claimed the silver; Scott Williams of the United States the bronze. The women's competition was full of surprises and results that were all over the place. 16-year-old Andrea Rohm of Vienna, a student of Olympic Gold Medallist Wolfgang Schwarz, won the figures but dropped to seventh overall with a disastrous short program. Japan's Midori Ito won the free skate, executing the first triple/triple combination by a woman in an ISU Championship, but placed one spot behind Rohm. Though she didn't win any phase of the competition, Frank Carroll's student Tiffany Chin's second-place showing in both the short program and free skate was enough to win the gold. A pair of talented young Soviet women, Marina Serova and Anna Antonova, took the silver and bronze. Canada's two entries, Diane Mae Ogibowski and Charlene Wong, both achieved top-ten finishes. The big controversy of this event was the CFSA's decision to send only six skaters, though ten spots were available. Canadian team leader Barbara Graham told reporters, "We can field any number of 15-year-olds who can end up in the top half. We're not talking about mass participation, we're talking about elite performance." The decision angered Canadian coaches and students, but many were hesitant to speak up for fear of reprisals from the CFSA. One skater anonymously told *MacLean's* contributor Bill Glaister, "I could have beaten half of the men out there, and I finished third in my region behind younger people." That skater's coach threatened to drop him as a student if his name appeared in the magazine. CFSA President David Dore thought that only skaters "going to the podium" should be sent to major competitions and that this approach would "encourage skaters".

**1981 WORLD JUNIOR CHAMPIONSHIPS**
(London, ON, December 8-14, 1980)

Men:

1. Paul Wylie (USA)
2. Yuri Bureiko (SOV)
3. Scott Williams (USA)
4. Masaru Ogawa (JPN)
5. Thomas Wieser (FRG)
6. Saak Mkhitarian (SOV)
7. Cameron Medhurst (AUS)
8. Oliver Höner (SUI)
9. Paul Robinson (GRB)
10. Thomas Hlavik (AUT)

Women:

1. Tiffany Chin (USA)
2. Marina Serova (SOV)
3. Anna Antonova (SOV)
4. Maria Causey (USA)
5. Cornelia Tesch (FRG)
6. Diane Mae Ogibowski (CAN)
7. Andrea Rohm (AUT)
8. Midori Ito (JPN)
9. Eva Drometer (FRG)
10. Charlene Wong (CAN)

Pairs:

1. Larisa Selezneva and Oleg Makarov (SOV)
2. Lorri Baier and Lloyd Eisler (CAN)
3. Marina Nikitiuk and Rashid Kadyrkaev (SOV)
4. Inna Bekker and Sergei Likhanski (SOV)
5. Julie Wasserman and Robert Davenport (USA)
6. Deborah Lynch and Keith Green (USA)
7. Carol and Carl Nelson (GRB)
8. Danielle and Stephen Carr (AUS)

Ice Dance:

1. Elena Batanova and Andrei Antonov (SOV)
2. Natalia Annenko and Vadim Karkachev (SOV)
3. Karyn and Rod Garossino (CAN)
4. Karan Giles and Russell Green (GRB)
5. Tatiana Gladkova and Igor Shpilband (SOV)
6. Sophie Schmidt and Eric Desplats (FRA)
7. Sharon Jones and Paul Askham (GRB)
8. Sandra Frabrocini and James Yorke (USA)
9. Sophie Merigot and Philippe Berthe (FRA)
10. Kathrin and Christoff Beck (AUT)

**World Professional Championships.** Over 18 000 spectators attended the first World Professional Championships in Landover, Maryland in December. Organized by Candid Productions, the event started as a team competition, pitting the *Stars of the 1980 Winter Olympic Games* against a team of *World and Olympic Professional Stars*. Dick Button devised the team format after recognizing the reluctance of former champions to risk their reputations by losing in head-to-head competition. Skaters had to perform two individual programs - a compulsory free skating program with six required elements and a free skating program emphasizing artistry. Both counted for just over 35 percent of their score. The remainder of each team's score was determined by the marking of an ensemble number, with skaters performing in groups of eight. The winning team split 120 000 dollars; the 'losers' divvied up 60 000. In 1998, Dick Button recalled, "My favourite memory is of Toller Cranston and Dorothy Hamill doing a Fourteenstep around the end of the rink in the team number - each carefully counting out the steps in the Fourteenstep dance - a basic dance. It was like Pavarotti and Streisand trying to sing in a chorus! Everybody realized they were not embarrassed by returning to competition and competing in a World Pro competition. They were still great champions." By four-tenths of a point, the *Stars of the 1980 Winter Olympic Games* team, which consisted of Robin Cousins, Charlie Tickner, Linda Fratianne, Emi Watanabe, Tai Babilonia and Randy Gardner and Krisztina Regőczy and András Sallay, were victorious. John 'Misha' Petkevich was the commentator on the NBC Sports World broadcast in the competition. The judges were Richard Dwyer, Ricky Harris, Norman Fuller, Carol Heiss Jenkins, David Jenkins, Janet Lynn and Ron Ludington.

**Canadian Championships.** For the first time in history, the Canadian Championships were held in Nova Scotia. To the delight of the knowledgeable crowd at the Halifax Metro Centre, hometown favourites Marie McNeil and Rob McCall made history in the ice dance event, becoming the first skaters from the Maritimes to win a senior national title in any discipline. McNeil and McCall represented the Halifax Skating Club and were coached by Janet Purdy and choreographed by Mary Turnbull. They wore costumes designed by Bob Doyle from the Neptune Theatre for their Gershwin free dance. Kelly Johnson and Kris Barber and Joanne French and John Thomas rounded out the ice dance podium, with another Nova Scotia duo, Gina Aucoin of Glace Bay and Hans-Peter Ponikau of New Glasgow, placing fourth. Barbara Underhill and Paul Martini won their third consecutive national pairs title despite suffering a fall early in their free skating program. Lorri Baier and Lloyd Eisler claimed the silver; Rebecca Gough and Mark Rowsom the bronze. An unusual event unfolded in the men's competition. The ISU's new judging system was put to the test when reigning champion Brian Pockar won the figures and short program and Brian Orser the free skate, resulting in a virtual tie. Under the revised system, the free skate result was used to break ties, resulting in Orser winning. Had the previous system of ordinals and points been used, Pockar would have won by a small margin. Orser's free skate featured six triples and the only triple Axel in the competition and earned him a standing ovation and five scores of 5.9. Gordon Forbes defeated Gary Beacom to take the bronze. Pockar handled his loss with grace, telling reporters, "Brian was fantastic. No one has ever done a triple Axel and a triple Lutz and combinations with triples coming out all over the place. It was great. In this competition, the new system went against me. I don't want to sound like I'm bitter against Brian, because I'm not. He was fantastic but I am upset because I lost my title. I think I was ahead of Brian more in figures and he was ahead of me in the long program but the new system doesn't give credit when a skater is better in one department - except in free skating."

**1980 WORLD PROFESSIONAL CHAMPIONSHIPS (Landover, MD, December 15, 1980)**

Team:

1. Stars Of The 1980 Winter Olympics: Robin Cousins, Charlie Tickner, Linda Fratianne, Emi Watanabe, Tai Babilonia and Randy Gardner, Krisztina Regőczy and András Sallay
2. World And Olympic Professional Stars: John Curry, Toller Cranston, Gordon McKellen Jr., Dorothy Hamill, Peggy Fleming, Janet Lynn, JoJo Starbuck and Ken Shelley, Sandra and Val Bezic, Colleen O'Connor and Jim Millns

**1981 CANADIAN CHAMPIONSHIPS (Halifax, NS, January 26-February 1, 1981)**

Men:

1. Brian Orser
2. Brian Pockar
3. Gordon Forbes
4. Gary Beacom
5. Daniel Béland
6. Kevin Hicks
7. Dennis Coi
8. Kevin Parker
9. Campbell Sinclair
10. Gary Paterson

Women:

1. Tracey Wainman
2. Kay Thomson
3. Elizabeth Manley
4. Charlene Wong
5. Kathryn Osterberg
6. Kerry Smith
7. Nonie Robertson
8. Lisa Spadafore
9. Karen Connolly
10. Patti Nieth

Pairs:

1. Barbara Underhill and Paul Martini
2. Lorri Baier and Lloyd Eisler
3. Becky Gough and Mark Rowsom
4. Katherina Matousek and Eric Thomsen
5. Mary Jo Fedy and Tim Mills

Ice Dance:

1. Marie McNeil and Rob McCall
2. Kelly Johnson and Kris Barber
3. Joanne French and John Thomas
4. Gina Aucoin and Hans Peter Ponikau
5. Lillian Heming and Murray Carey
6. Tracy Wilson and Mark Stokes
7. Christine and Dominic Pike
8. Karen and Leonard Warkentin

With Heather Kemkaran and Janet Morrissey moving on from the amateur ranks, the door was wide open in the women's event and Tracey Wainman skated right through it. Expanding upon an early lead in the figures, Wainman delivered two dynamic programs and won the gold. Kay Thomson and Elizabeth Manley finished second and third. Wainman's youth and fearless style of skating made her a star in Halifax. World Champion Donald Jackson told reporters, "She already has the quality, dynamic personality, that makes her skating look easy". At thirteen, Wainman was the youngest skater in history to win the Canadian senior women's title. A fours competition was held for the first time since 1967, inspired by fours exhibitions by Soviet pairs at the previous season's Olympics and World Championships. Melinda Kunhegyi, Rebecca Gough, Lyndon Johnston and Mark Rowsom bested eight other teams to claim the title. One of the most remarkable stories of the Championships was the win of Karyn and Rod Garossino in the junior ice dance event. Rod Garossino was recovering from an especially rough bout of mononucleosis and had subsisted on nothing more than instant breakfast drinks and soup the week in the competition. The team considered withdrawing ten minutes before they skated their free dance. Less than two weeks after the event, Tracey Wainman became one of the first Canadian women to land a triple loop in practice... on Friday the 13th.

**U.S. Championships.** San Diego, California played host to the U.S. Championships for the very first time, having previously hosted both Regional and Sectional events in the 70s. Judy Blumberg and Michael Seibert became the new national champions in ice dance, defeating perennial medal winners Carol Fox and Richard Dalley and Kim Krohn and Barry Hagan. Blumberg and Seibert's road to victory wasn't without its trials and tribulations. Just before they started their OSP, Seibert lost one of his contact lenses. He had to skate the program without it and almost hit the boards a couple of times. In the free dance, they were stopped by the referee when the bootstrap on Seibert's pants came loose. They were given the choice of starting their program from the top or picking up where they left off and chose the latter. The audience was behind them every step of the way and gave them the first standing ovation in the competition. In the women's event, two medal hopefuls, Sandy Lenz of Rockford, Illinois and 13-year-old Tiffany Chin of the host club, were forced to withdraw for the same reason: stress fractures in their left ankles. 15-year-old Elaine Zayak of Paramus, New Jersey came from behind to defeat Priscilla Hill, who had the overall lead after the short program. 1980 Olympian Lisa-Marie Allen and short program winner Vikki de Vries finished third and fourth. Zayak's winning free skate featured seven triple jumps – an unprecedented feat in the women's event at the U.S. Championships. Kitty and Peter Carruthers unanimously won the pairs competition, impressing spectators and judges alike with their athletic free skating program that included two triple twist lifts and a throw triple Salchow. The silver and bronze went to Lea Ann Miller and Bill Fauver and siblings Beth and Ken Flora.

*Marie McNeil and Rob McCall. Courtesy of the Dalhousie University Photographic Collection, PC 1, Box 36, Folder 24, Item 8.*

Fours:

1. Melinda Kunhegyi, Becky Gough, Lyndon Johnston and Mark Rowsom
2. Lorri Baier, Lynn Frasson, Lloyd Eisler and Mark Bystrek
3. Mary Jo Fedy, Penny Wilson, Tim Mills and William Thompson
4. Rosemary Barth, Lawrie Emerson, Sydney Shanks and Scott Douglas
5. Michelle Resch, Chantal Poirier, David Howe and Blair Matthewson
6. Christine Hough, Carol Wheeler, Kevin Wheeler and Michael Koshilka
7. Kim Hanford, Mary Ellen Roy, Sean Milligan and Michael Brown
8. Brooke Petersmeyer, Kristy Shippam, Kevin Playle and Ben Russenholt
9. Barbara Hellyer, Joanne Yates, Paul Coley and Cory Watson

Junior Winners:

Neil Paterson (men)
Diane Mae Ogibowski (women)
Melinda Kunhegyi and Lyndon Johnston
Karyn and Rod Garossino (ice dance)

Novice Winners:

Lauren Patterson (men)
Tracey Robertson (women)
Lynn Frasson and Mark Bystrek (pairs)
Deanna Poirier and Brett Schrader (ice dance)

**1981 U.S. CHAMPIONSHIPS (San Diego, CA, February 3-7, 1981)**

Men:

1. Scott Hamilton
2. David Santee
3. Robert Wagenhoffer
4. Brian Boitano
5. Mark Cockerell
6. Jimmie Santee
7. Bobby Beauchamp
8. Allen Schramm
9. Jim White
10. Tom Dickson

Women:

1. Elaine Zayak
2. Priscilla Hill
3. Lisa-Marie Allen
4. Vikki de Vries
5. Rosalynn Sumners
6. Jacki Farrell
7. Lynn Smith
8. Kristy Hogan
9. Melissa Thomas
10. Stephanie Anderson

The men's competition was a thrilling showdown from start to finish. Scott Hamilton led the way after the figures and short program and in the free skate, David Santee, Hamilton and Robert Wagenhoffer skated the performances of their lives back-to-back, each earning standing ovations. Hamilton's two 6.0s put him in first over Santee and Wagenhoffer but all three performances were truly memorable and worthy of gold. In a report featured in both the *Canadian Skater* and *Skating*, Gloria Williams aptly noted, "All the veterans of the sport on hand agreed they'd never seen anything like it before - three competitors in succession giving the best performances of their careers to three thundering standing ovations from a suddenly wide-awake audience. The specific moves, the number of triples each man performed - and there were many - became incidental to the overall experience of those three back-to-back nearly perfect programs."

**European Championships.** Snow blanketed the historic Tyrolean city of Innsbruck, Austria as the competition heated up in the Olympia Hall, the official venue of the European Championships. Practices were held in a balloon rink installed alongside the main stadium. 95 skaters from 18 countries were represented. The pairs competition in Innsbruck in 1981 had only six entries... the lowest in three decades. Extra ice dance practices were scheduled to give pairs ticket holders their money's worth of entertainment. World Champions Marina Cherkasova and Sergei Shakhrai entered the competition as favourites but Leningrad couple Irina Vorobieva and Igor Lisovsky took an early lead over their more experienced teammates in the short program. Cherkasova and Shakhrai dropped to third in the final standings behind Vorobieva and Livoski and Christina Riegel and Andreas Nischwitz. Riegel and Nischwitz's medal win was the first for a West German pair at the European Championships in a decade. In the men's event, France's Jean-Christophe Simond won the figures, West Germany's Norbert Schramm the short program and the Soviet Union's Igor Bobrin the free skate. Bobrin and Simond's overall consistency throughout the competition earned them the top two spots over Schramm and East Germany's Hermann Schulz. Bobrin's win was the second ever for a Soviet man at the European Championships, the first being Vladimir Kovalev in 1975. Reigning European Champion Anett Pötzsch withdrew from the women's competition, paving the way for Denise Biellmann's victory over Yugoslavia's Sanda Dubravčić and figures winner Claudia Kristofics-Binder of Austria. Biellmann won both the short program and free skate as expected, but her improved showing of fourth in the figures played an important factor in her win this time around. She became the first Swiss woman in history to claim a European title and the first Swiss skater in any discipline to win a European title since Silvia and Michel Grandjean were victorious in the pairs event back in the 50s. Sanda Dubravčić's silver medal win was also historically significant. No other skater from Yugoslavia had ever medalled at the European Championships and in Innsbruck, Dubravčić landed more triple jumps than the winner in the free skate. Jayne Torvill and Christopher Dean finally ascended to the top of the podium in the ice dance event, earning six marks of 5.9 for presentation for their masterful *Fame* free dance. Their victory was nothing less than an upset: they defeated World Champions Irina Moiseeva and Andrei Minenkov and Olympic Gold Medallists Natalia Linichuk and Gennadi Karponosov. Torvill and Dean's victory was the first for a British couple at the European Championships since Diane Towler and Bernie Ford won their fourth title in 1969. As was the fashion in judging circles at the time, the results of the nineteen teams remained the same in the compulsories, OSP and free dance.

**U.S. CHAMPIONSHIPS (continued)**

Pairs:

1. Kitty and Peter Carruthers
2. Lea Ann Miller and Bill Fauver
3. Beth and Ken Flora
4. Maria Di Domenico and Burt Lancon
5. Sheryl Franks and Michael Botticelli
6. Vicki Heasley and Peter Oppegard
7. Tricia Burton and Larry Schrier
8. Lynne and Jay Freeman
9. Dana Graham and Paul Wylie

Ice Dance:

1. Judy Blumberg and Michael Seibert
2. Carol Fox and Richard Dalley
3. Kim Krohn and Barry Hagan
4. Elisa Spitz and Scott Gregory
5. Nancy Berghoff and Jim Bowser
6. Ellen Pulver and Donald Adair
7. Susan Dymecki and Anthony Bardin
8. Robi Shepard and Kelly Witt
9. Cathleen Marron and Jay Pinkerton
10. Janice Kindrachuk and Blake Hobson

Junior Winners:

Paul Wylie (men)
Jill Frost (women)
Deborah Lynch and Keith Green (pairs)
Anne Spiewak and Keith Lichtman (ice dance)

Novice Winners:

Thomas Cierniak (men)
Kathleen Haines (women)

**1981 EUROPEAN CHAMPIONSHIPS**
(Innsbruck, Austria, February 3-8, 1981)

Men:

1. Igor Bobrin (SOV)
2. Jean-Christophe Simond (FRA)
3. Norbert Schramm (FRG)
4. Hermann Schulz (GDR)
5. Jozef Sabovčík (CZE)
6. Vladimir Kotin (SOV)
7. Grzegorz Filipowski (POL)
8. Falko Kirsten (GDR)
9. Alexandr Fadeev (SOV)
10. Patrice Macrez (FRA)

Women:

1. Denise Biellmann (SUI)
2. Sanda Dubravčić (YUG)
3. Claudia Kristofics-Binder (AUT)
4. Kristiina Wegelius (FIN)
5. Katarina Witt (GDR)
6. Debbie Cottrill (GRB)
7. Kira Ivanova (SOV)
8. Karin Riediger (FRG)
9. Carola Paul (GDR)
10. Manuela Ruben (FRG)

# PERSONALITIES

*Denise Biellmann. Contributor: United Archives GmbH / Alamy Stock Photo.*

*DENISE BIELLMANN*

Date of Birth: December 11, 1962
Place of Birth: Zürich, Switzerland
Coach: Otto Hügin, Jacques Gerschwiler
Choreographer: Patricia Neary, Denise Biellmann
Home Club: EC Zürich

*LISA-MARIE ALLEN*

Date of Birth: September 16, 1960
Place of Birth: Glendale, CA
Coach: Barbara Roles, Carlo and Christa Fassi
Choreographer: Darlene Garlutzo
Home Club: Broadmoor SC

*KRISTIINA WEGELIUS*

Date of Birth: October 17, 1960
Place of Birth: Helsinki, Finland
Coach: Carlo and Christa Fassi, Pia Saikkonen
Choreographer: Christa Fassi

*IRINA VOROBIEVA AND IGOR LISOVSKY*

Date of Birth: June 30, 1958/June 25, 1954
Place of Birth: Leningrad, Soviet Union
Coach: Tamara Moskvina
Choreographer: Valentina Vigant
Home Club: Burevestnik Leningrad

*BARBARA UNDERHILL AND PAUL MARTINI*

Date of Birth: June 24, 1963/November 2, 1960
Place of Birth: Pembroke, ON/Weston, ON
Coach: Judy Henderson, Anna Forder McLaughlin, Louis Stong
Choreographer: André Denis, Sandra Bezic
Home Club: Oshawa FSC/Woodbridge FSC

*VERONIKA PERSHINA AND MARAT AKBAROV*

Date of Birth: April 5, 1966/February 3, 1961
Place of Birth: Sverdlovsk, Soviet Union/Moscow, Soviet Union
Coach: Stanislav Zhuk, Irina Rodnina
Choreographer: Elena Cherkasskaya
Home Club: Dynamo Moscow

*MARIE MCNEIL AND ROB MCCALL*

Date of Birth: April 22, 1961/September 14, 1958
Place of Birth: Halifax, NS
Coach: Janet Dunnet Purdy, David Dunnet
Choreographer: Mary Turnbull, Bernard Ford
Home Club: Halifax SC

**EUROPEAN CHAMPIONSHIPS (continued)**

Pairs:

1. Irina Vorobieva and Igor Lisovsky (SOV)
2. Christina Riegel and Andreas Nischwitz (FRG)
3. Marina Cherkasova and Sergei Shakhrai (SOV)
4. Birgit Lorenz and Knut Schubert (GDR)
5. Veronika Pershina and Marat Akbarov (SOV)
6. Susan Garland and Robert Daw (GRB)

Ice Dance:

1. Jayne Torvill and Christopher Dean (GRB)
2. Irina Moiseeva and Andrei Minenkov (SOV)
3. Natalia Linichuk and Gennadi Karponosov (SOV)
4. Natalia Bestemianova and Andrei Bukin (SOV)
5. Karen Barber and Nicky Slater (GRB)
6. Nathalie Hervé and Pierre Béchu (FRA)
7. Jana Beránková and Jan Barták (CZE)
8. Birgit Goller and Peter Klisch (FRG)
9. Wendy Sessions and Stephen Williams (GRB)
10. Judit Péterfy and Csaba Bálint (HUN)

*Christopher Dean, Jayne Torvill and Lawrence Demmy. Photo by Fred & Joan Dean, courtesy Paul Dean, "Ice & Roller Skate" magazine archive.*

**World Championships.** 114 competitors from 25 countries participated in the World Championships in Hartford, Connecticut. Though the USFSA had hosted the World Championships several times, the Hartford Worlds were the first not held in Colorado Springs since the very first Worlds the country hosted in New York City in 1930. ABC's coverage of the event reached a record audience – 25 000 000 on each of the four days it was broadcast. Highlights were syndicated to 50 other countries. An all-event ticket to the event, including the Exhibition of Champions, was only 95 dollars. A lower-level seat for the women's free skate was only 12 dollars. The price point resulted in record ticket sales, with nearly 15 000 spectators showing up for each of the four finals. ISU officials and past champions lived it up at a lavish banquet, where Beef Bordelaise and Tarragon Lobster Salad were on the menu. Pairs from the Soviet Union had won fifteen out of the last sixteen World Championships, so it was of little surprise that 22-year-old Irina Vorobieva and 26-year-old Igor Lisovsky dominated the pairs event from start to finish. Sabine Baeß and Tassilo Thierbach of East Germany took the silver, with Christina Riegel and Andreas Nischwitz capturing the bronze - West Germany's first medal in the discipline since 1967. Defending champions Marina Cherkasova and Sergei Shakhrai also made a first in Hartford - but it wasn't a pleasant one. Going back to the Edwardian era, no other defending World Champions in pairs had ever finished off the podium the year after they won. Canada's Barbara Underhill and Paul Martini finished a creditable seventh, their first top-ten finish in three trips to the World Championships. With over 30 entries in the women's event, it took eight hours to complete the school figures. Claudia Kristofics-Binder of Austria led the way in the first phase of the competition, ahead of the UK's Debbie Cottrill, Finland's Kristiina Wegelius and Switzerland's Denise Biellmann. In the short program, Biellmann doubled a planned triple in her combination jump. Frau Müller's latest prodigy Katarina Witt won that phase of the competition with an exuberant and youthful display set to the theme from *The Muppet Show*. In the free skate, Biellmann rebounded with a masterful performance to become the first Swiss woman in history to win the World Championships. Following the event, she had a tulip named after her in Switzerland. Elaine Zayak came from behind to win the silver with an athletic program that featured a slew of triple jumps, including a dazzling double Axel/triple toe-loop combination. Kristofics-Binder earned the bronze, ahead of Cottrill, Witt and Wegelius. Canada's Tracey Wainman, the youngest skater in the event, skated the best figures of her career but a rough short program contributed to her drop to sixth overall. When asked for an opinion about the state of women's figure skating, 1937 World Champion Cecilia Colledge responded that there was too much emphasis on "how many turns [one] can do in the air, land on one foot, and hope [they're] going to stand up." British sportswriter John Henessy pulled no punches either, remarking in his review of the competition in the *Canadian Skater*, "No one would deny that Elaine [Zayak] is an extraordinary jumping machine, with a triple Axel lying in wait next year apparently, but surely Denise [Biellmann's] performance – and incidentally, a wonderfully generous reception from an American audience - points to a different, more rewarding, way ahead. I can recall that Denise was, in her time, regarded as a jumping prodigy before all else, but she has outgrown that. So should Elaine, especially as Katarina Witt, another from Jutta Müller's conveyor belt at Karl-Marx-Stadt, shows every evidence of matching Elaine in jumps, trading quality for quantity."

**1981 WORLD CHAMPIONSHIPS (Hartford, CT, March 3-8, 1981)**

Men:

1. Scott Hamilton (USA)
2. David Santee (USA)
3. Igor Bobrin (SOV)
4. Fumio Igarashi (JPN)
5. Jean-Christophe Simond (FRA)
6. Brian Orser (CAN)
7. Norbert Schramm (FRG)
8. Brian Pockar (CAN)
9. Vladimir Kotin (SOV)
10. Robert Wagenhoffer (USA)

Women:

1. Denise Biellmann (SUI)
2. Elaine Zayak (USA)
3. Claudia Kristofics-Binder (AUT)
4. Debbie Cottrill (GRB)
5. Katarina Witt (GDR)
6. Kristiina Wegelius (FIN)
7. Priscilla Hill (USA)
8. Carola Paul (GDR)
9. Karin Riediger (FRG)
10. Tracey Wainman (CAN)

Pairs:

1. Irina Vorobieva and Igor Lisovsky (SOV)
2. Sabine Baeß and Tassilo Thierbach (GDR)
3. Christina Riegel and Andreas Nischwitz (FRG)
4. Marina Cherkasova and Sergei Shakhrai (SOV)
5. Kitty and Peter Carruthers (USA)
6. Veronika Pershina and Marat Akbarov (SOV)
7. Barbara Underhill and Paul Martini (CAN)
8. Susan Garland and Robert Daw (GRB)
9. Birgit Lorenz and Knut Schubert (GDR)
10. Lea Ann Miller and Bill Fauver (USA)

Ice Dance:

1. Jayne Torvill and Christopher Dean (GRB)
2. Irina Moiseeva and Andrei Minenkov (SOV)
3. Natalia Bestemianova and Andrei Bukin (SOV)
4. Judy Blumberg and Michael Seibert (USA)
5. Olga Volozhinskaya and Alexandr Svinin (SOV)
6. Carol Fox and Richard Dalley (USA)
7. Karen Barber and Nicky Slater (GRB)
8. Nathalie Hervé and Pierre Béchu (FRA)
9. Jana Beránková and Jan Barták (CZE)
10. Birgit Goller and Peter Klisch (FRG)

Olympic Gold Medallists Natalia Linichuk and Gennadi's Karponosov's retirement made the newly crowned European Champions Jayne Torvill and Christopher Dean heavy favourites in Colorado Springs. They skated to an early lead in the Paso Doble, Rhumba and Westminster Waltz and Cha Cha OSP over former World Champions Irina Moiseeva and Andrei Minenkov and U.S. Judy Blumberg and Michael Seibert. The Americans found adapting their OSP to the Hartford rink difficult because the rounded corners were more sharply cut than their home rink. Torvill and Dean's *Fame* was the talk of the town in Hartford and the judges awarded them a slew of 5.8s and 5.9s and the gold medal over 'Min and Mo'. Natalia Bestemianova and Andrei Bukin won their first of many medals at the World Championships when Blumberg and Seibert tumbled early in their free dance. Kelly Johnson and Kris Barber reversed the result of the Canadian Championships, overtaking Marie McNeil and Rob McCall in the free dance to finish 12th to the Nova Scotian duo's 13th. Though a Belgian couple had competed in the second 'unofficial' World Championships for ice dance in 1951, Karen and Douglas Mankovich officially became the first team to represent Belgium in ice dancing at the World Championships. They finished 19th out of 21 teams. Following in John Curry's footsteps by coming to America to train with the Fassi's, Jean-Christophe Simond of France's hard work paid off when he won the figures, ahead of David Santee, Brian Pockar, Scott Hamilton and Igor Bobrin. Hamilton, Japan's Fumio Igarashi and Santee took the top three spots in the short program but it was Hamilton's athletic and crowd-pleasing free skate, choreographed by Ricky Harris, that stole the show and won the gold medal. Robin Cousins predicted that Hamilton would be the next World Champion a year earlier. Santee's *Rocky* program was a huge hit with the Connecticut crowd and he won the silver - a career-best for the two-time Olympian. Bobrin settled for bronze, but was also a crowd favourite. His avant-garde free skate to Rick Wakeman's "Journey to the Centre of the Earth" was a study in contrast to Hamilton's fleet footwork. After the competition was over, Bobrin got a standing ovation for his signature exhibition to "A Cowboy's Work Is Never Done". It was the first standing ovation for any Soviet skater in the entire event. Another crowd favourite was West Germany's Norbert Schramm, who was competing for the first time in thirteen months after breaking his leg. Schramm finished only seventh, but his quirky style, coupled with the fact he wore "I Love Hartford" shirts all week in practices, endeared to him to audiences. Brian Orser and Brian Pockar finished sixth and eighth respectively. It was the first time Canada had two men in the top ten since the last World Championships held in America in 1975. Though Vern Taylor was credited with landing a triple Axel in the 70s, Orser's triple Axel was the first one to be landed effortlessly. Orser wasn't the only man to push technical boundaries in Hartford. Robert Wagenhoffer attempted quadruple toe-loops in practice but did not include the jump in his free skate in the competition. One of the most amusing stories of the Championships happened off the ice. In the spring of 1980, members of the U.S. Olympic team made an unusual request at the USFSA Governing Council Meeting - that the World Team be provided with a hairdresser. In Hartford, their wish came true when Arline Voepel and her staff at Total Image provided complimentary makeovers to all competitors at a makeshift salon set up in the host hotel. Winners Scott Hamilton, Irina Vorobieva and Igor Lisovsky were among the dozens of skaters who had their hair and make-up done by Voepel's team. A particular amusing story about this program was shared in *Skating*: "Total Image received a call from the ladies' dressing room on the first night in the competition. [China's] Luan Bo was going to be skating before the television cameras in fifteen minutes and she had no make-up. Jeff [Jones] grabbed his make-up bag and rushed to the arena only to find that the Chinese interpreter had just left the side of her charge. Luan Bo took one look at Jeff and quickly mistook him for a dentist. Terrified, she refused to let him near her. Jeff finally managed to apply some blusher and lip gloss to Luan Bo before she was called to the ice." Bo and her interpreter arrived at the makeshift hotel salon before it opened the next morning and she ended up getting a full makeover.

# 1981-1982 SEASON

Hit Songs: "Physical" by Olivia Newton-John, "Eye of the Tiger" by Survivor, "I Love Rock 'n' Roll" by Joan Jett & The BlackHearts, "Tainted Love" by Soft Cell, "Don't You Want Me" by The Human League
Hit Movies: E.T. The Extra-Terrestrial, Tootsie, Rocky III, Poltergeist, Annie
Hit TV: Dallas, Three's Company, Alice, The Facts of Life, Laverne & Shirley
News: Royal Wedding of Prince Charles and Lady Diana Spencer, Falklands War, Capsize of The Ocean Ranger Drill Rig, Sandra Day O'Connor becomes first woman to serve as U.S. Supreme Court judge, Arab-Israeli Wars

## PEOPLE

Only a handful of the world's best amateur skaters retired following the 1980-1981 season. Denise Biellmann turned professional to tour with *Holiday on Ice*, while Lisa-Marie Allen joined the cast of the *Ice Capades*. Marina Cherkasova and Sergei Shakhrai turned also professional, with Cherkasova joining the Moscow Ice Ballet and Shakhrai taking up coaching. Marie McNeil retired and divided her time between coaching at three clubs and studying at Mount Saint Vincent University. McNeil later worked as an Administrative Assistant to Howard Crosby, the Progressive Conservative M.P. for Halifax West and became a skating judge and referee. Injured and traumatized after years of coach Karel Fajfr's physical abuse, Christina Riegel called it quits and took a job with the ARD television network. Her partner Andreas Nischwitz also retired to focus on his dentistry studies at the University of Tübingen. Hermann Schulz of East Germany, who withdrew from the 1981 World Championships due to injury, also retired.

Barry Hagan was seriously injured while working at his part-time job as a security guard at Bullock's Department Store in Lakewood, California in July. Hagan and another security guard escorted a disgruntled 37-year-old woman suspected of shoplifting and her 13-year-old daughter outside the store and jotted down the woman's license plate number. On his way to return to the store, the woman ran Hagan down with her car, throwing him through the store's plate glass window. He suffered serious injuries, including a broken leg and ankle, facial lacerations and several missing teeth. He told reporters he was "very lucky to be alive." The woman was charged with attempted murder.

Olympic Gold Medallist Maxi Herber Baier, who was inducted into the World Figure Skating Hall of Fame two years prior, received her plaque and medal at a ceremony held at the closing banquet of the Nebelhorn Trophy in Oberstdorf, West Germany in August, on behalf of her husband and partner Ernst Baier. The Presentation was made by ISU Historian Ben Wright and President of Deutsche Eislauf-Union Dr. Wolf-Dieter Montag.

In New York City in October, Peggy Fleming became the first figure skater to be inducted into the Hall of Fame of the Women's Sports Foundation.

John Curry made his British stage debut in the Nottingham Playhouse's modern interpretation of Shakespeare's *A Midsummer Night's Dream* in October. Curry starred as Puck alongside Imelda Staunton, who would go on to win a Screen Actors Guild Award for her role in the film *Shakespeare in Love*.

Norman Mackie Scott, who won both the Canadian and U.S. Championships in the early twentieth century, passed away in Montreal in October at the age of 89. A champion in both singles and pairs skating, Scott served with the Royal Canadian Engineers, the Royal Naval Air Service and the Royal Air Force in The Great War.

Jayne Torvill and Christopher Dean were invited to Buckingham Palace in October, where they were invested as Members of the Order of the British Empire (MBE) by Her Majesty Queen Elizabeth II. The following month, they were given the Team of the Year Award by the Sports Writers' Association. Torvill also was voted Sportswoman of the Year.

Donald B. Cruikshank officially retired as a figure skating judge and was honoured with a special Award of Excellence from CFSA President David Dore. Cruikshank, a Canadian Champion in Waltzing and North American Champion in fours skating, had been involved in figure skating since 1914. In 1947, he made history as the first Canadian to serve as a judge at the European Championships and in 1972, he was Canada's judge in the men's event at the Olympics.

Linda Fratianne decided to give Jane Fonda and Richard Simmons a run for their money when she capitalized on the fitness boom by releasing "Dance and Exercise with the Hits" and "Tune Up the Hits" records and cassettes. Both featured warm-up, aerobic and cool-down routines, accompanied by instructions from Fratianne. The albums sold over 300 000 copies.

A tragic house fire claimed the lives of Sonja Currie Jacobson and her teenage daughter and son in November in Lethbridge, Alberta. The wife of a provincial court judge, Currie Jacobson won the Canadian junior women's title in 1953. She coached at several clubs in the province over the years.

In December, Scott Hamilton made history as the first male figure skater to receive the USOC's Athlete of the Year Award. Linda Fratianne was the first female winner in 1977.

Pierre Baugniet died in December. With partner Micheline Lannoy, Baugniet made history as the first pairs team from Belgium to win gold medals at the Winter Olympic Games and World Championships in the 40s. After his skating career ended, Baugniet worked as an average adjuster at the Antwerp firm of Martroye, Baugniet and Varlez.

Two-time Olympian Mitsuru Matsumura made a valiant comeback at the Japanese Championships in December after missing the previous season due to a hernia operation in the summer of 1980.

Tracey Wainman became only the fourth figure skater in history to win the prestigious Bobbie Rosenfeld Award for Canada's Female Athlete of the Year. She was presented with the award at a black-tie dinner hosted by the Sports Federation of Canada in Toronto in January.

Natalia Linichuk and Gennadi Karponosov weren't the only well-known skaters to tie the knot during the 1981-1982 season. In December, Dr. Tenley Albright, who was serving as a consultant to the President's Council on Physical Fitness and Sports, was remarried in Boston, to hotelier Gerald Blakeley. Dorothy Hamill was married to actor Dean Paul Martin in January.

Long-time coach Peter Dunfield was honoured with the Professional Skaters Guild of America's Lifetime Achievement Award, as well as an honourary membership with the organization. With wife Sonya (Klopfer), Peter coached several elite skaters in the 80s, including Elizabeth Manley and Charlene Wong.

On New Year's Day, Anne Ewan Drummond passed away in Georgeville, Quebec at the age of 103. Ewan was remembered as the first woman to win a Canadian title in 1905, back in the days when men and women competed against one another.

Olympic Gold Medallist and World Champion Irina Rodnina was honoured as the first recipient of the ISU's new Jacques Favart Trophy, awarded to figure and speed skaters who made remarkable contributions to their sports. The award was presented at the 1982 World Championships in Copenhagen.

Edwin H. Mosler Jr. passed away in March. The President and CEO of The Mosler Safe Company, Mosler was the organizer of the annual Superskates benefit for the USOC, but also as the quiet benefactor of a who's who of figure skating. Mosler's financial support helped make Dorothy Hamill and John Curry's Olympic dreams a reality.

In April, Clarence Hislop passed away in Seattle at the age of 67. Hislop coached numerous elite skaters in his native Australia, Canada and the United States, including his son Brad, who won the U.S. junior ice dance title in 1968.

To the delight of his parents and long-time coach Winnie Silverthorne, Brian Pockar was awarded the Government of Canada Sport Excellence Award. At the CFSA's annual Bursary Dinner at the Westbury Hotel in Toronto, Pockar was also presented with the CFSA's Skater of the Year Award.

Everett McGowan passed away in Monticello, New York in May at the age of 83. A champion speed skater, McGowan was a pioneer of adagio pairs skating with his partner Ruth Mack. The duo toured with the *Ice Capades*, *Ice Follies* and *Holiday on Ice* and appeared in a dizzying series of shows in hotels and nightclubs across America. McGowan was also a professional boxer and baseball player at one time.

Chinese Champions Zhenhua Bao and Xu Zhaoxiao were sent to America to train with Carlo Fassi at the Broadmoor in Colorado Springs for two weeks. In an interview for *Skating* conducted through an interpreter, Bao remarked, "We are both aware of our low level. The standards set are high. All we can do is our best, and try to steadily improve. We will."

Herma Szabo was inducted into the World Figure Skating Hall of Fame. The first Olympic Gold Medallist to win their medal at a Winter Games in 1924 won a total of seven World titles (five in singles and two in pairs) in the roaring 20s. After retiring from competition in 1927, Szabo took up competitive skiing until a serious accident left her bedridden for a time. Szabo was widowed in the late 60s. She spent her golden years living alone in a gabled mountain house in the quiet Upper Styrian market town of Admont, southwest of Vienna. She had to use two canes to get around. When she was in her early 80s, she remarked, "All that remains of my youth is the discipline of a sportswoman. Every day, rain or shine, I force myself to walk ten rounds in the garden."

Dr. James Koch passed away at the age of 78 in June. The Swiss-born skating official served as the ISU's President in the 50s and 60s, tackling several delicate issues including judging controversies, internal corruption and skaters defecting from behind the Iron Curtain while attending ISU Championships. More than a decade after his death, he was inducted into the World Figure Skating Hall of Fame. Koch wasn't the only Swiss-born member of the skating community to pass away during the season. Armand Perren also passed away, having coached countless elite skaters in the UK, South Africa and Australia during his lengthy career as a professional.

Her Majesty Queen Elizabeth II visited Canada in April, to officially sign Canada's first Constitution. Brian Pockar, Brian Orser and Elizabeth Manley were invited to a gala dinner for Canada's Young Achievers, attended by The Queen. Upon her return to England, Her Majesty bestowed the title of OBE (Officer of the Order of the British Empire) on Eileen Mary Anderson "for services to ice-skating" in her Birthday Honours List in June. Anderson served as Vice-President of the British Olympic Association and was a long-time Honourary Secretary to the National Skating Association's Ice Dance Committee. Anderson served as Team Leader for the British team at numerous international competitions, including the Innsbruck, Lake Placid and Sarajevo Olympics where John Curry, Robin Cousins and Torvill and Dean won Olympic gold.

## AROUND THE WORLD

**Canada.** The fourth time was the charm for Calgary. After three previous unsuccessful bids, Alberta's capital city was awarded the 1988 Winter Olympics. Government funding for Canadian figure skating had more than tripled from 1973 to 1982. At a historic meeting in April, CFSA officials made several important decisions that would ultimately help grow the Association significantly. A marketing strategy was developed, as was a plan to seek corporate sponsorship through television packages with rink boards, program ads and on-ice cheque presentations. Tensions ran high between the CFSA and Canada's short-lived answer to the Professional Skater's Guild of America - Figure Skating Coaches' of Canada. Many recreational coaches affiliated with the latter organization, and in turn, the clubs where they taught, felt a disconnect with the sport's governing body.

**Japan.** Japanese figure skating celebrated a historic milestone in December when the country's National Championships were held for the fiftieth time in Tokyo. The sport's popularity in Japan had grown significantly in recent years, thanks to the country hosting the Winter Olympics and World Championships for the first time in the 70s and advertising campaigns featuring the darling of the 1972 Games, Janet Lynn. The darling of an Olympics held decades prior, Etsuko Inada, was a prominent coach in Tokyo and the country's top skaters were already becoming minor celebrities. Minoru Sano competed in a star-studded television bowling competition and the *Viva! Ice World* shows at the Shinagawa Skate Center, featuring Nobuo Satō and Miwa Fukuhara, drew large audiences. Ryusuke Arisaka, one of the first Japanese skaters to represent Japan at the World Championships after World War II, was interviewed for *Skating*. He philosophized, "We Japanese are good disciplinarians, but lack expression - or shall I say at least occidental expression - and judgment of that expression is also a Western value judgment. We must try to express ourselves in a Japanese way - in costuming, in music, and not feel thwarted by our lack of Western showmanship. We must take advantage of our inane characteristics and develop our technicality to an expressive level."

**United States.** The USFSA's National Headquarters got a fancy new computer with a printer, which organized the records of tests, club memberships and judge's statuses. The USFSA also outlined a new 'body of work' system for selecting entries for the 1984 Winter Olympics. In selecting members for the team, the results of three U.S. and World Junior Championships and two World Championships and National Sports Festivals would be taken into consideration.

## MUSIC

The USFSA began offering the Stephenson Cassette Music Library of skating music on TDK SA C-90 cassettes. Coaches and skaters could borrow copies of pre-cut skating music and 90-minute tapes of out-of-print music suitable for skating through the mail.

## ART AND HISTORY

The U.S. Figure Skating Museum and Hall of Fame presented two new exhibits. *The Wonderful World of Figure Skating* showcased antique skates from the Shipstad Collections, pins and medals. *The Legendary Gillis Grafström* highlighted the career of the legendary Olympic Gold Medallist, featuring a handmade costume presented to Grafström by the Swedish government in the roaring 20s.

The balance of Gillis Grafström's collection arrived at the U.S. Figure Skating Museum, including antique skates belonging to 1898 World Champion Henning Grenander, prints by van de Velde, Honore Daumier and William Unger and a large collection of antique skating books and photographs.

# BEHIND THE SCENES

Several important milestones and anniversaries were celebrated during the 1981-1982 season. It was the ISU's ninetieth anniversary, the fiftieth anniversary of the first World Championships held in Canada and the twentieth anniversary of Donald Jackson's historic win at the 1962 World Championships, where he executed the first triple Lutz ever performed in competition.

The ISU struggled to deal with the high number of entries at its Championships. More than once, the possibility of using the European Championships and a Pacific Championship for non-European members as a qualifying competition was discussed and rejected. In 1982, the ISU voted to approve a "B" or consolation round if more than 24 skaters entered a competition. The combined results of the figures and short program (or the compulsory dances and OSP) determined which fifteen skaters or teams would make it to the final and which skated their free skating program or free dance separately in the "B" round. The "B" round was shortly thereafter changed to a semi-final, with seventeen skaters qualifying for the final by way of the combined figure and short program scores and the top three finishers in the semi-final earning the right to compete in the 'actual' competition. This short-lived attempt to separate the best from the rest was unpopular with competitors
and audiences alike and proved to be short-lived. It was ultimately decided at the 1986 ISU Congress that the top 24 entries after the initial rounds would advance to the final, with the remaining skaters being eliminated from the competition and placing 25th, 26th, etc. overall based on their rankings after the initial rounds.

The now-famous ISU rule that required skaters to hold "residence in a foreign country for at least one year before being eligible to compete for the national association of that country (with the consent of that country's national association)" was also instituted.

A logo developed for the 1981 World Championships in Hartford was accepted by the ISU as a permanent logo for all World Championships. The logo was created by the co-sponsors, the Travelers Insurance Companies and the Skating Club of Hartford, Connecticut.

The USFSA's Sports Medicine Committee proposed banning triple jumps to prevent injuries. Many felt that if any such ban should occur, it should be guided by the medical profession or ISU decisions. The proposal went nowhere. The USFSA also published its first Guidelines for Precision Team Skating its its Rulebook. These were the first rules ever published for precision skating, a discipline now of course known as synchro.

Shamp Industries in California invented the Jump Tender - a ceiling-mounted safety-suspension unit/ pulley system with a parachute-style harness for practicing double and triple jumps off the ice. It wasn't the only mail-order innovation of the season. A new freestyle skating training film was marketed by Wally Sahlin, featuring his famous student Charlie Tickner.

The new Pro-Skate Tour of figure skating competitions revolutionized the professional skating landscape. Prioritizing performance level, choreography and musicality or technique, the event's organizers took an unorthodox approach to selecting judges. In an article in the *Canadian Skater*, Carole Stafford explained, "There were eight regular judges and a ninth public judge. The eight included two former amateur judges, a skating coach and a professional skater, a choreographer, a musician, a member of the professional artistic community and a celebrity judge. Each was responsible for marking in his or her area of expertise, including such criteria as overall performance and impact of the audience. A panel of ten local celebrities (swimmers, football players, university professors, radio hosts, etc.) comprised the 'public judge', whose combined and averaged marks provided the ninth score. The high and low marks among the panel and among the eight regular judges were discarded." This approach to judging intentionally aimed to add more subjectivity to scoring, producing many surprising results at many Pro-Skate events held in the early 80s.

## FILMS AND TELEVISION

After a five-year stint, CTV's weekly figure skating series *Stars on Ice* came to an end. Produced on an ice rink set up at one of CFTO's studios in Scarborough, the series was first hosted by Alex Trebek. Over the years, the show was syndicated in over 40 countries, including Brazil, Hong Kong, Nigeria and Iran. Featured skaters included Donald Jackson, Toller Cranston, Karen Magnussen and Lynn Nightingale. At one point in the 70s, it was one of the top three highest-rated shows on the CTV network.

Denise Biellmann took a break from touring to film scenes for Thomas Gottschalk and Mike Krüger in Siggi Götz's comedy *Piratensender Powerplay*. Biellmann's role in the West German film was originally going to be expanded but her schedule with *Holiday on Ice* got in the way.
Dorothy Hamill was featured in ABC's *Perry Como's French-Canadian Christmas*. The made-for-television special was filmed in Montreal. Hamill skated to an original composition by Quebec pianist André Gagnon.

In January, WGBH Boston aired the television special *John Curry Skates Peter and The Wolf and Other Dances*, featuring music from Sergei Prokofiev's famous ballet and narration from actor Peter Ustinov. The skating ballet starred Curry and JoJo Starbuck and featured performances by Sarah Kawahara, Jack Courtney, Catherine Foulkes and Paul Toomey.

On Valentine's Day, ABC's Wide World of Sports aired *From Concept to Curtain Call*, a behind-the-scenes look at Peggy Fleming's show at Harrah's in Lake Tahoe.

In March, Peggy Fleming was a special guest on the popular children's program Mister Rogers' Neighbourhood. Fleming took Mister Rogers skated together and talked about the discipline involved in competitive figure skating.

Toller Cranston's CBC special Strawberry Ice received rave reviews. Cranston's coach Ellen Burka was the Artistic Skating Consultant for this innovative production directed by David Acomba, featuring brilliant costumes designed by Frances Dafoe. Performers included Peggy Fleming, Sandra and Val Bezic, Allen Schramm, Jamie-Lynn Kitching, Sarah Kawahara, Osborne Colson Shelley MacLeod and John S. Rait, Ted Barton and Bernie Ford. Musical guests were Chita Rivera and Shawn Jackson. The production won an ACTRA Award for Best TV Variety Production and international rights were sold to Brazilian producers for 7000 dollars - the most money Brazil had ever spent for one hour of television programming.

## THE AIDS EPIDEMIC

The U.S. Center for Disease Control (CDC) released an article in June of 1981 discussing the diagnosis and treatment of "5 young men, all active homosexuals" for Pneumocystis carinii pneumonia at Los Angeles hospitals. By the end of the year, there are over 300 cases of "individuals with severe immune deficiency" in the United States. 40 percent died by the end of 1981. In May of 1982, *The New York Times* published an article with the headline "NEW HOMOSEXUAL DISORDER WORRIES HEALTH OFFICIALS". The article claimed that researchers dubbed this 'new pneumonia' GRID - for "gay-related immunodeficiency." Though a doctor from the National Cancer Institute acknowledged that the epidemic was a problem "of concern to all Americans", there was already a very strong stigma that AIDS affected only gay men, a demographic hugely represented in figure skating.

## PERSONALITIES

### SCOTT HAMILTON

Date of Birth: August 28, 1958
Place of Birth: Toledo, OH
Coach: Don Laws
Choreographer: Ricky Harris
Home Club: Philadelphia SC & HS

### NORBERT SCHRAMM

Date of Birth: April 7, 1960
Place of Birth: Nuremberg, West Germany
Coach: Erich Zeller
Choreographer: Elfi Hansch, Michael Stylianos, Norbert Schramm
Home Club: EC Oberstdorf

### IGOR BOBRIN

Date of Birth: November 14, 1953
Place of Birth: Leningrad, Soviet Union
Coach: Igor Moskvin, Yuri Ovchinnikov
Choreographer: Yuri Potemkin, Natalia Volkova, Nikolay Tagunov
Home Club: "Burevestnik" Leningrad/Dynamo

### BRIAN POCKAR

Date of Birth: October 27, 1959
Place of Birth: Calgary, AB
Coach: Winnie Silverthorne, Barbara Roles
Choreographer: L. Abra
Home Club: Calgary WC, Glencoe WC

### MITSURU MATSUMURA

Date of Birth: April 9, 1957
Place of Birth: Yokohoma, Japan
Coach: Nobuo Satō
Home Club: Senshu University

### DAVID SANTEE

Date of Birth: July 22, 1957
Place of Birth: Oak Park, IL
Coach: Evy and Mary Scotvold
Choreographer: Mary Scotvold
Home Club: Chicago FSC

### FUMIO IGARASHI

Date of Birth: November 6, 1958
Place of Birth: Tokyo, Japan
Coach: Frank Carroll, Carlo and Christa Fassi
Choreographer: Frank Carroll, Christa Fassi

### ROBERT WAGENHOFFER

Date of Birth: July 5, 1960
Place of Birth: San Bernardino, CA
Coach: John Nicks
Home Club: Arctic Blades FSC

### ELENA VODOREZOVA

Date of Birth: May 21, 1963
Place of Birth: Moscow, Soviet Union
Coach: Stanislav Zhuk
Home Club: CSKA Moscow

### ROSALYNN SUMNERS

Date of Birth: April 20, 1964
Place of Birth: Palo Alto, CA
Coach: Lorraine Borman
Choreographer: Lorraine Borman, Barbara Tanory Flowers
Home Club: Seattle SC

### ELAINE ZAYAK

Date of Birth: April 4, 1965
Place of Birth: Paramus, NJ
Coach: Peter Burrows, Marylynn Gelderman
Choreographer: Marylynn Gelderman
Home Club: SC of New York

### TRACEY WAINMAN

Date of Birth: May 27, 1967
Place of Birth: Kirkland Lake, ON
Coach: Ellen Burka, Doug Leigh
Choreographer: Ellen Burka, Kevin Cottam
Home Club: Toronto Cricket, Skating and Curling Club

### KAY THOMSON

Date of Birth: February 18, 1964
Place of Birth: Toronto, ON
Coach: Louis Stong, Sandra Bezic, Doug Haw
Choreographer: Sandra Bezic
Home Club: Granite Club

# Fall Internationals

**1981 COUPES DES ALPES** (Saint Gervais, France and Oberstdorf, West Germany, August 19-23, 1981 and August 26-29, 1981)

Grand Prix de St. Gervais Winners:

Heiko Fischer (FRG) - men
Charlene Wong (CAN) - women
Melinda Kunhegyi and Lyndon Johnston (CAN) - pairs
Karen Roughton and Mark Reed (GRB) - ice dance

Nebelhorn Trophy (Oberstdorf) Winners:

Heiko Fischer (FRG) - men
Cornelia Tesch (FRG) - women
Elena Valova and Oleg Vasiliev (SOV) - pairs
Karen Roughton and Mark Reed (GRB) - ice dance

**1981 ASKÖ CUP OF VIENNA** (Vienna, Austria, September 21-25, 1981)

Men:

1. Norbert Schramm (FRG)
2. Kevin Parker (CAN)
3. Ivan Kralik (CZE)

Women:

1. Maria Causey (USA)
2. Diane Mae Obigowski (CAN)
3. Myriam Oberwiler (SUI)

**1981 ST. IVEL ICE INTERNATIONAL** (London, England, September 28-October 1, 1981)

Men:

1. Brian Orser (CAN)
2. David Santee (USA)
3. Rudi Cerne (FRG)

Women:

1. Tracey Wainman (CAN)
2. Jackie Farrell (USA)
3. Karen Wood (GRB)

Pairs:

1. Lorri Baier and Lloyd Eisler (CAN)
2. Vicki Heasley and Peter Oppegard (USA)
3. Susan Garland and Ian Jenkins (GRB)

Ice Dance:

1. Jayne Torvill and Christopher Dean (GRB)
2. Karen Barber and Nicky Slater (GRB)
3. Wendy Sessions and Stephen Williams (GRB)

**1981 SKATE AMERICA** (Lake Placid, NY, October 8-11, 1981)

Men:

1. Scott Hamilton (USA)
2. Robert Wagenhoffer (USA)
3. Brian Boitano (USA)

Women:

1. Vikki de Vries (USA)
2. Elaine Zayak (USA)
3. Claudia Kristofics-Binder (AUT)

Pairs:

1. Barbara Underhill and Paul Martini (CAN)
2. Kitty and Peter Carruthers (USA)
3. Elena Valova and Oleg Vasiliev (SOV)

Ice Dance:

1. Judy Blumberg and Michael Seibert (USA)
2. Elena Garanina and Igor Zavozin (SOV)
3. Karen Barber and Nicky Slater (GRB)

**1981 SKATE CANADA** (Kitchener, ON, October 29-November 1, 1981)

Men:

1. Norbert Schramm (FRG)
2. Brian Orser (CAN)
3. Jozef Sabovčík (SVK)

Women:

1. Tracey Wainman (CAN)
2. Rosalynn Sumners (USA)
3. Kira Ivanova (SOV)

Ice Dance:

1. Carol Fox and Richard Dalley (USA)
2. Karen Barber and Nicky Slater (GRB)
3. Natalia Karamysheva and Rostislav Sinitsyn (SOV)

**1981 PRAGUE SKATE** (Prague, Czechoslovakia, November 5-8, 1981)

Men:

1. Jozef Sabovčík (CZE)
2. Neil Paterson (CAN)
3. Gurgen Vardanjan (SOV)

Women:

1. Kerry Smith (CAN)
2. Juri Ozawa (JPN)
3. Alla Formicheva (SOV)

Pairs:

1. Melinda Kunhegyi and Lyndon Johnston (CAN)
2. Inna Volyanskaya and Valery Spiridonov (SOV)
3. Lynne and Jay Freeman (USA)

Ice Dance:

1. Jana Beránková and Jan Barták (CZE)
2. Terri Slater and Rick Berg (USA)
3. Julia Romanova and Juri Gaichenkov (SOV)

**1981 ENNIA CHALLENGE CUP INTERNATIONAL FREE SKATING COMPETITION** (The Hague, Netherlands, November 10-15, 1981)

Men:

1. Rudi Cerne (FRG)
2. Jimmie Santee (USA)
3. Dennis Coi (CAN)

Women:

1. Katarina Witt (GDR)
2. Elaine Zayak (USA)
3. Diane Mae Ogibowski (CAN)

Pairs:

1. Barbara Underhill and Paul Martini (CAN)
2. Larisa Selezneva and Oleg Makarov (SOV)
3. Vicki Heasley and Robert Wagenhoffer (USA)

Ice Dance:

1. Carol Fox and Richard Dalley (USA)
2. Jana Beránková and Jan Barták (CZE)
3. Tracy Wilson and Rob McCall (CAN)

**1981 POKAL DER BLAUEN SCHWERTER** (Karl-Marx-Stadt, East Germany, November 18-21, 1981)

Men:

1. Alexander König (GDR)
2. Jaochim Ehmann (FRG)
3. Thomas Wieser (FRG)

Women:

1. Katarina Witt (GDR)
2. Anna Kondrashova (SOV)
3. Carmen Hartfiel (FRG)

Pairs:

1. Birgit Lorenz and Knut Schubert (GDR)
2. Elena Kashinzeva and Alexei Pogodin (SOV)
3. Elena Bechke and Valeri Kornienko (SOV)

# Fall Internationals

**1981 GOLDEN SPIN OF ZAGREB (Zagreb, Yugoslavia, November 18-22, 1981)**

Men:

1. Heiko Fischer (FRG)
2. Jimmie Santee (USA)
3. Philippe Paulet (FRA)

Women:

1. Sanda Dubravčić (YUG)
2. Nathalie Hildesheimer (FRA)
3. Mercedes Roskam (FRG)

Ice Dance:

1. Judit Péterfy and Csaba Bálint (HUN)
2. Marina Klimova and Sergei Ponomarenko (SOV)
3. Birgit Goller and Peter Klisch (FRG)

**1981 GRAND PRIZE SNP (Banská Bystrica, Czechoslovakia, November 20-22, 1981)**

Men:

1. Yuri Bureiko (SOV)
2. Tomislav Čižmešija (YUG)
3. Nils Köpp (GDR)

Women:

1. Frankie Hermanson (USA)
2. Heike Gobbers (FRG)
3. Karin Hendschke (GDR)

Pairs:

1. Marina Avstriyskaya and Yuri Kvashnin (SOV)
2. Inna Bekker and Sergei Likhanski (SOV)
3. Babette Preußler and Torsten Ohlow (GDR)

Ice Dance:

1. Natalia Annekova and Vadim Karkasev (SOV)
2. Viera Mináríková and Ivan Havránek (CZE)
3. Jana Kašpárková and Pavel Laurenčík (CZE)

**1981 NHK TROPHY (Kobe, Japan, November 27-29, 1981)**

Men:

1. Fumio Igarashi (JPN)
2. Norbert Schramm (FRG)
3. Jean-Christophe Simond (FRA)

Women:

1. Kristiina Wegelius (FIN)
2. Vikki de Vries (USA)
3. Charlene Wong (CAN)

Pairs:

1. Kitty and Peter Carruthers (USA)
2. Birgit Lorenz and Knut Schubert (GDR)
3. Maria Di Domenico and Burt Lancon (USA)

Ice Dance:

1. Karen Barber and Nicky Slater (GRB)
2. Natalia Karamysheva and Rostislav Sinitsyn (SOV)
3. Jana Beránková and Jan Barták (CZE)

**1981 PRIZE OF MOSCOW NEWS (Moscow, Soviet Union, December 9-13, 1981)**

Men:

1. Vladimir Kotin (SOV)
2. Igor Bobrin (SOV)
3. Vitali Egorov (SOV)

Women:

1. Kay Thomson (CAN)
2. Kira Ivanova (SOV)
3. Kerstin Wolf (GDR)

Pairs:

1. Larisa Selezneva and Oleg Makarov (SOV)
2. Veronika Pershina and Marat Akbarov (SOV)
3. Lorri Baier and Lloyd Eisler (CAN)

Ice Dance:

1. Natalia Bestemianova and Andrei Bukin (SOV)
2. Irina Moiseeva and Andrei Minenkov (SOV)
3. Olga Volozhinskaya and Alexandr Svinin (SOV)

*Fumio Igarashi. Photo courtesy Elaine Hooper / St. Ivel Figure Skating Archive.*

*Brian Orser. Contributor: PA Images / Alamy Stock Photo. Photographer: Don Morley.*

# Professional Competitions

**1982 CANADIAN PROFESSIONAL CHAMPIONSHIPS (Toronto, ON, March 20, 1982)**

Men:

1. Henri April
2. Jean-Pierre Martin

Women:

1. Heather Kemkaran
2. Carol-Ann Simon
3. Susan Wilson

Pairs:

1. Shelley Winters and Keith Davis
2. Leslie Rupp and Dennis Johnston

Ice Dance:

1. Susan Carscallen and Marty Fulkerth
2. Diana Flynn and Tom Kalweit
3. Bambi Schaff and Ruark Roswell Smith

**1982 LABATT'S PRO-SKATE MONTREAL (Montreal, QC, March 28-29, 1982)**

Men:

1. Toller Cranston (CAN)
2. Robin Cousins (GRB)
3. Gordon McKellen Jr. (USA)

Women:

1. Simone Grigorescu (ROM)
2. Heather Kemkaran (CAN)
3. Jamie Lynn Kitching (CAN)

Pairs:

1. Candy Jones and Don Fraser (CAN)
2. Shelley Winters and Keith Davis (CAN)
3. Janet and Mark Hominuke (CAN)

Ice Dance:

1. Kim Krohn and Barry Hagan (USA)
2. Judie Jeffcott and Keith Swindlehurst (CAN)
3. Shelley MacLeod and John Rait (CAN)

**1982 LABATT'S PRO-SKATE VANCOUVER (Vancouver, British Columbia, April 5-6, 1982)**

Men:

1. Fumio Igarashi (JPN)
2. Toller Cranston (CAN)
3. Robin Cousins (GRB)

Women:

1. Janet Lynn (USA)
2. Dianne de Leeuw (HOL)
3. Kath Malmberg (USA)

Pairs and Ice Dance Winners: Candy Jones and Don Fraser (CAN), Kim Krohn and Barry Hagan (USA)

**1982 CAMPEONATOS DEL MUNDO DE PATINAJE ARTÍSTICO PROFESIONAL SOBRE HIELO (Jaca, Spain, April 8-11, 1982)**

Men:

1. Robert Wagenhoffer (USA)
2. Henri April (CAN)
3. Billy Schober (AUS)

Women:

1. Angela Greenhow (GRB)
2. Simone Grigorescu (ROM)
3. Editha Dotson (BEL)

Pairs:

1. Rulona Roland and Jack Campbell (USA)
2. Suzy and Jeffrey Nolt (USA)
3. Natascha Devish and Rudi Matysik (FRG)

Ice Dance:

1. Anna Pisánská and Jiří Musil (CZE)
2. Natascha Devish and Rudi Matysik (FRG)
3. Susi and Peter Handschmann (AUT)

**1982 LABATT'S PRO-SKATE EDMONTON (Edmonton, Alberta, April 9-10, 1982)**

Men:

1. Toller Cranston (CAN)
2. Ron Shaver (CAN)
3. Fumio Igarashi (JPN)

Women:

1. Lynn Nightingale (CAN)

Pairs:

1. Candy Jones and Don Fraser (CAN)
2. Shelley Winters and Keith Davis (CAN)
3. Janet and Mark Hominuke (CAN)

Ice Dance:

1. Kim Krohn and Barry Hagan (USA)
2. Colleen O'Connor and Jim Millns (USA)
3(t). Shelley MacLeod and John Rait (CAN)
3(t). Judie Jeffcott and Keith Swindlehurst (CAN)

**1982 LABATT'S PRO-SKATE TORONTO (Toronto, Ontario, April 18, 1982)**

Men:

1. Toller Cranston (CAN)
2. David Santee (USA)
3. Ron Shaver (CAN)

Women:

1. Janet Lynn (USA)
2. Simone Grigorescu (ROM)
3. Lynn Nightingale (CAN)

Pairs:

1. Candy Jones and Don Fraser (CAN)
2. Shelley Winters and Keith Davis (CAN)
3. Janet and Mark Hominuke (CAN)

Ice Dance:

1. Kim Krohn and Barry Hagan (USA)
2. Judie Jeffcott and Keith Swindlehurst (CAN)
3. Shelley MacLeod and John Rait (CAN)

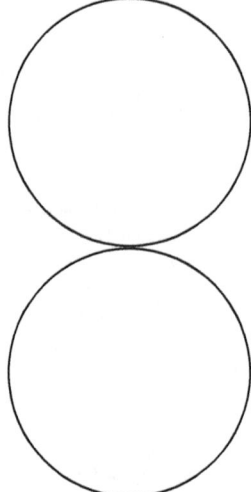

## SHOWS AND TOURS

*Walt Disney's World on Ice* made its debut at the Meadowlands Arena in East Rutherford, New Jersey in July. The first show starred Linda Fratianne and was staged by Irvin and Kenneth Feld, the producers of *Ice Follies* and *Holiday on Ice*.

Streatham Ice Rink in London, England celebrated its fiftieth anniversary with the *Private Patients Plan International Ice Skating Gala* starring John Curry and Jayne Torvill and Christopher Dean, broadcast on BBC in November.

In November, Madison Square Garden staged the eighth *Superskates* benefit show. Though the headliners were Tai Babilonia and Randy Gardner, one of the biggest stories of this show was the comeback of Belita Jepson-Turner, at the age of 58. A triple threat who had excelled in skating, acting and dancing, Jepson-Turner represented the UK at the 1936 Winter Olympics and starred in a series of film noirs for Monogram Pictures in the 40s, including *Suspense, The Gangster* and *The Hunted*. Jepson-Turner told reporters that she wanted to "prove to anybody who's had cancer that they don't have to pack up."

During the holiday season, the Warfield Theatre in San Francisco played host to *The Nutcracker: A Fantasy on Ice*. Choreographed by Karen Kresge and starring Dorothy Hamill, the production was a fundraiser for the Examiner-YMCA Christmas Camp fund. The production returned the following two years and was eventually adapted for an HBO special and mail-order video release starring Hamill and Robin Cousins.

Harrah's Headliner Room in Reno, Nevada presented *Hot Ice*, a production directed by Dick Foster and Willy Bietak and choreographed by Cathy Steele and Sarah Kawahara. The show featured a dozen skaters, alongside comedian Mike Neun and magician Dick Arthur. Gail Gilbert was the show's star. The production cost over 300 000 dollars to stage and featured an outer space number and an act with live birds.

For the first time, all competitors at the World Championships were required to sign a form stating that they would agree to take part in the ISU's 41-day post-Worlds tour of Europe if invited. John Curry was vocal in his opposition to these tactics, calling the tour "exploitative" due to its rushed schedule. Jayne Torvill and Christopher Dean, Scott Hamilton and Elaine Zayak the tour and in July, the trio were invited to perform alongside Robin Cousins in Bournemouth's *Hot Ice* show. While the ISU's European tour was going on, Cousins was starring in *Ice Revue '82* in Birmingham, Nottingham and Blackpool.

# National Championships and Other Competitions

**SENIOR NATIONAL CHAMPIONS BY COUNTRY**

**Men**

AUS - Cameron Medhurst
AUT - Thomas Hlavik
BUL - Atanas Ognyanov
CZE - Jozef Sabovčík
DEN - Todd Sand
FRA - Jean-Christophe Simond
FRG - Heiko Fischer
GRB - Mark Pepperday
HOL - Edward van Campen
HUN - András Száraz
ITA - Bruno Delmaestro
JPN - Fumio Igarashi
NZL - John Walkingshaw
POL - Grzegorz Filipowski
SAF - Rick Simons
SOV - Igor Bobrin
SUI - Oliver Höner
SWE - Lars Åkesson

**Women**

AUS - Vicki Holland
AUT - Claudia Kristofics-Binder
BUL - Tsvetanka Alexandrova
CZE - Hana Veselá
DEN - Anette Nygaard
FIN - Kristiina Wegelius
FRA - Béatrice Farinacci
FRG - Manuela Ruben
GDR - Katarina Witt
GRB - Debbie Cottrill
HOL - Ingrid Aalders
HUN - Nóra Miklósy
ITA - Karin Telser
JPN - Mariko Yoshida
KOR - Hye-kyung Lim
NOR - Tine Mai Krian
NZL - Kathy Lindsay
POL - Barbara Kaźmierczak
SOV - Elena Vodorezova
SUI - Myriam Oberwiler
SWE - Catarina Lindgren

**Pairs**

AUS - Danielle and Stephen Carr
FIN - Maija and Pekka Pekkala
FRA - Nathalie Tortel and Xavier Videau
FRG - Bettina Hage and Stefan Zins
GDR - Sabine Baeß and Tassilo Thierbach
GRB - Susan Garland and Ian Jenkins
POL - Ewa Czyż and Tadeusz Jankowski
SOV - Marina Pestova and Stanislav Leonovich
SUI - Gaby and Jörg Galambos

**Ice Dance**

AUS - Bridget Watson and Mark Hochmann
AUT - Maria Kniffer and Manfred Hübler
BUL - Hristina Boyanova and Yavor Ivanov
CZE - Jana Beránková and Jan Barták
FRA - Nathalie Hervé and Pierre Béchu
FRG - Birgit Goller and Peter Klisch
GRB - Jayne Torvill and Christopher Dean
HUN - Judit Péterfy and Csaba Bálint
ITA - Isabella Micheli and Roberto Pelizzola
JPN - Noriko Sato and Tadayuki Takahashi
POL - Jolanta Wesołowska and Andrzej Alberciak
SOV - Natalia Bestemianova and Andrei Bukin
SUI - Graziella and Marco Ferpozzi

**1982 NORDISKA MÄSTERSKAPEN (Helsinki, Finland)**

Men:

1. Antti Kontiola (FIN)
2. Todd Sand (DEN)
3. Peter Söderholm (SWE)

Women:

1. Nina Östman (FIN)
2. Susanna Peltola (FIN)
3. Elise Ahohen (FIN)

Pairs:

1. Maija and Pekka Pekkala (FIN)

Ice Dance:

1. Saila Saarinen and Kim Jacobson (FIN)
2. Ulla Örnmarker and Thomas Svedberg (SWE)
3. Karin Eliasson and Sten-Olof Eliasson (SWE)

**1982 MERANO SPRING TROPHY (Merano, Italy, March 27-28, 1982)**

Women:

1. Staci McMullin (USA)
2. Ingrid Karl (FRG)
3. Tracy Moore (USA)

**1982 MORZINE AVORIAZ (Morzine, France, April 8-10, 1982)**

Ice Dance:

1. Carol Fox and Richard Dalley (USA)
2. Natalia Karamysheva and Rostislav Sinitsyn (SOV)
3. Nathalie Hervé and Pierre Béchu (FRA)

*Claudia Kristofics-Binder. Photo courtesy Elaine Hooper / St. Ivel Figure Skating Archive.*

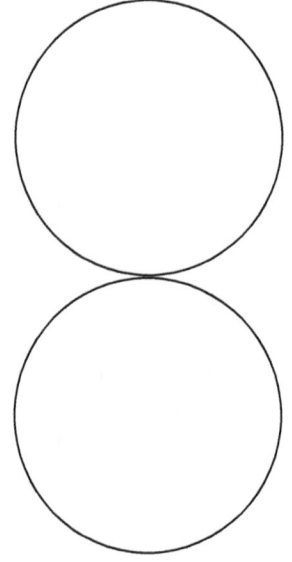

# MAJOR COMPETITIONS

**World Junior Championships.** Oberstdorf, West Germany was the site of the World Junior Championships in December. 106 skaters from 22 countries participated. Visitors from all around the world praised the three-rink facility, which housed a pool, sauna, weight room, classrooms, a cafeteria and dormitory. The Canadian contingent had an amusing trip to West Germany, being mistakenly announced by the pilot as the Canadian Ski Team. In the pairs event, Marina Avstriyskaya and Yuri Kvashnin of the Soviet Union came from behind with a technically difficult free skate to defeat their teammates Inna Bekker and Sergei Likhanski, who won the short program. East Germany's Babette Preußler and Torsten Ohlow took the bronze and Canadian siblings Lynda and John Ivanich finished sixth. Avstriyskaya and Kvashnin were coached by Stanislav Zhuk; Bekker and Likhanski by Zhuk's former student Irina Rodnina, who made her international debut as a coach at this event. Natalia Annenko and Vadim Karkatchev led the ice dance event from start to finish, defeating teammates Tatiana Gladkova and Igor Shpilband and Lydia Malek and Alexander Millier III of Michigan to win the gold medal. Canada's two teams, Deanna Poirier and Brett Schrader and Christine Horton and Michael Farrington, placed ninth and 13th. Beata Kawełczyk and Tomasz Politański withdrew at the very last minute when martial law was declared in Poland just a day before their departure. In the women's event, West Germany's Cornelia Tesch won the school figures and Japan's Midori Ito was the winner of both the short program and free skating. There was so much jostling in the standings that the overall winner ended up being East Germany's Janina Wirth, who finished fourth in the figures, second in the short and third in free skating. Cornelia Tesch took the silver and Canada's Elizabeth Manley, who landed two different triples in the free skate, won the bronze. Ito was only able to finish sixth as a result of a disastrous 19th place showing in the figures. Marina Serova of the Soviet Union, the runner-up the year prior, finished a disappointing ninth. The men's event was a completely different story to the women's. 16-year-old Scott Williams of Redondo Beach, California dominated the competition from start to finish, winning the figures, short program and free skate over his teammate Paul Guerrero and becoming the third American man to claim the World Junior title. Alexander König of East Germany had a disappointing short program but landed a triple Lutz in the free skate to win the bronze. Canada's Lauren Patterson placed ninth, just ahead of Ukrainian brothers Viktor and Vladimir Petrenko. One of the most remarkable aspects of the competition was the remarkable technical content Midori Ito included in her programs. She performed a triple flip, two triple loops, a triple toe-loop/triple toe-loop and double Axel/triple toe-loop combination, triple Salchow and two double Axels in her free skating program. In her exhibition, she performed a triple Lutz for good measure. Paul Guerrero's coach Debbie Stoery remarked that Ito "is not the first female to have mastered all the triples...but certainly is the youngest and the most blasé. She seems to have the healthy attitude that a triple is only another turn in the air. How embarrassing it would be to tell her that skating officials decided to limit the number of triples that could be included in a program, as some have contemplated... If she had to limit her amount of her triples, she'd probably just add a few quads."

**1982 WORLD JUNIOR CHAMPIONSHIPS**
(Oberstdorf, West Germany, December 15-20, 1981)

Men:

1. Scott Williams (USA)
2. Paul Guerrero (USA)
3. Alexander König (GDR)
4. Yuri Bureiko (SOV)
5. James Cygan (USA)
6. Makoto Kano (JPN)
7. Oliver Höner (SUI)
8. Philippe Roncoli (FRA)
9. Lauren Patterson (CAN)
10. Viktor Petrenko (SOV)

Women:

1. Janina Wirth (GDR)
2. Cornelia Tesch (FRG)
3. Elizabeth Manley (CAN)
4. Jill Frost (USA)
5. Kelly Webster (USA)
6. Midori Ito (JPN)
7. Heike Gobbers (FRG)
8. Parthena Sarafidis (AUT)
9. Marina Serova (SOV)
10. Mirella Grazia (SUI)

Pairs:

1. Marina Avstriyskaya and Yuri Kvashnin (SOV)
2. Inna Bekker and Sergei Likhanski (SOV)
3. Babette Preußler and Torsten Ohlow (GDR)
4. Marina Nikitiuk and Rashid Kadyrkaev (SOV)
5. Bettina Hage and Stefan Zins (FRG)
6. Lynda and John Ivanich (CAN)
7. Natalie and Wayne Seybold (USA)
8. Gaby and Jörg Galambos (SUI)
9. Amy Grossmann and Robert Davenport (USA)
10. Carol and Carl Nelson (GRB)

Ice Dance:

1. Natalia Annenko and Vadim Karkachev (SOV)
2. Tatiana Gladkova and Igor Shpilband (SOV)
3. Lynda Malek and Alexander Miller (USA)
4. Sophie Merigot and Philippe Berthe (FRA)
5. Viera Mináríková and Ivan Havránek (CZE)
6. Elena Novikova and Oleg Bliakhman (SOV)
7. Alison Perrigo and Michael Harding (GRB)
8. Isabelle Cousin and Gilles Vandenbroeck (FRA)
9. Deanna Poirier and Brett Schrader (CAN)
10. Kathrin and Christoff Beck (AUT)

**World Professional Championships.** Landover, Maryland played host to the second edition of the World Professional Championships in December. Tickets were only ten dollars and The Capital Centre was packed to the gills with 19 000 spectators. The star-studded event again had a team format, pitting a team of *All-Stars* (John Curry, Toller Cranston, Dorothy Hamill, Janet Lynn, Ludmila and Oleg Protopopov and JoJo Starbuck and Ken Shelley) up against a group of *Pro-Stars* (Robin Cousins, Charlie Tickner, John Carlow Jr., Tai Babilonia, Linda Fratianne, Dianne de Leeuw, Audrey King and Sandra and Val Bezic). Denise Biellmann withdrew before the event due to illness and Tai Babilonia was injured and had to pull out of the event at the last minute, forcing Randy Gardner to skate solo. Audrey King (Weisiger) was brought in to make up the numbers for the *All-Stars'* group number. Many memorable performances were given, including John Curry's "Scheherazade", Toller Cranston's "Pagliacci" and Janet Lynn's "The Sound of Music". Helen Maxson from the Ice Follies choreographed the wonderful group numbers. The *Pro-Stars* team came out on top by three-quarters of a point, though the *All-Stars* team received four perfect scores of 10.0.

**U.S. Championships.** In January, America's best figure skaters could be found skating up a storm at Market Square Arena in Indianapolis. Despite frigid temperatures, skating lovers showed up in droves. Huge crowds even showed up to watch the compulsory dances and figures! Scott Hamilton was allotted an awful patch of ice, with fresh paint leaking through, to perform his figures. He lodged a complaint with the referee, Claire Ferguson, before the competition but nothing was done. The ice conditions ended up being so problematic that Hamilton was forced to stop his paragraph double-three midway through and ask for a reskate. He was granted this, but some of his competitors complained openly about the situation. Despite the hullabaloo, Hamilton ended up winning over David Santee and Mark Cockerell. In the short program, Hamilton landed his double flip/triple toe-loop combination but he took an uncharacteristic fall on the double Axel. Robert Wagenhoffer won that phase of the competition, ahead of Hamilton, Brian Boitano, Santee and Cockerell. The free skate turned out to be almost as thrilling as the one at the previous year's Nationals, with Hamilton, Boitano and Santee all landing five triples. Boitano landed a difficult triple Axel in combination. Wagenhoffer, too, had an outstanding skate featuring an excellent triple Lutz. When the scores were tallied, Hamilton was first, followed by Wagenhoffer, Santee, Boitano and Cockerell. Boitano was third in both the short program and free skate but his sixth-place finish in figures kept him off the podium. Kitty and Peter Carruthers were flawless in the short program but made two mistakes in their free. Their performances were still strong enough to claim the gold in the pairs event, ahead of Maria DiDomenico and Burt Lancon and Lea Ann Miller and Bill Fauver. In the ice dance event, there was zero movement in the standings amongst the fourteen teams in the compulsories, OSP and free dance. Blumberg and Seibert's Fred and Ginger free dance to "Top Hat", "Dancing in the Dark" and "Puttin' on the Ritz" earned them a standing ovation and Carol Fox and Richard Dalley's "Zorba the Greek" free dance had the audience clapping along as well. In a close contest for third, Elisa Spitz and Scott Gregory defeated Kim Krohn and Barry Hagan. Krohn and Hagan were making an incredible comeback with very little training time after the horrific attack Hagan endured in the summer.

**1981 WORLD PROFESSIONAL CHAMPIONSHIPS (Landover, MD, December 17, 1981)**

Team:

1. All Stars: John Curry, Toller Cranston, Dorothy Hamill, Janet Lynn, Ludmila and Oleg Protopopov, JoJo Starbuck and Ken Shelley
2. Pro Stars: Robin Cousins, Charlie Tickner, John Carlow Jr., Linda Fratianne, Dianne de Leeuw, Audrey King, Randy Gardner, Sandra and Val Bezic

**1982 U.S. CHAMPIONSHIPS (San Diego, CA, Indianapolis, IN, January 25-31, 1982)**

Men:

1. Scott Hamilton
2. Robert Wagenhoffer
3. David Santee
4. Brian Boitano
5. Mark Cockerell
6. Jimmie Santee
7. Bobby Beauchamp
8. Tom Dickson
9. Jim White
10. Scott Williams

Women:

1. Rosalynn Sumners
2. Vikki de Vries
3. Elaine Zayak
4. Jacki Farrell
5. Tiffany Chin
6. Priscilla Hill
7. Jill Frost
8. Simone Grigorescu
9. Kelly Webster
10. Melissa Thomas

Pairs:

1. Kitty and Peter Carruthers
2. Maria Di Domenico and Burt Lancon
3. Lea Ann Miller and Bill Fauver
4. Vicki Heasley and Peter Oppegard
5. Lynne and Jay Freeman
6. Maryan and Bryan Amaral
7. Karyl Kawaichi and Larry Schrier
8. Cara and Craig Gill
9. Dawn and Dale Roberge

Ice Dance:

1. Judy Blumberg and Michael Seibert
2. Carol Fox and Richard Dalley
3. Elisa Spitz and Scott Gregory
4. Kim Krohn and Barry Hagan
5. Nancy Berghoff and Jim Bowser
6. Renée Roca and Donald Adair
7. Janice Kindrachuk and Blake Hobson
8. Terri Slater and Rick Berg
9. Susie Wynne and Joseph Druar
10. Eva Hunyadi and Jay Pinkerton

After the figures in the women's event, Priscilla Hill led the way over Elaine Zayak, Jacki Farrell, Vikki de Vries and Rosalynn Sumners. Like Scott Hamilton in the men's event, Elaine Zayak took an unfortunate tumble on the double Axel in her short program and wound up third, behind Sumners and de Vries, who both skated clean. Everybody expected Zayak to come back in the free skate and win, but it was not to be. She started strong with two triples and then made several unfortunate errors. Skating through the open door, Sumners perfectly executed one triple and five double Axels on the way to winning her first national title. de Vries made fewer mistakes than Zayak, to claim the silver behind Sumners. It was also a disappointing night for Priscilla Hill, who skated brilliantly in the short but received low marks and then had a rough free skate to finish sixth overall in her final Nationals. A historic milestone took place in the novice ranks in Indianapolis, when 12-year-old Rudy Galindo became the first skater of Latino heritage to win the U.S. novice men's title, following in the footsteps of Armando 'Pancho' Rodriguez, who medalled in the junior ranks at Nationals in the 1950s. At the end of the week, Maria Causey made her way onto the ice in a wheelchair to receive the City of Indianapolis Award for Sportsmanship. She was forced to withdraw after being hospitalized with a serious ankle injury. A blizzard started just after the final event ended, stranding many skaters in Indianapolis. No one seemed to mind being snowed in because everyone in Indianapolis was so nice.

**Canadian Championships.** Over 200 of Canada's best figure skaters showed off their best chassés and camel spins at the Keystone Centre in Brandon, Manitoba in January. Barbara Underhill and Paul Martini decisively won the pairs short program, earning unanimous first-place ordinals. In the free skate, Martini fell on a side-by-side double Salchow, but the duo's triple twist and whopping throw triple Salchow were more than enough to secure mostly 5.8s and another national title. The silver and bronze medals went to Lorri Baier and Lloyd Eisler and Rebecca Gough and Mark Rowsom. fourth-place team Melinda Kunhegyi and Lyndon Johnston were major crowd favourites, as Johnston hailed from Manitoba. Three judges rewarded fifth-place team Katherina Matousek and Eric Thomsen's clean "Swan Lake" free skate higher marks than the teams above them. Kunhegyi, Gough, Johnston and Rowsom took top honours in the fours event. Marie McNeil's retirement forced Rob McCall to look for a new partner and he found an absolute gem in Tracy Wilson. Wilson and McCall had only been skating together for five and a half months when they arrived in Brandon but under Bernie Ford's tutelage had already earned a medal at the Ennia Challenge Cup and won the Western Divisional Championships. In the Blues and Viennese Waltz, Wilson and McCall squeaked out a tiny lead, with Joanne French and John Thomas and Kelly Johnson and Kris Barber tied for second. In the third compulsory dance, Wilson and McCall increased their lead and French and Thomas dropped to third. All teams excelled in the Blues OSP, but those who gave a more bawdy interpretation of the Blues seemed to garner higher marks from the panel of seven judges. Wilson and McCall won their first Canadian title with their *Slaughter On Tenth Avenue* free dance, described by Greg Young as "nothing short of a masterpiece." Despite performing a charismatic free dance to "Rhapsody In Blue", French and Thomas remained in third behind Johnson and Barber.

**U.S. CHAMPIONSHIPS (continued)**

Junior Winners:

James Cygan (men)
Lorilee Pritchard (women)
Natalie and Wayne Seybold (pairs)
Amanda Newman and Jerry Santoferrara (ice dance)

Novice Winners:

Rudy Galindo (men)
Kathryn Adams (women)

**1982 CANADIAN CHAMPIONSHIPS**
(Brandon, MB, January 25-31, 1982)

Men:

1. Brian Orser
2. Brian Pockar
3. Dennis Coi
4. Gary Beacom
5. Gordon Forbes
6. Kevin Parker
7. Neil Paterson
8. Neil Giroday
9. Shaun McGill
10. Louis Lasorsa

Women:

1. Kay Thomson
2. Elizabeth Manley
3. Tracey Wainman
4. Diane Mae Ogibowski
5. Charlene Wong
6. Andrea Hall
7. Kathryn Osterberg
8. Kerry Smith
9. Anissa Gurchin
10. Colette Brabant

Pairs:

1. Barbara Underhill and Paul Martini
2. Lorri Baier and Lloyd Eisler
3. Becky Gough and Mark Rowsom
4. Melinda Kunhegyi and Lyndon Johnston
5. Katherina Matousek and Eric Thomsen
6. Vanessa Howe and Jeffrey Mawle

Ice Dance:

1. Tracy Wilson and Rob McCall
2. Kelly Johnson and Kris Barber
3. Joanne French and John Thomas
4. Karyn and Rod Garossino
5. Tracy Michael and Kerry Spong
6. Donna Martini and John Coyne
7. Karen Taylor and Robert Burk
8. Teri-Lynn Black and Mirko Savic
9. Catherine Cardiff and Keith Baker

In the women's event, something quite unexpected occurred - Tracey Wainman didn't win. Despite suffering from a bad stomach flu, Wainman managed to perform some of the best figures of her career to take an early lead. Things unraveled as the event went on, with Wainman falling three times in the free skate. 16-year-old Elizabeth Manley of Ottawa rose to the occasion with very strong performances, but her sixth-place finish in the figures kept her behind Kay Thomson overall. Wainman settled for bronze just ahead of Manitoba's own Diane Mae Ogibowski. Wainman took her defeat very hard but in a show of great sportsmanship, many of her competitors went out of their way to try to cheer her up. After losing his national title in Halifax in 1981 and placing behind Brian Orser at the World Championships that followed, Brian Pockar had missed Skate America after suffering complications following an operation for a ruptured appendix. Then came the two stress fractures in his left leg in practice that caused him to miss the NHK Trophy in Japan. With only about two months of training, he arrived in Brandon unprepared and fueled by determination. Pockar won the school figures with first-place ordinals from six of the seven judges. The seventh tied Pockar and 21-year-old Gary Beacom, who won the second figure. Orser, Gordon Forbes and Dennis Coi followed in the standings. In the short program, Pockar missed his double flip/triple toe combination. It was his first time falling in a short program at the Canadian Championships in seven years. Orser won with a clean performance, earning a slew of 5.8s and 5.9s. After the first two phases in the competition, Pockar and Orser were in a tie with 2.2 points each. Coi was second in the short program, skating cleanly though almost running into the boards after landing a required double Salchow. In the free skate, Brian Orser skated very well, landing a triple Axel but was slightly off balance on the landings of his triple Lutz and triple Salchow. Pockar upped his game with a more technically demanding program than usual, despite injuring himself a third time - spiking his right foot in practice before the free skate. Two of the seven judges tied Orser and Pockar, but the rest gave Orser top marks and for a second year in a row, Orser won the gold. Coi skated brilliantly to move up and take the bronze over Beacom. World Champion Donald Jackson called Pockar's gutsy free skate the "biggest surprise... [and] the most exciting event of the Canadian Championships."

**European Championships.** At the Charlemagne Ice Rink in Lyon, France, history was made in all four disciplines - but not without putting the safety of many of the skaters in jeopardy. To the pleasure of the French audience, Jean-Christophe Simond won the compulsory figures ahead of defending champion Igor Bobrin, Heiko Fischer, Norbert Schramm and Vladimir Kotin. Simond earned marks as high as 4.4 in the figures but in the short program, he singled a double Axel. Bobrin stumbled on his jump combination as well. Their errors opened the door for Jozef Sabovčík, only seventh in the figures, to win that phase of the event ahead of Schramm, Rudi Cerne and Alexandr Fadeev. In the free skate, the ordinals were all over the place and it was 21-year-old Schramm who came out on top. He nailed four triples including the Lutz and his only major error was a fall on a triple loop attempt. His victory was not only particularly significant in that he had only placed third at that year's West German Championships: he became the first German skater to take the European men's title since the Berlin Wall was erected. Skating last in the free skate, Simond rallied back with a jam-packed program with six clean triples (including a Lutz and flip) but fell attempting a second triple toe-loop. Bobrin claimed the bronze, followed by Cerne, Fadeev, Fischer, Kotin and Sabovčík. Poland's sole entry at the competition Grzegorz Filipowski finished ninth, skating to "The Impossible Dream" after taking a 36-hour train ride to the event.

### CANADIAN CHAMPIONSHIPS (continued)

Fours:

1. Melinda Kunhegyi, Becky Gough, Lyndon Johnston and Mark Rowsom
2. Susan Kinai, Cheryl Susick, David Howe and William Thompson
3. Lynn Frasson, Lawrie Emerson, Mark Bystreck and Sidney Shanks
4. Christine Hough, Laurene Collin, Kevin Wheeler and Sean Milligan
5. Isabelle Laverdure, Isabelle Brasseur, Pascal Courchesne and Jean-Michel Bombardier

Junior Winners:

Lyndon Johnston (men)
Monica Lipson (women)
Julie Brault and Richard Gauthier (pairs)
Teri-Lynn Black and Mirko Savic (ice dance)

Novice Winners:

Marc Ferland (men)
Melissa Murphy (women)
Christine Hough and Kevin Wheeler (pairs)
Jo-Anne Borlase and Scott Chalmers (ice dance)

### 1982 EUROPEAN CHAMPIONSHIPS (Lyon, France, February 2-7, 1982)

Men:

1. Norbert Schramm (FRG)
2. Jean-Christophe Simond (FRA)
3. Igor Bobrin (SOV)
4. Rudi Cerne (FRG)
5. Alexandr Fadeev (SOV)
6. Heiko Fischer (FRG)
7. Vladimir Kotin (SOV)
8. Jozef Sabovčík (CZE)
9. Grzegorz Filipowski (POL)
10. Didier Monge (FRA)

Women:

1. Claudia Kristofics-Binder (AUT)
2. Katarina Witt (GDR)
3. Elena Vodorezova (SOV)
4. Debbie Cottrill (GRB)
5. Claudia Leistner (FRG)
6. Kristiina Wegelius (FIN)
7. Carola Paul (GDR)
8. Karen Wood (GRB)
9. Janina Wirth (GDR)
10. Anna Antonova (SOV)

Pairs:

1. Sabine Baeß and Tassilo Thierbach (GDR)
2. Marina Pestova and Stanislav Leonovich (SOV)
3. Irina Vorobieva and Igor Lisovsky (SOV)
4. Veronika Pershina and Marat Akbarov (SOV)
5. Birgit Lorenz and Knut Schubert (GDR)
6. Susan Garland and Robert Daw (GRB)
7. Bettina Hage and Stefan Zins (FRG)
8. Nathalie Tortel and Xavier Videau (FRA)
9. Gaby and Jörg Galambos (SUI)

In 1972, Trixi Schuba didn't win the free skate at the European Championships. However, she won the gold based on a massive lead in the school figures. The same thing happened exactly ten years later in the women's event in Lyon when Vienna's Claudia Kristofics-Binder became the first Austrian woman since Schuba to take the European title. Kristofics-Binder was only third in the short program and free skate, both of which were won by Katarina Witt. Witt skated last in the free skate and managed three clean triples - two toe-loops and a Salchow. Kristofics-Binder had the skate of her life, matching Witt's effort with three clean triple Salchows, but the judges preferred the verve and vitality of Witt and West Germany's Claudia Leistner. Witt's sixth-place finish in the figures kept her in second overall. Elena Vodorezova of the Soviet Union finished third. History was made in the pairs event when Sabine Baeß and Tassilo Thierbach became the first East German team to win the European title. They were also the first non-Soviet team to win in eighteen years. Baeß and Thierbach's path to victory wasn't easy. Defending champions Irina Vorobieva and Igor Lisovsky narrowly defeated them in the short program. However, when an injured Vorobieva fell twice in the free skate, it opened the door for Baeß and Thierbach. They met the challenge with an athletic free skate. Another Soviet pair, Marina Pestova and Stanislav Leonovich took the silver and Vorobieva and Livoski were forced to settle for bronze. Nineteen teams competed in the ice dance event in Lyon but Jayne Torvill and Christopher Dean were in a class of their own. They danced their way to their second European title with a stunning Blues OSP to "Summertime" and their iconic *Mack and Mabel* free dance. The Britons received eleven 6.0s throughout the competition, setting a new European record. Natalia Bestemianova and Andrei Bukin overshadowed their more experienced Soviet teammates Irina Moiseeva and Andrei Minenkov with their interpretation of Stravinsky's "The Firebird" to claim the silver. The real drama at the event had absolutely nothing to do with figure skating. The night before the men's free skate, a bomb went off in the parking lot of the rink. During the warmup for the men's free skate, demonstrators supporting the solidarity movement in Poland stormed the rink and jumped over the boards onto the ice holding 'Solidarity' banners. The demonstrators began to throw bottles, shattering glass over the ice. The skaters were quickly led off the warm-up and security took control of the situation, but not all the glass shards were removed and the ice was not resurfaced as a precaution. The final flight of men had to rework their programs to avoid the shards. The frightening incident affected the competitors significantly and was unnerving for everyone in attendance.

**World Championships.** In March, many of the world's best figure skaters gathered at the Brøndby-Hallen in Copenhagen, Denmark. The event was the first (and to this day only) World Championships held in Denmark. The event was covered widely in the international media, with CTV, ABC, Eurosport, BBC, ITV and NHK all televising the action to millions around the world. A who's who of figure skating was in attendance either as commentators, coaches or spectators, including Dick Button, the Protopopovs, Irina Rodnina and Alexander Zaitsev, Peggy Fleming and Emmerich Danzer. Though visitors raved about the warm Danish hospitality, the event wasn't without its hiccups. The official hotel was 25 minutes away from the main rink and the practice rink (which was bigger than the competition rink and bone-chillingly cold) was even further away. Skaters and coaches spent upwards of five hours a day travelling back and forth. The British and American teams were paired for practice sessions, and there were complaints that the American skaters were too aggressive on the ice. Betty Callaway made a complaint through the British team leader to their American counterpart, and the U.S. ice dancers were warned to give teams the right of way when they were doing run-throughs.

**EUROPEAN CHAMPIONSHIPS**
(continued)

Ice Dance:

1. Jayne Torvill and Christopher Dean (GRB)
2. Natalia Bestemianova and Andrei Bukin (SOV)
3. Irina Moiseeva and Andrei Minenkov (SOV)
4. Olga Volozhinskaya and Alexandr Svinin (SOV)
5. Karen Barber and Nicky Slater (GRB)
6. Nathalie Hervé and Pierre Béchu (FRA)
7. Jana Beránková and Jan Barták (CZE)
8. Judit Péterfy and Csaba Bálint (HUN)
9. Wendy Sessions and Stephen Williams (GRB)
10. Birgit Goller and Peter Klisch (FRG)

**1982 WORLD CHAMPIONSHIPS**
(Copenhagen, Denmark, March 9-14, 1982)

Men:

1. Scott Hamilton (USA)
2. Norbert Schramm (FRG)
3. Brian Pockar (CAN)
4. Brian Orser (CAN)
5. Jean-Christophe Simond (FRA)
6. Robert Wagenhoffer (USA)
7. Igor Bobrin (SOV)
8. David Santee (USA)
9. Fumio Igarashi (JPN)
10. Alexandr Fadeev (SOV)

Women:

1. Elaine Zayak (USA)
2. Katarina Witt (GDR)
3. Claudia Kristofics-Binder (AUT)
4. Claudia Leistner (FRG)
5. Elena Vodorezova (SOV)
6. Rosalynn Sumners (USA)
7. Vikki de Vries (USA)
8. Kay Thomson (CAN)
9. Kristiina Wegelius (FIN)
10. Debbie Cottrill (GRB)

Pairs:

1. Sabine Baeß and Tassilo Thierbach (GDR)
2. Marina Pestova and Stanislav Leonovich (SOV)
3. Kitty and Peter Carruthers (USA)
4. Barbara Underhill and Paul Martini (CAN)
5. Irina Vorobieva and Igor Lisovsky (SOV)
6. Veronika Pershina and Marat Akbarov (SOV)
7. Birgit Lorenz and Knut Schubert (GDR)
8. Lea Ann Miller and Bill Fauver (USA)
9. Lorri Baier and Lloyd Eisler (CAN)
10. Maria Di Domenico and Burt Lancon (USA)

A new trial judging system that ultimately never got off the ground was tested in Copenhagen. Each discipline was judged by two panels. One panel judged men's figures and short and women's long; the other women's figures and short and men's long. Pairs and dance also had two panels - one for the short program or compulsory dances and OSP and another for the finals. The purpose of the trial was to curb the opportunity for bloc judging, but judges complained there was an imbalance of assignments. The ISU ultimately surmised that the experiment didn't change the results in the competition significantly. An unlucky thirteen pairs vied for gold in the pairs event in Copenhagen. A month before the event, it was announced that World Champions Irina Vorobieva and Igor Lisovsky would not compete due to injury and many were surprised when they showed up. Vorobieva had torn cartilage in her knee and skated with a bandaged leg. Lisovsky was also nursing an injury which made lifts a challenge. In the short program, clean performances put East Germans Sabine Baeß and Tassilo Thierbach and Tassilo Thierbach and Soviets Marina Pestova and Stanislav Leonovich in the top two positions, ahead of the defending Champions, who botched their closing pair spin combination. Baeß and Thierbach delivered a technically demanding free skate and in winning, made history as the first East German pair to win a World title. Pestova and Leonovich held on to the second position, but it was very close between them and Kitty and Peter Carruthers. The American pair skated superbly, nailing a triple twist, throw triple Salchow and throw double Axel. Their goal was to make the top five and they only lost the silver by one ordinal placing. Canada's Barbara Underhill and Paul Martini moved up to fourth, their performance marred by a freak fall 20 seconds before the end of an otherwise fabulous effort that included a triple twist and throw triple Salchow. The Canadians chalked it all up to a loss of concentration when their music was drowned out by applause. Their result was Canada's best finish in pairs skating at the World Championships since Maria and Otto Jelinek won in 1962, and they beat the reigning World Champions in the process. A fall on a throw triple loop and singed side-by-side double flip dropped Canada's second pair, Lorri Baier and Lloyd Eisler down to ninth, four places behind Vorobieva and Livosky. before the men's event, Scott Hamilton and Norbert Schramm shared practiced ice in Oberstdorf, West Germany. The defending World Champion and the dynamic army corporal and painter both had charisma, but their skating styles couldn't have been any more different. When the West German press got word of this, they went to town, pegging Hamilton as 'the athlete' and Schramm as 'the artist'. By the time the two young men arrived in Copenhagen, Schramm's stock had risen and Hamilton was ready to rumble. Because of a record 30 entries, the men had to be up at four o'clock in the morning and on the ice for their first school figures at six o'clock, despite an ISU recommendation that competitions shouldn't start before eight. This unfortunate situation led the ISU to expand the schedule of the World Championships by an extra day in 1983. Scott Hamilton was second to skate and had to wait four and a half hours between performing his first and second figure. After the rocker, paragraph double three and change loop were skated, France's Jean-Christophe Simond led the way, ahead of Hamilton, David Santee, Igor Bobrin, Brian Pockar and Schramm, Philippe Paulet and Fumio Igarashi. Brian Orser had hoped to improve upon his sixth-place finish at his first World Championships the year prior, but buried himself on the first figure, receiving scores in the 3.0 to 3.7 range. He managed to move up to 12th after the second and third figures. He wasn't the only excellent free skater to struggle in the figures either.

**WORLD CHAMPIONSHIPS (continued)**

Ice Dance:

1. Jayne Torvill and Christopher Dean (GRB)
2. Natalia Bestemianova and Andrei Bukin (SOV)
3. Irina Moiseeva and Andrei Minenkov (SOV)
4. Judy Blumberg and Michael Seibert (USA)
5. Carol Fox and Richard Dalley (USA)
6. Olga Volozhinskaya and Alexandr Svinin (SOV)
7. Karen Barber and Nicky Slater (GRB)
8. Elisa Spitz and Scott Gregory (USA)
9. Jana Beránková and Jan Barták (CZE)
10. Tracy Wilson and Rob McCall (CAN)

Jozef Sabovčík placed 18th. In the short program, the required flip combination had many of the men tumbling like dominos. Simond, Bobrin, Igarashi, Pockar and Santee all struggled with their combinations. Hamilton, Schramm, Orser, Robert Wagenhoffer, Rudi Cerne and Sabovčík were among the handful of contenders that were successful. Orser, delivering a career-best short program, placed third in that segment in the competition, behind Hamilton and Schramm. Schramm nailed his free skate, whipping the crowd into a frenzy with his new age style. Hamilton landed six triples and also had the audience in the palm of his hand with his energy and athleticism. Hamilton received five 5.9s for technical merit; Schramm five 5.9s for artistic impression. When the final scores were calculated, Hamilton came out on top, becoming the first American man in over a decade to win two consecutive World titles. Despite two minor errors in his free skating performance Pockar won the bronze medal. Though Pockar didn't place in the top three in any phase of the competition, his overall consistency earned Canada's first medal in the men's event at the World Championships in eight years. It was a sweet redemption after his trials and tribulations. Orser landed a triple Axel in his free skate and finished fourth overall. Though he placed eighth in both the short program and free skate, Simond placed fifth overall, one spot ahead of Wagenhoffer, who many felt gave two of the most underscored and underrated performances in the competition. Bobrin, Santee, Igarashi and Alexandr Fadeev rounded out the top ten. A record 34 women from 22 nations participated in the women's figures, which also started at six in the morning. Soviet skater Elena Vodorezova started her double threes on the wrong foot. Referee Elemér Terták only stopped her after a spectator called out "wrong foot!" It threw her off, and she had to reskate the double three without another warmup or any reference points to align the figure. Canada's Elizabeth Manley had an equally disastrous showing on the rocker, missing her center entirely. After all three figures were skated, Austria's Claudia Kristofics-Binder led the pack, ahead of Kristina Wegelius, Debbie Cottrill, Elaine Zayak, Vodorezova, Kay Thomson, Sonja Stanek, Vikki de Vries and Katarina Witt. Elizabeth Manley was 23rd. Witt won the short program, nailing a double flip/triple toe-loop combination. Claudia Leistner, only 14th in figures, placed second. Vodorezova was third despite doing only a single loop in her combination. Some speculated was 'a gift' after the refereeing mishap in the figures as Rosalynn Sumners and Wegelius, who placed fourth and fifth, performed clean combination jumps. Kristofics-Binder, the leader after the figures, had a step between her double flip and double loop, placing ninth in the short. Kay Thomson placed sixth, earning marks ranging from 5.1 to 5.7. It was an impressive showing, considering she had injured both her back and hip in practice. Elizabeth Manley placed 11th in the short and moved up to 17th overall. The biggest controversy surrounded Cottrill, who was ranked eighth in the short after being in the top three after figures. Canadian judge Margaret Berezowski gave her a 4.8 for required elements, while the other judges gave her 5.2s and 5.3s. Cottrill's coach Emmerich Danzer felt all of her marks had been too low and claimed that there was an Austrian conspiracy to 'hold up' Kristofics-Binder. The fact that another Canadian judge, Joyce Hisey, had given low marks to Torvill and Dean in the OSP only fueled the fire. Manley tumbled on a triple toe-loop early in her free skate but recovered well and landed two triple Salchows. She later joked to a reporter that playing the catch-up game after that disastrous first figure was "a bit like trying to eat peanut butter through a straw". Thomson stepped out of her triple Lutz but rebounded with three beautiful double Axels. Wegelius and Cottrill both gave disappointing performances, while Kristofics-Binder had one of her better skates at the Worlds in recent years. Witt landed a double Lutz/triple toe-loop combination, triple Salchow, triple toe-loop and two double Axels and squeaked out a rare triple flip but stepped out a triple Salchow and double Axel. Leistner landed five triples - two toe-loops, two Salchows and a loop. Zayak was so distraught after her disappointing short program that she cried in the dressing room before taking the ice. She ended up skating brilliantly, landing a record six triple jumps. Her remarkable effort, coupled with the flip-flopping results of skaters who excelled in the figures and the short program, was enough for her to move up and claim the gold medal. Witt's placement over Leistner in the free skate helped secure the silver, while Kristofics-Binder's figures win and comeback free skate were enough for the bronze. Leistner, Vodorezova, Sumners, Vikki de Vries, Thomson, Wegelius and Cottrill rounded out the top ten. Manley was an unlucky 13th. Manley would have been one spot higher had 14-year-old Janina Wirth of East Germany not been allowed to compete. Though she was a year younger than the minimum age, she entered because of a loophole that permitted the reigning World Junior Champions to compete even if they were underage. In winning both singles titles, Zayak and Hamilton were the first American singles skaters to win World titles in the same year since 1959, when David Jenkins and Carol Heiss took top honours. Zayak was also the first former World Junior Champion to translate their past success to a victory in the women's event at the World Championships.

In the ice dance event, the compulsories were the Blues, Yankee Polka and Viennese Waltz. Christopher Dean took an uncharacteristic tumble in the warmup for the Yankee Polka. He and Jayne Torvill received marks up to 5.9 for that dance but were placed second behind Judy Blumberg and Michael Seibert by Canadian judge Joyce Hisey. After winning all compulsories, Torvill and Dean had a strong lead ahead of Natalia Bestemianova and Andrei Bukin, Blumberg and Seibert and Irina Moiseeva and Andrei Minenkov. Canada's lone entry, Tracy Wilson and Rob McCall were tenth. In her report of the event for the *Canadian Skater*, Sandra Stevenson observed, "Ludwig Gassner was the reason for a judges' huddle in the first compulsory dance, the Blues. When it came time for the Hungarian champions [Judit Péterfy and Csaba Bálint] to skate, the third Russians took the ice because the [Hungarians] had to withdraw due to illness. Olga [Volozhinskaya] and her partner did a relatively good Blues and earned marks from 5.0 to 5.4 but Herr Gassner gave them a 4.4, which is probably what the Hungarian couple would have got had they competed. Of course, Herr Gassner was on the lookout for the Russians when they did their other two compulsories and gave them their highest marks for these portions." Torvill and Dean's haunting Blues OSP to "Summertime" had the slowest tempo permitted by ISU. It brought the house down in Copenhagen and helped the Brits expand their already monumental lead entering the free dance. The audience was so moved by Torvill and Dean's performance that John Hennessy recalled one spectator turning to him crying and shaking their head saying, "I just can't believe it." They earned six 6.0s, including a perfect set from French judge Lysiane Lauret. It was a new record of perfect marks for the OSP at the Worlds. Torvill and Dean's *Mack and Mabel* free dance brought the house down too and Torvill accidentally ripping open Dean's jacket only made the audience love it more. They earned a standing ovation before their program was even finished and another five perfect 6.0s helped them claim their second World title with ease. It is interesting to note that there was no British judge on either of the panels used in the event and that Torvill and Dean's 6.0s were the only perfect scores of the entire competition. They likely would have even received more 6.0s had they not been the first couple to skate in their free dance group. The BBC postponed the nine o'clock news to show Torvill and Dean's free dance live. Bestemianova and Bukin took the silver, while 'Min and Mo' moved ahead of Judy Blumberg and Michael Seibert to claim the bronze. Carol Fox and Richard Dalley finished fourth and Tracy Wilson and Rob McCall were tenth. Fox and Dalley's strong showing was remarkable, in that the day before leaving for Copenhagen, Dalley slid into the boards at Ron Ludington's feet, suffering a concussion, hairline fracture and lumbar vertebra injury and Fox pulled a muscle in her neck. Though they finished in the last two places, Saila Saarinen and Kim Jacobson and Ulla Örnmarker and Thomas Svedberg made history as the first ice dance teams from Finland and Sweden to compete at the World Championships. The competition was the first World Championships in 18 years in which a skater from the Soviet Union didn't win a gold medal. At the closing banquet, Christopher Dean gave a speech referencing the fairy tales Hans Christian Andersen wrote in Copenhagen and remarked that many skaters at the Worlds created their own fairy tale moments. A sellout crowd attended the Exhibition Gala. Among the attendees was Queen Margrethe II of Denmark. Scott Hamilton had a rough skate to "New York, New York" and joked to Dick Button, "It was my first queen." On the ISU tour that followed the World Championships, Christopher Dean traded his tickets for the Bolshoi Ballet with Brian Pockar for tickets to the Moscow State Circus... and so the concept for *Barnum* was born.

*Jayne Torvill and Christopher Dean. Photo by Fred & Joan Dean, courtesy Paul Dean, "Ice & Roller Skate" magazine archive.*

*Jayne Torvill and Christopher Dean. Photo by Fred & Joan Dean, courtesy Fred Dean, "Ice & Roller Skate" magazine archive.*

# 1982-1983 SEASON

Hit Songs: "Every Breath You Take" by The Police, "Sweet Dreams (Are Made Of This)" by The Eurythmics, "Blue Monday" by New Order, "Total Eclipse of the Heart" by Bonnie Taylor, "Maniac" by Michael Sembello
Hit Movies: Return of the Jedi, Flashdance, Risky Business, Terms of Endearment, Yentl
Hit TV: The Littlest Hobo, M*A*S*H, Dynasty, Newhart, Mr. Dressup
News: AIDS Epidemic recognized by CDC, Margaret Thatcher re-elected as British Prime Minister, Death of Princess Grace, Pope John Paul II signs new Roman Catholic Code, Bertha Wilson makes history as first woman to serve in Canada's Supreme Court of Justice

## PEOPLE

Following the 1981-1982 season, several top skaters turned professional or retired. David Santee joined John Curry's company and competed on the professional circuit. Robert Wagenhoffer joined the *Ice Capades*. Claudia Kristofics-Binder and Debbie Cottrill joined the cast of *Holiday on Ice*. Fumio Igarashi and Priscilla Hill toured as competitors in the Pro-Skate series, as did Brian Pockar, who also scored a gig as a commentator for CTV. Irina Moiseeva and Andrei Minenkov officially retired from competitive skating in November of 1983 in a ceremony at the Prize Of Moscow News competition at the Luzhniki Palace of Sports. Moiseeva was pregnant with the couple's daughter Elena at the time.

Before the United States Olympic Hall of Fame's official home was not even constructed, Dick Button and Peggy Fleming made history as the first figure skaters to be inducted. They were selected by members of the National Sportswriters and Sportscasters Association.

55-year-old André Calame suffered a fatal heart attack at the Orly airport in Paris in November. Calame founded the international skating school in St. Gervais, France and worked with several elite skaters over the years, including Jean-Christophe Simond, Claudia Kristofics-Binder and Rita Trapanese. In 1950, Calame and his partner Elyane Steinemann made history as the first pairs team from Switzerland to medal at the European Championships.

Natalia Bestemianova became a wife and a stepmother when she married Igor Bobrin, who had a 6-year-old son from his first marriage. Andrei Bukin, the other half of 'B and B', was married to his former partner Olga Abankina.

At the figure skating competition at the Spartakiad of the Peoples of the USSR in Krasnoyarsk in January, Kira Ivanova won the women's event but was stripped of her title when she didn't show up at the doping test afterward because she had been drinking. Ivanova was subsequently pulled from the Soviet national team.

Elaine Zayak was named Dial High School Athlete of the Year at the Touchdown Club in Washington D.C.'s annual black-tie dinner in January. The event was attended by Vice-President George H.W. Bush and afterwards, Zayak was given a tour of The White House.

Broadway and television producer Paul Feigay passed in February in Brewster, New York. Though well-remembered for bringing Leonard Bernstein's *On The Town* to Broadway and producing *Omnibus* in the 50s, Feigay played an important role in figure skating history, co-founding Candid Productions with Dick Button in 1959.

The newest inductees to the U.S. Figure Skating Hall of Fame were George Henry Browne and Eugene Turner. Browne, the Headmaster at Browne and Nichols School in Cambridge, Massachusetts, helped bring the Continental Style of skating to America and penned several important books on the sport. Browne was inducted posthumously. Turner, a U.S. Champion in both singles and pairs and a national medallist in ice dance, received his award at the Los Angeles Figure Skating Club's Golden (50th) Anniversary Revue in June. The timing was fitting for the first skater from the club to be so honoured.

Former USFSA President Harry N. Keighley of Chicago passed away at the age of 81. A long-time judge, referee and accountant, Keighley chaired six different USFSA Committees and led the Association during the rebuilding years following World War II.

World Champion and legendary coach John Nicks married Yvonne Littlefield. Nicks and Littlefield both taught at *Ice Capades* Chalets in Costa Mesa and North Hollywood, California.

George Takashi Yonekura was elected as the USFSA's first Asian American President. Yonekura's road to the top of the largely white American skating administration was a really big deal. During World War II, he and his parents Katsuzo and Masako were among the thousands of Japanese families interned at The Topaz War Relocation Center in Utah. It was in this 'camp' that he met and married his wife Margaret Wakayama in 1945. George first became interested in skating in 1958, when his daughter Lynn took up the sport. He was first elected to the USFSA Executive Committee nearly a decade later, after having served for many years on the board of the St. Moritz Ice Skating Club. He also served as an international judge and America's Team Leader at both the 1978 and 1979 World Championships. Off the ice, George was President of Blaco Printers, Inc. He used his connections to create and print World Team booklets as well as test and competition forms. It was during George's term as USFSA President that Tiffany Chin made history in 1985, as the first Asian American figure skater to win a U.S. senior title and medal at the World Championships.

## FASHION

UnicornSport kept with figure skating's fashion trends, designing a *Star Wars*-inspired skating jumper with cap sleeves and Flash Dance suspender trunks with attached skirt. Spandex and sequins were all the rage, as were garage doors, rouge, hairspray and mousse.

Robin Cousins donated the costume he wore in the free skate at the 1980 Winter Olympics to the U.S. Figure Skating Museum and Hall of Fame.

# AROUND THE WORLD

**Canada.** Though the CFSA saw a decline of over three percent in its membership, the country had over 1300 registered clubs and over 157 000 members. 8000 of those members were registered precision teams. The new Canadian Precision Team Championships afforded skaters from coast to coast wonderful new opportunities. Three newly launched learn-to-skate programs, CANSKATE, CANFIGURESKATE and CANPOWERSKATE, transformed the way Canadians were first introduced to the sport.

**Soviet Union.** The Figure Skating Section of the USSR Skating Federation greatly expanded its training programs for elite skaters. In years past, only three or four coaches worked with national team coaches. By 1983, there was a pool of more than 20 experts to choose from. This growth could be attributed to a new department for training figure skating coaches and choreographers that was established at the Institute of Theatre Arts in Moscow. Elena Tchaikovskaya, who coached Lyudmila Pakhomova and Aleksandr Gorshkov and Vladimir Kovalev, explained to a *Soviet Life* reporter, "We must rejuvenate our team. This is the only way Soviet figure skating will again be able to display all of its best qualities."

**Sweden.** One of the country's oldest sports associations, the Stockholm Allmänna Skridskoklubb, celebrated its 100th anniversary in 1983. SASK had the unusual distinction of being one of only two skating clubs in the world to have its own ISU membership, independent of any national governing body. The Svenska Konståkningsförbundet rebranded its magazine *Konståkningsnytt* to *Svensk Konståkning*. Along with the name change came a new full-size format. The magazine was the only one at that time that chronicled the sport of figure skating in the country.

**United Kingdom.** The NSA submitted a bid to host the 1986 World Championships at the National Exhibition Centre in Birmingham, with Solihull and Birmingham used as practice rinks. The UK had not hosted the World Championships since 1950 due to a lack of suitable facilities. Despite the hard work of Peter Jordan, Eileen Anderson, Cliff Dobbins and Harry Lauder, the bid was unsuccessful and the 1986 World Championships were awarded to Geneva.

**United States.** By 1983, the USFSA had over 40 000 skaters and 450 clubs. Precision skating was growing by leaps and bounds and plans were already underway for the first official U.S. Precision Team Skating Championships the following season in Bowling Green, Ohio. The USOC opened a second Olympic Training Center at Lake Placid. The USFSA got a new Executive Director, Larry McCollum, a former Assistant Director of Operations for the USOC. Having previously secured a five-year sponsorship deal from The Campbell Soup Company, the USFSA approved another new contract with General Foods. Skaters appeared in a national ad campaign for Maxwell House, with a percentage of sales contributed to the Memorial Fund. The rise in popularity of professional competitions, along with the new U.S. Professional Championships, led the USFSA to officially pass a new policy that firmly stated, "The USFSA does not endorse or support Professional Figure Skating Competitions."

## BEHIND THE SCENES

The Chinese Taipei Amateur Skating Association and Hong Kong Ice Activities Association joined the ISU, bringing the total number of members to 34.

Lawrence Demmy, the Chairman of the ISU Ice Dance Committee, acknowledged the difficulty that dancers faced finding instrumental rock 'n roll music for the OSP theme used during the 1982-1983 season, but didn't budge on allowing vocals, nor did the Committee allow toe-steps, extended hand-in-hand positions, pulling the lady through the man's legs, skating on one spot, jumping or lifting. Teams were instructed to "create the atmosphere and interpret the character of the music... by creating step movements, leg and body movements, which express and interpret the music of the Rock and Roll." Concerning costumes, dancers were urged to dress in theme but keep it "modest and dignified [as] we are staging a sport and not exhibition or ice revue."

Smoking was far more socially acceptable in the 80s than it is today. However, coaches and judges started to come under fire for lighting up while giving lessons. World Champion Cecilia Colledge wrote a letter to the editor of *American Skating World* complaining, "A number of professionals do not seem to realize that their behaviour, while teaching, is an example to their students. The manner in which a lesson is given is in itself a lesson. Smoking should not be permitted in ice rinks."

## THE AIDS EPIDEMIC

The CDC used the term AIDS (Acquired Immune Deficiency Syndrome) for the first time, noting that women had been infected but continuing to perpetuate the stigma by noting that those of highest risk were "sexually active homosexual or bisexual men with multiple partners; Haitian entrants to the United States; present or past abusers of IV drugs; patients with hemophilia; and sexual partners of individuals at increased risk for AIDS." By May, almost 1500 cases were reported and 38 percent had passed away.

One of the very first prominent skaters to pass away as a result of HIV/AIDS was Phil Romayne, in Los Angeles on March 21, 1983, at the age of 54. Born Philip Romanchuk Jr. to Polish immigrants from Newark, New Jersey, Romayne grew up in the working-class Brooklyn neighbourhood of Greenpoint, known to locals as 'Little Poland'. He first learned to skate at the age of fourteen on a tennis court that had been flooded and frozen in winter. Largely self-taught, he turned professional in 1943 to skate in one of Sonja Henie and Arthur M. Wirtz's ice revues at the Center Theatre. With partners Terry Brent and Cathy Steele, Phil established himself as one of the top adagio pairs skaters in the world in the 50s and 60s. He toured with Tom Arnold's Continental Company and the *Ice Capades* and appeared in ice shows at the Lido in Paris, Stoll Ice Theatre in London, Hotel New Yorker and Hotel Roosevelt in New Orleans. He also appeared on *The Ed Sullivan Show*. After he stopped performing, Phil worked as a coach and choreographer for the *Ice Capades* and taught skating in Burbank, California.

## FILMS AND TELEVISION

Figure skaters lit up the small screen during the 1982-1983 season. Toller Cranston's CTV special *The Magic Planet* was another successful collaboration with director David Acomba and costume designer Frances Dafoe, featuring Brian Pockar, Sandra and Val Bezic and Wendy Burge. Cranston also appeared in the popular television special *The Snow Queen: A Skating Ballet*, alongside John Curry, Dorothy Hamill, Janet Lynn, JoJo Starbuck and Sandra Bezic. Dorothy Hamill was on *Fantasy Island* and *Diff'rent Strokes*, as well as Andy Williams' *New England Christmas* special. Robin Cousins showed up on Jimmy Savile's *Jim'll Fix It*.

In December, the film *Six Weeks* was released by PolyGram Pictures. Katherine Healy played a twelve-year old dying of leukemia in the drama, which starred Mary Tyler Moore and Dudley Moore. For her role, Healy was nominated for Best New Female Star of the Year at the Golden Globe Awards.

In January, Richard Ciupka's Canadian slasher flick *Curtains* made history as the first horror film to feature a figure skating scene. A stunt double named Jo-Anne Hannah was brought in to shoot the scene, playing both the part of a skater and a masked killer chasing her on the ice. The low-budget film became a classic amongst fans of the genre.

The Travelers Corporation produced a 30-minute film narrated by Dick Button called *Skating Now and Then*, featuring footage of some of skating's early champions and today's stars. The film was available for loan free of cost to all U.S. skating clubs.

## ART AND HISTORY

Judy Blumberg and Michael Seibert took their skates to canvas to design the logo for the 1983 U.S. Championships program and souvenir poster. The unique art piece was created using blades and paint.

The U.S. Figure Skating Museum unveiled a new exhibition called *Beauty, Fantasy, and Fun on Ice*, featuring a new permanent collection of porcelain, bronze and glass figurines donated by collector Gladys McFerron.

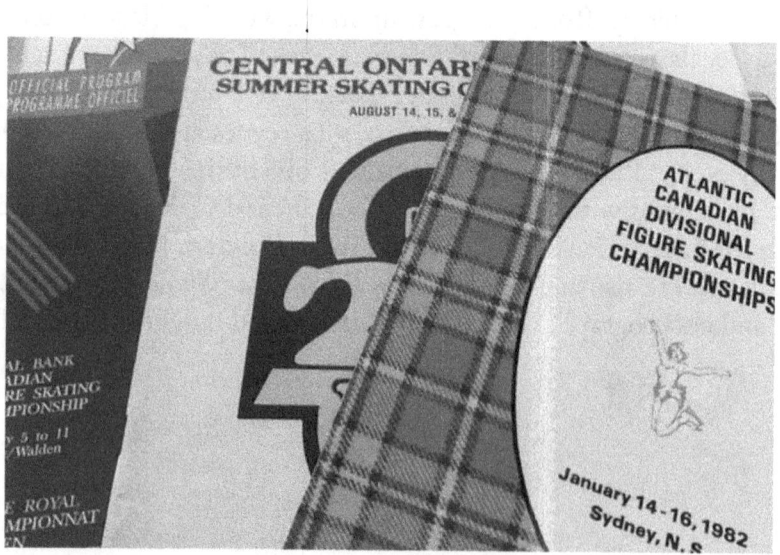

*1980s skating programs, donated to the author's collection by Yvonne Butorac. Author photograph.*

# Fall Internationals

**1982 COUPES DES ALPES (Saint Gervais, France and Oberstdorf, West Germany, August 18-22, 1982 and August 25-28, 1982)**

Grand Prix de St. Gervais Winners:

Fernand Fédronic (FRA) - men
Manuela Ruben (FRG) - women
Inna Volyanskaya and Valery Spiridonov (SOV) - pairs
Marina Klimova and Sergei Ponomarenko (SOV) - ice dance

Nebelhorn Trophy (Oberstdorf) Winners:

Leonardo-Christian Azzola (FRG) - men
Manuela Ruben (FRG) - women
Inna Volyanskaya and Valery Spiridonov (SOV) - pairs
Marina Klimova and Sergei Ponomarenko (SOV) - ice dance

**1982 ASKÖ CUP OF VIENNA (Vienna, Austria, September 20-24, 1982)**

Women:

1. Rosanna Tovi (USA)
2. Melissa Thomas (USA)
3. Natalia Lebedeva (SOV)

**1982 ST. IVEL ICE INTERNATIONAL (London, England, September 27-30, 1982)**

Men:

1. Brian Orser (CAN)
2. Norbert Schramm (FRG)
3. Tom Dickson (USA)

Women:

1. Elaine Zayak (USA)
2. Tracey Wainman (CAN)
3. Cornelia Tesch (FRG)

Pairs:

1. Lyudmila Koblova and Andrei Kalitin (SOV)
2. Melina Kunhegyi and Lyndon Johnston (CAN)
3. Susan Garland and Ian Jenkins (GRB)

Ice Dance:

1. Judy Blumberg and Michael Seibert (USA)
2. Karen Barber and Nicky Slater (GRB)
3. Elena Batanova and Alexei Soloviev (SOV)

**1982 SKATE AMERICA (Lake Placid, NY, October 7-10, 1982)**

Men:

1. Scott Hamilton (USA)
2. Heiko Fischer (FRG)
3. Jozef Sabovčík (CZE)

Women:

1. Rosalynn Sumners (USA)
2. Claudia Leistner (FRG)
3. Kristiina Wegelius (FIN)

Pairs:

1. Elena Valova and Oleg Vasiliev (SOV)
2. Lea Ann Miller and Bill Fauver (USA)
3. Nellie Chervotkina and Victor Teslia (SOV)

Ice Dance:

1. Elisa Spitz and Scott Gregory (USA)
2. Elena Garanina and Igor Zavozin (SOV)
3. Karyn and Rod Garossino (CAN)

**1982 TOURS INTERNATIONAL - JACQUES FAVART TROPHY (Tours, France, October 14-17, 1982)**

Men:

1. Daniel Doran (USA)
2. Laurent Depouilly (FRA)
3. Craig Henderson (USA)

Women:

1. Agnès Gosselin (FRA)
2. Susanne Gschwend (AUT)
3. Sophie Cuissot (FRA)

**1982 GRAND PRIX SNP (Banská Bystrica, Czechoslovakia, October 18-21, 1982)**

Men:

1. Nils Köpp (GDR)
2. Andrzej Strzelec (POL)
3. Alain Miquel (FRA)

Women:

1. Simone Koch (GDR)
2. Gabriela Ballová (CZE)
3. Ingrid Karl (FRG)

**1982 SKATE CANADA (Kitchener, ON, October 28-30, 1982)**

Men:

1. Brian Boitano (USA)
2. Brian Orser (CAN)
3. Heiko Fischer (FRG)

Women:

1. Vikki de Vries (USA)
2. Kristiina Wegelius (FIN)
3. Rosalynn Sumners (USA)

Ice Dance:

1. Elisa Spitz and Scott Gregory (USA)
2. Tracy Wilson and Rob McCall (CAN)
3. Natalia Annenko and Genrikh Sretenski (SOV)

**1982 PRAGUE SKATE (Prague, Czechoslovakia, November 4-6, 1982)**

Men:

1. Jozef Sabovčík (CZE)
2. André Bourgeois (CAN)
3. Makoto Kano (JPN)

Women:

1. Agnès Gosselin (FRA)
2. Natalia Lebedeva (SOV)
3. Karin Hendschke (GDR)

Pairs:

1. Babette Preußler and Torsten Ohlow (GDR)
2. Elena Bechke and Valeri Kornienko (SOV)
3. Jana Havlová and René Novotný (CZE)

**1982 ENNIA CHALLENGE CUP INTERNATIONAL FREE SKATING COMPETITION (The Hague, Netherlands, November 9-14, 1982)**

Men:

1. Brian Boitano (USA)
2. Norbert Schramm (FRG)
3. Jozef Sabovčík (CZE)

Women:

1. Vikki de Vries (USA)
2. Claudia Leistner (FRG)
3. Anna Antonova (SOV)

Pairs:

1. Larisa Selezneva and Oleg Makarov (SOV)
2. Birgit Lorenz and Knut Schubert (GDR)
3. Susan Garland and Ian Jenkins (GRB)

Ice Dance:

1. Karen Barber and Nicky Slater (GRB)
2. Marina Klimova and Sergei Ponomarenko (SOV)
3. Natalia Karmysheva and Rostislav Sinitsyn (SOV)

# Fall Internationals and Other Competitions

**1982 GOLDEN SPIN OF ZAGREB (Zagreb, Yugoslavia, November 16-21, 1982)**

Men:

1. Masaru Ogawa (JPN)
2. Jaochim Ehmann (FRG)
3. Miljan Begović (YUG)

Women:

1. Sanda Dubravčić (YUG)
2. Natalia Ovchinnikova (SOV)
3. Katrien Pauwels (BEL)

Ice Dance:

1. Natalia Annenko and Genrikh Sretenski (SOV)
2. Susie Wynne and Joseph Druar (USA)
3. Judit Péterfy and Csaba Bálint (HUN)

**1982 POKAL DER BLAUEN SCHWERTER (Karl-Marx-Stadt, East Germany, November 24-27, 1982)**

Men:

1. Falko Kirsten (GDR)
2. Fernand Fédronic (FRA)
3. Didier Manaud (FRA)

Women:

1. Janina Wirth (GDR)
2. Petra Schruf (AUT)
3. Kerstin Wolf (GDR)

Pairs:

1. Birgit Lorenz and Knut Schubert (GDR)
2. Inna Volyanskaya and Valery Spiridonov (SOV)
3. Lyudmila Koblova and Andrei Kalitin (SOV)

**1982 NHK TROPHY (Tokyo, Japan, November 26-28, 1982)**

Men:

1. Scott Hamilton (USA)
2. Alexandr Fadeev (SOV)
3. Grzegorz Filipowski (POL)

Women:

1. Katarina Witt (GDR)
2. Rosalynn Sumners (USA)
3. Tiffany Chin (USA)

Pairs:

1. Barbara Underhill and Paul Martini (CAN)
2. Irina Vorobieva and Igor Lisovsky (SOV)
3. Marina Avstriskaya and Yuri Kvashnin (SOV)

Ice Dance:

1. Elena Batanova and Alexei Soloviev (SOV)
2. Carol Fox and Richard Dalley (USA)
3. Wendy Sessions and Stephen Williams (GRB)

**1982 PRIZE OF MOSCOW NEWS (Moscow, Soviet Union, December 1-5, 1982)**

Men:

1. Alexandr Fadeev (SOV)
2. Vladimir Kotin (SOV)
3. Jozef Sabovčík (CZE)

Women:

1. Kira Ivanova (SOV)
2. Anna Kondrashova (SOV)
3. Anna Antonova (SOV)

Pairs:

1. Veronika Pershina and Marat Akbarov (SOV)
2. Larisa Selezneva and Oleg Makarov (SOV)
3. Elena Valova and Oleg Vasiliev (SOV)

Ice Dance:

1. Natalia Bestemianova and Andrei Bukin (SOV)
2. Olga Volozhinskaya and Alexandr Svinin (SOV)
3. Marina Klimova and Sergei Ponomarenko (SOV)

**1983 NORDISKA MÄSTERSKAPEN (Gothenburg, Sweden)**

Men:

1. Fini Ravn (DEN)
2. Lars Dresler (DEN)
3. Peter Söderholm (SWE)

Women:

1. Hanne Gamborg (DEN)
2. Anette Olsson (SWE)
3. Nina Östman (FIN)

Ice Dance:

1. Annika Persson and Johan Formgren (SWE)
2. Maria Ström and Owe Ridderstråle (SWE)

**1983 WORLD UNIVERSITY GAMES (Sofia, Bulgaria, February 17-27, 1983)**

Men:

1. Takashi Mura (JPN)
2. Vitali Egorov (SOV)
3. Grzegorz Głowania (POL)

Women:

1. Natalia Ovchinnikova (SOV)
2. Natalia Lebedeva (SOV)
3. Hana Veselá (CZE)

Pairs:

1. Nelli Chervotkina and Viktor Teslia (SOV)
2. Anna Malgina and Sergei Korovin (SOV)
3. Bo Luan and Yao Bin (CHN)

Ice Dance:

1. Natalia Annenko and Genrikh Sretenski (SOV)
2. Jindra Holá and Karol Foltán (CZE)
3. Isabella Micheli and Roberto Pelizzola (ITA)

**1983 MERANO SPRING TROPHY (Merano, Italy, March 25-27, 1983)**

Women:

1. Yvonne Gomez (USA)
2. Véronique Degardin (FRA)
3. Claudia Villiger (SUI)

**1983 MORZINE AVORIAZ (Morzine, France, April 7-9, 1983)**

Ice Dance:

1. Marina Klimova and Sergei Ponomarenko (SOV)
2. Wendy Sessions and Stephen Williams (GRB)
3. Jindra Holá and Karol Foltán (CZE)

**1983 WILKIE ICE DANCE INTERNATIONAL (Peterborough, England, May 5-6, 1983)**

Ice Dance:

1. Wendy Sessions and Stephen Williams (GRB)
2. Kelly Johnson and John Thomas (CAN)
3. Jindra Holá and Karol Foltán (CZE)

# National Championships and Precision Competitions

**SENIOR NATIONAL CHAMPIONS BY COUNTRY**

### Men

AUS - Perry Meek
AUT - Thomas Hlavik
CZE - Jozef Sabovčík
DEN - Todd Sand
FIN - Antti Kontiola
FRA - Jean-Christophe Simond
FRG - Heiko Fischer
GDR - Falko Kirsten
GRB - Mark Pepperday
HOL - Edward van Campen
HUN - András Száraz
ITA - Bruno Delmaestro
JPN - Shinji Someya
KOR - Hye-kyung Lim
POL - Grzegorz Filipowski
SAF - Rick Simons
SOV - Alexandr Fadeev
SPN - Fernando Soria
SUI - Richard Furrer
SWE - Lars Åkesson

### Women

AUS - Vicki Holland
AUT - Sonja Stanek
BUL - Tsvetanka Alexandrova
CZE - Hana Veselá
DEN - Hanne Gamborg
FIN - Kristiina Wegelius
FRA - Agnès Gosselin
FRG - Manuela Ruben
GDR - Katarina Witt
GRB - Karen Wood
HOL - Li Scha Wang
HUN - Nóra Miklósy
ITA - Karin Telser
JPN - Juri Ozawa
KOR - Hye-kyung Lim
NOR - Ellen Cathrine Hyrum
NZL - Denyse Adam
POL - Mirella Gawłowska
SOV - Elena Vodorezova
SPN - Charo Esteban
SUI - Sandra Cariboni

### Pairs

AUS - Danielle and Stephen Carr
CZE - Jana Havlová and René Novotný
FRA - Nathalie Tortel and Xavier Douillard
FRG - Claudia Massari and Leonardo-Christian Azzola
GDR - Sabine Baeß and Tassilo Thierbach
GRB - Susan Garland and Ian Jenkins
SOV - Marina Pestova and Stanislav Leonovich

### Ice Dance

AUS - Liane Telling and Michael Fisher
AUT - Kathrin and Christoff Beck
BUL - Hristina Boyanova and Yavor Ivanov
CZE - Jindra Holá and Karol Foltán
FRA - Nathalie Hervé and Pierre Béchu
FRG - Petra Born and Rainer Schönborn
GRB - Jayne Torvill and Christopher Dean
HUN - Judit Péterfy and Csaba Bálint
ITA - Isabella Micheli and Roberto Pelizzola
JPN - Noriko Sato and Tadayuki Takahashi
POL - Bożena Wierzchowska and Robert Kazanowski
SOV - Natalia Bestemianova and Andrei Bukin
SUI - Graziella and Marco Ferpozzi

**1983 LAKE PLACID INTERNATIONAL PRECISION SKATING COMPETITION** (Lake Placid, NY, February 26-27, 1983)

Team:

1. The Supremes (CAN)
2. K-W Queens (CAN)
3. Fraserettes (USA)

Other Winners:

Ilderton Silver Jets (CAN) - junior
Eis Fraus (USA) - veteran

**1983 CANADIAN PRECISION TEAM CHAMPIONSHIPS** (London, ON, April 3, 1983)

Team:

1. The Supremes
2. K-W Queens
3. Les Pirouettes de Laval

Other Winners:

Edmonton Junior Precision Team (junior)
London Ice Picks (novice)

*Elaine Zayak. Contributor: PA Images / Alamy Stock Photo. Photographer: Don Morley.*

# Professional Competitions

**1982 INTERNATIONAL PROFESSIONAL CHAMPIONSHIPS - PRO-SKATE NEW YORK** (New York City, NY, December 18-19, 1982)

Men:

1. Robin Cousins (GRB)
2. Toller Cranston (CAN)
3. Brian Pockar (CAN)

Women:

1. Janet Lynn (USA)
2. Lynn Nightingale (CAN)
3. Angela Greenhow (GRB)

Pairs:

1. Candy Jones and Don Fraser (CAN)
2. JoJo Starbuck and Ken Shelley (USA)
3. Shelley Winters and Keith Davis (CAN)

Team:

1. Peggy Fleming and John Curry's team: Peggy Fleming, John Curry, Toller Cranston, Fumio Igarashi, Bob Rubens, Billy Schober, Lorna Brown, Wendy Burge, Lynn Nightingale, Shelley Winters and Keith Davis, Janet and Mark Hominuke, Nancy Berghoff and Jim Bowser, Kim Krohn and Barry Hagan
2. Dorothy Hamill and Robin Cousins' team: Dorothy Hamill, Robin Cousins, Allen Schramm, David Santee, Gordon McKellen Jr., Karen Magnussen, Angela Greenhow, Emi Watanabe, Elizabeth Chabot and Bruce Hurd, Candy Jones and Don Fraser, Colleen O'Connor and Jim Millns, Judie Jeffcott and Keith Swindlehurst, Lillian Heming and Murray Carey

**1983 U.S. PROFESSIONAL CHAMPIONSHIPS** (Troy, OH, February 18-19, 1983)

Men:

1. Glenn Replogle (USA)

Women:

1. Melissa Jeanne Thomas (USA)
2. Kathleen Schmelz (USA)

Pairs:

1. Laurie Johnson and Glenn Replogle (USA)
2. Sue Kearney and Chuck Stafford (USA)
3. Cynthia Van Valkenberg and Phillipp Grout (USA)

**1983 PRO-SKATE CALGARY** (Calgary, AB, March 3, 1983)

Men:

1. Robin Cousins (GRB)
2. Brian Pockar (CAN)
3. Fumio Igarashi (JPN)

Women:

1. Denise Biellmann (SUI)
2. Wendy Burge (USA)
3. Priscilla Hill (USA)

**1983 PRO-SKATE VANCOUVER** (Vancouver, BC, March 4, 1983)

Men:

1. Robin Cousins (GRB)
2. Fumio Igarashi (JPN)
3. Brian Pockar (CAN)

Women:

1. Wendy Burge (USA)
2. Denise Biellmann (SUI)
3. Lynn Nightingale (CAN)

**1983 PRO-SKATE EDMONTON** (Edmonton, AB, March 5, 1983)

Men:

1. Robin Cousins (GRB)
2. Brian Pockar (CAN)
3. Fumio Igarashi (JPN)

Women:

1. Denise Biellmann (SUI)
2. Wendy Burge (USA)
3. Lynn Nightingale (CAN)

**1983 PRO-SKATE TORONTO** (Toronto, ON, March 20, 1983)

Men:

1. Robin Cousins (GRB)
2. Toller Cranston (CAN)
3. David Santee (USA)

Women:

1. Denise Biellmann (SUI)
2. Wendy Burge (USA)
3. Janet Lynn (USA)

Ice Dance:

1. Kim Krohn and Barry Hagan (USA)
2. Nancy Berghoff and Jim Bowser (USA)
3. Lillian Heming and Murray Carey (CAN)

**1983 CAMPEONATOS DEL MUNDO DE PATINAJE ARTÍSTICO PROFESSIONAL SOBRE HIELO** (Jaca, Spain, March 31-April 3, 1983)

Men:

1. Daniel Béland (CAN)
2. Billy Schober (AUS)
3. Michael Shinniman (CAN)

Women:

1. Editha Dotson (BEL)
2. Lori Nichol (CAN)
3. Kathleen Schmelz (USA)

Pairs:

1. Penny Booth and Michael Nemec (GRB/AUT)
2. Lynne Begin and Mark Gignac (CAN)
3. Natascha Devish and Rudi Matysik (FRG)

Ice Dance:

1. Nancy Berghoff and Jim Bowser (USA)
2. Lillian Heming and Murray Carey (CAN)
3. Joanne French and Kris Barber (CAN)

# SHOWS AND TOURS

There was an all-star lineup for the ninth annual *Superskates* show at Madison Square Garden in November. Olympic Medallists 'past and future' who performed included Janet Lynn, Scott Hamilton, Brian Boitano, Toller Cranston and Kitty and Peter Carruthers. 29-year-old Lynn had a lot to celebrate. She was a mother of three, it was the tenth anniversary of her bronze medal win at the 1972 Winter Olympics in Sapporo and she was back on the ice after overcoming ongoing respiratory problems, which were traced to an allergy and successfully managed by a change in her diet. When she decided to return to the ice, she saw two rainbows over the mountains on the drive to the rink and knew she had made the right decision.

Jayne Torvill and Christopher Dean starred in the *Newcastle upon Tyne Sports Council Ice Spectacular* in December, featuring Angela Greenhow, Mark Pepperday, Lorna Brown and Paul Robinson. Durham and Whitley Bay Ice Rinks were both packed to the gills, with funds raised benefiting Sports for the Disabled. Torvill and Dean also starred in a charity ice show staged by the Nottingham City Council, which raised almost 5000 pounds for two local hospital appeals.

*Paradise on Ice* was a popular attraction at La Ronde, the cabaret room of the Sheraton Center in New York. The show was performed on 'plastic ice' rolled out onto the dance floor with a cast of less than ten, including the always fabulous Stephanee Grosscup.

In February, Olympic Medallists John Curry, Peggy Fleming and Toller Cranston starred in the ice show *Ice* at Radio City Music Hall in New York. The 90-minute show, choreographed by Sarah Kawahara, received rave reviews from critics and featured 35 skaters backed by a 46-piece live orchestra.

Tom Collins' *World Figure Skating Tour* returned after a one-year hiatus. The seventeen-city tour kicked off at Boston Garden in late April and travelled westward, finishing in Oakland, California in May. The cast featured skaters from the United States, Canada, Great Britain, the Soviet Union and West Germany.

*Prime Minister Margaret Thatcher with Olympic Gold Medallists Duncan Goodhew, Sebastian Coe, Jayne Torvill and Christopher Dean. Contributor: PA Images / Alamy Stock Photo.*

# MAJOR COMPETITIONS

**World Junior Championships.** In a test run for the 1984 Olympics, the Zetra Ice Rink in Sarajevo, Yugoslavia was the scene of the World Junior Championships in December. Skaters from 24 nations and four continents were in attendance. Although Sarajevo was surrounded by mountains, thick industrial smog permeated the damp, rainy air, made more unpleasant by high winds. Soviet ice dancers Tatiana Gladkova and Igor Shpilband moved up a notch from the previous year to claim the gold in Sarajevo over teammates Elena Novikova and Oleg Bliakhman, leading the event from start to finish and earning high marks for their spirited free dance set to music from *Fiddler On The Roof*. Americans Christina and Keith Yatsuhashi finished seventh in the compulsory dances but moved up to fourth with strong performances in the OSP and free dance. The bronze medallists, Christine Chiniard and Martial Mette, were later disqualified in the ISU's first case of a failed doping test in an ISU Championship. Chiniard was taking a weight loss drug that was on the banned list. The Yatsuhashis found out they had been elevated to the bronze medal position upon their return to America when a member of their skating club happened to read the ISU bulletin. In winning the bronze, the siblings made history as the first Asian American dance team to win a medal at an ISU Championship. Canadians Christine Horton and Michael Farrington and Jo-Anne Borlase and Scott Chalmers finished fifth and sixth. The pairs event was not especially well-skated, with all the top teams being dinged by the judges for falls on jumps and mishaps on side-by-side spins and step sequences. The Soviet pair of Marina Avstryskaya and Yuri Kvashnin were the winners, followed by the East German pair of Peggy Seidel and Ralf Seifert. Short program winners Inna Bekker and Sergei Likhanski finished third. Canada didn't have an entry, as Christine Hough and Kevin Wheeler withdrew the day before they were to depart for Sarajevo due to Hough's injury. In the men's event, Christopher Bowman became the third American skater in a row to claim the World Junior title, executing five triples in his free skating performance. France's Philippe Roncoli moved up from fifth in figures to take the silver. East Germany's Nils Köpp held on to claim the bronze in a close battle with Beauport, Quebec's Marc Ferland, though neither finished in the top three in either the short program or free skate. Canada's second entry Jeff Partrick, who was one of the youngest competitors in the event, placed 16th.

## 1983 WORLD JUNIOR CHAMPIONSHIPS
(Sarajevo, Yugoslavia, December 14-19, 1982)

Men:

1. Christopher Bowman (USA)
2. Philippe Roncoli (FRA)
3. Nils Köpp (GDR)
4. Marc Ferland (CAN)
5. Yuri Bureiko (SOV)
6. Makoto Kano (JPN)
7. Erik Larson (USA)
8. Andrzej Strzelec (POL)
9. Frédéric Harpagès (FRA)
10. Vladimir Petrenko (SOV)

Women:

1. Simone Koch (GDR)
2. Karin Hendschke (GDR)
3. Parthena Sarafidis (AUT)
4. Nelli Dvalishvili (SOV)
5. Sachie Yuki (JPN)
6. Monica Lipson (CAN)
7. Melissa Murphy (CAN)
8. Claudia Villiger (SUI)
9. Susan Bohring (FRG)
10. Elise Ahonen (FIN)

Pairs:

1. Marina Avstryskaya and Yuri Kvashnin (SOV)
2. Peggy Seidel and Ralf Seifert (GDR)
3. Inna Bekker and Sergei Likhanski (SOV)
4. Manuela Landgraf and Ingo Steuer (GDR)
5. Irina Shishova and Alexei Suleimanov (SOV)
6. Susan and Jason Dungjen (USA)
7. Danielle and Stephen Carr (AUS)
8. Lisa and Neil Cushley (GRB)
9. Sun Jihong and Fan Jun (CHN)

Ice Dance:

1. Tatiana Gladkova and Igor Shpilband (SOV)
2. Elena Novikova and Oleg Bliakhman (SOV)
3. Christina and Keith Yatsuhashi (USA)*
4. Christine Horton and Michael Farrington (CAN)*
5. Jo-Anne Borlase and Scott Chalmers (CAN)*
6. Colleen McGuire and Bill Lyons (USA)*
7. Svetlana Liapina and Gorsha Sur (SOV)*
8. Stefania Calegari and Pasquale Camerlengo (ITA)*
9. Klára Engi and Attila Tóth (HUN)*
10. Doriane Bontemps and Charles-Henri Paliard (FRA)*

*Christine Chiniard and Martial Mette of France finished third but were stripped of their medals due to a doping violation. Bronze medals were later awarded to Christina and Keith Yatsuhashi and the results were elevated.

An unfortunate situation played out in the women's event when America's Staci McMullin was eliminated from the event during the draw due to an ISU rule specifying that if there were more than 24 entries, skater(s) whose names weren't drawn would be cut. McMullin wasn't allowed to be substituted for South Korean skater Ji Hyun-jung, whose name was drawn in absentia because her country's team had sent word they were "on the way". Ji arrived late in Sarajevo and two skaters, one being the other American, withdrew after the draw due to injury. The U.S. delegation believed that McMullin would be allowed to compete and to add to the confusion, organizers let her attend official practices after the draw. The situation caused many hurt feelings and the organizers tried to smooth things over by inviting her to perform two exhibitions. The debacle ultimately resulted in an ISU rule change allowing substitutions after the draw, but before the start in the competition, in ISU Championships. Sandra Stevenson lamented how the situation could have been easily avoided. Referee Sonia Bianchetti Garbato was held up in Milan by an air traffic controllers strike and had she been there, she would have managed the situation more gracefully. Leading the way in the first phase of the event was Austria's Parthena Sarafidis, followed by East Germans Simone Koch and Karin Hendschke. Koch delivered two strong programs to coast to the gold medal ahead of Hendschke and Sarafidis. Japan's Midori Ito, who had been the talk of the competition the year prior in Oberstdorf, missed the competition due to a broken ankle. Another young Japanese skater, Sachie Yuki, caused a similar sensation in Sarajevo, placing second in both the short program and free skate with technically demanding programs. Canada's two entries, Monica Lipson and Melissa Murphy placed fifth and seventh. Switzerland's Karl Enderlin made a return to the judging fold after a ten-year absence. Enderlin had been the referee at the 1973 World Championships in Bratislava, the event when Rodnina and Zaitsev's music stopped playing and they famously continued skating on. Enderlin turned heads in Sarajevo by giving Yugoslavia's Željka Čižmešija an insultingly low mark of 1.0 in the figures. When Čižmešija again received low marks in the short program, Enderlin and the other judges were audibly booed. Following the event, Soviet ice dance judge Irina Nechkina received a three-year suspension for "the violation of the basic principle of good sportsmanship, having attempted to influence other Judges in an attempt to obtain their support for skaters." Nechkina was later reinstated, only to be suspended again for misconduct at the 1993 World Championships.

**World Professional Championships.** More than 180 000 dollars in prize money was at stake in Landover, Maryland at the World Professional Championships in December. Almost 17 000 people showed up to watch the competition. For the third year, skaters were divided in two teams - the *All-Stars* and *Pro-Stars*. The winners in 1982 were the *Pro-Stars* team, consisting of Donald Jackson, Charlie Tickner, Linda Fratianne, Janet Lynn, Sandra Bezic and Krisztina Regőczy and András Sallay. Jackson was a last-minute replacement for Val Bezic, who was seriously injured during a practice at the event, when a television boom camera fell on top of him. Right after the event, many of the skaters headed right to the airport to head to New York and compete in the finals of the rival Pro-Skate series. At the New York event, John Curry gave a beautiful speech and presented Janet Lynn with the very first Professional Skater of the Year Award, presented by *American Skating World*. The award consisted of a lifetime subscription to the newspaper and a trophy mounted on a pair of blades.

## 1982 WORLD PROFESSIONAL CHAMPIONSHIPS (Landover, MD, December 17, 1982)

Team:

1. Pro Stars: Donald Jackson, Charlie Tickner, Linda Fratianne, Janet Lynn, Sandra and Val Bezic, Krisztina Regőczy and András Sallay
2. All Stars: Toller Cranston, John Carlow Jr., Dorothy Hamill, Dianne de Leeuw, Ludmila and Oleg Protopopov, JoJo Starbuck and Ken Shelley, Lorna Wighton and John Dowding

## 1983 CANADIAN CHAMPIONSHIPS (Montreal, QC, February 2-6, 1983)

Men:

1. Brian Orser
2. Gary Beacom
3. Gordon Forbes
4. Kevin Parker
5. Dennis Coi
6. Campbell Sinclair
7. Neil Paterson
8. André Bourgeois
9. Lyndon Johnston
10. Brad McLean

Women:

1. Kay Thomson
2. Charlene Wong
3. Cynthia Coull
4. Elizabeth Manley
5. Kerry Smith
6. Diana Mae Ogibowski
7. Tracey Wainman
8. Lana Sherman
9. Patricia Schmidt
10. Andrea Hall

Pairs:

1. Barbara Underhill and Paul Martini
2. Cynthia Coull and Mark Rowsom
3. Katherina Matousek and Lloyd Eisler
4. Melinda Kunhegyi and Lyndon Johnston
5. Lynda and John Ivanich
6. Melanie Buzek and Eric Thomsen

Ice Dance:

1. Tracy Wilson and Rob McCall
2. Kelly Johnson and John Thomas
3. Karyn and Rod Garossino
4. Isabelle and Paul Duchesnay
5. Karen Taylor and Robert Burk
6. Donna Martini and John Coyne
7. Teri Lynn Black and Mirko Savic
8. Kim Campbell and David Islam
9. Anna Griffith and Loch MacDonald

Junior Winners:

Patrick Greasley (men)
Melissa Murphy (women)
Lynda and John Ivanich (pairs)
Michelle McDonald and Patrick Mandley (ice dance)

**Canadian Championships.** In early February, a who's who of Canadian figure skating descended upon the Maurice Richard Arena in Montreal for the first Canadian Championships held in Quebec in almost a decade. The fact it had been so long since the Canadians were held in the province was no coincidence. Thanks to a snowstorm, the 1975 Canadians in Québec City were a serious financial failure - in fact, the event had ended with a 15 000 dollar deficit. Things weren't nearly so grim in 1983. There were some lovely moments in the lower ranks. Nathalie Sasseville made history as the first Quebec skater to win the national novice women's title. A very young Kurt Browning didn't know he won the novice men's title until Donald Jackson asked him in a CTV interview how it felt to a Canadian Champion. In the senior pairs, Barbara Underhill and Paul Martini won their fifth consecutive Canadian title with a confident and charismatic free skate to Gershwin's "Concerto In F", choreographed by Sandra Bezic. Cynthia Coull and Mark Rowsom took the silver; Katherina Matousek and Lloyd Eisler the bronze. The fours competition was cancelled due to a lack of entries. Tracy Wilson and Rob McCall led the ice dance competition from start to finish. They received a perfect 6.0 for artistic impression for their *Stray Cat Strut* OSP. It was the first 6.0 of their career, as well as the first awarded in any discipline at the Canadian Championships since 1976. In the fall at St. Ivel, judges had argued that *Stray Cat Strut* didn't fit the Rock 'n Roll theme. CFSA officials got behind it because singer/songwriter Paul Anka wrote a letter asserting that the piece was indeed Rock. Wilson and McCall received a second 6.0 for their dramatic free dance to selections from the French film "Les Uns et Les Autres", also earning the Bursary Award for the best performance of the entire competition. Kelly Johnson and John Thomas, who shared a coach (Bernie Ford) with Wilson and McCall, placed second. The bronze went to Karyn and Rod Garossino. Paul Duchesnay almost withdrew due to illness but persevered to finish fourth in his senior debut at Canadians with sister Isabelle. In the men's event, Gary Beacom won the figures, ahead of Brian Orser and Gordon Forbes. Orser skated brilliantly to win the short program with marks ranging from 5.6 to 5.9 for technical merit and 5.7 to 5.9 for artistic impression. However, Beacom maintained his overall lead with one of his finest competitive performances, landing a difficult triple flip/double toe-loop combination and igniting the crowd with innovative footwork, spins and exuberant choreography. Beacom faltered in the free skate, while Orser delivered another outstanding performance, landing a triple Axel and his first triple flip in competition. He was delighted to earn his first perfect mark of 6.0 for technical merit from Ontario judge Diane Jamieson, on his way to winning the gold over Beacom. Forbes missed both triple Lutz attempts in his free skate, but executed four other triples to take the bronze ahead of Kevin Parker and Dennis Coi. The road to Montreal was an extremely rocky one for several of the women competing. After the 1982 World Championships, Kay Thomson had cracked a vertebra when she landed on her tailbone in practice. After missing the entire summer, she returned to the ice in September only to tear ligaments in her right knee. Despite only two months of training, she arrived at the competition with three new tricks in her arsenal: the triple flip, triple Lutz and Hawson spin - named after coach Doug Haw and herself because they were the ones that came up with it. Elizabeth Manley was at the lowest point of her career. Training in America under World Champion Emmerich Danzer, she was struggling desperately with depression. She had gained over 30 pounds and was suffering from alopecia. Manley was asked not to compete because of how she looked but refused. She later recalled how people treated her like she was crazy: "People, when they'd walk down the hallway of the arena, ran into other rooms. They didn't want to talk to me, they didn't know what to say to me... It was like I had leprosy." Backstage before the short program, a particularly bitchy older skater handed Elizabeth Manley a can of hairspray, taunting her by saying "Want to borrow it?" Tracey Wainman comforted her, saying, "Don't let it get to you, Elizabeth. I think you look just fine. Just go out there and break a leg." Sadly, both Manley and Wainman struggled in the short program and ended up in seventh and eighth places. Thomson won all three phases in the competition to defend her national title, making history by landing a triple Lutz/double toe-loop combination (the first executed by a Canadian woman in competition) in the short program. Charlene Wong won the silver; Cynthia Coull the bronze. Coull's medal win was a historic one - she became the first woman since Jane Kirby in 1951 to medal in both senior women's and pairs in the same year. Manley finished fourth; Wainman was a shocking tenth in the free skate and seventh overall. Before the week was even over, CFSA officials were at Manley's hotel room door, asking for her world team uniform back. She quit skating for a time and started working with psychologist Terry Orlick. Manley is truly to commended for being one of the only skaters to talk openly about mental health in an era when people in skating only talked about The Blues in an ice dance context.

**U.S. Championships.** In February, the Mount Lebanon Recreation Center and Pittsburgh Civic Arena played host to the first Nationals held in The Steel City. The 1983 Nationals shattered an attendance record of 87 000 spectators that had been set the previous year in Indianapolis. 92 000 skating lovers showed up and the high attendance was attributed not only to the rising popularity of the sport but the fact the weather had held out quite well. It only snowed once during the event and skaters were able to walk from the hotel to the arenas. The event's theme was 'The Great Skate' and its mascot was Patches - an unfortunate skater relegated to suffocating in a very warm panda bear costume. In keeping with the panda theme were the local precision team, The Pittsburgh Pandettes, who gave an exhibition performance during the Opening Ceremonies. It was the first year that Campbell's Soup was a sponsor for the U.S. Championships - and soup was everywhere. Skaters, officials and members of the press were all served pots of chicken noodle and cream of mushroom and 'Campbelled eggs' were served to the attendees at the farewell breakfast. Judy and Jim Sladky dressed up as 'The Campbell Kids' - complete with eight-pound heads - to waltz around the rink extolling the virtues of Sodium-rich broth. It wasn't the first time the Sladky's had skated in mascot-style costumes. They had appeared as Bert and Ernie from Sesame Street in the Ice Follies. A historic milestone occurred in the novice women's event. Suggie Oh, the youngest competitor in any discipline at the Championships, struck gold in the novice women's event, making history as the first skater of South Korean descent to win a gold medal at Nationals. In the senior pairs event, siblings Kitty and Peter Carruthers skated brilliantly in both the short program and free skate to repeat as U.S. Champions. Lea Ann Miller and Bill Fauver came from behind to take the silver, dropping the new partnership of Jill Watson and Burt Lancon down from second to third. fourth place went to Gillian Wachsman and Robert Daw. Daw was a 1980 Olympian, representing the UK with Susan Garland. The Carruthers road to victory in Pittsburgh hadn't been an easy one. Kitty had a bout of chicken pox that caused them to miss a fall international event and they'd ditched their short program after poor reviews at the Eastern Championships, coming up with a new one in a matter of weeks. In the men's event, Scott Hamilton took an early lead by winning all three figures. All the men in the event attempted triple jumps in the short program, with Hamilton, Brian Boitano and Mark Cockerell completing triple Lutz combinations. The men's free skate was sold out, with scalpers selling 11-dollar tickets for double their value. Hamilton defended his national title with a dazzling performance that featured a double Axel/triple toe-loop combination and four other triples. His flashy effort earned near-perfect marks from all nine judges and a standing ovation from the packed arena. Boitano and Cockerell's programs were more technically demanding than Hamilton's. Boitano performed five clean triples including a triple Lutz and triple flip/double toe-loop combination. Cockerell landed six triples but fell on a triple toe-loop attempt. When the marks were tallied, Boitano was second; Cockerell third. Boitano and Paul Wylie (who finished fifth) were the only two men to attempt the triple Axel. Boitano rotated but landed on two feet; Wylie landed one in the warm-up but fell in his program. Judy Blumberg and Michael Seibert were huge favourites with the crowd in the ice dance event. They had only recently started representing the Pittsburgh Figure Skating Club and their participation made for many new dance fans. They won the Quickstep and Argentine Tango but finished third in the Ravensburger Waltz after falling on the double twizzle section right in front of the judges. Blumberg and Seibert rebounded in the Rock N' Roll OSP with an entertaining performance to "Shake, Rattle And Roll", replete with letter sweaters and saddle shoes, to secure their lead over Elisa Spitz and Scott Gregory and Carol Fox and Richard Dalley.

**CANADIAN CHAMPIONSHIPS (continued)**

Novice Winners:

Kurt Browning (men)
Nathalie Sasseville (women)
Penny Schultz and Scott Grover (pairs)
Debbie Horton and Curtis Moore (ice dance)

**1983 U.S. CHAMPIONSHIPS (Pittsburgh, PA, February 1-6, 1983)**

Men:

1. Scott Hamilton
2. Brian Boitano
3. Mark Cockerell
4. Bobby Beauchamp
5. Paul Wylie
6. Scott Williams
7. Tom Dickson
8. J. Scott Driscoll
9. James White
10. James Cygan

Women:

1. Rosalynn Sumners
2. Elaine Zayak
3. Tiffany Chin
4. Vikki de Vries
5. Melissa Thomas
6. Kelly Webster
7. Jill Frost
8. Jacki Farrell
9. Staci McMullin
10. Jennifer Newman

Pairs:

1. Kitty and Peter Carruthers
2. Lea Ann Miller and Bill Fauver
3. Jill Watson and Burt Lancon
4. Gillian Wachsman and Robert Daw
5. Lynne and Jay Freeman
6. Katy Keeley and Gary Kemp
7. Maria Di Domenico and Peter Oppegard
8. Debra Fahy and Craig Maurizi
9. Natalie and Wayne Seybold
10. Cara and Craig Gill

Ice Dance:

1. Judy Blumberg and Michael Seibert
2. Elisa Spitz and Scott Gregory
3. Carol Fox and Richard Dalley
4. Renée Roca and Donald Adair
5. Susie Wynne and Joseph Druar
6. Susan Jorgensen and Robert Yokabaskas
7. Eleanor De Vera and James Yorke
8. Eva Hunyadi and Jay Pinkerton
9. Lois Luciani and Russ Witherby
10. Karen Knieriem and Philip Plasecki

In the free dance, the audience booed low marks for Fox and Dalley but delighted in Blumberg and Seibert's classic Fred and Ginger free dance, which they had altered to add a tap dance section. Despite a stumble from Blumberg late in the program, the defending champions earned the only 6.0s awarded in any discipline in Pittsburgh: one for technical merit and five for style and composition. There was some criticism over the perfect marks because they hadn't skated perfectly. Blumberg and Seibert took the gold and in a five-four split, Spitz and Gregory the silver ahead of veterans Fox and Dalley, shutting them out of the World Team for the first time since 1980. In the women's event, Melissa Thomas of Massapequa, Long Island (who had finished dead last at Nationals in 1982) led the pack in the compulsory figures. Sumners sat in second, Vikki de Vries third and Elaine Zayak fourth. After the women skated their figures, a television crew came onto the use and painted Sumners and Zayak's patches turquoise, so that their paragraph loops would show up better on camera. They completely ignored the flawless loop skated by the winner. Rosalynn Sumners skated a wonderful short program to move up to first ahead of de Vries, Thomas and Zayak. Twelve of the fifteen competitors attempted triple jumps in combination and almost all of them were successful. While most of the competitors did the Salchow or toe-loop, fifth place Kelly Webster landed a triple loop in combination. Strangely enough, the element that seemed to give several of the women grief was the flying sit spin. In the free skate, Zayak landed six triples in one of the best skates of her career. Sumners responded with an ambitious skate of her own but took a tumble on a triple Salchow. Her early lead and high marks (all 5.8s and 5.9s for artistic impression) kept her in first. Zayak moved up to second. Tiffany Chin took the bronze in only her second year at the senior level, skating brilliantly and earning marks ranging from 5.4 to 5.7. Her only mistake was a fall on a triple toe-loop attempt. Though Thomas placed fifth overall behind Vikki de Vries, she gave one of the finest performances of her career in the free skate, landing three double Axels and staying upright on the triple toe-loop that had eluded her the previous year at Nationals. Sumners and Zayak accused the press of manufacturing a rivalry between them and issued a joint statement to the press: "We are not enemies! We are friends! We both have a job to do and we both do it to the best of our ability. We really are more friendly than most competitors." Sumners and Zayak both had to contend with a rather disturbing aspect of the press coverage of their careers - an unhealthy, bizarre focus on weight. It was a topic reporters constantly seemed to fixate on. Sports Illustrated even ran a story on the two entitled "The Thinner is the Winner". An article on the event in Skating named and praised the 'lightest' female pairs skaters and a nutrition and fitness seminar was held in Pittsburgh by two food scientists from - you guessed it - The Campbell Soup Company.

**European Championships.** The Große Westfalenhalle in Dortmund, West Germany was the place to be for European skating fans in 1983. One of the biggest topics of discussion during the Championships was the encouraging sign that pairs entries had doubled from six at the 1981 event. East German pair Sabine Baeß and Tassilo Thierbach dominated in Dortmund from start to finish, decisively defending their title. With clean side-by-side triple-toe-loops, the Soviet pair of Elena Valova and Oleg Vasiliev moved up from fourth after the short program to claim the silver, knocking a second East German pair, Birgit Lorenz and Knut Schubert, down to third. Siblings Naija and Pekka Pekkala placed dead last, but were the first pairs team from Finland to compete at the European Championships since 1965.

**U.S. CHAMPIONSHIPS (continued)**

Junior Winners:

Christopher Bowman (men)
Kathryn Adams (women)
Susan and Jason Dungjen (pairs)
Suzanne Semanick and Alexander Miller III (ice dance)

Novice Winners:

Christopher Mitchell (men)
Suggie Oh (women)

### 1983 EUROPEAN CHAMPIONSHIPS
(Dortmund, West Germany, February 1-6, 1983)

Men:

1. Norbert Schramm (FRG)
2. Jozef Sabovčík (CZE)
3. Alexandr Fadeev (SOV)
4. Heiko Fischer (FRG)
5. Vladimir Kotin (SOV)
6. Jean-Christophe Simond (FRA)
7. Rudi Cerne (FRG)
8. Grzegorz Filipowski (POL)
9. Laurent Depouilly (FRA)
10. Fernand Fédronic (FRA)

Women:

1. Katarina Witt (GDR)
2. Elena Vodorezova (SOV)
3. Claudia Leistner (FRG)
4. Manuela Ruben (FRG)
5. Anna Kondrashova (SOV)
6. Kristiina Wegelius (FIN)
7. Anna Antonova (SOV)
8. Janina Wirth (GDR)
9. Sonja Stanek (AUT)
10. Sanda Dubravčić (YUG)

Pairs:

1. Sabine Baeß and Tassilo Thierbach (GDR)
2. Elena Valova and Oleg Vasiliev (SOV)
3. Birgit Lorenz and Knut Schubert (GDR)
4. Veronika Pershina and Marat Akbarov (SOV)
5. Marina Avstriskaya and Yuri Kvashnin (SOV)
6. Babette Preußler and Torsten Ohlow (GDR)
7. Claudia Massari and Leonardo-Christian Azzola (FRG)
8. Susan Garland and Robert Daw (GRB)
9. Jana Havlová and René Novotný (CZE)
10. Nathalie Tortel and Xavier Douillard (FRA)

Ice Dance:

1. Natalia Bestemianova and Andrei Bukin (SOV)
2. Olga Volozhinskaya and Alexandr Svinin (SOV)
3. Karen Barber and Nicky Slater (GRB)
4. Marina Klimova and Sergei Ponomarenko (SOV)
5. Nathalie Hervé and Pierre Béchu (FRA)
6. Petra Born and Rainer Schönborn (FRG)
7. Wendy Sessions and Stephen Williams (GRB)
8. Isabella Micheli and Roberto Pelizzola (ITA)
9. Jindra Holá and Karol Foltán (CZE)
10. Judit Péterfy and Csaba Bálint (HUN)

The women's school figures were won by Elena Vodorezova, with Katarina Witt second and Switzerland's Sandra Cariboni third. Placing first in both the short program and free skate, Witt won her first European title over Vodorezova and West Germany's Claudia Leistner. However, it wasn't a win without its controversies. The East German skating sensation was criticized by skating officials for flaunting the ISU's dated rules surrounding costumes and wearing knickerbockers for her Mozart-themed short program. After being "advised", she ended up adding a skirt to the costume when she competed at the Worlds, even though she thought the rule that "ladies must wear skirts" was ridiculous. Incidentally, the dress Witt wore for the free skate in Dortmund was a hand-me-down from Anett Pötzsch. A controversial consolation round of sorts was also tested, with skaters who didn't place in the top fifteen after the figures and short program being relegated to a 'B' Final. Sportswriter Howard Bass called it "a pointless exercise" after France's Agnès Gosselin won the 'B' group with a clean triple Lutz combination - an element a total of zero 'A' group skaters even attempted. British Karen Wood had to pull out after the short program after being diagnosed with a viral throat infection. She conceded that she would not have passed the doping test anyway based on what the doctor gave her. Jayne Torvill and Christopher Dean were forced to withdraw from the ice dance event after Torvill injured her shoulder while working on a lift for their Barnum free dance. Natalia Bestemianova and Andrei Bukin rose to the occasion, winning all three phases in the competition by a wide margin over teammates Olga Volozhinskaya and Alexandr Svinin and the British team of Karen Barber and Nicky Slater. Former European Champions Angelika and Erich Buck criticized 'B and B' in the West German press, claiming "80 percent [of their] moves could be accomplished in the theatre, that they did not really ice dance." After the men's school figures, France's Jean-Christophe Simond led the pack ahead of Jozef Sabovčík, Heiko Fischer and Norbert Schramm - a victory that was bittersweet for Simond as he botched his final figure. Simond's lead evaporated when Norbert Schramm spectacularly won the short program, to the delight of the West German audience. The shuffling in the standings put Sabovčík into first place entering the free skate, but in winning the free skate, Schramm took home the title ahead of Sabovčík and Alexandr Fadeev, who wasn't even in the top eight after the figures. Some felt that Vladimir Kotin, who finished only fifth, had the skate of the night in the final round of the competition. Schramm's come-from-behind win wasn't the only thing that had audiences in Dortmund talking. Sabovčík, Fadeev and 17-year-old Austrian skater Thomas Hlavik all landed triple Axels. Fadeev's was the first ever performed in combination in an ISU Championship and his attempt at a quadruple toe-loop, though failed, marked the beginning of the quad race. He wasn't alone either. Czechoslovakia's Petr Barna was also attempting the quad in practices in Dortmund. Suitably impressed with the skaters who followed in his footsteps, three-time World Champion Emmerich Danzer remarked, "I have never seen a more impressive free program. The medals were awarded to three completely different types of skater."

**World Championships.** When Finnish skating official Jane Erkko gave a tour of the Helsinki Jäähalli to a visiting television crew, she was asked what the seating area where skaters received their marks was called. Her response, the "Kiss and Cry", became part of the skating lexicon. The World Championships in Helsinki marked the first time a World title had been decided on Finnish soil since 1934 when Hungarians Emília Rotter and László Szollás claimed the pairs crown.

**1983 WORLD CHAMPIONSHIPS** (Helsinki, Finland, March 8-13, 1983)

Men:

1. Scott Hamilton (USA)
2. Norbert Schramm (FRG)
3. Brian Orser (CAN)
4. Alexandr Fadeev (SOV)
5. Jean-Christophe Simond (FRA)
6. Jozef Sabovčík (CZE)
7. Brian Boitano (USA)
8. Heiko Fischer (FRG)
9. Vladimir Kotin (SOV)
10. Rudi Cerne (FRG)

Women:

1. Rosalynn Sumners (USA)
2. Claudia Leistner (FRG)
3. Elena Vodorezova (SOV)
4. Katarina Witt (GDR)
5. Anna Kondrashova (SOV)
6. Kristiina Wegelius (FIN)
7. Kay Thomson (CAN)
8. Manuela Ruben (FRG)
9. Tiffany Chin (USA)
10. Sandra Cariboni (SUI)

Pairs:

1. Elena Valova and Oleg Vasiliev (SOV)
2. Sabine Baeß and Tassilo Thierbach (GDR)
3. Barbara Underhill and Paul Martini (CAN)
4. Kitty and Peter Carruthers (USA)
5. Veronika Pershina and Marat Akbarov (SOV)
6. Marina Pestova and Stanislav Leonovich (SOV)
7. Lea Ann Miller and Bill Fauver (USA)
8. Birgit Lorenz and Knut Schubert (GDR)
9. Cynthia Coull and Mark Rowsom (CAN)
10. Katherina Matousek and Lloyd Eisler (CAN)

Ice Dance:

1. Jayne Torvill and Christopher Dean (GRB)
2. Natalia Bestemianova and Andrei Bukin (SOV)
3. Judy Blumberg and Michael Seibert (USA)
4. Olga Volozhinskaya and Alexandr Svinin (SOV)
5. Karen Barber and Nicky Slater (GRB)
6. Tracy Wilson and Rob McCall (CAN)
7. Elisa Spitz and Scott Gregory (USA)
8. Elena Batanova and Alexei Soloviev (SOV)
9. Petra Born and Rainer Schönborn (FRG)
10. Kelly Johnson and John Thomas (CAN)

No Hungarian pair competed in 1983 but the pairs event was certainly as dramatic as one of Liszt's symphonies. Coming from behind, Soviets Elena Valova and Oleg Vasiliev bested Sabine Baeß and Tassilo Thierbach to take the pairs crown, with a technically difficult free skate featuring side-by-side triple toe-loops. Underhill and Martini's bronze was the first medal at the World Championships for a Canadian pair in almost 20 years. Canada's other two pairs, Cynthia Coull and Mark Rowsom and Katherina Matousek and Lloyd Eisler, also had strong top-ten showings. The CFSA's offices were inundated with phone calls from fans who felt Underhill and Martini should have won after the CTV broadcast of the pairs event. CFSA President David Dore responded, "There is no doubt the country you come from determines your score. If you come from Russia or if you come from the United States, that means something. If you come from Canada, it doesn't help at all." Though still recovering from injury, Jayne Torvill and Christopher Dean's skating certainly didn't show it. The golden duo from Nottingham were skating better than ever in Helsinki. Dominating the ice dance competition from start to finish, they broke all previous records by receiving seven perfect 6.0s for their OSP (one for composition and six for presentation) and a 6.0s from every single judge for artistic impression for their Barnum free dance. Swiss judge Jürg Wilhelm held the distinction of being the only one to give them three 6.0s. 'T and D' also got a shocking seventeen 5.9s in the three compulsory dances - nine for the Argentine Tango, six for the Ravensburger Waltz and two for the Quickstep. This was a very rare distinction in itself, as judges were notoriously harsh in their scoring of compulsory dances. Judy Blumberg and Michael Seibert seemed to have a lock on the silver after the compulsories and OSP but dropped to third overall behind Natalia Bestemianova and Andrei Bukin. Blumberg and Seibert's medal was the first for an American couple at the Worlds since Colleen O'Connor and Jim Millns won the bronze in 1976. Canada had two teams in the top ten for the first time since 1977. Tracy Wilson and Rob McCall finished a strong sixth; Kelly Johnson and John Thomas were tenth. Rosalynn Sumners, Kristiina Wegelius and Elena Vodorezova (three of the finest proponents of compulsory figures of the day) led the way after the first phase of the women's events. In a shocking development, Elaine Zayak placed 11th after the first two figures and then withdrew. She was suffering from a badly swollen right ankle and skate issues which made doing paragraph loops especially difficult. Sumners had troubles of her own in the short program, two-footing a jump and placing fourth. Katarina Witt delivered an outstanding short program to win that phase of the competition, ahead of Claudia Leistner and Vodorezova. Sumners rebounded with an outstanding free skate featuring three triples, winning a very worthy gold medal over Leistner and Vodorezova, who both had falls. Held back by an eighth-place showing (and a mark of 2.7 from one judge) in the figures, Katarina Witt placed a disappointing fourth. Kay Thomson placed seventh, making history as the first Canadian woman to land a triple Lutz at the World Championships. Charlene Wong placed a very strong 12th in her debut at the Worlds. The winner of the unpopular 'B' Final was Italy's Karin Telser. As a gift for winning the World title, Rosalynn Sumners' father presented her with an expensive fur coat. Monaco-born figures specialist Jean-Christophe Simond was again a dominant force in the compulsories, asserting a hefty lead over Scott Hamilton, Jozef Sabovčík and Norbert Schramm. Simond had two of his better showings in the short program and free skate but still dropped in the standings to fifth. Scott Hamilton won his third consecutive World title with apparent ease, nailing a triple Lutz/double toe-loop combination in the short program and a free skate that featured six triples, flashy footwork, solid spins and a splendid sense of humour. Though beaten by Brian Orser in both the short program and free skate, the always eclectic Norbert Schramm won the silver and the Finnish audience's hearts. Brian Orser's silver medal-winning effort was very strong indeed, though imperfect as he missed his triple Axel attempt. Gary Beacom, Canada's second representative, had an unlucky kind of competition, fittingly placing 13th. Interestingly, the only two out of the five men who successfully landed a triple Axel in their free skate (Brian Boitano and Thomas Hlavik) placed outside of the top six. Foreshadowing the 'quad race' that was to come, Alexandr Fadeev, Brian Orser and Mark Cockerell each landed quadruple toe-loops in practice in Helsinki. Of the 123 skaters from 23 countries that participated, only 2 could claim they were representing their country for the first time at the World Championships. Ice dancers Hristina Boyanova and Iavor Ivanov had the distinction of being the first Bulgarians to compete in any discipline at the Worlds.

# PERSONALITIES

## COMPULSORY DANCES - CFSA STRUCTURE

Preliminary: Dutch Waltz, Canasta Tango, Swing Dance
Junior Bronze: Ten Fox, Fiesta Tango, Willow Waltz
Senior Bronze: European Waltz, Fourteenstep, Foxtrot
Junior Silver: Tango, American Waltz, Rocker Foxtrot
Senior Silver: Paso Doble, Starlight Waltz, Blues, Kilian
Gold: Viennese Waltz, Westminster Waltz, Quickstep, Argentine Tango, Rhumba
No Tests: Yankee Polka, Ravensburger Waltz, Tango Romantica

### KAREN BARBER AND NICKY SLATER

Date of Birth: June 21, 1961/April 6, 1958
Place of Birth: Manchester, England/Liverpool, England
Coach: Joan Slater, Jimmy Young, Betty Callaway
Choreographer: Joan Slater, Jimmy Young, Yan Yeadon

### JUDY BLUMBERG AND MICHAEL SEIBERT

Date of Birth: September 13, 1957/January 1, 1960
Place of Birth: Santa Monica, CA/Pittsburgh, PA
Coach: Doreen Denny MacSalka, Bobby Thompson, Kay Barsdell
Choreographer: Ricky Harris, Terry Rudolph, Georgianna Parkinson
Home Club: Broadmoor SC/ISC of Indianapolis/Pittsburgh FSC

### PETRA BORN AND RAINER SCHÖNBORN

Date of Birth: August 1, 1965/May 26, 1962
Place of Birth: Zweibrücken, West Germany
Coach: Martin Skotnický, Betty Callaway
Home Club: ERCH Zweibrücken, Würzburger ERV

### ISABELLA MICHELI AND ROBERTO PELIZZOLA

Date of Birth: March 30, 1962/October 13, 1958
Place of Birth: Como, Italy/Milan, Italy
Coach: Paola Mezzadri, Joan Slater
Home Club: Club Pattinaggio Ritmico Milano

### JEAN-CHRISTOPHE SIMOND

Date of Birth: April 29, 1960
Place of Birth: Les Contamines-Montjoie, France
Coach: Didier Gailhaguet, Carlo and Christa Fassi, Robert Dureville
Home Club: CSG Saint-Gervais

### GARY BEACOM

Date of Birth: February 23, 1960
Place of Birth: Calgary, AB
Coach: Gary Beacom, Ellen Burka, Helen Ann Shields
Choreographer: Gary Beacom
Home Club: Toronto Cricket, Skating and Curling Club

### RUDI CERNE

Date of Birth: September 26, 1958
Place of Birth: Wanne-Eickel, West Germany
Coach: Christa and Carlo Fassi, Günter Zöller
Home Club: Herner Eislauf Verein

### LAURENT DEPOUILLY

Date of Birth: October 26, 1963
Place of Birth: Asnières-sur-Seine, France
Coach: Robert Dureville
Home Club: Le Club des sports de Glace de Saint-Ouen

### KEVIN PARKER

Date of Birth: July 7, 1961
Place of Birth: Campbellville, ON
Coach: John Caughell, Louis Stong
Choreographer: Margo Hartley
Home Club: Kitchener-Waterloo SC, Granite Club

### DENNIS COI

Date of Birth: August 11, 1961
Place of Birth: North Vancouver, BC
Coach: Ellen Burka, Linda Brauckmann
Choreographer: Dennis Coi
Home Club: North Shore WC, Vancouver SC

### MANUELA RUBEN

Date of Birth: January 14, 1964
Place of Birth: Lauda-Königshofen, West Germany
Coach: Erich Zeller
Home Club: Eiskunstlaufclub Frankfurt EV

### JILL WATSON AND BURT LANCON

Date of Birth: March 29, 1963/November 13, 1960
Place of Birth: Bloomington, IN/Morgan City, LA
Coach: John Nicks, Johnny Johns
Home Club: Los Angeles FSC

### LEA ANN MILLER AND BILL FAUVER

Date of Birth: January 22, 1961/March 2, 1954
Place of Birth: Kirkwood, MO/Cleveland, OH
Coach: Ron Ludington, Pauline Williams Daw, John Bryant Renn
Choreographer: John Bryant Renn
Home Club: SC of Wilmington

### MELINDA KUNHEGYI AND LYNDON JOHNSTON

Date of Birth: December 1, 1965/December 4, 1961
Place of Birth: Guelph, ON/Hamiota, MB
Coach: Kerry Leitch
Home Club: Preston FSC/Hamiota FSC

### JAYNE TORVILL AND CHRISTOPHER DEAN

Date of Birth: October 7, 1957/July 27, 1958
Place of Birth: Clifton, England/Calverton, England
Coach: Betty Callaway
Choreographer: Christopher Dean, Michael Stylianos
Home Club: Nottingham Ice Dance and FSC

### NATALIA BESTEMIANOVA AND ANDREI BUKIN

Date of Birth: January 6, 1960/June 10, 1957
Place of Birth: Moscow, Soviet Union
Coach: Tatiana Tarasova
Choreographer: Tatiana Tarasova, Elena Matveeva, Galina Koenig, Dmitry Bryantsev, Irina Chubarets, Stanislav Shklyar, Natalya Ulyanova, Svetlana Alekseeva, Natalia Bestemianova, Andrei Bukin
Home Club: CSKA Moscow/Trade Union Moscow

### CAROL FOX AND RICHARD DALLEY

Date of Birth: July 11, 1956/August 2, 1957
Place of Birth: Ypsilanti, MI/Detroit, MI
Coach: Sandy Hess, Ron Ludington
Home Club: Wyandotte FSC

### OLGA VOLOZHINSKAYA AND ALEXANDR SVININ

Date of Birth: May 18, 1962/July 7, 1958
Place of Birth: Tallinn, Soviet Union/Leningrad, Soviet Union
Coach: Elena Tchaikovskaya
Choreographer: Valeria Kokhanovskaya
Home Club: Dynamo Moscow

### ELISA SPITZ AND SCOTT GREGORY

Date of Birth: May 17, 1963/July 31, 1959
Place of Birth: Short Hills, NJ/Auburn, NY
Coach: Ron Ludington, Tom Leczinsky
Choreographer: Ron Ludington, Diane Agle, Jill Cosgrove
Home Club: SC of New Jersey/SC of Wilmington

*Jayne Torvill and Christopher Dean. Photo by Fred & Joan Dean, courtesy Fred Dean, "Ice & Roller Skate" magazine archive.*

*Michael Schanze and Norbert Schramm. Contributor: United Archives GmbH / Alamy Stock Photo. Photographer: ZIK Images.*

# 1983-1984 SEASON

Hit Songs: "Smalltown Boy" by Bronski Beat, "Karma Chameleon" by Culture Club, "All Night Long (All Night)" by Lionel Richie, "What's Love Got To Do With It" by Tina Turner, "Girls Just Want To Have Fun" by Cyndi Lauper
Hit Movies: Ghostbusters, Indiana Jones and The Temple of Doom, The Karate Kid, Beverly Hills Cop, Gremlins
Hit TV: Dallas, Dynasty, Kate & Allie, Knots Landing, Cagney & Lacey
News: Terrorist explosion in Beirut, South Korean jetliner shot down over Soviet Union, Syria frees captured U.S. Navy pilot, Marc Garneau makes history as first Canadian in space, Jeanne Sauvé appointed as Canada's first female Governor-General

Igor Bobrin retired from competitive figure skating to direct the department of figure skating choreographers at the Russian Institute of Theater Arts in Moscow. Irina Vorobieva and Igor Lisovsky turned professional to perform with Tatiana Tarasova and Yuri Ovchinnikov's ice theatre, while Marina Pestova and Stanislav Leonovich turned to coaching. Kristiina Wegelius joined the cast of Walt Disney's World on Ice. Mark Pepperday turned professional in January, making his debut in London with *Holiday on Ice* after defending his British title but being snubbed for the Olympic team.

William and Caroline Grimditch organized a special dinner in Lake Placid to celebrate Gustave Lussi's 85th birthday and 62nd year as a coach, which coincided with his coronation as 'King Winter'. The dinner was attended by a who's who of figure skating, including Dick Button, Dorothy Hamill, Donald Jackson, Suzanne Morrow Francis and Maria Jelinek.

Alexia (Schøien) Bryn, the first woman from Norway to win an Olympic figure skating medal in 1920, passed away in July at the age of 94. Bryn's husband and pairs partner was part of Norway's very first Olympic team in 1900, competing as a runner in the Summer Games in Paris.

The Canadian figure skating community felt a huge loss in July when Canadian and North American Champion Mary Rose Thacker Temple passed away at the age of 61. The first woman from Western Canada to win the Canadian senior women's title, Thacker Temple went on to become a very well-respected coach in British Columbia. She was also one of the founders of the Canada Ice Dance Theatre.

"To skate or not to skate, that is the question..." In August, John Curry appeared in Regent's Park in London in the Open Air Theatre's presentation of the Shakespearian comedy *As You Like It*.

Margaret Bland Jameson, an Honourary Life Member of the National Skating Association who earned the Association's Gold Medal during the Edwardian era, passed away in August, just a few months shy of her 100th anniversary. Bland Jameson was one of the few surviving links to British figure skating in the Edwardian era.

Scott Hamilton received the Southland Olympia Award in Atlantic City, New Jersey. The award was given to amateur athletes in 31 different Olympic sports "in recognition of their achievements in athletics and their support of the amateur ideal." Other winners included Greg Louganis and Carl Lewis.

Olympic Silver Medallist and European Champion Eva Pawlik passed away in Vienna in July at the age of 55. After she turned professional, Pawlik toured with the Wiener and Scala Eisrevues and worked as a commentator for figure skating broadcasts on European television.

Two very important milestones were achieved in fall international competitions. Bobby Beauchamp made history as the first skater of colour to win a medal at Skate America, while Debi Thomas made history as the first woman of colour to win an international competition - the International Sugar Criterium in Tours, France. When asked about her achievement in an interview for *Skating*, Thomas responded, "When I skate, I strive to be the best - that's what I think about. Being black hasn't really affected me as a skater that much. I think it's affected other people more. After I won for instance, I got a fan letter from a young skater in Ohio who said that she was black and proud of my achievement."

Her Majesty Queen Elizabeth II bestowed the title of Member of the Most Excellent Order of the British Empire (MBE) to Lawrence Demmy for "services to Ice Dancing" in her New Year's Honours. Demmy, a former World Champion, long-time judge and ISU official, was an outspoken advocate for the fact that the judging of the compulsory dances, OSP/original dance and free dance should be completely independent of one another - something he acknowledged rarely happened. He was an advisor to Torvill and Dean and a big fan of 'Min and Mo' and the Duchesnays.

Just nineteen days before Jayne Torvill and Christopher Dean made history with their stunning *Bolero* at the Olympics, NSA President Len Seagrave, OBE passed away in Harrow at the age of 76. Seagrave's service to the NSA spanned four decades. He served on every single one of the Association's Committees and was a long-term member of the Ice Dance Committee. He was elected Treasurer in 1951 and Vice-Chairman in 1966. He served as the Association's representative to the British Olympic Association for many years. He was also a respected judge and World War II veteran.

Ollie Haupt Jr. passed away in New York City in February at the age of 91, just three days after Torvill and Dean won Olympic gold. Haupt was the runner-up at the U.S. Championships in 1938 and 1939 and had been selected to represent the United States at the 1940 Olympic Winter Games, which were cancelled due to World War II.

Betty Callaway-Fittall was invested a Member of the Order of the British Empire (MBE) in Her Majesty Queen Elizabeth II's Birthday Honours in June, for "services to ice dancing". Callaway was the coach of World Champions Jayne Torvill and Christopher Dean and Krisztina Regőczy and András Sallay.

Canadian figure skating pioneers Louis Rubenstein, Frances Dafoe and Norris Bowden and Swiss skater Werner Groebli (half of the famous comedic ice show duo 'Frick and Frack') were the latest inductees to the World Figure Skating Hall of Fame.

# AROUND THE WORLD

**Canada.** The Olympic season was the first time that Canadian figure skating coaches participated in CAC's apprenticeship program. This program allowed up-and-coming coaches to apprentice under high-level ones. British Columbia coach Nancy Glerup was one of the first to participate, going to Toronto to work under Valerie Jones Merrick and Sheldon Galbraith. The CFSA accepted a 10 000 dollar donation from Imperial Tobacco, which helped cover the costs of sending skaters' coaches to the Olympics and World Championships. The donation later became controversial when Otto Jelinek, Minister of State for Fitness and Amateur Sport, threatened to cut funding to any amateur sports association that accepted money from the tobacco industry. Ultimately, Jelinek named a national marketing council to help secure corporate sponsorship for amateur sports. Former CFSA Executive Director Lou Lefaive was the President and CTV Vice-President of Sports Johnny Esaw was the chairman.

**Mexico.** The USFSA sent a group of judges to test Eduardo Burguete's skaters at the Deportivo San Agustin in Monterrey. A major factor in figure skating's slow development in the country was a lack of qualified coaches.

**Romania.** With less than half a dozen covered ice rinks in the country, Romanian skaters struggled to make an impact on the world stage. Things started to look up in 1984 when the Federatia Romana de Patinaj opened its Junior Olympics Training Center, where young skaters could have centralized access to coaching. Within a couple of years, the Romanian federation started seeing a marked improvement in the results of its skaters in international competitions.

# THE AIDS EPIDEMIC

In September, a New York City physician filed a lawsuit after he was threatened with eviction for treating HIV-positive patients in his office. Two months later, the World Health Organization held its first meeting to study the global impact of the epidemic. A photograph of 32-year-old public health nurse and AIDS activist Bobbi Campbell and his partner Bobby Hilliard appeared on the cover of *Newsweek*. It was time a picture of two gay men embracing was featured on a mainstream magazine cover. Both men ultimately passed away from AIDS-related complications. At the time, AIDS continued to be framed as the 'gay cancer' and it wouldn't be long before the epidemic began devastating the figure skating community.

# BEHIND THE SCENES

The Cold War spilled out onto the ice in the fall. Several Russian diplomats and VIPs from Washington planned to attend Skate America in Rochester and when they found out that the USSR Skating Federation hadn't accepted the invitation yet, they reached out to the powers that be and the USFSA received a telegram letting them know that a 'B list' team of skaters would be sent, miffing the organizers who were expecting the national champions. A few days later, the USSR Skating Federation sent another telegram informing them that no one would be coming after all. The timing was an interesting coincidence, as this was not long after the Soviets had shot down Korean Air Lines Flight 007, killing all 269 passengers aboard. Among the passengers were several Kodak employees, whose headquarters were in Rochester, so there was speculation that the Soviet team may have been booed in light of the tragedy. It wasn't the first time there had been last-minute changes when it came to the Soviet team. In 1980, the USSR Skating Federation accepted an invitation to send skaters to perform at the Cendrillon Figure Skating Club in Cap-de-la-Madeleine's skating carnival. The Soviets applied for visas for the wrong skaters and Irina Rodnina and Aleksandr Zaitsev and Natalia Linichuk and Gennadi Karponosov ended up being detained at the Montreal airport for two hours because their visas and passports didn't match. At one St. Ivel competition in England, the USSR Skating Federation sent a woman to compete who wasn't on the list of entries, who posed as the skater who was. The sponsors in the competition insisted that the NSA distribute a tersely worded letter to all invited federations the next year, making it clear they wouldn't pay travel costs for any skater who was substituted at the last minute. The letter, very much aimed at the USSR Skating Federation, had the unintended consequence of ticking off the USFSA, who refused to send a team that year.

The Broadmoor in Colorado Springs played host to the first ISU Congress ever held outside of Europe. At the Fortieth Congress, Olaf Poulsen was re-elected for another four years. The ISU recognized the USFSA's Museum and Hall of Fame as the World Figure Skating Hall of Fame. A whole new ISU Constitution, drafted by a Committee led by Benjamin T. Wright, was adopted. The 'old boys club' of the ISU was shaken up when Sonia Bianchetti Garbato was elected Chair of the Figure Skating Committee and Joyce Hisey became the first woman to serve on the Ice Dancing Technical Committee. A particularly interesting proposal, which was shot down, was the introduction of a third program in pairs so that the discipline would mirror ice dance. With another proposal for a Pacific Championship as a qualifier for the World Championships shot down, the rules for Semi-Finals at the European and World Championships were slightly revised. Going forward, if there were more than 20 entries in an event, the top seventeen would automatically advance to the free skate, with the remainder of skaters competing in a 'B Final'. The top three skaters from the 'B Final' qualified to compete in the free skate as well. A major factor in this revision was no doubt Agnès Gosselin's outstanding effort in the 'B Final' at the 1983 World Championships in Helsinki.

The ISU adopted a new retirement age for all international figure skating judges and referees and reduced the maximum age for initial appointments from 55 to 45. New rules were also put in place requiring any judge suspended for "incompetence or unsatisfactory judging" to attend a judges' seminar, pass an examination and demonstrate satisfactory judging before being allowed to return to the fold.

The "Zayak Rule" was introduced in ISU Communication No. 596. The new rule limited the repetition of triple jumps for men's and women's free skating and also made changes with regard to spins and footwork sequences. Henceforth, each triple jump could be "executed either as individual jumps, in jump sequences or in jump combinations, but only one of these triple jumps can be repeated in one jump combination." The communication also specified that "at least four spins of a different nature are required, one of which must be a spin combination, but there can of course be more. The skaters have the complete freedom in selecting the kind of spin they intend to execute; in the spin combination the change of foot is not compulsory and the number of different positions is free." Men were required to do two different step sequences; women one. All step sequences, whether they be straight line, circular or serpentine, had to "fully utilize the ice surface."

## BOOKS AND MAGAZINES

*Dorothy Hamill: On and Off the Ice* hit bookstores in November. Written in collaboration with Elva Clairmont (Oglanby), the producer of the Pro-Skate events, the 'tell-all' biography failed to knock Erma Bombeck's *Motherhood: The Second Oldest Profession* off the top of *The New York Times* bestseller list.

Just before the Olympics, the BBC partnered with intrepid British figure skating journalist Sandra Stevenson to release *The BBC Book of Skating*. Stevenson, a long-time ice skating correspondent for the *Guardian* and regular contributor to *Skating, Ice & Roller Skate* and the *Canadian Skater*, was at her very best in this behind-the-scenes look at 80s figure skating. Another excellent figure skating book that hit the stands just before the Olympics was John 'Misha' Petkevich's *The Skater's Handbook*, published by Charles Scribner's Sons in New York.

Meredith Phillips' figure skating-themed murder mystery *Death Spiral: Murder at the Winter Olympics* also came out just in time for the Sarajevo Games. The self-published whodunit was set at a fictional Olympics in Squaw Valley. At the height of The Cold War, a British skating sleuth tried to solve the murder of her lover, a World Champion skater from the Soviet Union.

Rosalynn Sumners was the first skater to be interviewed by a muppet when Gonzo tested his journalism chops in the Winter edition of *Muppet* magazine.

After sixteen years of publication, the CFSA scrapped the *Canadian Skater*. Though hugely popular, the glossy magazine had been extremely expensive to produce. The discontinuation of the *Canadian Skater* left a huge gap in coverage of the sport in Canada.

## FILMS AND TELEVISION

Robin Cousins and members of the cast of his *Electric Ice* show appeared on BBC, live from the Richmond Ice Rink, in November in a program to raise funds for the British Olympic Fund. Cousins set two Guinness World records that still stand to this day: the longest Axel jump (nineteen feet, one inch) and the longest backflip (eighteen feet).

Sandra Bezic's choreography was at its best in the television special *Romeo and Juliet on Ice*. Filmed on a tiny ice surface installed at a CFTO studio in Toronto, the production starred Brian Pockar as Romeo, Dorothy Hamill as Juliet and Toller Cranston as Tybalt. It took fifteen minutes to film the kissing scene because Pockar's lips started quivering when he had to go in for the smooch and Hamill couldn't stop laughing.

"Elementary, my dear pairs team..." Tai Babilonia and Randy Gardner appeared on an episode of *Hart to Hart* in January, recruited to help solve a mysterious assassination attempt of a figure skater destined for Olympic stardom. JoJo Starbuck made an appearance on an episode of *Webster*. Ice Castles star Lynn-Holly Johnson was on *Trapper John, M.D.*

In March, Global Television aired a star-studded documentary called *The Golden Age of Canadian Skating*, hosted by Jan Tennant. The documentary was researched by David Young, the producer of *The Silver Years* and *The Race of Champions*. Young also released a companion book the same year. The one-hour special featured previously unseen footage of Canadian skating royalty and interviews with Barbara Ann Scott, Sheldon Galbraith, Frances Dafoe and Norris Bowden, Barbara Wagner and Bob Paul, Maria and Otto Jelinek, Donald Jackson, Donald McPherson, Petra Burka and Karen Magnussen.

## FASHION

Lycra and Spandex revolutionized figure skating fashions in the 80s and no stretchy skating costume was complete without a week's worth of beading. Glitz and glam were all the rage, as were shoulder pads and sequins. Skaters no longer only dressed for success with the judges. They dressed up for the television cameras.

World Champion and NSA President Courtney Jones and his partner Bobby Thompson designed all of Jayne Torvill and Christopher Dean's costumes. Michael Seibert usually designed his and Judy Blumberg's costumes, but in the Olympic season, they sported dramatic costumes by award-winning designer Mary McFadden. Karen Barber and Nicky Slater took to the ice in the 80s in fashions by Elizabeth and David Emanuel, who designed Princess Diana's wedding dress.

Canadian skaters got a glow-up, when the CFSA sparked a deal with Sears to outfit the National Team for the Olympic season. The new team uniform colours were black and grey.

# Fall Internationals

**1983 COUPES DES ALPES** (Saint Gervais, France and Oberstdorf, West Germany, August 17-21, 1983 and August 23-27, 1983)

Grand Prix de St. Gervais Winners:

Philippe Paulet (FRA) - men
Katrien Pauwels (BEL) - women
Inna Bekker and Sergei Likhanski (SOV) - pairs
Marina Klimova and Sergei Ponomarenko (SOV) - ice dance

Nebelhorn Trophy (Oberstdorf) Winners:

Heiko Fischer (FRG) - men
Staci McMullin (USA) - women
Inna Bekker and Sergei Likhanski (SOV) - pairs
Marina Klimova and Sergei Ponomarenko (SOV) - ice dance

**1983 ASKÖ CUP OF VIENNA** (Vienna, Austria, September 19-23, 1983)

Women:

1. Leslie Sikes (USA)
2. Maradith Feinberg (USA)
3. Natalia Ovchinnikova (SOV)

**1983 ST. IVEL ICE INTERNATIONAL** (London, England, September 27-29, 1983)

Men:

1. Heiko Fischer (FRG)
2. Gary Beacom (CAN)
3. Falko Kirsten (GDR)

Women:

1. Tiffany Chin (USA)
2. Manuela Ruben (FRG)
3. Karen Wood (GRB)

Pairs:

1. Birgit Lorenz and Knut Schubert (GDR)
2. Cynthia Coull and Mark Rowsom (CAN)
3. Lea Ann Miller and Bill Fauver (USA)

Ice Dance:

1. Karen Barber and Nicky Slater (GRB)
2. Carol Fox and Richard Dalley (USA)
3. Wendy Sessions and Stephen Williams (GRB)

**1983 SKATE AMERICA** (Rochester, NY, October 10-16, 1983)

Men:

1. Brian Boitano (USA)
2. Rudi Cerne (FRG)
3. Bobby Beauchamp (USA)

Women:

1. Tiffany Chin (USA)
2. Jill Frost (USA)
3. Kelly Webster (USA)

Pairs:

1. Kitty and Peter Carruthers (USA)
2. Jill Watson and Burt Lancon (USA)
3. Melinda Kunhegyi and Lyndon Johnston (CAN)

Ice Dance:

1. Elisa Spitz and Scott Gregory (USA)
2. Kelly Johnson and John Thomas (CAN)
3. Wendy Sessions and Stephen Williams (GRB)

**1983 SKATE CANADA** (Halifax, NS, October 27-29, 1983)

Men:

1. Brian Orser (CAN)
2. Grzegorz Filipowski (POL)
3. Masaru Ogawa (JPN)

Women:

1. Katarina Witt (GDR)
2. Kay Thomson (CAN)
3. Tiffany Chin (USA)

Ice Dance:

1. Tracy Wilson and Rob McCall (CAN)
2. Wendy Sessions and Stephen Williams (GRB)
3. Natalia Annenko and Genrikh Sretenski (SOV)

**1983 PRAGUE SKATE** (Prague, Czechoslovakia, November 3-5, 1983)

Men:

1. Takashi Mura (JPN)
2. Jimmie Santee (USA)
3. Campbell Sinclair (CAN)

Women:

1. Midori Ito (JPN)
2. Sachie Yuki (JPN)
3. Constanze Gensel (GDR)

Pairs:

1. Inna Bekker and Sergei Likhanski (SOV)
2. Peggy Seidel and Ralf Seifert (GDR)
3. Toshimi Ito and Takashi Mura (JPN)

Ice Dance:

1. Jindra Holá and Karol Foltán (CZE)
2. Maya Usova and Alexandr Zhulin (SOV)
3. Lois Luciani and Russ Witherby (USA)

**1983 ENNIA CHALLENGE CUP INTERNATIONAL FREE SKATING COMPETITION** (The Hague, Netherlands, November 8-13, 1983)

Men:

1. Brian Orser (CAN)
2. Takashi Mura (JPN)
3. Rudi Cerne (FRG)

Women:

1. Katarina Witt (GDR)
2. Midori Ito (JPN)
3. Sachie Yuki (JPN)

Pairs:

1. Birgit Lorenz and Knut Schubert (GDR)
2. Cynthia Coull and Mark Rowsom (CAN)
3. Katherina Matousek and Lloyd Eisler (CAN)

Ice Dance:

1. Marina Klimova and Sergei Ponomarenko (SOV)
2. Elena Batanova and Alexei Soloviev (SOV)
3. Tracy Wilson and Rob McCall (CAN)

**1983 GOLDEN SPIN OF ZAGREB** (Zagreb, Yugoslavia, November 17-20, 1983)

Men:

1. Scott Hamilton (USA)
2. Norbert Schramm (FRG)
3. Makoto Kano (JPN)

Women:

1. Sanda Dubravčić (YUG)
2. Rosalynn Sumners (USA)
3. Karin Telser (ITA)

Ice Dance:

1. Petra Born and Rainer Schönborn (FRG)
2. Tatiana Gladkova and Igor Shpilband (SOV)
3. Eva Hunyadi and Jay Pinkerton (USA)

# Fall Internationals and Other Competitions

**1983 GRAND PRIZE SNP** (Banská Bystrica, Czechoslovakia, November 17-20, 1983)

Men:

1. Daniel Weiss (FRG)
2. Pavel Vančo (CZE)
3. Karel Kovář (CZE)

Women:

1. Jana Sjodin (USA)
2. Ingrid Karl (FRG)
3. Inga Gauter (GDR)

Pairs:

1. Olga Neizvestnaya and Sergei Khudiakov (SOV)
2. Manuela Landgraf and Ingo Steuer (GDR)
3. Ekaterina Gordeeva and Sergei Grinkov (SOV)

Ice Dance:

1. Stefania Calegari and Pasquale Camerlengo (ITA)
2. Honorata Górna and Andrzej Dostatni (POL)
3. Dana Jendrisková and Roman Sabol (CZE)

**1983 POKAL DER BLAUEN SCHWERTER** (East Berlin, East Germany, November 23-26, 1983)

Men:

1. Boris Uspenski (SOV)
2. Falko Kirsten (GDR)
3. Pierre Seveno (FRA)

Women:

1. Janina Wirth (GDR)
2. Beatrice Gelmini (ITA)
3. Marion Krause (GDR)

Pairs:

1. Birgit Lorenz and Knut Schubert (GDR)
2. Babette Preußler and Tobias Schröter (GDR)
3. Tatiana Chozko and Oleg Efimov (SOV)

**1983 PRIZE OF MOSCOW NEWS** (Moscow, Soviet Union, November 23-27, 1983)

Men:

1. Vladimir Kotin (SOV)
2. Gary Beacom (CAN)
3. Alexandr Fadeev (SOV)

Women:

1. Kira Ivanova (SOV)
2. Anna Kondrashova (SOV)
3. Natalia Lebedeva (SOV)

Pairs:

1. Larisa Selezneva and Oleg Makarov (SOV)
2. Veronika Pershina and Marat Akbarov (SOV)
3. Elena Bechke and Valeri Kornienko (SOV)

Ice Dance:

1. Natalia Bestemianova and Andrei Bukin (SOV)
2. Marina Klimova and Sergei Ponomarenko (SOV)
3. Olga Volozhinskaya and Alexandr Svinin (SOV)

**1983 INTERNATIONAL SUGAR CRITERIUM - JACQUES FAVART TROPHY** (Tours, France, November 25-27, 1983)

Men:

1. Daniel Doran (USA)
2. Angelo D'Agostino (USA)
3. James Cygan (USA)

Women:

1. Debi Thomas (USA)
2. Agnès Gosselin (FRA)
3. Cornelia Renner (FRG)

Pairs:

1. Sandy Hurtubise and Karl Kurtz (USA)
2. Margo Shoup and Patrick Page (USA)
3. Luan Bo and Yao Bin (CHN)

**1984 NORDISKA MÄSTERSKAPEN** (Oslo, Norway)

Men:

1. Henrik Walentin (DEN)
2. Antti Kontiola (FIN)
3. Fini Ravn (DEN)

Women:

1. Elina Hänninen (FIN)
2. Nina Östman (FIN)
3. Lotta Falkenbäck (SWE)

**1984 MERANO SPRING TROPHY** (Merano, Italy, March 30-April 1, 1984)

Women:

1. Rosemarie Sakic (CAN)
2. Jill Trenary (USA)
3. Susanne Becher (FRG)

**1984 MORZINE AVORIAZ** (Morzine, France, April 5-7, 1984)

Ice Dance:

1. Carol Fox and Richard Dalley (USA)
2. Kelly Johnson and John Thomas (CAN)
3. Isabella Micheli and Roberto Pelizzola (ITA)

**1984 WILKIE ICE DANCE INTERNATIONAL** (Peterborough, England, May 3-5, 1984)

Ice Dance:

1. Marianne Van Bommel and Wayne Deweyert (HOL)
2. Karyn and Rod Garossino (CAN)
3. Sharon Jones and Paul Askham (GRB)

*Marina Klimova and Sergei Ponomarenko. Contributor: PA Images / Alamy Stock Photo.*

# National Championships and Precision Competitions

## SENIOR NATIONAL CHAMPIONS BY COUNTRY

### Men

AUS - Cameron Medhurst
AUT - Thomas Hlavik
BUL - Boyko Aleksiev
CZE - Jozef Sabovčík
DEN - Lars Dresler
FIN - Antti Kontiola
FRA - Jean-Christophe Simond
FRG - Norbert Schramm
GDR - Falko Kirsten
GRB - Mark Pepperday
HOL - Edward van Campen
HUN - András Száraz
ITA - Alessandro Riccitelli
JPN - Masaru Ogawa
POL - Grzegorz Filipowski
SAF - Rick Simons
SOV - Vitali Egorov
SUI - Oliver Höner

### Women

AUS - Amanda James
AUT - Parthena Sarafidis
BUL - Svetla Staneva
CZE - Hana Veselá
DEN - Hanne Gamborg
FIN - Susanna Peltola
FRA - Agnès Gosselin
FRG - Manuela Ruben
GDR - Katarina Witt
GRB - Susan Jackson
HOL - Li Scha Wang
HUN - Tamara Téglássy
ITA - Karin Telser
JPN - Masako Kato
KOR - Hae-sung Kim
NOR - Vibecke Sørensen
NZL - Denyse Adam
POL - Helena Chwila
SOV - Natalia Lebedeva
SPN - Cristina Haas
SUI - Myriam Oberwiler

### Pairs

AUS - Danielle and Stephen Carr
CHN - Sun Dan and Shan Zhen Yuan
CZE - Dagmar Kovářová and Jozef Komár
FIN - Maija and Pekka Pekkala
FRA - Sylvie Vaquero and Didier Manaud
FRG - Claudia Massari and Leonardo-Christian Azzola
GDR - Sabine Baeß and Tassilo Thierbach
GRB - Susan Garland and Ian Jenkins
SOV - Larisa Selezneva and Oleg Makarov
SUI - Gaby and Jörg Galambos

### Ice Dance

AUS - Liane Telling and Michael Fisher
AUT - Kathrin and Christoff Beck
CZE - Jindra Holá and Karol Foltán
FIN - Virpi Kunnas and Petri Kokko
FRA - Nathalie Hervé and Pierre Béchu
FRG - Petra Born and Rainer Schönborn
GRB - Jayne Torvill and Christopher Dean
HUN - Gabriella Remport and Sándor Nagy
ITA - Isabella Micheli and Roberto Pelizzola
JPN - Noriko Sato and Tadayuki Takahashi
NZL - Clare Shave and Chris Laurie
POL - Bożena Wierzchowska and Robert Kazanowski
SOV - Elena Batanova and Alexei Soloviev
SUI - Graziella and Marco Ferpozzi

## 1984 CANADIAN PRECISION TEAM CHAMPIONSHIPS (London, ON, April 1, 1984)

Team:

1. The Supremes
2. K-W Queens
3. Edmonton Senior Precision Teams

Other Winners:

Ilderton Silver Jets (junior)
London Ice Picks (novice)

## 1984 U.S. PRECISION TEAM SKATING CHAMPIONSHIPS (Bowling Green, OH, May 6, 1984)

Team:

1. Fraserettes
2. Ice Crystalettes
3. Ann Arbor Hockettes

Other Winners:

Hot Fudge Sundaes (junior)
Hot Fudge Sundaes (novice)
Acton-Ups (adult)

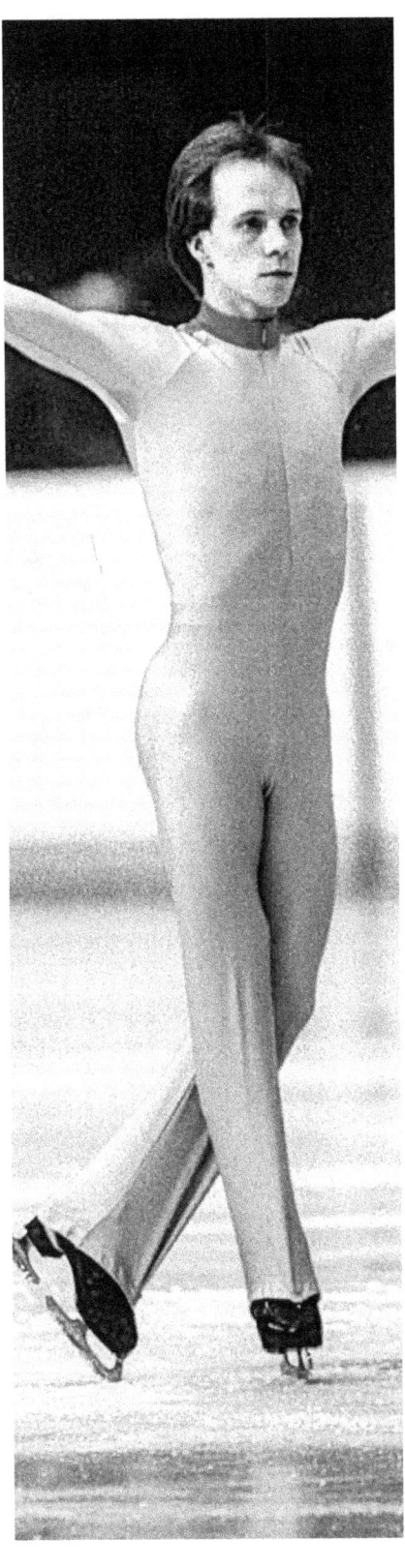

*Scott Hamilton. Contributor: PCN Photography / Alamy Stock Photo.*

# Professional Competitions

**THE 1983 INTERNATIONAL PROFESSIONAL CHAMPIONSHIPS - MITA PRO-SKATE NEW YORK (New York City, NY, December 10-11, 1983)**

Men:

1. Robin Cousins (GRB)
2. Allen Schramm (USA)
3. Toller Cranston (CAN)

Women:

1. Angela Greenhow (GRB)
2. Denise Biellmann (SUI)
3. Simone Grigorescu (ROM)

Pairs:

1. Candy Jones and Don Fraser (CAN)
2. Elina Viola and Keith Green (USA/CAN)
3. JoJo Starbuck and Ken Shelley (USA)

Team:

1. John Curry and Dorothy Hamill's team: John Curry, Dorothy Hamill, Katherine Healy, David Santee and others*
2. Robin Cousins and Denise Biellmann's team: Robin Cousins, Denise Biellmann, Toller Cranston, Brian Pockar, Angela Greenhow, Wendy Burge, Tai Babilonia and Randy Gardner, Elina Viola and Keith Green

**1984 PRO-SKATE TOKYO (Tokyo, Japan, February 25-26, 1984)**

Men:

1. Robin Cousins (GRB)
2. Allen Schramm (USA)
3. David Santee (USA)

Women:

1. Denise Biellmann (SUI)
2. Wendy Burge (USA)
3. Lynn Nightingale (CAN)

Pairs:

1. Candy Jones and Don Fraser (CAN)
2. JoJo Starbuck and Ken Shelley (USA)
3. Elina Viola and Keith Green (USA/CAN)

Ice Dance:

1. Kim Krohn and Barry Hagan (USA)
2. Lillian Heming and Murray Carey (CAN)
3. Shelley McLeod and John Rait (CAN)

**1984 PRO-SKATE SAPPORO (Sapporo, Japan, March 3-4, 1984)**

Men:

1. Robin Cousins (GRB)
2. Fumio Igarashi (JPN)
3. Allen Schramm (USA)

Women:

1. Denise Biellmann (SUI)
2. Wendy Burge (USA)
3. Simone Grigorescu (ROM)

Pairs:

1. Candy Jones and Don Fraser (CAN)
2. JoJo Starbuck and Ken Shelley (USA)
3. Elina Viola and Keith Green (USA/CAN)

Ice Dance:

1. Lillian Heming and Murray Carey (CAN)
2. Kim Krohn and Barry Hagan (USA)
3. Shelley MacLeod and John Rait (CAN)

**1984 CANADIAN PROFESSIONAL CHAMPIONSHIPS (Toronto, ON, March 10, 1984)**

Men:

1. Mitch Giffin
2. Jack Frizelle
3. John Knight

Women:

1. Susan Smith
2. Gia Guddat
3. Suzanne Dionne

Ice Dance:

1. Karen Taylor and Robert Burk
2. Marie McNeil and Hans-Peter Ponikau
3. Lenore Kay and Danny Sorley

**1984 RIEDELL OPEN UNITED STATES PROFESSIONAL CHAMPIONSHIP (Troy, OH, March 16-17, 1984)**

Men:

1. J. Scott Driscoll
2. Scott Cramer
3. Kevin Bryzek

Women:

1. Vicki Heasley
2. Priscilla Hill
3. Roslynn van Horn

Pairs:

1. Katie Baxter and Greg Taylor
2. Lauren Laakso and Bob Young
3. Heidi Meissner and Kevin Bryzek

Ice Dance:

1. Kim Krohn and Barry Hagan
2. Moira North and Patrick Dean
3. Carol Schultz and Kevin Poit

**1984 CAMPEONATOS DEL MUNDO DE PATINAJE ARTÍSTICO PROFESSIONAL SOBRE HIELO (Jaca, Spain, April 16-22, 1984)**

Men:

1. Brian Pockar (CAN)
2. Adam Leib (USA)
3. Daniel Béland (CAN)

Women:

1. Simone Grigorescu (ROM)
2. Claudia Kristofics-Binder (AUT)
3. Karen Wood (GRB)

Pairs:

1. Barbara Underhill and Paul Martini (CAN)
2. Lea Ann Miller and Billy Fauver (USA)
3. Candy Jones and Don Fraser (CAN)

Ice Dance:

1. Karen Taylor and Robert Burk (CAN)
2. Wendy Sessions and Stephen Williams (GRB)
3. Moira North and Patrick Dean (USA)

# SHOWS AND TOURS

The Ice Castle in Blue Jay, California officially opened in June with a star-studded ice spectacular and 500-dollar-a-plate dinner, raising funds for a local hospital. Produced by Eddie Shipstad and directed by Paul Wahlberg, *Symphony on Skates* featured a 69-piece orchestra and performances by Robin Cousins, Toller Cranston, Tai Babilonia and Randy Gardner and Judy Blumberg and Michael Seibert.

Precision skating met hockey when Les Étincelles de Charlesbourg and Tourbillons de Sillery performed at the opening ceremonies of the Quebec Nordiques first home game of the season. The Edmonton Oilers also requested a precision team for one of their games.

*Superskates* celebrated its tenth anniversary at Madison Square Garden in October. Giving performances to raise funds for the 1984 Olympic team were Dorothy Hamill, Scott Hamilton, Rosalynn Sumners, Elaine Zayak and Kitty and Peter Carruthers.

Following in the footsteps of John Curry, Olympic Gold Medallist Robin Cousins developed a repertory ice skating company of his own, opening a UK tour of *Electric Ice* in London's West End in August. Electric Ice was directed by Brian Foley and choreographed by Cousins, who was also the headliner. The supporting cast included Brian Pockar, Allen Schramm, Simone Grigorescu, Angela Greenhow, Bob Rubens and Elina Viola and Keith Green. When the tour came to Cousins' hometown of Bristol in May, Cousins received a five-minute standing ovation. A subsequent run of the show on Broadway was cancelled when the funding to produce the show wasn't raised in time.

In April, history was made when the entire stage of the Royal Albert Hall in London was frozen over for the first time. The Royal Philharmonic Orchestra provided the music for *Symphony on Ice*, starring John Curry, Janet Lynn, JoJo Starbuck, David Santee and Katherine Healy. The show featured choreography by Laura Dean and Peter Martins, the ballet master of the New York City Ballet. The fall before the Royal Albert Hall show, The John Curry Skating Company presented a Canadian tour with the same name.

Thousands lined the streets of Nottingham to cheer on Jayne Torvill and Christopher Dean in a parade in April. Less than a week later, they performed all their signature numbers at the Nottingham Ice Rink in *The Best of Torvill and Dean*, which raised 30 000 pounds. Torvill and Dean presented the proceeds to the city council, who in turn donated it to charity. The gesture was Torvill and Dean's way of saying thanks for the 53 000 pounds the city had contributed to their training costs over the years. In May, Torvill and Dean were named Pye Colour Television's Personalities of the Year at a lunch at the Hilton Hotel in London. They gave their farewell performance as amateurs at a gala ice show at Richmond Ice Rink in London, where "The Iron Lady" (Prime Minister Margaret Thatcher) lauded them in a speech, admitting she was one of their "great fans". Torvill and Dean then embarked on the *International Ice Gala*, a nineteen-show tour of Australia, which also featured Elena Valova and Oleg Vasiliev, Barbara Underhill and Paul Martini, Natalia Bestemianova and Andrei Bukin, Alexandr Fadeev, Gary Beacom and Anna Kondrashova.

The '84 *Tour of Olympic & World Figure Skating Champions* featured skaters from the United States, Canada, East and West Germany, the Soviet Union and Great Britain. The only Gold Olympic Medallists from Sarajevo missing from the line-up were Jayne Torvill and Christopher Dean. The tour drew large crowds in 22 shows, returning to Canada for performances in Toronto and Montreal.

# MAJOR COMPETITIONS

**World Junior Championships.** The Makomanai Ice Arena in Sapporo, the site of the figure skating events at the 1972 Winter Olympics, played host to the first World Junior Championships ever held in Asia in early December. The event's timing forced the Japan Skating Federation to cancel the NHK Trophy that year. Though brothers Viktor and Vladimir Petrenko generated much buzz in practices with triple Lutzes and triple/triple combinations, their performances in the competition failed to live up to expectations. Viktor ultimately moved up from third to take the the gold over 15-year-old Canadian Marc Ferland and America's Thomas Ciernak and Vladimir finished fifth, one spot ahead of Canada's second entry, Matthew Hall. On the whole, the men's event was unfortunately characterized by many falls and two-footed landings on jumps. In the ice dance event, Christina and Keith Yatsuhashi returned to take the silver, sandwiched between two Soviet couples, Elena Krykanova and Evgeni Platov and Svetlana Liapina and Gorsha Sur. Canada's two teams Christine Horton and Michael Farrington and Jo-Anne Borlase and Scott Chalmers, were a very strong fourth and fifth. Austria's Gigi Siegert won the figures but was clearly outclassed in the free skating events and dropped to seventh overall. East Germany's Karin Hendschke and Simone Koch were the eventual winners of gold and silver, though neither came first in any phase of the competition. Both the short program and free skate were unanimously won by Japan's Midori Ito, who made a remarkable comeback to the event after missing the previous season due to injury, sporting a huge triple Lutz to boot. Ito's 13th-place finish in the figures held her down in third place. Canada's Melissa Murphy and Nathalie Sasseville finished the event in ninth and 13th. Though the pairs event was very well-skated, it did not go unnoticed that the Soviet Union and East Germany continued to enter 'rag doll' teams with clear height, weight and age differences. The unanimous winners of the short program, Olga Neizvestnaya and Sergei Hudyakov, fell twice in the free skate, setting the stage for a unanimous win for the East German pair of Manuela Landgraf and Ingo Steuer. American siblings Susan and Jason Dungjen won the silver and Canada's Penny Schultz and Scott Grover finished sixth, one spot behind Stanislav Zhuk's team Ekaterina Gordeeva and Sergei Grinkov, who were making their debut at Junior Worlds.

**World Professional Championships.** Over 18 000 spectators watched an exemplary group of professional figure skating's most eminent stars at the World Professional Championships in Landover, Maryland in December. The kitty at stake was 210 000 dollars. Though the team format of *All-Stars* .vs. *Pro-Stars* for the Avon Cup and group number remained, skaters received individual scores and placements for the first time. before this, only combined scores of two members from each team at a time were announced. The big winners in 1983 were the *All-Stars* team, consisting of Toller Cranston, John Carlow Jr., Dorothy Hamill, Dianne de Leeuw, Ludmila and Oleg Protopopov, JoJo Starbuck and Ken Shelley and Lorna Wighton and John Dowding. The first individual winners of the event were Charlie Tickner, Janet Lynn, the Protopopovs and Wighton and Dowding. Lynn's good luck charms were her children, who held up signs saying "Go Mom!" The prestigious *American Skating World* Professional Skater of the Year Award was presented to the Protopopovs. They were the first pairs team to be so honoured. Toller Cranston did 'double duty' as commentator of the CBC broadcast of the event.

## 1984 WORLD JUNIOR CHAMPIONSHIPS (Sapporo, Japan, December 5-11, 1983)

Men:

1. Viktor Petrenko (SOV)
2. Marc Ferland (CAN)
3. Thomas Cierniak (USA)
4. Erik Larson (USA)
5. Vladimir Petrenko (SOV)
6. Matthew Hall (CAN)
7. Alain Miquel (FRA)
8. Noritomo Taniuchi (JPN)
9. Frédéric Lipka (FRA)
10. Henrik Walentin (DEN)

Women:

1. Karin Hendschke (GDR)
2. Simone Koch (GDR)
3. Midori Ito (JPN)
4. Kathryn Adams (USA)
5. Heike Gobbers (FRG)
6. Irina Klimova (SOV)
7. Gigi Siegert (AUT)
8. Constanze Gensel (GDR)
9. Melissa Murphy (CAN)
10. Claudia Villiger (SUI)

Pairs:

1. Manuela Landgraf and Ingo Steuer (GDR)
2. Susan and Jason Dungjen (USA)
3. Olga Neizvestnaya and Sergei Hudyakov (SOV)
4. Irina Shishova and Alexei Suleymanov (SOV)
5. Ekaterina Gordeeva and Sergei Grinkov (SOV)
6. Penny Schultz and Scott Grover (CAN)
7. Danielle and Stephen Carr (AUS)
8. Sonja Hoefler and Marc Druener (FRG)
9. Lisa and Neil Cushley (GRB)
10. Jan and Todd Waggoner (USA)

Ice Dance:

1. Elena Krykanova and Evgeni Platov (SOV)
2. Christina and Keith Yatsuhashi (USA)
3. Svetlana Liapina and Gorsha Sur (SOV)
4. Christine Horton and Michael Farrington (CAN)
5. Jo-Anne Borlase and Scott Chalmers (CAN)
6. Doriane Bontemps and Charles-Henri Paliard (FRA)
7. Stefania Calegari and Pasquale Camerlengo (ITA)
8. Honorata Górna and Andrzej Dostatni (POL)
9. Corinne Paliard and Didier Courtois (FRA)
10. Christine Goettler and Michael Loefflad (FRG)

## 1983 WORLD PROFESSIONAL CHAMPIONSHIPS (Landover, MD, December 16, 1983)

Men:

1. Charlie Tickner (USA)
2. Toller Cranston (CAN)
3. John Carlow Jr. (USA)
4. Donald Jackson (CAN)

**U.S. Championships.** In January, the Salt Palace and Bountiful Recreation Center in Salt Lake City, Utah played host to the U.S. Championships for the first time. There was a record entry of 86 entries in the senior events. Doping control tests were conducted on all potential Olympic competitors at the Championships for the first time. "Absolutely Banned" drugs included anabolic steroids, a painkiller called Darvon, high quantities of caffeine and any stimulants or narcotics. Alcohol and marijuana were not banned but the USOC recommended against" their use. As expected, Judy Blumberg and Michael Seibert dominated the senior ice dance event from start to finish, earning a total of three perfect marks of 6.0 - one in the OSP and two in the free dance. Blumberg and Seibert developed their theatrical "Scheherazade" free dance with a choreographer from the American Ballet Theater. Carol Fox and Richard Dalley took the silver ahead of Elisa Spitz and Scott Gregory, reversing the order from the previous year's Nationals. While most of the top teams skated relatively cleanly in the short program, every single one of the senior pairs made at least one mistake in their free skate. Kitty and Peter Carruthers (who had been practicing throw quadruple Salchows) fell on a throw triple Salchow but finished strongly to take the gold over Lea Ann Miller and Bill Fauver and Jill Watson and Burt Lancon. Scott Hamilton, Brian Boitano and Tom Dickson took the top three spots in the men's figures, with Hamilton receiving applause from the audience for his excellent rocker and loop. Hamilton skated brilliantly in the short program, earning unanimous first-place marks. Boitano and Mark Cockerell, who finished second and third, both landed triple Lutz/double loop combinations, whereas Hamilton chose to do the required double loop as the first jump in a combination with an easier triple toe-loop. A capacity crowd cheered on during the men's free skate as Hamilton had one of the best performances of his career in his final trip to Nationals. He landed five triples in his program and earned four perfect marks of 6.0 for composition and style to win his fourth consecutive national title. Boitano edged Cockerell for the silver in a five-four split of the judging panel. This result that was somewhat ironic as Boitano did not skate his best and many felt in the past, he had been 'held down' by the judges after giving much stronger performances. Cockerell, in contrast, skated very well, only struggling on one jump late in his program. Paul Wylie finished fourth but received a standing ovation for his outstanding free skate. There was a great deal and excitement over the women's competition. As the defending World and U.S. Champion Rosalynn Sumners was the favourite, but Tiffany Chin was the star of the practices. Vikki de Vries was forced to withdraw due to injury. Elaine Zayak arrived at Nationals with a new attitude. Reflecting on the loss of her U.S. and World titles in the weeks leading up to Nationals, she remarked, "When I lost the Nationals, I thought it was the end of the world. I would get hysterical, crying, and I wanted to quit. I was a spoiled brat and I probably still am, but now I can handle the problems. I learned you have to feel good about yourself and not worry how many people in the audience think you're a sweetheart." The judging was all over the place in the figures, with five different skaters receiving at least one first-place ordinal on the paragraph bracket and a five-four split between Sumners and Zayak occurring in the paragraph loop. However, when the results were tallied Sumners won the figures with first-place ordinals from eight of the nine judges over Zayak, Jill Frost and Chin. All four of the leaders in the figures skated clean short programs. Chin was both the audience and judge's favourite, earning a standing ovation and first-place marks. Sumners finished second ahead of Zayak and Frost, though she executed only a double Axel/double loop combination and the other three top women did combinations with a triple toe-loop.

**WORLD PROFESSIONAL CHAMPIONSHIPS (continued)**

Women:

1. Janet Lynn (USA)
2. Dorothy Hamill (USA)
3. Linda Fratianne (USA)
4. Dianne de Leeuw (HOL)

Pairs:

1. Ludmila and Oleg Protopopov (SOV)
2. JoJo Starbuck and Ken Shelley (USA)
3. Tai Babilonia and Randy Gardner (USA)

Ice Dance:

1. Lorna Wighton and John Dowding (CAN)
2. Krisztina Regőczy and András Sallay (HUN)

Team:

1. All Stars: Toller Cranston, John Carlow Jr., Dorothy Hamill, Dianne de Leeuw, Ludmila and Oleg Protopopov, JoJo Starbuck and Ken Shelley, Lorna Wighton and John Dowding
2. Pro Stars: Charlie Tickner, Donald Jackson, Linda Fratianne, Janet Lynn, Tai Babilonia and Randy Gardner, Krisztina Regőczy and András Sallay

**1984 U.S. CHAMPIONSHIPS (Salt Lake City, UT, January 17-22, 1984)**

Men:

1. Scott Hamilton
2. Brian Boitano
3. Mark Cockerell
4. Paul Wylie
5. Tom Dickson
6. Daniel Doran
7. Scott Williams
8. Bobby Beauchamp
9. Christopher Bowman
10. Craig Henderson

Women:

1. Rosalynn Sumners
2. Tiffany Chin
3. Elaine Zayak
4. Jill Frost
5. Kathryn Adams
6. Debi Thomas
7. Sara MacInnes
8. Yvonne Gómez
9. Maradith Feinberg
10. Kelly Webster

Unfortunately, as in the pairs event, all the top women made mistakes when the pressure was on during ABC's *Wide World of Sports* broadcast of the free skate. Chin included three triples, including a rare flip, to earn another standing ovation and a win in the free skate. Sumners landed three triples of her own but fell on a double Axel to finish second in the free skate. Her lead in the figures was just enough to keep her in first overall. The overall results were remarkably close between Sumners and Chin - a five-four split. Had Chin finished third in figures, instead of fourth, she may have won the title. Zayak and Frost both had numerous mistakes in their free skate, but two triple combinations early in her program were enough to keep Zayak ahead and earn her the final berth on the Olympic team. In the junior women's event, Allison Oki of Montclair, New Jersey made history as the first Asian American skater to win the national junior women's title. Oki's father, a dentist, was a first-generation American with roots in Japan. The junior pairs and ice dance events were also won by talented young Asian American skaters, Ginger and Archie Tse and Christina and Keith Yatsuhashi.

**Canadian Championships.** The Agridome in Regina, Saskatchewan played host to the Canadian Championships in January. Given the controversy surrounding the Olympic entries four years prior, the CFSA specified well in advance that the Canadian Olympic Association had "final say as to the size and composition of the Olympic team" and that the national team would be selected based on "potential to be an international calibre contender, fitness profile... [and] attitude such that the skater will benefit from national seminar participation." Though 4000 spectators showed up to watch the senior compulsory dances - a new record, by a mile - Tracy Wilson and Rob McCall's road to victory in Regina wasn't a cakewalk. They lost the first compulsory dance (the Starlight Waltz) to Kelly Johnson and John Thomas and some judges had Johnson and Thomas first in the Kilian and Tango Romantica as well. Wilson and McCall asserted their dominance in the fiery Paso Doble OSP and ultimately defended their national title with a dramatic film noir-style free dance set to music from the film *Staccato*. Kelly Johnson and John Thomas took the silver ahead of Karyn and Rod Garossino, earning the second spot on the Olympic team. The fifth-place team from 1983, Karen Taylor and Robert Burk, were forced to withdraw when the couple fell and Taylor dislocated her knee during the Kilian. Barbara Underhill and Paul Martini withdrew and were given a bye to the Olympics and Worlds. Underhill tore a ligament in her left ankle a week before the competition. A trio of Kerry Leitch's pairs from the Preston Figure Skating Club ended up sweeping the pairs podium. Katherina Matousek and Lloyd Eisler won the gold, followed by Melinda Kunhegyi and Lyndon Johnston and Cynthia Coull and Mark Rowsom. The top two pairs joined forces to win the fours competition as well. Gary Beacom won the compulsory figures by a considerable margin for the third year in a row. Brian Orser faltered on the first two figures but moved up to finish second in the first phase of the competition. Orser was at his very best in the short program. Though his free skate featured a triple Axel, he made uncharacteristic errors on both the triple Lutz and flip. The quality of his skating and the content of his programs were still more than enough to take the title. Beacom predictably finished second behind Orser in both the short program and free skate, despite delivering two outstanding performances and earning a standing ovation in the free skate. The bronze medal went to Gordon Forbes, but the CFSA successfully recommended to the COA that Jaimee Eggleton, the junior men's champion, be named to the Olympic team. Forbes was given the 'consolation prize' of being selected for the World team.

**U.S. CHAMPIONSHIPS (continued)**

Pairs:

1. Kitty and Peter Carruthers
2. Lea Ann Miller and Bill Fauver
3. Jill Watson and Burt Lancon
4. Gillian Wachsman and Robert Daw
5. Natalie and Wayne Seybold
6. Lynne and Jay Freeman
7. Katy Keeley and Gary Kemp
8. Susan and Jason Dungjen
9. Maria Lako and Michael Blicharski
10. Margo Shoup and Patrick Page

Ice Dance:

1. Judy Blumberg and Michael Seibert
2. Carol Fox and Richard Dalley
3. Elisa Spitz and Scott Gregory
4. Renée Roca and Donald Adair
5. Susie Wynne and Joseph Druar
6. Susan Jorgensen and Robert Yokabaskas
7. Lois Luciani and Russ Witherby
8. Eva Hunyadi and Jay Pinkerton
9. Kristan Lowery and Chip Rossbach
10. Eleanor De Vera and James Yorke

Junior Winners:

Billy Lawe (men)
Allison Oki (women)
Ginger and Archie Tse (pairs)
Christina and Keith Yatsuhashi (ice dance)

Novice Winners:

Patrick Brault (men)
Sharon Barker (women)

**1984 CANADIAN CHAMPIONSHIPS**
(January 9-15, 1984, Regina, SK)

Men:

1. Brian Orser
2. Gary Beacom
3. Gordon Forbes
4. Dennis Coi
5. Kevin Parker
6. Mark MacVean
7. André Bourgeois
8. David Watson
9. Lloyd Eisler
10. Neil Paterson

Women:

1. Kay Thomson
2. Elizabeth Manley
3. Cynthia Coull
4. Charlene Wong
5. Barbara Butler
6. Kerry Smith
7. Diane Mae Ogibowski
8. Patricia Schmidt
9. Lana Sherman
10. Merriam Twinn

The move was seen as somewhat controversial at the time, but David Dore asserted it was important to push "forth younger skaters that may not have made their mark so that international judges may remember them the year after the Olympics - when many older, top skaters quit." An interesting footnote about the men's competition was the fact that the skater who finished dead last in the short program landed a triple Axel. Neil Paterson's result was a classic case of a skater getting too excited after successfully landing a jump they didn't expect to. He botched the second part of his combination and later missed a double Axel. In the women's event, Kay Thomson decisively won the figures over Andrea Hall, receiving scores ranging from 3.8 to 4.3 - the highest marks she had ever received in figures. Elizabeth Manley, who had switched coaches to Sonya and Peter Dunfield in Ottawa after her harrowing experience at Canadians the previous season, was third - her best finish ever in the figures at a major event. Thomson fell on her triple flip/double loop combination in the short program and finished third. The short program winner was Cynthia Coull, who was the first to skate and performed a clean program. Coull unfortunately placed only eighth in the figures. Manley placed third after falling on the double loop in her triple Salchow combination. She had to restart her program after children threw flowers intended for Thomson, who had skated before her, on the ice during her program. Thomson came back in the vengeance with a triple Lutz in the free skate, defending her national title with a dramatic performance to "Swan Lake". She became the first woman to win three consecutive national titles since Lynn Nightingale in 1977. With renewed confidence, Manley finished second over Coull and Charlene Wong, earning the second coveted spot on the Olympic team. Missing in action was Tracey Wainman, who was suffering from tendinitis.

**European Championships.** In January, the Budapest Sportcsarnok played host to 108 skaters from 19 countries at the European Championships. Only two years old at the time, the largest indoor sports hall in Hungary had two ice rinks, conveniently allowing both the figures, free skating and practices to all take place under one roof. In the pairs event, World Champions Elena Valova and Oleg Vasiliev defeated the reigning European Champions Sabine Baeß and Tassilo Thierbach by a wide margin, receiving two perfect marks of 6.0 for artistic impression in the free skate. Birgit Lorenz and Knut Schubert defeated Larisa Selezneva and Oleg Makarov to win the bronze, marking the first time since 1975 that East Germany had two pairs on the podium at the event. Elena Vodorezova, Katarina Witt and Manuela Ruben led the way after the women's compulsory figures. Vodorezova played it safe in the short program, opting to do a double Axel combination instead of a triple, but ultimately withdrew before the free skate and rushed home to Moscow upon learning that her mother was extremely ill. Witt delivered two outstanding performances, both featuring fine triple jumps, to easily win the gold medal in Budapest. Despite falling on a triple loop in the free skate, West Germany's Manuela Ruben took the silver medal. Anna Kondrashova fell twice in the free skate and finished behind Kira Ivanova in that segment of the competition, but Kondrashova's second-place finish in the short program to Ivanova's sixth was enough for the bronze. Jean-Christophe Simond won the men's figures, as was expected, by a wide margin over Jozef Sabovčík, Rudi Cerne, Alexandr Fadeev, Heiko Fischer and Norbert Schramm.

**CANADIAN CHAMPIONSHIPS (continued)**

Pairs:

1. Katherina Matousek and Lloyd Eisler
2. Melinda Kunhegyi and Lyndon Johnston
3. Cynthia Coull and Mark Rowsom
4. Lynda and John Ivanich
5. Laurene Collin and David Howe
6. Lynn Frasson and Doug Ladret

Ice Dance:

1. Tracy Wilson and Rob McCall
2. Kelly Johnson and John Thomas
3. Karyn and Rod Garossino
4. Isabelle and Paul Duchesnay
5. Christine Horton and Michael Farrington
6. Kim Campbell and David Islam
7. Michelle McDonald and Patrick Mandley
8. Teri-Lynn Black and Toivo Heinsaar
9. Gayle Coughtry and Steve Percival
10. Shirley Dublanko and Leslie Hills

Fours:

1. Katherina Matousek, Melinda Kunhegyi, Lloyd Eisler and Lyndon Johnston
2. Cynthia Coull, Laurene Collin, Mark Rowsom and David Howe

Junior Winners:

Jaimee Eggleton (men)
Rosemary Sakic (women)
Penny Schultz and Scott Grover (pairs)
Christine Horton and Michael Farrington (ice dance)

Novice Winners:

Craig Burns (men)
Trudy Treslan (women)
Denise Benning and Alan Kerslake (pairs)
Melanie Cole and Donald Godfrey (ice dance)

**1984 EUROPEAN CHAMPIONSHIPS**
(Budapest, Hungary, January 9-14, 1984)

Men:

1. Alexandr Fadeev (SOV)
2. Rudi Cerne (FRG)
3. Norbert Schramm (FRG)
4. Jozef Sabovčík (CZE)
5. Heiko Fischer (FRG)
6. Vladimir Kotin (SOV)
7. Vitali Egorov (SOV)
8. Grzegorz Filipowski (POL)
9. Falko Kirsten (GDR)
10. Petr Barna (CZE)

Though Schramm stumbled in his straight-line step sequence in the short program, he placed second behind a flawless Fadeev. Simond was suffering from the flu and withdrew after the short program. In the free skate, Fadeev demonstrated his technical prowess with a taxing performance that included two difficult combinations - the triple Axel/double toe-loop and triple Lutz/triple toe-loop. Cerne finished second in the free skate with an elegant performance featuring four triples. Fadeev won the gold, receiving two 5.9s for technical merit and Cerne the silver, with three 5.9s for artistic impression. Schramm held on to win the bronze medal, unsuccessfully attempting the only other triple Axel in the free skate and accidentally crashing into the barrier at another point. In the ice dance, it was Torvill and Dean and then, everybody else. The Brits started strongly in the compulsory dances and earned perfect 6.0s for presentation from six of the judges for their impeccable Paso Doble OSP. Soviet judge Irina Absaliamova was the lone dissenter, defiantly awarding Torvill and Dean a 5.6 for composition because she could, earning a well-deserved chorus of boos. A capacity crowd of 8500 spectators showed up to watch Torvill and Dean's theatrical free dance, which ended in them lying flat on the ice in a move that was symbolic of a double suicide in a volcano crater. Their marks were unprecedented in any discipline at Europeans - three perfect 6.0s for technical merit and eight for artistic impression. The only judge to award Torvill and Dean a 5.9 instead of a six was West Germany's Heinz Müllenbach. Natalia Bestemianova and Andrei Bukin, who had won the year prior when Torvill and Dean were absent, took the silver. In a close contest for third, Marina Klimova and Sergei Ponomarenko came out ahead of Karen Barber and Nicky Slater. Barber unfortunately pulled ligaments in her left leg the day before the free dance.

**EUROPEAN CHAMPIONSHIPS (continued)**

Women:

1. Katarina Witt (GDR)
2. Manuela Ruben (FRG)
3. Anna Kondrashova (SOV)
4. Kira Ivanova (SOV)
5. Sanda Dubravčić (YUG)
6. Sandra Cariboni (SUI)
7. Simone Koch (GDR)
8. Karin Telser (ITA)
9. Agnès Gosselin (FRA)
10. Cornelia Tesch (FRG)

Pairs:

1. Elena Valova and Oleg Vasiliev (SOV)
2. Sabine Baeß and Tassilo Thierbach (GDR)
3. Birgit Lorenz and Knut Schubert (GDR)
4. Larisa Selezneva and Oleg Makarov (SOV)
5. Marina Avstriskaya and Yuri Kvashnin (SOV)
6. Babette Preußler and Torsten Ohlow (GDR)
7. Dagmar Kovářová and Jozef Komár (CZE)
8. Claudia Massari and Leonardo-Christian Azzola (FRG)
9. Susan Garland and Ian Jenkins (GRB)
10. Gaby and Jörg Galambos (SUI)

Ice Dance:

1. Jayne Torvill and Christopher Dean (GRB)
2. Natalia Bestemianova and Andrei Bukin (SOV)
3. Marina Klimova and Sergei Ponomarenko (SOV)
4. Karen Barber and Nicky Slater (GRB)
5. Olga Volozhinskaya and Alexandr Svinin (SOV)
6. Petra Born and Rainer Schönborn (FRG)
7. Wendy Sessions and Stephen Williams (GRB)
8. Nathalie Hervé and Pierre Béchu (FRA)
9. Jindra Holá and Karol Foltán (CZE)
10. Isabella Micheli and Roberto Pelizzola (ITA)

*Jayne Torvill and Christopher Dean. Photo by Fred & Joan Dean, courtesy Fred Dean, "Ice & Roller Skate" magazine archive.*

**Olympic Games.** 114 skaters from 20 countries participated in the figure skating and ice dancing competitions at the Olympics in Sarajevo. Not everyone was thrilled about the event being held in the Yugoslavian capital. The city had few hotel rooms and limited parking. It was perpetually smoky, causing athletes to come down with what they called 'Yugo Throat'. During the Opening Ceremony, which paid homage to the first Winter Olympics 60 years prior, the Olympic flame was lit by Yugoslavian figure skater Sanda Dubravčić. Christopher Dean and Tadayuki Takahashi carried the flags of the United Kingdom and Japan. In the pairs short program, 1983 World Champions Elena Valova and Oleg Vasiliev performed exceptionally well to Russian folk music, very much in the style that Irina Rodnina and Aleksandr Zaitsev had made famous. Both Larisa Selezneva and Oleg Makarov and Kitty and Peter Carruthers skated exceptionally well and though the Americans received two 5.8s and the Soviets received none, when the marks were tallied the two teams ended up in a tie for second. 1982 World Champion Tassilo Thierbach popped the required side-by-side double loop jump into a single, finishing a disappointing fourth with partner Sabine Baeß. Disaster struck at the worst possible time for Canada's Barbara Underhill and Paul Martini. After starting their program strongly with a lasso lift and clean solo jumps, Underhill lost her edge during the side-by-side spins and crashed into Martini, resulting in him falling as well. The mishap dashed any hopes for an Olympic gold medal for the Canadian Champions, leaving them in sixth place. Valova and Vasiliev chose a very unusual mix of music for their free skate - sandwiching Beethoven's "Für Elise" between orchestral versions of The Beatles' "Get Back" and Led Zeppelin's "Stairway to Heaven". The Soviet favourites were not perfect, with Valova two-footing the landing of a side-by-side double Axel and the throw triple Salchow, but they were very strong indeed - landing side-by-side triple toe-loops and two 'big ticket' throws cleanly. Their marks of 5.8 and 5.9 earned them the gold medal, though the Carruthers flawless silver medal-winning free skate was the favourite of the Sarajevo crowd. The Americans opted not to attempt the throw quad Salchow but they didn't put a foot wrong, showcasing gorgeous throws and their superb lateral twist and hydrant lift. It was the first time in over 30 years a U.S. pair won an Olympic silver medal and after the competition, they received a telegram from Karol and Peter Kennedy, the last Americans to achieve the honour, who were by coincidence also a sibling pair. Selezneva and Makarov weren't perfect, but they executed a throw triple Salchow and double Axel and side-by-side triple toe-loops to claim the bronze. Underhill and Martini's free skate was perhaps even more disappointing than their short and certainly not indicative of their skill level. They missed two key throws and Underhill singled a side-by-side jump. The pressure was immense for the Canadians, who were featured on the cover of *MacLean's* in the lead-up to the Games with the byline "Underhill and Martini: The Olympic Promise". Their heartbreaking performances left them in seventh. Canada's two other teams, Katherina Matousek and Lloyd Eisler and Melinda Kunhegyi and Lyndon Johnston were eighth and 12th. Ever the 'class clown', Scott Hamilton was spotted in the stands in Sarajevo wearing a pair of glasses with tiny windshield wipers that went back and forth. In the men's compulsory figures, Hamilton, Jean-Christophe Simond and Rudi Cerne finished 1-2-3, but what is best remembered about the men's figures in Sarajevo was an incident that had absolutely nothing to do with the leaders. After skating his third figure, Canada's Gary Beacom was given marks lower than the first two figures he skated, which he felt weren't of the same strength.

**1984 WINTER OLYMPIC GAMES (Sarajevo, Yugoslavia, February 10-18, 1984)**

Men:

1. Scott Hamilton (USA)
2. Brian Orser (CAN)
3. Jozef Sabovčík (CZE)
4. Rudi Cerne (FRG)
5. Brian Boitano (USA)
6. Jean-Christophe Simond (FRA)
7. Alexandr Fadeev (SOV)
8. Vladimir Kotin (SOV)
9. Norbert Schramm (FRG)
10. Heiko Fischer (FRG)

Women:

1. Katarina Witt (GDR)
2. Rosalynn Sumners (USA)
3. Kira Ivanova (SOV)
4. Tiffany Chin (USA)
5. Anna Kondrashova (SOV)
6. Elaine Zayak (USA)
7. Manuela Ruben (FRG)
8. Elena Vodorezova (SOV)
9. Claudia Leistner (FRG)
10. Sanda Dubravčić (YUG)

Pairs:

1. Elena Valova and Oleg Vasiliev (SOV)
2. Kitty and Peter Carruthers (USA)
3. Larisa Selezneva and Oleg Makarov (SOV)
4. Sabine Baeß and Tassilo Thierbach (GDR)
5. Birgit Lorenz and Knut Schubert (GDR)
6. Jill Watson and Burt Lancon (USA)
7. Barbara Underhill and Paul Martini (CAN)
8. Katherina Matousek and Lloyd Eisler (CAN)
9. Marina Avstriskaya and Yuri Kvashnin (SOV)
10. Lea Ann Miller and Bill Fauver (USA)

Ice Dance:

1. Jayne Torvill and Christopher Dean (GRB)
2. Natalia Bestemianova and Andrei Bukin (SOV)
3. Marina Klimova and Sergei Ponomarenko (SOV)
4. Judy Blumberg and Michael Seibert (USA)
5. Carol Fox and Richard Dalley (USA)
6. Karen Barber and Nicky Slater (GRB)
7. Olga Volozhinskaya and Alexandr Svinin (SOV)
8. Tracy Wilson and Rob McCall (CAN)
9. Petra Born and Rainer Schönborn (FRG)
10. Elisa Spitz and Scott Gregory (USA)

Instead of going back to the boards, Beacom stood directly in front of the judges and gave them a good old-fashioned Barbara Fusar-Poli death stare. One of the judges gave him a dirty look and then he skated away and kicked the boards, sending a thunderous boom through the eerily silent arena. Although not officially reprimanded by Donald Gilchrist, the first Canadian to referee the men's event at the Olympics, Beacom was hauled into a meeting on the day of the free dance with Robert Hindmarch, Canada's Olympic chef de mission and warned that disciplinary action would be forthcoming if his behaviour continued. Beacom finished tenth in the figures, three spots behind Brian Orser, whom he had soundly beaten in the figures at Canadians. Beacom later reminisced, "My back change loop at Olympics was a personal achievement in spite of the temperamental conflict that ensued. It was the only loop in the competition that came close to rulebook specs. Yet, I suspect because it stood out and because I was reputed to be a renegade, I was not justly rewarded." Scott Hamilton was suffering from an ear infection at the time, though no one knew it when he went out and skated a flawless short program. The winner of the short program, however, was Brian Orser, who performed a triple Lutz/double loop combination that was far more difficult than Hamilton's double loop/triple toe-loop. A surprise third in the short program was Brian Boitano, who was only eighth in figures. Both Simond and Cerne skated very well indeed in the short program, placing in the top six and keeping themselves in the medal conversation. Scott Hamilton truly wasn't feeling well on the day of the free skate, but he gave it everything he had. Though he singled a planned triple flip and doubled a triple Salchow, he landed three triples, one of them a Lutz, and two fine double Axels. In contrast, Brian Orser's performance to the music of Vangelis and The Salsoul Orchestra was really that 'Olympic dream skate', featuring a smorgasbord of triple jumps, including the Axel and Lutz. Though Orser won both the short program and free skate, his seventh-place showing in the figures kept him in second overall. Jozef Sabovčík landed six triples, including a triple Axel of his own, to move up and win a surprise bronze medal over Cerne, Boitano and Simond. Gary Beacom settled for 11th and Canada's third entry Jaimee Eggleton was 20th. Reflecting on his experience in Sarajevo, Eggleton later recalled how unwelcome he felt and how his roommate said to him, "I don't know what you're doing here, Eggleton." He remarked, "It was pure hell. It took me two years to recover from that. I told the Olympic Committee that was the worst thing they could do to a young athlete."

*Kitty and Peter Carruthers. Contributor: PCN Photography / Alamy Stock Photo.*

In winning, Scott Hamilton became the first American man to win an Olympic gold medal since David Jenkins in 1960. Jozef Sabovčík and Brian Orser made history as the first skaters to land triple Axels in Olympic medal-winning performances. Though unsuccessful, seventh-place finisher Alexandr Fadeev was the first skater to attempt a quad at the Olympics. Noteworthy was the ninth-place finish of Norbert Schramm, who had twice won the gold medal at the European Championships and the silver medal at the Worlds. Schramm later claimed that the day before the men's figures, the Vice-President of the West German Olympic Committee came to the German House in the athlete's village and told his parents he was going to place ninth in the figures - exactly where he ended up. Two months before the competition, Schramm began working with Carlo Fassi in America. He believed that any 'funny business' that went on with the judging in Sarajevo may have been connected to this coaching change and his Federation backing Rudi Cerne instead of him. In the women's compulsory figures, Rosalynn Sumners pulled ahead of Elena Vodorezova to take an early lead, with Katarina Witt, who skated the second and third figures with an upset stomach, placing third. Witt won the short program with a faultless display to Monti's "Csárdás", earning marks of 5.8 and 5.9. Sumners made a costly mistake, two-footing her double Axel, and placed only fifth in the short behind Tiffany Chin, Ivanova and Anna Kondrashova. In an outstanding free skate set to a medley of Gershwin tunes, Katarina Witt landed a double Lutz/triple toe-loop combination and two other triples, earning marks ranging from 5.7 to 5.9. She became the second student of Jutta Müller in a row to win the Olympic gold medal. Sumners turned a planned triple toe-loop and double Axel into a double and single late in her program, settling for silver but receiving the only perfect mark awarded to a singles skater at the Games - a 6.0 for artistic impression from Italian judge Giorgio Siniscalco. Kira Ivanova won the bronze - a first for a Soviet woman at the Olympics - but placed only fifth in the free skate behind Tiffany Chin and Elaine Zayak, who both delivered superb performances. Chin and Zayak only finished fourth and sixth, hampered by 12th and 13th place finishes in the figures. Elena Vodorezova dropped from second to eighth. Canada's two representatives in the women's event, Kay Thomson and Elizabeth Manley, finished 12th and 13th. Jayne Torvill and Christopher Dean dominated the ice dance event from the very beginning, earning an unprecedented three 6.0s for their Westminster Waltz from the Hungarian, British and Japanese judges. Interestingly, the Paso Doble was skated twice in Sarajevo - as a compulsory dance and as the OSP. Torvill and Dean's dramatic Paso OSP to Rimsy-Korsakov's "Capriccio Espagnol" earned them four more 6.0s, including perfect marks for both composition and presentation from Hungarian judge István Sugár. In the free dance, the audience was mesmerized as Torvill and Dean weaved a spell with their dramatic free dance to Ravel's "Bolero", a tale of two doomed lovers fittingly performed on Valentine's Day. The Brits earned a record-breaking 12 perfect 6.0s on their way to winning the UK's first Olympic gold medal in ice dancing. The Hungarian, British and Japanese judges were the three to give them 6.0s for both technical merit and artistic impression. Though Torvill and Dean's performances in Sarajevo will go down in history as some of the finest Olympic performances on record, the rest of the field in Sarajevo was very strong too. To the disappointment of American skating fans, Judy Blumberg and Michael Seibert finished fourth after being in third in both the compulsories and OSP, behind Natalia Bestemianova and Andrei Bukin. Some felt the Americans were robbed of a medal and that a 5.5 given by Italian judge Cia Bordogna had been unduly harsh. Canada's Tracy Wilson and Rob McCall and Kelly Johnson and Kris Barber were eighth and 12th. Brian Boitano's coach Linda Leaver and Scott Hamilton's choreographer Ricky Harris sat right in the middle of a huge British delegation during the ice dance competition. They were surprised when a member of the group asked them if they felt uncomfortable with their seating arrangement. It was none other than Her Royal Highness Princess Anne. Several other important firsts were recorded at the Sarajevo Games. Several countries were represented in figure skating disciplines for the first time. Grzegorz Filipowski and Milgan Begovic were the first Polish and Yugoslavian men to compete, while Luan Bo and Yao Bin were China's first pair. In the ice dance event, Bulgaria, China, France and Japan were represented for the first time at the Olympics by Hristina Boyanova and Javor Ivanov, Xi Hongyan and Zhao Xiaolei, Nathalie Hervé and Pierre Béchu and Noriko Sato and Tadayuki Takahashi. Ida Tetsuko Shimizu Tateoka made history as the first Asian American judge at the Olympics, representing the United States as an official in the men's event.

*Rosalynn Sumners, Katarina Witt and Kira Ivanova. Contributor: PCN Photography / Alamy Stock Photo*

**World Championships.** The Civic Centre in Ottawa was thrilled to 'welcome home' many of the World's best figure skaters at the World Championships in March... 115 from 21 countries, to be precise. When the capital was last awarded Worlds in 1978, the event had been a huge success, netting nearly 500 000 in profit for skater development in Canada). The 1984 event proved to be incredibly successful as well. A record 7000 spectators showed up to watch the compulsory dances and sell-out crowds of 10 000 watched each of the four finals. An unusual situation presented itself in the women's event, when Tiffany Chin withdrew due to an ankle injury and Rosalynn Sumners announced her intention to turn professional at the last minute, leaving Elaine Zayak as the only U.S. entry in the women's event. The last time there was only one American woman at the Worlds was in 1948 - the year Barbara Ann Scott won the Olympic gold medal. The pressure to earn two spots for the following year seemed too much for the 1982 World Champion at first. Zayak finished only 13th in the first figure but moved up to finish ninth after the other two, still well behind the leaders Katarina Witt, Kira Ivanova and Manuela Ruben. Witt won the short program, proving her Olympic gold medal win had been no fluke. Zayak finished fifth with a clean program, behind Anna Kondrashova, Ivanova and Japan's Midori Ito. With a very strong performance in the free skate, Witt won the gold medal. There were three other clear stars: Ito, Zayak (who each landed five triples) and Elizabeth Manley, who brought down the house in front of a hometown audience and earned a standing ovation. Many felt Manley and Ito, in particular, were lowballed with their marks and that Anna Kondrashova, who ultimately finished second over Zayak, was given the marks she received on a silver platter. At a press conference after the event, one reporter straight up asked Kondrashova if she felt she deserved the silver medal. She responded, "I'm satisfied. I apologize to the spectators for missing some early jumps, but I came back to land some triples." Zayak's come-from-behind medal win was a testament to her determination. At a press conference after the event, she told reporters, "I wanted to show everybody I was not a freak. I wanted to prove I could come back every year. I wanted to see the American flag go up." Kay Thomson's fifth-place finish, coupled with Manley's eighth marked the first time since 1973 that Canada had two women in the top ten at the Worlds. In each of the three previous World Championships, Scott Hamilton had won the gold medal but lost the figures to France's Jean-Christophe Simond. Simond's decision to retire and take up coaching after the Olympics cleared the path for Hamilton's victory in the figures. West Germany's Rudi Cerne and Heiko Fischer finished second and third in that phase of the competition, but it was the actions of their more experienced teammate that gained international attention in the first phase of the men's event. Norbert Schramm, 11th and 14th in the first two figures, skated onto his patch to perform his third. He spread his arms to align his figure, started his tracing and then put his free foot down. Referee Sonia Bianchetti Garbato went over to Schramm and offered him an opportunity to restart. He shook her hand and said he could not continue. She tried to convince him to but he said he couldn't and was quitting out of frustration. He bowed to the crowd, received a standing ovation and left the ice, effectively ending his amateur career. It was an unhappy time for Schramm, but years later he still felt it was the right decision. Scott Hamilton was outstanding in the short program, skating a clean program and receiving 5.8s and 5.9s. Orser had a shaky landing on his triple Lutz but squeaked out the double loop to complete his combination. He finished second ahead of Alexandr Fadeev. In the free skate, Hamilton was not perfect, landing a triple Lutz very close to the boards and touching down on a triple flip.

**1984 WORLD CHAMPIONSHIPS (Ottawa, ON, March 20-25, 1984)**

Men:

1. Scott Hamilton (USA)
2. Brian Orser (CAN)
3. Alexandr Fadeev (SOV)
4. Jozef Sabovčík (CZE)
5. Rudi Cerne (FRG)
6. Brian Boitano (USA)
7. Heiko Fischer (FRG)
8. Vladimir Kotin (SOV)
9. Gordon Forbes (CAN)
10. Gary Beacom (CAN)

Women:

1. Katarina Witt (GDR)
2. Anna Kondrashova (SOV)
3. Elaine Zayak (USA)
4. Kira Ivanova (SOV)
5. Kay Thomson (CAN)
6. Manuela Ruben (FRG)
7. Midori Ito (JPN)
8. Elizabeth Manley (CAN)
9. Sanda Dubravčić (YUG)
10. Sandra Cariboni (SUI)

Pairs:

1. Barbara Underhill and Paul Martini (CAN)
2. Elena Valova and Oleg Vasiliev (SOV)
3. Sabine Baeß and Tassilo Thierbach (GDR)
4. Larisa Selezneva and Oleg Makarov (SOV)
5. Katherina Matousek and Lloyd Eisler (CAN)
6. Birgit Lorenz and Knut Schubert (GDR)
7. Cynthia Coull and Mark Rowsom (CAN)
8. Veronika Pershina and Marat Akbarov (SOV)
9. Babette Preußler and Tobias Schröter (GDR)
10. Lea Ann Miller and Bill Fauver (USA)

Ice Dance:

1. Jayne Torvill and Christopher Dean (GRB)
2. Natalia Bestemianova and Andrei Bukin (SOV)
3. Judy Blumberg and Michael Seibert (USA)
4. Marina Klimova and Sergei Ponomarenko (SOV)
5. Karen Barber and Nicky Slater (GRB)
6. Tracy Wilson and Rob McCall (CAN)
7. Elena Batanova and Alexei Soloviev (SOV)
8. Carol Fox and Richard Dalley (USA)
9. Petra Born and Rainer Schönborn (FRG)
10. Elisa Spitz and Scott Gregory (USA)

Brian Orser delivered an outstanding free skate, replete with a triple Axel, to win the free skate over Hamilton and finish second overall. Orser received 5.9s for both technical merit and artistic impression from Yugoslavian judge Vladimir Amsel and Polish judge Maria Zuchowicz and credited his success in Ottawa to a new visualization program called Psybrovision. A week before the Olympics, a television crew filmed him performing every element in both his short program and figures perfectly. The film repeated each element ten times, reinforcing a positive image in his mind. The other big star of the men's event was Alexandr Fadeev, who landed a string of triples including a triple Lutz/triple toe-loop combination and only finished behind Hamilton in the free skate by the marks of one judge. Canada's other two men, Gordon Forbes and Gary Beacom, finished ninth and tenth. Canada had not had three men in the top ten at the Worlds since 1954, a fact not lost on Forbes, who had been excluded from the Olympic team in favour of Jaimee Eggleton, who had not fared well in Sarajevo. Nearing the end of his career and with little to lose, Forbes not so cryptically called out the CFSA, which had been behind the COA decision, telling reporters, "The idea of the Olympics is to compete, rather than to win. That's part of the Olympic oath... yet they say they won't send you if you're not good enough. That seems to be hypocritical to me." The Carruthers opted to skip the World Championships and Jill Watson and Burt Lancon withdrew after a very scary fall in the short program, leaving Lea Ann Miller and Bill Fauver as the lone American entries - the same situation Elaine Zayak faced in the women's event. After their Olympic disappointment, Barbara Underhill and Paul Martini had a similarly disastrous performance in an exhibition in Toronto attended by several local judges. They seriously considered withdrawing from the World Championships. Brian Orser suggested that Underhill try an old pair of boots, so she pulled out a pair she had worn for a year and a half and Martini put the blades she had worn at the Olympics on them. Almost instantly, everything clicked and they realized that their performances in Sarajevo couldn't be chalked up to pressure. There had been an equipment issue all along. Underhill and Martini were flawless in the short program, finishing a close second to Olympic Gold Medallists Elena Valova and Oleg Vasiliev. In the free skate, Underhill and Martini had the skate of their lives. The audience cheered so loudly that their music could barely be heard during the final seconds of their program. With marks ranging from 5.7 to 5.9, they pulled off a major upset, winning Canada's first gold medal at the World Championships in pairs skating since the Jelineks in 1962 and becoming the first former winners of the World Junior Championships to capture a World pairs title. Valova and Vasiliev two-footed a throw and settled for silver. East Germany's Sabine Baeß and Tassilo Thierbach redeemed themselves by winning the bronze medal in their final trip to the World Championships, defeating Larisa Selezneva and Oleg Makarov, who finished third in Sarajevo. Canada's other two teams, Katherina Matousek and Lloyd Eisler and Cynthia Coull and Mark Rowsom were fifth and seventh. Miller and Fauver suffered the disappointment of finishing last, but the withdrawal of Watson and Lancon and a West German team meant there were only ten teams, assuring America a second spot the following year anyway. Jayne Torvill and Christopher Dean's swan song in the amateur ranks blew their record-breaking Olympic record out of the water. A perfect 6.0 had never been awarded at the World Championships in the compulsory dances and Torvill and Dean received seven of them - three for the Westminster Waltz and four for the Rhumba. Their Paso Doble OSP received 6.0s for presentation from every single judge - another first at the Worlds. Their winning *Bolero* free dance received another thirteen 6.0s, four for technical merit and nine for artistic impression. In total, they received 29 6.0s, ten more than they had earned in Sarajevo. Natalia Bestemianova and Andrei Bukin won the silver, as they had in Sarajevo, but Judy Blumberg and Michael Seibert reversed the result from the Olympics, winning the bronze over Marina Klimova and Sergei Ponomarenko. The Americans were delighted to win bronze but Blumberg and Seibert both noted the irony of their success, as they had skated much better at the Olympics. Canada's Tracy Wilson and Rob McCall and Kelly Johnson and John Thomas ended the event in sixth and 11th. Though they finished dead last, Liane Telling and Michael Fisher made history as the first ice dance team to represent Australia at the Worlds. Incredibly, the free dance was delayed by six hours due to a power failure at the Civic Centre. The rescheduling of the event became a complicated mess, as the ISU had no less than 22 television contracts to consider, but it was simply unavoidable. The night after Torvill and Dean won Olympic gold, a fire alarm went off in the host hotel, sending a who's who of figure skating down to the lobby in their pajamas. It ended up being a false alarm, but there were no doubt some very tired skaters the next day at the Parade of Champions.

*Jayne Torvill and Christopher Dean. Photos by Fred & Joan Dean, courtesy Fred Dean, "Ice & Roller Skate" magazine archive.*

# 1984-1985 SEASON

Hit Songs: "Like A Virgin" by Madonna, "Wake Me Up Before You Go-Go" by Wham!, "Everybody Wants To Rule The World" by Tears For Fears, "Take On Me" by a-ha, "Smooth Operator" by Sade
Hit Movies: Clue, The Goonies, Back to the Future, Out of Africa, The Color Purple
Hit TV: Murder She Wrote, Cheers, Family Ties, Dynasty, Dallas
News: Crash of Air India Flight 182, Desmond Tutu wins Nobel Peace Prize, Mikhail Gorbachev elected President of Soviet Union, Brian Mulroney elected Prime Minister of Canada, Assassination of Indira Gandhi

## PEOPLE

Jayne Torvill and Christopher Dean were not the only high-profile skaters to move on after the Olympic season. Rosalynn Sumners turned professional to tour with *Walt Disney's World on Ice*, while Norbert Schramm and Rudi Cerne joined *Holiday on Ice*. Scott Hamilton, Barbara Underhill and Paul Martini, Carol Fox and Richard Dalley, Kitty and Peter Carruthers and Kay Thomson performed with the *Ice Capades*. Lea Ann Miller turned professional to tour with Torvill and Dean. Elena Vodorezova got married, graduated from the Moscow Institute of Physical Education and Sports and took up coaching in Moscow. Stephen Williams took up coaching at Solihull Ice Rink. He and his partner Wendy Sessions also skated professionally in shows in England. Gary Beacom, Kelly Johnson and John Thomas all competed at Skate Canada but turned professional to tour with Torvill and Dean mid-season. Other skaters who retired or turned professional after the Olympic season included Sabine Baeß and Tassilo Thierbach, Vikki de Vries, Manuela Ruben, Sanda Dubravčić, Babette Preußler, Catarina Lindgren and Tom Dickson.

Vivi-Anne Hultén, an Olympic Bronze Medallist behind Sonja Henie in 1936, called out skaters, coaches and judges in a damning article in *Skating*. Hultén called the standards of the world's top skaters in compulsory figures "a disgrace to the sport", making it clear that standards would only improve if judges went by the rulebook to the letter and were far harsher. In turn, coaches would be forced to teach better posture and technique. Hultén aptly noted that the low marks received in the figures in international competitions would fail them on tests.

Olympic Gold Medallists Elena Valova and Oleg Vasiliev were married in Leningrad, where they were both students at the Institute of Physical Culture. Valova and Vasiliev had been skating for approximately fifteen years and they were talented singles skaters before being paired by Tamara Moskvina. Olympic Silver Medallists Marina Klimova and Sergei Ponomarenko also tied the knot. Klimova was only 18 years old when she married Ponomarenko.

Though the first ice dance event held at an ISU Championship officially recognized as a World Championship didn't occur until 1952, international ice dance competitions were held at the Worlds in both 1950 and 1951. Michael McGean, one of the winners of the 1950 competition, was honoured at a special Ivy League dinner in Boston for former Dartmouth athletes, *Wearers of the Green*. I

In his speech, the College's President remarked, "There are many 'Wearers of the Green' here tonight (or with us in spirit) who have performed feats of magic in their sports. But probably only you - with the indispensable help of your wife, Lois - actually helped give birth to your sport as a World and Olympic event."

In November, the figure skating community lost a legend when Charlotte Oelschlägel passed away in Berlin at the age of 86. Known to audiences simply by the mononym Charlotte, the skating queen got her start in the Eisballets at the Admiralspalast, taking Broadway by storm during The Great War and starring in a silent skating film called *The Frozen Warning* before touring Mexico and Cuba in the roaring 20s. Charlotte was one of the first women to include an Axel in her program and she created a back spiral variation named after her. Charlotte was posthumously inducted into the World Figure Skating Hall of Fame in the spring, along with another skating legend - coach Arnold Gerschwiler.

Jayne Torvill and Christopher Dean flew in from Australia to appear as surprise special guests at the Royal Variety Performance in November at London's Victoria Palace Theatre. A sneak peek of their new "Song of India" routine, filmed down under, was shown on a huge screen on stage. When the screen was raised to reveal them in the flesh, they received a thunderous round of applause. The Queen Mother, Prince Charles and Princess Diana were in attendance. Afterward, Torvill and Dean met the royals for the first time. Princess Diana told them, "At last we have got to meet you. I have been looking forward to it."

The influence of Jayne Torvill and Christopher Dean was immediately felt in the ice dance world, with over half of the world's top ice dance teams presenting one-concept free dances during the 1984-1985 season. However, West German ice dancers Petra Born and Rainer Schönborn drew criticism for their free dance to music from the film *Slow Dancing in the Big City*. Many felt the theme of the program's theme, which ended in Born's character committing suicide, 'borrowed' too liberally from Torvill and Dean's Bolero. Born and Schönborn were coached by Martin Skotnický in Oberstdorf, the same mountain town where Torvill and Dean trained for much of their amateur career.

At the castle of Thibeuf in the Bournezeau commune in Vendée, France, Jeanne Chevalier passed away in December at the age of 93. Chevalier was one of Canada's biggest skating stars in the early twentieth century, winning multiple national titles in singles, pairs and fours skating. Chevalier also won the first U.S. pairs title in 1914, with partner Norman Mackie Scott.

Georg Häsler died in January at the age of 78. Häsler was an officer of the ISU for 29 years, serving as Secretary from 1947 to 1975 when the ISU bestowed him the title of Honourary Secretary. Häsler was also an Honourary Life Member of the National Skating Association, Union Suisse de Patinage and Oslo Skøiteklub. January also marked the death of Howard Craker, the owner of Van Nuys Ice Rink in California and the official cinematographer of the USFSA. Craker was responsible for capturing some of the earliest video footage of the U.S. Championships, preserving for posterity the history of many great figure skating champions.

Olympic and World Medallist Dr. Georges Gautschi passed away in February at the age of 80. The first skater from Switzerland to win an Olympic medal, Gautschi helped make Zürich's first artificial outdoor ice rink a reality in the 30s.

Natalia Linichuk and Gennadi Karponosov became parents in February. Their daughter Anastasiya was born in Moscow, where the Olympic Gold Medallists were working as coaches.

Several important figures in the skating world passed away in the spring. Marcus Nikkanen, the first man from Finland to win a medal at the World Championships, passed away in March. Nikkanen taught skating for many years in Canada and the United States and founded the Suomen Taitoluisteluvalmentajat (Finnish Figure Skating Coaches Association) not long before his death. In April, pioneering professional skater Norman A. Falkner, who toured North America giving ice shows after losing his leg during The Great War, passed away in British Columbia. Svea Norén passed away in May at the age of 89. Norén was one of Sweden's first Olympic and World Medallists in the early twentieth century. In June, the first skater from British Columbia to win the senior men's title at the Canadian Championships passed away. Only 58 years old at the time he suffered a fatal heart attack, Roger Wickson helped put the West Coast on the map.

JoJo Starbuck and Ken Shelley celebrated their 25th year as pair partners with a special anniversary program called *You Are My Best Friend*, an original piece arranged by Starbuck's partner Jordan Bennett. Starbuck and Shelley were first paired up for an ice show at a studio ice rink in Downey, California.

In April, Barbara Underhill and Paul Martini were inducted into the Canadian Amateur Sports Hall of Fame at the annual meeting of the Canadian Olympic Association in Montreal. They were the first figure skaters in nine years to be so honoured.

In June, Toronto teacher and librarian Kenneth Zeller was beaten to death by five youths in Toronto's High Park. The tragedy forced the Toronto District School Board to implement a program to end discrimination based on sexual orientation. In his youth, Kenneth was an enthusiastic member of the Stouffville Figure Skating Club.

## BOOKS AND MAGAZINES

In May came Stein and Day's long-anticipated release of *Queen of Ice, Queen of Shadows: The Unsuspected Life of Sonja Henie*, penned by Raymond Strait and Henie's brother Leif. Though panned by Boston book reviewer Fanny Howe, the book sparked a mini-Henie revival in Massachusetts when the Coolidge Corner Theatre in Brookline dusted off old copies of *Sun Valley Serenade* and *Second Fiddle*.

# AROUND THE WORLD

**Canada.** The province of Newfoundland and Labrador played host to the CFSA's Annual General Meeting for the first time in June at the Hotel St. John's. Bruce Miller was elected as the new President, though David Dore continued to sit on the Association's executive for the rest of the decade.

**East Germany.** Under Socialist rule, the people of the German Democratic Republic lived in a 'Big Brother' state, sheltered from Western civilization and routinely monitored and manipulated by their government like hamsters in a cage. The country's top skaters were hailed by their government as examples of the essence of 'socialist personalities', their success stories manipulated by politicians and the state-controlled media to drum up support for and/or justify 'the system'. In reality, the price many East German skaters paid for success was significant and their fates, in many ways, were very much out of their control. Skaters were recruited by the DEV through advertisements in state-sponsored newspapers, offering ten weeks of free instruction to any child interested in skating. These young recruits had to practice for four weeks off the ice before they were allowed on. Coaches acted as talent identification scouts, selecting which youngsters showed enough talent to be allowed to continue in the program. Skaters were required to pass tests four times a year. If they didn't, they were redirected to another sport or kicked out of the program. Young skaters were also required to pass rigorous mandatory physical fitness tests. If they couldn't run 1000 meters in five minutes, for instance, they were also out. Those that remained in East Germany's figure skating program enjoyed low coach-to-student ratios, recognition through sport badge programs, competitions for youth called Spartakiads and a regimented training program consisting of on-ice practice, off-ice conditioning (including running a track for 45 minutes) and modified education programs with little time for leisure. Recreational skating and ice dancing weren't even in the Deutscher Eislauf-Verband's vocabulary. Young skaters were either funneled into competitive singles or pairs skating... and it all came at a terrible cost. Staatsplanthema 14.25 was a state-organized forced doping program that affected over 12 000 elite East German athletes. The program 'officially' started in 1974, but there were certainly documented instances of forced doping in the German Democratic Republic recorded as early as the mid-to-late late 60s. Katrin Kanitz, who won the bronze medal in the pairs event at the 1987 European Championships claimed to have been prescribed Oral-Turinabol, an androgenic anabolic steroid, by a sports doctor while she was competing. She was given the "vitamins" for seven or eight years but trusted her coach was doing the right thing at the time. Today, she is unable to have children. In her excellent dissertation *The East German Sports System: Image And Reality*, Barbara Carol Cole argued, "We do not now know, nor probably ever will know, the extent of the drug usage of the GDR's competitors, because, there too, no records exist. [Dr. Werner] Franke adheres, in the meantime, to the conviction that 'universal' doping was applied in all realms by 1980. This does not mean, however, that there were not numerous cases and disciplines or even institutes where doping played no factor at all, or that only selective usage at certain levels was the rule." Although many of the documents related to Staatsplanthema 14.25 were destroyed at the time of German unification, at least 50 examples of athletes being doped were found in a 1994 inquiry. We will likely never know the true extent to which doping affected East German skaters.

East German skaters were also subject to video surveillance at the rinks they trained and manipulated by the coaches, officials, athletes, doctors and scientists they trusted most. A collection of files in the STASI Records Agency noted the existence of 'training plans' for Jan Hoffmann, Anett Pötzsch, Sabine Baeß and Tassilo Thierbach and many other top East German skaters of the 80s. STASI infiltration of the East German figure skating world ran deep. Pairs coach Monica Scheibe once went by the alias "Anna-Ros". After turning to coaching, Gaby Seyfert was "Pearl". Jutta Müller allegedly was alleged to have worked with a network of several spies "to inform immediately on special occasions". Some claimed Katarina Witt was a beneficiary of the system; others a victim. Her file was extensive, consisting of dozens upon dozens of file folders. The 'monitoring' began when she was 8 years old and continued until the fall of The Wall. In 2002, *Der Spiegel* reported at length on the contents of her STASI files, revealing dozens of members of the skating community who spied on her during her life. There was a whole file on two minutes she spent alone in a room with West German skater Norbert Schramm in Dortmund at the 1983 European Championships, and an anecdote about how she was sent to bed without dinner in 1983 during a tour in Oslo because of a poor performance. "Klaus Peter", "Sagittarius", "Gerhard", "Torsten", "Paul Schmidt", "Benno" and "Maria" all weaved their way into her life, acting as informers, reading her correspondence, watching her abroad and assessing and manipulating her relationship with Jutta Müller, love life and friendships. At the 1985 World Championships in Tokyo, East German officials reportedly shared a threatening letter from a Japanese murderer and cannibal with Witt and told her she needed to shape up for the next East German Championships. Numerous gifts and concessions to Witt were made in hopes of scaring her away from defection and limiting her contact with 'the West'. When Anett Pötzsch married Katarina Witt's brother Axel, the Pötzsch and Witt families wanted to invite relatives from West Germany to the wedding. The District Director of the DTSB threatened both families, telling them it was "highly undesirable" for athletes to have contact with citizens of "non-socialist economic territories." What East German skaters went through at the hands of their government was nothing short of horrifying. In addition to doping, routine spying and manipulation, they were exposed to grueling training regimens and immense pressure to succeed, often at great cost if they didn't produce the desired results on the international system. The successes of East German skaters in the 80s were all the more remarkable considering the immense stress they were under.

**United States.** The USFSA had almost 450 member clubs and over 36 000 registered skaters. The first U.S. Collegiate Championships were slated for August in Lake Placid and the Los Angeles Figure Skating Club's annual Showcase for Skaters celebrated its decade anniversary. The success of this event led to similar artistic competitions being held in Sacramento, Texas, Arizona, Nevada, Missouri and other states.

## BEHIND THE SCENES

For the first time, the Quickstep was selected as the rhythm for the OSP in ice dance. In an official communication, the ISU clarified, "The Ice Dance Committee is aware that toe steps are an integral part of the dance and therefore to express the character and rhythm of the dance... toe steps will be accepted."

## FILMS AND TELEVISION

A performance by Tai Babilonia and Randy Gardner, filmed at the Ice Rink at Rockefeller Center, was featured in the NBC Christmas special *A Christmas Dream*, alongside Mr. T and *Webster* star Emmanuel Lewis.

The ISU released a new instructional film which was produced at the 1984 European Championships in Budapest. The film featured videos of eighteen international compulsory dances with detailed explanations and slow-motion segments. It was available through mail-order in English and German in VHS, BETA and Video 2000 formats. The same year, the ISU also released a new three-record set of compulsory dance music by Hugo Strasser.

## ART AND HISTORY

The World Figure Skating Museum and Hall of Fame in Colorado Springs suffered extensive water damage when the seal on a water pump broke. Miraculously, not a single artifact, print or costume was damaged. Figure skating history aficionados thanked the Skate Gods that these treasured were spared.

## HOMOPHOBIA

The media's hyperfocus on trying to butch up skating was already in full swing. Phil Hersh published an article in the Chicago Sun-Times, which quoted American skater Mark Cockerell: "The No. 1 I want to stress is masculinity on the ice. My long program is blood and guts and speed... It's been known as a feminine sport for years, but some of us are out to really change that... It's more exciting to see a man give all he's got and barrel down the ice rather than see someone on his toes flaunting around."

*American Skating World* applauded a Letter to the Editor which they felt "summed up what many thought." William Simms of Chicago wrote: "Mark Cockerell [wishes] to appease homophobic jocks and spectators by changing the very nature of figure skating competitions. It is a sad commentary on our maturity... Even pro football players don't barrel down the field. They recognized long ago that grace, speed and intelligence superseded sheer brawn as the keystones of competitive athletics. To change style and uniform to assuage their imagined fears is the least macho action they could take."

# THE AIDS EPIDEMIC

Blood banks began screening blood supplies and the World Health Organization held its first International AIDS Conference in Atlanta, Georgia. The stories of those living with AIDS are brought to life on New York City stages in the plays *As Is* and *The Normal Heart*.

Frank Tyler, a figure skating coach who toured with the *Ice Follies*, co-founded the Alaskan AIDS Assistance Association, which provided financial and emotional support to people living with HIV and AIDS. Born in Iowa, Tyler took up figure skating at the Broadmoor Skating Club while attending Colorado State University in the 60s. He passed his USFSA Silver Test in figures and remained active in the sport as a coach, passing away of AIDS-related complications in Anchorage on April 28, 1992, at the age of 47.

Douglas J. Norwick passed away on November 7, 1984 in Mount Vernon, New York at the age of 42. Born in White Plains, New York, Norwick got his start in figure skating at the Metropolitan Figure Skating Club. In 1961, he won the bronze medal in the junior men's event at the Eastern Championships and competed in the novice men's event at the U.S. Championships. The following year, he competed in the senior men's event against Tommy Litz and Scott Ethan Allen. Norwick went on to study drama at Michigan State University and make his mark in the entertainment industry as an actor, dancer and choreographer. He appeared on Broadway in the Tony Award-winning play *Rosencrantz and Guildenstern are Dead*. As a choreographer, he toured with the Paper Bag Players and developed works for countless stage productions. In 1978, he adapted a work he did for Paper Bag Players to the ice for John Curry's *Ice Dancing*.

Charles Dale Copenhaver received the distressing news that he was HIV positive. Born in Ulm, West Germany, Dale (born Erwin Zimmerman) got his start skating at the Broadmoor Skating Club in Colorado Springs. With partner Dana Jo Boles, he won the novice pairs title at the Midwestern Championships in Denver in 1976. Three years later, he won the same title with his second partner Kelly Herman. Herman and Copenhaver were also the 1979 Upper Great Lakes Champions. After retiring from competitive skating, he attended the University of Colorado. He worked as a night manager and coached figure skating at the Sertich Ice Center for five years.

Copenhaver's partner Mark recalled, "He was born in Germany. His parents put him and his twin sister Donna up for adoption and they were adopted by the Copenhaver family. They started in Kansas and they moved to Colorado Springs. I met him in 1984. I worked at a local hospital and his partner was admitted with AIDS. That's how I met Dale. We were all gowned up and PPE'd. His partner died shortly thereafter and he and I got together. I knew he was likely HIV positive at the time we met, but that was not a player in how our relationship evolved... I was negative and he was positive. I remember coming out of the treatment center and it was a pretty stunning situation. He was very healthy for a long time but he dealt with fevers and other issues... We were lucky enough to go to Alaska and camp with a couple of friends of ours. He worked at Hewlett-Packard full-time for quite a while assembling chip boards. He would occasionally go down to the arena and skate, but that was something he did on his own. He was a big fan of Toller Cranston and he had some of his prints, which I have hanging today... In 1988-89, he started getting sicker. We had four or five good years and then things went south. It was a very miserable, devastating end of life for him. I wish he would have got back to Germany. He was connecting with his family there when we were together." Copenhaver passed away at the age of 34 on April 1, 1991.

## Personalities

BRIAN ORSER

Date of Birth: December 18, 1961
Place of Birth: Belleville, ON
Coach: Doug Leigh
Choreographer: Suzanne Russell Philip, Uschi Keszler Boornazian
Home Club: Midland FSC

JOZEF SABOVČÍK

Date of Birth: December 4, 1963
Place of Birth: Bratislava, Czechoslovakia
Coach: Agnesa Búřilová
Choreographer: Frantisek Blaťák

VLADIMIR KOTIN

Date of Birth: March 28, 1962
Place of Birth: Moscow, Soviet Union
Coach: Elena Tchaikovskaya
Choreographer: Elena Tchaikovskaya, Valentina Vigant, Y. Potemkin
Home Club: Dynamo

ALEXANDR FADEEV

Date of Birth: January 4, 1964
Place of Birth: Kazan, Soviet Union
Coach: Stanislav Zhuk, Sergei Volkov, Stanislav Leonovich, Gennady Tarasov
Choreographer: R. Semyonova, Marina Zoueva
Home Club: Spartak/CSKA Moscow

BRIAN BOITANO

Date of Birth: October 22, 1963
Place of Birth: Mountain View, CA
Coach: Linda Leaver
Choreographer: Sandra Bezic, Ricky Harris
Home Club: Peninsula FSC

NEIL PATERSON

Date of Birth: April 21, 1964
Place of Birth: Ottawa, ON
Coach: Wendy Sawchuk, Gary Paterson
Home Club: North Shore WC

HEIKO FISCHER

Date of Birth: February 25, 1960
Place of Birth: Stuttgart, West Germany
Coach: Karel Fajfr

KATARINA WITT

Date of Birth: December 3, 1965
Place of Birth: Falkensee, East Germany
Coach: Jutta Müller
Choreographer: Rudi Suchy
Home Club: SC Karl-Marx-Stadt

TIFFANY CHIN

Date of Birth: October 3, 1967
Place of Birth: Oakland, CA
Coach: John Nicks, Don Laws, Frank Carroll
Choreographer:
Home Club: San Diego FSC

DEBI THOMAS

Date of Birth: March 25, 1967
Place of Birth: Poughkeepsie, NY
Coach: Alex McGowan
Choreographer: Debi Thomas, Robin Cousins, Mikhail Baryshnikov, George de la Peña
Home Club: Crystal Springs ISC/Los Angeles FSC

KIRA IVANOVA

Date of Birth: January 10, 1963
Place of Birth: Moscow, Soviet Union
Coach: Viktor Kudriavtsev, Vladimir Kovalev, Eduard Pliner
Choreographer: Alla Kapranova
Home Club: Spartak/Dynamo

CLAUDIA LEISTNER

Date of Birth: April 15, 1965
Place of Birth: Ludwigshafen, West Germany
Coach: Günter Zöller, Ondrej Nepela, Martin Skotnický
Choreographer: Uschi Keszler Boornazian
Home Club: Mannheimer ERC

CARYN KADAVY

Date of Birth: December 7, 1967
Place of Birth: Erie, PA
Coach: Carlo and Christa Fassi
Choreographer: Christa Fassi, Toller Cranston
Home Club: Broadmoor SC

ANNA KONDRASHOVA

Date of Birth: June 30, 1965
Place of Birth: Moscow, Soviet Union
Coach: Eduard Pliner, Stanislav Zhuk, Stanislav Leonovich
Choreographer: Elena Matveeva, Nina Domanovskaya
Home Club: CSKA Moscow

ELIZABETH MANLEY

Date of Birth: August 7, 1965
Place of Birth: Belleville, ON
Coach: Bob McAvoy, Emmerich Danzer, Sonya Dunfield, Peter Dunfield
Choreographer: Anne Schelter, Sonya Dunfield
Home Club: Minto SC/Gloucester SC

# Fall Internationals

**1984 COUPES DES ALPES (Saint Gervais, France and Oberstdorf, West Germany, August 22-26, 1984 and August 29-September 1, 1984)**

Grand Prix de St. Gervais Winners:

Craig Henderson (USA) - men
Debi Thomas (USA) - women
Elena Bechke and Valeri Kornienko (SOV) - pairs
Irina Zhuk and Oleg Petrov (SOV) - ice dance

Nebelhorn Trophy (Oberstdorf) Winners:

Richard Zander (FRG) - men
Debi Thomas (USA) - women
Elena Bechke and Valeri Kornienko (SOV) - pairs
Lois Luciani and Russ Witherby (USA) - ice dance

**1984 ASKÖ CUP OF VIENNA (Vienna, Austria, September 24-28, 1984)**

Women:

1. Nathalie Sasseville (CAN)
2. Marina Tweretinova (SOV)
3. Ingrid Karl (FRG)

**1984 ST. IVEL ICE INTERNATIONAL (London, England, September 25-27, 1984)**

Men:

1. Brian Boitano (USA)
2. Victor Petrenko (SOV)
3. Grzegorz Filipowski (POL)

Women:

1. Kathryn Adams (USA)
2. Cynthia Coull (CAN)
3. Claudia Villiger (SUI)

Pairs:

1. Inna Bekker and Sergei Likhansky (SOV)
2. Katy Keeley and Joseph Mero (USA)
3. Laurene Collin and David Howe (CAN)

Ice Dance:

1. Tracy Wilson and Rob McCall (CAN)
2. Natalia Annenko and Genrikh Sretenski (SOV)
3. Susie Wynne and Joseph Druar (USA)

**1984 SKATE CANADA (Victoria, BC, October 25-27, 1984)**

Men:

1. Brian Orser (CAN)
2. Grzegorz Filipowski (POL)
3. Masaru Ogawa (JPN)

Women:

1. Midori Ito (JPN)
2. Tiffany Chin (USA)
3. Natalia Lebedeva (SOV)

Pairs:

1. Elena Bechke and Valery Kornienko (SOV)
2. Cynthia Coull and Mark Rowsom (CAN)
3. Katherina Matousek and Lloyd Eisler (CAN)

Ice Dance:

1. Olga Volozhinskaya and Alexandr Svinin (SOV)
2. Petra Born and Rainer Schönborn (FRG)
3. Kelly Johnson and John Thomas (CAN)

**1984 PRAGUE SKATE (Prague, Czechoslovakia, November 8-11, 1984)**

Men:

1. Petr Barna (CZE)
2. Richard Zander (FRG)
3. Gurgen Vardanjan (SOV)

Women:

1. Cornelia Renner (FRG)
2. Leslie Sikes (USA)
3. Simone Koch (GDR)

Pairs:

1. Yulia Bystrova and Alexander Tarasov (SOV)
2. Dagmar Kovářová and Jozef Komár (CZE)
3. Maria Lako and Michael Blicharski (USA)

Ice Dance:

1. Noriko Sato and Tadayuki Takahashi (JPN)
2. Kathrin and Christoff Beck (AUT)
3. Margaret Bodo and Rick Berg (USA)

**1984 AEGON CUP (The Hague, Netherlands, November 13-18, 1984)**

Men:

1. Petr Barna (CZE)
2. Viktor Petrenko (SOV)
3. Christopher Bowman (USA)

Women:

1. Constanze Gensel (GDR)
2. Yukari Yoshimori (JPN)
3. Yvonne Gómez (USA)

Pairs:

1. Larisa Selezneva and Oleg Makarov (SOV)
2. Melinda Kunhegyi and Lyndon Johnston (CAN)
3. Natalie and Wayne Seybold (USA)

Ice Dance:

1. Marina Klimova and Sergei Ponomarenko (SOV)
2. Maya Usova and Alexander Zhulin (SOV)
3. Kathrin and Christoff Beck (AUT)

**1984 POKAL DER BLAUEN SCHWERTER (East Berlin, East Germany, November 15-17, 1984)**

Men:

1. Vladimir Petrenko (SOV)
2. Rudy Luccioni (FRA)
3. Daniel Weiss (FRG)

Women:

1. Inga Gauter (GDR)
2. Natalia Skrabnevskaya (SOV)
3. Evelyn Großmann (GDR)

Pairs:

1. Irina Mironenko and Dmitri Shkidchenko (SOV)
2. Antje Schramm and Jens Müller (GDR)
3. Katrin Kanitz and Alexander König (GDR)

**1984 GOLDEN SPIN OF ZAGREB (Zagreb, Yugoslavia, November 22-24, 1984)**

Men:

1. Scott Williams (USA)
2. Grzegorz Filipowski (POL)
3. Fernand Fédronic (FRA)

Women:

1. Agnès Gosselin (FRA)
2. Kelly Webster (USA)
3. Claudia Villiger (SUI)

Ice Dance:

1. Petra Born and Rainer Schönborn (FRG)
2. Isabella Micheli and Roberto Pelizzola (ITA)
3. Kandi Amelon and Alec Binnie (USA)

**1984 GRAND PRIZE SNP (Banská Bystrica, Czechoslovakia, November 22-25, 1984)**

Men:

1. Rudy Galindo (USA)
2. Axel Médéric (FRA)
3. Jaroslav Suchý (CZE)

Women:

1. Inga Gauter (GDR)
2. Elena Taranenko (SOV)
3. Iveta Voralová (CZE)

Pairs:

1. Antje Schramm and Jens Müller (GDR)
2. Elena Gud and Evgeni Koltoun (SOV)
3. Ginger and Archie Tse (USA)

Ice Dance:

1. Jodie Balogh and Jerod Swallow (USA)
2. Irina Stavrovskaya and Andrei Antonov (SOV)
3. Isabelle Marcellin and Pascal Lavanchy (FRA)

# Fall Internationals and Other Competitions

**1984 NHK TROPHY (Tokyo, Japan, November 23-25, 1984)**

Men:

1. Alexandr Fadeev (SOV)
2. Brian Orser (CAN)
3. Brian Boitano (USA)

Women:

1. Midori Ito (JPN)
2. Debi Thomas (USA)
3. Juri Ozawa (JPN)

Pairs:

1. Veronika Pershina and Marat Akbarov (SOV)
2. Birgit Lorenz and Knut Schubert (GDR)
3. Cynthia Coull and Mark Rowsom (CAN)

Ice Dance:

1. Karen Barber and Nicky Slater (GRB)
2. Elena Batanova and Alexei Soloviev (SOV)
3. Kelly Johnson and John Thomas (CAN)

**1984 INTERNATIONAL SUGAR CRITERIUM - JACQUES FAVART TROPHY (Tours, France, November 29-December 2, 1984)**

Men:

1. Philippe Roncoli (FRA)
2. David Fedor (USA)
3. Jaimee Eggleton (CAN)

Women:

1. Constanze Gensel (GDR)
2. Laura Steele (USA)
3. Tonya Harding (USA)

Pairs:

1. Melinda Kunhegyi and Lyndon Johnston (CAN)
2. Manuela Landgraf and Ingo Steuer (GDR)
3. Jeanine and Tony Jones (USA)

**1984 PRIZE OF MOSCOW NEWS (Moscow, Soviet Union, December 5-9, 1984)**

Men:

1. Alexandr Fadeev (SOV)
2. Vladimir Kotin (SOV)
3. Viktor Petrenko (SOV)

Women:

1. Kira Ivanova (SOV)
2. Natalia Lebedeva (SOV)
3. Anna Kondrashova (SOV)

Pairs:

1. Larisa Selezneva and Oleg Makarov (SOV)
2. Veronika Pershina and Marat Akbarov (SOV)
3. Elena Bechke and Valeri Kornienko (SOV)

Ice Dance:

1. Marina Klimova and Sergei Ponomarenko (SOV)
2. Natalia Bestemianova and Andrei Bukin (SOV)
3. Olga Volozhinskaya and Alexandr Svinin (SOV)

**1985 BÄSLER CUP (Basel, Switzerland, January 26-27, 1985)**

Ice Dance:

1. Maya Usova and Alexandr Zhulin (SOV)
2. Irina Zhuk and Oleg Petrov (SOV)
3. Stefania Calegari and Pasquale Camerlengo (ITA)

**1985 NORDISKA MÄSTERSKAPEN (Copenhagen, Denmark, February 14-17, 1985)**

Men:

1. Lars Åkesson (SWE)
2. Lars Dresler (DEN)
3. Henrik Walentin (DEN)

Women:

1. Lotta Falkenbäck (SWE)
2. Maria Bergquist (SWE)
3. Karin Starzman (SWE)

**1985 UNIVERSITY WINTER GAMES (Belluno, Italy, February 16-24, 1985)**

Men:

1. Shubin Zhang (CHN)
2. Robert Rosenbluth (USA)
3. David Jamison (USA)

Women:

1. Juri Ozawa (JPN)
2. Debbie Walls (USA)
3. Deborah Tucker (USA)

Pairs:

1. Sandy Hurtubise and Craig Maurizi (USA)
2. Julia Bystrova and Alexander Tarasov (SOV)
3. Svetlana Frantsuzova and Oleg Gorshkov (SOV)

Ice Dance:

1. Maya Usova and Alexandr Zhulin (SOV)
2. Jindra Holá and Karol Foltán (CZE)
3. Kathrin and Christoff Beck (AUT)

Pairs:

1. Gillian Wachsman and Todd Waggoner (USA)
2. Christine Hough and Doug Ladret (CAN)
3. Isabelle Brasseur and Pascal Courchesne (CAN)

Ice Dance:

1. Isabelle and Paul Duchesnay (CAN)
2. Lois Luciani and Russ Witherby (USA)
3. Michelle McDonald and Patrick Mandley (CAN)

**1985 MERANO SPRING TROPHY (Merano, Italy, March 29-30, 1985)**

Women:

1. Tracey Damigella (USA)
2. Linda Florkevich (CAN)
3. Tracey Seliga (USA)

**1985 MORZINE AVORIAZ (Morzine, France, April 4-5, 1985)**

Ice Dance:

1. Suzanne Semanick and Scott Gregory (USA)
2. Irina Zhuk and Oleg Petrov (SOV)
3. Isabella Micheli and Roberto Pelizzola (ITA)

**1985 WILKIE ICE DANCE INTERNATIONAL (Nottingham, England, May 7-9, 1985)**

Ice Dance:

1. Kathrin and Christoff Beck (AUT)
2. Susie Wynne and Joseph Druar (USA)
3. Dorianne Bontemps and Charles-Henri Paliard (FRA)

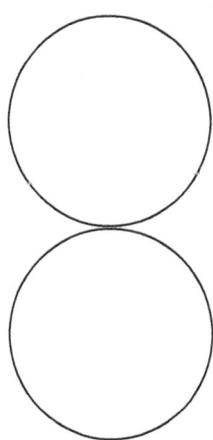

# National Championships

## SENIOR NATIONAL CHAMPIONS BY COUNTRY

### Men

AUS - Cameron Medhurst
AUT - Ralph Burghart
BUL - Boyko Aleksiev
CZE - Petr Barna
DEN - Lars Dresler
FIN - Oula Jääskeläinen
FRA - Fernand Fédronic
FRG - Heiko Fischer
GDR - Falko Kirsten
GRB - Stephen Pickavance
HOL - Edward van Campen
HUN - Imre Raábe
ITA - Alessandro Riccitelli
JPN - Masaru Ogawa
NZL - Christopher Blong
POL - Grzegorz Filipowski
SAF - Daniel 'Buddy' Voges
SOV - Vladimir Kotin
SPN - Fernando Soria
SUI - Oliver Höner
SWE - Lars Åkesson

### Women

AUS - Diana Zovko-Nicolic
AUT - Sabine Paal
BUL - Petya Gavazova
CZE - Gabriela Ballová
DEN - Connie Sjøholm Jørgensen
FIN - Elise Ahonen
FRA - Agnès Gosselin
FRG - Claudia Leistner
GDR - Katarina Witt
GRB - Susan Jackson
HOL - Tjin Li Wang
HUN - Tamara Téglássy
ITA - Paola Tosi
JPN - Midori Ito
NOR - Vibecke Sørensen
NZL - Jane Clifford
POL - Mirella Gawłowska
SOV - Anna Kondrashova
SPN - Marta Olozagarre
SUI - Claudia Villiger
SWE - Lotta Falkenbäck

### Pairs

AUS - Danielle and Stephen Carr
CZE - Lenka Knapová and René Novotný
FIN - Maija and Pekka Pekkala
FRA - Sylvie Vaquero and Didier Manaud
FRG - Claudia Massari and Daniele Caprano
GDR - Birgit Lorenz and Knut Schubert
GRB - Lisa and Neil Cushley
POL - Iwona Oliwa and Piotr Szczerbowski
SOV - Larisa Selezneva and Oleg Makarov

### Ice Dance

AUS - Monica MacDonald and Rodney Clarke
AUT - Kathrin and Christoff Beck
BUL - Hristina Boyanova and Yavor Ivanov
CZE - Jindra Holá and Karol Foltán
FIN - Virpi Kunnas and Petri Kokko
FRA - Sophie Mérigot and Philippe Berthe
FRG - Petra Born and Rainer Schönborn
GRB - Karen Barber and Nicky Slater
HUN - Klára Engi and Attila Tóth
ITA - Isabella Micheli and Roberto Pelizzola
JPN - Noriko Sato and Tadayuki Takahashi
POL - Honorata Górna and Andrzej Dostatni
SOV - Marina Klimova and Sergei Ponomarenko
SUI - Gaby Schuppli and Markus Merz
SWE - Johanna Elfving and Pontus Krantz

### 1985 CANADIAN PRECISION TEAM CHAMPIONSHIPS (Thunder Bay, ON, April 5-7, 1985)

Team:

1. The Supremes
2. Edmonton Senior Precision
3. Les Pirouettes

Other Winners:

Whitby Ice Crystals (junior)
Whitby Ice Angels (novice)

### 1985 U.S. PRECISION TEAM CHAMPIONSHIPS (Lakewood, OH, April 20, 1985)

Team:

1. Fraserettes
2. Ice Crystalettes
3. Minneapplettes

Other Winners:

Hot Fudge Sundaes (junior)
Hot Fudge Sundaes (novice)
Acton-Ups (adult)

## THE DEFINITION OF AN AMATEUR

From the *CFSA Rulebook* (1984)

a) An amateur in skating is a person is a person who participates in the sport as an avocation, for pleasure and not as a means of livelihood, and who is not disqualified as an amateur by any regulation of the I.S.U. or any of the following provisions:

b) A person is not an amateur if he has:

(I) practiced, taught, or signed a contract to practice or teach skating for gain (excepting teachers in schools who teach skating as a subsidiary part of their duties without receiving specific additional renumeration)
(II) participated, in any capacity, in a skating competition or exhibition not sanctioned by the C.F.S.A. or other member of the I.S.U.
(III) skated or appeared with a professional in a skating exhibition except as permitted under Rule 1708, or for those special purposes as may be authorized by the Association
(IV) displayed advertising for any commercial product, service or enterprise during any C.F.S.A. or I.S.U. sanctioned competition without the express approval of the Association. Precision skating teams may wear warm-up outfits bearing the name of a sponsor, but these may not be worn during the actual performance.
IV) accepted expenses in excess of those allowed under Section 2300.

### GIFTS TO AMATEUR SKATERS - 2307

a) The total value of all gifts to one participant in a figure skating exhibition shall not exceed $100.00 or the amount allowable under I.S.U. Rules (200 Swiss Francs), whichever is less. An exhibition for purposes of this rule shall be interpreted as being all of the performances held on one day.
b) The gift may take the form of a gift-certificate or purchase voucher provided that such certificate may not be sold or converted (wholly or in part) for cash.
c) An honourary membership in a skating club, whch does not include any financial benefits other than ordinary membership, shall not be affected by this rule.

*Kevin Parker. Photo courtesy Elaine Hooper / St. Ivel Figure Skating Archive.*

# PERSONALITIES

ELENA VALOVA AND OLEG VASILIEV

Date of Birth: January 4, 1963/November 22, 1959
Place of Birth: Leningrad, Soviet Union
Coach: Tamara Moskvina
Choreographer: Natalia Volkova, Valentina Vigant
Home Club: Trud Leningrad

CYNTHIA COULL AND MARK ROWSOM

Date of Birth: August 14, 1965/April 15, 1959
Place of Birth: Greenfield Park, QC/Waterloo, ON
Coach: Kerry Leitch
Choreographer: Gabby Micelli
Home Club: CPA St-Jean/Preston FSC

EKATERINA GORDEEVA AND SERGEI GRINKOV

Date of Birth: May 28, 1971/February 4, 1967
Place of Birth: Moscow, Soviet Union
Coach: Stanislav Zhuk, Stanislav Leonovich
Choreographer: Nina Domanovskaya, Marina Zoueva
Home Club: CSKA Moscow

LARISA SELEZNEVA AND OLEG MAKAROV

Date of Birth: September 12, 1963/October 22, 1962
Place of Birth: Leningrad, Soviet Union
Coach: Andrei Suraikin, Igor Moskvin, Tamara Moskvina
Choreographer: V. Pechersky
Home Club: Zenit Leningrad

KATHERINA MATOUSEK AND LLOYD EISLER

Date of Birth: April 20, 1964/April 28, 1963
Place of Birth: Prague, Czechoslovakia/
Seaforth, ON
Coach: Kerry Leitch
Choreographer: Gabby Micelli
Home Club: North Shore WC/Preston FSC

*Dennis L. Bird, Arnold Gerschwiler, Cecilia Colledge, Benjamin T. Wright and Courtney Jones. Photo by Fred & Joan Dean, courtesy Fred Dean, "Ice & Roller Skate" magazine archive.*

*Louis Stong, Joan Dean and Tracy Wilson. Photo by Fred & Joan Dean, courtesy Fred Dean, "Ice & Roller Skate" magazine archive.*

*Karen Barber and Nicky Slater. Photo by Fred & Joan Dean, courtesy Fred Dean, "Ice & Roller Skate" magazine archive.*

# SHOWS AND TOURS

In the heat of the summer, a 8000 square-foot ice rink was installed on the stage of the Metropolitan Opera House in New York City. John Curry, Dorothy Hamill and members of Curry's Skating Company performed 24 pieces conceived by such esteemed choreographers as Jean-Pierre Bonnefoux, Lar Lubovitch, Twyla Tharp and Eliot Feld. It was the first time an ice show was ever presented on the stage of The Met. The John Curry Skating Company also gave performances at the Opera House at the Kennedy Center for the Performing Arts in Washington, D.C. during the summer.

The 11th edition of *Superskates* was held at Madison Square Garden in November. Performers included Robin Cousins, Rosalynn Sumners, Barbara Underhill and Paul Martini, Richard Dwyer, Judy Blumberg and Michael Seibert and Tiffany Chin.

After a successful stint in Australia, Jayne Torvill and Christopher Dean took their World Tour on the road to New Zealand, attracting thousands of Kiwis for their performances with the Moscow Ice Circus. The Auckland shows were held at the Wiri Woolstore in Auckland; the Christchurch shows under a canvas tent in Hagley Park. The Brits were so popular in Christchurch that after the local ice rink closed, the location was renamed Torvill and Dean Lane.

The Ice Theatre of New York was founded by Moira North, in collaboration with Marjorie Kouns, Marc Bogaerts and Cecily Morrow. The much-loved performance company got its start with a series of experimental ice shows and only grew in popularity throughout the 80s after offering free lunchtime concerts at The Rink at Rockefeller Plaza.

Tai Babilonia and Randy Gardner and JoJo Starbuck and Ken Shelley gave special exhibitions in March during the Closing Ceremonies of the International Winter Special Olympic Games in Salt Lake City, Utah, inspiring a generation of young figure skaters involved in the Special Olympics program.

## Professional Competitions

**1985 PRO-SKATE TOKYO (Tokyo, Japan, February 2, 1985)**

Men:

1. Robin Cousins (GRB)
2. Toller Cranston (CAN)
3. David Santee (USA)

Women:

1. Denise Biellmann (SUI)
2. Wendy Burge (USA)
3. Simone Grigorescu (ROM)

Pairs:

1. Candy Jones and Don Fraser (CAN)
2. JoJo Starbuck and Ken Shelley (USA)
3. Elina Viola and Keith Green (USA/CAN)

**1985 PRO-SKATE SAPPORO (Sapporo, Japan, February 3, 1985)**

Men:

1. Robin Cousins (GRB)
2. Toller Cranston (CAN)
3. Mitsuru Matsumura (JPN)

Women:

1. Denise Biellmann (SUI)
2. Wendy Burge (USA)
3. Simone Grigorescu (ROM)

Pairs:

1. Candy Jones and Don Fraser (CAN)
2. JoJo Starbuck and Ken Shelley (USA)
3. Elina Viola and Keith Green (USA/CAN)

*Jayne Torvill meeting a koala down under. Photo by Fred & Joan Dean, courtesy Fred Dean, "Ice & Roller Skate" magazine archive.*

# MAJOR COMPETITIONS

**World Junior Championships.** In December, skaters from 21 countries competed at the World Junior Championships, hosted by the Broadmoor Skating Club in Colorado Springs. In the men's event, 13-year-old Vladimir Petrenko of the Soviet Union won both the figures and short program but fell four times in the free skate to drop to second behind American skater Erik Larson, who skated a flawless program featuring four different triple jumps. Rudy Galindo delivered a four-triple performance of his own to move up to third, having placed only ninth in the figures. Canada's Craig Burns, who had been third in figures, dropped to fourth after making errors in both the short program and free skate. Canada's second man, Jeff Partrick finished ninth. A trio of Soviet pairs, led by Ekaterina Gordeeva and Sergei Grinkov, dominated the pairs event from start to finish. Canada's two teams, Penny Schultz and Scott Grover and Isabelle Brasseur and Pascal Courchesne placed fifth and sixth. Speed and assurance were qualities that stood out in the performances of the top two teams in the ice dance event, Elena Krykanova and Evgeni Platov and Svetlana Liapina and Gorsha Sur. However, some felt that the young Soviet teams were all carbon copies of Natalia Bestemianova and Andrei Bukin. The French team of Doriane Bontemps and Charles-Henri Paliard placed third with a dramatic interpretation of *West Side Story*. Canada's two teams, Melanie Cole and Donald Godfrey and Catherine Pal and Kelly Marshall were seventh and ninth. The third Soviet team, Svetlana Serkeli and Andrei Zharkov caused a raucous when Zharkov performed an Arabian cartwheel in the free dance. In the women's competition, America's Jana Sjodin won the compulsory figures, ahead of West Germany's Susanne Becher. Tatiana Andreeva of the Soviet Union won both the short program and free skate to take the gold over Becher and another Soviet skater, Natalia Gorbenko. Andreeva landed three triple jumps in the free skate. Sjodin dropped to fifth after falling on the only triple jump she attempted in the free skate. Canada's two representatives, Rosmarie Sakic and Susan MacKay, finished a respectable eighth and ninth in a large field.

**World Professional Championships.** More than 200 000 dollars in prize money was at stake in Landover, Maryland at the fifth World Professional Championships, sponsored by NutraSweet for the first time. The format from the previous year altered slightly. The skaters were still divided into two teams (the *All-Stars* and *Pro-Stars*) and all skaters performed three times but the final choreographed group number was not judged. Jayne Torvill and Christopher Dean, Scott Hamilton, Rosalynn Sumners, Kitty and Peter Carruthers, Elaine Zayak, Norbert Schramm, and Carol Fox and Richard Dalley all made their debut in professional competition at the event, which was won by the *All-Stars* team. The individual winners were Hamilton, Dorothy Hamill, Barbara Underhill and Paul Martini and Torvill and Dean. Torvill and Dean earned perfect 10.0's across the board for their new program *Encounter*, set to George Winston's "January Stars". Hamill was awarded the *American Skating World* Professional Skater of the Year Award, which *USA Today* called "skating's equivalent to the Oscar." In the CBC broadcast of the event, Toller Cranston remarked that "there was great camaraderie and everybody was rooting for everybody" at this event.

**1985 WORLD JUNIOR CHAMPIONSHIPS (Colorado Springs, CO, December 11-16, 1984)**

Men:

1. Erik Larson (USA)
2. Vladimir Petrenko (SOV)
3. Rudy Galindo (USA)
4. Craig Burns (CAN)
5. Michael Shmerkin (SOV)
6. Daniel Weiss (FRG)
7. Oula Jääskeläinen (FIN)
8. Axel Médéric (FRA)
9. Jeff Partrick (CAN)
10. Hiroshi Sugiyama (JPN)

Women:

1. Tatiana Andreeva (SOV)
2. Susanne Becher (FRG)
3. Natalia Gorbenko (SOV)
4. Tracy Ernst (USA)
5. Jana Sjodin (USA)
6. Izumi Aotani (JPN)
7. Cornelia Renner (FRG)
8. Rosemarie Sakic (CAN)
9. Susan MacKay (CAN)
10. Yukiko Kashihara (JPN)

Pairs:

1. Ekaterina Gordeeva and Sergei Grinkov (SOV)
2. Irina Mironenko and Dmitri Shkidchenko (SOV)
3. Elena Gud and Evgeni Koltoun (SOV)
4. Shelly Propson and Jerod Swallow (USA)
5. Penny Schultz and Scott Grover (CAN)
6. Isabelle Brasseur and Pascal Courchesne (CAN)
7. Lisa and Neil Cushley (GRB)
8. Ginger and Archie Tse (USA)

Ice Dance:

1. Elena Krykanova and Evgeni Platov (SOV)
2. Svetlana Liapina and Gorsha Sur (SOV)
3. Doriane Bontemps and Charles-Henri Paliard (FRA)
4. Jodie Balogh and Jerod Swallow (USA)
5. Svetlana Serkeli and Andrei Zharkov (SOV)
6. Corinne Paliard and Didier Courtois (FRA)
7. Melanie Cole and Donald Godfrey (CAN)
8. Michela Malingambi and Andrea Gilardi (ITA)
9. Catherine Pal and Kelly Marshall (CAN)
10. Éva Száraz and László Partos (HUN)

**1984 WORLD PROFESSIONAL CHAMPIONSHIPS (Landover, MD, December 14, 1984)**

Men:

1. Scott Hamilton (USA)
2. Toller Cranston (CAN)
3. Charles Tickner (USA)
4. Norbert Schramm (FRG)

**European Championships.** It was a case of déjà vu for a handful of the skaters at the Scandinavium in Gothenburg in January, who had competed in the same rink just five years prior but there were few surprise results at the European Championships. Unfortunately, the Swedish city was experiencing its coldest weather in 40 years and ticket sales suffered greatly as a result. In the ice dance event, Natalia Bestemianova and Andrei Bukin easily reclaimed the European title they had last won in 1983 when Jayne Torvill and Christopher Dean were absent due to injury. Bestemianova and Bukin's winning free dance was no *Bolero*, but it was arguably the best interpretation of "Carmen" to date. The judges rewarded them with eight perfect marks in the free dance, including a set of perfect 6.0s for both technical merit and artistic impression from Swiss judge Lily Klapp. Marina Klimova and Sergei Ponomarenko won the silver and Petra Born and Rainer Schönborn's controversial free dance helped them climb up three spots from their sixth-place finish at Europeans in 1984 to win the bronze, ahead of Brits Karen Barber and Nicky Slater. Veteran British sportswriter Howard Bass openly criticized the fact that Bestemianova and Bukin received a slew of 6.0s, stating that by doing so "the once cherished maximum mark has been devalued and no longer implies perfection". He also pointed out that all the top teams had "abused the rules intended to curb moves more suited to pair skating and each should have been penalized accordingly." Olympic Gold Medallists Elena Valova and Oleg Vasiliev successfully defended their pairs title over Larisa Selezneva and Oleg Makarov and Veronika Pershina and Marat Akbarov in the first Soviet sweep of the pairs podium at Europeans since the event was last held in Gothenburg in 1980. Valova and Vasiliev's strong free skate earned five 5.9s for presentation from the judges. Katarina Witt's path to victory in the women's event was apparent when she won the compulsory figures over Kira Ivanova and Anna Kondrashova. However, in the short program, Witt cautiously chose to do a double toe-loop instead of a triple in her combination and was marked down to fourth. Ivanova had one of the best skates of her career to win that phase of the event, with Claudia Leistner, who had missed the 1984 World Championships due to injury, finishing second and Simone Koch third. In the free skate, Witt missed her opening triple toe-loop and singled a planned double Axel, but landed three other triples to move up and take the gold over Ivanova, who only landed two triples. Leistner took the bronze, ahead of Koch and Kondrashova. In the men's compulsory figures, defending European Champion Alexandr Fadeev was notably absent, having sprained a tendon in practice the month prior. France's Fernand Fédronic made history as the first person of colour to win the figures in a senior ISU Championship, topping Jozef Sabovčík and Heiko Fischer. Vladimir Kotin led after the first two figures but botched the third quite badly to drop to fourth. Both Sabovčík and Kotin performed masterfully in the short program, landing triple Lutz combinations. Sabovčík won the short program over Kotin and Viktor Petrenko, who was competing in his first Europeans. In the free skate, Sabovčík and Kotin each landed four triples. Sabovčík touched down on a triple Axel, which Kotin didn't attempt, and finished second in the free skate but first overall, earning Czechoslovakia its first gold medal in the men's event at Europeans in twelve years. Kotin's fourth place in the figures kept him in second overall. A strong free skate, coupled with mistakes from others, allowed Grzegorz Filipowski to move up and win the bronze over Fischer, East Germany's Falko Kirsten, Petrenko and Fédronic. Filipowski's bronze was the first medal won by a Polish man at Europeans in over 75 years and it was a controversial one indeed. As the only skater to land a triple Axel and the only one to do five different triples, many felt he should have won the free skate.

**WORLD PROFESSIONAL CHAMPIONSHIPS (continued)**

Women:

1. Dorothy Hamill (USA)
2. Elaine Zayak (USA)
3. Linda Fratianne (USA)
4. Rosalynn Sumners (USA)

Pairs:

1. Barbara Underhill and Paul Martini (CAN)
2. Ludmila and Oleg Protopopov (SOV)
3. Kitty and Peter Carruthers (USA)
4. Tai Babilonia and Randy Gardner (USA)

Ice Dance:

1. Jayne Torvill and Christopher Dean (GRB)
2. Carol Fox and Richard Dalley (USA)
3. Lorna Wighton and John Dowding (CAN)
4. Kim Krohn and Barry Hagan (USA)

Team:

1. All-Stars: Scott Hamilton, Norbert Schramm, Rosalynn Sumners, Elaine Zayak, Kitty and Peter Carruthers, Barbara Underhill and Paul Martini, Jayne Torvill and Christopher Dean, Carol Fox and Richard Dalley
2. Pro-Stars: Toller Cranston, Charlie Tickner, Dorothy Hamill, Linda Fratianne, Ludmila and Oleg Protopopov, Tai Babilonia and Randy Gardner, Lorna Wighton and John Dowding, Kim Krohn and Barry Hagan

**1985 EUROPEAN CHAMPIONSHIPS**
(Budapest, Hungary, January 9-14, 1985)

Men:

1. Jozef Sabovčík (CZE)
2. Vladimir Kotin (SOV)
3. Grzegorz Filipowski (POL)
4. Heiko Fischer (FRG)
5. Falko Kirsten (GDR)
6. Viktor Petrenko (SOV)
7. Fernand Fédronic (FRA)
8. Richard Zander (FRG)
9. Lars Åkesson (SWE)
10. Petr Barna (CZE)

Women:

1. Katarina Witt (GDR)
2. Kira Ivanova (SOV)
3. Claudia Leistner (FRG)
4. Simone Koch (GDR)
5. Anna Kondrashova (SOV)
6. Natalia Lebedeva (SOV)
7. Claudia Villiger (SUI)
8. Patricia Neske (FRG)
9. Agnès Gosselin (FRA)
10. Susan Jackson (GRB)

**U.S. Championships.** Kansas City, Missouri was the site of the U.S. Championships in late January and early February. Single event tickets were twelve dollars at most, with a portion of the proceeds benefiting the local Crittenton Center For Disturbed Youths. A key sponsor pulled out of the event at the last minute leaving organizers scrambling. Then there was the matter of the ice. Although the King Louie Ice Chateau and Fox Hill Ice Arena were ready to go for practices and compulsory figures, the main venue, the Kemper Arena, had been scheduled for a basketball game the night before the very first practices 'on the big rink' were to be held. Rink employees worked overtime through the night to ensure the ice was ready. The people of Kansas City went all out to ensure the event was a success. For the first time, the Christmas lights at the Alameda Plaza Hotel were turned on at a time other than the holiday season in a special ceremony in celebration of the event. In the junior pairs event, Kristi Yamaguchi made her debut at Nationals. In the novice men's event, 16-year-old Aren Nielsen made history as the first skater from the Kansas City area to win a medal at the U.S. Championships. An unlucky thirteen teams vied for top honours in the senior pairs event, which seemed doomed from the get-go. Margo Shoup and Patrick Page of the Broadmoor Skating Club withdrew after she crashed into the boards during a warm-up; Karen Courtland was taken to a local hospital after skating her short program with partner Robert Daw and treated for an upper respiratory infection. Many of the other teams suffered mishaps on key elements in their programs and judges were tasked with deciding which pair had made the fewest mistakes. Ultimately, that team was Jill Watson and Peter Oppegard. Only skating together for a few months, Watson and Oppegard trained in Canada with Louis Stong. Winning both the short program and the free skate, Watson and Oppegard went for the gusto, attempting both the throw triple Salchow and throw double Axel in their winning free skate, earning marks ranging from 5.2 to 5.8. Siblings Natalie and Wayne Seybold settled for silver, ahead of Gillian Wachsman and Todd Waggoner. With Rosalynn Sumners and Elaine Zayak out of the picture, many expected that Tiffany Chin would be a shoo-in for gold in Kansas City. In reality, she would end up facing some very legitimate competition in her quest for the national title. Although she took a strong lead in the school figures ahead of Debi Thomas and Jill Frost, Chin struggled in the short program, botching the triple toe-loop in her combination and losing her balance on the change foot sit spin. Bolstered by her early lead, Chin managed to hold on to the top spot entering the free skate despite a very strong performance by Thomas. Rebounding with a clean program that featured two triple toe-loops and three double Axels, Chin showed verve and confidence in clinching the gold medal. In her first U.S. Championships, Caryn Kadavy delivered a flawless free skate that featured a triple loop, triple toe-loop and three double Axels, receiving marks ranging from 5.5 to 5.8. It was enough for the bronze, behind Thomas, who landed a double Axel/triple toe-loop in her free skate but stepped out of a triple Salchow and double Axel and put her hand down on a triple loop. Jill Frost dropped to fifth, having endured a stress fracture, tonsilitis, strep throat and the flu in the months leading up to the event. Chin became the first Chinese American woman to win the U.S. senior women's crown, while Thomas became the first African American skater to win a medal in the senior women's event at Nationals. Judy Blumberg and Michael Seibert were the only reigning U.S. Champions to defend their title in Kansas City. Leading the dance event from start to finish, Blumberg and Seibert won their fifth consecutive national title and earned high praise for their flashy new *Fire on Ice* free dance set to music composed for them by Joel Silberman. Renée Roca and Donald Adair won the silver over Suzanne Semanick and Scott Gregory, earning a standing ovation for their *42nd Street* Quickstep OSP.

### EUROPEAN CHAMPIONSHIPS (continued)

Pairs:

1. Elena Valova and Oleg Vasiliev (SOV)
2. Larisa Selezneva and Oleg Makarov (SOV)
3. Veronika Pershina and Marat Akbarov (SOV)
4. Birgit Lorenz and Knut Schubert (GDR)
5. Manuela Landgraf and Ingo Steuer (GDR)
6. Claudia Massari and Daniele Caprano (FRG)
7. Lenka Knapová and René Novotný (CZE)

Ice Dance:

1. Natalia Bestemianova and Andrei Bukin (SOV)
2. Marina Klimova and Sergei Ponomarenko (SOV)
3. Petra Born and Rainer Schönborn (FRG)
4. Karen Barber and Nicky Slater (GRB)
5. Natalia Annenko and Genrikh Sretenski (SOV)
6. Kathrin and Christoff Beck (AUT)
7. Isabella Micheli and Roberto Pelizzola (ITA)
8. Jindra Holá and Karol Foltán (CZE)
9. Klára Engi and Attila Tóth (HUN)
10. Antonia and Ferdinand Becherer (FRG)

### 1985 U.S. CHAMPIONSHIPS (Kansas City, MO, January 29-February 3, 1985)

Men:

1. Brian Boitano
2. Mark Cockerell
3. Scott Williams
4. Christopher Bowman
5. Paul Wylie
6. Daniel Doran
7. Bobby Beauchamp
8. Craig Henderson
9. Angelo D'Agostino
10. David Fedor

Women:

1. Tiffany Chin
2. Debi Thomas
3. Caryn Kadavy
4. Kathryn Adams
5. Jill Frost
6. Leslie Sikes
7. Jana Sjodin
8. Yvonne Gómez
9. Sara MacInnes
10. Tracy Ernst

Pairs:

1. Jill Watson and Peter Oppegard
2. Natalie and Wayne Seybold
3. Gillian Wachsman and Todd Waggoner
4. Susan and Jason Dungjen
5. Katy Keeley and Joseph Mero
6. Sandy Hurtubise and Craig Maurizi
7. Maria Lako and Michael Blicharski
8. Karen Courtland and Robert Daw
9. Tammy Crowson and Jay Freeman
10. Ginger and Archie Tse

With Scott Hamilton out of the picture, the men's competition in Kansas City was really between Brian Boitano and Mark Cockerell. Taking an early lead over in the figures, Boitano skated brilliantly as James Bond in his short program to music from the soundtrack of *The Spy Who Loved Me*. Miming a gunshot in his choreography, Boitano joked to reporters that his intended victim was coach Linda Leaver. She laughed, "I was glad to be shot. It was great!" Cockerell's short program was set to the *Lone Ranger* theme. After his program, a girl came down to the railing and plopped a black cowboy hat with a silver star badge on his head. Seven of the nine judges preferred Boitano's program, expanding his figures lead to 50 percent. In the free skate, Cockerell landed five triples, including a triple Lutz and triple toe-loop/triple toe-loop combination. His gutsy performance was rewarded with marks ranging from 5.6 to 5.9. Boitano did one better, landing six triples, including a triple Axel, triple Lutz and three-jump double flip/triple toe-loop/triple toe-loop combination. Boitano's marks ranged from 5.6 to 5.9 for both technical merit and artistic impression, earning him his first U.S. title as a senior, seven years after he had won the national junior title. 18-year-old Scott Williams of Redondo Beach, California was outstanding in his bronze medal-winning performance, as was Christopher Bowman, who moved up from eighth after figures to finish fourth. After winning, Boitano, told reporters, "The frustration is finally over. It's like I've made it over the mountain."

**Canadian Championships.** In February, the Moncton Coliseum played host to the Canadian Championships. It was only the second time in history that Canadians had been held in the province of New Brunswick. In the lead-up to the competition, the media focused heavily on the story of 17-year-old Tracey Wainman's return to the sport after an injury forced her off the ice entirely for half a year. 'The Comeback Kid' started her journey in the women's event on a high by winning the figures ahead of Elizabeth Manley, Charlene Wong and Meredith Owen. Manley won the first figure; Wainman the second and third. Wainman's comeback arc ended when she took a tumble early in her short program, finishing a discouraging eighth. Manley skated a strong performance to win the short program, ahead of Cynthia Coull and Wong. Coull had the skate of her life to win the free skate, landing three triples and earning a standing ovation. Her seventh-place finish in the figures was not enough to overtake Manley, who popped a triple Lutz early in her program but skated well enough to finish second in the free skate and first overall. Wong took the bronze and it was revealed that both she and Manley had suffered injuries in practice in the fall. Wainman's free skate was not a walk in the park. She fell on a triple Salchow and missed two double Axels but her program was good enough to finish fifth in the free skate and fourth overall. Brian Orser was suffering from a cold in Moncton, but his victory in the compulsory figures in the men's event was enough to give anyone the sniffles. It was the first time he ever won the figures in a senior event. Orser continued his dominance by winning the short program with a clean triple Lutz/double toe-loop combination, earning a perfect mark of 6.0 for technical merit from judge Sally Rehorick. Entering the free skate, Neil Paterson was in second and Gordon Forbes was tied for third with a hometown favourite, André Bourgeois of Dieppe. A capacity crowd of 6800 spectators showed up to watch the men's free skate, where Orser skated brilliantly, receiving a standing ovation on the way to winning his fifth straight Canadian men's title. He received seven perfect 6.0s, with judges Sally Rehorick and Dorothy MacLeod giving him perfect marks for both technical merit and artistic impression.

**U.S. CHAMPIONSHIPS (continued)**

Ice Dance:

1. Judy Blumberg and Michael Seibert
2. Renée Roca and Donald Adair
3. Suzanne Semanick and Scott Gregory
4. Lois Luciani and Russ Witherby
5. Susie Wynne and Joseph Druar
6. Susan Jorgensen and Robert Yokabaskas
7. Eva Hunyadi and Jay Pinkerton
8. Kristan Lowery and Chip Rossbach
9. Kandi Amelon and Alec Binnie
10. April Sargent and John D'Amelio

Junior Winners:

Doug Mattis (men)
Jill Trenary (women)
Deveny Deck and Luke Hohmann (pairs)
Jodie Balogh and Jerod Swallow (ice dance)

Novice Winners:

Todd Eldredge (men)
Katie Wood (women)

**1985 CANADIAN CHAMPIONSHIPS**
(Moncton, NB, February 6-10, 1985)

Men:

1. Brian Orser
2. Neil Paterson
3. Gordon Forbes
4. André Bourgeois
5. Kevin Parker
6. Marc Ferland
7. Brad McLean
8. Scott Rachuk
9. Jaimee Eggleton
10. Patrick Greasley

Women:

1. Elizabeth Manley
2. Cynthia Coull
3. Charlene Wong
4. Tracey Wainman
5. Diane Mae Ogibowski
6. Patricia Schmidt
7. Anissa Gurchin
8. Melinda Kunhegyi
9. Rosemarie Sakic
10. Meredith Owen

Pairs:

1. Cynthia Coull and Mark Rowsom
2. Melinda Kunhegyi and Lyndon Johnston
3. Christine Hough and Doug Ladret
4. Penny Schultz and Scott Grover
5. Isabelle Kourie and Guy Trudeau
6. Laurene Collin and David Howe

Paterson, the only other skater to successfully complete a triple Axel, won the silver. Bourgeois fell on a triple Axel attempt of his own, losing the bronze to Forbes, whose program was interrupted when the foot strap of his costume came free. Forbes delighted the audience by successfully landing a combination jump he previously missed when he restarted his program. Jaimee Eggleton, who had been selected for the Olympic team in 1984, finished only ninth. This time around, the CFSA avoided controversy by naming the top three senior men to the World team, though they certainly wouldn't have done poorly with that year's up-and-coming junior men's champion Kurt Browning. The pairs event was anyone's to win. Barbara Underhill and Paul Martini had turned professional and Katherina Matousek and Lloyd Eisler withdrew after Matousek aggravated an ankle injury she had incurred in the fall while practicing in Moncton. Cynthia Coull and Mark Rowsom skated clean and led the way in the short program, with Melinda Kunhegyi and Lyndon Johnston second and Christine Hough and Doug Ladret and Peggy Schultz and Scott Grover in a tie for third. Coull and Rowsom were up and down in the free skate, but they skated strongly enough to win their first national title ahead of Kunhegyi and Johnston and Hough and Ladret. Ultimately, Matousek and Eisler were given a bye to Worlds in Tokyo, bumping Hough and Ladret off the team. Coull made history in Moncton as the first Canadian woman to be named to the World team in both singles and pairs since Marlene Smith, 35 years prior. With six entries, the fours event boasted the largest field since its reintroduction to Canadians in Halifax in 1981. The winners were Kunhegyi, Hough, Johnston and Ladret. Tracy Wilson and Rob McCall's road to the Canadians hadn't been an easy one. Wilson caught the flu in December, and then was diagnosed with asthma. They missed an entire month of training time at the National Ice Dance Centre in Richmond Hill in the lead-up to the competition. Wilson and McCall persevered, winning all three of the compulsories in the senior ice dance event - the Blues, Yankee Polka and Viennese Waltz. In the Quickstep OSP, Wilson and McCall were so impressive that one judge gave them a 6.0. Their technically demanding free dance to "Mouvements" by André Gagnon earned them a standing ovation and their fourth consecutive national title - McCall's fifth. Sibling duos Karyn and Rod Garossino and Isabelle and Paul Duchesnay were second and third, with the Garossinos defeating the Duchesnays four judges to three. The Garossinos faced an unusual situation in the free dance when they took the ice to skate but were stopped by the referee, who ordered the ice to be flooded again because it was covered in sequins that had fallen off the last team to skate's costumes. Many lamented the fact that Canada had only two spots in ice dance at the Worlds because all three teams were of a high calibre.

**CANADIAN CHAMPIONSHIPS** (continued)

Ice Dance:

1. Tracy Wilson and Rob McCall
2. Karyn and Rod Garossino
3. Isabelle and Paul Duchesnay
4. Kim Campbell and Michael Farrington
5. Jo-Anne Borlase and Scott Chalmers
6. Michelle McDonald and Patrick Mandley
7. Deanna Poirier and Paul MacIntosh
8. Margo Hoyt and Mark Mitchell
9. Erica Davenport and Keith Baker
10. Teri-Lynn Black and Toivo Heinsaar

Fours:

1. Melinda Kunhegyi, Christine Hough, Lyndon Johnston and Doug Ladret
2. Cynthia Coull, Penny Schultz, Mark Rowsom and Scott Grover
3. Laurene Collin, Brooke Petersmeyer, David Howe and Jim Blackburn
4. Denise Benning, Katherina Matousek, Alan Kerslake and Lloyd Eisler
5. Lynda, Laura, John and Jamie Ivanich
6. Isabelle Kourie, Barbara Martin, Guy Trudeau and John Penticost

Junior Winners:

Kurt Browning (men)
Nathalie Sasseville (women)
Isabelle Brasseur and Pascal Courchesne (pairs)
Penny Mann and Richard Perkins (ice dance)

Novice Winners:

Cory Watson (men)
Shannon Allison (women)
Lara Carscadden and Steve Akins (pairs)
Sheryl Baker and Derrick Gaede (ice dance)

*Isabelle and Paul Duchesnay. Photo courtesy Elaine Hooper / St. Ivel Figure Skating Archive.*

**World Championships.** In March, Tokyo played host to the second World Championships ever held in Asia. The Yoyogi National Gymnasium was an unconventional choice as a venue for a world-class figure skating competition. The Gymnasium had played host to the swimming and diving events at the 1964 Summer Olympics. A last-minute effort to construct a rink over a swimming pool resulted in less-than-ideal ice conditions and the ten-meter diving board was a bizarre sight. The skaters complained that the rink was too cold and that the ice was too hard and watery. To get from the host Prince Hotel Takanawa to the Yoyogi National Gymnasium and the other two rinks utilized for the competition (Shinagawa-ku and Meiji Jingu Gaien), they had to take very long bus rides through congested traffic. Finnish judge Giordano Abbondati was running late after attending a reception and decided to take a taxi to the rink instead of the long bus ride. The driver misunderstood his directions and took him first to the wrong rink, then to a swimming pool and finally to a police station where, with the help of officers, he was able to communicate to the taxi driver where he needed to be. He almost didn't make it in time to judge the women's short program. A group of American skating fans had the trip of a lifetime when Far West Tours International in Santa Monica, CA organized a trip to Tokyo called *Fabulous Oriental Odyssee,* which included tickets to all skating events, a motorcoach tour of Japan with a private guide and three days in Hong Kong. The cost of the eighteen-day vacation was less than 2300 dollars per person. In Tokyo, several countries had representation on the World stage for the first time. Hong Kong sent a contingent of the skaters for the first time. Cheukfai Lai entered the men's event. Shuk-Ching Ngai competed in both the women's and pairs competitions, entering the latter with partner Kwokyung Mak. China's Liu Luyang and Zhao Xiaolei became the first Chinese ice dance team to compete at the Worlds and Petya Gavazova was Bulgaria's first representative in the women's event. Olympic Gold Medallists and World Champions Elena Valova and Oleg Vasiliev made an uncharacteristic error in the short program when Valova popped the required side-by-side double Lutz jump into a single. This mistake allowed their teammates Larisa Selezneva and Oleg Makarov to take the lead, though their timing was off on the side-by-side jumps. Katherina Matousek and Lloyd Eisler finished a strong third ahead of their training mates Cynthia Coull and Mark Rowsom. In the free skate, Valova and Vasiliev rebounded with a very strong performance to take the win, landing side-by-side triple toe-loops, two different throw triple jumps and earning four 5.9s for artistic impression. Selezneva and Makarov had to settle for silver. Matousek and Eisler made mistakes on side-by-side double Salchows and a throw double Axel, but their program was strong enough to hold on for the bronze. Though the Canadians were disappointed with their performance, it was a remarkable comeback after being out of competition for four months due to Matousek's injury. Kunhegyi and Johnston moved up to fifth, with Coull and Rowsom dropping to seventh with a disappointing free skate where they missed both of their throws. Olympic Silver Medallists Natalia Bestemianova and Andrei Bukin dominated the ice dance competition from the beginning, winning the Viennese Waltz, Yankee Polka and Blues with first-place ordinals from eight of the nine judges. In a close second were, of course, their teammates Marina Klimova and Sergei Ponomarenko, who had won the bronze medal behind B&B in Sarajevo. Judy Blumberg and Michael Seibert stood in third in their fifth trip to Worlds, followed by Tracy Wilson and Rob McCall, who earned particular praise from reporters for their Viennese Waltz. In true 80s ice dance fashion, not a single placement changed from the compulsory dances through the OSP except for the teams in 15th and 16th places swapping spots.

**1985 WORLD CHAMPIONSHIPS (Tokyo, Japan, March 3-10, 1985)**

Men:

1. Alexandr Fadeev (SOV)
2. Brian Orser (CAN)
3. Brian Boitano (USA)
4. Jozef Sabovčík (CZE)
5. Vladimir Kotin (SOV)
6. Heiko Fischer (FRG)
7. Grzegorz Filipowski (POL)
8. Mark Cockerell (USA)
9. Viktor Petrenko (SOV)
10. Neil Paterson (CAN)

Women:

1. Katarina Witt (GDR)
2. Kira Ivanova (SOV)
3. Tiffany Chin (USA)
4. Anna Kondrashova (SOV)
5. Debi Thomas (USA)
6. Claudia Leistner (FRG)
7. Natalia Lebedeva (SOV)
8. Agnès Gosselin (FRA)
9. Elizabeth Manley (CAN)
10. Cynthia Coull (CAN)

Pairs:

1. Elena Valova and Oleg Vasiliev (SOV)
2. Larisa Selezneva and Oleg Makarov (SOV)
3. Katherina Matousek and Lloyd Eisler (CAN)
4. Jill Watson and Peter Oppegard (USA)
5. Melinda Kunhegyi and Lyndon Johnston (CAN)
6. Veronika Pershina and Marat Akbarov (SOV)
7. Cynthia Coull and Mark Rowsom (CAN)
8. Manuela Landgraf and Ingo Steuer (GDR)
9. Natalie and Wayne Seybold (USA)
10. Claudia Massari and Daniele Caprano (FRG)

Ice Dance:

1. Natalia Bestemianova and Andrei Bukin (SOV)
2. Marina Klimova and Sergei Ponomarenko (SOV)
3. Judy Blumberg and Michael Seibert (USA)
4. Tracy Wilson and Rob McCall (CAN)
5. Petra Born and Rainer Schönborn (FRG)
6. Karen Barber and Nicky Slater (GRB)
7. Natalia Annenko and Genrikh Sretenski (SOV)
8. Isabella Micheli and Roberto Pelizzola (ITA)
9. Kathrin and Christoff Beck (AUT)
10. Karyn and Rod Garossino (CAN)

Bestemianova and Bukin earned ten 5.9s for their *Carnival Night* Charleston-inspired Quickstep. Klimova and Ponomarenko's *Hello Dolly!* OSP was well received by judges and audience alike, giving them the nod over Blumberg and Seibert and Wilson and McCall. Bestemianova and Bukin's "Carmen" was regarded by many as the finest free dance of their eligible career. The program earned them no less than thirteen 5.9s and two 6.0s (the only two perfect marks awarded at the event) and their first World title. In *Tracings*, Frank Loeser Nowosad described B&B's "Carmen" as "a frenzy of movement, the least dominant feature being the carving, gliding edge that traditionalists so seek. Conventional ice dance steps pop up in this Soviet pair's programs as though in parentheses - as traditional passages between extended poses, crossovers and perilous toe-runs... [Natalia's] performing ferocity makes her a terror to be subdued... Gloomy Bukin can appear as the perfect nemesis, a malevolent force accepting the challenge of a redhead fury." Klimova and Ponomarenko's Latin American free dance earned the silver over Blumberg and Seibert and Wilson and McCall. Canada's second team, Karyn and Rod Garossino, ended up in tenth. After the event, a meeting of coaches and ISU officials addressed the acrobatic direction ice dance was headed. It was made very clear that while theatrics were in, acrobatics were out. Japanese fans expressed sorrow over the fact that Midori Ito was unable to compete in Tokyo. The young jumping phenom from Nagoya had the terrible luck of injuring her ankle a second time working on the triple Axel. Kira Ivanova's decisive win in the women's figures was a shock to no one, but the fact Tiffany Chin placed second over Katarina Witt was certainly a surprise. Canadians Elizabeth Manley and Cynthia Coull had a very disappointing outing, placing only tenth and 18th. In the short program, Witt gave a strong performance to take the lead over a clean Chin and Ivanova, with Coull and Manley in ninth and tenth. Debi Thomas and Claudia Leistner, the only two women to attempt and execute a triple as the second jump in their combination, placed fourth and sixth. The combined standings had Ivanova in first entering the final phase of the competition. Witt gave an outstanding performance in the free skate, landing four triples to best Chin, who singled a triple Salchow attempt and fell on her double Axel. Ivanova faltered as well, but her lead was enough to hold on to the silver. Chin's medal win in Tokyo was a historic milestone - the first medal at the Worlds ever won by an Asian American skater. Manley and Coull ended up in ninth and tenth. Manley was disappointed with her free skate, where she fell on the triple Lutz and aggravated an existing injury to her left ankle. The men's compulsory figures took seven and a half hours to complete and when the dust settled, Alexandr Fadeev was atop the leaderboard, followed by Jozef Sabovčík (who was recovering from a 104-degree fever), France's Fernand Fédronic, Brian Orser (who was also sick), Brian Boitano and Vladimir Kotin. Hong Kong's Cheukfai Lai had the unfortunate distinction of receiving the lowest score in the competition. Losing his balance eight times on one figure, he placed dead last and received a score of 0.1 from one judge. ISU Representative Josef Dědič told reporters that the ISU was "apparently... a little premature" in permitting him to enter. In front of 2000 spectators, Fadeev dazzled and maintained his lead with a flawless short program, earning four 5.9s, three 5.8s and two 5.7s. Orser, who finished second in the short program with five 5.8s, moved up to third overall behind Sabovčík. In the free skate, Fadeev gave one of the finest performances of his career in front of a crowd of 4000, landing his triple Axel in combination, as well as a triple Lutz/triple toe-loop. He earned 5.8s and 5.9s from all but one judge for his effort. In winning, he became the first man to translate a previous win at the World Junior Championships to a win at senior Worlds. Orser's results in the figures and short program meant that he was skating for silver, not gold, and second is exactly where he finished. A third-place finish in the free skate to Sabovčík's disappointing sixth gave Brian Boitano the bronze. There could be no accusation of bias from Canadian judge Norris Bowden, who placed Boitano ahead of Orser in the free skate. Judges from the U.S., France and Finland joined him in giving Boitano second-place ordinals, resulting in a five-four split. Sabovčík landed a quadruple toe-loop both in practice and the warm-up for the free skate, but omitted it from his program after missing his triple Axel. Canada's other two entries, Neil Paterson and Gordon Forbes, ended up in tenth and 17th overall. After the event, the *Montreal Gazette* reported on Canadian allegations that Soviet, American and Swiss officials were involved in a back-room deal, where American judge Dr. Franklin S. Nelson would promote Fadeev in exchange for favours for Chin from Soviet judge Sergei Kononykhin in the women's event. To support their claim, Canadian officials pointed out how Swiss judge Maja Reinhart had Orser 18th in the first figure, in which he finished fifth and eighth overall in the figures, where he finished fourth. Chin's second-place finish in the figures was also a point of contention, as she had placed only 12th in figures the previous year at the Olympics and Katarina Witt had been third. Soviet and American officials denied the claims but it didn't go unnoticed that the Soviet delegation rented almost an entire floor at the Takanawa Prince Hotel, dubbed 'Caviar Row', as it was openly suggested at the time that Soviet officials would offer officials from other countries lavish gifts like caviar, Stoli and jewelry.

*Jayne Torvill and Christopher Dean. Photo by Fred & Joan Dean, courtesy Fred Dean, "Ice & Roller Skate" magazine archive.*

# 1985-1986 SEASON

Hit Songs: "How Will I Know" by Whitney Houston, "Running Up That Hill (A Deal With God)" by Kate Bush, "West End Girls" by Pet Shop Boys, "Kiss" by Prince and The Revolution, "Sledgehammer" by Peter Gabriel
Hit Movies: Crocodile Dundee, Top Gun, Ferris Bueller's Day Off, The Mission, Platoon
Hit TV: Murder She Wrote, Family Ties, Who's The Boss?, Kate & Allie, Night Court
News: The Chernobyl Disaster, Wreckage of Titanic found, Live Aid Concert, Challenger Disaster, Italian government toppled as a result of PLO terrorist hijacking of cruise ship

## PEOPLE

Following the 1984-1985 season, several skaters decided to leave the amateur world behind them. Karen Barber and Nicky Slater made their swan song at the opening gala of the Swindon Ice Rink in July. Slater got married in October, started commentating figure skating events with Betty Callaway on ITV and developed a comedy act for shows with a life-sized doll with pink hair, called Doris. Barber joined the cast of Torvill and Dean's tour, as did West German ice dancers Petra Born and Rainer Schönborn. Judy Blumberg and Michael Seibert, Gordon Forbes and Kevin Parker joined the cast of the *Ice Capades*.

"Up, up and away!" Christopher Dean took to the blue skies in the summer. When the *Torvill and Dean: The World Tour* was in Nottingham, Dean was invited to go flying with Richard Thomas, the Squadron Leader of the famous Red Arrow RAF acrobatic team. After leaving the runway at the Arrows' base in Scrampton, Dean was allowed to take over the controls of the plane for a bit.

Debi Thomas and her coach Alex McGowan made a trip Down Under in the summertime. Thomas was invited to give exhibitions at the Australian Championships and McGowan conducted skating clinics in Brisbane, Melbourne and Sydney. Thomas emerged as a truly popular exhibition skater during the 1985-1986 season and her hilarious Wanda Beazel number was a huge hit with audiences around the world.

In August, Helene Engelmann passed away in Vienna at the age of 87. Engelmann won Austria's first Olympic gold medal in figure skating in 1924 and three World Championships in pairs with partner Alfred Berger.

Gossip in the skating world? Say it ain't so! By 1985, word had spread throughout the skating community that Tiffany Chin had landed triple Axels in practice, but people had a lot more than that in their mouths. Marjorie Chin claimed to have heard it all after it was announced that her daughter was withdrawing from Skate America and Skate Canada: that she was in jail or going through a divorce, that her family was struggling financially, that her son was in a car accident and that both of Tiffany's legs were broken. The truth was after the 1985 Nationals, tests revealed that several of Tiffany's leg joints were out of alignment and she was suffering from an extreme muscle imbalance. Tiffany withdrew from fall competitions at her mother's insistence, spending several months off the ice undergoing physical therapy to rebuild her leg muscles. She also left coach John Nicks for Don Laws.

After a contentious relationship with the CFSA, Isabelle and Paul Duchesnay announced their decision to skate for France in an October press reference. The FFSG agreed to pay the couple's training expenses under the condition that they placed first at the French Championships. The Duchesnays received the cold shoulder from other skaters in their first French Nationals but won the gold.

Dame Gladys Hogg, MBE passed away in London at the age of 75 in October. Miss Hogg, as she was known to her students, was 'the' ice dance coach in England in the 50s and 60s, when British ice dance teams first dominated international competition. Her students included Diane Towler and Bernie Ford, John Curry, Robin Cousins, Jean Westwood and Lawrence Demmy. She also worked with many skaters who went on to be international coaches, including Betty Callaway, John Nicks, Carol and Jon Lane and Peter Burrows.

Olympic Bronze Medallist Scott Ethan Allen married Anne Grace Binford in Hillsdale, New Jersey in February. Binford was a writer and producer for NBC News; Allen the Vice-President of Research and Development for the men's clothing company Corbin Ltd.

In May, the figure skating community said goodbye to two formidable women. Herma Szabo passed away in Austria just ten days before Lyudmila Pakhomova lost her battle with leukemia in Moscow at the age of 39. Between them, they won thirteen gold medals at the World Championships. Szabo was the first women's champion of the Winter Games in figure skating in 1924 and the only skater to hold World titles in both singles and pairs simultaneously; Pakhomova was the first Olympic Gold Medallist in ice dancing in 1976 and she worked at the Department of Sports Choreographers of the Theater Arts Institute of Moscow.

American ice dancers Kandi Amelon and Alec Binnie were the first recipients of the USOC's Fair Play Award in April. They were chosen after demonstrating wonderful sportsmanship at the Golden Spin of Zagreb competition in the fall, where they sportingly attempted to give their bronze medals to Hungarians Klára Engi and Attila Tóth, who withdrew from the event after suffering injuries in a collision in the warmup for the free dance. Though the referee told them that under ISU rules, the medals were theirs, their generous gesture earned praise from President Ronald Reagan and the Governors of Michigan and Delaware, their home state and the state where they trained.

In Nepean, Ontario in June, Peter Mumford lost a long battle with cancer at the age of 66. Mumford served as the Vice-President of the CFSA for ten years and was the chairman of the 1978 World Championships in Ottawa, which raised almost 500 000 dollars for skater development in Canada. He also played a key behind-the-scenes role in the organization of the second Ottawa Worlds in 1984.

The newest inductees to the World Figure Skating Hall of Fame were World Champion Courtney Jones and former USFSA President F. Ritter Shumway. The honour couldn't have come at a better time for Shumway, who celebrated his eightieth birthday not long before the announcement was made.

## AROUND THE WORLD

**Canada.** The CFSA unveiled a new logo with a modern design, similar to the logo used at the 1984 World Championships in Ottawa. Bruce Miller's time as the CFSA's President came to an end in May. Miller was succeeded by Bob Howard, who had chaired the Marketing Committee since 1981.

**China.** China had indoor ice rinks in Beijing and Harbin but the growth of its figure skating program was hampered by a lack of government funding and the fact its facilities were not open year-round. The construction of a new sports complex with a year-round ice rink in Beijing meant that the country's top skaters no longer had to go abroad to train in the summer.

**Greece.** The Stadio Eirinis kai Filias in Piraeus was the first big stadium in Greece to install an ice rink. A smaller-scale touring production called *Fantasy on Ice* was set to perform there in 1985, but not long after arriving, the event's promoter bolted for an airport with the money, leaving the skaters stranded. The city denied the organizers access to the rink for weeks. Despite this unfortunate situation, the Hellenic Ice Sports Federation was founded in June and became a provisional ISU member the following year.

**South Africa.** History was made in July when Pro-Skate staged the first professional figure skating competition in Africa. The competition was held at the Sun City resort in Bophuthatswana, a territory under South African control whose independence was recognized by the apartheid government but decried by the United Nations. A who's who of professional figure skating made the trip, including Scott Hamilton, Toller Cranston, Elaine Zayak, David Santee and Brian Pockar. several skaters from South Africa also competed. Days after the skaters left, the area exploded into terrible riots that made front-page news around the world.

**United States.** George T. Yonekura ended his three-year term as the USFSA's President and was succeeded by Dr. Hugh C. Graham Jr., a Tulsa pediatrician who was a former medallist in both singles and pairs at the U.S. Championships in the 50s. At the end of the season, elite coach Ron Ludington also announced the move of his coaching center from the Skating Club of Wilmington to the University of Delaware.

## FUN AND GAMES

Computer nerds were finally able to 'figure skate' from the comfort of their living rooms when Epyx released *Winter Games*, an Olympic-themed computer game, first released on floppy disc for Commodore 64. The game sold 250 000 copies in the 80s and was later released for Amiga, Atari and Nintendo.

## BEHIND THE SCENES

In September, IOC President Juan Antonio Samanarch was present in Indiana for the signing of the Memorandum of Mutual Understanding and Cooperation in Sports, a historic agreement binding the USOC and the National Olympic Committee of the Soviet Union in mutual support of amateur sports and Olympic ideals. The signing was a symbolic gesture of goodwill amid The Cold War.

The ISU introduced some important rule changes at its June Congress in Vienna. Pairs could include a maximum of five lifts in their free skating programs, with no more than two twist lifts. The rules surrounding deductions for falls and interruptions in ice dancing were revised to add mandatory deductions for the compulsory dances and OSP. A rule change in the junior ranks requiring both partners in a pairs or ice dance team to be under the age of eighteen the July before entering international competitions posed a challenge to some federations with small pools of emerging talent. However, the Soviet Union had no less than 36 promising dance couples under the age of 14.

## BOOKS AND MAGAZINES

Karen Barber and Nicky Slater partnered with Sandra Stevenson to write their autobiography *Spice on Ice*, released by Sidgwick and Jackson. NSA Historian Dennis L. Bird praised the book, but noted that 75 percent of the book "consists of Nicky's own forthright words, and another 25% is his partner's."

Brian Pockar caused a minor scandal in March by appearing in *Playgirl* magazine. Pockar's agent Michael Rosenberg hoped the tasteful pictures would lead to movie work.

## FILMS AND TELEVISION

In September, figure skating made one of its first appearances on *Jeopardy*. In the Double Jeopardy round, contestants are asked, "Of 6, 10, or 100, a perfect score in figure skating". The host of the show, the late Alex Trebek, previously hosted the Canadian figure skating series *Stars On Ice*.

Just in time for the holidays, CBC aired the marvelously off-kilter television special *The True Gift of Christmas*. Starring Toller Cranston and award-winning actress Martha Gibson, the special featured an outstanding cast of skaters including Robin Cousins, Kitty and Peter Carruthers, JoJo Starbuck and Ken Shelley, Norbert Schramm, Sarah Kawahara, Shelley MacLeod and John S. Rait and Simone Grigorescu. Film critic Rick Groen praised the special for its "holiday myths... ancient legends... resplendent costumes... nifty visual effects... [and] virtuoso skating."

# THE AIDS EPIDEMIC

Governments empowered health officials to close gay bars, clubs and bathhouses and showcasing the public ignorance about HIV and AIDS at the time, a poll in the *Los Angeles Times* revealed that the majority of Americans were in favour of quarantining AIDS patients. The CDC reported an 89 percent increase in cases and when actor Rock Hudson, one of the first celebrities to openly talk about his diagnosis, died in October, the world took notice.

Alastair Munro passed away in Ottawa in July at the age of 44. Born in Ottawa, Munro got his start in figure skating at the Minto Skating Club. With Judith Rudd, he won the junior pairs title at the 1958 Canadians. At the age of 20, while studying English at Carleton University, he took his first ballet class. He joined the National Ballet of Canada in 1964 and later studied with the Joffrey Ballet company in New York. He was a principal dancer with the Metropolitan Opera Ballet at Lincoln Center from 1973 to 1978 and later taught with the Washington School of Ballet and Ottawa School Of Dance.

John Curry's one-time lover Brian Grant passed away in January at the age of 39. A talented all-around entertainer, Grant (born Brian Granzow) danced alongside Twiggy in the film *The Boy Friend* and modeled with the McDonald/Richards agency. He took up skating in the late 60s, appearing in *Winter Romance On Ice* with Peggy Fleming and in plastic ice shows at Studio 54 and the Nanuet Star Theatre. With partner Darlene (Gilbert) Parent, he skated in numerous plastic ice shows around the country, including *Fashion On Ice*, a fundraiser for the Viennese Opera Ball and a series of productions at the Rainbow Grill. He also appeared in skating scenes in the film *Splash*, television series *Kate & Allie* and in John Curry's show *Ice Dancing*. He was a pioneering member of the Ice Theatre of New York and taught skating for several years at the Sky Rink. Mary Gaillard remembered, "Brian was very ambitious and loved to skate, but he was a skater who learned as an adult. He didn't grow up as a skater. It was really wonderful that John [Curry] took him under his wing and he was able to skate in his show. He was my group class teacher at Sky Rink and then I started taking private lessons from him. We'd walk to the subway together and talk after lessons and he became a good friend. He was diagnosed with pneumonia on April 26, 1985, and was sick for nine months before he passed away. During that time, I ended up living with him and taking care of him. This was in the days when AIDS was just popping up a little bit and nobody knew much about it. He was going to lick this thing. He went into this with vitamins and was taking good care of himself. He was going to be the first one to not die from it. His outlook was strong. He kept it very much to himself and didn't tell anyone what he had. People might have guessed but he was adamant that he didn't want everybody's negativity impacting his trying to get better. Another reason he didn't tell anyone was that his family didn't know he was gay. Certainly, after he died everybody knew. He had a memorial service here in New York and his funeral was in Syracuse... He was really good-looking. You'd go into a restaurant and you could see people looking at him because he was very attractive. That, of course, got him very far in life. His biggest money-making was certainly modeling and entertaining. He was outgoing, very friendly and definitely had a sense of humour."

Canadian skating coach Guy Nick passed away in May in Vancouver at the age of 51. Nick got his start in skating at the Tacoma Figure Skating Club in Washington. After disappointing results in his first three trips to the Pacific Coast Championships, he represented the Lakewood Winter Club in the junior men's event at the U.S. Championships twice, placing ninth in 1951 and fourth in 1952. At the 1953 U.S. Championships in Hershey, he won the school figures in the junior men's event and placed second overall, sandwiched between future Olympians David Jenkins and Tim Brown. He won his second and final medal at the U.S. Championships, a bronze in junior men's, in 1954, and passed both the USFSA and CFSA's Gold (Eighth) Tests. He made his mark as a coach in British Columbia in the 50s and 60s, teaching at the Capilano Winter Club, Racquet Club of Victoria and Connaught Skating Club.

## ART AND HISTORY

History was made at the PSGA and ISIA's annual trade show when skates worn by Queen Victoria and Prince Albert were displayed in the United States at a booth shared by John Wilson Blades and Riedell's Boots.

The World Figure Skating Museum and Hall of Fame undertook an ambitious expansion project, introducing new displays, a special 'Sonja Henie corner' and an expansive library of figure skating reference books.

1986 marked the 25th anniversary of the crash of Sabena Flight 548 in February of 1961, which tragically killed an entire generation of American figure skaters, coaches and officials en route to that year's World Championships in Prague. The USFSA issued a sterling silver commemorative pin and encouraged donations to its Memorial Fund in memory of those who perished.

*Guy Nick. Photo courtesy B.C. Gay and Lesbian Archives.*

# Fall Competitions

**1985 COUPES DES ALPES (Saint Gervais, France and Oberstdorf, West Germany, August 20-25, 1985 and August 27-31, 1985)**

Grand Prix de St. Gervais Winners:

Doug Mattis (USA) - men
Tracey Damigella (USA) - women
Christine Hough and Doug Ladret (CAN) - pairs
Maya Usova and Alexandr Zhulin (SOV) - ice dance

Nebelhorn Trophy (Oberstdorf) Winners:

Richard Zander (FRG) - men
Cornelia Tesch (FRG) - women
Lyudmila Koblova and Andrei Kalitin (SOV) - pairs
Maya Usova and Alexandr Zhulin (SOV) - ice dance

**1985 ASKÖ CUP OF VIENNA (Vienna, Austria, September 16-20, 1985)**

Men:

1. Daniel Doran (USA)
2. Andrei Torosian (SOV)
3. Thomas Wieser (FRG)

Women:

1. Marina Tweretinova (SOV)
2. Sara MacInnes (USA)
3. Simone Lang (GDR)

**1985 ST. IVEL ICE INTERNATIONAL (London, England, September 24-26, 1985)**

Men:

1. Brian Orser (CAN)
2. Grzegorz Filipowski (POL)
3. Christopher Bowman (USA)

Women:

1. Debi Thomas (USA)
2. Susan Jackson (GRB)
3. Joanne Conway (GRB)

Pairs:

1. Natalie and Wayne Seybold (USA)
2. Christine Hough and Doug Ladret (CAN)
3. Julia Brystova and Aleksandr Tarasov (SOV)

Ice Dance:

1. Natalie Annenko and Genrikh Sretenski (SOV)
2. Suzanne Semanick and Scott Gregory (USA)
3. Klára Engi and Attila Tóth (HUN)

**1985 SKATE AMERICA (St. Paul/Minneapolis, MN, October 14-20, 1985)**

Men:

1. Jozef Sabovčík (CZE)
2. Brian Boitano (USA)
3. Viktor Petrenko (SOV)

Women:

1. Debi Thomas (USA)
2. Tracey Wainman (CAN)
3. Katrien Pauwels (BEL)

Pairs:

1. Jill Watson and Peter Oppegard (USA)
2. Elena Bechke and Valeri Kornienko (SOV)
3. Gillian Wachsman and Todd Waggoner (USA)

Ice Dance:

1. Renée Roca and Donald Adair (USA)
2. Irina Zhuk and Oleg Petrov (SOV)
3. Antonia and Ferdinand Becherer (FRG)

**1985 SKATE CANADA (London, ON, October 23-27, 1985)**

Men:

1. Jozef Sabovčík (CZE)
2. Scott Williams (USA)
3. Grzegorz Filipowski (POL)

Women:

1. Caryn Kadavy (USA)
2. Elizabeth Manley (CAN)
3. Patricia Neske (FRG)

Pairs:

1. Ekaterina Gordeeva and Sergei Grinkov (SOV)
2. Veronika Pershina and Marat Akbarov (SOV)
3. Denise Benning and Lyndon Johnston (CAN)

Ice Dance:

1. Renée Roca and Donald Adair (USA)
2. Olga Volozhinskaya and Alexandr Svinin (SOV)
3. Kathrin and Christoff Beck (AUT)

**1985 DANUBIUS THERMAL TROPHY (Budapest, Hungary, October 30-November 3, 1985)**

Men:

1. Angelo D'Agostino (USA)
2. Yuri Bureiko (SOV)
3. Laurent Depouilly (FRA)

Women:

1. Yvonne Gómez (USA)
2. Izumi Aotani (JPN)
3. Sachie Yuki (JPN)

Ice Dance:

1. Maya Usova and Alexandr Zhulin (SOV)
2. Klára Engi and Attila Tóth (HUN)
3. Lois Luciani and Russ Witherby (USA)

**1985 PRAGUE SKATE (Prague, Czechoslovakia, November 8-9, 1985)**

Men:

1. Petr Barna (CZE)
2. Ralf Lewandowski (GDR)
3. Philippe Roncoli (FRA)

Women:

1. Inga Gauter (GDR)
2. Sachie Yuki (JPN)
3. Izumi Aotani (JPN)

Pairs:

1. Lori Blasko and Todd Sand (USA)
2. Svetlana Frantsuzova and Oleg Goshkov (SOV)
3. Laurene Collin and David Howe (CAN)

**1985 INTERNATIONAL SUGAR CRITERIUM - JACQUES FAVART TROPHY (Tours, France, November 13-17, 1985)**

Men:

1. Christopher Bowman (USA)
2. Leonid Kaznakov (SOV)
3. Richard Zander (FRG)

Women:

1. Constanze Gensel (GDR)
2. Cornelia Tesch (FRG)
3. Debbie Walls (USA)

Pairs:

1. Elena Kvitchenko and Rashid Kadrykaev (SOV)
2. Kristin Kriwanek and Doug Williams (USA)
3. Isabelle Kourie and Guy Trudeau (CAN)

Ice Dance:

1. Svetlana Liapina and Gorsha Sur (SOV)
2. Karen Knieriem and Leif Erickson (USA)
3. Jo-Anne Borlase and Scott Chalmers (CAN)

# Fall and Spring Competitions

**1985 GOLDEN SPIN OF ZAGREB (Zagreb, Yugoslavia, November 20-24, 1985)**

Men:

1. Heiko Fischer (FRG)
2. John Filbig (USA)
3. Nils Köpp (GDR)

Women:

1. Constanze Gensel (GDR)
2. Manuela Tschupp (SUI)
3. Heike Gobbers (FRG)

Ice Dance:

1. Antonia and Ferdinand Becherer (FRG)
2. Pronkina and Igor Shpilband (SOV)
3. April Sargent and John D'Amelio (USA)

**1985 POKAL DER BLAUEN SCHWERTER (Karl-Marx-Stadt, East Germany, November 20-24, 1985)**

Men:

1. Vladimir Petrenko (SOV)
2. Rudy Galindo (USA)
3. Yuri Tsimbaliuk (SOV)

Women:

1. Natalia Gorbenko (SOV)
2. Inga Gauter (GDR)
3. Cornelia Renner (FRG)

Pairs:

1. Antje Schramm and Jens Müller (GDR)
2. Mandy Hannebauer and Marno Kreft (GDR)
3. Ekaterina Murugova and Artem Torgashev (SOV)

**1985 GRAND PRIZE SNP (Banská Bystrica, Czechoslovakia, November 21-24, 1985)**

Men:

1. Roman Koudriatsev (SOV)
2. Pavel Tchernoussov (SOV)
3. Jaroslav Suchý (CZE)

Women:

1. Jana Petrusková (CZE)
2. Iveta Voralová (CZE)
3. Patricia Firth (FRG)

Pairs:

1. Elena Leonova and Gennadi Krasnitski (SOV)
2. Fleur Armstrong and Mark Edney (AUS)

Ice Dance:

1. Corinne Paliard and Didier Courtois (FRA)
2. Dominique Yvon and Frédéric Palluel (FRA)
3. Michela Malingambi and Andrea Gilardi (ITA)

**1985 NHK TROPHY (Kobe, Japan, November 21-24, 1985)**

Men:

1. Brian Boitano (USA)
2. Brian Orser (CAN)
3. Viktor Petrenko (SOV)

Women:

1. Midori Ito (JPN)
2. Cynthia Coull (CAN)
3. Juri Ozawa (JPN)

Pairs:

1. Gillian Wachsman and Todd Waggoner (USA)
2. Veronika Pershina and Marat Akbarov (SOV)
3. Denise Benning and Lyndon Johnston (CAN)

Ice Dance:

1. Marina Klimova and Sergei Ponomarenko (SOV)
2. Karyn and Rod Garossino (CAN)
3. Sharon Jones and Paul Askham (GRB)

**1985 TSK-PIRUETTEN (Trondheim, Norway, December 1985)**

Men:

1. Alessandro Riccitelli (ITA)
2. Thomas Hlavik (AUT)
3. Emanuele Ancorini (SWE)

Women:

1. Katrien Pauwels (BEL)
2. Sabine Paal (AUT)
3. Jayne Taylor (GRB)

**1985 PRIZE OF MOSCOW NEWS (Moscow, Soviet Union, December 4-8, 1985)**

Men:

1. Alexandr Fadeev (SOV)
2. Vladimir Kotin (SOV)
3. Vitali Egorov (SOV)

Women:

1. Caryn Kadavy (USA)
2. Anna Kondrashova (SOV)
3. Natalia Lebedeva (SOV)

Pairs:

1. Larisa Selezneva and Oleg Makarov (SOV)
2. Veronika Pershina and Marat Akbarov (SOV)
3. Elena Bechke and Valeri Kornienko (SOV)

Ice Dance:

1. Natalia Bestemianova and Andrei Bukin (SOV)
2. Marina Klimova and Sergei Ponomarenko (SOV)
3. Natalia Annenko and Genrikh Sretenski (SOV)

**1986 NORDISKA MÄSTERSKAPEN (Turku, Finland, February 21-23, 1986)**

Men:

1. Lars Åkesson (SWE)
2. Peter Johansson (SWE)
3. Henrik Walentin (DEN)

Women:

1. Lotta Falkenbäck (SWE)
2. Elise Ahohen (FIN)
3. Elina Hänninen (FIN)

**1986 MERANO SPRING TROPHY (Merano, Italy, March 28-30, 1986)**

Women:

1. Tonia Kwiatkowski (USA)
2. Shannon Allison (CAN)
3. Cornelia Renner (FRG)

**1986 CANADIAN PRECISION TEAM CHAMPIONSHIPS (Vancouver, BC, March 28-30, 1986)**

Team:

1. Edmonton Precision Skating Team
2. Les Pirouettes
3. The First Edition

Other Winners:

Whitby Ice Crystals (junior)
Whitby Ice Angels (novice)

**1986 MORZINE AVORIAZ (Morzine, France, April 3-5, 1986)**

Ice Dance:

1. Maya Usova and Alexandr Zhulin (SOV)
2. Renée Roca and Donald Adair (USA)
3. Isabella Micheli and Roberto Pelizzola (ITA)

**1986 U.S. PRECISION TEAM CHAMPIONSHIPS (Boston, MA, April 11-12, 1986)**

Team:

1. Hot Fudge Sundaes
2. Haydenettes
3. Detroit Capets

Other Winners:

The Figurettes (junior)
Hot Fudge Sundaes (novice)
Acton-Ups (adult)

# National Competitions

**SENIOR NATIONAL CHAMPIONS BY COUNTRY**

**Men**

AUS - Cameron Medhurst
AUT - Thomas Hlavik
BUL - Boyko Aleksiev
CHN – Shubin Zhang
CZE - Jozef Sabovčík
DEN - Lars Dresler
FIN - Oula Jääskeläinen
FRA - Laurent Depouilly
FRG - Heiko Fischer
GDR - Falko Kirsten
GRB - Stephen Pickavance
HOL - Alcuin Schulten
HUN - András Száraz
ITA - Alessandro Riccitelli
JPN - Masaru Ogawa
NZL - Christopher Blong
POL - Grzegorz Filipowski
ROM – Cornel Gheorghe
SAF - Rick Simons
SOV - Alexandr Fadeev
SUI - Oliver Höner
SWE - Lars Åkesson

**Women**

AUS - Tracy-Lee Brook
AUT - Sabine Paal
BUL - Biliana Vladimirova
CHN – Fu Chai Shu
CZE - Gabriela Ballová
DEN - Tina Hegner
FIN - Elina Hänninen
FRA - Agnès Gosselin
FRG - Claudia Leistner
GDR - Katarina Witt
GRB - Joanne Conway
HOL - Li Scha Wang
HUN - Tamara Téglássy
ITA - Beatrice Gelmini
JPN - Midori Ito
KOR - Sung-jin Byun
NOR - Anita Thorenfeldt
NZL - Carey Shepherd
POL - Mirella Gawłowska
SOV - Anna Kondrashova
SUI - Claudia Villiger
SWE - Lotta Falkenbäck

**Pairs**

AUS - Danielle and Stephen Carr
CHN - Mei Zhibin and Li Wei
CZE - Lenka Knapová and René Novotný
FRA - Sylvie Vaquero and Didier Manaud
FRG - Kerstin Kiminus and Stefan Pfrengle
GDR - Katrin Kanitz and Tobias Schröter
GRB - Cheryl Peake and Andrew Naylor
ITA - Isabella Micheli and Roberto Pelizzola
POL - Iwona Oliwa and Piotr Szczerbowski
SOV - Elena Valova and Oleg Vasiliev

**Ice Dance**

AUS - Monica MacDonald and Rodney Clarke
AUT - Kathrin and Christoff Beck
BUL - Hristina Boyanova and Yavor Ivanov
CHN - Liu Luyang and Zhao Xiaolei
CZE - Viera Řeháková and Ivan Havránek
FIN - Susanna Peltola and Kim Jacobson
FRA - Isabelle and Paul Duchesnay
FRG - Antonia and Ferdinand Becherer
GRB - Sharon Jones and Paul Askham
HUN - Klára Engi and Attila Tóth
ITA - Isabella Micheli and Roberto Pelizzola
JPN - Tomoko Tanaka and Hiroyuki Suzuki
NZL - Denise Borcoskie and Kelvin Nicolle
POL - Beata Kawelczyk and Tomasz Politański
SOV - Marina Klimova and Sergei Ponomarenko
SUI - Claudia and Daniel Schmidlin

*Tomoko Tanaka and Hiroyuki Suzuki. Photo courtesy Elaine Hooper / St. Ivel Figure Skating Archive.*

# Personalities

**PERSONALITIES**

*JAIMEE EGGLETON*

Date of Birth: June 26, 1964
Place of Birth: Montreal, QC
Coach: Doug Leigh, Louise Séguin
Choreographer: Uschi Keszler
Home Club: CPA St. Bruno

*GILLIAN WACHSMAN AND TODD WAGGONER*

Date of Birth: September 19, 1966
Place of Birth: Riverside, CT/ Arlington Heights, IL
Coach: Pauline Williams Daw
Home Club: SC of Wilmington/ DuPage FSC

*JILL WATSON AND PETER OPPEGARD*

Date of Birth: March 29, 1963/August 23, 1959
Place of Birth: Bloomington, IN/ Knoxville, TN
Coach: Rita Lowery, Louis Stong
Choreographer: Rita Lowery
Home Club: Los Angeles FSC

*DENISE BENNING AND LYNDON JOHNSTON*

Date of Birth: September 1, 1967/ December 4, 1961
Place of Birth: Windsor, ON/ Hamiota, MB
Coach: Kerry Leitch, Mark Rowsom
Choreographer: John Briscoe
Home Club: South Windsor FSC// Hamiota FSC

*NATALIE AND WAYNE SEYBOLD*

Date of Birth: September 18, 1965/ September 5, 1963
Place of Birth: Orlando, FL
Coach: Ron Ludington
Choreographer: Jill Cosgrove, Lea Ann Miller, Bill Fauver
Home Club: University of Delaware FSC

*MARINA KLIMOVA AND SERGEI PONOMARENKO*

Date of Birth: July 28, 1966/October 6, 1960
Place of Birth: Sverdlovsk, Soviet Union/Balkhash, Soviet Union
Coach: Natalia Dubova, Tatiana Tarasova
Choreographer: Elena Kholina, Elena Matveeva, Natalia Dubova
Home Club: Spartak Moscow

## Professional Competitions

**1985 PRO-SKATE SUN CITY**
(Bophuthatswana, South Africa, July 1985)

Men:

1. Scott Hamilton (USA)
2. Toller Cranston (CAN)
3. Norbert Schramm (FRG)

Women:

1. Lynn Nightingale (USA)
2. Kay Thomson (CAN)
3. Elaine Zayak (USA)

Pairs:

1. Candy Jones and Don Fraser (CAN)
2. Almut Lehmann and Herbert Weisinger (FRG)
3. Lisa Carey and Chris Harrison (USA)

Ice Dance:

1. Carol Fox and Richard Dalley (USA)
2. Lorna Wighton and John Dowding (CAN)
3. Susan Jorgenson and Robert Yokabaskas (USA)

**1985 PROFESSIONAL FIGURE SKATING'S WORLD CHALLENGE OF CHAMPIONS**
(Paris, France, December 1985)

Men:

1. Robin Cousins (GRB)
2. Scott Hamilton (USA)
3. Toller Cranston (CAN)
4. Norbert Schramm (FRG)

Women:

1. Dorothy Hamill (USA)
2. Linda Fratianne (USA)
3. Denise Biellmann (SUI)
4. Rosalynn Sumners (USA)

Pairs:

1. Kitty and Peter Carruthers (USA)
2. Barbara Underhill and Paul Martini (CAN)
3. Ludmila and Oleg Protopopov (SOV)
4. Tai Babilonia and Randy Gardner (USA)

## Shows and Tours

*Torvill and Dean: The World Tour* opened at Wembley Ice Arena in London in the summer. The second show, a charity benefit for Help the Hospices, was attended by Princess Diana. Despite mixed reviews and complaints about high ticket prices, the Wembley show drew capacity crowds for seven weeks in the summer. The Wembley shows were followed by a series of performances in The Forrest in Nottingham in the fall, performed under a custom-designed blue tent the size of a football field that was made in New Zealand at a cost of 1 000 000 pounds. In Nottingham, Torvill and Dean were presented with a very unique gift indeed - a rose named after them, created by rose growers in Cheshire. In the spring, the tour weaved its way through Canada and the United States, making its first appearance in the United States in Los Angeles, before returning to Australia for shows in Hobart and Perth. Graeme Murphy of the Sydney Dance Company choreographed and directed the tour in collaboration with Torvill and Dean, with World Champion Courtney Jones (who created the costumes for *Bolero*) designing the costumes. The cast included Gia Guddat, Karen Barber, Lea Ann Miller and Bill Fauver, Shaun McGill, Lilian Heming and Murray Carey, Kelly Johnson and John Thomas and an ensemble of aerial artists. Gary Beacom starred as The Devil in the controversial *Hell* number.

Scott Hamilton, Robin Cousins, Rosalynn Sumners, Barbara Underhill and Paul Martini, Kitty and Peter Carruthers, Toller Cranston, Charlie Tickner, Judy Blumberg and Michael Seibert, Debi Thomas, David Santee and Ron Shaver were among the stars in Sun Valley's summer ice shows. It was in the 80s that the summer shows in Sun Valley started consistently featuring A-list professional skaters. Over two dozen Olympic Medallists and World Champions performed in Sun Valley over the decade.

Robin Cousins' *Ice Majesty* tour was cancelled after four shows at the Hippodrome in Bristol after The Musicians' Union caused a stink over the alleged unauthorized use of recorded music by 150 different artists in the show. The Union insisted that the show should use "live music - provided by its members." The show's cast included Cousins, Allen Schramm, Angela Greenhow, Simone Grigorescu, Jean Yun, John S. Rait, Reggie Raiford and Garnet Ostermeier.

Cypress Gardens in Winter Haven, Florida presented *Southern Ice*, a daily show on a 12 000-square-foot rink installed in the theme park's Ice Palace. The 25-minute show, choreographed by Debbie Casanzio, featured adagio pair Carrie Buddecke and Don Yontz and a cast of skaters in crocodile costumes.

# SHOWS AND TOURS

The John Curry Skating Company returned to the Opera House at the Kennedy Center for the Performing Arts in Washington, D.C. in August for a three-week run. The cast of *The John Curry Skaters* included Curry, David Santee, Patricia Dodd, Catherine Foulkes, Nathan Birch, Editha Dotson, Mark Hominuke and Shaun McGill. Highlights of the show were Curry's trademark *Afternoon of a Faun* and a brilliant avant-garde piece *Burn* set to music by Jean-Michel Jarre. Choreographed by Laura Dean, *Burn* was first performed in Vancouver in the fall of 1983. Curry also debuted two new ensemble pieces (*Skating Class* and *Six Debussy Pieces*) and a duet with Dodd called *Remember Me*. On the show's opening night, one of the skater's blades cut through one of the plastic pipes in the ice and green cooling liquid came up from the ice in a fountain during Curry and Dodd's duet and the show was delayed until the problem was fixed. During the show's run, the Opera House threw an ice skating and ice cream party, where 45 gallons of ice cream was served to guests and the show's crew took to the ice to skate with the cast.

In England, the *Hot Ice* show at Blackpool Pleasure Beach's Ice-Drome celebrated its Golden Jubilee with a tribute to Doctor Who, starring Leslie Robinson, Linda Dean and Karen Wood. A world away in Japan, the popular *Viva! Ice World* show, later renamed *Prince Ice World*, expanded from Tokyo to other cities, including Kyoto, Sapporo, Fukuoka and Nagoya.

The long-running *Evening with Champions* show at Harvard University's Bright Arena continued to raise much-needed capital for the Jimmy Fund. The 1985 show brought 80s pop music to the fore. Scott Williams performed to Prince's "Purple Rain", while Suzanne Semanick and Scott Gregory skated to "We Are The World" wearing USA/Africa t-shirts over their costumes.

Dorothy Hamill, Tai Babilonia and Randy Gardner toured with Willy Bietak's Broadway-style theatre ice show *Festival on Ice*. Babilonia and Randy Gardner also took to the ice in *City Lites*, a multi-million dollar show at Trump's Castle Hotel & Casino. The production featured performances by acrobats, comedians, singers, showgirls and a skating ensemble. In the 80s, Bietak also staged ice shows at Knott's Berry Farm, Busch Gardens, King's Island and Great America.

Igor Bobrin's *Theater of Ice Miniatures* gave its debut performance in Chelyabinsk in April. The ice theatre's first production *The Silent Movies* was a futuristic take on Charlie Chaplin's silent pictures with choreography by Elena Valova and Oleg Vasiliev's Leningrad-based choreographer Natalia Volkova. The troupe's first members included Irina Vorobieva and Igor Lisovsky, Natalia Karamysheva and Rostislav Sinitsyn and Elena Vasyukova. At the time of the show's debut, Bobrin was studying at the State Institute of Dramatic Art.

# SHOWS AND TOURS

13 000 spectators showed up to see *Ice Classics* in California in April. Peggy Fleming, Charlie Tickner, Debi Thomas and Brian Boitano performed to the music of Johann Strauss, Aaron Copeland, Igor Stravinsky and Leonard Bernstein, performed live by the 87-member Oakland Symphony. The production was choreographed by Karen Kresge and Wanda Guntert and directed by Don Laws.

Nicky Slater organized the *Skate Electric Sport Aid Gala* at the National Exhibition Center in Marston Green in May to raise funds for famine relief in Africa. The show, a joint effort between Bob Geldof's Band Aid Trust and UNICEF, was telecast worldwide, featuring a star-studded cast including Jayne Torvill and Christopher Dean, Robin Cousins, Toller Cranston, Barbara Underhill and Paul Martini, Tai Babilonia and Randy Gardner, Scott Hamilton, Elaine Zayak and Kitty and Peter Carruthers. 750 000 dollars was raised. A second Sport Aid event, *Skate with the Stars: The Race Against Time* in Edmonton, brought together top Canadian skaters and NHL hockey players.

*Brian Boitano. Contributor: Robert Clay / Alamy Stock Photo.*

*Elizabeth Manley. Photo courtesy Elaine Hooper / St. Ivel Figure Skating Archive.*

*Vladimir Kotin. Photo courtesy Elaine Hooper / St. Ivel Figure Skating Archive.*

# MAJOR COMPETITIONS

**World Junior Championships.** Talented young skaters from all around the world flocked to the Zetra Ice Rink in Sarajevo, Yugoslavia in December to compete in the World Junior Championships. Almost all the skaters took to the ice to compete on Friday the 13th, an unlucky omen that seemed amplified by the events that transpired before and during the competition. The long and stressful journeys many skaters, coaches and officials took to get to the site of the 1984 Olympics were unfortunate. Heavy fog meant that almost everybody had to travel by train from Belgrade or Zagreb. The trains didn't have restaurant cars. The Americans flew on a red-eye from Copenhagen only to get stuck in Belgrade for several hours waiting for the train. When they got on, they found themselves surrounded by drunk people puking their guts up everywhere. The Australians had it even worse. The team had all been in Banská Bystrica, Czechoslovakia competing in an international junior event. They had received a Telex invitation to participate in a similar event in Poland but when they got to the border, the guards pulled them all off the train and told them they had to go back to Ostrava. In the hullabaloo, Tracy-Lee Brook's skates disappeared. The skaters slept on benches while they waited five hours to go back to Ostrava. After receiving their visas, they made it to Poland, where Brook managed to get a new pair of skates. While breaking them in, she fell and sprained her ankle. Bad weather forced the Aussies to take a six-hour train ride to Warsaw where they boarded a Lufthansa flight to Vienna via Frankfurt. After boarding their flight in Austria, their plane was met on the runway by fire trucks because the brakes were on fire. They deplaned and took two more train trips before arriving in Sarajevo. Odesa teenagers Elena Krykanova and Evgeni Platov dominated the ice dance event in Sarajevo from start to finish, easily defeating their teammates Svetlana Serkeli and Andrei Zharkov and the French duo of Corinne Paliard and Didier Courtois. It was Krykanova and Platov's third consecutive win at the World Junior Championships - a feat that has not been repeated to this day in dance. Canada was well-represented by Melanie Cole and Martin Smith and Catherine Pal and Donald Godfrey, who placed fourth and seventh. The unfortunate fact about the dance event in Sarajevo was that the stands of the Zetra Ice Rink were practically empty and those who did show up had the awkward habit of loudly clapping to encourage a skater when they fell. The young athletes, many not used to dealing with audiences period, were quite thrown off by it. Sessions with the Canadian team's physiotherapist allowed Australia's Tracy Lee Brook to compete in the women's event. However, a heavily wrapped foot coupled with a brand-new pair of skates put her down in 23rd in the figures, taking her completely out of the running. The figures were won by 16-year-old Jana Sjodin of St. Paul, Minnesota who trained at the Broadmoor with Carlo and Christa Fassi. West Germany's Susanne Becher won the short program over East Germany's Inga Gauter and Natalia Gorbenko of the Soviet Union. A 15th place finish in the short took Jana Sjodin out of the running for the title. During the short program, the Belgian judge was noticeably ill and struggled to keep up with his duties. After the event, it was finally realized that he was having a heart attack. He was taken to the hospital and replaced by substitute judge Therese Maisel of France in the free skate. Linda Florkevich, a 17-year-old who trained at the North Shore Winter Club in North Vancouver, aspired to be the next Elizabeth Manley. It showed in her plucky *Oklahoma!* free skate which featured three clean triples - two toe-loops and a Salchow. However, Gorbenko had the edge on difficulty, landing a triple loop, Salchow and toe-loop to take the win. Becher held on to the silver despite placing only fourth in the free.

**1985 WORLD JUNIOR CHAMPIONSHIPS** (Sarajevo, Yugoslavia, December 9-14, 1985)

Men:

1. Vladimir Petrenko (SOV)
2. Rudy Galindo (USA)
3. Yuri Tsimbaliuk (SOV)
4. Michael Shmerkin (SOV)
5. Todd Eldredge (USA)
6. Sean Abram (AUS)
7. Jaroslav Suchý (CZE)
8. Sung-il Jung (KOR)
9. Jochen Dachtler (FRG)
10. Tomoaki Koyama (JPN)

Women:

1. Natalia Gorbenko (SOV)
2. Susanne Becher (FRG)
3. Linda Florkevich (CAN)
4. Inga Gauter (GDR)
5. Mari Asanuma (JPN)
6. Natalia Skrabnevskaya (SOV)
7. Gina Fulton (GRB)
8. Holly Cook (USA)
9. Masako Kawai (JPN)
10. Ekaterina Denisenko (SOV)

Pairs:

1. Elena Leonova and Gennadi Krasnitski (SOV)
2. Irina Mironenko and Dmtri Shkidchenko (SOV)
3. Ekaterina Murugova and Artem Torgashev (SOV)
4. Mandy Hannebauer and Marno Kreft (GDR)
5. Kristi Yamaguchi and Rudy Galindo (USA)
6. Ginger and Archie Tse (USA)
7. Isabelle Brasseur and Pascal Courchesne (CAN)
8. Laura and James Ivanich (CAN)
9. Penny Schultz and Scott Grover (CAN)
10. Fleur Armstrong and Mark Edney (AUS)

Ice Dance:

1. Elena Krykanova and Evgeni Platov (SOV)
2. Svetlana Serkeli and Andrei Zharkov (SOV)
3. Corinne Paliard and Didier Courtois (FRA)
4. Melanie Cole and Martin Smith (CAN)
5. Dominique Yvon and Frédéric Palluel (FRA)
6. Michela Malingambi and Andrea Gilardi (ITA)
7. Catherine Pal and Donald Godfrey (CAN)
8. Anna Croci and Luca Mantovani (ITA)
9. Andrea Juklová and Martin Šimeček (CZE)
10. Jennifer and Jeffrey Benz (USA)

**1985 WORLD PROFESSIONAL CHAMPIONSHIPS** (Landover, MD, December 1985)

Men:

1. Robin Cousins (GRB)
2. Scott Hamilton (USA)
3. Norbert Schramm (FRG)
4. Toller Cranston (CAN)

Florkevich's bronze was the first women's medal at the World Junior Championships since Manley's in 1982. Canada's second entry, Diane Takeuchi, placed 14th. Dnipropetrovsk's Irina Mironenko and Dmitri Shkidchenko took the lead in the pairs short program, although their own judge had them third behind the other two Soviet couples. In the free skate, Mironenko and Shkidchenko dropped to second while 12-year-old Elena Leonova and 17-year-old Gennadi Krasnitski moved up from third to claim the gold with a technically difficult free skate to *My Fair Lady*. The bronze went to 12-year-old Ekaterina Murugova and 16-year-old Artem Torgashev. Both Leonova and Krasnitski and Murugova and Torgashev attempted side-by-side triple jumps in the free skate. Canada's three pairs, Isabelle Brasseur and Pascal Courchesne, Laura and James Ivanich and Penny Schultz and Scott Grover, were seventh, eighth and ninth. Sandwiched between them were a third Canadian pair, Laura and James Ivanich from Vancouver, who had Yugoslavian roots. In the men's event, the figures were won by Soviet skater Vladimir Petrenko. The men, like the women, were required to include a double loop in their combination jump in the short program. Rudy Galindo did a double loop/triple toe-loop combination and Vladimir Petrenko played it safer, doing the triple toe-loop as the first jump. Despite this - and the fact he finished after his music - he still earned first-place ordinals from seven of the nine judges, enough for first. Petrenko won the free and the gold with a less-than-stellar performance. He managed to stay upright throughout but had problems with the landings of his triple Lutz, flip and Salchow. Galindo placed third in the free and second overall with a five-triple free skate. Second in the free but fourth overall due to a poor showing in the figures was Michael Shmerkin, then 15 years old, living in Kharkiv and representing the Soviet Union. Michael landed five triples of his own, including a triple Salchow/triple toe-loop, but fell on a double Axel. Yuriy Tsymbalyuk took the bronze despite landing only one clean triple jump. Canada's two men, Brent Frank and Cory Watson, placed 12th and 16th. The Canadian Press misidentified Brent Frank as 'Frank Bent'. South Korean skater Jung Sung-il surprised many by showing off his triple Lutz and placed sixth. It was the first top-ten finish by a South Korean man in the event's history. Another interesting little piece of history about this event is the fact that Rudy Galindo added himself to the record books as only the fourth skater in history to compete in more than one discipline at the World Junior Championships. The first was Canada's Lorri Baier, who competed in singles and pairs in 1978. The second was Australia's Stephen Carr, who competed in singles and pairs in 1983. The third was Jerod Swallow, who competed in pairs and dance in 1985 - with different partners. When the event was over, several skaters skipped the exhibitions and closing banquet to try to get on trains before the fog set in. Those who waited to fly out on Monday morning found their flights were cancelled. They were forced to leave the city by train.

**World Professional Championships.** In December, some of the best professionals in the business were in Landover vying for top honours at the World Professional Championships. The total kitty was 210 000 thousand dollars, in addition to hefty appearance fees. When the event was first held five years prior, many top pros were reluctant to participate as they were worried their reputations would be sullied if they lost, so a team format was used. By 1985, the competition's prestige was well-established and so the team format was incorporated into the competition for the last time. The judging panel was composed of David Jenkins, Ája Zanová, Bernie Ford, Carol Heiss Jenkins, Norman Fuller, Maria Jelinek and Hayes Alan Jenkins. The judges were generous, awarding no mark lower than a 9.6.

**WORLD PROFESSIONAL CHAMPIONSHIPS (continued)**

Women:

1. Dorothy Hamill (USA)
2. Linda Fratianne (USA)
3. Rosalynn Sumners (USA)
4. Elaine Zayak (USA)

Pairs:

1(t). Tai Babilonia and Randy Gardner (USA)
1(t). Ludmila and Oleg Protopopov (SOV)
3. Barbara Underhill and Paul Martini (CAN)
4. Kitty and Peter Carruthers (USA)

Ice Dance:

1. Jayne Torvill and Christopher Dean (GRB)
2. Judy Blumberg and Michael Seibert (USA)

Team:

1. All Stars: Robin Cousins, Toller Cranston, Dorothy Hamill, Linda Fratianne, Ludmila and Oleg Protopopov, Tai Babilonia and Randy Gardner, Judy Blumberg and Michael Seibert
2. Pro Stars: Scott Hamilton, Norbert Schramm, Rosalynn Sumners, Elaine Zayak, Barbara Underhill and Paul Martini, Kitty and Peter Carruthers, Jayne Torvill and Christopher Dean

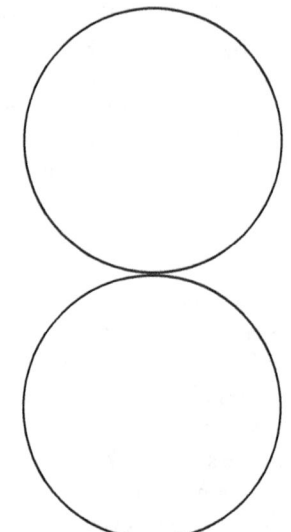

The big winners were the *All-Stars* team, consisting of Robin Cousins, Toller Cranston, Dorothy Hamill, Linda Fratianne, Ludmila and Oleg Protopopov, Tai Babilonia and Randy Gardner and Judy Blumberg and Michael Seibert. Cousins, Hamill and Jayne Torvill and Christopher Dean took top honours in singles and ice dance. Outstanding performances in the pairs event resulted in a surprising result, with the Protopopovs and Babilonia and Gardiner finishing in a tie for first, ahead of Barbara Underhill and Paul Martini and Kitty and Peter Carruthers. Though third, Underhill and Martini made history in Landover as the first Canadian pair to successfully perform a throw triple jump in a professional competition. Two highlights in the competition were Robin Cousins' positively delightful and cleverly choreographed program to Larry Clinton's "Satan Takes a Holiday" and Torvill and Dean's cheeky burlesque to Janko Nilovic's "Diabolo Tango", which earned perfect 10.0s from six of the seven judges. Scott Hamilton received the coveted Professional of the Year Award, presented by *American Skating World*. In December, many of the same skaters also travelled to Paris to compete in the World Professional Championships' brand-new sister event, the World Challenge of Champions.

**European Championships.** In late January and early February, 103 skaters representing 20 countries competed at the European Championships at the Brøndbyhallen in Copenhagen, Denmark, which had last hosted the Europeans in 1975. In the pairs event, Larisa Selezneva and Oleg Makarov were initially slated to compete, but they did not show up because Makarov was suffering from a groin injury. The Soviet federation had both Selezneva and Makarov and Veronika Pershina and Marat Akbarov listed as entries, but never bothered to update the list, causing much confusion among the press. Elena Valova and Oleg Vasiliev won the short program despite a fall from Vasiliev. The British, Czechoslovakian and Hungarian judges placed Valova and Vasiliev behind their young teammates, Ekaterina Gordeeva and Sergei Grinkov. In the free skate, Valova and Vasiliev delivered a very strong program, though Valova missed the side-by-side double Axel. The World Champions retained their title with four marks of 5.9 for artistic impression, but the Soviet, Czechoslovakian and West German judges had them behind Gordeeva and Grinkov, who took the silver ahead of Elena Bechke and Valeri Kornienko. It was the second year in a row that Soviet pairs swept the podium at Europeans. In the ice dance event, many were surprised when Marina Klimova and Sergei Ponomarenko defeated the winners of the compulsories, World Champions Natalia Bestemianova, in a five-four split in the Polka OSP. Though Bestemianova was suffering from a knee injury, 'B and B' rebounded to successfully defend their European title in the free dance, defeating Klimova and Ponomarenko with first-place marks from all but the British judge. They earned perfect 6.0s for artistic impression from the Bulgarian, French, Italian and Soviet judges. Natalia Annenko and Genrikh Sretenski won the bronze in the first Soviet medal sweep in ice dance at Europeans in a decade. In their first trip to Europeans, Isabelle and Paul Duchesnay were told by the FFSG that they needed to place in the top eight in order to continue receiving funding. They finished eighth and the audience booed the low marks their Gyspy folk free dance received. One of the most heartwarming stories was the top-ten finish of Czechoslovakian ice dancers Viera Řeháková and Ivan Havránek. Řeháková was the proud mother of a 4-month-old baby and had precious little training time before the competition.

**1986 EUROPEAN CHAMPIONSHIPS**
(Copenhagen, Denmark, January 27-February 1, 1986)

Men:

1. Jozef Sabovčík (CZE)
2. Vladimir Kotin (SOV)
3. Alexandr Fadeev (SOV)
4. Viktor Petrenko (SOV)
5. Grzegorz Filipowski (POL)
6. Falko Kirsten (GDR)
7. Petr Barna (CZE)
8. Laurent Depouilly (FRA)
9. Richard Zander (FRG)
10. Lars Åkesson (SWE)

Women:

1. Katarina Witt (GDR)
2. Kira Ivanova (SOV)
3. Anna Kondrashova (SOV)
4. Natalia Lebedeva (SOV)
5. Claudia Leistner (FRG)
6. Claudia Villiger (SUI)
7. Susan Jackson (GRB)
8. Constanze Gensel (GDR)
9. Agnès Gosselin (FRA)
10. Susanne Becher (FRG)

Pairs:

1. Elena Valova and Oleg Vasiliev (SOV)
2. Ekaterina Gordeeva and Sergei Grinkov (SOV)
3. Elena Bechke and Valeri Kornienko (SOV)
4. Katrin Kanitz and Tobias Schröter (GDR)
5. Manuela Landgraf and Ingo Steuer (GDR)
6. Lenka Knapová and René Novotný (CZE)
7. Marianne Ocvirek and Holger Maletz (FRG)
8. Sylvie Vacquero and Didier Manaud (FRA)
9. Kerstin Kimminus and Stefan Pfrengle (FRG)
10. Cheryl Peake and Andrew Naylor (GRB)

Ice Dance:

1. Natalia Bestemianova and Andrei Bukin (SOV)
2. Marina Klimova and Sergei Ponomarenko (SOV)
3. Natalia Annenko and Genrikh Sretenski (SOV)
4. Kathrin and Christoff Beck (AUT)
5. Antonia and Ferdinand Becherer (FRG)
6. Klára Engi and Attila Tóth (HUN)
7. Isabella Micheli and Roberto Pelizzola (ITA)
8. Isabelle and Paul Duchesnay (FRA)
9. Sharon Jones and Paul Askham (GRB)
10. Viera Řeháková and Ivan Havránek (CZE)

Kira Ivanova dominated in the women's compulsory figures, soundly defeating Katarina Witt, Claudia Leistner, Anna Kondrashova and Natalia Lebedeva. A group of children shouting during one of the competitor's figures were kicked out of the rink for causing a disturbance. In the short program, Witt erred on the landing of a double loop in her combination and Kondrashova and Ivanova took the top two spots. In the free skate, almost all the contenders did not skate up to their full potential. Ivanova fell on a triple Salchow, while Witt stepped out of a triple toe-loop and doubled a planned triple Salchow. When the marks were tallied, Witt's effort was enough to move up and overtake Ivanova. Kondrashova won the bronze, ahead of Lebedeva and Leistner. Though Witt was not at her best in Copenhagen, she was debuting a brand-new program and suffering from bursitis, which necessitated her wearing special padding in her right boot. In the men's event, Jozef Sabovčík won the compulsory figures in a close contest with World Champion Alexandr Fadeev. In the short program, Fadeev two-footed the double loop in his combination jump to place third. Sabovčík defeated Vladimir Kotin in a five-four split of the judging panel. Both men successfully landed triple Lutz combinations. West Germany's Heiko Fischer, who was third in the figures and fourth in the short, withdrew after pulling a groin muscle in the warm-up for the men's free skate. Kotin and Fadeev both landed five triples in their programs but were forced to settle for silver and bronze behind Sabovčík, who went for broke attempting a quadruple toe-loop and successfully defended the title he'd won in Fadeev's absence the year prior. Many believed that Sabovčík had successfully landed the quad because the referee of the event, Elemér Terták, initially confirmed that the attempt was successful. After the event, officials reviewed videotape footage and changed their minds. There was considerable controversy over this ruling, both at the time and well after the fact. The fact remained that the attempt itself was historic. Never before had a skater stayed on their feet when attempting to rotate four times in the air in an ISU Championship. Far more controversial were the marks Sabovčík received for his free skate - seven firsts, one second place ordinal and a fifth from British judge Sally-Anne Stapleford. He received five 5.9s and a perfect 6.0 from the Soviet judge for technical merit, though he botched a triple Lutz and doubled three other planned triples after the quad attempt. Sabovčík later revealed that while he was performing a spread eagle during the slow section of his program, a bandage on his right knee came undone and he spent the rest of his program deciding whether or not to stop or carry on. He had been hampered by a knee injury for three years.

**Canadian Championships.** In February, the small Northern Ontario mining city of North Bay played host to the Canadian Championships for the first time since 1964. 225 skaters participated and two rinks in were utilized for the competition - the North Bay Memorial Gardens and Doublerinks Arena. The ice was painted black at the latter rink, which was used for the compulsory figures, to allow judges a much clearer look at skater's tracings. Denise Benning, Isabelle Kourie, Lyndon Johnston and Guy Trudeau won the fours event. Eight of the ten couples entered in the pairs event trained at the Preston Figure Skating Club and were coached by Kerry Leitch. At the previous year's Nationals in Moncton, Cynthia Coull and Mark Rowsom had won the title but at the World Championships in Tokyo, they were the lowest-ranked of the three Canadian pairs. Lloyd Eisler, who won the bronze medal in Tokyo, had since broken up with partner Katherina Matousek and teamed up with Peterborough's Karen Westby, who placed fifth place in the junior women's event at Canadians in 1985. Melinda Kunhegyi and Lyndon Johnston, fifth at the Tokyo Worlds, had also broken up.

**1986 CANADIAN CHAMPIONSHIPS**
(North Bay, ON, February 2-9, 1986)

Men:

1. Brian Orser
2. Neil Paterson
3. Jaimee Eggleton
4. Kevin Parker
5. Kurt Browning
6. Mark MacVean
7. André Bourgeois
8. David Watson
9. Brad McLean
10. Rob Lenarduzzi

Women:

1. Tracey Wainman
2. Elizabeth Manley
3. Patricia Schmidt
4. Charlene Wong
5. Linda Florkevich
6. Cynthia Coull
7. Rosemarie Sakic
8. Dianne Takeuchi
9. Nathalie Sasseville
10. Lindsay Fedosoff

Pairs:

1. Cynthia Coull and Mark Rowsom
2. Denise Benning and Lyndon Johnston
3. Karen Westby and Lloyd Eisler
4. Christine Hough and Doug Ladret
5. Isabelle Brasseur and Pascal Courchesne
6. Penny Schultz and Scott Grover
7. Laurene Collin and David Howe
8. Lynda and John Ivanich
9. Barbara Martin and John Penticost
10. Isabelle Kourie and Guy Trudeau

Ice Dance:

1. Tracy Wilson and Rob McCall
2. Karyn and Rod Garossino
3. Jo-Anne Borlase and Scott Chalmers
4. Michelle McDonald and Michael Farrington
5. Penny Mann and Richard Perkins
6. Kim Hanford and Julien Lalonde
7. Erica Davenport and Mark Mitchell
8. Kimberley Weeks and Curtis Moore
9. Carolyn Drummond and Keith Baker

Fours:

1. Denise Benning, Isabelle Kourie, Lyndon Johnston and Guy Trudeau
2. Cynthia Coull, Christine Hough, Mark Rowsom and Doug Ladret
3. Barbara Martin, Karen Westby, John Penticost and Lloyd Eisler
4. Penny Schultz, Laurene Collin, Scott Grover and David Howe
5. Lynda, Laura, John and Jamie Ivanich

Johnston teamed up with 18-year-old Denise Benning only five months before the competition. North Bay Nationals. On paper, Coull and Rowsom were the favourites but Rowsom had lost twelve weeks of valuable training time heading into the event due to a groin injury and Coull arrived in North Bay with a nasty cold. In the short program, Benning and Johnston delivered a clean performance to take the lead over Westby and Eisler and Coull and Rowsom. Rebounding with a spirited, technically demanding performance, Coull and Rowsom vaulted from third to first in the free skate and earned a standing ovation from the packed audience at the Memorial Gardens. Benning and Johnston and Westby and Eisler settled for silver and bronze. In the lead-up to the men's event, there were rumours that Brian Orser would attempt a quad in his free skating performance after Jozef Sabovčík attempted one in his free skate at the European Championships only a week prior. Orser quashed the rumours but confirmed he was "playing with the quad... [and landing] it on an average of three out of ten times." Orser placed first in all three compulsory figures, ahead of Neil Paterson and Mark MacVean. It was the first time he managed to win all three figures at the Canadian Championships and only the second time he'd won that phase of the event at Canadians. Orser was brilliant in his *Hungarian Dance* short program, earning a perfect 6.0 for artistic impression and a standing ovation. Jaimee Eggleton was second best in the short program but was seventh in the figures and his result only moved him up to fifth behind Paterson, MacVean and Kevin Parker. Orser earned eleven 5.9s for his free skate to the theme from *Ladyhawke*. Though he landed five of his seven planned triples, it wasn't a perfect performance. After landing his opening triple Lutz, he tripped on the boards, stumbled and fell to his knee. Though his first triple Axel/double toe-loop combination was clean as a whistle, his second triple Axel had a faulty landing. Many were so used to seeing Orser skate clean that a couple of errors provided the typical fodder for reporters to overdramatize his mistakes. In reality, his performance was quite strong, especially compared to his rivals. Paterson, who claimed the silver, landed a triple Axel early in his program but fell or doubled most of the rest of his jumps. Bronze medallist Eggleton tried a triple Axel but landed on his stomach. Kurt Browning placed an impressive fifth in his senior debut, behind Kevin Parker, despite a back injury that required acupuncture. A disappointing free skate from MacVean dropped him out of the top five entirely. In the ice dance event, Tracy Wilson and Rob McCall were clear favourites but Wilson's acute tendinitis had forced them to withdraw from the NHK Trophy in the fall. In the compulsory dances, Wilson and McCall were outstanding, easily taking a commanding lead over their Richmond Hill training mates Karyn and Rod Garossino and Roy Bradshaw's students Jo-Anne Borlase and Scott Chalmers. The results from the compulsories remained the same in the Polka OSP, with Wilson and McCall's performance to "Shall We Dance?" from *The King and I* earning top marks. More than 4000 spectators turned up to watch the free dances. Wilson and McCall earned eleven 5.9s and three 5.8s for their difficult samba, waltz, quickstep and jive free dance choreographed by Bernie Ford, where they portrayed entrants in a ballroom dance competition. The Garossinos skated to silver with an elegant free dance to "Romeo and Juliet". Borlase and Chalmers took the bronze. In the women's compulsory figures, Elizabeth Manley won the first figure but Tracey Wainman won the second two. Although many weren't surprised by Wainman's win because of her history as a whiz in compulsories, few expected her to be able to retain her lead through the short program and free skate. The real shocker in the compulsories was Cynthia Coull. Sick with a cold and burdened with the daunting task of participating in the women's, pairs and fours events, she placed a shocking 12th out of 14 skaters and took herself out of the medal equation entirely.

**CANADIAN CHAMPIONSHIPS** (continued)

Junior Winners:

Michael Slipchuk (men)
Pamela Giangualano (women)
Melanie Gaylor and Lee Barkell (pairs)
Melanie Cole and Martin Smith (ice dance)

Novice Winners:

Darran Leaker (men)
Joelle Batten (women)
Sarah Fry and Kris Wirtz (pairs)
Kellie Lynn Bradshaw and Juan Carlos Noria (ice dance)

*Christine Hough and Doug Ladret. Photo courtesy Elaine Hooper / St. Ivel Figure Skating Archive.*

In the short program, Manley skated brilliantly, safely choosing to change a planned triple Lutz/double loop combination to a triple Salchow/double loop. However, Wainman more than held her own, working the audience into a frenzy with her sassy, upbeat program to an instrumental version of "Relax" by Frankie Goes To Hollywood. A less difficult double Axel/double loop combination kept her behind Manley in that phase of the event, but she maintained her overall lead on the strength of her figures result, ahead of Manley, Patricia Schmidt and Charlene Wong. Both Manley and Wainman skated quite well in the free skate, but several shaky landings on triple jumps kept Manley behind Wainman in a four-three split of the judging panel. Wainman's exuberant display and comeback win was a wonderful moment but the result was seen as controversial by some. Hoping to ease the pain of losing her national title, a stranger sent Manley a letter that read, "When I was a young girl in my 20's, I had a major disappointment in my life. I was in tears and my father was watching me. He quietly said to me: You must remember that life is like a streetcar. You have just missed one. Another will be along soon and you will be right there to catch it. Pressing money into my hand, he said: 'Go out and buy a new hat.' In the 40 years since that time, many hats have been bought... So now I say to you Elizabeth, go out and buy a nice hat and I enclose a small cheque so you may do so. That streetcar will be there for you, and you will catch it." Manley was deeply touched by the letter, went out and bought the hat and as we all know, eventually caught that streetcar.

**U.S. Championships.** In February, a who's who of American figure skating gathered in Uniondale on Long Island, New York for the U.S. Championships. Figures were skated at the chilly, dimly lit Newbridge Road Park rink in Hempstead and free skating events at the Nassau Veterans Memorial Coliseum. The organizers had a hard time getting sponsors and coaches were scattered in hotels throughout the area, making transportation to and from practice rinks and scheduling a challenge. One of the practice rinks, home to the Nassau High School hockey team, had paint and plaster falling from the ceiling. Attendance was comparatively poor to Nationals in years past - with less than 29 000 tickets sold over nine sessions. A snowstorm on the Friday night of the competition didn't help matters, nor did the fact that the evening sessions started so late that those travelling from New York City and Westchester County had to make their way to Long Island in rush-hour traffic. To top things off, the *Ice Capades* were playing at Madison Square Garden. Rudy Galindo made history in the junior pairs event, as the first skater of Latino heritage to win the title. With Judy Blumberg and Michael Seibert having turned professional, the senior ice dance crown was very much up for grabs. Suzanne Semanick and Scott Gregory won the first compulsory dance, the Kilian, but Gregory got cut in a rut and fell in the Starlight Waltz. With wins in the Starlight and Tango Romantica, Roca and Adair won the compulsories with first-place marks from all but one judge. Semanick and Gregory won the Polka OSP by one judge and one-tenth of a point, setting the stage for a dramatic showdown in the free dance. Hoping for an edge with the judges, Roca and Adair had reworked their *Valentino* program just before Nationals, adding brief Charleston and Tango sections to liven up a program that had been critiqued as overly dramatic. Semanick and Gregory took theatre and mask classes to up the expression in their lively Russian-inspired program, set to music specially composed for them by the Delaware Symphony Orchestra. In a five-four split of the judging panel, Roca and Adair took the gold. The bronze went to crowd favourites Lois Luciani and Russ Witherby. In winning, Roca made history as the first skater of Latin American ancestry to win the U.S. senior ice dance title. Her father, an ophthalmologist, was born in Cuba.

**1986 U.S. CHAMPIONSHIPS (Uniondale, NY, February 4-9, 1986)**

Men:

1. Brian Boitano
2. Scott Williams
3. Daniel Doran
4. Angelo D'Agostino
5. Paul Wylie
6. James Cygan
7. Doug Mattis
8. Craig Henderson
9. Scott Kurttila
10. Bobby Beauchamp

Women:

1. Debi Thomas
2. Caryn Kadavy
3. Tiffany Chin
4. Tracey Damigella
5. Jill Trenary
6. Tonya Harding
7. Yvonne Gómez
8. Kelly Ann Szmurlo
9. Leslie Sikes
10. Holly Cook

Pairs:

1. Gillian Wachsman and Todd Waggoner
2. Jill Watson and Peter Oppegard
3. Natalie and Wayne Seybold
4. Katy Keeley and Joseph Mero
5. Maradith Feinberg and Craig Maurizi
6. Susan and Jason Dungjen
7. Lori Blasko and Todd Sand
8. Kellee Muchison and Bob Pellaton
9. Ginger and Archie Tse
10. Kristin Kriwanek and Doug Williams

Ice Dance:

1. Renée Roca and Donald Adair
2. Suzanne Semanick and Scott Gregory
3. Lois Luciani and Russ Witherby
4. Susie Wynne and Joseph Druar
5. Kristan Lowery and Chip Rossbach
6. April Sargent and John D'Amelio
7. Karen Knieriem and Leif Erickson
8. Dorothi Rodek and Robert Nardozza
9. Jill Aleisa Heiser and Michael Verlich
10. Jodie Balogh and Jerod Swallow

Junior Winners:

Mark Mitchell (men)
Cindy Bortz (women)
Kristi Yamaguchi and Rudy Galindo (pairs)
Colette Huber and Ron Kravette (ice dance)

Novice Winners:

Cameron Birky (men)
Liane Moscato (women)

In the pairs event, Jill Watson and Peter Oppegard suffered a serious setback just two weeks before Nationals. While training in Detroit with coach Johnny Johns, Oppegard slashed Watson in the face while they were practicing a side-by-side camel spin. She suffered a broken nose and contusions under her eye and had to have stitches. Their bad luck continued in the short program with a miss on the side-by-side jumps, allowing Gillian Wachsman and Todd Waggoner, who had only been skating together for fourteen months, to move into the lead. Despite a crash into the boards early in their free skate, Wachsman and Waggoner rebounded to deliver an otherwise strong free skate and won the gold. Watson and Oppegard missed both throws and were forced to settle for silver. Wachsman and Waggoner's training mates Natalie and Wayne Seybold moved up to take the bronze, though they had several false starts to their program because their tape malfunctioned. Shelly Propson and Jerod Swallow, the only senior skater to compete in two disciplines in 1986, had a serious fall on a lift in practice. Propson was rushed to the Nassau County Medical Center in East Meadow, where it was revealed she had a slight skull fracture and the team was forced to withdraw. In the men's event, Brian Boitano arrived in Uniondale in excruciating pain, suffering from a serious case of tendinitis in his ankle. He missed practice sessions in the lead-up to the event and there was talk of him withdrawing. In the end, he opted to push through the pain and compete, winning the figures over Christopher Bowman. Boitano won the short program as well, landing a solid triple Lutz/double loop combination and earning five 5.8s for composition and style. Bowman was also injured, suffering from a bone bruise on his landing leg. The injury was the result of breaking in new skates at the Prize of Moscow News event in December. After finishing third in the short, he withdrew. He quipped to reporters, "My heart ached but my leg ached a lot harder." In the free skate, Boitano pushed through the pain with a gutsy performance that featured the only clean triple Axel of the Championships, performed in combination with a double toe-loop. Though he fell on a triple flip attempt, he still received marks ranging from 5.6 to 5.8 and managed to defend his title. Scott Williams and Daniel Doran won the silver and bronze. Despite his withdrawal, Bowman received a bye to Worlds. The rules at the time allowed an 'exemption' for any skater who finished in the top four at the previous year's Nationals and officials were impressed both by his showing in the figures (a previous weakness of his) and the fact he'd earned a 6.0 at the National Sports Festival in the summer. Ultimately, Bowman's injury didn't allow him to compete and Doran, who was originally named first alternate, got the third spot anyway. Like Boitano, Tiffany Chin was on the comeback trail after injury. Her training was limited in the lead-up to Nationals and she admitted that she lacked consistency on some of her triple jumps. Many were surprised she even planned to compete. Stanford pre-med student Debi Thomas took top honours in the compulsory figures, six judges to three, but it was Chin who won the second figure. The short program was won by Caryn Kadavy, who trained with the Fassi's in Colorado Springs. Kadavy performed a triple loop/double loop combination, while Debi Thomas did the double loop/triple toe-loop. In the free skate, Chin drew first to skate in the final group and skated surprisingly well. The ice was littered with flowers after her performance and Thomas collided with one of the flower girls before her program. Thomas' performance was outstanding. She landed two triple toe-loops, two triple Salchows and the triple loop to earn first-place marks from seven of the nine judges. Kadavy skated right after Thomas and landed her opening triple loop but almost fell on the triple toe-loop and doubled a planned triple Salchow to settle for silver over Chin. In winning the gold, Thomas made history as the first person of colour to win the U.S. senior women's title. The most remarkable fact is that she almost didn't compete out of frustration. After getting two B's and a C for chemistry in her first exams at Stanford, she tore up her entry form to the competition. After talking through it with her mother, she taped the form back up and sent it in. At the time, twice a week Thomas had what she called 'suicide days' with six and a half hours of skating after lectures and classes in the morning. Studying kept her up until three in the morning on those days. After winning in Uniondale, she told reporters, "It was the most exhilarating thing I've ever experienced in my life. I hadn't been skating worth beans all week and I amazed myself. I'm speechless... I went through a lot to get here and it feels good. This is the pot at the end of the rainbow but it was a bumpy rainbow."

**World Championships.** In March, Geneva played host to the first World Championships in Switzerland in eighteen years. Though the weather was unseasonably mild, the event was unfortunately timed in conjunction with a nine-day emergency conference of The Organization of the Petroleum Exporting Countries (OPEC) and the host Intercontinental Hotel had to be shared by the world's top figure skaters, coaches, judges, government heads of state, the press corps and armed Swiss militia. At least no one could say the security wasn't good! It was anticipated that the men's event would be a four-way battle between reigning World Champion Alexandr Fadeev, Olympic Medallists Brian Orser and Jozef Sabovčík and U.S. Champion Brian Boitano. In the first phase of the competition, Fadeev won the first two figures and Sabovčík the second to finish one-two. The oldest and tallest skater in the competition, West Germany's Heiko Fischer, finished third, ahead of Boitano and Orser. The standard in the short program was very high, with most of the competitors electing to do triple Lutz combinations. In a five-four split of the judging panel, Orser won the short ahead of Fadeev, Vladimir Kotin, Sabovčík and Boitano. The combined standings entering the free skate had Fadeev in first, ahead of Sabovčík, Orser and Boitano. In the free skate, many of the top men made uncharacteristic errors. Sabovčík, clearly in pain from his ankle injury and only competing because his federation did not believe he was injured, popped a triple Axel, fell on a triple flip and omitted the quadruple jump that had made him the talk of the town at Europeans. Orser missed both of his triple Axel attempts but skated an otherwise strong program. Fadeev fell apart, taking a fall on a triple Axel and unsuccessfully attempting a quad of his own. Boitano was clean as a whistle, landing five triples including the only clean triple Axel performed in the free skate, which he combined with a double toe-loop. Boitano received 5.8s or 5.9s from every judge for both technical merit and artistic impression. He won his first World title in a six-three split of the judges over Orser and Fadeev. Sabovčík ended the competition in sixth place. Canada's second entry, Neil Paterson, placed a discouraging 18th. Boitano's come-from-behind win was somewhat overshadowed by the shameless national bias exhibited by some of the judges. Soviet judge Tatiana Danilchenko blatantly ignored an ISU rule requiring judges to deduct 0.1 for falls, awarding Fadeev - who fell twice and missed a third jump - a 5.9 for technical merit. She was the only judge to place Fadeev first. No other judge had him higher than third and he finished fifth in the free skate. The audience booed Danilchenko's marks and before she even left Geneva, a member of the ISU Council reached out to the USSR Skating Federation's headquarters in Moscow. They were informed that the Federation had taken the unprecedented move of banning Danilchenko for two years for national bias. It was believed that the Federation made this decision so quickly in fear that all Soviet judges would be banned outright, as they had been during the 1977/1978 season. Two months after the competition at the ISU Congress in Austria, Danilchenko was given a three-year suspension. She was back in the fold at the 1992 Winter Olympic Games in Albertville, placing Paul Wylie, who won the silver medal, outside of the top three in both programs. Another Soviet judge, Ludmila Kubashevskaya, was also suspended for national bias that year. Lawrence Demmy called Danilchenko's marking of Fadeev in Geneva "one of the worst pieces of judging [he] had ever seen."

**1986 WORLD CHAMPIONSHIPS** (Geneva, Switzerland, March 17-23, 1986)

Men:

1. Brian Boitano (USA)
2. Brian Orser (CAN)
3. Alexandr Fadeev (SOV)
4. Vladimir Kotin (SOV)
5. Viktor Petrenko (SOV)
6. Jozef Sabovčík (CZE)
7. Heiko Fischer (FRG)
8. Daniel Doran (USA)
9. Scott Williams (USA)
10. Masaru Ogawa (JPN)

Women:

1. Debi Thomas (USA)
2. Katarina Witt (GDR)
3. Tiffany Chin (USA)
4. Kira Ivanova (SOV)
5. Elizabeth Manley (CAN)
6. Claudia Leistner (FRG)
7. Anna Kondrashova (SOV)
8. Caryn Kadavy (USA)
9. Tracey Wainman (CAN)
10. Natalia Lebedeva (SOV)

Pairs:

1. Ekaterina Gordeeva and Sergei Grinkov (SOV)
2. Elena Valova and Oleg Vasiliev (SOV)
3. Cynthia Coull and Mark Rowsom (CAN)
4. Larisa Selezneva and Oleg Makarov (SOV)
5. Denise Benning and Lyndon Johnston (CAN)
6. Jill Watson and Peter Oppegard (USA)
7. Gillian Wachsman and Todd Waggoner (USA)
8. Natalie and Wayne Seybold (USA)
9. Katrin Kanitz and Tobias Schröter (GDR)
10. Lenka Knapová and René Novotný (CZE)

Ice Dance:

1. Natalia Bestemianova and Andrei Bukin (SOV)
2. Marina Klimova and Sergei Ponomarenko (SOV)
3. Tracy Wilson and Rob McCall (CAN)
4. Natalia Annenko and Genrikh Sretenski (SOV)
5. Suzanne Semanick and Scott Gregory (USA)
6. Renée Roca and Donald Adair (USA)
7. Kathrin and Christoff Beck (AUT)
8. Antonia and Ferdinand Becherer (FRG)
9. Karyn and Rod Garossino (CAN)
10. Isabella Micheli and Roberto Pelizzola (ITA)

Natalia Bestemianova and Andrei Bukin, Marina Klimova and Ponomarenko and Natalia Annenko and Genrikh Sretenski earned the top three spots in the compulsory dances and many wondered if the Soviets might pull off a podium sweep. Tracy Wilson and Rob McCall finished fourth and were visibly rattled by their scores. In the second dance, eight judges had them third and West German judge Gerhard Frey placed them ninth. Wilson called out Frey, remarking, "That was a direct result of him feeling that the Canadian judge didn't mark his German pair [Antonia and Ferdinand Becherer] high enough in the first dance, so he put us ninth. Now to me, that's just like a slap in the face. I find there's no excuse for that." Klimova and Ponomarenko's clever OSP to the "Thunder & Lighting" polka by Strauss earned them a perfect 6.0 from Hungarian judge Judit Fürst. They won that phase of the competition in a five-four split over 'B and B', who scrapped their OSP after Europeans and quickly came up with a new program with Tatiana Tarasova after receiving criticisms about both their music choice and choreography. The free dance was extremely well-skated, from the top group down to the bottom. Bestemianova and Bukin won the gold with their free dance to Rachmaninoff's "Rhapsody on a Theme of Paganini", earning perfect 6.0s for artistic impression from the Soviet, French and Hungarian judges. Klimova and Ponomarenko finished second, earning a 6.0 of their own from Swiss judge Lily Klapp for their classical free dance set to the music of Strauss. Wilson and McCall rebounded after finishing fourth in the OSP to win Canada's first medal at the World Championships in ice dance in 22 years, tying Annenko and Sretenski on ordinals but defeating them seven judges to two. The judges who voted in favour of Annenko and Sretenski were from the Soviet Union and The United States. Canada's Karyn and Rod Garossino finished ninth in their second trip to Worlds, three spots ahead of the Duchesnays. Though dead last, Park Kyeung-sook and Han Seung-jong made history first South Korean ice dancers to compete at the Worlds. Fifteen teams from nine countries competed in the pairs event. In the short program, Ekaterina Gordeeva and Sergei Grinkov pulled off an upset by defeating their far more experienced rivals Elena Valova and Oleg Vasiliev. Larisa Selezneva and Oleg Makarov finished a strong third, coming back after an injury that kept them out of Europeans. In the free skate, Gordeeva and Grinkov were outstanding, executing a high triple twist, two sets of side-by-side double Axels and a throw triple Salchow. Their only error was a step out on the landing of a throw double Axel. Their marks ranged from 5.7 to 5.9. Though Valova was skating with a bandaged knee, she and Vasiliev put up a valiant fight, executing side-by-side triple toe-loops and double Axels and two different throw triple jumps. However, they visibly tired late in their program, missing a lift and making other small errors. Eight out of the nine judges had Gordeeva and Grinkov first, with the Soviet judge putting Valova and Vasiliev in a tie for second with Selezneva and Makarov, who dropped to fourth behind Canada's Cynthia Coull and Mark Rowsom. The other Canadian pair entered, Denise Benning and Lyndon Johnston, placed a very strong fifth. Viktor Rhyzkin, a coach at the Central Army Sports Club in Moscow and former partner of Lyudmila Pakhomova, later remarked that the win of 'G and G' over 'V and V' was "a sensation... in the Soviet Union. It is usual for our Olympic Champions to retire before they are beaten." In the women's event, Kira Ivanova won all three compulsory figures to take an early lead over Debi Thomas, Katarina Witt, Tiffany Chin and Tracey Wainman. Elizabeth Manley placed a disappointing 11th, seven spots ahead of Midori Ito, who felt that the fact she had to wear glasses was a hindrance during figures. The day of the short program, an article in the Swiss newspaper *Sport* quoted Jacqueline Itschner, the Swiss judge in the women's event. Itschner expressed her opinion that figures should be abolished because there was too much pressure on judges to give the best free skaters higher marks than they deserved. Itschner named specific skaters who didn't excel in figures - Witt being one. The article led to scrutiny over Itschner's second-place marks for Witt, who finished third. Thomas and Wainman had the crowd going in the short program, both choosing the same music - an instrumental version of "Relax" by Frankie Goes to Hollywood. Thomas' double loop/triple toe-loop combination gave her the lead, while Wainman's easier double Axel combination left her down in 11th place. Chin and Anna Kondrashova both skated clean short programs with triple toe-loop/double loop combinations to finish in a rare tie for second. Manley and Ito had outstanding skates of their own, gaining ground in the standings. The apple cart was knocked over when the two leaders after the figures had errors in the short program. Ivanova had to put her foot on the landing of her double Axel to keep from falling, while Witt lost control on the double loop in her triple toe-loop combination, stumbling and sliding into the boards. Entering the free skate, Thomas had enough of a lead that she could afford to finish second to Witt and still win. Only four-tenths of a point separated Ivanova, Chin and Witt. Kondrashova was a full point behind the four, having placed only sixth in the figures. In the free skate, Witt rebounded with a strong performance featuring four triples - two toe-loops and two Salchows. The East and West German judges, well aware that she was too far behind after the short to win, awarded her two 6.0s for artistic impression - the first perfect marks she ever received and the first 6.0s given to an East German skater at the Worlds since her coach Jutta Müller's daughter Gaby Seyfert received one in 1970.

Thomas skated exceptionally well, with four triples of her own, to finish second in the free and first overall. In winning, she made history as the first African American woman to win a gold medal at the World Championships - a remarkable achievement that earned international attention. Winning the bronze for the second year in a row at the Worlds was Tiffany Chin, who delivered a confident but cautious performance. Ivanova and Kondrashova were not at their best in the free skate, finishing the competition in fourth and seventh places. Manley, who was one of many skaters fighting a stomach virus that was making its rounds in Geneva, had one of the best skates of her career to finish third in the free, landing four different triple jumps including the Lutz. She ended the competition in a very strong fifth, though the popular consensus was that she should have won the free skate. Wainman was disappointed to take a fall on the only triple jump in her program but jostling in the standings, coupled with her strong showing in the figures, left her in ninth overall. Two spots behind Wainman, Ito was in a class of her own technically, landing no less than six triples, including a triple toe-loop/triple toe-loop combination. Ito finished sixth in the free skate, receiving technical merit marks as high as 5.8 from the Yugoslavian and West German judges, but only 11th overall. Taiwan made its debut at the World Championships, with the ISU following the IOC's lead and taking special measures to avoid causing issues with China. The delegation was announced as the Republic of Taipei instead of Taiwan and a special flag and anthem were created especially for the event. Taiwan's man got sick on the flight over from the United States, where he had been training, and unbeknownst to officials, a reserve skater who had not been named to the team was allowed to skate in an official practice session because the organizers thought he was the original skater. Completely unaccustomed to skating on such a large rink, the skater got muscle cramps and withdrew, leaving the women's competitor Pauline Lee as the one to make history as the first skater to represent the Chinese Taipei at the Worlds.

*Debi Thomas. Contributor: Sueddeutsche Zeitung Photo / Alamy Stock Photo. Photograph by Horstmüller/Süddeutsche Zeitung.*

# 1986-1987 SEASON

Hit Songs: "Everybody Have Fun Tonight" by Wang Chung, "Walk Like An Egyptian" by The Bangles, "Alone" by Heart, "I Wanna Dance With Somebody (Who Loves Me)" by Whitney Houston, "Livin' On A Prayer" by Bon Jovi
Hit Movies: Three Men and a Baby, Good Morning Vietnam, Moonstruck, Lethal Weapon, The Witches of Eastwick
Hit TV: The Golden Girls, Cheers, Who's The Boss?, Murder She Wrote, Matlock
News: Margaret Thatcher makes history as first British Prime Minister since 1820 to lead a party to three consecutive victories, Gestapo official Klaus Barbie sentenced in France for crimes during World War II, Iraqi attack on U.S. frigate Stark, American hostage in Lebanon killed

## PEOPLE

Veronika Pershina and Marat Akbarov and Olga Volozhinskaya and Alexandr Svinin joined Tatiana Tarasova's *Russian All-Stars*. Jozef Sabovčík underwent his third operation for his ankle injury and announced he would not compete during the 1986-1987 season. He announced that he planned to come back and compete during the Olympic season once he recovered, but he ultimately turned professional. Both he and Tracey Wainman were offered contracts with *Holiday on Ice* in South America but the couple turned down the offer and taught in Stuttgart instead as Sabovčík dealt with immigration passport issues. Also retiring from the amateur ranks were Birgit Lorenz, Isabella Micheli and Laurent Depouilly.

After winning a medal at the World Championships in Geneva in the spring, Cynthia Coull decided to give up singles and focus on pairs. In addition to competing in singles, pairs - and quite often fours, as well - Coull studied sports medicine at the University of Guelph.

Debi Thomas was named ABC Wide World of Sports Athlete of the Year in 1986. The only other figure skater to receive the honour was Peggy Fleming, in 1967. Thomas was also named McDonald's Amateur Sportswoman of the Year by the Women's Sport Foundation and the official 'spokesathlete' of the Campbell Soup Company, the title sponsor of the U.S. Championships.

In October, the Minto Skating Club announced the appointment of World Champion Donald Jackson as the Club's new Executive Director of Skating. Jackson had been living and coaching in Toronto. In his new role, he would oversee skating programs at the Ottawa club's new state-of-the-art three-rink facility. Jackson wasn't the only big-name skater given an appointment during the 1986-1987 season. Robin Cousins was hired as the new Vice-President, Head Coach and Director of the Blue Jay Ice Castle in California.

Olympic Gold Medallist and two-time World Champion Ria (Baran) Falk passed away in November at the age of 64. Ria and her husband Paul had the rare distinction of being World Champions on both ice and rollers. Baran was inducted into the World Figure Skating Hall of Fame posthumously in 1993.

The Asian-American Alliance and Chinese Cultural Association of Pierce County, Washington honoured Tiffany Chin at a reception in Tacoma during the U.S. Championships, attended by the local mayor.

Dénes Pataky passed away in Toronto in April at the age of 70. A medallist at both the European and World Championships representing Hungary in the 30s, Pataky was decorated for his military service during the Resistance in the Seige of Budapest during World War II. After a harrowing wartime experience, Pataky and his family emigrated to Canada, where he worked as a figure skating coach for many years.

In May, Tracy Wilson married Brad Kinsella, a former rugby player turned restauranteur whom she first met on a blind date after moving from British Columbia to Toronto six years prior.

The British figure skating community mourned the losses of two of its most beloved members in the spring. Just two weeks before her 21st birthday, Susan Garland was killed in a horrific car accident on the MI5, near Bristol, in April. At the time of her death, Garland had been teaching at the new ice rink in Cardiff, Wales. In June, Mildred 'Wag' Richardson passed away at the age of 93. Richardson represented Great Britain in the pairs event at the 1924 Olympics with her late husband and was an international judge, member of the Ice Skating Committee of the NSA and long-time skating correspondent for *The Observer*.

## AROUND THE WORLD

**Austria.** The WEV in Vienna celebrated its 120th anniversary the same year the ISU celebrated its 95th. Members of the WEV still performed the old Rundtanz (round dances) where six skaters performed dance steps in unison, holding hands. The history of skating was kept alive in the historic skating capital where Jackson Haines was a sensation in the Victorian era.

**Canada.** The Ontario Ministry of Education gave approval for a private academic school at the Mariposa School of Skating. Skaters could attend regular classes and receive tutoring at the school from teachers from the Simcoe County Board of Education. Members of Canada's national team received 650 dollars per month for living expenses. The CFSA covered approximately 10 000 dollars per year for training costs. ISU rules permitted each skater to earn up to 250 Swiss francs (approximately 210 dollars) per exhibition without losing their amateur status.

**Hong Kong.** Hong Kong only had one small rink with a broken Zamboni. The ice surface was flooded the old-fashioned way each day with buckets of water. To make matters worse, the rink was shared with local merchants, who used the ice for refrigeration. A Canadian coach who visited the country complained that her "biggest problem was getting the chicken coups off the ice." Aside from occasional visits from Australian and Canadian coaches, the country's skaters were entirely self-taught until 1985. The country's national champions had to pay eighteen dollars every time they practiced in a crowded public session.

**United States.** The USOC instituted a new Drug Hotline, where skaters, coaches and parents could call in to listen to recorded information on banned substances, medications and drug interactions. The Colorado Ice Arena in Lakewood, outside Denver, closed in August. The two-rink facility served national and Olympic competitors for fourteen years. Don Laws blamed the closure on rising insurance and utility costs.

## BEHIND THE SCENES

There was absolute mayhem in September when the Organizing Committee for the 1988 Winter Olympic Games in Calgary received 53 000 orders on the first day tickets were made available. The figure skating events sold out before all the ticket orders could even be processed, as large blocks of seats were reserved for dignitaries. 11 000 people were put on a waiting list and the CFSA and USFSA's Headquarters were inundated with calls. In June, the number of tickets allotted to dignitaries was reduced and several tickets opened up for the most riveting figure skating events of all... the compulsory figures.

At the IOC's October meeting in Lausanne, Switzerland, Albertville, France was selected as the site of '92 Olympics, defeating Sofia, Bulgaria in the final round of voting. The IOC also voted to alternate the Summer and Winter Olympics every two years, meaning an 'extra' Winter Games would be added in 1994 to reset the cycle.

Out with the old, in with the new... The final year the Yankee Polka was skated at the World Championships, a brand-new compulsory dance was invented by Marina Klimova, Sergei Ponomarenko and Natalia Dubova - the Golden Waltz.

The ISU Council and Technical Committees met in Toronto in May to discuss proposals to reduce the compulsory dances from three to one and abolish the compulsory figures altogether. The arguments for both proposals were that the time skaters spent training on compulsory dances and figures "has not contributed to the further development of free skating with its beauty, artistry and athleticism" and that figures and compulsory figures added increased lengths, costs and organizational challenges to the organizers of ISU Championships. An original program for singles and pairs was also proposed as a replacement for the short program. The elimination of figures was a hot and very decisive topic for many years leading up to this meeting and everyone from skaters, coaches and judges to skating associations, television producers and rink owners would be affected by the ISU's decision, which would be voted on at the next ISU Congress the following May in Davos.

## ART AND HISTORY

During the World Championships, the Taft Museum presented a special exhibition called *Ice Skating in 17th Century Art*. The exhibition featured 40 works on loan from Dutch and American institutions and private collections, as well as antique skates and 20 Regency-era prints loaned from the World Figure Skating Museum and Hall of Fame's Grafström *Skating in Art* Collection.

## FUN AND GAMES

Typographics in Cordova, Tennessee produced a board game called *Ice Skating Trivia*. Two to six players could work their way through 400 question-and-answer cards. The first player to correctly answer questions in each of the Bronze, Silver, Gold and Professional rounds became the Grand Champion.

# THE AIDS EPIDEMIC

Princess Diana made international headlines when she was photographed holding the hand of an AIDS patient at London's Middlesex Hospital. The People's Queen opened the UK's first unit dedicated to treating HIV and AIDS patients during that visit. The first panel of the AIDS Memorial Quilt was created, the FDA approved the first medication for AIDS (AZT) and a report from the office of the United States Surgeon General called for a national education campaign on safe sex and voluntary HIV testing.

In October, Tom Steinruck passed away in San Diego, California at the age of 39. Born in Colorado, Steinruck got his start in figure skating at the Seattle Skating Club. In 1969, he and his partner Nina Emden won the Northwest Pacific junior pairs title, the silver medal at the Pacific Coast Championships and competed at the U.S. Championships. During his competitive career, he studied zoology at the University of Washington. Steinruck later skated professionally with the *Ice Follies*. His obituary in the *Bay Area Reporter* recalled, "His smile, his enthusiasm, his dedication to things he believed in made life better for many of us. His contribution to our community through his devotion of AIDS research will be greatly missed."

In January, Ian Knight passed away at the age of 51 in Oakland, California. Knight got his start in skating at the Lachine Figure Skating Club. He made his national debut at the 1956 Canadian Championships in Galt and won a pair of medals in the junior pairs events the following two years with partners Patricia Scott and Lise Petit. In 1959, Knight won the Quebec junior men's title and the bronze medal in the senior pairs event at the Canadian Championships. He went on to teach skating in Montreal, California and Utah.

Famed pianist Liberace passed away of an AIDS-related illness in February, just four months after he appeared as a special guest at a golden anniversary ice show organized to celebrate The Rink at Rockefeller Plaza's fiftieth anniversary. One of the show's stars was Brian Pockar.

Greg Welch passed away at the age of 29 in April, leaving behind his partner Dennis Coi. Welch got his start in skating at the Skaneateles Figure Skating Club at the age of twelve. At the 1972 Middle Atlantic Figure Skating Championships, he won the bronze medal in pairs with Kathy Edmonds. Two years later, he won the New England Regional novice pairs title with Susan Gundersen. Gunderson and Welch went on to win the bronze medal in novice pairs at the 1974 Eastern Championships. Welch went on tour professionally with the *Ice Capades* and performed at Knott's Berry Farm and Radio City Music Hall.

*Greg Welch. Photos courtesy Laurie Welch.*

Welch's sister Laurie recalled, "He was a great brother. He was six years older and was extremely creative. He was the reason I got into skating because I wanted to be just like him. He would babysit for my brother and I because he was older than us. Whenever he would babysit for us... he would organize a huge production. He knew where my Dad's video camera was and would save his money and go buy a blank tape. He would have these elaborate productions and I was always the star. He would do set design, costumes, make-up and run rehearsals. The people that were in his 'shows' or movies were all my friends, my other brother Chris' friends and neighbour kids... We performed at Radio City Music Hall together for two years - 1985 and 1986. The funny story there was that when we auditioned, we heard it was on synthetic ice. We didn't really skate together ever but we put together this nice little routine. When we got to the audition, we realized it was being held on real ice. We had our other blades on that we would wear for synthetic ice. We were an absolute disaster! We left there and were just horrified and we thought, 'Oh my gosh, how embarrassing! That was the worst audition ever.' We went back to our apartment, and the phone rang and we were offered the job. We both said, 'Are you sure you called the right people?' Robin Cousins and Peggy Fleming came in and they filmed the Radio City Christmas show and they cut where our skating segment was and put Robin and Peggy at Rockefeller Center in our spot. Greg was so mad! If you look closely at that video, there are snowmen and trees on the stage at Radio City. If you look behind the trees, you'll see Greg standing up. We were told to crouch down behind the trees so that they could film that part and cut to Rockefeller Center but because Greg was so mad he was like, 'I'm not crouching, damn it!'... He was just such a phenomenal person and he and Dennis were the funniest couple. They adored each other."

## BOOKS AND MAGAZINES

In partnership with the ISU, Tamara Moskvina and Igor Moskvin published the book *Pair Skating as Sport and Art*. Designed as a companion work to Dr. Josef Dědič's *Single Figure Skating*, the book was an extremely valuable contribution to figure skating literature - the first modern book of its kind geared specifically towards the coaching of elite level pairs skaters.

The first issue of *Patinage* was published in France in December, with Jean-Christophe Berlot as editor-in-chief. After the French edition of the *Canadian Skater* was scrapped, the magazine was the only French-language figure skating periodical in the world.

## FILMS AND TELEVISION

Scott Hamilton appeared as a celebrity guest on the *$100,000 Pyramid*. Hamilton was a perennial favourite on American game shows in the 80s, also appearing on *Blackout* and *Win, Lose or Draw*. Debi Thomas, Jill Watson and Peter Oppegard also made game show appearances during the decade.

"On the first day of Christmas, my true love gave to me, Torvill and Dean on the telly". On Boxing Day, ITV aired the world premiere of *Fire and Ice*, a one-hour ice skating drama starring Jayne Torvill and Christopher Dean and Michael Crawford, featured choreography by Graeme Murphy and music composed by Carl Davis and performed by the London Philharmonic Orchestra. The production, which featured both dancers and skaters, was filmed in Stuttgart, West Germany.

World Champions Tai Babilonia and Randy Gardner teamed up with their coach John Nicks and executive producer Michael Rosenberg to present *How To Ice Skate*, a 60-minute VHS instructional video. The USFSA sold the video by mail-order.

Video Image Products in Etna, California released a five-volume set on BETA and VHS called *25 Years of National Champions*, featuring rare videos from U.S. Figure Skating Championships in years past from the collections of Howard Craker. Video Sports Productions released a mail-order video of Tom Collins' *Tour of Olympic & World Figure Skating Champions*.

Jill Trenary and Caryn Kadavy were guests on NBC's *Today Show* in May. The American skating stars were interviewed by Jane Pauley in a segment highlighting Colorado as a major training center for sports.

*Gillian Wachsman and Todd Waggoner. Photo courtesy Elaine Hooper / St. Ivel Figure Skating Archive.*

*Falko Kirsten. Photo courtesy Elaine Hooper / St. Ivel Figure Skating Archive.*

*Kathrin and Christoff Beck. Photo courtesy Elaine Hooper / St. Ivel Figure Skating Archive.*

*Richard Zander. Photo courtesy Elaine Hooper / St. Ivel Figure Skating Archive.*

# Fall Internationals

**1986 COUPES DES ALPES (Saint Gervais, France and Oberstdorf, West Germany, August 20-24, 1986 and August 26-30, 1986)**

Grand Prix de St. Gervais Winners:

Erik Larson (USA) - men
Holly Cook (USA) - women
Melanie Gaylor and Lee Barkell (CAN) - pairs
Karen Knieriem and Leif Erickson (USA) - ice dance

Nebelhorn Trophy (Oberstdorf) Winners:

Vitali Egorov (SOV) - men
Holly Cook (USA) - women
Melanie Gaylor and Lee Barkell (CAN) - pairs
Antonia and Ferdinand Becherer (FRG) - ice dance

**1986 ASKÖ CUP OF VIENNA (Vienna, Austria, September 1986)**

Men:

1. Michael Slipchuk (CAN)
2. Nils Köpp (GDR)
3. Thomas Hlavik (AUT)

Women:

1. Tamara Téglássy (HUN)
2. Stéfanie Schmid (SUI)
3. Iveta Voralová (CZE)

**1986 ST. IVEL ICE INTERNATIONAL (London, England, September 23-25, 1986)**

Men:

1. Daniel Doran (USA)
2. Oliver Höner (SUI)
3. Richard Zander (FRG)

Women:

1. Elizabeth Manley (CAN)
2. Jill Trenary (USA)
3. Inga Gauter (GDR)

Pairs:

1. Christine Hough and Doug Ladret (CAN)
2. Michelle Menzies and Kevin Wheeler (CAN)
3. Gillian Wachsman and Todd Waggoner (USA)

Ice Dance:

1. Kathrin and Christoff Beck (AUT)
2. Sharon Jones and Paul Askham (GRB)
3. Isabelle and Paul Duchesnay (FRA)

**1986 FUJI FILM TROPHY (Frankfurt, West Germany, October 1986)**

Men:

1. Petr Barna (CZE)
2. Alessandro Riccitelli (ITA)
3. Shubin Zhang (CHN)

Women:

1. Dianne Takeuchi (CAN)
2. Caishu Fu (CHN)
3. Cornelia Renner (FRG)

Pairs:

1. Melanie Gaylor and Lee Barkell (CAN)
2. Colette May and Carl Nelson (GRB)
3. Kerstin Kiminus and Stefan Pfrengle (FRG)

Ice Dance:

1. Lia Trovati and Roberto Pelizzola (ITA)
2. Elizabeth Coates and Alan Abretti (GRB)
3. Dominique Yvon and Frédéric Palluel (FRA)

**1986 SKATE AMERICA (Portland, ME, October 16-19, 1986)**

Men:

1. Brian Boitano (USA)
2. Viktor Petrenko (SOV)
3. Daniel Doran (USA)

Women:

1. Tiffany Chin (USA)
2. Tonya Harding (USA)
3. Agnès Gosselin (FRA)

Pairs:

1. Katy Keeley and Joseph Mero (USA)
2. Denise Benning and Lyndon Johnston (CAN)
3. Ludmila Koblova and Andrey Katlin (SOV)

Ice Dance:

1. Isabelle and Paul Duchesnay (FRA)
2. Suzanne Semanick and Scott Gregory (USA)
3. Jo-Anne Borlase and Scott Chalmers (CAN)

**1986 SKATE CANADA (Regina, SK, October 30-November 1, 1986)**

Men:

1. Vitali Egorov (SOV)
2. Christopher Bowman (USA)
3. Grzegorz Filipowski (POL)

Women:

1. Elizabeth Manley (CAN)
2. Claudia Leistner (FRG)
3. Joanne Conway (GRB)

Pairs:

1. Cynthia Coull and Mark Rowsom (CAN)
2. Ekaterina Gordeeva and Sergei Grinkov (SOV)
3. Natalie and Wayne Seybold (USA)

Ice Dance:

1. Natalia Annenko and Genrikh Sretenski (SOV)
2. Suzanne Semanick and Scott Gregory (USA)
3. Karyn and Rod Garossino (CAN)

**1986 PRAGUE SKATE (Prague, Czechoslovakia, November 7-9, 1986)**

Men:

1. Petr Barna (CZE)
2. Henrik Walentin (DEN)
3. Daniel Weiss (FRG)

Women:

1. Susanne Becher (FRG)
2. Jana Přibylová (CZE)
3. Inna Krundysheva (SOV)

Pairs:

1. Peggy Schwarz and Alexander König (GDR)
2. Elena Bechke and Valeri Kornienko (SOV)
3. Lyudmila Koblova and Andrei Kalitin (SOV)

**1986 NOVARAT TROPHY (Budapest, Hungary, October 30-November 2, 1986)**

Men:

1. Brian Orser (CAN)
2. Doug Mattis (USA)
3. Mark Mitchell (USA)

Women:

1. Cindy Bortz (USA)
2. Charlene Wong (CAN)
3. Tonia Kwiatkowski (USA)

Ice Dance:

1. Tracy Wilson and Rob McCall (CAN)
2. Klára Engi and Attila Tóth (HUN)
3. Larisa Fedorinova and Evgeni Platov (SOV)

# Fall Internationals

**1986 GOLDEN SPIN OF ZAGREB (Zagreb, Yugoslavia, November 12-16, 1986)**

Men:

1. Viktor Petrenko (SOV)
2. Philippe Roncoli (FRA)
3. James Cygan (USA)

Women:

1. Caryn Kadavy (USA)
2. Anna Kondrashova (SOV)
3. Željka Čižmešija (YUG)

Ice Dance:

1. Susie Wynne and Joseph Druar (USA)
2. Andrea Juklová and Martin Šimeček (CZE)
3. Kimberley Weeks and Curtis Moore (CAN)

**1986 POKAL DER BLAUEN SCHWERTER (Karl-Marx-Stadt, East Germany, November 13-15, 1986)**

Men:

1. Yuri Tsimbaliuk (SOV)
2. Rico Krahnert (GDR)
3. Mirko Eichhorn (GDR)

Women:

1. Inga Gauter (GDR)
2. Tanja Krienke (GDR)
3. Alina Pisarenko (SOV)

Pairs:

1. Mandy Hannebauer and Marno Kreft (GDR)
2. Antje Schramm and Jens Müller (GDR)
3. Irina Saifutinova and Andrei Bardykin (SOV)

**1986 NHK TROPHY (Tokyo, Japan, November 27-30, 1986)**

Men:

1. Angelo D'Agostino (USA)
2. Makoto Kano (JPN)
3. Philippe Roncoli (FRA)

Women:

1. Katarina Witt (GDR)
2. Midori Ito (JPN)
3. Juri Ozawa (JPN)

Pairs:

1. Elena Valova and Oleg Vasiliev (SOV)
2. Jill Watson and Peter Oppegard (USA)
3. Natalie and Wayne Seybold (USA)

Ice Dance:

1. Natalia Bestemianova and Andrei Bukin (SOV)
2. Suzanne Semanick and Scott Gregory (USA)
3. Kathrin and Christoff Beck (AUT)

**1986 GRAND PRIZE SNP (Banská Bystrica, Czechoslovakia)**

Men:

1. Mirko Eichhorn (FRG)
2. Attila Sekillioglu (FRG)
3. Roman Koudriatsev (SOV)

Women:

1. Elena Kushnir (SOV)
2. Tanja Krienke (GDR)
3. Song-sul Kim (KOR)

Pairs:

1. Antje Schramm and Jens Müller (GDR)
2. Elena Gud and Evgeni Koltoun (SOV)
3. Ginger and Archie Tse (USA)

Ice Dance:

1. Ivana Střondalová and Milan Brzý (CZE)
2. Monika Mandiková and Dalibor Joura (CZE)
3. Meike and Frank Dehne (FRG)

**1986 PRIZE OF MOSCOW NEWS (Moscow, Soviet Union, December 3-7, 1986)**

Men:

1. Vladimir Kotin (SOV)
2. Vitali Egorov (SOV)
3. Vladimir Petrenko (SOV)

Women:

1. Kira Ivanova (SOV)
2. Jill Trenary (USA)
3. Anna Kondrashova (SOV)

Pairs:

1. Elena Kvitchenko and Rashid Kadyrkaev (SOV)
2. Elena Bechke and Valeri Kornienko (SOV)
3. Lyudmila Koblova and Andrei Kalitin (SOV)

Ice Dance:

1. Marina Klimova and Sergei Ponomarenko (SOV)
2. Natalia Annenko and Genrikh Sretenski (SOV)
3. Maya Usova and Alexandr Zhulin (SOV)

**a987 WINTER UNIVERSITY GAMES (Poprad, Czechoslovakia, February 21-28, 1987)**

Men:

1. Petr Barna (CZE)
2. Vitali Egorov (SOV)
3. Paul Wylie (USA)

Women:

1. Larisa Zamotina (SOV)
2. Stefanie Schmid (SUI)
3. Yvonne Gómez (USA)

Pairs:

1. Elena Kvitchenko and Rashid Kadyrkaev (SOV)
2. Elena Bechke and Valeri Kornienko (SOV)
3. Calla Urbanski and Michael Blicharski (USA)

Ice Dance:

1. Kathrin and Christoff Beck (AUT)
2. Maya Usova and Alexandr Zhulin (SOV)
3. Svetlana Liapina and Gorsha Sur (SOV)

**1987 NORDISKA MÄSTERSKAPEN (Upplands Väsby, Sweden, February 27-March 1, 1987)**

Men:

1. Henrik Walentin (DEN)
2. Jari Kauppi (FIN)
3. Kim Ketelsen (SWE)

Women:

1. Lotta Falkenbäck (SWE)
2. Elina Hänninen (FIN)
3. Birgitta Andersson (SWE)

Ice Dance:

1. Åsa Agblad and Owe Ridderstråle (SWE)
2. Susanna Peltola and Kim Jacobson (FIN)
3. Johanna Elfving and Pontus Krantz (SWE)

**1987 MERANO SPRING TROPHY (Merano, Italy, March 28-29, 1987)**

Women:

1. Kristi Yamaguchi (USA)
2. Sandra Garde (FRA)
3. Joelle Batten (CAN)

**1987 DANSE SUR GLACE DE GRENOBLE (Grenoble, France)**

Ice Dance:

1. Kathrin and Christoff Beck (AUT)
2. Klára Engi and Attila Tóth (HUN)
3. Lia Trovati and Roberto Pelizzola (ITA)

# National Championships and Other Competitions

## SENIOR NATIONAL CHAMPIONS BY COUNTRY

### Men

AUS - Cameron Medhurst
AUT - Ralph Burghart
BUL - Boyko Aleksiev
CHN - Shubin Zhang
CZE - Petr Barna
DEN - Lars Dresler
FIN - Oula Jääskeläinen
FRA - Philippe Roncoli
FRG - Richard Zander
GDR - Falko Kirsten
GRB - Paul Robinson
HOL - Alcuin Schulten
HUN - András Száraz
ITA - Alessandro Riccitelli
JPN - Masaru Ogawa
KOR - Sung-il Jung
NZL - Christopher Blong
POL - Przemysław Noworyta
ROM - Cornel Gheorghe
SOV - Alexandr Fadeev
SUI - Oliver Höner
SWE - Peter Johansson

### Women

AUS - Tracy-Lee Brook
AUT - Sabine Paal
BUL - Svetla Staneva
CHN - Jiang Yi Bing
CZE - Iveta Voralová
DEN - Connie Sjøholm Jørgensen
FIN - Tiia-Riikka Pietikäinen
FRA - Agnès Gosselin
FRG - Claudia Leistner
GDR - Katarina Witt
GRB - Joanne Conway
HOL - Li Scha Wang
HUN - Tamara Téglássy
ITA - Beatrice Gelmini
JPN - Midori Ito
KOR - Sung-jin Byun
NOR - Anita Thorenfeldt
NZL - Rosanna Blong
POL - Mirella Gawłowska
SOV - Anna Kondrashova
SUI - Claudia Villiger
SWE - Hélène Persson

### Pairs

AUS - Danielle and Stephen Carr
CHN - Mei Zhi Bin and Li Wei
CZE - Lenka Knapová and René Novotný
FRA - Charline Mauger and Benoît Vandenberghe
FRG - Sonja Adalbert and Daniele Caprano
GDR - Katrin Kanitz and Tobias Schröter
GRB - Cheryl Peake and Andrew Naylor
JPN - Akiko Nogami and Yoichi Yamazaki
POL - Anna Wikłacz and Piotr Szczerbowski
SAF - Delene McKenzie and B. Voges
SOV - Ekaterina Gordeeva and Sergei Grinkov

### Ice Dance

AUS - Monica MacDonald and Rodney Clarke
AUT - Kathrin and Christoff Beck
BUL - Hristina Boyanova and Yavor Ivanov
CHN - Luyang Liu and Xiaolei Zhao
CZE - Viera Řeháková and Ivan Havránek
FIN - Susanna Rahkamo and Petri Kokko
FRA - Isabelle and Paul Duchesnay
FRG - Antonia and Ferdinand Becherer
GRB - Sharon Jones and Paul Askham
HUN - Klára Engi and Attila Tóth
ITA - Lia Trovati and Roberto Pelizzola
JPN - Tomoko Tanaka and Hiroyuki Suzuki
POL - Honorata Górna and Andrzej Dostatni
SOV - Natalia Bestemianova and Andrei Bukin
SUI - Désirée Schlegel and Patrick Brecht
SWE - Lillemor Lööf and Rickard Renholm

## 1987 INTERNATIONAL PRECISION SKATING COMPETITION (Lake Placid, NY, January 17-18, 1987)

Team:

1. Les Pirouettes de Laval (CAN)
2. The Haydenettes (USA)
3. K-W Kweens on Ice (CAN)

Other Winners:

Burlington Ice Images (CAN) - junior
Hot Fudge Sundaes (USA) - novice
Second Edition (CAN) - adult

## 1987 CANADIAN PRECISION TEAM CHAMPIONSHIPS (Laval, QC, March 27-29, 1987)

Team:

1. Les Pirouettes de Laval
2. K-W Kweens on Ice
3. Second Edition

Other Winners:

Whitby Ice Crystals (junior)
Les Altesses - St-Leonard (novice)

## 1987 U.S. PRECISION TEAM CHAMPIONSHIPS (Tulsa, OK, April 10-11, 1987)

Team:

1. Fraserettes
2. The Haydenettes
3. The Figurettes

Other Winners:

The Superettes (junior)
Hot Fudge Sundaes (novice)
Fabulous 40s (adult)

## 1987 LA COUPE EXCELLENCE (Montreal, QC, April 3-5, 1987)

Men:

1. Daniel Doran (USA)
2. Matthew Hall (CAN)
3. Jaimee Eggleton (CAN)

Women:

1. Tonya Harding (USA)
2. Patricia Neske (FRG)
3. Dianne Takeuchi (CAN)

Pairs:

1. Laureen Collin and John Penticost (CAN)
2. Natalie and Wayne Seybold (USA)
3. Cheryl Peake and Andrew Naylor (GRB)

Ice Dance:

1. Sharon Jones and Paul Askham (GRB)
2. April Sargent and Russ Witherby (USA)
3. Penny Mann and Richard Perkins (CAN)

*Daniel Doran. Photo courtesy Elaine Hooper / St. Ivel Figure Skating Archive.*

*Stefania Calegari and Pasquale Camerlengo. Photo courtesy Elaine Hooper / St. Ivel Figure Skating Archive.*

## Professional Competitions

**1986 WORLD CHALLENGE OF CHAMPIONS (Paris, France, December 16, 1986)**

Men:

1. Scott Hamilton (USA)
2. Robin Cousins (GRB)
3. Norbert Schramm (FRG)
4. Toller Cranston (CAN)

Women:

1. Rosalynn Sumners (USA)
2. Dorothy Hamill (USA)
3. Denise Biellmann (SUI)
4. Linda Fratianne (USA)

Pairs:

1. Barbara Underhill and Paul Martini (CAN)
2. Ludmila and Oleg Protopopov (SOV)
3. Lea Ann Miller and Bill Fauver (USA)
4. JoJo Starbuck and Ken Shelley (USA)

**1986 UNITED STATES OPEN PROFESSIONAL CHAMPIONSHIP (Rochester, MN, December 19-21, 1986)**

Men:

1. Brian Pockar (CAN)
2. Charlie Tickner (USA)
3. Bobby Beauchamp (USA)

Women:

1. Kathleen Schmelz (USA)
2. Kay Thomson (CAN)
3. Kacey Yoreson (USA)

Pairs:

1. Tricia Burton and Burt Lancon (USA)
2. Lisa Carey and Chris Harrison (USA)
3. Sandy Lenz and Keith Green (USA/CAN)

Ice Dance:

1. Judy Blumberg and Michael Seibert (USA)
2. Nina Newby and Rick Berg (USA)
3. Micheline Coyne and John Sally (CAN)

Challenge Cup Winners:

Stewart Sturgeon (USA) - men
Tracy Shulman (USA) - women
Tricia Burton and Burt Lancon (USA) - pairs
Nina Newby and Rick Berg (USA) - ice dance

## Shows and Tours

At the inaugural edition of the Goodwill Games in Moscow in July, some of the world's best figure skaters were on hand to give two exhibitions at the Luzhniki Palace of Sports. The cast of skaters, all American and Soviet except for Czechoslovakia's Petr Barna, included all four of the reigning World Champions - Natalia Bestemianova and Andrei Bukin, Ekaterina Gordeeva and Sergei Grinkov, Debi Thomas and Brian Boitano. For many of the American skaters taking part, it was their first time visiting the Soviet Union. In between shows, they went to see the Moscow Circus. Thomas and Soviet rhythmic gymnast Galina Beloglazova were both awarded the honourary title Miss Goodwill Games.

Billed as the "largest gathering of Senior U.S. Figure National Figure Skating Champions ever assembled", *Celebration... America on Ice!* took place in Indianapolis, Indiana in September. The event marked the 65th anniversary of the USFSA and the 25th anniversary of the Memorial Fund. The star-studded show, directed by JoJo Starbuck and Ken Shelley, included photos and video clips of every U.S. Champion dating back to the early years, projected on giant screens. Dick Button, Peggy Fleming, Carol Heiss Jenkins, Hayes and David Jenkins and John 'Misha' Petkevich acted as host commentators. Performers included recent World Champions Scott Hamilton, Tai Babilonia and Randy Gardner, Elaine Zayak and Charlie Tickner, as well as performances Suzanne Davis, Joan Tozzer and Marjorie Parker, who all won gold medals at the U.S. Championships before World War II. All funds raised from the show benefited the Memorial Fund.

A cast of 61 performers, many from the Kyiv Ice Ballet, performed in *Soviet Stars on Ice*. The six-week tour kicked off in Cape Breton in October, visiting 38 Canadian cities and towns along the way. It was the first time members of the Kyiv Ice Ballet had performed in Canada since 1974. Performers included Elena and Vladimir Bogolyubov, Galina Grzhibovskaya and Vyacheslav Baboshin.

After being unceremoniously dumped from the *Ice Capades* and told "Men don't sell tickets in figure skating", Scott Hamilton teamed up with Bob Kain and Don Laws to present the *Scott Hamilton America Tour*, which visited five cities on the Eastern Seaboard in October. Rosalynn Sumners left Walt Disney's World on Ice to star in the tour with Hamilton, which also featured Toller Cranston, Judy Blumberg and Michael Seibert, Brian Pockar, Sandy Lenz and Lisa Carey and Chris Harrison. Dorothy Hamill, Robin Cousins and JoJo Starbuck and Ken Shelley joined a second stint of the tour in December, which made its first Canadian appearance in Hamilton. In January, the tour got its now iconic name - *Stars on Ice*.

*Torvill & Dean: The World Tour* kicked off an American tour in the fall. After a show in Portland, Maine, only a few weeks into the 60-city tour, Christopher Dean tripped and fell leaving the ice after posing for photographers and fractured his wrist. The tour was unfortunately cancelled in December before they made it to Madison Square Garden.

In November, World Champions Dick Button and Ája Zanová teamed up to produce *A Party on the Pond* - a gala reopening after six years of "Donald Trump's gift to New York" - Wollman Rink in Central Park. Performers included Jayne Torvill and Christopher Dean, Dorothy Hamill, Robin Cousins, Scott Hamilton, Peggy Fleming, Debi Thomas and Judy Blumberg and Michael Seibert.

John Curry was the special guest star in the 12th edition of *Superskates* in November. Joining Curry on the ice at Madison Square Garden were Scott Hamilton, Elaine Zayak, JoJo Starbuck and Ken Shelley and Debi Thomas. The most expensive ticket for the show was eighteen dollars.

*Disney on Ice* made its international debut in Japan with a show called *Walt Disney's World on Ice - Happy Birthday Donald*. There were five different *Disney on Ice* tours running concurrently by the following season, including Walt Disney's Magic Kingdom on Ice and Snow White on Ice.

In May, the Minto Skating Club celebrated the grand opening of its new Canadian-American Friendship Arena with a star-studded gala featuring Brian Orser, Elizabeth Manley, Donald Jackson, Lynn Nightingale and Isabelle and Paul Duchesnay. The guest of honour was Barbara Ann Scott King - dressed to the nines as always!

In June, over 180 000 people showed up to watch the first professional ice revue in the southern mainland of China. *Skate Festival China '87* was held in conjunction with the Shanghai International Arts Festival and produced by Stephen Goldberg, through Marco Entertainment. Ice equipment was rented from Australia for the production and the production was put together in ten days. All eight shows sold out and received standing ovations. The cast was treated "like The Beatles". Performers included Barbara Underhill and Paul Martini, Judy Blumberg and Michael Seibert, JoJo Starbuck and Ken Shelley, Gary Beacom, Lorna Wighton and John Dowding, Brian Pockar, Bobby Beauchamp, Sandra Bezic, Karen Kresge and Lisa Carey and Chris Harrison.

*Fernand Fédronic. Photo courtesy Elaine Hooper / St. Ivel Figure Skating Archive.*

*Norbert Schramm. Photo courtesy Sarina Stützer.*

### PERSONALITIES

*TRACY WILSON AND ROB MCCALL*

Date of Birth: September 25, 1961/September 14, 1958
Place of Birth: Lachine, Quebec/Halifax, Nova Scotia
Coach: Bernie Ford, Marijane Stong, John Briscoe
Choreographer: Bernie Ford, Marijane Stong, André Denis, Vanessa Harwood
Home Club: Hollyburn CC/North Shore WC/ Vancouver SC/Inlet SC/Halifax SC

*NATALIA ANNENKO AND GENRIKH SRETENSKI*

Date of Birth: April 17, 1964/July 23, 1962
Place of Birth: Moscow, Soviet Union
Coach: Lyudmila Pakhomova, Tatiana Tarasova, Gennady Akkerman
Choreographer: Elena Matveeva
Home Club: CSKA Moscow

*SUZANNE SEMANICK AND SCOTT GREGORY*

Date of Birth: May 18, 1967/July 31, 1959
Place of Birth: Bridgesville, PA/Auburn, NY
Coach: Ron Ludington, Robbie Kaine
Choreographer: Diane Agle, Jill Cosgrove, Robbie Kaine
Home Club: SC of Wilmington/University of Delaware SC

**World Junior Championships.** The Kitchener Memorial Auditorium played host to the first World Junior Championships in Canada in six years in December. Ticket sales were very disappointing, owing somewhat to the fact that organizers only had a year and a half to put the event together. The ISU originally awarded the competition to Östersund, Sweden, but the Scandinavian organizers had to rescind it because they only had one suitable ice surface, instead of the two that were required. Though only ten young teams entered the pairs event, the standard of skating was exceptionally high from a technical standpoint. The Soviet pair of Elena Leonova and Gennadi Krasnitski won both the short program and free skate to take the gold ahead of their teammates Ekaterina Murugova and Artem Torgashev, including a very rare split quadruple twist in their free skate. Americans Kristi Yamaguchi and Rudy Galindo took the bronze, landing the first-ever side-by-side triple flips at the World Junior Championships. Canada's two entries did not fare well against the Eastern Bloc and American pairs. Jodi Barnes and Rob Williams finished seventh; Marie-Josée Fortin and Jean-Michel Bombardier ended up in eighth. Odesa's Ilona Melnichenko and Gennadi Kaskov dominated the ice dance event from start to finish, winning the gold medal for the Soviet Union in their first trip to the World Junior Championships. Ontario's Catherine Pal and Donald Godfrey finished second in the compulsories but dropped a spot in the OSP and free dance, finishing third behind a second Soviet pair, Oksana Grishuk and Alexandr Chichkov. Pal and Godfrey's goal was to finish in the top three, and they were delighted to win the bronze on their third try. Canada's second pair, Jacqueline Petr and Mark Janoschak finished seventh of the 15 couples entered - a remarkable result considering they had only been skating together since June. West Germany's Susanne Becher led Americans Cindy Bortz and Holly Cook and Coquitlam, British Columbia's Shannon Allison in the women's compulsory figures. Canada's second skater, Angie Folk, placed a solid sixth. Cook did very well to finish third. She arrived in Kitchener only nine hours before the competition started as a last-minute replacement for an injured Tonya Harding. Cook only had one practice session to reacquaint herself with the figures that were being skated in the junior event, having just come back from the NHK Trophy in Japan where she performed figures from a different group altogether. Bortz was a class ahead of the rest of the field in both the short program and free skate, winning the gold with a program that Toller Cranston, commentating for CBC, remarked could have easily contended with any top senior skater in the world. Bortz's free skate included a triple Lutz, flip, Salchow, two triple toe-loops and two double Axels. Her only error wasn't even on a jump - she tripped on the boards and fell after landing the triple Lutz. Becher skated a clean program to win the silver, while Allison landed three triples and moved up to take the bronze over Cook. Folk placed a disastrous 18th in the free skate, dropping down to 12th overall. Yuri Tsimbaliuk of the Soviet Union led Americans Todd Eldredge and Rudy Galindo in the men's compulsory figures, with North Battleford, Saskatchewan's Brent Frank finishing a solid eighth out of 24 entries. Galindo was solid as a rock to win the short program over Tsimbaliuk. The fact that Eldredge even competed, let alone placed third in the short program, was quite courageous. He took a serious fall on a triple Lutz in one of the practices, injuring his tailbone, and had missed practices for two days. With an outstanding performance featuring four triple jumps, Galindo won the free skate. Eldredge fell on his triple Lutz but added it back in late in his program along with four other triples to take the silver. Tsimbaliuk doubled many of his planned triples after taking a hard fall on his triple Lutz and finished third. A particularly rough free skate dropped Frank down to ninth overall.

**1987 WORLD JUNIOR CHAMPIONSHIPS**
(Kitchener, ON, December 2-7, 1986)

Men:

1. Rudy Galindo (USA)
2. Todd Eldredge (USA)
3. Yuri Tsimbaliuk (SOV)
4. Cameron Birky (USA)
5. Daniel Weiss (FRG)
6. Michael Shmerkin (SOV)
7. Sergei Dudakov (SOV)
8. Éric Millot (FRA)
9. Brent Frank (CAN)
10. Jaroslav Suchý (CZE)

Women:

1. Cindy Bortz (USA)
2. Susanne Becher (FRG)
3. Shannon Allison (CAN)
4. Holly Cook (USA)
5. Natalia Skrabnevskaya (SOV)
6. Inga Gauter (GDR)
7. Junko Yaginuma (JPN)
8. Kyoko Ina (JPN)
9. Ylia Kuzmina (SOV)
10. Claude Péri (FRA)

Pairs:

1. Elena Leonova and Gennadi Krasnitski (SOV)
2. Ekaterina Murugova and Artem Torgashev (SOV)
3. Kristi Yamaguchi and Rudy Galindo (USA)
4. Mandy Hannebauer and Marno Kreft (GDR)
5. Irina Saifutdinova and Andrei Bardykin (SOV)
6. Ginger and Archie Tse (USA)
7. Jody Barnes and Rob Williams (CAN)
8. Marie-Josée Fortin and Jean-Michel Bombardier (CAN)
9. Catherine Barker and Neil Herring (GRB)
10. Liling Chen and Wenjun Qiu (CHN)

Ice Dance:

1. Ilona Melnichenko and Gennadi Kaskov (SOV)
2. Oksana Grishuk and Alexandr Chichkov (SOV)
3. Catherine Pal and Donald Godfrey (CAN)
4. Anna Croci and Luca Mantovani (ITA)
5. Sophie Moniotte and Pascal Lavanchy (FRA)
6. Ivana Strondalová and Milan Brzý (CZE)
7. Jacqueline Petr and Mark Janoschak (CAN)
8. Krisztina Kerekes and Csaba Szentpétery (HUN)
9. Elizabeth Punsalan and David Shirk (USA)
10. Vera Zietemann and Andreas Ullmann (FRG)

In winning the gold medal, his fourth medal at the Championships in three years, Galindo became the first skater of Latino heritage to win the World Junior title and the first skater in history to win medals in more than one discipline at the event. Galindo's victory in Kitchener was also remarkable because he had almost given up the sport out of sheer frustration. At the 1986 U.S. Championships, the judges placed him third even though he landed a triple flip/triple toe-loop combination in the junior men's event - an element the seniors weren't even attempting.

**World Professional Championships.** Less than two weeks before Christmas, eighteen of the biggest stars in professional figure skating brought tidings of comfort and joy to the Capital Centre in Landover, Maryland. With Jayne Torvill and Christopher Dean unable to defend their title because of Dean's injury, there were only two couples entered in the ice dance event. In the artistic program, Judy Blumberg and Michael Seibert stumbled in their program to the Talking Heads' "Once In A Lifetime" and Carol Fox and Richard Dalley pulled off an upset win, earning a set of perfect 10.0s for their classical performance to Zamfir's interpretation of "The Pearl Fishers' Duet". Kitty and Peter Carruthers were forced to pull out of the pairs event at the last minute when Kitty injured her ankle. Barbara Underhill and Paul Martini were the only team to do a triple twist and a throw triple jump in the pairs technical program, but they only earned a three-tenths of a point advantage over Lea Ann Miller and Bill Fauver, Ludmila and Oleg Protopopov and JoJo Starbuck and Ken Shelley. With a strong performance to "American Hymn", Underhill and Martini soared to victory in the pairs artistic program, regaining the title they had lost the year prior. The standings of the rest of the pairs remained the same as they did in the technical program, though it didn't go unnoticed that the Protopopovs upped their technical game to include side-by-side double Salchows in their program - a considerable feat considering Ludmila was 51 and Oleg 54. In the men's technical program, Scott Hamilton was a cut above the competition, landing a triple Lutz, triple Salchow, three double Axels and a backflip in his jazzy program to "Flight" by David Sanborn. He earned perfect 10.0s from every judge but Canada's Kerry Leitch. Robin Cousins finished second of Norbert Schramm and Toller Cranston, landing a triple toe-loop, double Axel and backflip in a gorgeous program set to music from the soundtrack album *Country*. He earned five perfect tens, trailing Hamilton by only one-tenth-of-a-point as the high and low scores were thrown out. There were some unusual choices in the artistic program. Cranston left the opera records at home, skating to Billy Joel and Ray Charles' ballad "Baby Grand" and Schramm skated to Dixieland music in a costume better suited for Oktoberfest than a figure skating competition. Cousins earned 10.0s across the board for a modern program to Aussie rock group Models' "Out of Sight, Out of Mind". Hamilton earned a set of perfect 10.0s of his own for his patriotic program to the old Civil War standard "Battle Hymn of The Republic". When the marks were tallied, Hamilton regained the title he lost to Cousins the year before based on his one-tenth of a point lead in the technical program. Three of the four men performed backflips in both programs. Dorothy Hamill won the women's technical program with an elegant program to the strains of Prokofiev that featured a double flip, double toe-loop and two single Axels. The result was controversial as Rosalynn Sumners and Linda Fratianne, who placed second and third, both skated clean, more technically difficult programs featuring double Axels. Sumners skated to the "Russian Dance" from Tchaikovsky's "Swan Lake"; Fratianne went for a modern vibe with a program to David Foster's "tapDANCE".

**1986 WORLD PROFESSIONAL CHAMPIONSHIPS (Landover, MD, December 12, 1986)**

Men:

1. Scott Hamilton (USA)
2. Robin Cousins (GRB)
3. Norbert Schramm (FRG)
4. Toller Cranston (CAN)

Women:

1. Dorothy Hamill (USA)
2. Rosalynn Sumners (USA)
3. Linda Fratianne (USA)
4. Elaine Zayak (USA)

Pairs:

1. Barbara Underhill and Paul Martini (CAN)
2. Lea Ann Miller and Bill Fauver (USA)
3. Ludmila and Oleg Protopopov (SOV)
4. JoJo Starbuck and Ken Shelley (USA)

Ice Dance:

1. Carol Fox and Richard Dalley (USA)
2. Judy Blumberg and Michael Seibert (USA)

In the artistic program, Linda Fratianne and Rosalynn Sumners' programs to Puccini's "O Mio Babbino Caro" and Andrea Bofill's "This Time I'll Be Sweeter" were beautifully skated, but they weren't a match for Dorothy Hamill. With a departure in style, Hamill skated a clever comedy number to "Bigger Isn't Better" from *Barnum*, dressed as General Tob Thumb in a military costume with epaulets, tails and trousers. Receiving perfect marks from all but three judges (Arthur Bourque, Ája Zanová and Bernie Ford), Hamill won her third World Professional women's title in a row, which was a record in any discipline at that point at the event. In Landover, *American Skating World* awarded its annual Professional Skater of the Year Award to JoJo Starbuck and Ken Shelley.

**U.S. Championships.** Attendance records were shattered in February when 87 000 spectators showed up to watch the U.S. Championships, held at the Sprinker Recreation Center and Tacoma Dome in Washington. The sell-out crowd of 20 000 at the Exhibition of Champions set a record of its own, as it was the largest audience ever for any kind of sporting event at the Tacoma Dome. The most popular spectators were those of the feathered variety. The mascot in Tacoma was Gooey the Duck and, coincidentally, sparrows somehow made their way into the rink during the competition. For many, the sparrows brought back memories of the flock of birds that made their way into the Riverfront Coliseum at the 1979 Nationals in Cincinnati. John Baldwin Jr. won the novice men's title in Tacoma, a title his father and coach John Baldwin Sr. had won exactly 20 years prior. It was the first time in history that a father and son won the same U.S. title. In the senior ice dance event, Renée Roca and Donald Adair led after the compulsories, winning the Westminster Waltz and Rhumba and finishing a close second to Suzanne Semanick and Scott Gregory in the Yankee Polka. Semanick and Gregory won the Viennese Waltz OSP, six judges to three, but Roca and Adair still held a narrow lead entering the free dance. Scott and Gregory pulled ahead to take the gold over Roca and Adair, again six judges to three, with a fast, crowd-pleasing free dance set to the music "Waiting for the Robert E. Lee", "Carny" and "Dueling Banjos". Susie Wynne and Joseph Druar won the bronze. Semanick and Gregory's victory over Roca and Adair in Tacoma marked the first time that the defending Champions in dance at Nationals had been dethroned the subsequent year since 1963. Defending U.S. Champions Gillian Wachsman and Todd Waggoner delivered a clean short program to unanimously lead the pairs field of fifteen in the first phase of the competition. Jill Watson and Peter Oppegard moved up from second after the short to take the gold with a dramatic free skate to Stravinsky's "The Firebird", which earned them nine 5.9s from the judges. Watson and Oppegard's winning program featured a triple twist, throw triple Salchow, throw double Axel and a unique headstand-style lift. Wachsman and Waggoner executed an excellent triple twist and throw double Axel, but two-footed a throw triple Salchow to finish third in the free skate, but second overall. Katy Keeley and Joseph Mero landed side-by-side double Axels and finished third overall, earning first-place ordinals in the free from three judges. Southern California's Sherri and Michael Kern finished dead last, but they had the distinction of being the only married couple in the competition. Before the women's event, coach Alex McGowan was livid over rumours that Debi Thomas was out of shape, not practicing and planning on withdrawing after the compulsory figures and petitioning for a bye to Worlds. McGowan claimed that judges even came up to him to ask if the rumours were true. In reality, Thomas was suffering from tendinitis and a leg strain resulting from off-ice exercises. Despite her injury, Thomas took a decisive lead over Jill Trenary, Caryn Kadavy and Tiffany Chin.

**1987 U.S. CHAMPIONSHIPS (Tacoma, WA, February 1-8, 1987)**

Men:

1. Brian Boitano
2. Christopher Bowman
3. Scott Williams
4. Daniel Doran
5. Paul Wylie
6. Angelo D'Agostino
7. Scott Kurttila
8. Rudy Galindo
9. James Cygan
10. Doug Mattis

Women:

1. Jill Trenary
2. Debi Thomas
3. Caryn Kadavy
4. Tiffany Chin
5. Tonya Harding
6. Cindy Bortz
7. Tracey Damigella
8. Holly Cook
9. Kathryn Adams
10. Yvonne Gómez

Pairs:

1. Jill Watson and Peter Oppegard
2. Gillian Wachsman and Todd Waggoner
3. Katy Keeley and Joseph Mero
4. Natalie and Wayne Seybold
5. Kristi Yamaguchi and Rudy Galindo
6. Calla Urbanski and Michael Blicharski
7. Ashley Stevenson and Scott Wendland
8. Heidi Franks and Luke Hohmann
9. Maria Lako and Joel McKeever
10. Karen Courtland and Joshua Roberts

Ice Dance:

1. Suzanne Semanick and Scott Gregory
2. Renée Roca and Donald Adair
3. Susie Wynne and Joseph Druar
4. April Sargent and Russ Witherby
5. Karen Knieriem and Leif Erickson
6. Ann Hensel and James Yorke
7. Jill Heiser and Michael Verlich
8. Dorothi Rodek and Robert Nardozza
9. Colette Huber and Ron Kravette
10. Jodie Balogh and Jerod Swallow

Junior Winners:

Todd Eldredge (men)
Jeri Campbell (women)
Kellie Lynn Creel and David McGovern (pairs)
Jennifer and Jeffrey Benz (ice dance)

Novice Winners:

John Baldwin Jr. (men)
Amy Holberg (women)

In the short program, Thomas was outstanding, attacking her program to "Relax" by Frankie Goes To Hollywood and taking a very strong lead. Trenary finished a unanimous second, landing a more difficult combination than Thomas - the triple flip/double toe-loop. Chin took a slip on her triple toe-loop combination but held on to third, while Kadavy botched both her combination and double Axel to place a disappointing ninth. Entering the free skate, Thomas, Trenary, Chin and Kadavy held the top four spots. In the free skate, Thomas had problems on her opening triple toe-loop but rebounded with an otherwise strong program to earn marks ranging from 5.5 to 5.9. Trenary and Kadavy both delivered two of their finest programs, landing multiple triple jumps and showcasing their grace and style. Chin fell on a triple toe-loop and two-footed two jumps, paling in comparison to Tonya Harding, who landed three triples. The overall standard of skating meant that the judges had their work cut out for them. when the marks were calculated, Trenary defeated Thomas both in the free and overall and Kadavy moved up to win the bronze. Chin finished fourth over Harding, though their positions were reversed in the free skate. In winning, Trenary was the first skater since Elaine Zayak to win the U.S. senior women's title two years after winning the junior women's title. Only five other women in history had accomplished the feat, one of them being Dr. Tenley Albright. Defending U.S. Champion Brian Boitano led the field following the compulsory figures. Skating to Henry Mancini's score from the film *Oklahoma Crude*, Boitano landed one of the first triple Axel/double toe-loop combinations in the short program at the U.S. Championships to earn unanimous first-place ordinals from the judges. Christopher Bowman, only fifth in figures, landed a triple Lutz/double toe-loop combination and earned two 5.9s for presentation, finishing second ahead of Scott Williams, who skated a clean program to "St. Louis Blues". Entering the free skate, Boitano had a decisive lead ahead of Daniel Doran, who was second in figures and fourth in the short, Williams and Bowman. The audience went berserk when Boitano landed a quadruple toe-loop in the warmup for the final flight of the men's free skate. He had been working on the quad in practice since 1983 and claimed to be successful on about 85 percent of his attempts. During his program, he touched down on the landing of the quad and popped a triple Axel into a single, but otherwise skated very well, earning sixteen 5.9s from the judges. In winning, Boitano was only the 11th man in the history of the U.S. Championships to win three consecutive senior national titles and, notably, he earned first-place ordinals from every judge in all three phases in the competition. Bowman's technically demanding program to classical music moved him up to second - his first podium finish at Nationals since winning the junior men's event in 1983. Scott Williams' entertaining program to "Zorba the Greek" featured an array of strong jumps and his trademark piston rolls, but the marks were only enough to earn him the bronze. Doran dropped to fourth overall, one spot behind Paul Wylie, who finished third in the free skate. All three of the medallists earned standing ovations - a testament not only to the standard of skating but the generosity of the Tacoma crowd. Enthusiasm wasn't the only thing that was catching, though. Todd Reynolds had to withdraw from the senior men's event in Tacoma because he'd caught chicken pox. He unknowingly passed the itch on to Paul Wylie, who brought them to the Winter University Games in Czechoslovakia.

**European Championships.** 104 skaters from 18 countries competed at the European Championships at the Zetra Ice Rink in Sarajevo, the site of the 1984 Olympics. Though snow blanketed the city, the event drew capacity crowds of 18 000 spectators for the free skating events.

**1987 EUROPEAN CHAMPIONSHIPS**
(Sarajevo, Yugoslavia, February 3-8, 1987)

Men:

1. Alexandr Fadeev (SOV)
2. Vladimir Kotin (SOV)
3. Viktor Petrenko (SOV)
4. Grzegorz Filipowski (POL)
5. Falko Kirsten (GDR)
6. Richard Zander (FRG)
7. Philippe Roncoli (FRA)
8. Petr Barna (CZE)
9. Oliver Höner (SUI)
10. Frédéric Harpagès (FRA)

Women:

1. Katarina Witt (GDR)
2. Kira Ivanova (SOV)
3. Anna Kondrashova (SOV)
4. Claudia Leistner (FRG)
5. Susanne Becher (FRG)
6. Claudia Villiger (SUI)
7. Tamara Téglássy (HUN)
8. Natalia Skrabnevskaya (SOV)
9. Iveta Voralová (CZE)
10. Agnès Gosselin (FRA)

Pairs:

1. Larisa Selezneva and Oleg Makarov (SOV)
2. Elena Valova and Oleg Vasiliev (SOV)
3. Katrin Kanitz and Tobias Schröter (GDR)
4. Lenka Knapová and René Novotný (CZE)
5. Cheryl Peake and Andrew Naylor (GRB)
6. Sonja Adalbert and Daniele Caprano (FRG)
7. Lisa and Neil Cushley (GRB)
8. Charline Mauger and Benoît Vandenberghe (FRA)

Ice Dance:

1. Natalia Bestemianova and Andrei Bukin (SOV)
2. Marina Klimova and Sergei Ponomarenko (SOV)
3. Natalia Annenko and Genrikh Sretenski (SOV)
4. Kathrin and Christoff Beck (AUT)
5. Isabelle and Paul Duchesnay (FRA)
6. Klára Engi and Attila Tóth (HUN)
7. Antonia and Ferdinand Becherer (FRG)
8. Sharon Jones and Paul Askham (GRB)
9. Lia Trovati and Roberto Pelizzola (ITA)
10. Viera Řcháková and Ivan Havránek (CZE)

In the ice dance event, Natalia Bestemianova and Andrei Bukin skated assuredly in the Starlight Waltz, Yankee Polka, Argentine Tango and Viennese Waltz OSP and full throttle in their *Cabaret* free dance to win their fourth European title, earning five 6.0s for presentation in the free dance. Marina Klimova and Sergei Ponomarenko and Natalia Annenko and Genrikh Sretenski took the silver in the bronze for a second year in a row in another Soviet podium sweep. It was the very first time since 1975 that the same couples had finished in the same order on the podium in ice dance at the European Championships in consecutive years. The Duchesnays moved up from seventh after compulsories to finish a strong fifth, three places higher than they had in their European debut the season prior. Their free dance to Aranjuez's "Concierto de Aranjuez" and Lecuona's "Malaguena" had been conceived after a family trip to Spain and polished through many hours of practice in Oberstdorf with Martin Skotnický and trips to London to work with Betty Callaway. In the pairs short program, Elena Valova and Oleg Vasiliev and Larisa Selezneva and Oleg Makarov bested World Champions Ekaterina Gordeeva and Sergei Grinkov, setting the stage for an exciting three-way battle in the free skate. The surprise victors were Selezneva and Makarov, whose electrifying program featured side-by-side triple toe-loops, a throw double Axel into side-by-side a double Axel/double toe-loop, a triple twist and throw triple toe-loop, all performed at breakneck speed. Valova and Vasiliev were unable to match their performance and settled for the silver ahead of East Germany's Katrin Kanitz and Tobias Schröter. A highly unusual situation presented itself quite early in Gordeeva and Grinkov's free skate. After performing a split quadruple twist, the bootstrap on Grinkov's costume broke. The American referee of the event, Benjamin T. Wright, signaled for them to stop their program by blowing his whistle, but their coach, Stanislav Leonovich, gestured for them to continue. Wright then had the music operator stop their music, as another signal they should stop their program. The Sarajevo audience did not understand what was going on and clapped in encouragement as 'G and G' continued their entire program without their music, while Wright continued to blow his whistle. Many viewed the pair's choice to continue skating as an act of defiance at the time. After they finished their program, Wright conferred with Gordeeva and Grinkov's coach Stanislav Leonovich and Soviet skating officials, offering the pair the option of either reskating their entire program after the final pair in the group or starting their program again at the point in which they were interrupted. Ultimately, 'G and G' declined both offers, stating they were too tired, and didn't think they could perform their free skate any better than they had. As a result, they were declared to have withdrawn, though the media incorrectly reported that they were disqualified from the competition. Aleksandr Gorshkov supported Wright's decision to stop their program, but other members of the Soviet delegation argued that 'G and G' should have been marked on their performance. Soviet officials cited the example of Irina Rodnina and Aleksandr Zaitsev continuing their program after their music stopped at the 1973 World Championships in Bratislava, either being forgetful or ignorant of the fact that ISU rules were revised after that incident, making it mandatory for skaters to stop their program at a referee's behest. Gordeeva later claimed that though she and Grinkov heard the whistle, they didn't know that it meant for them to stop because their former coach Stanislav Zhuk had always told them to continue their program until the end and to only listen to instructions from their coach. Gordeeva and Grinkov both took the unfortunate situation quite hard, accepting responsibility for their actions but also blaming their coach for not instructing them to stop their program or being more insistent that they reskate their program. In the women's competition, Kira Ivanova won the compulsory figures for the second year in a row at Europeans, with Katarina Witt finishing a disappointing fourth behind Claudia Leistner and Anna Kondrashova. Witt's short program to a synthesizer version of Gershwin's "In The Mood" may have been hard on the ears, but it wasn't hard on the eyes. She skated brilliantly to win the second phase of the competition over Kondrashova, Ivanova and Leistner but entered the free skate in third place overall. Witt more than rose to the occasion, executing four triple jumps, two toe-loops and two Salchows - in her *West Side Story* free skate. The rest of the contenders skated poorly. Ivanova fell on a triple Salchow and stepped out of a triple loop, while Kondrashova two-footed the landings of three triples. When the marks were tallied, Witt was first, Ivanova second and Kondrashova third - the same podium finish from Europeans a year prior. Claudia Leistner finished fourth and afterwards, her coach Ondrej Nepela was vocal about his disagreement with the result. British judge Vanessa Riley cautioned, "You have to be careful with coaches. A coach is not going to say his girl is worse, or she will go to another trainer. This is his living. It's very easy to make the judges the scapegoat. It's very easy to say, 'Yes, dear, you were wonderful. The judges didn't know what they were doing.'" With 1986 European Champion Jozef Sabovčík out due to injury, the men's event in Sarajevo was the only title left undefended. Alexandr Fadeev, who had won the title in 1984, took the lead over Vladimir Kotin in the figures. In the first two figures, the judges were split five-four between Fadeev and Kotin, but in the third figure, the loop, five of the nine judges had Kotin in fifth. In the short program, the top three positions were attained by Fadeev, Viktor Petrenko and Kotin. Fadeev and Petrenko both landed triple Axel/double toe-loop combinations. Two men landing triple Axels in the short program was a first at Europeans.

In the free skate, Fadeev executed no less than seven triple jumps in the first two and a half minutes of his program, including a triple Axel and triple Lutz/triple toe-loop combination, receiving three 6.0s from the judges - one for technical merit and two for presentation. Kotin delivered a strong performance to win the silver ahead of Petrenko. Both Petrenko and Poland's Grzegorz Filipowski, who finished third in the free but fourth overall after falling on a triple Axel attempt in the short program, performed triple Axels in the free skate. Fadeev, Kotin and Petrenko's podium sweep was the first ever in the men's event at the European Championships for the Soviet Union, underscoring the dominance of the country that won ten of the twelve medals in Sarajevo.

**Canadian Championships.** In February, Ottawa's Civic Centre played host to the first Canadian Championships in the nation's capital in 29 years. Though attendance was less-than-ideal early in the week, 7000 spectators showed up in the middle of a blizzard to watch the men's and women's free skating. The competition marked the first time in history that the Canadian Championships had a title sponsor. Sugar-free sweetener company NutraSweet was the ironic choice since reporters boasted of the seemingly endless supply of sugar-laden donuts and plates of candy that were served up by members of the Nepean Skating Club in the media room. Tracy Wilson and Rob McCall had a tumultuous season leading up to Canadians. They parted ways with long-time coach Bernie Ford and were working primarily with Marijane Stong and John Briscoe. After a mixed reaction from the judges at the Novarat Trophy in Hungary in the fall, they ditched their Viennese Waltz OSP and put together a tongue in cheek 'prince and pauper' themed parody of a traditional waltz to Strauss' "Tales from the Vienna Woods". At 28, McCall was the oldest of the 243 skaters in Ottawa. Wilson and McCall took a strong lead in the compulsory dances ahead of Karyn and Rod Garossino and Jo-Anne Borlase and Scott Chalmers, but their biggest test of the event would be the OSP. The new program earned them marks from 5.6 to 5.8 and expanded their already healthy lead. Disaster struck Jo-Anne Borlase and Scott Chalmers when they finished a shocking sixth in the OSP after a fall and a stumble. They dropped to fifth overall, behind the Garossinos, Penny Mann and Richard Perkins and Michelle McDonald and Michael Farrington, who placed third in that segment in the competition. Wilson and McCall had a slight stumble late in their free dance to the strains of Duke Ellington, but their intricate footwork and clever choreography were a cut above the rest. The Garossinos took the silver with a circus-inspired march program to Henry Mancini's soundtrack to *The Great Waldo Pepper*. Borlase and Chalmers moved up to take the bronze with an energetic free dance to South American rhythms. For the fourth year in a row, Lyndon Johnston found himself atop the podium in the fours competition at the Canadian Championships. In 1987, he shared the victory with his pairs partner Denise Benning, Laureen Collin and John Penticost. Cynthia Coull and Mark took the lead in the pairs short program. Though they couldn't seem to put a foot wrong, their efforts were overshadowed by the second-place team, whose story was the talk of the competition. A very serious fall on a lift in practice the autumn before the competition left Doug Ladret in the hospital with a skull fracture and a concussion. Ladret arrived in Ottawa with an addition to his costume: a hockey helmet. CFSA officials claimed it was the first time a skater ever wore a helmet at Canadians. Ladret hadn't just been practicing with a helmet for his own safety. He was concerned about his partner, Christine Hough, who had suffered a serious concussion a couple of years prior. Ladret sported his black helmet for the first half of his short program, but after performing the same lasso lift that caused him his injury, he took it off mid-performance, handed it to coach Dave Howe and kept going. The crowd went bananas.

**1987 CANADIAN CHAMPIONSHIPS**
(Ottawa, ON, February 2-7, 1987)

Men:

1. Brian Orser
2. Kurt Browning
3. Michael Slipchuk
4. Neil Paterson
5. Brad McLean
6. Matthew Hall
7. Mark MacVean
8. Rob Lenarduzzi
9. Martin Marceau
10. Jeff Partrick

Women:

1. Elizabeth Manley
2. Patricia Schmidt
3. Linda Florkevich
4. Dianne Takeuchi
5. Charlene Wong
6. Joelle Tustin
7. Shannon Allison
8. Lindsay Fedosoff
9. Pamela Giangualano
10. Shelley Ann Smith

Pairs:

1. Cynthia Coull and Mark Rowsom
2. Denise Benning and Lyndon Johnston
3. Christine Hough and Doug Ladret
4. Laureen Collin and John Penticost
5. Katherine and Rob Kates
6. Melanie Gaylor and Lee Barkell
7. Lori Rissling and Scott Grover
8. Lynda and John Ivanich
9. Laura and Jamie Ivanich
10. Nathalie Rodrigue and Jim Blackburn

Ice Dance:

1. Tracy Wilson and Rob McCall
2. Karyn and Rod Garossino
3. Jo-Anne Borlase and Scott Chalmers
4. Penny Mann and Richard Perkins
5. Michelle McDonald and Michael Farrington
6. Erica Davenport and Mark Mitchell
7. Melanie Cole and Martin Smith
8. Kimberley Weeks and Curtis Moore
9. Nathalie Lessard and Darcy Pleckham
10. Gayle Coughtry and Jeff Fish

Fours:

1. Denise Benning, Laureen Collin, Lyndon Johnston and John Penticost
2. Christine Hough, Michelle Menzies, Doug Ladret and Kevin Wheeler
3. Cynthia Coull, Melanie Gaylor, Mark Rowsom and Lee Barkell

A fall on footwork by Hough was the only thing to detract from their gutsy performance. Benning and Johnston, together for only a year, finished third after Benning fell on a side-by-side double loop. In a classical free skate set to the music of Riccardo Drigo, Coull and Rowsom were again spectacular. Their only major error was a miss by Rowsom on a side-by-side double Axel attempt. When Rowsom retired, he hoped to become a professional singer. He was a music major at the University of Waterloo and sang the national anthem at the Opening Ceremonies of the 1984 World Championships and a Toronto Blue Jays game. He was also a pro at knitting sweaters. Benning and Johnston wowed the crowd with their signature statue lift, a variation on the platter lift where she flipped in the air on the exit, but the team struggled on their jumping passes. Hough fell on a throw triple Salchow and both she and Ladret unfortunately lost steam in the latter half of their program. In the end, it was Coull and Rowsom first, Benning and Johnston second, and Hough and Ladret third. A notable face missing in Ottawa was Lloyd Eisler. After the retirement of Karen Westby, he had just teamed up with a new partner, Isabelle Brasseur. The duo planned to make their debut in competition the following season. In the women's event, Elizabeth Manley got a bye to Ottawa through the Eastern Divisionals as she had a flu over Christmas that laid her up for three weeks. Manley finished second to Patricia Schmidt on the first compulsory figure but won the other two. A surprising third was Joelle Tustin, who had missed the 1986 Canadian Championships and placed 11th in 1985. Linda Florkevich, who had beaten Schmidt at the Western Divisionals, was fourth and Charlene Wong was sixth. An unlucky 13th and last was Mississauga's Lindsay Fedosoff, who arrived at the Nepean Sportsplex for the school figures with a mismatched pair of skates - a left free skating boot and a right figures boot. In the short program, Manley expanded her lead with a clean but cautious program. Instead of going for her planned triple Lutz combination, she performed a gorgeous triple toe-loop/double loop combination and ended up with marks ranging from 5.6 to 5.8. Schmidt and Florkevich also skated cleanly to finish second and third. An overrotation on a triple toe-loop attempt only allowed Charlene Wong to climb one spot in the standings. Dressed in black and gold for the free skate, Manley reclaimed her Canadian title despite errors on four of the five triples she attempted. It was not the skate Manley wanted to have, but the mistakes she made were quite understandable. After doubling a planned triple flip, the double knot in the lace on her right skate came undone. She could feel the other knot loosening after she fell on the loop, but pressed on and lost focus. She looked at the situation as a learning experience - if the same thing were to happen at the World Championships, she would stop her program. 16-year-old Dianne Takeuchi finished second ahead of Florkevich and Schmidt in the free skate with excellent spins and the only two triple performance in the competition, but Patricia Schmidt's strong performances in the figures and short program kept her in second overall ahead of Florkevich. Takeuchi, only ninth in figures, placed fourth overall. In the men's event, Brian Orser skated three of the best figures of his career to take an early lead over Neil Paterson (who won the loop), Kurt Browning and Michael Slipchuk. After badly spraining his right ankle in a pre-competition practice, 1986 Canadian Bronze Medallist Jaimee Eggleton finished a disastrous 11th and withdrew from the competition. Orser credited his improvement in the figures to his work with sports psychologist Peter Jensen and former Olympic Medallists Karol Divín and Jimmy Grogan. Orser was spectacular in the short program, landing a triple Axel and earning 5.9s from all seven judges for technical merit and one 5.9 and six 6.0s for artistic impression. Paterson remained in second, ahead of Browning, who landed a chose the triple Lutz as his combination jump. Orser skated his *Ladyhawke* program lights out. He landed two triple Axels, one after the four-minute mark, and four other triples to earn ten 5.9s and four perfect 6.0s.

**CANADIAN CHAMPIONSHIPS** (continued)

Junior Winners:

Norm Proft (men)
Angie Folk (women)
Michelle Menzies and Kevin Wheeler (pairs)
Catherine Pal and Donald Godfrey (ice dance)

Novice Winners:

Glenn Fortin (men)
Margot Bion (women)
Stacey Ball and Jeffrey Gavin (pairs)
Brigitte Richer and Michel Brunet (ice dance)

*Kurt Browning. Photo courtesy Elaine Hooper / St. Ivel Figure Skating Archive.*

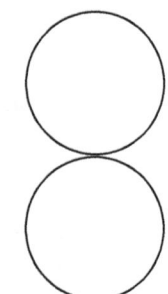

In winning, Orser became the first person since Montgomery Wilson to win seven consecutive Canadian senior men's titles. In his second year as a senior, Browning moved up to take the silver with a five-triple program - his best performance in competition to date. At the time, Browning had been landing the quadruple toe-loop in practice, but he caught an edge on the entry to the toe-loop in his free skate and did not attempt it. After landing a triple Axel, Paterson overrated almost every other jump in his program and tumbled off the podium behind Slipchuk.

**World Championships.** In March, the Riverfront Coliseum and Albert B. Sabin Convention Center in Cincinnati, Ohio played host to the first World Championships on American soil since 1981. 132 skaters from 14 countries participated in the event. The explosive popularity of figure skating over the decade led to unprecedented ticket sales. 170 000 people jammed their way into the facilities over the course in the competition, with free skating events sold out months in advance. The demand for tickets was so great that the Organizing Committee started selling tickets to the practice sessions at three dollars a pop. 3000 spectators showed up just to watch one of the women's practices. The event wasn't without its minor snafus. Thousands of programs had to be recalled after they were printed because a full-page photo of Katarina Witt listed her country as East Germany. Volunteers spent hours doctoring the programs with stickers that said 'G.D.R.' There were also problems with the ice at the Albert B. Sabin Convention Center. A Zamboni mishap caused refrigeration fluid to spill onto the ice. Some practices had to be moved to another facility, the Northland Ice Center. Olympic Gold Medallists Jayne Torvill and Christopher Dean were honoured at the event as recipients of the ISU's prestigious Jacques Favart Trophy. The competition's official mascot was Blades, a white tiger with a long neck scarf knitted with flags of the countries that participated. The pairs event started on quite a high with all the top six teams skating clean programs. Defending World Champions Ekaterina Gordeeva and Sergei Grinkov won the short program with first-place ordinals from seven of the nine judges. They skated with assurance and speed to Honky Tonk style music clearly chosen with the American audience in mind. Elena Valova and Oleg Vasiliev placed second, demonstrating the same level of speed and perhaps more maturity in their program set to Georgian folk music. Jill Watson and Peter Oppegard's energetic program kept them just ahead of Canada's Cynthia Coull and Mark Rowsom, who skated to Ravel's "Spring Quartet in F Major". Americans Gillian and Wachsman and Todd Wagonner and Canadians Denise Benning and Lyndon Johnston rounded out the top six teams, all of whom executed double twists and side-by-side double loop jumps without issue. Larisa Selezneva and Oleg Makarov finished down in seventh, just ahead of the third Canadian pair Christine Hough and Doug Ladret. Selezneva and Makarov started their program with side-by-side spins, but Makarov abruptly stopped mid-spin and went over to the judges, complaining that there was a problem with their tape. After some discussion, the referee allowed them to start their program from the beginning. In the reskate, their side-by-side jumps were not in good unison and Makarov stumbled, coming out of the side-by-side spins. Shuk-Ching Ngai and Cheuk-Fai Lai, the pairs team from Hong Kong that placed last in the competition, were so out of their league in their short program to "Romeo and Juliet" that one judge gave them a 0.2 for technical merit. Their highest mark was a 2.7 for presentation. Most of their technical merit marks were around 0.8 and most of their presentation marks were around 1.8.

**1987 WORLD CHAMPIONSHIPS**
(Cincinnati, OH, March 10-15, 1987)

Men:

1. Brian Orser (CAN)
2. Brian Boitano (USA)
3. Alexandr Fadeev (SOV)
4. Vladimir Kotin (SOV)
5. Grzegorz Filipowski (POL)
6. Viktor Petrenko (SOV)
7. Christopher Bowman (USA)
8. Petr Barna (CZE)
9. Richard Zander (FRG)
10. Scott Williams (USA)

Women:

1. Katarina Witt (GDR)
2. Debi Thomas (USA)
3. Caryn Kadavy (USA)
4. Elizabeth Manley (CAN)
5. Kira Ivanova (SOV)
6. Claudia Leistner (FRG)
7. Jill Trenary (USA)
8. Midori Ito (JPN)
9. Anna Kondrashova (SOV)
10. Joanne Conway (GRB)

Pairs:

1. Ekaterina Gordeeva and Sergei Grinkov (SOV)
2. Elena Valova and Oleg Vasiliev (SOV)
3. Jill Watson and Peter Oppegard (USA)
4. Larisa Selezneva and Oleg Makarov (SOV)
5. Denise Benning and Lyndon Johnston (CAN)
6. Cynthia Coull and Mark Rowsom (CAN)
7. Gillian Wachsman and Todd Waggoner (USA)
8. Christine Hough and Doug Ladret (CAN)
9. Cheryl Peake and Andrew Naylor (GRB)
10. Lenka Knapová and René Novotný (CZE)

Ice Dance:

1. Natalia Bestemianova and Andrei Bukin (SOV)
2. Marina Klimova and Sergei Ponomarenko (SOV)
3. Tracy Wilson and Rob McCall (CAN)
4. Natalia Annenko and Genrikh Sretenski (SOV)
5. Suzanne Semanick and Scott Gregory (USA)
6. Kathrin and Christoff Beck (AUT)
7. Antonia and Ferdinand Becherer (FRG)
8. Klára Engi and Attila Tóth (HUN)
9. Isabelle and Paul Duchesnay (FRA)
10. Karyn and Rod Garossino (CAN)

Though the team's training conditions were very poor, they had actually come a long way since they started working with Australian coach Kathy Kitchner. She told reporters, "When I came six months ago, they were teaching themselves. I'm here to support them, but I don't feel they are ready for this." American pairs coach Pieter Kollen took the struggling team under his wing in practice, reminding, "The fun of sports is more than the competition; it's the sportsmanship involved." In the free skate, Gordeeva and Grinkov again selected music with the American crowd in mind - "Caravan", "Mack the Knife", "In The Mood" and "St. Louis Blues". Making it look easy, 'G and G' showed North American audiences the fabulous quadruple twist they performed in Sarajevo at Europeans, as well as two sets of side-by-side double Axels and a throw triple Salchow. The judges rewarded them with two 5.9s for technical merit and one for presentation. In contrast to the youthful exuberance of 'G and G', Valova and Vasiliev's program to well-known polka, waltz and march music by Strauss was in the more traditional style of Soviet pairs skating. They included their trademark side-by-side triple toe-loops, throw triple Salchow and throw triple toe-loop but had an awkward catch on their triple twist late in the program. The judges rewarded 'V and V' with one more 5.9 for artistic impression than 'G and G' but they were placed second. Selezneva and Makarov rallied back with a technically demanding free skate featuring side-by-side triple toe-loops, a throw double Axel and a throw triple toe-loop. Their comeback effort was only enough to finish fourth behind Watson and Oppegard, who earned a standing ovation in their home country for a flawless program set to Stravinsky's "The Firebird". A fall on a throw and a botched triple twist proved costly errors for Coull and Rowsom, who dropped to sixth behind Benning and Johnston. Though their eighth-place finish was the lowest of the Canadian pairs, Hough and Ladret arguably had the cleaner skate. They made history in Cincinnati as the first Canadian pair to land the throw triple toe-loop at the World Championships. In the ice dance event, it was over for Hong Kong's team before it even started. There were two different skating associations in the country and the ISU sent the regulations for Worlds to the wrong one. Cheung Lai-yuk and Chan Chiu-keung showed up with an OSP that was the wrong rhythm and a free dance that was only two minutes and fifteen seconds long. To make matters worse, Cheung became very ill after eating Western food for the first time. To their dismay, Cheung and Chan were forced to withdraw. There were no great revelations or judging revolutions in the compulsory dances. Natalia Bestemianova and Andrei Bukin won all three dances - the Westminster Waltz, Yankee Polka and Blues. At 29, Bukin was the oldest skater in any category at the Championships. Marina Klimova and Sergei Ponomarenko and Tracy Wilson and Rob McCall placed second and third, the same order they had finished in at the previous year's Worlds in Geneva. The Duchesnays sat in tenth, one spot behind their old Canadian rivals Karyn and Rod Garossino. Canada's number three team, Jo-Anne Borlase and Scott Chalmers were well down the ladder in 17th. The most amusing part of the compulsories was when the referee, Hans Kutschera, pulled "Oh! Susanna" from the rotation for the Yankee Polka because the crowd was getting boisterous with their applause and causing a distraction. Confident and consistent as ever, Bestemianova and Bukin delivered a very strong OSP to one of the quintessential waltz tunes of all time - Strauss' "Emperor Waltz". Their marks - all 5.8s and 5.9s - seemed unbeatable. Marina Klimova and Sergei Ponomarenko put a spanner in the works when they received marks even higher than 'B and B', including a perfect 6.0 from American judge Jean Robinson, to place first in OSP. The only other changes in the standings were the 12th and 13th place and 20th and 21st place teams switching positions. The status quo of ice dance judging was alive and well. In the free dance, Bestemianova and Bukin were as theatrical as ever, delivering their romping *Cabaret* program with as much gusto as they could muster. As fully expected, they won their third consecutive World title with high marks indeed, including six perfect 6.0s from the Austrian, French, Hungarian, Italian, Polish and Soviet judges. Klimova and Ponomarenko's free dance to Liszt's "Hungarian Rhapsody" finished second as predicted, but the French judge Daniel de Paix generously gave the couple his second 6.0 of the night. Wilson and McCall took the bronze for the second year in a row, skating even better than they had at Canadians. The Duchesnays and Garossinos finished ninth and tenth; Borlase and Smith remained in 17th. The men's event began with the compulsory figures. Alexandr Fadeev was the early leader, winning both the RFI-LBI counter and LFO-RFI paragraph bracket. The surprise winner of the third figure, a RBO-LBI paragraph loop, was Brian Orser, who had never won a figure at the Worlds in the six times he had competed. Entering the short program, the overall standings in the figures had Fadeev in first, followed by defending World Champion Brian Boitano, Orser, Vladimir Kotin and Viktor Petrenko. Only four-tenths of a point separated the top three skaters. Brian Orser won over both the judges and crowd in the short program, landing a triple Axel/double toe-loop combination and earning seven 5.9s for technical merit and six for artistic impression. All but the American judge, Janet Allen, had him in first place over Boitano and Fadeev, who both skated clean programs featuring less difficult triple Lutz combinations. Orser's technical prowess was evident even in the practices in Cincinnati. Though he had no intention of including the jump in his free skate, he landed four quadruple toe-loops to show people he could do it. In the warm-up for the final flight of the men's free skate, Boitano landed a quad of his own, but an attempt in his program was underrotated.

Though he executed a clean triple Axel/double toe-loop combination and his trademark 'Tano Lutz, Boitano erred on a triple flip combination late in his program. Fadeev, who was suffering from a groin injury, had problems on his triple Axel attempt and turned a planned triple Lutz/triple toe-loop combination into a triple/double, but skated an otherwise dynamic program to Russian folk music. Orser was electric, making history as the first skater to land two triple Axels in one program and three triple Axels in one competition on the way to winning Canada's first gold medal in the men's event at the World Championships in 24 years. Boitano and Fadeev settled for silver and bronze, making for an exceptionally rare podium where all the medallists had the title World Champion on their proverbial résumé. Though hampered by a fall on the combination in the short program, Kurt Browning landed a triple/triple combination in the free skate and finished 15th in his first trip to the World Championships. Browning's Royal Glenora training mate, Michael Slipchuk, placed a disappointing twentieth, rattled by an unfortunate incident where he had to restart his free skate when a photographer accidentally dropped a plastic film container on the ice. At the medal ceremony for the men, ISU officials awarded the wrong medals - the small medals for figures instead of the championship ones. A security guard raced to the vault to get the correct ones and Orser, Boitano and Fadeev blocked the medals with flowers in the official photograph of the winners. The women's event began with the compulsory figures. In the first figure, a RFI-LBI counter, reigning World Champion Debi Thomas carved out an early lead over Kira Ivanova, Elizabeth Manley and Claudia Leistner. Katarina Witt finished sixth. On the LFO-RFI paragraph bracket, Ivanova fell behind Thomas, Caryn Kadavy, Leistner and Witt. Ivanova rebounded to win the final figure, a RBO-LBI paragraph bracket, by a wide margin over Kadavy, Leistner, Manley and Witt. Thomas' tendinitis flared up and she finished ninth on the final figure. When the marks were tallied, Ivanova won the figures, ahead of Thomas, Leistner, Kadavy, Witt and Manley. Hong Kong's Edith Poon was placed dead last, having practiced the wrong figures until someone set her straight upon her arrival in Cincinnati. Poon was a roller skater who had only been skating on ice for three months. The judges had their work cut out for them in the short program. Thomas had the crowd on her side and seemed poised to take the top spot until, after landing a solid double toe-loop/triple toe-loop combination, she put a hand down on her double Axel. On any other day, the mistake wouldn't have necessarily been overly costly. However, every single one of her challengers couldn't have skated better and if you asked who should have been placed first, you would have gotten a different answer from everyone. Seven of the nine judges preferred Witt's boppy "In The Mood" program, placing her in first over superb performances by Manley, Midori Ito, Trenary, Kadavy and Ivanova. Thomas finished a disappointing seventh - which was a generous result as Leistner, who placed eighth, skated a clean program. Entering the free skate, Ivanova remained the leader, followed by Witt, Thomas, Manley, Kadavy and Leistner. It was so close at the top one reporter called it "a traffic jam". A capacity crowd watched the women's free skate and, for the first time, CBS covered the event in prime time. The television coverage received the highest ratings since the Superbowl. The event was full of surprises. Skating earlier than the leaders because she had placed only 14th in the figures, Ito attempted the most ambitious program of the night. Though she fell on a triple Lutz attempt, she landed no less than six triples, including a triple flip and two difficult combinations - the triple toe-loop/triple toe-loop and double Axel/half loop/triple Salchow. Trenary was solid as well, landing her trademark one-foot-Axel/triple Salchow and a triple flip. Organizers told the women skating in the final flight that due to the television broadcast, which of course featured commercials, they would have to wait anywhere from two to twenty minutes before they could get on the ice. The first two skaters in the final group, Leistner and Ivanova, both made costly errors on jumps. Kadavy had the skate of her life, landing two triple loops and earning a standing ovation from the American crowd. Rattled by Kadavy's high marks and distracted after picking up flower petals left on the ice, Manley lost focus and had a very disappointing skate, landing only one triple and falling on her triple Lutz. Thomas delivered an exceptional program, her only error being a two-footed landing on a triple loop, and received a standing ovation even louder than Kadavy's. Thomas' performance was particularly remarkable in that missed a week of training in the lead-up to the competition due to injury. The final skater of the night, Witt delivered one of her finer performances in competition, landing five triples including the loop on which Thomas had faltered. She was rewarded with marks ranging from 5.7 to a perfect 6.0 for artistic impression from East German judge Reinhard Mirmseker. In the end, Witt took the gold, Thomas the silver and Kadavy the bronze. Manley finished fourth, followed by Ivanova, Leistner, Trenary and Ito. Patricia Schmidt, Canada's second woman, placed an impressive 11th. It was the first time two American women had been on the podium at the Worlds since Carol Heiss Jenkins and Barbara Roles Williams in 1960.

*Katarina Witt. Contributor: PCN Photography / Alamy Stock Photo.*

*Ekaterina Gordeeva and Sergei Grinkov. Contributor: PCN Photography / Alamy Stock Photo.*

# 1987-1988 SEASON

Hit Songs: "Faith" by George Michael, "Never Gonna Give You Up" by Rick Astley, "Hands To Heaven" by Breathe, "Fast Car" by Tracy Chapman, "Don't Worry, Be Happy" by Bobby McFerrin
Hit Movies: Who Framed Roger Rabbit, Big, Twins, Rain Man, A Fish Called Wanda
Hit TV: The Golden Girls, ALF, L.A. Law, A Different World, Cheers
News: Sinking of Doña Paz is the deadliest peacetime Maritime Disaster in history, Yellowstone Fires, U.S. And Canada reach Free Trade Agreement

## PEOPLE

Following injuries and a disappointing 1986-1987 season, Tiffany Chin decided to turn professional and accept a lucrative offer to tour with *Holiday on Ice*'s Asian tour, giving guest performances with the *Ice Capades* as well in select cities. After years of suffering from a groin injury, Mark Rowsom had surgery with the knowledge that the recovery time wouldn't allow him and Cynthia Coull to be contenders at the Olympics. He announced his retirement in the summer and focused on his studies at Wilfrid Laurier University. He also coached part-time with Kerry Leitch at the national pairs center in Cambridge. Coull moved to Toronto to go to York University. She continued to train there in singles for a couple of weeks, then decided to hang up her skates as well. Other skaters retiring after the 1986-1987 season included Donald Adair, Falko Kirsten, Tobias Schröter and Masaru Ogawa.

Wedding bells rang in Bratislava when Jozef Sabovčík and Tracey Wainman said "I do". Linda Fratianne traded her Blue Fairy costume from *Walt Disney's World on Ice* for a wedding dress when she walked down the aisle to marry Nick Maricich, a ski racer who was a stunt skater with the tour. Just before competing in the World Championships in March, Debi Thomas quietly married Brian Vanden Hogen in Boulder, Colorado. Thomas and Vanden Hogen met at the University of Colorado at Boulder, where Debi had been training and attending classes. Brian was a senior majoring in sports medicine and physical therapy.

At the United States Olympic Festival in Greensboro, North Carolina in July, Grammy Award-winning singer Roberta Flack performed at the Opening Ceremonies. At the event, Flack met her second cousin Rory, who won a gold medal at the event, for the first time.

In September, Tracey Damigella had the unusual distinction of being the first American skater to finish in first place in the senior women's event at the Australian Championships. The NISAA often invited skaters from abroad to compete in its Championships as special guests, but never before had any of them won. Though she won all three phases in the competition, per the rules of the event she was not awarded the title because she was a guest.

After the cancellation of their American tour the previous season, Jayne Torvill and Christopher Dean took some time away from the gruelling life of their World Tour. After Dean had recovered from their injury, the duo performed as special guests with the *Ice Capades* in select cities in Canada and the United States and acted as guest commentators for Australian television coverage of the Calgary Olympics.

Terry Kubicka, best remembered for performing a backflip at the 1976 Olympics, received his Doctorate of Veterinary Medicine from the University of California. Kubicka went on to work with the Sacramento Animal Medical Group, specializing in small animal medicine and surgery. The same year, Scott Cramer received his Doctor of Chiropractic degree from the Los Angeles College of Chiropractic and opened a practice in Colorado Springs.

Two of the greatest skating duos of the 70s received long-overdue recognition. Lyudmila Pakhomova and Aleksandr Gorshkov were the latest inductees to the World Figure Skating Hall of Fame. Gorshkov accepted plaques for himself and the family of his late wife Pakhomova at a banquet at the ISU Congress in Davos in May. *American Skating World* bestowed its coveted Professional Skater of the Year Award on Tai Babilonia and Randy Gardner. Babilonia and Gardner and Scott Hamilton were also honoured as the winners of the USOC's Maxwell House Coffee Olympic Spirit Awards at a special ceremony at the Hart Senate Office in Washington, D.C.

Figure skating took center stage on Parliament Hill in Ottawa in April when the COA inducted Brian Orser and Suzanne Morrow-Francis to the Canadian Amateur Sports Hall of Fame at a special luncheon ceremony. The timing was fitting, as Orser had just won a silver medal at the Calgary Olympics, where Morrow-Francis made history as the first woman to give the Judge's Oath in the Opening Ceremony.

Following the Olympic Games and World Championships, there was a massive exodus of skaters to the professional ranks. While some skaters flocked to ice revues like *Holiday on Ice* and the *Ice Capades*, a great deal more were starting to be "freelance professionals" and work with agents to piece together a schedule that included a mixture of touring, one-off shows and competitions. It was announced that Katarina Witt, Tracy Wilson and Rob McCall, Elizabeth Manley, Brian Orser, Debi Thomas, Elena Valova and Oleg Vasiliev and Kira Ivanova were all moving on before the summer.

In the spring, the American figure skating community mourned the deaths of Edith and John Shoemaker, just two months apart. John was the USFSA's President in the 60s. He was the ISU's first Vice-President for a decade in the 70s and played an instrumental role in the development of skating on the West Coast. Edith was an esteemed judge and referee who served as an official at two Olympics, nine World Championships and no less than 20 U.S. Championships over the years. The couple's contributions to American figure skating over the years were immeasurable.

Dr. Tenley Albright was one of four American athletes inducted into the U.S. Olympic Hall of Fame in May. The induction ceremony was held aboard the ocean liner M.S. Seaward, docked in New York Harbor.

George J. Blundun, the first Canadian to become an Honourary Member of the ISU, passed away in Calgary in May. A former President of the CFSA, Blundun served as a judge at two World Championships and served on the ISU's Ice Dance Committee. He played an instrumental role in the development of the Skate Canada competition and served as the General Chairman of the 1972 World Championships in Calgary. Just months before his death, Blundun came out of retirement to help with the organization of the figure skating events at the Olympics.

## AROUND THE WORLD

**New Zealand.** Kiwi skaters rejoiced as the NZISA celebrated its fiftieth anniversary. The country had four indoor ice rinks in operation by the 1987-1988 season - two in Auckland, one in Christchurch and one in Gore, as well as an outdoor artificially frozen rink at Alexandra in Central Otago. Three of the country's skating officials were certified to judge at the international level. The development of the sport was bolstered by several Canadian and American coaches and the keen interest and involvement of the CFSA's Technical Director, Barbara Graham. Rhona Whitehouse, a long-time NZISA Figure Committee member, penned a meticulous history of the Association for its Jubilee.

**United States.** The estimated annual expenses of U.S. World Team skaters exceeded 40 000 dollars a year. Nearly 6000 dollars are spent on costumes alone. For the first time, the USFSA organized a seminar for elite ice dancers where American ice dancers could benefit from instruction from Soviet coaches. Ron Ludington and Carlo Fassi collaborated on the project with Natalia Dubova and Aleksandr Gorshkov and Marina Klimova and Sergei Ponomarenko and Maya Usova and Alexandr Zhulin gave demonstrations for the elite U.S. teams in attendance. The Skating Association for the Blind and Handicapped, based out of Buffalo, NY, became an Associate Member of the USFSA. Olympic Gold Medallist Dr. Kurt Oppelt was a passionate advocate for accessibility in the sport, reminding people that anyone could "benefit from therapeutic ice skating." Long before the idea of World Ice Skating Day was conceived by the ISU, the USFSA, PSGA and ISIA partnered with NutraSweet to present the first National Ice Skating Awareness Week in November. The week's goal was to celebrate the beauty of skating and introducing new people to the sport. Over 100 rinks in the country offered NutraSweet Skate Days where skating, skate rentals and group lessons were free. Wollman Park in New York City staged an ice show featuring performances by Dorothy Hamill and Richard Dwyer. Hamill did public service announcements on radio and television and national team members like Debi Thomas, Suzanne Semanick and Scott Gregory and Jill Watson and Peter Oppegard all made appearances to promote the week's events. The Week was so successful that it became an annual affair in subsequent years.

## FUN AND GAMES

Up In The Air Inc., a stuffed animal company based out of Alpharetta, Georgia, released a line of 'Stuffed Stunts' based on figure skating elements. There was a Flying Camel, Double-toe Wally the Walrus, a two-headed cow called Double Salchow and a 'wild and crazy bird' called Spread Eagle. At nearly 30 dollars a pop, the Stuffed Stunts were not the kind of toys you found in a cereal box.

# BEHIND THE SCENES

The Federación Mexicana de Patinaje Sobre Hielo and the Thailand Ice Skating Association became the latest skating federations to join the ISU.

At the ISU Congress in Davos, Sonia Bianchetti Garbato became the first woman to be elected to the ISU Council. Benjamin T. Wright became the first American to be elected chairman of a major ISU Committee - the Technical Committee for Figure Skating. It was also announced that F. Ritter Shumway would be honoured as a recipient of the Georg Häsler medal. Shumway was also honoured by the PSGA with a National Recognition of Achievement Award for his lifelong support of the sport.

The ISU voted to approve several sweeping and historic rule changes at its May Congress, first and foremost being the gradual elimination of compulsory figures in both junior and senior international competitions. Effective July 1, 1988, the number of figures skated was reduced from three to two, with figures being worth 20 percent, a new original program worth 30 percent and free skating worth 50. On July 1, 1990, figures would be eliminated, with the original program worth just over 33 percent and free skating almost 67. Four federations (the CFSA, NISA, USFSA and NZISA) voted against figures being abolished. Interestingly, the CFSA submitted a proposal that three-part compound figures be added to the schedule to make them more difficult, which was shot down. The USFSA unsuccessfully submitted an equally unpopular proposal to have a short program skated first, then two figures, followed by a free skating program. Opinions remained very divided on the issue, with many strong opinions from the sport's leaders, officials, coaches and skaters expressed in the press. Shadowing the North America .vs. Europe debate about figures, Canada's Elizabeth Manley and Brian Orser were adamant figures should stay, while Katarina Witt felt just as strongly they should go. Dick Button believed the elimination of figures had everything to do with the demands of television producers, remarking, "There is no flair, no originality in them [but] I would hate to see a very interesting activity lost because it is expensive or it doesn't make good TV." The guidelines for the original program were outlined. Skaters would perform for a maximum of 2 minutes and 40 seconds, including eight required elements in their programs. The men were required to perform a double Axel, a triple jump preceded by steps or other free skating movements, a jump combination of two doubles, a double and a triple or two triples, a flying spin, spin with at least two changes of foot, spin combination and two different types of step sequences - either straight line, circular or serpentine. Women did a double as the solo jump, were not permitted to do a triple/triple and did a layback or sideways leaning spin instead of the spin with at least two changes of foot. Instead of two step sequences, they did one step sequence and a spiral sequence. Curiously, men were allowed to do any triple jump as their solo jump, but women and junior men were allowed to any double except the Axel. In the junior women's event, the double Axel was not allowed to be repeated. In pairs, the original program required elements were an overhead lift, double twist lift, double solo jump, side-by-side spins with or without a change of foot, a pair spin combination with at least one change of position and only one change of foot, death spiral, spiral sequence and step sequence. Kerry Leitch thought the elements of the pairs original should have been more difficult, suggesting a throw jump be added. A revised schedule for deductions required all judges to penalize skaters from to two to five-tenths of a point for all errors on a jump combination or prescribed jump. Errors on all other elements or extra or repeated elements ranged ranged from one to three-tenths of a point.

In pairs, the deduction for failed lifts or side-by-side jumps ranged from two to four-tenths of a point, with a mandatory six-tenths-of-a-point deduction for omissions of these elements. For the 1988-1989 season, only the top 20 skaters after the figures and original program would advance to the free skate. In ice dance, the number of compulsory dances was reduced from two to three, with compulsory dances worth 20 percent, the OSP 30 and free dance 50. This rule change was opposed vehemently by the USFSA. For the 1988/89 season, a draw would be done at each Championship from a group of four dances - the Westminster Waltz, Yankee Polka, Rhumba and Argentine Tango. The OSP rhythm was announced as the Charleston. Age rules for juniors were revised, with the minimum age for all categories being twelve and the maximum for women being seventeen and for men, pairs and ice dance eighteen, by July 1 before the competition. The second mark (artistic impression or presentation) became the tie-breaker in free skating and free dancing and a new 'Call to Start' rule was also instituted to ensure all ISU Championships ran like clockwork. The new rule stated, "Every competitor must begin each part in the competition (compulsory figure, dance, short program, original set pattern dance, free skating, and free dancing) no later than two minutes after his name has been announced, failing which such competitor shall be considered withdrawn."

A hot topic during the 1987-1988 season was the IOC's rules surrounding amateurism. Two years prior, the first changes to the Olympic Charter in more than 90 years had been made, gradually paving the way for professional athletes to compete at the Olympics in sports like hockey, track and field and tennis. IOC President Juan Antonio Samaranch was a staunch believer that "the best athletes" should be able to compete in the Games, regardless of their amateur status. Many in the skating world were already pondering the possibility that professional skaters might have the opportunity to be reinstated to the amateur ranks in time for the 1992 Winter Olympics in Albertville. Dick Button was all for it, providing compulsory figures remained a part of the Games telling reporters, "It is fraudulent now. You either cancel the Olympics or you open it up so that the best person wins." One of the first skaters to publicly announce they would love to come back, in the fall of 1987, was Elaine Zayak.

## ART AND HISTORY

In an Olympic season, historical skating buffs couldn't help but look back at two very important milestones. 1988 marked the twentieth anniversary of Peggy Fleming's win at the 1968 Olympics in Grenoble and the fortieth anniversary of Barbara Ann Scott and Dick Button's victories at the 1948 Olympics in St. Moritz.

## FILMS AND TELEVISION

In October, CBC aired Randy Bradshaw's made-for-television drama *Skate!*, which was later released on BETA and VHS under the title *Blades of Courage*. The film's plot centered around a Canadian figure skater's road to stardom. Leading actress Christiane Hirt was a former competitive figure skater. Debbi Wilkes worked with Suzette Couture on the script and choreographed the skating scenes and Lynn Nightingale was Hirt's mentor and stunt double. The film was criticized for its inaccuracies but won three Gemini Awards, including Best TV Movie.

In November, WGBH Boston aired the ice skating ballet *The Sleeping Beauty: A Ballet on Ice*, featuring choreography by Lars Lubovitch and Tchaikovsky's iconic score performed by the London Symphony Orchestra. The on-ice retelling of the classic Charles Perreault fairy tale featured performances by Robin Cousins, Rosalynn Sumners, Shaun McGill, Patricia Dodd, Lea Ann Miller and Bill Fauver, Nathan Birch, Catherine Foulkes, Stephen Pickavance and Karen Barber.

Inga Schilling, a former star of the Wiener Eisrevue and *Ice Follies*, released a new mail-order instructional video called *Skating Beautifully*, featuring demonstrations by Barry Hagan and Maria Causey. *Skating Beautifully* was unique as compared to many other instructional skating videos, as it focused primarily on how skaters could apply off-ice dance exercises to their on-ice training regimens.

"Skinnamarinky dinky dink... Skinnamarinky do. I love you!" Toller Cranston was a very special guest on Sharon, Lois and Bram's beloved children's program *The Elephant Show* in December.

In January, HBO aired a made-for-television skating special called *World Figure Skating Champions Salute Dorothy Hamill*. The special featured an all-star cast, with performances by Hamill, Scott Hamilton, Robin Cousins, Rosalynn Sumners, Kitty and Peter Carruthers, Judy Blumberg and Michael Seibert and Tiffany Chin. The show ended with a group number to "Hello Dorothy!", a specially recorded take on an old standard made famous by Carol Channing.

## FASHION

A trend towards more theatrical costuming, particularly in the ice dance and women's events, led the ISU to institute new guidelines on skating fashions in May. The ISU's new costume rules stated, "Costumes for Men cannot be theatrical in nature or sleeveless, must have a neckline which does not expose the chest and be without excessive decoration, such as beads, sequins and the like... Costumes for Ladies cannot be theatrical in nature. They must have skirts and pants covering the hips and posterior. A bare midriff is not acceptable. Costumes must be without excessive decoration, such as beads, sequins, feathers and the like. Any ornamentation attached to the costume must be firmly fastened, so as not to fall off while skating under normal competitive conditions." A mandatory two-tenths of a point deduction was instituted for those who flaunted the rules. Katarina Witt's showgirl costume came under the most fire, but Debi Thomas' short program unitard would have broken the rules too as it didn't have a skirt. Toller Cranston quipped, "There are many countries in the world that have horrific taste. East Germany would head the list; chartreuse and orange is heaven for them... But who's going to wield the whip? Your gorgeous might be my grotesque." The media's focus on Katarina Witt's costumes at the Olympics helped to bring figure skating costume designers out of the sewing room and into the spotlight.

Lauren MacDonald Sheehan designed the costumes Debi Thomas, Jill Trenary and Christopher Bowman wore in Calgary. A self-taught seamstress who got an "F" in sewing in high school, MacDonald Sheehan's first Olympic costumes were the dresses she made for Elaine Zayak in 1984. She proudly took credit for being the first to use flesh-coloured cutouts and spandex and lamé appliques and credited Linda Fratianne as the skater who helped put glitzy costumes on the map.

Frances Dafoe was not only a World Champion skater and distinguished judge - she was the queen of Canadian skating fashion. Dafoe designed the costumes worn by Brian Orser and Elizabeth Manley in Calgary, which were created by Margit Sándor. She also created 85 different costume designs for the Closing Ceremony of the Games. In addition to her work with individual skaters and her 'day job' as a designer for CBC, Dafoe also designed costumes for Toller Cranston, Elizabeth Manley and Brian Orser's television specials. Before design fees, Orser's costumes for the Olympics cost 1500 dollars each.

## THE AIDS EPIDEMIC

There were over 132 000 reported cases of AIDS worldwide, 59 000 of which were reported in 1988 alone. The AIDS Memorial Quilt went on display for the first time and the U.S. Surgeon General's Office took the unprecedented step of educating the public about AIDS prevention by mailing an eight-page booklet called *Understanding AIDS* to all American households. It was the largest public health mail campaign in history.

Nearly four months to the day of the death of his partner, Dennis Coi lost his battle with AIDS in British Columbia on September 1, 1987. Coi was only 26 years old when he passed away. Born in North Vancouver, Coi started skating at the age of ten at the North Shore Winter Club. His earliest success in figure skating came at the 1974 Canadians in Moncton, when he won the bronze medal in novice pairs with Julie Mutcher. By the age of fifteen, he passed his Gold tests in figures and free skating. In 1978, he won the Canadian junior men's title and the World Junior Championships in Megève, defeating both Brian Boitano and Brian Orser. He won the bronze medal at the 1982 Canadians in Brandon and narrowly missed a spot on the 1984 Canadian Olympic team. He is remembered for his dramatic style of skating and killer sense of humour.

*Calgary Sun* journalist Christie Blatchford uncovered that in the fall of 1987, after it was learned that Dennis Coi passed away of AIDS-related complications, a suggestion to CFSA officials that "we'd better start preparing to deal with AIDS" was greeted with "a hands-off attitude".

Larry Rost passed away at the age of 50 on May 27, 1988, in Texas. Born in London, England, Rost got his start in figure skating at the Ice Club of Greater Winnipeg in Manitoba. He made his competitive debut in 1952 at the Western Canadian Championships in Vancouver, as part of the silver-medal-winning Winnipeg Four. In 1955, Rost won the Western Canadian junior pairs title with Jane Sinclair. The following year, Sinclair and Rost won their first of three silver medals in the junior pairs event at the Canadians in Galt.

At the 1957 Canadians, Rost was fourth in the junior men's event. Sinclair and Rost won the silver medal in the senior pairs event at the 1959 Canadians and represented Canada at that year's North American Championships. Rost went on to tour with *Holiday on Ice* before teaching skating for 25 years at the Houston Figure Skating Club in Texas.

John Curry received the terrible news that no one wanted to hear - he was HIV-positive. By this point, two of his recent lovers were also positive and another had passed away. Though Curry won an Olympic gold medal, his most important contributions to skating were undoubtedly his performances as a professional. Throughout the 80s, Curry mesmerized audiences with his unique and otherworldly style in performances on stage, ice and television. His contributions to the art of skating were ahead of their time and his performances set a gold standard of excellence that will never be duplicated. Curry's dear friend and former skating partner Lorna Brown remembered, "John and I would talk about our dream of having an ice ballet company when we were very young. We were both winning competitions together but then I turned pro and John went out to the USA and eventually won Europeans, Olympics and Worlds on the trot and that enabled him to do what he really wanted to do and that was to dance on the ice in theaters and do things his way: the way he always dreamed of from being a child. He was hugely inspired by Vaslav Nijinsky as I was with Isadora Duncan. He was a perfectionist and was very dedicated in everything he did for his work. His shows were incredible. We had people like Diana Ross, Mikhail Baryshnikov and Natalia Makarova attending... all of these amazing people were in the audiences and they were amazed that John was bringing ballets to the ice. We used to laugh a lot. We would sit on the bed and I would sing 'Life' by Shirley Bassey to him. We would go into the park pretending we were Romeo and Juliet. We were going to do Midsummer Night's Dream someday and he wanted me to play Puck on the ice. We were like brother and sister: very close... There are many stories but really he was also very loving and deeply involved with the work we were doing and tried to live out his dreams as much as possible in reality until the dreaded end to his life began." Curry developed full-blown AIDS in 1991 and tragically passed away in England on March 15, 1994 at the age of 44.

*John Curry. Contributor: Trinity Mirror / Mirrorpix / Alamy Stock Photo.*

# Fall Internationals

**1987 COUPES DES ALPES (Saint Gervais, France and Oberstdorf, West Germany, August 26-30 and September 1-5, 1987)**

Grand Prix de St. Gervais Winners:

Todd Eldredge (USA) - men
Shannon Allison (CAN) - women
Michelle Menzies and Kevin Wheeler (CAN) - pairs
Anna Croci and Luca Mantovani (ITA) - ice dance

Nebelhorn Trophy (Oberstdorf) Winners:

Todd Eldredge (USA) - men
Shannon Allison (CAN) - women
Michelle Menzies and Kevin Wheeler (CAN) - pairs
Ilona Melnichenko and Gennadi Kaskov (SOV) - ice dance

**1987 ST. IVEL ICE INTERNATIONAL (London, England, October 6-8, 1987)**

Men:

1. Paul Wylie (USA)
2. Kurt Browning (CAN)
3. Heiko Fischer (FRG)

Women:

1. Caryn Kadavy (USA)
2. Patricia Neske (FRG)
3. Joanne Conway (GRB)

Pairs:

1. Denise Benning and Lyndon Johnston (CAN)
2. Peggy Schwarz and Alexander König (GDR)
3. Gillian Wachsman and Todd Waggoner (USA)

Ice Dance:

1. Maya Usova and Alexandr Zhulin (SOV)
2. Sharon Jones and Paul Askham (GRB)
3. Lia Trovati and Roberto Pelizzola (ITA)

**1987 KARL SCHÄFER MEMORIAL (Vienna, Austria, October 22-26, 1987)**

Men:

1. Rudy Galindo (USA)
2. Matthew Hall (CAN)
3. Yuri Tsimbaliuk (SOV)

Women:

1. Natalia Gorbenko (SOV)
2. Holly Cook (USA)
3. Katrien Pauwels (BEL)

Ice Dance:

1. Natalia Annenko and Genrikh Sretenski (SOV)
2. Kathrin and Christoff Beck (AUT)
3. Corinne Paliard and Didier Courtois (FRA)

**1987 SKATE CANADA (Calgary, AB, October 29-31, 1987)**

Men:

1. Brian Orser (CAN)
2. Brian Boitano (USA)
3. Viktor Petrenko (SOV)

Women:

1. Debi Thomas (USA)
2. Elizabeth Manley (CAN)
3. Joanne Conway (GRB)

Pairs:

1. Christine Hough and Doug Ladret (CAN)
2. Elena Kvitchenko and Rashid Kadyrkaev (SOV)
3. Katy Keeley and Joseph Mero (USA)

Ice Dance:

1. Tracy Wilson and Rob McCall (CAN)
2. Kathrin and Christoff Beck (AUT)
3. Lia Trovati and Roberto Pelizzola (ITA)

**1987 PRAGUE SKATE (Prague, Czechoslovakia, November 4-8, 1987)**

Men:

1. Petr Barna (CZE)
2. Heiko Fischer (FRG)
3. Dmitri Gromov (SOV)

Women:

1. Lotta Falkenbäck (SWE)
2. Yvonne Pokorny (AUT)
3. Julie Wasserman (USA)

Pairs:

1. Mandy Wötzel and Axel Rauschenbach (GDR)
2. Natalia Mishkutenok and Artur Dmitriev (SOV)
3. Isabelle Brasseur and Lloyd Eisler (CAN)

Ice Dance:

1. Renée Roca and James Yorke (USA)
2. Michela Malingambi and Andrea Gilardi (ITA)
3. Viera Řeháková and Ivan Havránek (CZE)

**1987 PRIZE OF MOSCOW NEWS (Moscow, Soviet Union, November 10-15, 1987)**

Men:

1. Alexandr Fadeev (SOV)
2. Daniel Doran (USA)
3. Viktor Petrenko (SOV)

Women:

1. Cindy Bortz (USA)
2. Natalia Gorbenko (SOV)
3. Natalia Skrabnevskaya (SOV)

Pairs:

1. Ekaterina Gordeeva and Sergei Grinkov (SOV)
2. Elena Valova and Oleg Vasiliev (SOV)
3. Larisa Selezneva and Oleg Makarov (SOV)

Ice Dance:

1. Marina Klimova and Sergei Ponomarenko (SOV)
2. Maya Usova and Alexandr Zhulin (SOV)
3. Natalia Annenko and Genrikh Sretenski (SOV)

**1987 GOLDEN SPIN OF ZAGREB (Zagreb, Yugoslavia, November 10-15, 1987)**

Men:

1. Scott Kurttila (USA)
2. Cameron Medhurst (AUS)
3. Martin Marceau (CAN)

Women:

1. Jeri Campbell (USA)
2. Charlene Wong (CAN)
3. Katrien Pauwels (BEL)

Ice Dance:

1. Stefania Calegari and Pasquale Camerlengo (ITA)
2. Jodie Balogh and Jerod Swallow (USA)
3. Nathalie Lessard and Darcy Pleckham (CAN)

**1987 POKAL DER BLAUEN SCHWERTER (Karl-Marx-Stadt, East Germany, November 11-14, 1987)**

Men:

1. Ronny Winkler (GDR)
2. Philippe Candeloro (FRA)
3. Elvis Stojko (CAN)

Women:

1. Karen Preston (CAN)
2. Atsuko Suda (JPN)
3. Kathleen Fenske (GDR)

Pairs:

1. Inna Svetacheva and Vladimir Shapov (SOV)
2. Mandy Hannebauer and Marno Kreft (GDR)
3. Jodi Barnes and Rob Williams (CAN)

# Fall and Spring Internationals

**1987 GRAND PRIX INTERNATIONAL DE PARIS (Paris, France, November 11-15, 1987)**

Men:

1. Petr Barna (CZE)
2. Angelo D'Agostino (USA)
3. Paul Robinson (GRB)

Women:

1. Jill Trenary (USA)
2. Agnès Gosselin (FRA)
3. Patricia Neske (FRG)

Pairs:

1. Natalie and Wayne Seybold (USA)
2. Yulia Bystrova and Alexander Tarasov (SOV)
3. Laurene Collin and John Penticost (CAN)

Ice Dance:

1. Lia Trovati and Roberto Pelizzola (ITA)
2. Susie Wynne and Joseph Druar (USA)
3. Corinne Paliard and Didier Courtois (FRA)

**1987 FUJI FILM TROPHY (Frankfurt, West Germany, November 18-22, 1987)**

Men:

1. Christopher Bowman (USA)
2. Vladimir Petrenko (SOV)
3. Makoto Kano (JPN)

Women:

1. Midori Ito (JPN)
2. Jill Trenary (USA)
3. Natalia Gorbenko (SOV)

Pairs:

1. Jill Watson and Peter Oppegard (USA)
2. Laurene Collin and John Penticost (CAN)
3. Brigitte Groh and Holger Maletz (FRG)

Ice Dance:

1. Marina Klimova and Sergei Ponomarenko (SOV)
2. Antonia and Ferdinand Becherer (FRG)
3. Michela Malingambi and Andrea Gilardi (ITA)

**1987 NOVARAT TROPHY (Budapest, Hungary, November 19-22, 1987)**

Men:

1. Brian Boitano (USA)
2. Cameron Medhurst (AUS)
3. Neil Paterson (CAN)

Women:

1. Tracey Damigella (USA)
2. Carola Wolff (FRG)
3. Evelyn Großmann (GDR)

Ice Dance:

1. Klára Engi and Attila Tóth (HUN)
2. Ilona Melnichenko and Gennadi Kaskov (SOV)
3. Stefania Calegari and Pasquale Camerlengo (ITA)

**1987 NHK TROPHY (Kushiro, Japan, November 27-29, 1987)**

Men:

1. Christopher Bowman (USA)
2. Paul Wylie (USA)
3. Makoto Kano (JPN)

Women:

1. Katarina Witt (GDR)
2. Midori Ito (JPN)
3. Tonya Harding (USA)

Pairs:

1. Elena Leonova and Gennadi Krasnitski (SOV)
2. Gillian Wachsman and Todd Waggoner (USA)
3. Katy Keeley and Joseph Mero (USA)

Ice Dance:

1. Natalia Bestemianova and Andrei Bukin (SOV)
2. Svetlana Liapina and Gorsha Sur (SOV)
3. Susie Wynne and Joseph Druar (USA)

**1987 GRAND PRIZE SNP (Banská Bystrica, Czechoslovakia)**

Men:

1. Mirko Eichhorn (FRG)
2. Steven Cousins (GRB)
3. Vadim Shebeco (SOV)

Women:

1. Sandra Garde (FRA)
2. Kathleen Fenske (GDR)
3. Kateřina Mrázová (CZE)

**1988 NORDISKA MÄSTERSKAPEN (Asker, Norway, March 4-6, 1988)**

Men:

1. Peter Johansson (SWE)
2. Henrik Walentin (DEN)
3. Jari Kauppi (FIN)

Women:

1. Hélène Persson (SWE)
2. Susanne Säger (SWE)
3. Anisette Torp-Lind (DEN)

**1988 MERANO SPRING TROPHY (Merano, Italy, March 25-27, 1988)**

Women:

1. Surya Bonaly (FRA)
2. Lisa Cornelius (USA)
3. Yuka Sato (JPN)

**1988 GRAND PRIX INTERNATIONAL DE FRANCE SUR GLACE (Grenoble, France, April 6-9, 1988)**

Ice Dance:

1. Kathrin and Christoff Beck (AUT)
2. Klára Engi and Attila Tóth (HUN)
3. Lia Trovati and Roberto Pelizzola (ITA)

**1988 SKATE ELECTRIC INTERNATIONAL CHALLENGE (Berkshire, England, May 3-4, 1988)**

Men:

1. Daniel Doran (USA)
2. Jaimee Eggleton (CAN)
3. Dmitri Gromov (SOV)

Women:

1. Jeri Campbell (USA)
2. Natalia Skrabnevskaya (SOV)
3. Marie-Claude Tremblay (CAN)

Pairs:

1. Kristi Yamaguchi and Rudy Galindo (USA)
2. Elena Kvitchenko and Rashid Kadyrkaev (SOV)
3. Katherine and Rob Kates (CAN)

Ice Dance:

1. Svetlana Liapina and Gorsha Sur (SOV)
2. Sharon Jones and Paul Askham (GRB)
3. April Sargent and Russ Witherby (USA)

*Marina Klimova and Sergei Ponomarenko. Photo courtesy Sarina Stützer.*

# National Championships

## SENIOR NATIONAL CHAMPIONS BY COUNTRY

### Men

AUS - Cameron Medhurst
AUT - Ralph Burghart
BUL - Alexander Mladenov
CZE - Petr Barna
DEN - Lars Dresler
FIN - Jari Kauppi
FRA - Frédéric Lipka
FRG - Heiko Fischer
GDR - Michael Huth
GRB - Paul Robinson
HOL - Alcuin Schulten
HUN - András Száraz
ITA - Alessandro Riccitelli
JPN - Makoto Kano
POL - Przemysław Noworyta
ROM – Cornel Gheorghe
SAF - Dino Quattrocecere
SOV - Alexandr Fadeev
SUI - Oliver Höner
SWE - Peter Johansson

### Women

AUS - Tracy-Lee Brook
AUT - Yvonne Pokorny
BUL - Asia Aleksieva
CZE - Iveta Voralová
DEN - Anisette Torp-Lind
FIN - Elina Hänninen
FRA - Agnès Gosselin
FRG - Claudia Leistner
GDR - Katarina Witt
GRB - Joanne Conway
HOL - Astrid Winkelman
HUN - Tamara Téglássy
JPN - Midori Ito
KOR - Sung-jin Byun
NOR - Anita Thorenfeldt
NZL - Justine Brownlee
POL - Mirella Gawłowska
SAF - Barbara-Anne Hawkes
SOV - Kira Ivanova
SUI - Stéfanie Schmid
SWE - Lotta Falkenback

### Pairs

AUS - Danielle and Stephen Carr
CZE - Lenka Knapová and René Novotný
FRA - Valérie Binsse and Jean-Christophe Mbonyinshuti
FRG - Brigitte Groh and Holger Maletz
GDR - Peggy Schwarz and Alexander König
GRB - Cheryl Peake and Andrew Naylor
JPN - Akiko Nogami and Yoichi Yamazaki
POL - Anna Wikłacz and Piotr Szczerbowski*
SOV - Larisa Selezneva and Oleg Makarov
SUI - Saskia and Guy Bourgeois

* The Polish pairs title was not awarded as the only team entered did not reach the required standard of marks.

### Ice Dance

AUS - Monica MacDonald and Rodney Clarke
AUT - Kathrin and Christoff Beck
BUL - Anna Raykova and Pavel Dimitrov
CZE - Viera Řeháková and Ivan Havránek
FIN - Susanna Rahkamo and Petri Kokko
FRA - Corinne Paliard and Didier Courtois
FRG - Antonia and Ferdinand Becherer
GRB - Sharon Jones and Paul Askham
HOL - Joanne and Eerde van Leeuwen
HUN - Klára Engi and Attila Tóth
ITA - Lia Trovati and Roberto Pelizzola
JPN - Tomoko Tanaka and Hiroyuki Suzuki
POL - Honorata Górna and Andrzej Dostatni
SAF - Leesa Mostert and Clinton King
SOV - Marina Klimova and Sergei Ponomarenko
SUI - Désirée Schlegel and Patrick Brecht
SWE - Ulla-Stina Johansson and Andreas Hein

### 1988 CANADIAN PRECISION TEAM CHAMPIONSHIPS (Toronto, ON, April 1-3, 1988)

Team:

1. Whitby Ice Fyre
2. K-W Kweens on Ice
3. Les Pirouettes de Laval

Other Winners:

Unique Express Unionville (junior)
Brampton Angelettes (novice)
Classics Wynward (adult)

### 1988 U.S. PRECISION TEAM CHAMPIONSHIPS (Reno, NV, April 16-17, 1988)

Team:

1. The Haydenettes
2. Fraserettes
3. Detroit Capets

Other Winners:

Hot Fudge Sundaes (junior)
Fraser Juniorettes (novice)
Fabulous 40s (adult)

*Claudia Leistner. Photo courtesy Sarina Stützer.*

*Oliver Höner. Photo courtesy Elaine Hooper / St. Ivel Figure Skating Archive.*

*Marina Klimova and Sergei Ponomarenko. Photo courtesy Sarina Stützer.*

*Lars Dresler. Photo courtesy Danmarks Idrætsforbunds Museum.*

## Professional Competitions

**1987 CAMPEONATOS DEL MUNDO DE PATINAJE ARTÍSTICO PROFESSIONAL SOBRE HIELO** (Jaca, Spain, December 18-21, 1987)

Men:

1. Daniel Béland (CAN)
2. Shaun McGill (CAN)
3. Bobby Beauchamp (USA)

Women:

1. Vicky Heasley (USA)
2. Julie Brault (CAN)
3. Kathleen Schmelz (USA)

Pairs:

1. Tricia Burton and Burt Lancon (USA)
2. Tracey Solomons and Ian Jenkins (GRB)
3. Lea Ann Miller and Bill Fauver (USA)

Ice Dance:

1. Kelly Johnson and John Thomas (CAN)
2. Kristan Lowery and Chip Rossbach (USA)
3. Micheline Sally and John Coyne (CAN)

## Shows and Tours

America was ice show crazy! Harrah's at Lake Tahoe featured Willy Bietak's ice revue *Broadway on Ice*, which started as a touring production called *Festival on Ice*. The production featured a rotating cast of skating stars including John Curry, Scott Hamilton, Judy Blumberg and Michael Seibert, Tai Babilonia and Randy Gardner and Lynn-Holly Johnson of *Ice Castles* fame. *America on Ice* played to audiences at Kings Island in Cincinnati. Both Busch Gardens and Cypress Gardens in Florida included ice shows in their summer entertainment lineup.

*Stars on Ice* kicked off a 34-city American tour in September, presented by Plymouth and sponsored by Discover Card. The tour was choreographed by Karen Kresge and Sandra Bezic. The cast was comprised of Scott Hamilton, Dorothy Hamill, Rosalynn Sumners, Toller Cranston, Barbara Underhill and Paul Martini, Judy Blumberg and Michael Seibert, Brian Pockar, Lea Ann Miller and Bill Fauver and Kathleen Schmelz.

A fringe-style experimental skating production called *Hard Edge* was presented in Ottawa and Vancouver in March. The production starred Gary Beacom and Gia Guddat, in collaboration with members of Ottawa's skating ensemble Rainbow Ice, Vancouver's Canada Ice Dance Theatre and the Ice Theatre of New York. In one of the programs in the show, Beacom skated a solo that was over 20 minutes long. John Curry and Michael Seibert joined Beacom in May when the mini-tour visited Sky Rink in New York City.

Following the World Championships in Budapest, a who's who of figure skating embarked on the European leg of the World Champions tour, which included a gala exhibition at Richmond Ice Rink in London. Tom Collins' subsequent *'88 Tour of Olympic and World Champions* was such a draw that it sold out in almost every city. Ten additional cities had to be added at the last minute, taking the tour well into June. Performers included Katarina Witt, Brian Boitano, Ekaterina Gordeeva and Sergei Grinkov, Natalia Bestemianova and Andrei Bukin, Brian Orser, Debi Thomas, Elizabeth Manley, Tracy Wilson and Rob McCall, Christopher Bowman, Caryn Kadavy and the Duchesnays.

In April, Minnesota hosted an international ice extravaganza by Command Performance for King Carl XVI Gustaf and Queen Silvia of Sweden. Dick Button and Peggy Fleming hosted the affair, which featured skating performances by Robin Cousins, Rosalynn Sumners, Brian Pockar and Judy Blumberg and Michael Seibert. 1936 Olympic Bronze Medallist Vivi-Anne Hultén of Sweden was a special guest of honour at the event.

*Natalia Bestemianova and Andrei Bukin. Photo courtesy Sarina Stützer.*

*Brian Orser. Photo courtesy Sarina Stützer.*

*Midori Ito. Photo courtesy Sarina Stützer.*

# Major Competitions

**World Junior Championships.** History was made in December, when the Brisbane Sports and Entertainment Centre and Iceworld Olympic Ice in Brisbane, Australia played host to the first ISU Championship ever held in the Southern Hemisphere. The ISAA lobbied the ISU for seven years before finally being awarded the event. After finishing second the year prior in Canada, Todd Eldredge struck gold in the men's event, though the short program was won by his teammate Shepherd Clark and the free skate by the Soviet Union's Viacheslav Zagorodniuk, who finished second. The technical standard of the men's event was exceptionally high for a junior competition, with Zagorodniuk landing a triple Axel and Korea's Sung-il Jung performing a triple/triple combination. Kristi Yamaguchi and Rudy Galindo, bronze medallists at the same event a year prior in Canada, came from behind after the short program and defeated three Soviet pairs, making history as the first American duo to win a gold medal in pairs skating at the World Junior Championships. Skating 'double duty' in singles, Yamaguchi pulled off a win over Japan's Junko Yaginuma and Yukiko Kashihara and Sandra Garde, an exceptionally artistic French skater whose style was reminiscent of Denise Biellmann. As Galindo had won the men's title the year prior, he and Yamaguchi had the unusual distinction of being the only skaters to win World Junior titles in both singles and pairs. Another milestone was achieved in the ice dance event when Oksana Grishuk and Alexandr Chichkov, Irina Antsiferova and Maxim Sevastianov and Maria Orlova and Oleg Ovsiannikov took gold, silver and bronze for the Soviet Union - the first podium sweep for one country in the history of the ice dance event. Canada's team had a very disappointing showing Down Under. Though Judith Tartal and Allison MacLean and Konrad Schaub finished fifth in the women's and ice dance events, the event marked only the third time since the inception of the World Junior Championships that Canadian skaters failed to win at least one medal.

**World Professional Championships.** A total purse of 300 000 dollars was at stake at the World Professional Championships in December, with winners of each category taking home 40 000 dollars each. In the ice dance competition, Carol Fox and Richard Dalley defended their title with a Fred and Ginger-inspired technical program and an exquisite interpretation of "Silent Night", which was understandably popular with the audience as the competition was held at the same time people were busy doing their Christmas shopping and baking. Their only competitors, Judy Blumberg and Michael Seibert, took a tumble in the technical program and were unable to make up ground. Though marred by the fall, Blumberg and Seibert's tango was an innovative program for the time. They were dressed as identical male tango dancers in Spanish tuxedos with slicked-back hair. In the pairs event, Barbara Underhill and Paul Martini successfully defended their title as well, earning a string of perfect 10.0s in their artistic program to "On My Own" from *Les Misérables*. Their perfect score made all the difference. They only beat Kitty and Peter Carruthers, who won the technical program, by one-tenth of a point. Lea Ann Miller and Bill Fauver edged the Protopopovs for third, winning over the crowd with a rousing rendition of John Kander's score from *The Rink*. In the women's event, three-time defending Champion Dorothy Hamill made history in the technical program as the first of many Olympic Medallists to interpret the iconic song "Music of the Night" from Andrew Lloyd Webber's brand-new musical *Phantom of the Opera* in competition. After facing criticism the previous year for a technical program that was light on content, she upped her game considerably, including four different double jumps in her program including the Lutz. Hamill's master class of a program, performed in a beautiful purple Victorian lace dress, earned a perfect 10.0 from judge Ája Zanová.

**1988 WORLD JUNIOR CHAMPIONSHIPS**
(Brisbane, Australia, December 8-13, 1987)

Men:

1. Todd Eldredge (USA)
2. Viacheslav Zagorodniuk (SOV)
3. Yuri Tsimbaliuk (SOV)
4. Shepherd Clark (USA)
5. Cameron Birky (USA)
6. Sung-il Jung (KOR)
7. Philippe Candeloro (FRA)
8. Michael Shmerkin (ISR)
9. Marcus Christensen (CAN)
10. Masakazu Kagiyama (JPN)

Women:

1. Kristi Yamaguchi (USA)
2. Junko Yaginuma (JPN)
3. Yukiko Kashihara (JPN)
4. Sandra Garde (FRA)
5. Judith Tartal (CAN)
6. Elizabeth Wright (USA)
7. Margot Bion (CAN)
8. Tatiana Klenina (SOV)
9. Evgenia Leonidova (SOV)
10. Susanne Mildenberger (FRG)

Pairs:

1. Kristi Yamaguchi and Rudy Galindo (USA)
2. Evgenia Chernyshova and Dmitri Sukhanov (SOV)
3. Yulia Liashenko and Andrei Bushkov (SOV)
4. Irina Saifutdinova and Andrei Bardykin (SOV)
5. Jennifer Heurlin and John Frederiksen (USA)
6. Ann-Marie and Brian Wells (USA)
7. Marie-Josée Fortin and Jean-Michel Bombardier (CAN)
8. Narelle Rolfe and Stephen Roberts (AUS)

Ice Dance:

1. Oksana Grishuk and Alexandr Chichkov (SOV)
2. Irina Antsiferova and Maxim Sevastianov (SOV)
3. Maria Orlova and Oleg Ovsiannikov (SOV)
4. Christelle Gautier and Alberick Dalongeville (FRA)
5. Allison MacLean and Konrad Schaub (CAN)
6. Lynn Burton and Andrew Place (GRB)
7. Meike and Frank Dehne (FRG)
8. Pascale Vrot and David Quinsac (FRA)
9. Rachel Mayer and Peter Breen (USA)
10. Jeannine Jones and Michael Shroge (USA)

Discouraged after placing a distant last the previous year, Elaine Zayak worked on her presentation with JoJo Starbuck and Ken Shelley. Zayak landed the triple toe-loop and double Axel in her program to "Kingdom of the Shades" by Marcus and the judges placed her in a tie with Hamill. 20-year-old Tiffany Chin, making her debut as the youngest skater in the competition, placed third ahead of Rosalynn Sumners. In the artistic program, Hamill broke out the Aquanet and corset for a unique bluesy number to "Do the Bearcat" by David Wilcox. Going out of her comfort paid off for Hamill, who won her fourth consecutive World Professional title over Zayak, who performed a sassy program to "Broadway Baby" from *Follies*. Though Chin did not look at all out of place in her pro debut, the judges weren't sold and she dropped to fourth behind Sumners. Scott Hamilton fractured a bone in his landing foot in the lead-up to the competition. He didn't seem hampered at all by his injury in the men's technical program, where he delivered a strong performance to selections from the Andrew Lloyd Webber musical *Song & Dance*, including two triples, a double Axel and backflip in his program. Robin Cousins slipped on the landing of his triple toe-loop and was forced to tack a single on the end, but he was otherwise absolutely fabulous in his crowd-pleasing program to Corky Siegel's "Street Music" - a piece best remembered by skating fans for its use in Torvill and Dean's *Hat Trick* program. Like Cousins, Toller Cranston lacked the triples but he produced a solid double Axel in his classical program. When the marks were tallied, Hamilton took the lead but all three men earned perfect at least one 10.0. Hamilton received three, from Ája Zanová, Maria Jelinek and David Jenkins. If anything, the standard of skating was even higher in the artistic program. Cranston's artistic program was classic Toller - an angular, unusual and dramatic program to Strauss' "Tales from The Vienna Woods". He was rewarded with perfect 10.0s from judges Arthur Bourque, Krisztina Regőczy and Ája Zanová. Hamilton was delightfully humourous in a playful character piece to "When I'm Sixty-Four" by The Beatles, replete with a pork-pie hat, windowpane plaid pants, a mouth full of bubblegum and skate covers that looked like black high-top sneakers. Cousins went in a completely different direction, performing a dynamic, modern self-choreographed program to "p:Machinery" by Propaganda that featured clever choreography, a double Axel, backflip and a moonwalk. Cousins won the artistic program, earning six perfect 10.0s to Hamilton's three, but with the score from the technical program added on, the two men tied in points. Per the rules in the competition, in the event of a tie the skater who won the artistic program won the title and so, Cousins was World Professional Champion once again.

**U.S. Championships.** The weather outside was frightful but the skating was just delightful in January, when McNichols Arena and the South Suburban Ice Center in Denver, Colorado played host to the U.S. Championships. Dick Button hosted the Opening Ceremonies, which featured a video retrospective celebrating Peggy Fleming's Olympic win 20 years prior, a performance by Richard Dwyer, precision skating and even fireworks. An ill-conceived 'clopen' schedule had the senior pairs skating their short program one night and their free skates the next morning. Rudy Galindo had it the worst as he had to skate the pairs short and men's free on the same day, with a pulled muscle in his leg to boot. Jill Watson and Peter Oppegard took the lead in the pairs short program over Gillian Wachsman and Todd Waggoner and Natalie and Wayne Seybold, with all three teams delivering clean performances. The pairs free skate suffered delays due to a computer malfunction. Judges had to hold up their scores on placards, which was an unfamiliar sight to newer fans. All the top teams made at least one costly error. Despite a fall on a throw triple Salchow, Watson and Oppegard's performance to the strains of Puccini's "Madama Butterfly" received high enough scores to earn them their third national title over Wachsman and Waggoner and the Seybolds.

**1987 WORLD PROFESSIONAL CHAMPIONSHIPS** (Landover, MD, December 11, 1987)

Men:

1. Robin Cousins (GRB)
2. Scott Hamilton (USA)
3. Toller Cranston (CAN)
4. Norbert Schramm (FRG)

Women:

1. Dorothy Hamill (USA)
2. Elaine Zayak (USA)
3. Rosalynn Sumners (USA)
4. Tiffany Chin (USA)

Pairs:

1. Barbara Underhill and Paul Martini (CAN)
2. Kitty and Peter Carruthers (USA)
3. Lea Ann Miller and Bill Fauver (USA)
4. Ludmila and Oleg Protopopov (SOV)

Ice Dance:

1. Carol Fox and Richard Dalley (USA)
2. Judy Blumberg and Michael Seibert (USA)

**1988 U.S. CHAMPIONSHIPS** (Denver, CO, January 4-10, 1988)

Men:

1. Brian Boitano
2. Paul Wylie
3. Christopher Bowman
4. Daniel Doran
5. Angelo D'Agostino
6. Scott Williams
7. James Cygan
8. Todd Eldredge
9. Doug Mattis
10. Rudy Galindo

Women:

1. Debi Thomas
2. Jill Trenary
3. Caryn Kadavy
4. Jeri Campbell
5. Tonya Harding
6. Holly Cook
7. Cindy Bortz
8. Tracey Damigella
9. Kelly Ann Szmurlo
10. Kristi Yamaguchi

Pairs:

1. Jill Watson and Peter Oppegard
2. Gillian Wachsman and Todd Waggoner
3. Natalie and Wayne Seybold
4. Katy Keeley and Joseph Mero
5. Kristi Yamaguchi and Rudy Galindo
6. Calla Urbanski and Michael Blicharski
7. Sharon Carz and Doug Williams
8. Lori Blasko and Todd Sand
9. Ginger and Archie Tse
10. Kellie Creel and Bob Pellaton

Interestingly enough, the placements of the top five pairs did not change from the short to the free. Of particular interest to the audience was a throw triple Lutz attempt by the Seybolds. Though unsuccessful, the throw was exceptionally rare in pairs skating in the 80s and with Olympic spots on the line, it was a particularly risky attempt. The organizers of the event faced criticism for scheduling the compulsory dances at the comparatively small South Suburban Arena used for compulsory figures. Many spectators were turned away because there weren't enough seats. Some wondered if defending Champion Scott Gregory would be able to compete, as he was suffering from a back injury. Gregory and partner Suzanne Semanick persevered through the Viennese Waltz, Tango Romantica and Paso Doble, winning the compulsories in a five-four split over Susie Wynne and Joseph Druar. Semanick and Gregory expanded their lead over Wynne and Druar in the Tango OSP. The third and fourth-place teams, April Sargent and Russ Witherby and Renée Roca and James Yorke, switched places but Sargent and Witherby were still third entering the free dance. Semanick and Gregory opened their free dance with Rondò Veneziano's dramatic "Sinfonia Per Un Addio" and finished it with Grigoras Dinicu's lightning-fast "Hora Staccato". They modified their program to accommodate Gregory's injury, taking out all the lifts. It was a move that paid off when the judges rewarded them their second national title, ahead of Wynne and Druar, who won over the crowd skating to "Boogie Woogie Bugle Boy". Sargent and Witherby outskated Roca and Yorke to win the bronze. The heavy favourite in the women's event, Debi Thomas, made major changes in her life during the Olympic season. She took a nine-month leave of absence from the pre-med program at Stanford and moved to Boulder to train with coach Alex McGowan. In Boulder, she enrolled in courses at the University of Colorado's Sports Medicine Department. Thomas' decision to move from California to Colorado was prompted by the closure of her home rink in Redwood City. The big move paid off when Thomas held the lead after the compulsory figures, tying with Caryn Kadavy on the first figure and winning the second and third outright. Inthe short program, Thomas skated exceptionally well, landing a double loop/triple toe-loop in her crowd-pleasing program to "Something In My House" by Dead or Alive. Kadavy was also outstanding, landing a difficult triple loop/double loop combination in her program to Stanley Black & His Orchestra's rendition of "Two Guitars", choreographed by Toller Cranston. Jill Trenary attempted a difficult triple flip/double loop combination in her short program but erred on the landing. In a five-four split, the judges placed Thomas first over Kadavy and Trenary. George de la Peña, a choreographer from the American Ballet Theatre who worked with Thomas on her program to Bizet's "Carmen", flew to Denver to watch the free skate. Ája Zanová had first arranged for Thomas to work with Mikhail Baryshnikov and Baryshnikov suggested that she work further with de la Peña. Despite intense pressure, Thomas delivered an outstanding performance, featuring a clean triple toe-loop/triple toe-loop combination and triple loop. Every single judge awarded her either 5.8s or 5.9s for both marks, allowing her to reclaim the national title she had lost in Tacoma the previous year. Trenary skated extremely well, landing four triple jumps and earning marks ranging from 5.6 to 5.9. Kadavy fell on a triple loop less than 25 seconds into her program but unfazed, skated the rest of her program quite well. Unfortunately, it wasn't enough and she dropped to third overall behind Trenary. One of the other standout performances of the evening came from Tonya Harding, who moved up from eighth in the figures and ninth in the short to finish fifth overall with gutsy triple Lutz and triple loop/triple toe-loop attempts. Kristi Yamaguchi had a disappointing debut as a senior at Nationals, placing tenth overall. Competing in both pairs and singles meant that she had to skate two senior free skating programs in a six-hour span.

**U.S. CHAMPIONSHIPS** (continued)

Junior Winners:

Christopher Mitchell (men)
Dena Galech (women)
Kenna Bailey and John Denton (pairs)
Elizabeth Punsalan and Shawn Rettstat (ice dance)

Novice Winners:

Chris Browne (men)
Caroline Lee (women)

*Brian Boitano. Photo courtesy Sarina Stützer.*

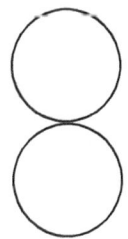

In the men's compulsory figures, Brian Boitano took a commanding lead over Christopher Bowman, Paul Wylie, Daniel Doran and Scott Williams. The men's short program was without a doubt the best skated short program at U.S. Nationals of the decade. Seventeen of the 20 men skated clean programs, giving the judges a very difficult time and leaving spectators' hands sore from clapping. The best of them all was Boitano, who landed a beautiful triple Axel/double loop in his masterful program to Meyerbeer's "Les Patineurs". Choreographed by Sandra Bezic, the program hearkened back to the 19th century and the grand style of Jackson Haines, The Father of Figure Skating. Boitano earned a standing ovation and no less than eight 6.0s from the judges for presentation. No doubt that the one holdout, Cleveland's Elaine DeMore, regretted not writing down that perfect mark. Bowman and Wylie finished second and third in the short program with outstanding performances. Due to more scheduling issues and delays caused by 'flower showers', the men's free skate went on until well after midnight. Boitano's free skate was another Sandra Bezic masterpiece, set to Gerald Fried's score from the miniseries *Napoleon and Josephine: A Love Story*. Unfortunately, Boitano had a couple of significant errors, including a step out of the landing of a triple Axel and hand down on a triple loop. However, he landed four other triples and received a standing ovation and a perfect 6.0 for composition and style from California judge Sherie Grimson on the way to defending his title. Paul Wylie moved up to win the silver medal, earning a standing ovation of his own with an exceptional six-triple program that some felt should have beaten Boitano. 'Bowman the Showman' skated what was probably the cleanest performance of the three contenders, landing a triple Lutz and four other triples in his beautifully constructed "Hungarian Rhapsody" program. However the judges, perhaps swayed by Wylie's extra triple or the fact he attempted a triple Axel which Bowman didn't, dropped him down a spot to third. Bowman's performance in Denver was very good considering the fact it was well-known that he was skating with a sprained ankle. Years later, he admitted that around the time of the event he spent time at the Betty Ford Center in treatment for his cocaine addiction.

**European Championships.** In January, the Sportovní hala in Prague, Czechoslovakia played host to sellout crowds at the first European Championships held in the Iron Curtain city in 40 years. When Prague last hosted the Europeans in 1948, North American skaters were allowed to compete and Barbara Ann Scott and Dick Button won gold medals. Notably absent in the pairs event were Elena Valova and Oleg Vasiliev. In the lead-up to the event, Valova was hospitalized with an injured left ankle that started to develop gangrene. They were replaced by 17-year-olds Natalia Mishkutenok and Artur Dmitriev. Defending European Champions Larisa Selezneva and Oleg Makarov were expected to face stiff competition from two-time World Champions Ekaterina Gordeeva and Sergei Grinkov. However, Gordeeva was recovering from a concussion and had lost weight, felt weak and was suffering from headaches. Skating to "Les Toreadores" and "La Garde Montante" from Bizet's "Carmen", Gordeeva and Grinkov delivered a strong short program, putting themselves ahead of Selezneva and Makarov. The two-time World Champions had several small errors in their free skate set to a medley of music by Mendelssohn, Chopin and Mozart, but still received marks in the 5.7-5.9 range and first-place ordinals from five of the nine judges, just enough to narrowly beat Selezneva and Makarov for the title. East German Champions Peggy Schwarz and Alexander König took the bronze, just ahead of Mishkutenok and Dmitriev. In the men's compulsory figures, Alexandr Fadeev led his Soviet teammate Vladimir Kotin and Heiko Fischer of West Germany by a comfortable margin.

**1988 EUROPEAN CHAMPIONSHIPS**
(Prague, Czechoslovakia, January 12-17, 1988)

Men:

1. Alexandr Fadeev (SOV)
2. Vladimir Kotin (SOV)
3. Viktor Petrenko (SOV)
4. Grzegorz Filipowski (POL)
5. Richard Zander (FRG)
6. Heiko Fischer (FRG)
7. Petr Barna (CZE)
8. Oliver Höner (SUI)
9. Paul Robinson (GRB)
10. Axel Médéric (FRA)

Women:

1. Katarina Witt (GDR)
2. Kira Ivanova (SOV)
3. Anna Kondrashova (SOV)
4. Claudia Leistner (FRG)
5. Simone Koch (GDR)
6. Natalia Gorbenko (SOV)
7. Agnès Gosselin (FRA)
8. Tamara Téglássy (HUN)
9. Marina Kielmann (FRG)
10. Joanne Conway (GRB)

Pairs:

1. Ekaterina Gordeeva and Sergei Grinkov (SOV)
2. Larisa Selezneva and Oleg Makarov (SOV)
3. Peggy Schwarz and Alexander König (GDR)
4. Natalia Mishkutenok and Artur Dmitriev (SOV)
5. Mandy Wötzel and Axel Rauschenbach (GDR)
6. Lenka Knapová and René Novotný (CZE)
7. Brigitte Groh and Holger Maletz (FRG)
8. Cheryl Peake and Andrew Naylor (GRB)
9. Anuschka Gläser and Stefan Pfrengle (FRG)
10. Lisa and Neil Cushley (GRB)

Ice Dance:

1. Natalia Bestemianova and Andrei Bukin (SOV)
2. Natalia Annenko and Genrikh Sretenski (SOV)
3. Isabelle and Paul Duchesnay (FRA)
4. Maya Usova and Alexandr Zhulin (SOV)
5. Kathrin and Christoff Beck (AUT)
6. Klára Engi and Attila Tóth (HUN)
7. Lia Trovati and Roberto Pelizzola (ITA)
8. Sharon Jones and Paul Askham (GRB)
9. Viera Řeháková and Ivan Havránek (CZE)
10. Corinne Paliard and Didier Courtois (FRA)

Fadeev landed a clean triple Axel/double loop combination in his short program, earning 5.8s and 5.9s for his effort. After the second phase of the competition, Fadeev had a strong lead over Kotin. Viktor Petrenko moved up to third with a triple Axel/double loop combination of his own. Fadeev landed four triples and three double Axels in his free skate but fell on his triple Axel, doubled and singled his triple loop attempts and opted to perform a double toe-loop instead of the quadruple he had been attempting in practices. Fadeev's program, set to a medley of Russian folk music, was jam-packed full of lightning-fast footwork and novel moves like a double Axel/sit spin and barrel rolls into a butterfly. He performed more than enough technical content to easily best Kotin and Petrenko and take the gold. Not only was this the second consecutive Soviet sweep of the men's podium at Europeans, but it was the first time since 1979 that the same three men finished in the same order on the podium at the event in consecutive years. For the third year in a row at Europeans, Kira Ivanova won the compulsory figures over Katarina Witt, Anna Kondrashova and Claudia Leistner. In the short program, Witt skated flawlessly, landing a triple toe-loop/double loop combination. She earned five perfect 6.0s, the most ever in a singles short program in an international competition. before that, the record was Brian Boitano's four at the Novarat Trophy in Budapest in autumn of 1987. The Yugoslavian judge gave her two 6.0s, while the Polish, Hungarian and East German judges gave her 6.0s for presentation. After her program, Witt was mobbed by fans seeking autographs in the hall outside the rink and she had to be whisked away. Though there was no huge outcry in Prague, the North American press made a big to-do about how revealing Witt's showgirl costume was. More feathers were strategically added in time for the Olympics in Calgary. Entering the free skate, Ivanova still held the overall lead over Witt. She and Kondrashova both fell in the final phase of the competition but managed to hold on to the silver and bronze medals. Witt landed four triple jumps in her "Carmen" free skate and earned a spate of 5.8s and 5.9s, as well as two 6.0s for artistic impression, from the Hungarian and East German judges. Witt's marks were more than enough to easily win her sixth European title, tying Sonja Henie's record from back in the 30s. A bout with hepatitis kept Sergei Ponomarenko and his partner Marina Klimova from competing in Prague. The Olympic Bronze Medallists were replaced by young Muscovites Maya Usova and Alexandr Zhulin. To the surprise of absolutely no one, Natalia Bestemianova and Andrei Bukin won the compulsory dances. Their "Hernando's Hideaway" OSP only expanded their lead, earning them three perfect scores of 6.0 for presentation from the Hungarian, Italian and Soviet judges. Heading into the free dance, Natalia Sretenski and Genrikh Sretenski sat in second, followed by Austria's Kathrin and Christoff Beck, Usova and Zhulin and France's Isabelle and Paul Duchesnay. Many in the audience thought the French siblings should have won the OSP. 29 500 spectators showed up for the free dance - more than for any other event in Prague. Bestemianova and Bukin were at their best, skating to Alexander Borodin's "Polovtsian Dances" in bold costumes designed by Soviet fashion designer Slava Zaitsev. They earned 6.0s for artistic impression from seven of the nine judges, easily winning their fifth European title. However, it was the Duchesnays *Savage Rites* free dance set to Mandingo's "War Dance" and Famey's "Kiss Of Death", choreographed by Christopher Dean, that stole the show. The performance was so big of a deal that Czechoslovakian periodicals that never reported on figure skating raved about it. The majority of the judges gave the French siblings 5.8s and 5.9s. Hungarian judge István Sugár gave them a set of 5.2s and Polish judge Maria Blazek-Miller gave them a 4.7 and 4.8. Referee Wolfgang Kunz asked Blazek-Miller if she wanted to change her marks but she repeated, "4.7, 4.8". This exchange delayed Annenko and Sretenski's performance. Despite the judging drama, the Duchesnays moved up to claim the bronze, while the Becks dropped to fifth behind Usova and Zhulin. Annenko and Sretenski took the silver, skating a very conservative, typically 80s program to an original composition.

*Natalia Bestemianova and Andrei Bukin. Photo courtesy Sarina Stützer.*

*Kira Ivanova. Contributor: PCN Photography / Alamy Stock Photo. Photographer: Paul Sutton.*

When a string of high marks including a '5.8, 5.8' from the Polish judge came up for Annenko and Sretenski, the Prague audience erupted into an emotional chorus of boos, perhaps not understanding how Annenko and Sretenski's second-place finish in the compulsories and OSP would have made it impossible for the Duchesnays to win the silver regardless of their marks in their free dance. Kunz later claimed that Blazek-Miller came up to him crying after the event saying that she made a mistake. She claimed that she wanted to give the Duchesnays a 5.7 and 5.8, but that she was so overcome with emotion after their performance that she had a mental blockage and repeated the incorrect marks.

**Canadian Championships.** The Victoria Memorial Arena played host to the first Canadian Championships in Victoria in a decade in January. The mild West Coast weather was a welcome change for most of the visiting skaters, coaches and judges and capacity crowds of 5500 spectators packed the Arena throughout the competition. In the women's compulsory figures, Elizabeth Manley carved out a healthy lead over Shannon Allison, Patricia Schmidt and Charlene Wong. Skating to Sir Richard Rodney Bennett's score from *Murder on the Orient Express*, Manley couldn't put a foot wrong in the short program. Landing a triple Salchow/double loop and double Axel with ease, she was rewarded with the first perfect 6.0 of her career from judge Jacquie Cassity. Lac Beauport, Quebec's Marie Tremblay, only 13th in figures, seemingly came out of nowhere to finish second in the short with a clean performance of her own. Schmidt doubled both jumps in her combination and singled her Axel, Allison fell on a rare triple Lutz/double loop attempt and Wong landed a double Axel but fell on her combination. When the marks were tallied, Schmidt, Allison and Wong were in a virtual tie for second entering the free skate, despite their mistakes, because Tremblay finished so low in the figures. Manley's free skate to "Dis-donc, Dis-donc" and "There Is Only One Paris For That" from the film "Irma La Douce" and Kurt Edelhagen's "Canadian Concerto" began strongly with a triple toe-loop, but things fell apart when she overrated her triple Lutz, fell on a triple loop and put both hands down on a triple Salchow. Fortunately for Manley and very unfortunately for her competitors, the women's free skate in Victoria was full of falls and underrotated jumps. She was able to earn first-place ordinals from every judge despite her mistakes. Wong skated well enough in her "Spartacus" program to finish second in the free skate over Allison, four judges to three, dropping Schmidt to fourth. Tremblay moved up from ninth after the short to finish sixth overall behind Diane Takeuchi. Manley and Wong were named to the Olympic team, to the great disappointment of Allison, who was a home province favourite at the event. She collided with another skater in a practice at the Hollyburn Country Club in West Vancouver a week and a half prior and was suffering from thigh and back problems. She was also taking an over-the-counter anti-spasm medication that wasn't on the IOC's banned substance list, but it made her very drowsy. In the warmup for the short program, she kept trying the triple Lutz and fell five times. To no one's surprise, Tracy Wilson and Rob McCall took a commanding lead in the Tango Romantica, Ravensburger Waltz and Quickstep and their Tango OSP received a string of 5.9s and a perfect 6.0 from judge Suzanne Morrow-Francis. Wilson and McCall's ragtime free dance, developed with Marijane Stong and John Briscoe with National Ballet of Canada dancer and choreographer Vanessa Harwood, brought down the house. Though they had a minor slip, five of the seven judges awarded them perfect 6.0s for artistic impression. Ironically, one of the two that awarded them a 5.9 instead was Morrow-Francis. Karyn and Rod Garossino skated one of their best performances and finished second. Melanie Cole and Michael Farrington capitalized on falls from three other teams to claim the final spot on the Olympic team. Isabelle Brasseur and Lloyd Eisler surprised many by skating clean in their debut performance at Canadians and winning the pairs short program over Denise Benning and Lyndon Johnston and Christine Hough and Doug Ladret.

**1988 CANADIAN CHAMPIONSHIPS**
(Victoria, BC, January 20-23, 1988)

Men:

1. Brian Orser
2. Kurt Browning
3. Neil Paterson
4. Michael Slipchuk
5. Matthew Hall
6. Jaimee Eggleton
7. Brad McLean
8. Jeff Partrick
9. Martin Marceau
10. Mark MacVean

Women:

1. Elizabeth Manley
2. Charlene Wong
3. Shannon Allison
4. Patricia Schmidt
5. Dianne Takeuchi
6. Marie Trembley
7. Tracey Robertson
8. Joelle Tustin
9. Josée Arsenault
10. Pamela Giangualano

Pairs:

1. Christine Hough and Doug Ladret
2. Isabelle Brasseur and Lloyd Eisler
3. Denise Benning and Lyndon Johnston
4. Laurene Collin and John Penticost
5. Michelle Menzies and Kevin Wheeler
6. Melanie Gaylor and Lee Barkell
7. Lori Rissling and Alan Kerslake
8. Katherine and Rob Kates
9. Laura and Jamie Ivanich
10. Lynda and John Ivanich

Ice Dance:

1. Tracy Wilson and Rob McCall
2. Karyn and Rod Garossino
3. Melanie Cole and Michael Farrington
4. Jo-Anne Borlase and Martin Smith
5. Michelle McDonald and Mark Mitchell
6. Penny Mann and Richard Perkins
7. Kimberley Weeks and Curtis Moore
8. Catherine Pal and Donald Godfrey
9. Nathalie Lessard and Darcy Pleckham
10. Carla Maillard and Julien Lalonde

Fours:

1. Denise Benning, Christine Hough, Lyndon Johnston and Doug Ladret
2. Melanie Gaylor, Michelle Menzies, Lee Barkell and Kevin Wheeler
3. Laureen Collin, Lori Rissling, John Penticost and Alan Kerslake
4. Nathalie Rodrigue, Jim Blackburn, Patricia MacNeil and Cory Watson
5. Lynda, Laura, Jamie and John Ivanich

With a cleverly choreographed program to music from *Slaughter On Tenth Avenue*, Hough and Ladret moved up to win the gold over Brasseur and Eisler in a four-three split of the judging panel. Both teams demonstrated their technical prowess by executing three different high-risk throw jumps - the double Axel, triple toe-loop and throw triple Salchow. Though 'Herbie and Fred' had only been skating together for a short time, their triple twist probably looked so easy because they were doing a quadruple in practice. Benning and Johnston, who had already been named to the Olympic team by the COA based on their finish at the 1987 World Championships, had a disappointing free skate to "Carmen" with two missed throws. The maturity of their skating, coupled with their strong lifts and unison, kept them in third overall. Five teams participated in the fours competition in 1988, with the gold deservedly going to Benning, Hough, Johnston and Ladret. Though Brian Orser managed to pull off a win over Neil Paterson and Kurt Browning in the men's compulsory figures, it was not decisive nor was he content with his performance. Orser was much happier when he knocked it out of the park with a flawless short program to "Sing Sing Sing", earning perfect 6.0s for artistic impression from all seven judges - a first in any discipline at Canadians. Browning skated a perfect short program of his own to "Tequila", nailing a triple Axel/double loop combination, to finish second in the short over Jaimee Eggleton, who had only been tenth in the figures. Paterson had an unfortunate fall on his step sequence and finished fourth. Like Elizabeth Manley in the women's event, Orser gave a performance that was not up to his usual standard in the free skate. Skating to Shostakovich's "The Bolt", he missed both of his triple Axel attempts and turned three planned triples into doubles. Browning popped a planned quadruple toe-loop into a double and fell on a triple Axel, but managed to hold on to second place over Paterson, who landed six triples but fell on a triple Lutz. Eggleton's comeback hopes dissolved in the free skate when he fell on his triple Axel attempt and finished sixth overall. Many of the skaters blamed their 'hot and cold' performances in Victoria on the bright television lights and soft ice. Rob McCall had a sense of humour about the event, quipping that he hadn't seen so many doubles since last call at the bar.

**CANADIAN CHAMPIONSHIPS**
(continued)

Junior Winners:

Craig Burns (men)
Tanya Bingert (women)
Cindy Landry and Sylvain Lalonde (pairs)
Jacqueline Petr and Mark Janoschak (ice dance)

Novice Winners:

Jason Mongrain (men)
Jennifer Lynne White (women)
Marie-Claude Savard-Gagnon and Luc Bradet (pairs)
Marie-France Dubreuil and Bruno Yvars (ice dance)

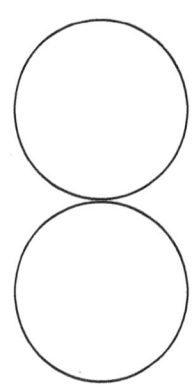

*Brian Orser. Photos courtesy Sarina Stützer.*

*Elizabeth Manley. Contributor: PCN Photography / Alamy Stock Photo. Photographer: Paul Sutton.*

**Olympic Games.** As the chair of the competition Committee at the Calgary Olympics, Joyce Hisey worked tirelessly to ensure the figure skating events ran like clockwork. The campus of the University of Calgary was transformed into a maximum security Olympic Village and four different venues were used for figure skating - The Olympic Saddledome, Stampede Corral, Father David Bauer Arena and Jimmie Condon Arena. The men's and women's figures were held at the Father David Bauer Arena, the compulsory dances, men's and pairs short at the Stampede Corral and all other events at the Saddledome. Practices were held at all four venues. Per the IOC Medical Commission and ISU Regulations, doping controls were carried out each day in the competition. The top four skaters from each discipline were tested, but "the man or the lady, not both" in pairs and dance were tested. Other skaters were selected based on random draws. Christopher Bowman recalled being "excited, nervous, scared, anxious and embarrassed" when IOC representatives handed him a free beer and awkwardly cheered him on to produce a urine sample in the Doping Control Lounge. At the Opening Ceremony, Brian Orser, Andrei Bukin, Lars Dresler, Attila Tóth, Katrien Pauwels, Shubin Zhang and Ricardo Olavarrieta carried the flags of Canada, the Soviet Union, Denmark, Hungary, Belgium, China and Mexico. Olavarietta and Diana Encinas-Evans made history as the first skaters from Mexico to compete at the Olympics. North Korea and Taiwan also had their first Olympic representatives in Ho Kang, Kim Song-suk, David Liu and Pauline Chen Lee. Bulgaria was represented in singles for the first time by Boyko Aleksiev and Petya Gavazova, while Australia had its first ice dance team, Monica MacDonald and Rodney Clarke. Fifteen couples from eight countries competed in the pairs short program at the Stampede Corral but only three teams arguably had a realistic shot at taking the top spot. Reigning World and European Champions Ekaterina Gordeeva delivered a first-rate performance in the short program to "The Toreador Song" from Bizet's "Carmen", perfectly executing each of the required elements in their program with great confidence and unison. The height of their split double twist, in particular, was outstanding. 1984 Olympic Gold Medallists Elena Valova and Oleg Vasiliev managed to pull off something of a miracle, considering Valova was in severe pain from the injury to her left ankle. 'V and V', like their rivals, perfectly executed every element in their lightning-fast "Zorba the Greek" program. The third team with the résumé to potentially serve as a spoiler if either 'G and G' or 'V and V' made a mistake was Larisa Selezneva and Oleg Makarov. When Makarov took a bad fall on the side-by-side double flip, he and Selezneva took themselves completely out of the running for the gold. Jill Watson and Peter Oppegard delivered a crisp, modern performance to Mezzoforte's "Check It In". The Calgary crowd was delighted when all three of the Canadian pairs skated more or less clean programs. Denise Benning and Lyndon Johnston were particular favourites with the crowd, as their polished and jazzy program to Max Greger's "Trumpet Blues" was perhaps the best-packaged of the three team's programs. When the marks were tallied, Gordeeva and Grinkov received unanimous first-place ordinals from all nine judges. The judges were completely divided on the rest of the field. The West German, American, Czechoslovakian and Polish judges had Watson and Oppegard second, the Soviet and British judges had Valova and Vasiliev second, the Canadian and East German judges had Benning and Johnston second the Australian judge gave their nod to Gillian Wachsman and Todd Waggoner. With a majority of third-place ordinals, Valova and Vasiliev narrowly squeezed ahead of Watson and Oppegard. Benning and Johnston were fifth, Selezneva and Makarov sixth, Brasseur and Eisler seventh and Hough and Ladret eighth.

**1988 WINTER OLYMPIC GAMES (Calgary, Alberta, February 14-27, 1988)**

Men:

1. Brian Boitano (USA)
2. Brian Orser (USA)
3. Viktor Petrenko (SOV)
4. Alexandr Fadeev (SOV)
5. Grzegorz Filipowski (POL)
6. Vladimir Kotin (SOV)
7. Christopher Bowman (USA)
8. Kurt Browning (CAN)
9. Heiko Fischer (FRG)
10. Paul Wylie (USA)

Women:

1. Katarina Witt (GDR)
2. Elizabeth Manley (CAN)
3. Debi Thomas (USA)
4. Jill Trenary (USA)
5. Midori Ito (JPN)
6. Claudia Leistner (FRG)
7. Kira Ivanova (SOV)
8. Anna Kondrashova (SOV)
9. Simone Koch (GDR)
10. Marina Kielmann (FRG)

Pairs:

1. Ekaterina Gordeeva and Sergei Grinkov (SOV)
2. Elena Valova and Oleg Vasiliev (SOV)
3. Jill Watson and Peter Oppegard (USA)
4. Larisa Selezneva and Oleg Makarov (SOV)
5. Gillian Wachsman and Todd Waggoner (USA)
6. Denise Benning and Lyndon Johnston (CAN)
7. Peggy Schwarz and Alexander König (GDR)
8. Christine Hough and Doug Ladret (CAN)
9. Isabelle Brasseur and Lloyd Eisler (CAN)
10. Natalie and Wayne Seybold (USA)

Ice Dance:

1. Natalia Bestemianova and Andrei Bukin (SOV)
2. Marina Klimova and Sergei Ponomarenko (SOV)
3. Tracy Wilson and Rob McCall (CAN)
4. Natalia Annenko and Genrikh Sretenski (SOV)
5. Kathrin and Christoff Beck (AUT)
6. Suzanne Semanick and Scott Gregory (USA)
7. Klára Engi and Attila Tóth (HUN)
8. Isabelle and Paul Duchesnay (FRA)
9. Antonia and Ferdinand Becherer (FRG)

After placing ninth in the short program with partner Lenka Knapová, Czechoslovakian skater René Novotný developed a bad migraine headache. The doctor of the Czechoslovakian ski jump team prescribed Novotný the drug Alnagon, which contained codeine, caffeine and phenobarbital. He later reflected, "I don't even want to remember what happened next. Before the competition, I was in the locker room putting on my skates when two 'gorillas' came and led me out of the hall. Then Lenka and I were locked up in the Olympic Village and interrogated until morning. The doctor denied everything and I had to take it. They pulled us from the competition." The incident led to amendments to rules surrounding doping controls the following season and more random tests were conducted. Skating to a medley of Mendelssohn, Chopin and Mozart, Gordeeva and Grinkov were exquisite in the free skate, performing a split triple twist, two sets of side-by-side double Axels, a throw double Axel and throw triple Salchow with security and speed. In the final minute of their program, Gordeeva exuded that joie de vivre that made her something of a media darling in Calgary and the standing ovation that they received was well-deserved. With the exception of a pair of 5.8s from British judge Sally-Anne Stapleford, every mark they received was a 5.9 and every judge had them first on their scorecards. Valova and Vasiliev certainly had the repertoire to give 'G and G' a run for their money but it was clear that making it through the program was the couple's main focus. Though 'V and V' included difficult elements, such as a throw triple toe-loop and a triple twist from an Axel entrance, Vasiliev stepped out of a side-by-side triple toe-loop and two key jumping passes were downgraded due to Valova's injury. Their program, a disjointed mix of Europe's "The Final Countdown" and Sviridov's "Blizzard", perhaps also did not do them justice. The judges unanimously placed them second but the fact they were able to pull off a performance worthy of an Olympic medal under the circumstances said much for their talent. Watson and Oppegard not only had to skate right after 'G and G' - they also had to contend with a very unusual distraction. Early in their program, a photographer dropped a camera bag on the ice. A volunteer took it upon themselves to walk on the ice while the pair were performing their trademark 'free fall' lift to retrieve the camera. The situation threw the team off but they skated extremely well, with the exception of a fall by Watson on the side-by-side double Axels. When later asked about the whole camera bag incident, Oppegard said, "I wish they just would have left it there. We saw it and we were aware of it, but suddenly there was a third person on the ice. I wondered if there was a comedy going on behind us while we were performing." The Hungarian referee Elemér Terták never intervened and the American public was completely unaware of what happened because it wasn't brought up by Dick Button or Peggy Fleming in the television broadcast. For their troubles and great performance, Watson and Oppegard took the bronze with third-place ordinals from six of the nine judges. Selezneva and Makarov showcased their technical prowess with side-by-side triple toe-loops and a throw triple toe-loop, but they made costly errors on the triple twist and throw double Axel. Though the West German, American and British judges had Selezneva and Makarov in sixth, the rest of the panel awarded them marks high enough for fourth overall. The Soviet judge predictably had them third but they also surprisingly received a third place ordinal from Canadian judge Suzanne Morrow-Francis. Benning and Johnston skated their stylish "Carmen" program much better than they had at Canadians, but a two-footed landing on the throw double Axel dropped them to sixth, though British judge Sally-Anne Stapleford had them third. Hough and Ladret and Brasseur and Eisler ended the competition in eighth and ninth, though one judge had each of them in the top five in the free skate. China's pair, Mei Zhibin and Li Wei, were the first victims of the 'Olympic curse'. Zhibin and Wei drew first to skate in both the pairs short program and free skate and finished dead last, as did the first skater in the men's short program and the compulsory dances. One of figure skating's oldest superstitions was that skating first, or early in the draw, doomed skaters to receive the lowest marks. After the pairs competition concluded, 'G and G' and 'V and V' gave an exhibition in the nearby town of Okotoks, where they had been training for two weeks before the Games. They suggested that the organizers charge admission and use the proceeds to purchase a new Zamboni. In the men's compulsory figures, Alexandr Fadeev had a decisive lead after the first two figures and to the surprise of many, Heiko Fischer was in second. Having missed much of the two previous seasons with a groin injury, Fischer was somewhat of an unknown quantity in Calgary. Fischer fell apart on the final loop, finishing seventh, and dropped to fourth overall behind Fadeev, Brian Boitano and Brian Orser. Canada's other two entries, Kurt Browning and Neil Paterson, finished 11th and 17th. Boitano's loop was so perfect that his coach Linda Leaver came out on the ice afterward to snap a picture of it.

*How would you have judged the figure skating competitions at the Calgary Olympics? Share your favourite performances on social media using the hashtag #TheSk80s*

The Battle of The Brians in the short program was an epic showdown, with both men skating flawless performances featuring triple Axel/double loop combinations. Orser's "Sing Sing Sing" and Boitano's "Les Patineurs" could not have been more different styles of programs. Fadeev stepped out of the triple Axel in his combination. Viktor Petrenko, Grzegorz Filipowski and Kurt Browning all skated clean programs with triple Axel combinations to make up considerable ground after lower rankings in the figures. Orser won the short program with first-place ordinals from seven of the nine judges, with the American and Soviet judges placing Boitano first. Petrenko and Filipowski finished third and fourth, Browning seventh, Fadeev ninth and Paterson 13th. Following in the footsteps of Fadeev four years earlier in Sarajevo, Browning tried to make history by attempting a quadruple toe-loop in the free skate. Though unsuccessful, it was a valiant attempt. Fadeev completed six triple jumps in his performance, including a triple Lutz/triple toe-loop combination, but missed both a triple Axel and Salchow. Filipowski's performance was quite similar - he missed the triple Axel but landed six other triples, including a triple flip/triple toe-loop. Petrenko executed seven triples, including the triple Axel, in a program that felt like an advanced class in jumping. In contrast, Orser and Boitano's programs were both master classes in great figure skating, balancing technical prowess and polished presentation with outstanding attention to detail. Both men landed triple Axel combinations but from a technical perspective, the mark that was still the tiebreaker at the time, Boitano had an edge with two triple Axels to Orser's one and a triple flip/triple toe-loop combination. A slight step out of a triple flip from Orser was the only error made by either man. Boitano also had an overall advantage in the triple jump count with eight to Orser's six. The judges were divided in a five-four split with the American, Danish, Soviet, Swiss and Japanese judges placing Boitano first in the free skate and the West and East German, Canadian and Czechoslovakian judges putting Orser in the number one position. The latter judge, Gerhardt Bubník, gave Orser the only 6.0 in either one of the singles events for artistic impression. The Battle of The Brians ended with Boitano first, Orser second and Petrenko pulling ahead of Fadeev and Filipowski to win the bronze. Browning finished an incredible eighth in his Olympic debut; Paterson 16th. Boitano's win was the first gold medal of the Calgary Games for the United States in any sport.

*Brian Boitano. Contributor: PCN Photography / Alamy Stock Photo.*

*Brian Orser. Contributor: PCN Photography / Alamy Stock Photo. Photographer: Paul Sutton.*

There were no surprises in the compulsory dances. Natalia Bestemianova and Andrei Bukin, Marina Klimova and Sergei Ponomarenko weaved their way through the Kilian, Paso Doble and Viennese Waltz with no hiccups, taking the top three places. As was par for the course, the only movement in the standings through all three dances were the 12th and 13th place couples swapping places. In the Tango OSP, Bestemianova and Bukin expanded their lead over Klimova and Ponomarenko and Wilson and McCall with a polished and dramatic performance. However, the performances of the leaders were overshadowed by the chorus of boos that the panel of judges received after the marks awarded to the Duchesnays, who delivered a particularly dramatic tango that truly stood out. While American judge Nancy Meiss awarded the Canadians skating for France a 5.7 and 5.8 - higher marks than she gave to the top American couple - the Duchesnays received marks as low as 5.1, with Soviet judge Irina Absaliamova and Austrian judge Heide Maritczak placing them tenth. They remained in eighth, as they had been in the compulsories. In the free dance, Bestemianova and Bukin were at their theatrical best, performing their program to Borodin's "Polovtsian Dances" with their usual panache and speed. The Soviet, Italian and French judges awarded them perfect 6.0s for artistic impression. They received unanimous first-place marks for the gold, though West German judge Willi Wernz nailed them with a 5.5 for presentation. Klimova and Ponomarenko took the silver with their interpretation of the story of Adam and Eve, set to a medley of music by The Beatles. Wilson and McCall, skating in their home country, had the skate of their lives and earned a standing ovation. Canadian judge Ann Shaw was the only one to dare place them second. Wilson and McCall's bronze medal win was the first Olympic medal in ice dancing for Canada. Canada's other two teams, Karyn and Rod Garossino and Melanie Cole and Michael Farrington ended the competition in 12th and 16th place. As in the OSP, the Duchesnays were audience favourites and the judging of their *Savage Rites* program - which earned a standing ovation - was extremely controversial and drew considerable media scrutiny of the discipline. Remaining in eighth place, the siblings from Quebec received top five marks from the American, British and French judges and 5.8s for artistic impression from both the American and Canadian judges. The Soviet and Hungarian judges lowballed them with marks only good enough for tenth place. Former World Champion Lawrence Demmy, the ISU Technical Delegate at the event, told the press that he would have had the Duchesnays second in the free dance. Not everyone agreed with Demmy's assessment of the Duchesnays. Ron Ludington and Roy Bradshaw felt some aspects of the Duchesnays programs violated the rules. Rob McCall thought that change was coming to the sport. He told veteran *Toronto Star* reporter Frank Orr, "I think we'll see ice dancing always in a state of evolution and change as people try new things and test the rules. It's growing very rapidly... That means more people with ideas they want to try, and maybe the rulebook will need to be changed often to keep up with what's really happening in the sport."

*Andrei Bukin, Betty Callaway and Natalia Bestemianova. Contributor. PA Images / Alamy Stock Photo.*

*Midori Ito. Contributor: PCN Photography / Alamy Stock Photo. Photographer: Paul Sutton.*

The media frenzy over The Battle of The Carmens in the women's event was at a ten. Katarina Witt and Debi Thomas were mobbed by photographers wherever they went and the rest of the top skaters weren't exactly left alone either. The Canadian press was relentless in their coverage of Elizabeth Manley and after her disappointing performance at the Canadian Championships, some of them were downright vicious. The compulsory figures were a restrained tug of war between some of the world's best. Kira Ivanova took a very strong lead in the first figure over Witt, Caryn Kadavy, Thomas and Manley. In the second figure, Ivanova faltered, finishing behind Thomas, Witt and Jill Trenary and just ahead of Claudia Leistner and Kadavy. Manley finished a discouraging eighth. In the final figure, Thomas took the win over Ivanova, Witt, Trenary and Manley. Kadavy finished a disastrous tenth. When the results were tallied, Ivanova squeaked out a narrow lead over Thomas, Witt, Manley, Trenary, Leistner and Kadavy. Midori Ito had one of her best results in figures, placing in the top ten in all three figures. Charlene Wong ended the figures in a disappointing 18th place. The highest mark awarded to any of the women in the figures was a 4.2, four-tenths a point lower than the marks 'the human scribe' Trixi Schuba received in her heyday in the early 70s. In the short program, Midori Ito stole the show from the top contenders with the most difficult program of the event, featuring a rare double loop/triple loop combination and a positively massive double Axel. The judges were very generous with their technical marks - all 5.7s and 5.8s. However, they were much more divided in their presentation marks. Swiss judge Jacqueline Itschner awarded Ito a 5.8 and had her in third place. Czechoslovakian judge Gerhardt Bubník had her in a tie for second. Ivanova made a costly error early on in her program, landing completely off balance on the triple toe-loop and stepping out of the double loop in her combination. A tenth-place finish eliminated any chance Ivanova had of relying on her figures lead to contend for a medal. Manley, who was already taking antibiotics for an ear infection, was one of its first victims of a nasty flu with a high fever that was making the rounds the Olympic Village. Kadavy then fell victim, missing practice the day before the short program. Despite their illnesses, both skaters managed to deliver outstanding performances in the short program. Kadavy's combination, the triple loop/double loop, was slightly more difficult than Manley's triple Salchow/double loop. Witt and Thomas both skated the best programs they could have possibly delivered, but their styles could not have been more different. Witt served glitz and glamour with her medley of show tunes from American musicals, while Thomas gave Europop energy with a punchy program to music by a British pop group. The judges had to consider that Thomas' double loop/triple toe-loop combination was more difficult than Witt's triple toe-loop/double loop, but strong performances from the rest of the field, coupled with artistic considerations, made for some interesting results. Witt won the short program with first-place marks from six of the nine judges. Thomas finished second, though the American and Japanese judges placed her first. Manley finished a solid third, though British judge Sally-Anne Stapleford had her in first. Kadavy and Jill Trenary finished a solid fifth and sixth, while Charlene Wong moved up to 14th. Based on her advantage in the figures, Thomas held the overall lead over Witt and Manley entering the final phase of the competition. Absolutely exhausted after attempting a few triple jumps in practice, Kadavy made the difficult decision to withdraw from the competition due to illness. The Battle of The Carmens in the free skate drew the highest Nielsen ratings in Winter Olympic history. 43 000 000 people tuned in to watch ABC's broadcast - significantly more than the Miracle on Ice hockey game in Lake Placid. Over half of all Americans who were watching television at the time tuned in. The broadcast had a higher share level than the 1987 Superbowl and was the highest on any network on a Saturday night since *Roots* aired in 1977. Midori Ito kicked things off in the free skate with another flawless performance, which Dick Button called "a triumph of athleticism." Her program included a triple toe-loop/triple toe-loop combination, triple Lutz and triple flip. Not only was Ito's technical content far more difficult than any of her competitors, but her performance proved a convincing argument for the elimination of compulsory figures, as her eighth-place finish entering the free skate made it impossible for her to win a medal. In front of thousands of avid fans in her home country, Manley delivered the skate of her life. Her electrifying performance featured four different triple jumps including a rare Lutz, excellent spins and wonderfully timed footwork. Manley was in shock when she finished her program to a standing ovation. As she donned a white cowboy hat thrown from the crowd, ABC commentator Jim McKay famously remarked, "Wouldn't it be great if every human being could have one moment like this once in their lives?" In The Battle of The Carmens, Witt's sophisticated program featured four triple jumps - two toe-loops and two Salchows - and two double Axels. In comparison, Thomas landed only two clean triples, stepping out of a triple toe-loop and triple loop and putting a hand down on a triple Salchow. In terms of artistic impression, Witt was clearly in a class of her own, but neither she nor Thomas could compare technically with either Ito or Manley. Seven of the nine judges placed Manley first in the free skate, with East German judge Reinhard Mirmseker and Soviet judge Sergey Kononykhin preferring Witt's performance. Ito finished third ahead of Thomas in the free skate, receiving second-place ordinals from the British, Japanese and West German judges. When the marks were tallied, Witt won the gold, Manley the silver and Thomas the bronze.

Ito finished fifth, Ivanova seventh and Wong 13th. Thomas' medal was a historic first. She was the first woman of colour to win a medal in any sport at the Winter Olympics. In the Exhibitions, Debi Thomas movingly skated to George Michael's "One More Try" in a gold dress, while Katarina Witt delighted the crowd with a program to Michael Jackson's "Bad". Brian Pockar was the Artistic Director of the final figure skating performances of the Calgary Games. Pockar collaborated with Kevin Cottam to stage a magnificent production on an ice rink constructed in the center of McMahon Stadium. Barbara Underhill and Paul Martini, Robin Cousins and Dorothy Hamill all gave outstanding performances. A magnificent group number highlighting Canada's rich Canadian skating history featured Barbara Ann Scott, Suzanne Morrow and Wally Distelmeyer, Frances Dafoe, Barbara Wagner and Bob Paul, Maria and Otto Jelinek, Donald Jackson, Petra Burka, Debbi Wilkes, Karen Magnussen, Toller Cranston and Brian Pockar. Never before had so many legends of Canadian figure skating all taken the ice together and the display was a deeply moving and appropriate finale to an unforgettable Olympic Games.

*Elizabeth Manley, Katarina Witt and Debi Thomas. Contributor: PCN Photography / Alamy Stock Photo.*

*Katarina Witt. Contributor: PCN Photography / Alamy Stock Photo.*

**World Championships.** In 1939, Budapest played host to the final World Championships held before the ISU suspended international competitions for seven years in the wake of World War II. In 1988, the Hungarian capital played host to the final World Championships before the announcement was officially made that compulsory figures were being eliminated. For many of the skaters participating, this would be their final trip to the Worlds before they turned professional or retired. The 12 500 seat Budapest Sportcsarnok had more than enough room for everyone to watch their favourite skaters in action. Unfortunately, attendance for certain events - the compulsory dances and pairs short program in particular - was quite poor. The free dance, in contrast, attracted a full house. The rink used for the compulsory figures only had room for approximately 200 spectators. A decision was made by the ISU and organizers to only allow those with official credentials admission to figure events, which only heightened speculation about the legitimacy of the judging. Joaquin Guerrero and Diana Marcos made history as the first skaters from Mexico to compete at the World Championships and Taiwan had its first man and ice dance team in David Liu and Yucca Liu and Jim Sun. The pairs event got underway with the short program. Ekaterina Gordeeva and Sergei Grinkov duplicated their perfect performance from the Olympics, earning a sea of 5.8s and 5.9s and first-place ordinals from all nine judges. Elena Valova and Oleg Vasiliev were flawless as well, finishing in a strong second. Larisa Selezneva and Oleg Makarov redeemed themselves after their disastrous short program in Calgary, beating Jill Watson and Peter Oppegard by just one ordinal placing to finish third. Denise Benning and Lyndon Johnston and Isabelle Brasseur and Lloyd Eisler both skated very strong programs to finish sixth and seventh. Canadian Champions Christine Hough and Doug Ladret ditched their program to Gross' "Epilogue" two days after the Olympics and went back to their old program to "Kalinka". A minor problem on the entrance to their lift and a lack of unison on the side-by-side spins left them in a disappointing ninth place. In their free skate to music from *Slaughter on Tenth Avenue*, Hough and Ladret had success on both the throw triple Salchow and double Axel, but bobbled the landings of the throw triple toe-loop and their side-by-side double Lutzes, remaining in ninth. Despite problems on the landings of both of their throw triple jumps, Brasseur and Eisler's speed, attack and high triple twist helped them move up to sixth place. Benning and Johnston's post-Olympic decision to take out one of their throws and a lift was a wise strategy. They fought their way through their "Carmen" program to remain in fifth. Americans Gillian Wachsman and Todd Waggoner had the skate of their lives, earning a standing ovation and finishing just off the podium in fourth. During the warmup for the final group, Selezneva and Makarov and Watson Oppegard collided and Oppegard was hit in the head. Selezneva and Makarov had several problems in their performance, the most notable being two-footed landings from Selezneva on the side-by-side triple toe-loop and throw triple toe-loop. Watson and Oppegard fared even worse. Watson took back-to-back hard falls on the side-by-side double Axels and throw double Axel and after the second fall, the two completely lost their concentration and stopped their program for almost forty seconds before continuing on. Walburga Grimm, the referee, did not intervene. It was unclear if Watson or Oppegard were suffering from concussions from the collision but the judges had to mark what they saw, even though the pair omitted a lift and a death spiral. They finished seventh in the free and sixth overall, a result that infuriated Hough and Ladret and Benning and Johnston's coach Kerry Leitch. In their final World Championships, 'V and V' had the skate of their lives, nailing their side-by-side triple toe-loops, throw triple Salchow and throw triple toe-loop. Between Valova's injury and the disappointment of being dethroned at the Olympics, the performance of 'V and V' was a truly remarkable swan song. When Grinkov took an uncharacteristic fall in the warmup, some wondered if 'G and G' would be able to repeat their brilliant free skate from the Olympics.

**1988 WORLD CHAMPIONSHIPS**
(Cincinnati, OH, March 10-15, 1988)

Men:

1. Brian Boitano (USA)
2. Brian Orser (CAN)
3. Viktor Petrenko (SOV)
4. Grzegorz Filipowski (POL)
5. Christopher Bowman (USA)
6. Kurt Browning (CAN)
7. Heiko Fischer (FRG)
8. Petr Barna (CZE)
9. Paul Wylie (USA)
10. Vladimir Petrenko (SOV)

Women:

1. Katarina Witt (GDR)
2. Elizabeth Manley (CAN)
3. Debi Thomas (USA)
4. Claudia Leistner (FRG)
5. Jill Trenary (USA)
6. Midori Ito (JPN)
7. Caryn Kadavy (USA)
8. Simone Koch (GDR)
9. Natalia Lebedeva (SOV)
10. Joanne Conway (GRB)

Pairs:

1. Elena Valova and Oleg Vasiliev (SOV)
2. Ekaterina Gordeeva and Sergei Grinkov (SOV)
3. Larisa Selezneva and Oleg Makarov (SOV)
4. Gillian Wachsman and Todd Waggoner (USA)
5. Denise Benning and Lyndon Johnston (CAN)
6. Jill Watson and Peter Oppegard (USA)
7. Isabelle Brasseur and Lloyd Eisler (CAN)
8. Mandy Wötzel and Axel Rauschenbach (GDR)
9. Christine Hough and Doug Ladret (CAN)
10. Natalie and Wayne Seybold (USA)

Ice Dance:

1. Natalia Bestemianova and Andrei Bukin (SOV)
2. Marina Klimova and Sergei Ponomarenko (SOV)
3. Tracy Wilson and Rob McCall (CAN)
4. Natalia Annenko and Genrikh Sretenski (SOV)
5. Kathrin and Christoff Beck (AUT)
6. Isabelle and Paul Duchesnay (FRA)
7. Klára Engi and Attila Tóth (HUN)
8. Antonia and Ferdinand Becherer (FRG)
9. Susie Wynne and Joseph Druar (USA)
10. Lia Trovati and Roberto Pelizzola (ITA)

It was not to be. Suffering from a nasty cold, Gordeeva took a hard fall on the throw triple Salchow. 'V and V' won their third gold medal at the World Championships, with 'G and G' second and Selezneva and Makarov third. It was the first podium sweep by Soviet pairs at the Worlds since 1969. In a press conference before the ice dance competition, Tracy Wilson and Rob McCall called out the fact that the top eight couples at the Olympics were placed in the same order during the entire competition, stating that they hoped "the judges in Budapest will be more liberal." Their hopes were dashed when the judges managed to place the top five teams from the Olympics in the same order in the compulsory dances. In the Tango Romantica, Quickstep and Viennese Waltz, Natalia Bestemianova and Andrei Bukin, Marina Klimova and Sergei Ponomarenko and Tracy Wilson and Rob McCall predictably took the top three positions. 'B and B' were looked after by Betty Callaway. Their coach Tatiana Tarasova was in the hospital in Moscow after suffering a serious heart attack. Bestemianova caused something of a stir in Budapest after dying her hair blonde. The Duchesnays moved up a spot from the Olympics to seventh but only because Semanick and Gregory didn't attend due to Gregory's back injury. Canadian judge Ann Shaw bucked convention, placing Wilson and McCall in a tie for first with 'B and B' in the Quickstep. The only other judge to go against the grain was Maria Blazek-Miller of Poland, who placed Klimova and Ponomarenko over 'B and B'. The Garossinos were very happy with how they skated but finished 11th. They had been tenth in 1987 and ninth in 1986. Melanie Cole and Michael Farrington had a fall in the Romantica but moved up with 15th place finishes in both the Quickstep and Viennese Waltz. In the Tango OSP, Bestemianova and Bukin were rewarded with a perfect 6.0 from French judge Lysiane Lauret. The Duchesnays and West Germany's Antonia and Ferdinand Becherer managed to each move up a spot when Attila Tóth took a tumble. Out of 25 teams, the only other two to switch positions were the Japanese and West German couples in 18th and 19th. In the free dance, the Duchesnays were once again brilliant, bringing the audience along for the journey. They were the only team to receive noisy standing ovations in both the OSP and free dance, both of which lasted for over two minutes. The judges remained divided over whether or not *Savage Rites* was an exhibition program or a free dance. Their lowest marks, a 5.3 from Canadian judge Ann Shaw and 5.4 from Hungarian judge Katalin Alpern received boos and hisses from the audience. Four judges dared to place them fourth in the free dance and one had them in seventh. They ended the competition in fifth and Isabelle told reporters at a press conference, "You don't know what [the judges] want and what they don't want. They tell you something is wrong, but not what it is. We've been through the rulebook so many times, I know it off by heart." As expected, 'B and B' won the gold, Klimova and Ponomarenko the silver and Wilson and McCall the bronze. The Soviet and French judges gave 'B and B' perfect 6.0s for artistic impression but of the top three teams, Wilson and McCall were the clear audience favourites and they skated their ragtime free dance even better than they had at the Olympics. The Garossinos and Cole and Farrington ended the competition where they started in 11th and 15th. The women's competition in Budapest was expected to be a particularly interesting one. Kira Ivanova, the skater who had so dominantly won the figures at the last three World Championships, had announced her retirement. Ivanova's teammate Anna Kondrashova opted not to compete due to injury and Caryn Kadavy was back in the fold after sadly withdrawing at the Olympics due to illness. Ivanova's absence, in particular, had the potential to shake up the results considerably. The figures, held away from prying eyes, saw some unexpected and controversial results. In the first figure, a rocker, Thomas received the highest mark in the competition - a 4.1 from the Yugoslavian judge, but Witt earned four first-place ordinals to Manley's three and Thomas' two. When the first and second-place ordinals were combined by the accountants, Manley moved ahead of Witt and Thomas by the narrowest of margins. The same thing happened on the second figure, with Manley beating Witt and Thomas with seven first and second-place ordinals to Witt and Thomas' six. Though Manley won the first two figures, Witt still managed to lead by one judge entering the final figure because her overall marks were higher. Witt defeated Manley in the final loop to take the win, six judges to three, with Thomas finishing third. The three judges who didn't have Witt first had her third. The scenario disgusted referee Sonia Bianchetti Garbato, who felt Witt had performed so poorly she had her sixth on her scorecard. In the judges' meeting, Bianchetti Garbato called out the Swiss judge and an Eastern Bloc of judges from Bulgaria, East Germany, Poland the Soviet Union and Yugoslavia for their scoring, letting them know in no uncertain terms that the result had been "unacceptable". The range in the marks of the judges marks was also concerning. On one figure, the judge's marks ranged from first to 16th for Soviet skater Natalia Lebedeva and first to 13th for Kadavy. Manley, who had never skated so well in the figures, told reporters, "I never thought I could ever be dissatisfied with placing second in figures at a World Championship, but I am... Everybody was surprised [by the result] - not just me."

When Manley went out to skate her short program, the cassette player started playing garbled nonsense. She abruptly stopped her program, went to referee Bianchetti Garbato, and asked for a restart. Once her tape went into a different player, it worked absolutely fine. Rattled by the unusual situation, she was off balance in both jumps in her triple Salchow combination. She finished fourth behind Midori Ito, who bounced back from a 14th place finish in the figures with a dynamic, clean program featuring a double loop/triple loop combination. Katarina Witt skated a clean program with a triple toe-loop/double loop combination and her coach Frau Jutta Müller thought she skated even better than she did at the Olympics. East German judge Reinhard Mirmseeker agreed, giving her a perfect 6.0 for presentation. Debi Thomas celebrated her 21st birthday with a flawless program featuring a double loop/triple toe-loop combination and a chorus of "Happy Birthday!" from the crowd. When the marks were tallied, Thomas won the short program in a five-four split. Three of the judges who placed Witt first were from the Eastern Bloc (East Germany, Bulgaria and the Soviet Union) while the fourth was surprisingly Canada's Audrey Moore. In the free skate, Ito didn't quite manage to reproduce her perfect performance from the Olympics. She demonstrated her technical prowess with a clean triple Lutz and double Axel/half loop/triple Salchow but had problems on her triple toe-loop/triple toe-loop combination and triple loop and doubled a planned triple flip. Thomas fared worse, falling on a triple Salchow and erring on the landings of two other triples. After an uncharacteristically poor warmup, Witt rebounded to perform three triple jumps in her program. However, she popped a fourth to a double and one of her double Axels into a single. There was a very noticeable difference in her presentation as compared to the Olympics. In her final competitive performance as an amateur, she worked the crowd and judges more than ever. Manley didn't quite recreate the same magic she did at the Olympics, but she came pretty darn close. Her only minor errors were a tight landing on her opening triple Lutz and a two-footed triple loop, added after she doubled her initial attempt. Like Witt, Manley looked more relaxed than she had been at the Olympics and sold her program to the audience. Witt received the only perfect mark in the free skate, a 6.0 from Bulgarian judge Evgenia Karnolska. Seven of the nine judges had Witt first in the free skate, with the Finnish and Canadian judges preferring Manley. Witt won the gold, Manley the silver and Thomas the bronze. Ito ended the competition in sixth and Canada's second entry, Charlene Wong, placed 17th. The event was the final time Witt, Manley and Thomas stood a podium together in an amateur competition. Their paths wouldn't cross in professional competition until 1991. The only top men's skater from the Olympics missing in Budapest was Vladimir Kotin, who was suffering from an injury. In the figures, Alexandr Fadeev and Brian Boitano led the way after the first two figures but in the third figure, the loop, Poland's Grzegorz Filipowski surprised many by moving up from fourth to second, dropping Boitano and Heiko Fischer to third and fourth. Brian Orser ended the figures in fifth, but Filipowski's finish over Boitano took a bit of the pressure off of him entering the short. As in the women's event, there was some controversy over the judging. Each of the top four men had at least one first-place ordinal on each of the figures. The highest mark awarded was a 4.5 for Boitano's loop by Australian judge Frank Parsons. Orser admittedly did not skate his first two figures as well as he did at the Olympics but he felt his loop did not get the marks it deserved. Orser wasn't the only excellent free skater to get dinged in the figures in Budapest - Kurt Browning, Petr Barna and Paul Wylie all placed outside of the top ten. The short program was not particularly well-skated. Boitano was the clear winner, with a flawless performance that received all 5.8s and 5.9s from the judges. Orser stumbled on both jumps in his combination but managed to hold on to second place because almost all the other contenders, third place Petrenko and fourth place Filipowski included, also botched their triple Axel combinations. Browning, who placed 12th in the figures, managed to gain some ground with a seventh-place finish, though he had a problem with his triple Axel combination as well. With two of the very few clean skates of the night, Czechoslovakia's Petr Barna and Canada's Neil Paterson received marks only good enough for fifth and 12th place. Fadeev, who arrived late in Budapest, took to the ice for the warmup of the final group in the short program. Aggravating a groin injury that had hampered him for much of the season, he withdrew from the competition. Magic was in the air as spectators looked forward to a much-anticipated sequel to The Battle of The Brians in the free skate. After several failed attempts, a group of Canadian fans managed to successfully get "the wave" to circle the Budapest Sportcsarnok four times. Orser landed the triple flip and second triple Axel that had eluded him at the Olympics in one of the finest performances of his career, while Boitano replaced his first triple Axel with another quad attempt, which was close but unsuccessful. He also popped his second triple Axel into a single. Orser won the free skate, receiving three perfect 6.0s for artistic impression from the Canadian, Soviet and Swedish judges. However, his showing in the figures and short program meant that no matter how he skated in the free, he was too far behind to win. Boitano took the gold, Orser the silver and Petrenko the bronze. Filipowski ended the event in fourth, Barna in eighth and Paterson in 13th. Boitano's win marked the first time a World Champion in the men's event successfully reclaimed the title after losing the previous year since 1979.

The performances of all three of the medallists were eclipsed by an incredible accomplishment from Browning, who finished third in the free skate and sixth overall... a quad. Browning's quadruple toe-loop was ratified by ISU Vice-President Josef Dědič as the first to be successfully landed in competition, erasing from the history books Jozef Sabovčík's previous attempt. Browning's achievement followed in the footsteps of fellow Canadians Donald Jackson and Vern Taylor, who made history of their own by breaking the triple Lutz and Axel barriers. After his program, Browning thanked Jackson for encouraging him to attempt the jump in Budapest. What made Browning's success even more remarkable was that it was only his second trip to the World Championships and fourth time attempting the jump in competition. Following the men's competition, the Skála-Coop department store, a corporate sponsor of the event, presented two very special awards. The first, for the skater who won the most gold medals in international competitions, was awarded to Witt. The second, "for the first skater who performed, for the first time in the history of figure skating, a perfect and high quadruple toe-loop in competition" went to Browning. After the event, the Royal Glenora Club presented Browning with a personalized license plate that said '1STQUAD'.

*Katarina Witt. Photo courtesy Sarina Stützer.*

*Scott Hamilton receiving the Jacques Favart Trophy. Photo courtesy Sarina Stützer.*

*Brian Boitano. Photo courtesy Sarina Stützer.*

*Brian Orser. Photo courtesy Sarina Stützer.*

# 1988-1989 SEASON

Hit Songs: "Love Shack" by The B-52's, "Straight Up" by Paula Abdul, "A Little Respect" by Erasure, "She Drives Me Crazy" by Fine Young Cannibals, "Like A Prayer" by Madonna
Hit Movies: Indiana Jones and the Last Crusade, Batman, Ghostbusters II, Honey I Shrunk The Kids, Uncle Buck
Hit TV: The Golden Girls, Empty Nest, Roseanne, Cheers, Murder She Wrote
News: Protests and demonstrations in Tiananmen Square, Crash of Pan-Am Flight 103, Benazir Bhutto makes history as first Islamic woman to serve as Prime Minister in Pakistan, Audrey McLaughlin makes history as first Canadian woman to lead a national political party, Author Salman Rushdie sentenced to death in Iran

## PEOPLE

Brian Boitano joined the growing list of skaters announcing their intention to turn professional or retire in the fall. Natalia Bestemianova joined her husband Igor Bobrin's ice theatre, while Andrei Bukin took a desk job with the USSR Skating Federation. 'B and B' continued to skate together in professional competitions and shows. Jill Watson and Peter Oppegard toured the cast of *Ice Capades*. Other skaters not returning to compete in the amateur ranks included Vladimir Kotin, Anna Kondrashova, Caryn Kadavy, Scott Williams, Gillian Wachsman and Todd Waggoner, Heiko Fischer, Scott Gregory, Antonia and Ferdinand Becherer, Neil Paterson, Kathrin and Christoff Beck, Denise Benning and Lia Trovati and Roberto Pelizzola.

There were weddings and babies galore during the 1988-1989 season. Catarina Lindgren and Tom Dickson tied the knot in July in Pitea, Sweden, honeymooning on the French Riviera. Alexandr Fadeev and his wife Svetlana became the proud parents of a baby boy named Vladimir. Peggy Fleming and Greg Jenkins, welcomed their second son, Todd. Dorothy Hamill's daughter Alexandra Hamill Forsythe was born. Kitty Carruthers announced her engagement to Brett Conrad. The couple met when she was performing with the *Ice Capades* at Summit Arena in Houston, where Conrad was the event coordinator. Kristi Yamaguchi's coach Christy Kjarsgaard married Dr. Andrew Ness in California in April. The best wedding story of the season was that of Lori Benton. During a performance at Sea World in the summer, Matt O'Donnell had a sign lowered from the rafters that said, "Lori, Will You Marry Me?" The answer was yes.

Frank J. Zamboni, the inventor of the revolutionary ice resurfacing machine that bore his name, passed away in California in July at the age of 87. The history of the Zamboni's rise in popularity was tied directly to figure skating - the machine took off in popularity after Sonja Henie bought the first one. Zamboni was posthumously inducted into the World Figure Skating Hall of Fame over fifteen years after his death.

In the summer, Natalia Bestemianova, Andrei Bukin and Tatiana Tarasova were honoured as recipients of The Order of the Red Banner of Labour, the third-highest civil honour in the Soviet Union.

1984 Olympian Pierre Béchu passed away at the age of 29 in a head-on car accident in France in August. His eighteen-month-old daughter was also killed in the accident, which spared the life of his wife and ice dance partner Nathalie Hervé.

In September, Katarina Witt was named the new Sports Ambassador of the United Nations International Children's Emergency Fund. In her role, Witt arranged skating performances to raise funds for UNICEF's National Committees in East Germany and Sweden.

Barbara Underhill and Paul Martini were inducted into Canada's Sports Hall of Fame at a gala dinner at the Royal York Hotel in Toronto in October, following in the footsteps of fellow pairs inductees Frances Dafoe and Norris Bowden, Barbara Wagner and Bob Paul and Maria and Otto Jelinek.

In October, Marina Kielmann won her first of three consecutive medals at the World Roller Skating Championships. West German figure skaters had a long history of success at the event. Ria Baran and Paul Falk, Marika Kilius, Franz Ningel, Freimut Stein, Sigrid Knake and Gunther Koch and Rita and Peter Kwiet were all West German Champions on the ice and World Champions on rollers.

Brian Boitano had a busy fall. In October, he received the Athlete of the Year Award from the Order Sons of Italy in America at Trump's Castle in Atlantic City. On his birthday, he was honoured as Young Italian American of the Year at the annual Italian American Dinner in Washington, D.C. In November, he commentated the men's event at the NHK Trophy for Japanese television.

In November, Midori Ito made history as the first woman to land a triple Axel in competition at the Japanese Championships. Later that same month, she became the first woman to land the jump in international competition at the NHK Trophy, earning a perfect 6.0 for technical merit in the process.

Elizabeth Manley was named Woman of the Year by *Chatelaine* in December. Previous winners included Margaret Atwood and k.d. Lang.

Esteemed American coach Arthur Bourque died in February at the age of 52. A member of the PSGA Board of Directors and USFSA Competitions Committee, Bourque worked with numerous top U.S. skaters over the years including John 'Misha' Petkevich, Kitty and Peter Carruthers, Gillian Wachsman and Todd Waggoner and Natalie and Wayne Seybold.

President George H.W. Bush was a surprise guest at The Broadmoor Arena in the spring. Aware of the Broadmoor's reputation as a first-class skating facility, he wanted to see what all the fuss was about. The President showed up unannounced at around six in the morning to watch a patch session and chatted with the shocked skaters for about fifteen minutes. He asked which ones would be "future Olympians".

Kristi Yamaguchi was announced as the very first recipient of *Skating*'s Readers' Choice Award for the Amateur Figure Skater of the Year at the USFSA's Governing Council Meeting in Anaheim, California in the spring. Ballots were received by mail from every U.S. state and seven different countries. Yamaguchi beat out 60 other nominees for the honour. The trophy consisted of a silver-plated antique skate mounted on ice-like lucite.

Richard Dwyer was the very first recipient of the PSGA's prestigious F. Ritter Shumway Award, presented to an individual "who has earned distinction for unending dedication and significant contribution to the world of figure skating."

Toller Cranston was the recipient of the *American Skating World* Professional Skater of the Year Award. One of the busiest pros on the circuit, Cranston's daily planner included painting and numerous art exhibitions in Europe, performing in professional shows and competitions and working for the CBC as a commentator on skating broadcasts.

The skating community was shocked and disturbed to learn that 13-year-old Ilene Misheloff went missing on her way to a practice session at the St. Moritz Skating Club in California in January. Misheloff finished third in the Pre-Juvenile Girls event at the Central Pacific Regional Championships. Her disappearance, which remains unsolved to this day, was featured on *Unsolved Mysteries*.

Lois Waring McGean passed away in Vermont in February at the age of 58. Waring McGean won the first ice dance event at the World Championships in 1950 with her husband, but through a technicality was not recognized as a World Champion, because the event was styled as an international ice dance competition held in conjunction with the event, not an ISU Championship in itself. Waring McGean was a coach and choreographer for many years after she retired from competing.

Elizabeth Manley, Tracy Wilson and Rob McCall were inducted into Canada's Olympic Hall of Fame at a ceremony in Montreal in April. Manley was invested as an Officer of the Order of Canada by Governor General Jeanne Sauvé the same month.

French President François Mitterrand awarded Pierre Brunet the title of Knight in The National Order of the Legion of Honour in April. The prestigious order was the highest order of merit in France, established in the 19th century by Napoleon Bonaparte. Brunet, a two-time Olympic Gold Medallist in pairs skating, had an equally illustrious career as a coach, working with great champions like Carol Heiss Jenkins, Donald Jackson, Alain Calmat, Alain Giletti and Janet Lynn.

Irina Rodnina, Jayne Torvill and Christopher Dean were the latest inductees to the World Figure Skating Hall of Fame. Between them, the trio won an incredible four Olympic gold medals, fourteen World titles and fifteen European titles.

Her Majesty Queen Elizabeth II bestowed the title of OBE (Officer of the Order of the British Empire) on Courtney Jones "for services to ice-skating" in her Birthday Honours List in June. A four-time World Champion, Jones was President of the NSA at the time he was inducted at Buckingham Palace.

In June, *Bild* published an eight-part story based on interviews with two East German doctors who had defected to the West. The articles claimed that Witt was involved in East Germany's doping program. The story made international headlines and Witt's picture ended up being plastered on the front page of a British tabloid. The first doctor, World Champion ski jumper Hans-Georg Aschenbach admitted to taking the drugs himself. He claimed that all East German sports stars were required to take drugs or "be forced out of the national squad and face great difficulties in private life." The second doctor, Hans-Jürgen Noczenski, a former head of the East German Judo Association said, "Every athlete who competes internationally for East Germany is doped, everyone."

The alleged drugs in question - blue and white pills - were said to have only remained in the bloodstream for five days. Athletes reportedly stopped taking the pills, which came from a distribution center in East Berlin, ten days before major sporting events. East German officials denied the claims and defended Witt. When asked for a comment, the ISU's General Secretary Beat Häsler responded that Witt had "taken every dope test and each one has been negative."

## AROUND THE WORLD

**Canada.** New Brunswick hosted the CFSA's Annual General Meeting for the first time in May, where fittingly the first President from Atlantic Canada was elected. Barbara Ryan was not only the first Newfoundlander to be elected President, she was also only the second woman to hold the position. Marco Entertainment and Baseline Productions of Canada teamed up to present a brand-new annual professional competition called The World Cup of Figure Skating. Offering 214 000 dollars in prize money, the event was judged by skating royalty like Barbara Ann Scott and Osborne Colson.

**Singapore.** Over 1000 people a day showed up to skate at the newly-opened Fuji Ice Palace Rink in Singapore. Figure skating had an explosion of popularity in the country in the 70s, holding its first National Championships in 1976. The closure of both of Singapore's ice rinks soon after had completely killed the sport for a decade. The sport had a long way to go to rebuild but people were just happy to be back on the ice.

**United States.** Franklin S. Nelson was elected as the USFSA's new President in the spring. The USFSA nominated three cities in a bid for the 1992 World Championships - San Francisco, Los Angeles and St. Louis. Officials were delighted when the ISU announced in June the San Francisco bid was successful.

## FUN AND GAMES

Distinctive Dolls of Canada released the Elizabeth Manley collector's doll, featuring the white cowboy hat and pink dress Manley famously wore at the Calgary Olympics. Manley's mini-me was designed by acclaimed British Columbia doll maker Jeanne Venton. An American company manufactured a collector's edition Peggy Fleming doll to celebrate the 20th anniversary of her Olympic victory.

## MUSIC

While in Australia, Jayne Torvill and Christopher Dean were persuaded to capitalize on their World Tour's popularity by singing up a storm. Partnering with music producer Kevin Stanton, they released the record "Here We Stand", featuring the (dare we say) cult classic "Cinderella Rockafella".

## FASHION

Toller Cranston was honoured at the Toronto Men of Style Awards in October. When asked about his fashion preferences, he told reporters, "My style is very much dependent on mixing pieces that have nothing to do with each other." Cranston didn't own a single pair of jeans, had over 50 coats and loved wearing quirky pins.

# BEHIND THE SCENES

An urgent meeting of the ISU Council scheduled to take place at the World Championships in Paris in March was cancelled due to scheduling concerns. Two very interesting proposals were to have been discussed at this meeting. The first was an impatient movement to bump up the July 1, 1990 date for the discontinuation of compulsory figures, so that they wouldn't be skated at the 1990 World Championships. The second was a proposal to formally recognize both precision and fours as disciplines in ISU Championships. CFSA officials were confident that both disciplines would be added to the World Championships and noted the ISU's keen interest in the addition of fours at Skate Canada.

The USFSA started actively discouraging the throwing of flowers onto the ice at competitions. President Hugh Graham cited the image the sport projected as part of the reason. He told reporters that "the TV interview area in competitions that we control will project a sporting image rather than a frilly flower garden." The delays in flower cleanup and hazards of foreign objects on the ice led organizers of the 1989 U.S. Championships to ban the selling of flowers at the Baltimore Arena. The flower girls were still in full force because some fans simply visited their friendly neighbourhood florist on their way to the rink.

World Champion Bernie Ford collaborated with Kelly Johnson, Laurie Palmer and Steven Belanger to invent a new compulsory dance, the Cha Cha Congelado.

Long before the days of Zoom, a new mail-order program called Sports Monitor was launched offering skaters "a personal evaluation and consultation with the expert of your choice." After sending in a VHS tape of their best Salchows and sit spins, the skater received back a 50-point scoring sheet and another VHS with advice from the expert they chose. The experts were Sandra Bezic, Ellen Burka, John Nicks, Frank Carroll, Linda Leaver, Doug Leigh, Ron Ludington, Kerry Leitch and Ron McCall. Sports Monitor cost 95 dollars a shot - no paltry sum in those days!

# BOOKS AND MAGAZINES

*Skating* celebrated its 65th anniversary. The magazine started as an experiment in 1923 and by 1988, it was the oldest continuously published figure skating periodical, with thousands of readers around the world. *Skating* had healthy competition from the new kid on the block, *Blades on Ice*, an independently published periodical based in Tucson, Arizona.

Julia Whedon's *The Fine Art of Figure Skating: An Illustrated History and Portfolio Of Stars* was released by Abrams in New York. Juxtaposing beautiful photography with a general overview of the sport's history, the coffee table book was a welcome addition to many skating libraries.

Brian Orser's autobiography *Orser: A Skater's Life* was released in November. The book was written in collaboration with sportswriter Steve Milton. Orser promoted the book with a Q&A and autograph session at the Ontario Science Centre. A children's book highlighting Orser's story was also published the same year.

# FILMS AND TELEVISION

You couldn't flip through the channels without stumbling upon a figure skater somewhere on television. Brian Boitano judged the Miss America Pageant and Rosalynn Sumners judged Miss Universe. Christopher Bowman was a contestant on *The Dating Game* and Debi Thomas was on *Win, Lose or Draw*. Tai Babilonia and Randy Gardner were interviewed on *Regis and Kathie Lee* and Brian Orser was a special guest performer on *Anne Murray's Family Christmas*. The telecast of the Christmas Tree lighting at Rockefeller Center featured performances by The Haydenettes and Natalie and Wayne Seybold. Christopher Bowman, Lori Blasko and Todd Sand skated on a float in Pasadena's 100th Rose Bowl Parade on New Year's Day.

In November, Paul Wylie made his television acting debut in an afterschool special called *Breaking the Ice* presented by WCVB, Boston's ABC affiliate. Wylie played a bullied figure skater who tried out for his high school's hockey team. The second lead in the special, the hockey player, was played by Jonathan Niles, the grandson of three-time Olympian Nathaniel Niles. The special was part of a public affairs series called *Use Your Smarts* and the skating scenes were filmed at The Skating Club of Boston.

In December, ABC aired *Brian Boitano's Canvas of Ice*. Produced and directed by Doug Wilson with choreography by Sandra Bezic and Linda Leaver, *Canvas of Ice* was the first American television special Brian Boitano, Brian Orser and Katarina Witt appeared in as professionals. The special was filmed over two months in the United States, Canada, France and East Germany. Boitano's iconic skating performance on an Alaska glacier was filmed in minus 23-degree temperatures. He said he was the best ice he ever skated on.

*Skating Free*, Brian Orser's first television special, aired on CBC in December. The production was filmed in Lake Louise, Alberta and featured performances by Brian Boitano, Toller Cranston, Tracy Wilson and Rob McCall and musical guests Glass Tiger and Kidd Sister. The special featured Orser's popular exhibition to Neil Diamond's "The Story of My Life".

In between Christmas and New Year's, ABC aired a television special featuring highlights from the *Ice Capades*, hosted by *Growing Pains* star Kirk Cameron. The special featured choreography by Sarah Kawahara, costumes by Jef Billings and performances by Scott Hamilton, Elizabeth Manley, Debi Thomas and Kitty Carruthers. The Smurfs and The California Raisins also made appearances.

Americans celebrated the New Year with fabulous skating when John Curry, JoJo Starbuck and Katherine Healy were featured performers on the PBS *Happy New Year U.S.A.* special, filmed in Baltimore. The star-studded affair featured musical legends like The Glenn Miller Orchestra, Rosemary Clooney and Mel Tormé. Also featured in the special was *The Next Ice Age*, a new skating ensemble company founded by Nathan Birch and Tim Murphy, former members of Curry's company. *The Next Ice Age* soon received a Baltimore City Arts Grant to develop work that combined dance and figure skating.

In February, Alan Thicke hosted the television broadcast of *From The Heart - A Gala On Ice*, a skating benefit for the Heart and Stroke Foundation of Ontario filmed at Maple Leaf Gardens. Performers included Brian Boitano, Dorothy Hamill, Robin Cousins, Brian Orser, Elizabeth Manley, Tracy Wilson and Rob McCall, Rosalynn Sumners and Barbara Underhill and Paul Martini. The special, choreographed by Sandra Bezic, included Boitano and Orser's popular duet to "King of the Road", which they debuted in Sun Valley in the summer.

In March, Elizabeth Manley's first television special *Dear Elizabeth* aired on CTV. Choreographed by Sandra Bezic and filmed at the Nepean Sportsplex, the special featured skating performances by Manley and Barbara Underhill and Paul Martini and special appearances from Alan Thicke, David Foster and Christopher Plummer. *Dear Elizabeth* was the highest-rated television special of the season on CTV and the second-highest-rated in Canada, behind an Anne Murray special.

In May, *CTV's Wide World of Sports* aired the first Canadian documentary about precision skating. The one-hour special documented the Whitby Ice Fyres team's path to victory at the Canadian Precision Team Skating Championships.

*Claudia Leistner. Photo courtesy Sarina Stützer.*

*Maya Usova and Alexandr Zhulin. Photo courtesy Sarina Stützer.*

*Marina Klimova and Sergei Ponomarenko. Photo courtesy Sarina Stützer.*

# THE AIDS EPIDEMIC

World AIDS Day was observed for the first time, two months after 176 members of the activist group ACT UP were arrested at a sit-in protest which successfully nudged the FDA into speeding up the process for approval of drug treatments for HIV/AIDS. Cross-border travel restrictions in many countries forced dozens of skaters who were living with HIV/AIDS to keep their diagnoses a closely guarded secret so that they could continue working in other countries.

Professional figure skater Gene Gant passed away at the age of 50 in Las Vegas in July. Born in Washington, D.C., Gant had no amateur career to speak of. He took up skating at the age of sixteen, while attending Cardozo High School, during the Jim Crow era. Though he wanted to receive lessons, he was turned down because he was a person of colour. "A guy named Vernon Jackson and I tried all over town, but no teachers would take us," he said in a 1970 interview. While working in his father's dry-cleaning business and running a coffee shop, he studied dancing. An impromptu audition resulted in a lengthy career skating with the *Ice Capades*.

Esteemed choreographer André Denis passed away in Quebec at the age of 46. Born in Saint-Jean-sur-Richelieu, Denis was an accomplished ballet, folk and tap dancer who toured with the *Les Feux-Follets* in the United States. He began working with figure skaters in 1973, at a time when choreographers or 'artistic coaches' and 'stylists', as they were then known, were few and far between in the amateur skating world. His successful partnership with American ice dancers Carol Fox and Richard Dalley led to a highly successful career in Canada. He worked with a who's who of figure skating, including Barbara Underhill and Paul Martini, Tracy Wilson and Rob McCall, Ron Shaver, Lori Nichol and Lorna Wighton and John Dowding. He led off-ice dance classes at the CFSA and Quebec section's seminars and the Canada Ice Dance Theatre in Victoria. He also worked with Doug Leigh's students in Barrie and Carlo Fassi's students in Colorado Springs. Coach Jean-Pierre Boulais recalled, "He was one of the people who influenced the artistic part of skating and brought it to another level. He was just such a great person and had such a good way of influencing us in the right way. All the skaters loved him. He pushed the envelope and we pushed him too, because he was getting into something he really didn't know. We got him out on the ice teaching us in skates. He was so agile and we told him, 'André, you need a pair of skates and we're going to show you how.' Within a few months, he was standing up on his skates. It was funny because sometimes he would try things and just let himself go. We'd laugh. Obviously, we didn't want him to hurt himself, but as a dancer he was so agile that skating was really easy for him to learn... He was a very timid person. He was very reserved, into himself. He was sick at a time when AIDS was just coming out and it was the worst disease to have. It was a great career going on for this guy who was living such a pitiful, hard life at the same time. Because of the connection we had - family wise and friendship - he was very open to us, so we got the chance to meet the real André. I went to see him on his deathbed in Toronto with David Wilson, who was my partner at the time. I was so happy because he was conscious. I held his hand. I talked to him. He was very, very happy that I went to see him. Two days later he was gone. If you would have known him, you would have fallen in love with him. He was so nice and positive. He was a source of inspiration and a big part of the reason I've achieved what I have in skating." Lorna (Wighton) Aldridge Gosvener remembered, "He had a wonderful sense of humour and working with him was always a fun-loving experience. He made our sessions so enjoyable and never entered the rink without a big grin on his face. I miss him so and I'm sure all those who were so fortunate to have worked with the Great André Denis feel the same way."

In February, Ondrej Nepela passed away in Mannheim, West Germany at the age of 38. The son of a driver and a seamstress, Nepela was born in Bratislava, Czechoslovakia. He made his international debut at the 1964 Winter Olympic Games in Innsbruck, Austria at the age of thirteen. Coached by Hilda Múdra, he won an incredible eight Czechoslovakian titles, eight medals at the European Championships (five of them gold), five medals at the World Championships (three of them gold) and the gold medal at the 1972 Winter Olympic Games in Japan. He went on to tour with *Holiday on Ice* and coach in West Germany. Nepela's square in the National AIDS Memorial Quilt features the Japanese flag and the Olympic logo with the words "Sapporo '72".

Ron Alexander passed away in April at the age of 46. Born in British Columbia, Alexander (born Ronald Verdun Slater) got his start in skating at the Willingdon Figure Skating Club. In 1964, he performed in Dick Button's *Icetravaganza* at the New York World's Fair. After years of touring abroad as an adagio skater in Europe and Africa and performing in a jazz dancing troupe, he joined John Curry's company, appearing in his *Theatre Of Skating II* show at the London Palladium and *Ice Dancing* on Broadway. He later worked at a gymnasium and acted as one of the founding members of AIDS Vancouver.

Donald Bonacci passed away at the age of 35 in Mamaroneck, New York in June. Born in Port Chester, New York, he got his start in skating as a youngster in the 60s at the Rye Figure Skating Club, later making a name for himself as a professional. He toured with the *Ice Follies* for many years and won the silver medal at the World Professional Championships in Jaca, Spain in 1977, with partner Cathy Mishkin. Before turning professional, Mishkin and Bonacci won the bronze medal in the junior pairs event at the U.S. Championships in 1970. All three of the men on the podium that year died of HIV/AIDS complications.

Bobby Black passed away in Boston in June at the age of 39. Black got his start in figure skating at the North Shore Skating Club. He went on to represent The Skating Club of Boston nationally, passing his Gold test and winning the 1964 U.S. novice men's title and the silver medal in the junior men's event at the 1965 U.S. Championships. He went on to teach at the Falmouth Ice Arena, North Shore Skating Club and The Skating Club of Boston. A graduate of Tufts University and Babson College, he also worked as the Vice-President of BayBank Boston.

*Toller Cranston and Ondrej Nepela. Photo by Fred & Joan Dean, courtesy Paul Dean, "Ice & Roller Skate" magazine archive.*

*Bobby Black. Photo courtesy Jane Piercy, The Skating Club of Boston. Contributor: Roger F. Turner.*

*Panel of the AIDS Quilt celebrating the life of René Vancampen. Photo courtesy Edward Vancampen.*

René Vancampen passed away in June at the age of 29. Born in Haarlem, The Netherlands, Vancampen moved to Southern California with his family when he was 4 years old. He took up figure skating at the South Bay Figure Skating Club at the age of sixteen. He represented the Arctic Blades Figure Skating Club several times at the Southwest Pacific Championships and passed his seventh figure and junior free skating tests. He and his twin brother Edward later opted to skate for their country of birth. René won the silver medal in the senior men's event at the Dutch Championships twice. His coaches were Jerry and Louella Rehfield, Kim McIsaac, Doug Chapman and Dianne de Leeuw. Off the ice, he worked in retail and modelling. He collected Dutch antiques and Delft Blue porcelain. Vancampen's brother Edward recalled, "René was beautiful. I was so jealous of his looks. I thought he had it all. Not realizing that he was also jealous of me. We fought a lot. Such a waste of valuable time. He was diagnosed with AIDS in 1988. He then moved back home with my mother. She took care of him for the last year he was alive. Remember, at that time, HIV and AIDS was a death sentence. There were no real medicines to combat this illness. AZT was a medication that my brother was taking. It is now believed that AZT and its horrible side effects did more damage than good. I would visit and spend time with René once or twice a week. We would just sit and watch a movie or TV. There were times when he spoke to me, and for a split second I would forget that he was dying of AIDS, and I would turn around to answer him and I would be shocked all over again. He was about 6 feet tall and weighed about 175 pounds. He passed away in his own room with my mother by his side. Losing my twin brother changed my life forever. After he passed, I started skating again and never stopped. You could say, because of my brother, that I have the life I have now."

## HOMOPHOBIA

At the same time the impact of the AIDS epidemic was truly starting to be felt in the skating community, Canadian reporter Christie Blatchford was one of the first members of the mainstream media to write about homophobia and AIDS in the figure skating world. Her article for the *Calgary Sun* discussed how LGBTQ+ skaters were forced to live double lives, bringing their partners along to competitions but introducing them as their cousins. When a reporter at the 1988 U.S. Championships tried to pull a gotcha question about the column on Dick Button, he quipped back, "Well, if they don't like it, they don't have to watch."

Not long after Blatchford's article made the rounds, USFSA President Hugh Graham went on a tirade about "the mixed image of the sport and the very real difficulty of attracting more participation by young men." Graham pontificated that figure skating should be a sport where athleticism was stressed, so that "parents, especially fathers, [would] feel this is a sport in which they would like their sons to participate in." Graham suggested making rule changes surrounding men's costuming and putting a stop to giving men bouquets on the podium. He felt so strongly about these issues that he brought them up in his acceptance speech when he was elected President.

An elite Canadian coach echoed Graham's sentiments: "The father in the rec room who sees an athlete sitting in the Kiss and Cry, surrounded by flowers, is not going to want to see his 10-year-old son get into skating. I don't know quite how we've created this monster... the flowers on the ice, the tuxes, the sequins."

A prominent skating official, who is still very much involved with the sport, remarked, "There's an enormous problem, no question. Some of our men appear to be effeminate or are effeminate. There are effeminate people in every walk of life but like ballet, we attract more gay people. Our image is good in as much as our kids are healthy, not into drugs and things, but there is no doubt it comes across as artsy. But skating is extremely athletic, a great sport, but it is not promoted in the proper fashion. We have to educate the public more. One thing we do... to attract boys is to encourage pairs skating. It is very demanding."

Remarks like these did little to make LGBTQ+ athletes feel welcome in the sport... and ironically, the cries of skating officials that "not enough men were skating" simply did not jive with the numbers. An analysis of the number of entries at the World, World Junior, Canadian and U.S. Championships revealed that the number of men participating in the sport at an elite level steadily increased from 1980 to 1990, with particularly strong growth at the grassroots level. The number of men competing in the novice men's event at the U.S. Championships actually doubled and in 95.4% of cases, the number of men entered in singles, pairs and ice dance events at all four competitions increased from the start of the decade to the end.

So if there was no shortage of men in figure skating, what were were people so worried about? It wasn't rocket science. It was homophobia.

*Brian Boitano. Photo courtesy Sarina Stützer.*

*Katarina Witt. Photo courtesy Sarina Stützer.*

*Brian Orser. Photo courtesy Sarina Stützer.*

# Fall Internationals

**1988 COUPES DES ALPES (Saint Gervais, France and Oberstdorf, West Germany, August 24-28, 1988 and August 30-September 3, 1988)**

Grand Prix de St. Gervais Winners:

Marcus Christensen (CAN) - men
Tonia Kwiatkowski (USA) - women
Cindy Landry and Lyndon Johnston (CAN) - pairs
Jacqueline Petr and Mark Janoschak (CAN) - ice dance

Nebelhorn Trophy (Oberstdorf) Winners:

Aren Nielsen (USA) - men
Tonia Kwiatkowski (USA) - women
Cindy Landry and Lyndon Johnston (CAN) - pairs
Ilona Melnichenko and Gennadi Kaskov (SOV) - ice dance

**1988 SKATE ELECTRIC UK INTERNATIONAL (London, England, October 4-6, 1988)**

Men:

1. Kurt Browning (CAN)
2. Christopher Bowman (USA)
3. Ronny Winkler (GDR)

Women:

1. Charlene Wong (CAN)
2. Joanne Conway (GRB)
3. Beatrice Gelmini (ITA)

Pairs:

1. Peggy Schwarz and Alexander König (GDR)
2. Elena Bechke and Denis Petrov (SOV)
3. Cheryl Peake and Andrew Naylor (GRB)

Ice Dance:

1. Maya Usova and Alexandr Zhulin (SOV)
2. Sharon Jones and Paul Askham (GRB)
3. Suzanne Semanick and Ron Kravette (USA)

**1988 NOVARAT TROPHY (Budapest, Hungary, October 6-9, 1988)**

Men:

1. Mark Mitchell (USA)
2. Peter Johansson (SWE)
3. Stéphane Yvars (CAN)

Women:

1. Nancy Kerrigan (USA)
2. Tamara Téglássy (HUN)
3. Kathrin Schröter (SUI)

Ice Dance:

1. Larisa Fedorinova and Evgeni Platov (SOV)
2. Jodie Balogh and Jerod Swallow (USA)
3. Krisztina Kerekes and Csaba Szentpétery (HUN)

**1988 KARL SCHÄFER MEMORIAL (Vienna, Austria, October 10-13, 1988)**

Men:

1. Viacheslav Zagorodniuk (SOV)
2. Rico Krahnert (GDR)
3. Mark Mitchell (USA)

Women:

1. Nancy Kerrigan (USA)
2. Evelyn Großmann (GDR)
3. Tamara Téglássy (HUN)

Ice Dance:

1. Larisa Fedorinova and Evgeni Platov (SOV)
2. Krisztina Kerekes and Csaba Szentpéteri (HUN)
3. Jodie Balogh and Jerod Swallow (USA)

**1988 SKATE AMERICA (Portland, ME, October 17-23, 1988)**

Men:

1. Christopher Bowman (USA)
2. Daniel Doran (USA)
3. Todd Eldredge (USA)

Women:

1. Claudia Leistner (FRG)
2. Midori Ito (JPN)
3. Kristi Yamaguchi (USA)

Pairs:

1. Natalia Mishkutenok and Artur Dmitriev (SOV)
2. Marina Eltsova and Sergei Zaitzev (SOV)
3. Natalie and Wayne Seybold (USA)

Ice Dance:

1. Susie Wynne and Joseph Druar (USA)
2. Svetlana Liapina and Gorsha Sur (SOV)
3. Renée Roca and James Yorke (USA)

**1988 SKATE CANADA (Thunder Bay, ON, October 29-31, 1988)**

Men:

1. Kurt Browning (CAN)
2. Viktor Petrenko (SOV)
3. Angelo D'Agostino (USA)

Women:

1. Natalia Lebedeva (SOV)
2. Jill Trenary (USA)
3. Patricia Neske (FRG)

Pairs:

1. Isabelle Brasseur and Lloyd Eisler (CAN)
2. Peggy Schwarz and Alexander König (GDR)
3. Ekaterina Murugova and Artem Torgashev (SOV)

Ice Dance:

1. Natalia Annenko and Genrikh Stretenski (SOV)
2. April Sargent and Russ Witherby (USA)
3. Melanie Cole and Michael Farrington (CAN)

**1988 PRIZE OF MOSCOW NEWS (Leningrad, Soviet Union, November 1-6, 1988)**

Men:

1. Vladimir Petrenko (SOV)
2. Yuri Tsimbaliuk (SOV)
3. Alexandr Fadeev (SOV)

Women:

1. Tonya Harding (USA)
2. Natalia Lebedeva (SOV)
3. Natalia Gorbenko (SOV)

Pairs:

1. Natalia Mishkutenok and Artur Dmitriev (SOV)
2. Elena Bechke and Denis Petrov (SOV)
3. Marina Eltsova and Sergei Zaitsev (SOV)

Ice Dance:

1. Marina Klimova and Sergei Ponomarenko (SOV)
2. Larisa Fedorinova and Evgeni Platov (SOV)
3. Ilona Melnichenko and Gennadi Kaskov (SOV)

*Natalia Mishkutenok and Artur Dmitriev. Photo courtesy Sarina Stützer.*

# Fall Internationals

## 1988 PRAGUE SKATE (Prague, Czechoslovakia, November 3-6, 1988)

Men:

1. Petr Barna (CZE)
2. Philippe Candeloro (FRA)
3. Zsolt Kerekes (ROM)

Women:

1. Simone Lang (GDR)
2. Sabine Contini (ITA)
3. Michèle Claret (SUI)

Pairs:

1. Mandy Wötzel and Axel Rauschenbach (GDR)
2. Karina Guchmazova and Sergei Petrovski (SOV)
3. Danielle and Stephen Carr (AUS)

Ice Dance:

1. Andrea Juklová and Martin Šimeček (CZE)
2. Stefania Calegari and Pasquale Camerlengo (ITA)
3. Susanna Rahkamo and Petri Kokko (FIN)

## 1988 GOLDEN SPIN OF ZAGREB (Zagreb, Yugoslavia, November 9-13, 1988)

Men:

1. Riko Krahnert (GDR)
2. András Száraz (HUN)
3. Norm Proft (CAN)

Women:

1. Lisa Sargeant (CAN)
2. Kelly Szmurlo (USA)
3. Anja Geissler (FRG)

Ice Dance:

1. Melanie Cole and Michael Farrington (CAN)
2. Dorothi Rodek and Robert Nardozza (USA)
3. Christelle Gautier and Alberick Dalongeville (FRA)

## 1988 POKAL DER BLAUEN SCHWERTER (East Berlin, East Germany, November 9-13, 1988)

Men:

1. Viacheslav Zagorodniuk (SOV)
2. Scott Davis (USA)
3. Mirko Eichhorn (GDR)

Women:

1. Tanja Krienke (GDR)
2. Tisha Walker (USA)
3. Stéphanie Ferrer (FRA)

Pairs:

1. Elena Nikonova and Nikolai Apter (SOV)
2. Sherry Ball and Christopher Bourne (CAN)
3. Angela Caspari and Marno Kreft (GDR)

## 1988 GRAND PRIX INTERNATIONAL DE PARIS (Paris, France, November 11-15, 1988)

Men:

1. Paul Wylie (USA)
2. Grzegorz Filipowski (POL)
3. Michael Slipchuk (CAN)

Women:

1. Claudia Leistner (FRG)
2. Natalia Gorbenko (SOV)
3. Evelyn Großmann (GDR)

Pairs:

1. Elena Bechke and Denis Petrov (SOV)
2. Mandy Wötzel and Axel Rauschenbach (GDR)
3. Katy Keeley and Joseph Mero (USA)

Ice Dance:

1. Susie Wynne and Joseph Druar (USA)
2. Sharon Jones and Paul Askham (GRB)
3. Oksana Grishuk and Alexander Chichkov (SOV)

## 1988 NHK TROPHY (Tokyo, Japan, November 24-27, 1988)

Men:

1. Alexandr Fadeev (SOV)
2. Petr Barna (CZE)
3. Kurt Browning (CAN)

Women:

1. Midori Ito (JPN)
2. Kristi Yamaguchi (USA)
3. Marina Kielmann (FRG)

Pairs:

1. Larisa Selezneva and Oleg Makarov (SOV)
2. Elena Bechke and Denis Petrov (SOV)
3. Kristi Yamaguchi and Rudy Galindo (USA)

Ice Dance:

1. Marina Klimova and Sergei Ponomarenko (SOV)
2. Maya Usova and Alexandr Zhulin (SOV)
3. April Sargent and Russ Witherby (USA)

## 1988 GRAND PRIZE SNP (Banská Bystrica, Czechoslovakia)

Men:

1. Sergey Minaev (SOV)
2. Cornel Gheorghe (ROM)
3. Thomas Dörmer (GDR)

Women:

1. Laetitia Hubert (FRA)
2. Katja Günther (GDR)
3. Tamara Heggen (AUS)

Pairs:

1. Iveta Svetacheva and Vladimir Shagov (SOV)
2. Beata Szymłowska and Mariusz Siudek (POL)
3. Angela Caspari and Marno Kreft (GDR)

Ice Dance:

1. Anjelika Krylova and Vladimir Leliukh (SOV)
2. Maria Anikanova and Samvel Gezalian (SOV)
3. Zuzana Slobodová and Tomas Morbacher (CZE)

## 1989 NORDISKA MÄSTERSKAPEN (Hvidovre, Denmark, February 24-26, 1989)

Men:

1. Peter Johansson (SWE)
2. Henrik Walentin (DEN)
3. Lars Dresler (DEN)

Women:

1. Hélène Persson (SWE)
2. Anisette Torp-Lind (DEN)
3. Ann-Marie Söderholm (SWE)

## 1989 MERANO SPRING TROPHY (Merano, Italy, March 24-26, 1989)

Women:

1. Geremi Weiss (USA)
2. Laetitia Hubert (FRA)
3. Tanja Krienke (GDR)

## 1989 CHALLENGE LYSIANE LAURET (Grenoble, France, April 13-15, 1989)

Ice Dance:

1. Klára Engi and Attila Tóth (HUN)
2. Suzanne Semanick and Ron Kravette (USA)
3. Svetlana Liapina and Gorsha Sur (SOV)

# National Championships and Other Competitions

## SENIOR NATIONAL CHAMPIONS BY COUNTRY

### Men

AUS - Cameron Medhurst
AUT - Ralph Burghart
BUL - Alexander Mladenov
CZE - Petr Barna
DEN - Henrik Walentin
FIN - Jari Kauppi
FRA - Axel Médéric
FRG - Richard Zander
GDR - Mirko Eichhorn
GRB - Christian Newberry
HOL - Alcuin Schulten
HUN - András Száraz
ITA - Alessandro Riccitelli
JPN - Makoto Kano
NOR - Jan Erik Digernes
NZL - Christopher Blong
POL - Przemysław Noworyta
SAF - Dino Quattrocecere
SOV - Alexandr Fadeev
SUI - Oliver Höner
SWE - Peter Johansson

### Women

AUS - Tracey Damigella*
AUT - Yvonne Pokorny
BUL - Tsvetelina Yankova
CZE - Iveta Voralová
DEN - Anisette Torp-Lind
FIN - Elina Hänninen
FRA - Surya Bonaly
FRG - Claudia Leistner
GDR - Evelyn Großmann
GRB - Joanne Conway
HOL - Jeltje Schulten
HUN - Tamara Téglássy
ITA - Sabine Contini
JPN - Midori Ito
KOR - Sung-jin Byun
NOR - Anita Thorenfeldt
NZL - Rosanna Blong
POL - Mirella Gawłowska
SOV - Natalia Gorbenko
SUI - Stéfanie Schmid
SWE - Hélène Persson

*Tracey Damigella won the figures, short and long programs at the Australian Championships but was not awarded the national title because she was an invited guest skater from America.

*Grzegorz Filipowski. Photo courtesy Sarina Stützer.*

### Pairs

AUS - Danielle and Stephen Carr
CZE - Radka Kovaříková and René Novotný
FRA - Surya Bonaly and Benoît Vandenberghe
FRG - Anuschka Gläser and Stefan Pfrengle
GDR - Mandy Wötzel and Axel Rauschenbach
GRB - Cheryl Peake and Andrew Naylor
JPN - Yuki Shoji and Takaya Usuda
POL - Anna Górecka and Arkadiusz Górecki**
SOV - Larisa Selezneva and Oleg Makarov
SUI - Saskia and Guy Bourgeois

**The Polish pairs title was not awarded as the winning team did not reach the required standard of marks.

### Ice Dance

AUS - Monica MacDonald and Duncan Smart
AUT - Ursula and Herbert Holik
BUL - Petya Gavazova and Nikolay Tonev
CZE - Andrea Juklová and Martin Šimeček
FIN - Susanna Rahkamo and Petri Kokko
FRA - Dominique Yvon and Frédéric Palluel
FRG - Andrea Weppelmann and Hendryk Schamberger
GRB - Sharon Jones and Paul Askham
HOL - Joanne and Eerde van Leeuwen
HUN - Klára Engi and Attila Tóth
ITA - Stefania Calegari and Pasquale Camerlengo
JPN - Kaoru and Kenji Takino
POL - Małgorzata Grajcar and Andrzej Dostatni
SOV - Marina Klimova and Sergei Ponomarenko
SUI - Diane Gerencser and Bernard Columberg
SWE - Ulla-Stina Johansson and Andreas Hein

## 1989 WINTER UNIVERSITY GAMES (Sofia, Bulgaria, March 2-12, 1989)

Men:

1. Makoto Kano (JPN)
2. James Cygan (USA)
3. Vladimir Petrenko (SOV)

Women:

1. Marina Kielmann (FRG)
2. Larisa Zamotina (SOV)
3. Nancy Kerrigan (USA)

Pairs:

1. Natalia Mishkutenok and Artur Dmitriev (SOV)
2. Sharon Carz and Doug Williams (USA)
3. Marina Eltsova and Sergei Zaitsev (SOV)

Ice Dance:

1. Svetlana Liapina and Gorsha Sur (SOV)
2. Ilona Melnichenko and Gennadi Kaskov (SOV)
3. Tracy Sniadach and Leif Erickson (USA)

## 1989 U.S. PRECISION TEAM CHAMPIONSHIPS (Providence, RI, March 31-April 1, 1989)

Team:

1. The Haydenettes
2. Goldenettes
3. Detroit Capets

Other Winners:

Shoreliners (junior)
Fraser Juniorettes (novice)
Fabulous 40s (adult)

## 1989 CANADIAN PRECISION TEAM CHAMPIONSHIPS (Edmonton, AB, April 7-9, 1989)

Team:

1. Whitby Ice Fyre
2. Les Pirouettes de Laval
3. K-W Kweens on Ice

Other Winners:

Burlington Ice Image (junior)
Les Altesses - St-Leonard (novice)
Edmonton Masters (adult)

*Maya Usova and Alexandr Zhulin. Photo courtesy Sarina Stützer.*

# Personalities

KURT BROWNING

Date of Birth: June 18, 1966
Place of Birth: Rocky Mountain House, AB
Coach: Michael Jiranek
Choreographer: Kurt Browning, Sandra Bezic, Kevin Cottam
Home Club: Royal Glenora SC

VIKTOR PETRENKO

Date of Birth: June 27, 1969
Place of Birth: Odesa, Soviet Union
Coach: Galina Zmievskaya
Home Club: Odesa

GRZEGORZ FILIPOWSKI

Date of Birth: July 28, 1966
Place of Birth: Łódź, Poland
Coach: Barbara Kossowska, Michael Jiranek

CHRISTOPHER BOWMAN

Date of Birth: March 30, 1967
Place of Birth: Hollywood, CA
Coach: Frank Carroll
Choreographer: Frank Carroll, Ricky Harris
Home Club: Los Angeles FSC

PAUL WYLIE

Date of Birth: October 24, 1964
Place of Birth: Dallas, TX
Coach: Carlo Fassi, Evy and Mary Scotvold
Choreographer: Robin Cousins, Mary Scotvold, Mark Militano
Home Club: Colorado SC/Broadmoor SC/SC of Boston

PETR BARNA

Date of Birth: March 9, 1966
Place of Birth: Prague, Czechoslovakia
Coach: František Pechar
Choreographer: Milada Šittová
Home Club: Rudá hvězda Praha

MICHAEL SLIPCHUK

Date of Birth: March 19, 1966
Place of Birth: Edmonton, AB
Coach: Michael Jiranek, Jan Ullmark
Choreographer: Sandra Bezic, Kevin Cottam
Home Club: Royal Glenora SC

MIDORI ITO

Date of Birth: August 13, 1969
Place of Birth: Nagoya, Japan
Coach: Machiko Yamada
Choreographer: Machiko Yamada, Michiko Matsumoto
Home Club: Chunichi Club (Nagoya)

HOLLY COOK

Date of Birth: December 1, 1971
Place of Birth: Bountiful, UT
Coach: Kris Sherard
Home Club: Utah FSC

JILL TRENARY

Date of Birth: August 1, 1968
Place of Birth: Minnetonka, MN
Coach: Carlo and Christa Fassi
Choreographer: Sandra Bezic, Christa Fassi, Renée Roca
Home Club: Broadmoor SC

CHARLENE WONG

Date of Birth: March 4, 1966
Place of Birth: Montreal, QC
Coach: Helen Ann Shields, Louis Stong, Sonya and Peter Dunfield
Choreographer: Sandra Bezic
Home Club: CPA Pierrefonds, Gloucester SC

KAREN PRESTON

Date of Birth: July 8, 1971
Place of Birth: Toronto, ON
Coach: Wally Distelmeyer, Osborne Colson
Choreographer: Osborne Colson
Home Club: Toronto Cricket, Skating and Curling Club

JOANNE CONWAY

Date of Birth: March 11, 1971
Place of Birth: Wallsend, England
Coach: Mildred Athlerly, Carlo and Christa Fassi, Robin Cousins
Home Club: Chester's Ice Club (Sunderland), Gillingham Ice Dance and FSC

LISA SARGEANT

Date of Birth: January 8, 1971
Place of Birth: Lacombe, AB
Coach: Michael Jiranek
Choreographer: Michael Jiranek
Home Club: Royal Glenora SC

EVELYN GROßMANN

Date of Birth: June 16, 1971
Place of Birth: Dresden, East Germany
Coach: Jutta Müller, Peter Meyer
Choreographer: Rudi Suchy
Home Club: SC Karl-Marx-Stadt/Chemnitz EV

CHRISTINE HOUGH AND DOUG LADRET

Date of Birth: October 9, 1969/November 13, 1961
Place of Birth: Renfrew, ON/Vancouver, BC
Coach: Kerry Leitch
Choreographer: Susan McGrigor
Home Club: Kitchener-Waterloo SC/Preston FSC/Vancouver SC

ISABELLE BRASSEUR AND LLOYD EISLER

Date of Birth: July 28, 1970/April 28, 1963
Place of Birth: Kingsburg, QC/Seaforth, ON
Coach: Josée Picard, Eric Gillies
Choreographer: Uschi Keszler Boornazian
Home Club: CPA St-Jean/Seaforth FSC

ELENA BECHKE AND DENIS PETROV

Date of Birth: January 7, 1966/March 3, 1968
Place of Birth: Leningrad, Soviet Union
Coach: Tamara Moskvina
Choreographer: Tamara Moskvina, Aleksandr Matveyev
Home Club: Leningrad

NATALIA MISHKUTENOK AND ARTUR DMITRIEV

Date of Birth: July 14, 1970/January 21, 1968
Place of Birth: Minsk, Soviet Union/Bila Tserkva, Soviet Union
Coach: Tamara Moskvina
Choreographer: Tamara Moskvina, Aleksandr Matveyev
Home Club: Trade Unions/Armed Forces Leningrad

ISABELLE AND PAUL DUCHESNAY

Date of Birth: December 18, 1963/July 31, 1961
Place of Birth: Aylmer, QC/Metz, France
Coach: Martin Skotnický, Betty Callaway
Choreographer: Christopher Dean, Bobby Thompson
Home Club: Minto SC

KARYN AND ROD GAROSSINO

Date of Birth: June 7, 1965/June 7, 1963
Place of Birth: Didsbury, AB
Coach: Bernie Ford, Marijane Stong, John Briscoe, Michael Jiranek, Roy Bradshaw
Choreographer: Bernie Ford, Marijane Stong, John Briscoe, Karyn and Rod Garossino
Home Club: Calalta FSC

MAYA USOVA AND ALEXANDR ZHULIN

Date of Birth: May 22, 1964/July 20, 1963
Place of Birth: Gorky, Soviet Union/Moscow, Soviet Union
Coach: Natalia Dubova
Choreographer: Elena Kholina
Home Club: Trade Union Moscow

MICHELLE MCDONALD AND MARK MITCHELL

Date of Birth: February 1, 1964/August 19, 1963
Place of Birth: Abbotsford, BC/Halifax, NS
Coach: Marijane Stong, John Briscoe
Choreographer: Gabby Kamino, Tracy Wilson, Rob McCall
Home Club: MSA FSC (Abbotsford)/Sackville SC

SUSIE WYNNE AND JOSEPH DRUAR

Date of Birth: March 6, 1965/September 5, 1962
Place of Birth: Syracuse, NY/Buffalo, NY
Coach: Sandy Hess
Choreographer: Phillip Mills
Home Club: Philadelphia SC & HS/Seattle SC

# Professional Competitions

**1988 CAMPEONATOS DEL MUNDO DE PATINAJE ARTÍSTICO PROFESSIONAL SOBRE HIELO (Jaca, Spain, December 5-7, 1988)**

Men:

1. Gary Beacom (CAN)
2. Shaun McGill (CAN)
3. Mark Cockerell (USA)

Women:

1. Julie Brault (CAN)
2. Lori Benton (USA)
3. Aimee Kravette (USA)

Pairs:

1. Tracey Solomons and Ian Jenkins (GRB)
2. Terry Pagano and Tony Paul Kudrna (USA)
3. Anita Hartshorn and Frank Sweiding (USA)

Ice Dance:

1. Micheline Sally and John Coyne (CAN)
2. Géraldine Inghelaere and Hervé Casier (FRA)
3. Nathalie Jaccard and Ronald Teyssot (SUI/FRA)

**1988 U.S. OPEN PROFESSIONAL CHAMPIONSHIPS (Daytona Beach, FL, December 17-19, 1988)**

Men:

1. Gary Beacom (CAN)
2. Shaun McGill (CAN)
3. Mark Cockerell (CAN)

Women:

1. Kathleen Schmelz (USA)
2. Lisa-Marie Allen (USA)
3. Aimee Kravette (USA)

Pairs:

1. Anita Hartshorn and Frank Sweiding (USA)
2. Carrie Buddecke and Don Yontz (USA)
3. Laurie Johnson and Gary Strangman (USA)

Ice Dance:

1. Judy Blumberg and Michael Seibert (USA)
2. Kristan Lowery and Chip Rossbach (USA)
3. Kelly Johnson and John Thomas (CAN)

Challenge Cup Winners:

Perry Meek (AUS) - men
Janet Lee (USA) - women
Anita Hartshorn and Frank Sweiding (USA) - pairs
Kristan Lowery and Chip Rossbach (USA) - ice dance

**1988 NUTRASWEET WORLD CHALLENGE OF CHAMPIONS (Paris, France, December 19, 1988)**

Men:

1. Brian Boitano (USA)
2. Brian Orser (CAN)
3. Scott Hamilton (USA)

Women:

1. Denise Biellmann (SUI)
2. Rosalynn Sumners (USA)
3. Debi Thomas (USA)
4. Elaine Zayak (USA)
5. Dorothy Hamill (USA)

Pairs:

1. Jill Watson and Peter Oppegard (USA)
2. Kitty and Peter Carruthers (USA)
3. Lea Ann Miller and Bill Fauver (USA)
4. Barbara Underhill and Paul Martini (CAN)

**1988 WORLD CUP OF FIGURE SKATING (Ottawa, Ontario, December 21, 1988)**

Men:

1. Toller Cranston (CAN)
2. Brian Pockar (CAN)
3. Gary Beacom (CAN)

Women:

1. Elizabeth Manley (CAN)
2. Rosalynn Sumners (USA)
3. Elaine Zayak (USA)

Pairs:

1. Jill Watson and Peter Oppegard (USA)
2. Barbara Underhill and Paul Martini (CAN)
3. Lisa Carey and Chris Harrison (USA)

Ice Dance:

1. Judy Blumberg and Michael Seibert (USA)
2. Lorna Wighton and John Dowding (CAN)

**1989 JEEP MAIN EVENT OF SKATING (Montreal, QC, April 7, 1989)**

Men:

1. Brian Orser (CAN)
2. Scott Hamilton (USA)
3. Gary Beacom (CAN)

*Norbert Schramm. Photo courtesy Sarina Stützer.*

*Denise Biellmann. Photo courtesy Sarina Stützer.*

*Scott Hamilton. Photo courtesy Sarina Stützer.*

# SHOWS AND TOURS

Jayne Torvill and Christopher Dean relaunched their World Tour, this time working with Tatiana Tarasova and her *Russian All-Stars* troupe. After performances in Moscow and St. Petersburg, the tour was a huge hit in Australia and New Zealand. In March, Dean was invited to perform in a ten-lap celebrity motor-racing event at Calder Park in Melbourne. His car crashed and he was lucky to escape with only neck and back injuries. The tour was put on hold as Dean had to spend two months in a cast.

The Broadmoor Skating Club in Colorado Springs celebrated its fiftieth anniversary with a sold-out summer ice revue in August, featuring a full orchestra and live singers. The cast included Brian Boitano, Jill Watson and Peter Oppegard, Jill Trenary and Susie Wynne and Joseph Druar.

David Dore was very open to the concept of pro-am shows and competitions and played an instrumental role in developing the CFSA's *Champions on Ice* tour - the first Canadian skating touring show to feature both amateurs and professionals. The three-month tour kicked off in Chatham in September, visiting 29 cities in Ontario, Quebec and Atlantic Canada in the fall. Brian Orser, Tracy Wilson and Rob McCall and Barbara Underhill and Paul Martini were the headliners. In each community the tour visited, the professional stars were joined by national team members and local amateur skaters. Funds raised benefited the CFSA's National Junior Development Program and local skating clubs.

Katarina Witt made special guest appearances in five cities with *Holiday on Ice* in Europe. rumours circulated that a 4 000 000 contract was involved, with East German officials keeping 80 percent of Witt's earnings. It was also reported that this figure was "grossly exaggerated."

Baily's Grand Hotel and Casino in Atlantic City presented Richard Porter's *Celebration on Ice*. Tai Babilonia and Randy Gardner, Brian Pockar and Lisa-Marie Allen starred in the show. Elizabeth Manley, Jill Watson and Peter Oppegard and Judy Blumberg and Michael Seibert made guest appearances. When the production made its way to the Castle Resort Hotel in Miami in December, Scott Hamilton and John Curry joined the cast as special guests.

In October, Scott Hamilton, Brian Orser, Rosalynn Sumners, Debi Thomas, Toller Cranston and Tracy Wilson and Rob McCall went on tour with the *Benson & Hedges Command Performance on Ice* tour. The tour featured live music by the American Symphony Orchestra. The skaters who participated received criticism, as many didn't feel that a tobacco company was an appropriate sponsor for a skating tour.

The Union Plaza Hotel and Casino in Las Vegas presented a dinner theatre ice show called *Nudes on Ice*. Choreographed by Ron Meren, the George Arnold production featured Canadian Champion Kay Thomson, adagio pairs skaters Kelly Greigo and Peter Gordon, a juggler, a comedian and The Latin Cowboys, a South American dance act. Despite the name, the skaters didn't do Biellmann spins in their birthday suits... but they didn't wear much either.

*Discover Card Stars on Ice* travelled the United States in the winter and spring, appearing in 30 cities in 23 states. Seasoned professionals like Scott Hamilton, Dorothy Hamill, Toller Cranston and Rosalynn Sumners were joined by new pros Brian Orser, Debi Thomas and Tracy Wilson and Rob McCall. The big finale to "Dancing In The Streets" had the audience dancing along in their seats. A portion of the proceeds from ticket sales were donated to Big Brothers and Big Sisters of America.

In April, the *Skate Electric Gala of World Champions* brought a glitzy cast of skating stars to Richmond Ice Rink in London. Katarina Witt, Brian Boitano, Ekaterina Gordeeva and Sergei Grinkov, Natalia Bestemianova and Andrei Bukin joined the UK's top skaters in the show.

Tom Collins' 1989 *Tour of Olympic & World Champions* opened in Baltimore in late May, playing 28 U.S. cities before ending in Dallas in late June. The all-star cast included Katarina Witt, Brian Boitano, Brian Orser, Ekaterina Gordeeva and Sergei Grinkov, Kurt Browning, Tracy Wilson and Rob McCall and Debi Thomas. Boitano had to skate his iconic "Music of the Night" program in various outfits. His costume fell out of an open storage compartment on the tour bus. It was later found on the side of the road and returned.

Figure skating and gymnastics made an unusual connection at two different events in the spring. In April at the John A. Dobson Arena in Vail, Colorado, Robin Cousins joined forces with gymnastics coach Paul Ziert to choreograph *A Symphony of Sports*, featuring performances by Cousins, Katherine Healy and Bart Conner, an Olympic Gold Medallist in gymnastics at the 1984 Summer Games in Los Angeles. The Economic Club of Chicago hosted its 35th annual Fifth Night in June, bringing together skaters and gymnasts in a show called *A Salute to Americana*. The latter production was the first cooperative venture between the USFSA and the U.S. Gymnastics Federation. Performers included Caryn Kadavy, Paul Wylie, Jessica Mills and Mills' sister Phoebe, an Olympic Bronze Medallist in gymnastics at the 1988 Summer Games in Seoul, South Korea.

*Maya Usova and Alexandr Zhulin. Photo courtesy Sarina Stützer.*

*Marina Klimova and Sergei Ponomarenko. Photo courtesy Sarina Stützer.*

*Alexandr Fadeev. Photo courtesy Sarina Stützer.*

*Karen Preston. Photo courtesy Elaine Hooper / St. Ivel Figure Skating Archive.*

*Petr Barna. Photo courtesy Sarina Stützer.*

*Natalia Mishkutenok and Artur Dmitriev. Photo courtesy Sarina Stützer.*

# Major Competitions

**World Junior Championships.** For the third time in the 80s, the Zetra Ice Rink in Sarajevo played host to the World Junior Championships in late November and early December. Attendance was not especially high, with only 3000 spectators showing up to watch the pairs final. Soviet teenagers Evgenia Chernyshova and Dmitri Sukhanov dominated the pairs event from start to finish, earning marks ranging from 5.0 to 5.5 for their classical free skate, which featured a split triple twist, clean throw double Axel and strong lifts. Canada's Marie-Josée Fortin and Jean-Michel Bombardier finished in a tie for third in the free skate. A fourth-place finish in the original program kept the Quebec team behind East Germany's Angela Caspari and Marno Kreft and Soviets Irina Saifutdinova and Alexei Tikhonov. Jennifer Leng of the United States won the women's figures, followed by East Germany's Tanja Krienke and West Germany's Patricia Wirth. All three of the leaders faltered in the original program, which was won by Japan's Junko Yaginuma. Jessica Mills, fourth in figures and second in the original program, won the free skate to take the title over Yaginuma. France's Surya Bonaly moved up to take the bronze, a monumental leap from her 14th place finish in her debut at the event the previous season. Bonaly attempted both a triple Lutz and triple toe-loop/triple toe-loop combination in the free skate, signaling to the judges that she was an ambitious skater to watch. Mills' victory was remarkable in that she was originally only named to the American team as an alternate. She was sent to Sarajevo at the last minute to replace Shenon Badre, the bronze medallist in the junior women's event at the 1988 U.S. Championships. Her goal was to skate well and place in the top six. Canada's two entries, Margot Bion and Jutta Cossette, had good showings in the figures but later fell out of contention, placing eighth and 12th overall. The ice dance event was a close competition between two Soviet duos, Angelika Kirkhmaier and Dmitri Lagutin and Liudmila Berezova and Vladimir Fedorov. The teams traded places in the compulsories and OSP, with Kirkhmaier and Lagutin coming out on top with a winning free dance set to the soundtrack of the Andrew Lloyd Webber musical *Cats*. France's Marina Morel and Gwendal Peizerat took the bronze, with Canada's two teams, Marie-France Dubreuil and Bruno Yvars and Brigitte Richer and Michel Brunet, finishing fifth and seventh. In the men's event, Ukrainian skater Viacheslav Zagorodniuk dominated from start to finish, winning the figures, original program and free skate by a wide margin to take the title for the Soviet Union, ahead of America's Shepherd Clark. Zagorodniuk's winning free skate featured two triple Axels, a triple Lutz and four other triple jumps - technical content that would easily contend at any senior event. Japan's Masakazu Kagiyama clawed his way back from eighth after figures to win the bronze. Elvis Stojko of Canada and Philippe Candeloro of France were fourth and fifth in figures. The teenagers who would grow up to become two of the best free skaters in the world were both let down by their jumps. Stojko finished sixth; Candeloro tenth. Canada's second entry, Herb Cherwoniak, placed an unlucky 13th.

**World Professional Championships.** 305 000 dollars was on the line at the World Professional Championships in Landover, Maryland in December. Doreen Denny, Ron Ludington, Colleen O'Connor, Hayes Alan Jenkins, Barbara Roles Williams, Fritz Dietl, Barbara Wagner, Irina Rodnina and John 'Misha' Petkevich served as judges at the competition. Brian Orser and Brian Boitano both made their professional competitive debuts in the men's event. In the technical program, Boitano made history by landing the first triple Axel and triple/triple combination ever performed at the World Professional Championships. His exquisite performance to Rodgers and Hammerstein's "Carousel Waltz" earned him perfect marks from every judge but Petkevich.

**1989 WORLD JUNIOR CHAMPIONSHIPS**
(Sarajevo, Yugoslavia, November 29-December 4, 1988)

Men:

1. Viacheslav Zagorodniuk (SOV)
2. Shepherd Clark (USA)
3. Masakazu Kagiyama (JPN)
4. Nicolas Pétorin (FRA)
5. Mirko Eichhorn (GDR)
6. Elvis Stojko (CAN)
7. Igor Pashkevich (SOV)
8. Gleb Boiky (SOV)
9. Alex Chang (USA)
10. Philippe Candeloro (FRA)

Women:

1. Jessica Mills (USA)
2. Junko Yaginuma (JPN)
3. Surya Bonaly (FRA)
4. Tanja Krienke (GDR)
5. Patricia Wirth (FRG)
6. Jennifer Leng (USA)
7. Sandra Garde (FRA)
8. Margot Bion (CAN)
9. Alma Lepina (SOV)
10. Yuka Sato (JPN)

Pairs:

1. Evgenia Chernyshova and Dmitri Sukhanov (SOV)
2. Angela Caspari and Marno Kreft (GDR)
3. Irina Sayfutdinova and Alexei Tikhonov (SOV)
4. Marie-Josée Fortin and Jean-Michel Bombardier (CAN)
5. Inna Svetacheva and Vladimir Shagov (SOV)
6. Ann-Marie and Brian Wells (USA)
7. Jennifer Heurlin and John Frederiksen (USA)
8. Catherine Barker and Michael Aldred (GRB)
9. Beata Szymłowska and Mariusz Siudek (POL)

Ice Dance:

1. Anjelika Kirchmayr and Dmitri Lagutin (SOV)
2. Ludmila Berezova and Vladimir Fedorov (SOV)
3. Marina Morel and Gwendal Peizerat (FRA)
4. Lynn Burton and Andrew Place (GRB)
5. Marie-France Dubreuil and Bruno Yvars (CAN)
6. Christine Chadufaux and Karim Zeriahem (FRA)
7. Brigitte Richer and Michel Brunet (CAN)
8. Sabine Baratelli and Paolo Ceccattini (ITA)
9. Holly Robbins and Kyle Schneble (USA)
10. Katherine and Ben Williamson (USA)

Orser's debut didn't go quite as planned. Though he landed a triple toe-loop, double Axel and backflip in his program to St-Saens' "Danse Macabre", he popped both triple and double Axel attempts into singles. Scott Hamilton skated a near-flawless performance, featuring three triples, a backflip and the fanciest footwork in town. Hamilton's choreography by Sarah Kawahara was outstanding but his music choice - a specially composed piece by Chick Corea called "Hamilton Fantasy" – was not to everyone's taste. Recovering from knee surgery and a back injury, Robin Cousins gave the most artistic and elegant performance performance of the men. However, without a double Axel or triple toe-loop in his program, he didn't have the technical content to compete with the others. Boitano won the technical program, followed by Orser, Hamilton and Cousins. In the artistic program, Cousins skated elegant and clean program to Michael Feinstein's "Where Do You Start", featuring four different double jumps including the Axel, which he didn't perform in the technical program. Skating his signature program to Gershwin's "In The Mood", Hamilton was at his very best. Landing a triple toe-loop, three double Axels in a row and a backflip, he received a standing ovation. Orser wore face paint and a jungle-inspired costume and went out of his comfort zone in his clean program to "The Lion Sleeps Tonight". Boitano's program to "Un Amor" by The Gipsy Kings was understated, sophisticated and the most technically demanding of the lot. Hamilton's crowd-pleasing performance earned perfect 10.0s from every judge but Ron Ludington. He won the artistic program but Boitano's lead in the first round in the competition was enough to win the title. Orser finished third; Cousins fourth. All four men received at least one perfect mark of 10.0 from the judges. The pairs technical program produced a very surprising result, with Kitty and Peter Carruthers taking a five-tenths of a point lead over defending Champion Barbara Underhill and Paul Martini. The Carruthers stepped out of their throw triple Salchow and Underhill and Martini skated a flawless program, with a clean throw triple Salchow. In the artistic program, Underhill and Martini rebounded to win their third World Professional title with a dramatic program to Elton John's "Tonight". The Carruthers crowd-pleasing program to "Hot, Hot, Hot" finished second, ahead of Lea Ann Miller and Bill Fauver and Jill Watson and Peter Oppegard. In the ice dance competition, compulsory dances were introduced instead of a technical program or OSP. The two teams, Tracy Wilson and Rob McCall and Judy Blumberg and Michael Seibert, performed the Blues, Kilian and Starlight Waltz in tandem, starting on opposite ends of the rink. The result was highly surprising. Blumberg and Seibert, who hadn't done compulsories in three years, defeated Wilson and McCall who were fresh out of the amateur ranks by three-tenths of a point. In the artistic program, Wilson and McCall's mambo program didn't wow the judges to the same degree as Blumberg and Seibert's gorgeous program to Patsy Cline's "Crazy" and Elvis Presley's "Are You Lonesome Tonight?" Blumberg and Seibert won their first World Professional title by a comfortable margin with a row of perfect 10.0s. In the women's technical program, Debi Thomas made her professional debut with a clever program to a James Bond medley, complete with a triple toe-loop, prop gun and two costume changes. Though she landed a triple toe-loop, she took an unfortunate fall on her first double Axel, but landed the second. Considering she flew on a red-eye flight after taking an exam at Stanford, it was a fine effort. Denise Biellmann gave roaring 20s vibes and landed two triples in her program to Liza Minnelli's "The Money Tree". Rosalynn Sumners showed a monumental improvement in her performance ability, skating a well-packaged, entertaining program to "Wilkommen", "Mein Herr" and "Maybe This Time" from *Cabaret*. A double Axel put her ahead of Dorothy Hamill and Elaine Zayak. Hamill skated a lovely program to Whitney Houston's "One Moment in Time", but her program was particularly light on the jumps as it was her first time competing after giving birth to her daughter.

**1988 WORLD PROFESSIONAL FIGURE SKATING CHAMPIONSHIPS** (Landover, MD, December 9, 1988)

Men:

1. Brian Boitano (USA)
2. Scott Hamilton (USA)
3. Brian Orser (CAN)
4. Robin Cousins (GRB)

Women:

1. Debi Thomas (USA)
2. Denise Biellmann (SUI)
3. Rosalynn Sumners (USA)
4. Dorothy Hamill (USA)
5. Elaine Zayak (USA)

Pairs:

1. Barbara Underhill and Paul Martini (CAN)
2. Kitty and Peter Carruthers (USA)
3. Lea Ann Miller and Bill Fauver (USA)
4. Jill Watson and Peter Oppegard (USA)

Ice Dance:

1. Judy Blumberg and Michael Seibert (USA)
2. Tracy Wilson and Rob McCall (CAN)

*Barbara Underhill, Paul Martini and footballer Don Loney at the Canada's Sports Hall of Fame induction. Photo courtesy Canada's Sports Hall of Fame.*

*Debi Thomas. Photo courtesy Sarina Stützer.*

The women could not have chosen more different styles for their artistic programs. Hamill was relaxed and charming in her performance to Louis Armstrong's version of "Zip-a-Dee-Doo-Dah", but she took an uncharacteristic tumble. Biellmann was high-energy in her program to "We Are The Katz Kids" by the Bo Katzmann Gang. Rosalynn Sumners brought down the house skating to "Walk Like an Egyptian" but she and Biellmann both 'only' received one perfect 10.0. Thomas won the title with an elegant performance to the music of Rachmaninoff, which earned 10.0s from four judges - her first perfect scores ever.

**European Championships.** In January, the National Exhibition Centre in Birmingham, England played host to the European Championships. The event was the first ISU Championship held in England since 1950. Fittingly, the program featured "best wishes to all concerned for an enjoyable and successful competition" from the NSA's Patron Her Majesty Queen Elizabeth II. The event was televised in 28 countries and 95 skaters from 20 nations participated. The Championships tied in with the City of Birmingham Centenary Festival. Visitors to the Venice of the North enjoyed a grand firework display, an organ recital at the town hall, a centenary service at St. Philip's Cathedral and an art exhibition presented by the Royal Birmingham Society of Artists. At the gala opening, there was a special number celebrating the UK's rich skating history, featuring Robin Cousins and children from Birmingham and four other clubs in the Midlands. At the closing exhibition, the skaters performed before Her Royal Highness The Princess Royal Anne. John Curry and Bobby Thompson acted as the British team's national coaches. There was confusion surrounding the entries for the Soviet team. Two different lists were sent by the USSR Skating Federation to the British organizers. One list had Viktor Petrenko and Ekaterina Gordeeva and Sergei Grinkov; another didn't. At the last minute, the hosts discovered the trio of Olympic Medallists were not competing. With Gordeeva and Grinkov out due to injury, the favourites in Birmingham were Larisa Selezneva and Oleg Makarov. It wasn't Selezneva and Makarov's first time at the rodeo and they skated strongly in the original program to music from *West Side Story*. They took the lead entering the free skate but the irony of a Soviet pair wearing stars and stripes and skating to a song about wanting to live in America at the height of The Cold War was not lost. With side-by-side triple toe-loops, a throw triple toe-loop and a vastly improved sense of presentation, Selezneva and Makarov narrowly defeated East Germany's Mandy Wötzel and Axel Rauschenbach in a five-four split of the judging panel in the free skate. The bronze went to Soviets Natalia Mishkutenok and Artur Dmitriev, who chose to take a risk by skating to Jewish folk music with vocals. British team Cheryl Peake and Andrew Naylor hung on to fifth place despite a couple of errors. If the crowd had Peake and Naylor's back, the British judge didn't. Mary Groombridge gave them their lowest marks - 4.8 and 4.9 – and had the other British pair, Lisa and Neil Cushley, ahead of them. In the men's event, Alexandr Fadeev was seeking his fourth European title in nine years, with little competition as Petrenko was out with a groin injury. In a major upset, Oregon-born West German skater Richard Zander won the compulsory figures over Fadeev. To give some context to that result, Fadeev won the figures at the Calgary Olympics and Zander had been ninth. Fadeev rebounded with a stellar original program, winning that phase of the event over Grzegorz Filipowski and Petr Barna. Zander finished only tenth, dropping to sixth in the overall standings entering the free skate. Unfortunately, he was forced to withdraw due to the same back injury that almost forced him to retire the previous season.

**1989 EUROPEAN CHAMPIONSHIPS**
(Birmingham, England, January 17-22, 1989)

Men:

1. Alexandr Fadeev (SOV)
2. Grzegorz Filipowski (POL)
3. Petr Barna (CZE)
4. Dmitri Gromov (SOV)
5. Daniel Weiss (FRG)
6. Viacheslav Zagorodniuk (SOV)
7. Axel Médéric (FRA)
8. Peter Johansson (SWE)
9. Lars Dresler (DEN)
10. Alessandro Riccitelli (ITA)

Women:

1. Claudia Leistner (FRG)
2. Natalia Lebedeva (SOV)
3. Patricia Neske (FRG)
4. Simone Lang (FDR)
5. Natalia Gorbenko (SOV)
6. Joanne Conway (GRB)
7. Evelyn Großmann (GDR)
8. Surya Bonaly (FRA)
9. Tamara Téglássy (HUN)
10. Yvonne Gómez (SPN)

Pairs:

1. Larisa Selezneva and Oleg Makarov (SOV)
2. Mandy Wötzel and Axel Rauschenbach (GDR)
3. Natalia Mishkutenok and Artur Dmitriev (SOV)
4. Elena Kvitchenko and Rashid Kadyrkaev (SOV)
5. Cheryl Peake and Andrew Naylor (GRB)
6. Anuschka Gläser and Stefan Pfrengle (FRG)
7. Lisa and Neil Cushley (GRB)
8. Sonja Adalbert and Daniele Caprano (FRG)
9. Anna Górecka and Arkadiusz Górecki (POL)

Ice Dance:

1. Marina Klimova and Sergei Ponomarenko (SOV)
2. Maya Usova and Alexandr Zhulin (SOV)
3. Natalia Annenko and Genrikh Sretenski (SOV)
4. Klára Engi and Attila Tóth (HUN)
5. Stefania Calegari and Pasquale Camerlengo (ITA)
6. Sharon Jones and Paul Askham (GRB)
7. Andrea Juklova and Martin Šimeček (CZE)
8. Dominique Yvon and Frédéric Palluel (FRA)
9. Małgorzata Grajcar and Andrzej Dostatni (POL)
10. Andrea Weppelman and Hendryk Schamberger (FRG)

Fadeev's costume for the original program was wild. He wore gloves with what one reporter referred to as "long, glittering Florence Griffith-Joyner style claws" and had a sequined parrot on the back of his outfit. The Bulgarian, French, Hungarian and Polish judges ignored the new mandatory 0.2 costume deduction rule and gave him 5.9s. In the free skate, Fadeev brought the house down with an eight-triple performance and won the gold medal, receiving four perfect 6.0s for artistic impression from the Bulgarian, French, Hungarian and Yugoslavian judges. Grzegorz Filipowski, Petr Barna, Dmitri Gromov, Daniel Weiss and Viacheslav Zagorodniuk rounded out the top six. British judge Vanessa Riley chose to give Fadeev the 0.2 costume deduction because his tight white costume didn't leave much to the imagination. She told reporters, "There's no point in having rules if you don't use them. The rules say costumes must be modest and dignified. Fadeev's clearly wasn't. I therefore deducted 0.2 from the artistic impression mark, making it 5.6. I still had him first." Fadeev avoided getting dinged for his dingle at the Worlds in Paris by wearing a pair of jockey shorts over his dance belt. In the women's event, East Germany's Simone Koch withdrew, leaving West Germany's Claudia Leistner as the odds-on favourite. Leistner took a strong lead in the figures, which had been reduced in number from three to two. Joanne Conway, Natalia Gorbenko, Natalia Lebedeva and Željka Čižmešija rounded out the top five. 17th in her debut at Europeans was a young Surya Bonaly. Vanessa Riley called the outfit Bonaly wore in the figures "a court jester's outfit." A different Simone from East Germany, Simone Lang, finished second to Leistner in the original program. Conway's fourth-place finish kept her in second overall entering the free skate, with Natalia Lebedeva in third. Leistner claimed the gold with an athletic free skating performance that included a triple loop, two triple Salchows and a triple toe-loop. Lebedeva and Patricia Neske took the silver and bronze, while Conway dropped down to sixth, two spots ahead of Bonaly. Leistner's victory was the first for a West German woman at Europeans since Gundi Busch in 1954. Her former coach Ondrej Nepela, dying in hospital, was able to watch her victory on television. After winning, she told reporters, "It's been a long wait. I hope I can do the same in Paris [at the World Championships]. I would have liked Katarina to have been here so I could have tried to beat her." She was on the payroll of Daimler's Untertürkheim plant, along with almost 50 other West German sporting stars. When she returned home to her country, she received a Mercedes 300 as a gift for winning. Conway was quite sick in Birmingham and threw up half an hour before taking the ice. She skated a clean original program, but as is so often the case in skating, many played her rough free skate off as nerves. The British press, hoping for a medal, weren't exactly kind to her. David Whaley, sports editor for the *Sandwell Evening Mail* wrote, "Jolly Joanne 'I can bottle it with the best' Conway has rarely shown she can handle pressure. Then, shock and horror, one round to go and in the silver medal spot. Surprise, surprise - down she went and down the drain went the forlorn medal dream." Marina Klimova and Sergei Ponomarenko were the favourites in the ice dance event for the first time. It was their sixth crack at the title and they had medalled every time except their first Europeans back in 1983, when they finished fourth. Notably absent were Isabelle and Paul Duchesnay. Isabelle underwent four surgeries (three on her knee and one on her throat) and had not recovered sufficiently to compete. The Duchesnays were bitterly disappointed that they were unable to compete because they had wanted to unveil their new free dance, choreographed by Christopher Dean, in front of a British audience. As expected, Klimova and Ponomarenko took a strong lead in the compulsories - the Yankee Polka and Rhumba. Maya Usova and Alexandr Zhulin finished second; Natalia Annenko and Genrikh Sretrenski third. There was an outcry when Usova's lime green bikini and body stocking for the Rhumba weren't penalized by many judges.

*Marina Klimova and Sergei Ponomarenko. Photo courtesy Sarina Stützer.*

*Viktor Petrenko. Photo courtesy Sarina Stützer.*

Joan Slater, the coach of British ice dancers Sharon Jones and Paul Askham, complained that Usova and Zhulin's costumes were "over the top" and that the NSA would never allow British ice dancers to wear costumes that were so revealing. Usova and Zhulin's coach Natalia Dubova responded, "We didn't realize the costume would create such a furor. The design at the World Championships will definitely be changed and will be fully in agreement with the new regulations." Klimova and Ponomarenko's "Ain't She Sweet" topped Usova and Zhulin's "Black Bottom" in the Charleston OSP. There was criticism over the fact that Annenko and Sretenski skated in pastel outfits that didn't say Charleston whatsoever, but still ended up ahead of teams that performed more classic Charlestons. Klimova and Ponomarenko finally won their first ISU Championship with an excellent free dance to Kurt Weill's "Mack the Knife", earning 6.0s from both the Soviet and Italian judges. The Soviet judge also gave a 6.0 to Usova and Zhulin, whose free dance to "The Planets" somewhat stole the show from their elder teammates. Annenko and Sretenski's lovely free dance made up for the criticisms over their OSP. The third Soviet sweep of the European dance podium of the 1980s did not go unnoticed, nor did the new level of athleticism that was permeating the discipline.

**U.S. Championships.** In February, the Baltimore Arena played host to the first U.S. Championships ever held in the state of Maryland. 183 competitors participated. For the first time since 1981, all four of the reigning Champions in the senior events did not return to defend their titles, though ice dance winner Suzanne Semanick was back with a new partner, Ron Kravette. The exodus of talent following the 1987-1988 Olympic season had little effect on the turnout or television viewership, with over 11 000 000 viewers tuning in to watch the live broadcast of the men's and women's finals on ABC's Wide World of Sports. The USFSA commissioned a special musical fanfare for the event called "Ice Champions", which was performed live by the United States Army Band. Unfortunately, the biggest fanfare in Baltimore had nothing to do with music. A respiratory infection was making the rounds in a big way and many of the skaters, coaches and judges fell victim. Natalie and Wayne Seybold, Katy Keeley and Joseph Mero and Kristi Yamaguchi and Rudy Galindo took the top three spots in the pairs original program. The result was somewhat controversial, as Yamaguchi and Galindo executed clean side-by-side double Axels and the top two teams did double loops. Keeley was one of those suffering from the virus that was making the rounds, which was evident when she and Mero started to lose steam near the end of their free skating program. Yamaguchi and Galindo skated a program jam-packed with incredibly difficult technical content - side-by-side triple flips and triple toe-loops and a throw triple Salchow. Disaster struck for the Seybolds. After a particularly hard fall on the throw triple loop, they abruptly stopped their program and skated over to show the judges that Natalie's lace had come loose. Referee Bette Snuggerud did not offer them the opportunity to start their program from the beginning and they picked up where they left off. Despite making numerous mistakes, the judges were surprisingly generous, awarding them two 5.8s for artistic impression. Yamaguchi and Galindo's marks were good enough to unanimously take the win, with the Seybolds controversially finishing second over Keeley and Mero, who skated a near-flawless performance. In winning, Yamaguchi and Galindo made history as the first skaters of Japanese and Latino heritage to win the U.S. pairs title. In the singles events, for the first time, competitors only had to skate two figures instead of three. Jill Trenary unanimously won both the RFO Paragraph Bracket and LBO Paragraph Loop to take an early lead over Jeri Campbell, Holly Cook and Tonya Harding. Kristi Yamaguchi placed a disappointing eighth.

**1989 U.S. CHAMPIONSHIPS (Baltimore, MD, February 7-12, 1989)**

Men:

1. Christopher Bowman
2. Daniel Doran
3. Paul Wylie
4. Erik Larson
5. Todd Eldredge
6. Angelo D'Agostino
7. James Cygan
8. Mark Mitchell
9. Doug Mattis
10. Craig Heath

Women:

1. Jill Trenary
2. Kristi Yamaguchi
3. Tonya Harding
4. Holly Cook
5. Nancy Kerrigan
6. Kelly Szmurlo
7. Cindy Bortz
8. Tonia Kwiatkowski
9. Tracey Damigella
10. Jenni Meno

Pairs:

1. Kristi Yamaguchi and Rudy Galindo
2. Natalie and Wayne Seybold
3. Katy Keeley and Joseph Mero
4. Sharon Carz and Doug Williams
5. Calla Urbanski and Mark Naylor
6. Kenna Bailey and John Denton
7. Kellie Creel and Bob Pellaton
8. Elaine Asanakis and Joel McKeever
9. Paula Visingardi and Jason Dungjen
10. Ginger and Archie Tse

Ice Dance:

1. Susie Wynne and Joseph Druar
2. April Sargent and Russ Witherby
3. Suzanne Semanick and Ron Kravette
4. Jeanne Miley and Michael Verlich
5. Elizabeth McLean and Ari Lieb
6. Jodie Balogh and Jerod Swallow
7. Tracy Sniadach and Leif Erickson
8. Elizabeth Punsalan and Shawn Rettstatt
9. Dorothi Rodek and Robert Nardozza
10. Lisa Grove and Scott Myers

Junior Winners:

Shepherd Clark (men)
Kyoko Ina (women)
Jennifer Heurlin and John Frederiksen (pairs)
Rachel Mayer and Peter Breen (ice dance)

Novice Winners:

Philip Dulebohn (men)
Casey Link (women)

Trenary had a scary moment in the warmup for the original program, crashing into the boards while practicing her spiral sequence. She and coach Carlo Fassi decided to take the triple flip combination out of her program and do a less difficult triple toe-loop/double toe-loop. Fassi pointed out how successful that strategy had been for Elizabeth Manley at the Calgary Olympics. Trenary skated a clean program to David Foster's "Winter Games" and the judges placed her first ahead of Harding and Yamaguchi who both executed triple Lutz/double toe-loop combinations. Campbell placed sixth in the original program and subsequently withdrew due to a painful foot injury. In the free skate, Trenary skated very well, executing four triple jumps including a triple flip, but as in the original program, she was very much challenged by Harding and Yamaguchi. Harding executed four triples, her only mistake being a two-footed landing on a triple Lutz. Yamaguchi's show-stealing program featured seven triple jumps including a triple Lutz/double toe-loop combination. Five judges preferred Yamaguchi's program and three Trenary's. Illinois judge Shirley Sherman was the sole dissenter, placing Harding first in the free skate. Trenary's lead from the figures and short program was more than enough to win her first U.S. title, ahead of Yamaguchi, Harding and Cook. Yamaguchi became the first skater to win medals in two senior events in over fifteen years and Trenary became only the fourth woman in history to regain a senior national title after losing it. In the ice dance event, Susie Wynne and Joseph Druar took a commanding lead after the two compulsories - the Yankee Polka and Westminster Waltz. Wynne and Druar captured the spirit of the roaring 20s better than most of the top teams in the world in the Charleston OSP to expand their lead over April Sargent and Russ Witherby, Suzanne Semanick and Ron Kravette. When it came time for the final flight of the free dance, fourth-place team Renée Roca and James Yorke were forced to withdraw after the warmup due to illness. Roca was one of the many skaters who'd caught the 'Baltimore bug'. Semanick and Gregory's program, which told the story of a young soldier leaving for War and leaving his lover behind, received marks ranging from 5.5 to 5.8 - only good enough for third. Sargent and Witherby chose a Fred and Ginger theme for their program. They had barely started when one of Sargent's laces came undone. Walter Lupke Jr. was more benevolent than the referee the Seybolds had in the pairs event and allowed them a restart. Though they skated very well, it was Wynne and Druar's high-energy Latin program that took the win in the free dance and the title. Incredibly, Sargent and Witherby and the Seybolds weren't the only skaters to have mid-program lace problems in Baltimore. The same thing happened to a lower-ranked senior dance couple and the junior dance winners, Kara Berger and Jay Barton. With Brian Boitano out of the picture, Paul Wylie and Christopher Bowman were heavy favourites in the men's event. The press described their rivalry as "Hollywood .vs. Harvard". The unexpected happened on the day of the compulsory figures when whoever was on the front desk at the hotel failed to give Wylie a wake-up call. He arrived at the rink at the last minute, with little warmup time. The results ended up being surprising, with Daniel Doran taking the lead over James Cygan, Todd Eldredge, Bowman, Doug Mattis and Wylie. Some attributed Bowman's poor showing to the fact he had missed several weeks of training time after spiking his leg in practice. The new original program format allowed the men to try triple/triple combinations for the first time. Eldredge and Bowman both successfully landed triple Lutz/triple toe-loop, while Cygan and Mitchell pulled off the triple flip/triple toe-loop. Wylie was the only skater to attempt a triple Axel combination, but he took a step between the Axel and double toe-loop, garnering a deduction. Bowman received a standing ovation and unanimously won the short program ahead of Doran and Larson, who did triple flip/double toe-loop and triple loop/double toe-loop combinations. Wylie finished fourth, while Mitchell was lowballed with marks ranging from 4.7 to 5.3 for a clean program and placed seventh.

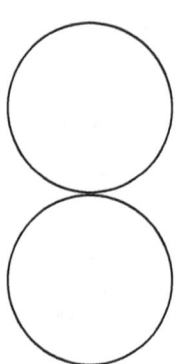

*Christopher Bowman. Photo by A. Raclare Kanal, courtesy Jaya Kanal.*

Bowman had some fun with reporters in a press conference before the free skate. When asked what he planned on doing in the free skate, he responded, "Jumps and spins." When asked how many jumps he would do at Skate America, his sarcastic response had been "hundreds". Entering the free skate, only eight-tenths of a point separated Doran, the overall leader, and Larson, who was fifth. Skating in the penultimate flight in the free skate, Mitchell delivered one of the cleanest skates in the competition, landing six triple jumps. His marks were again surprisingly low, ranging from 5.1 to 5.4. Bowman landed the triple Lutz/triple toe-loop combination in his program, along with a triple Axel, to earn all 5.8s and 5.9s from the judges. Larson followed with a strong performance that included five triples, including a triple loop/triple toe-loop combination. Doran opened his program with a solid triple Lutz but had problems on three other triples. Though Wylie downgraded his triple Axel into a double, he gave a show-stopping performance featuring six triple jumps, earning the only standing ovation in the competition. Eldredge, who was suffering from a serious back injury that caused him to miss several weeks of practice, followed with an outstanding performance of his own featuring six triples including a triple Axel. With so many of the men delivering strong performances, the judges had their work cut out for them. In the end, Bowman unanimously won the free skate and gold, Doran took the silver despite placing fifth in the free and Wylie claimed the bronze. Larson and Eldredge finished fourth and fifth and Mitchell ended the event in eighth.

**Canadian Championships.** In February, the Centre Georges-Vézina in Chicoutimi, Quebec was the site of the Canadian Championships. Ticket sales suffered in the absence of Brian Orser, Elizabeth Manley and Tracy Wilson and Rob McCall, with only 2600 tickets (out of 4000) sold for the men's free skate. There were also hiccups of another kind. Some of the practice sessions for the compulsory figures were held at a rink in nearby Jonquière and skaters were transported there on 'not so magic' school buses. Kurt Browning, Michael Slipchuk and Norm Proft all missed one of their practices because the bus failed to show up at their hotel. One of the biggest surprises in the competition was the winning performance of Charlesbourg's Pierre Gignac in the junior men's event. He landed seven triple jumps - an unheard-of accomplishment in the junior ranks in Canada. After the pairs original program, Lyndon Johnston and his new partner Cindy Landry led the way, ahead of Isabelle Brasseur and Lloyd Eisler and Christine Hough and Doug Ladret. The victory was a special one for Landry, who was celebrating her 17th birthday. Brasseur and Eisler unanimously won the free skate and the gold with a very up-and-down performance. Skating to Rimsky-Korsakov's "Scheherazade", they performed an impressive split triple twist and lateral triple twist but erred on the landings of two throw triple jumps and the side-by-side double Axels. Despite their mistakes, 'Herbie and Fred' were very popular with the audience, earning a standing ovation. Landry and Johnston landed a throw triple Salchow but they missed their side-by-side triple Salchows and took a bad fall on a throw double Axel. Hough had problems on three side-by-side double jumps, but she and Ladret executed a solid split triple twist and throw double Axel. Some felt that Hough and Ladret's errors weren't as egregious as Lyndon and Johnston's but the judges unanimously disagreed. Hough and Ladret got their taste of redemption in the fours event, where they teamed up with Patricia MacNeil and Cory Watson to take the gold over Landry and Johnston, Jodi Dawson and David Wood. After a disappointing 1987-1988 season, Karyn and Rod Garossino decided to make several changes to stand out and get noticed. Going for "a more mature look", Karyn grew her hair longer, Rod grew a beard and the duo put special care into choosing great costumes. They also made the move from the National Ice Dance Centre in Richmond Hill to Kitchener.

**1989 CANADIAN CHAMPIONSHIPS**
(Chicoutimi, QC, February 8-12, 1989)

Men:

1. Kurt Browning
2. Michael Slipchuk
3. Michael Hall
4. Norm Proft
5. Brent Frank
6. Stéphane Yvars
7. Martin Marceau
8. Patrick Brault
9. Jaimee Eggleton
10. Marcus Christensen

Women:

1. Karen Preston
2. Charlene Wong
3. Lisa Sargeant
4. Dianne Takeuchi
5. Shannon Allison
6. Tanya Bingert
7. Josée Chouinard
8. Angie Folk
9. Annie St. Hilaire
10. Leslie Anne White

Pairs:

1. Isabelle Brasseur and Lloyd Eisler
2. Cindy Landry and Lyndon Johnston
3. Christine Hough and Doug Ladret
4. Michelle Menzies and Kevin Wheeler
5. Melanie Gaylor and Lee Barkell
6. Katherine and Rob Kates
7. Jodi Barnes and Rob Williams
8. Alison Hughes and Jim Blackburn
9. Chantal Gagnon and Sylvain Lalonde

Ice Dance:

1. Karyn and Rod Garossino
2. Michelle McDonald and Mark Mitchell
3. Jo-Anne Borlase and Martin Smith
4. Penny Mann and Richard Perkins
5. Melanie Cole and Michael Farrington
6. Jacqueline Petr and Mark Janoschak
7. Pamela Watson and Aimé LeBlanc
8. Dara Failey and Curtis Moore
9. Nathalie Lessard and Donald Godfrey
10. Kimberley Weeks and Jeff Fish

Fours:

1. Patricia MacNeil, Christine Hough, Cory Watson and Doug Ladret
2. Cindy Landry, Jodi Dawson, Lyndon Johnston and David Wood
3. Michelle Menzies, Alison Hughes, Kevin Wheeler and Jim Blackburn

The Garossinos decisively won the compulsory dances over Jo-Anne Borlase and Martin Smith, Penny Mann and Richard Perkins, Michelle McDonald and Mark Mitchell and Melanie Cole and Michael Farrington. McDonald and Mitchell gave the Garossinos a run for their money in the OSP, with a crowd-pleasing and cleverly choreographed Charleston that moved them up to second in a four-three split for first. The Garossinos won their first national title with a stylish Spanish free dance to Rodrigo's "Concierto de Aranjuez" and Monty Kelly's "Fiesta Flamenca". McDonald and Mitchell proved their performance in the OSP was no fluke with a sultry blues program set to "Fever" and "Echoes of Harlem" and claimed the silver over Borlase and Smith. McDonald and Mitchell's silver medal win was not only significant in that moving up from fourth to second was rare in ice dance, but Mitchell was the first skater from New Brunswick in any discipline to win a medal in a senior event at Canadians. After narrowly losing a spot on the Olympic team in 1988, Shannon Allison made a major change, leaving longtime coach Bob Rubens to work with World Champion Karen Magnussen, who had just moved back home to British Columbia from Boston to teach at the North Shore Winter Club. Despite her best efforts, Allison finished third in the women's compulsory figures behind Charlene Wong and Dianne Takeuchi. Outside of the top three, the judge's scores were all over the place. Lisa Sargeant finished seventh of the 15 women but had scores ranging from sixth to 12th. Right behind her in eighth was Karen Preston. Wong's finish was a great story of perseverance. Though she made the Olympic and World teams in 1988, she was so discouraged by her results that she debated retiring. Preston was the spoiler in the original program, seemingly coming out of nowhere with a clean performance featuring a triple toe-loop/double toe-loop combination. She won the original program, ahead of Wong, who skated a clean program that featured a double Axel combination instead of a triple. Sargeant, Allison and Takeuchi rounded out the top five. Entering the free skate, Wong held the lead over Allison, with Preston and Takeuchi tied for third and Sargeant fifth. Preston shocked many, including herself, by landing three triple jumps in the free skate and winning the title, to the delight of her coach Osborne Colson. Her goal entering the event had been to make the top five. Wong held on to the silver but was only fourth in the free skate. Though her spins and presentation were lovely as always, she missed both of the triples she attempted. Sargeant skated a near-clean program to take the bronze in her very first trip to Canadians, never having qualified as a junior or novice. Takeuchi, Allison and Bingert rounded out the top five. Kurt Browning won the men's compulsory figures over Michael Slipchuk, Norm Proft and Jeff Partrick. Proft's strong finish came as a shock to many as he was only 12th in the figures at the 1988 Canadians. In the original program, Browning landed a triple Axel/double loop combination and triple flip but caught his heel and singled his double Axel. Matthew Hall jumped from fifth to second overall with an outstanding original program featuring a triple Lutz/double loop combination and triple loop. Jaimee Eggleton mounted a comeback from tenth after figures to fifth with an energetic third place original program to selections by John Miles. Though he was fifth in the original program, Slipchuk remained in third overall. In practice, Browning was living up to his 'quadtastic' reputation, landing quadruple toe-loops every day. He also landed two quadruple Salchows to boot! In the free skate, he proved his quad at the 1988 Worlds was no fluke by making history as the first skater to land a quadruple toe-loop at Canadians. Browning also landed a triple Axel but he wasn't perfect, falling on a triple Axel and touching down on a triple loop. A quad and a triple Axel, coupled with his wonderful presentation, skating skills and natural charm, was more than enough to win his first Canadian title. Slipchuk delivered a performance which, like Browning's, had its ups and downs. He landed a triple Axel and triple toe-loop/triple toe-loop combination but fell on a triple Salchow and popped two triple Lutz attempts.

**CANADIAN CHAMPIONSHIPS** (continued)

Junior Winners:

Pierre Gignac (men)
Margot Bion (women)
Marie-Josée Fortin and Jean-Michel Bombardier (pairs)
Julie Marcotte and Juan Carlos Noria (ice dance)

Novice Winners:

Stacy-Paul Healy (men)
Jacquie Taylor (women)
Sherry Ball and Christopher Bourne (pairs)
Amélie Dion and Alexandre Alain (ice dance)

*Kurt Browning. Photo courtesy Sarina Stützer.*

Hall fell on his triple Axel attempt but he landed six triple jumps to Slipchuk's four. However, every single judge placed him behind Slipchuk and he took the bronze over Proft. Eggleton had a disappointing performance, landing only one triple jump and dropping back down to ninth.

**World Championships.** Springtime in Paris may have been on the rainy side but the skating at the World Championships at the Palais Omnisports de Paris-Bercy was anything but dry either. France was delighted to hold their first World Championships in 18 years during the country's Bicentennial of the French Revolution. 133 skaters from 27 countries participated. Many were delighted to see Katarina Witt honoured as the latest recipient of the ISU's Jacques Favart Trophy. However, not every aspect in the competition went smoothly. Attendance was inconsistent, with only 3500 spectators showing up to watch the men's original program. Security was ramped up at the rink to the point that bomb-sniffing dogs were brought in, after a series of alarming incidents that seemed to target North American visitors. A Canadian television crew was assaulted by an unknown assailant on the street brandishing a knife. American judge Joan Gruber fainted midway though the men's figures and had to be replaced. She was under "severe strain" because her hotel room was burglarized twice in two days. An American skater had her dress damaged in the dressing room. Rumours circulated that bomb threats were called in at the airport. Susie Wynne and Joseph Druar's coach Phillip Mills was at the airport when security police exploded two suitcases that were left unattended. The occurrences seemingly came to a halt when the American Embassy got involved, but skaters from the United States were instructed not to wear uniforms with any insignia identifying they were Americans. The men's event started with the compulsory figures, where Alexandr Fadeev established a strong lead over Viktor Petrenko, Grzegorz Filipowski, Christopher Bowman and Kurt Browning. After finishing 12th in figures the previous year, Browning's goal was to make the top six and he was very pleased with the result. Skating to music by Duke Ellington, Browning rebounded to unanimously win the original program with an outstanding performance that earned a sea of 5.9s and a standing ovation. He also made history as the first skater to land two triple Axels in the original program at the World Championships. Bowman also earned a standing ovation, landing the only triple/triple combination of the event - a triple Lutz/triple toe-loop. Not everyone skated fared as well. Fadeev landed his triple Axel combination but fell on a triple loop. Filipowski two-footed the triple Axel and Petrenko fell on his attempt. Entering the free skate, Fadeev had a slight lead over Browning and Bowman but the three were almost tied. Browning won the hearts of the Parisian crowd in the free skate, skating to music by French composers Massenet and Offenbach, including the infamous "Can Can". He landed six triple jumps in his program, including a triple Axel/double toe-loop and triple toe-loop/triple toe-loop combination. His only errors were a slight two-footed landing on his quadruple toe-loop and a step out of his first triple Axel attempt. Bowman stepped out of his opening triple Axel but again landed the triple Lutz/triple toe-loop combination in an outstanding performance of his own. Petrenko and Fadeev both had costly falls and were not at their best, while Filipowski pulled off a convincing six-triple performance. Though the Bulgarian and Soviet judges awarded him only 5.7s, a sea of 5.8s and 5.9s was more than enough for Browning to win the free skate and his first gold medal at the World Championships. Filipowski finished second in the free skate and took the bronze behind Bowman. Fadeev finished just off the podium in fourth, Petrenko sixth and Canada's second man Michael Slipchuk bounced back from 13th in figures to place ninth. In winning gold, Browning became only the fourth Canadian in history to win the men's title at the Worlds. Scott Hamilton quipped that instead of The Battle of Brian's, the rivalry between Browning and Bowman should be called The Battle of The Killer B's.

**1989 WORLD CHAMPIONSHIPS (Paris, France, March 14-19, 1989)**

Men:

1. Kurt Browning (CAN)
2. Christopher Bowman (USA)
3. Grzegorz Filipowski (POL)
4. Alexandr Fadeev (SOV)
5. Petr Barna (CZE)
6. Viktor Petrenko (SOV)
7. Daniel Doran (USA)
8. Oliver Höner (SUI)
9. Michael Slipchuk (CAN)
10. Cameron Medhurst (AUS)

Women:

1. Midori Ito (JPN)
2. Claudia Leistner (FRG)
3. Jill Trenary (USA)
4. Patricia Neske (FRG)
5. Natalia Lebedeva (SOV)
6. Kristi Yamaguchi (USA)
7. Evelyn Großmann (GDR)
8. Natalia Gorbenko (SOV)
9. Beatrice Gelmini (ITA)
10. Surya Bonaly (FRA)

Pairs:

1. Ekaterina Gordeeva and Sergei Grinkov (SOV)
2. Cindy Landry and Lyndon Johnston (CAN)
3. Elena Bechke and Denis Petrov (SOV)
4. Peggy Schwarz and Alexander König (GDR)
5. Kristi Yamaguchi and Rudy Galindo (USA)
6. Elena Kvitchenko and Rashid Kadyrkaev (SOV)
7. Isabelle Brasseur and Lloyd Eisler (CAN)
8. Natalie and Wayne Seybold (USA)
9. Anuschka Gläser and Stefan Pfrengle (FRG)
10. Danielle and Stephen Carr (AUS)

Ice Dance:

1. Marina Klimova and Sergei Ponomarenko (SOV)
2. Maya Usova and Alexandr Zhulin (SOV)
3. Isabelle and Paul Duchesnay (FRA)
4. Klára Engi and Attila Tóth (HUN)
5. Susie Wynne and Joseph Druar (USA)
6. Larisa Fedorinova and Evgeni Platov (SOV)
7. Stefania Calegari and Pasquale Camerlengo (ITA)
8. Karyn and Rod Garossino (CAN)
9. Sharon Jones and Paul Askham (GRB)
10. Andrea Juklová and Martin Šimeček (CZE)

The fight for the vacant women's title at the World Championships began in the compulsory figures. Jill Trenary struggled on the first figure, a bracket, allowing Claudia Leistner to assert an early lead. The second figure, a loop, was problematic for Midori Ito, causing her to drop from fourth to sixth. Natalia Lebedeva, Natalia Gorbenko and Patricia Neske finished third, fourth and fifth in the first phase of the competition. Canada's two entries, Charlene Wong and Karen Preston, were eighth and 17th. The top contenders all skated well in the original program. Ito took the top spot with a double toe-loop/triple toe-loop combination, earning perfect 6.0s for technical merit from Hungarian judge Judit Fürst-Tombor and Bulgarian judge Italian judge Franco Benini. Trenary and Leistner finished second and third, both choosing to do the triple toe-loop as the first jump in the combination. Ito received five first-place ordinals to Trenary's three and Leistner's one. Kristi Yamaguchi executed the most difficult performance of the field, landing a triple Lutz combination, but was only awarded marks good enough for fifth place. Preston gained some ground with an excellent performance featuring a triple toe-loop combination, finishing 11th. With a double Axel combination instead of a triple, Wong placed a disappointing 15th. Though she finished dead last and was eliminated from the competition after the original program, Charuda Upatham made history as the first skater from Thailand to compete at the World Championships. On the day of the free skate, the pressure in the competition got the best of many of the skaters. Trenary had a disastrous practice session and Leistner's warmup was equally rough. Things didn't go well for Wong either. Losing her concentration halfway through her program, she made several errors and finished the competition in 16th. Preston's triple jumps did not fail her, allowing her to move up to ninth in the free skate and 11th overall. Leistner pulled off four triples in her program, but had a hard fall on a triple flip and very telegraphed entries to her jumps. Leistner's presentation also suffered in comparison to Trenary but the U.S. Champion gave a very tentative performance, landing only two triple jumps. Leistner's four triples allowed her to win the silver and Trenary was given marks high enough for third. Though Trenary was disappointed with her performance, her bronze was the twentieth consecutive medal won by an American medal at the Worlds. Ito trounced the competition with a flawless seven-triple performance, including a triple toe-loop/triple toe-loop combination and a huge triple Axel, a historic first at the World Championships for a woman. Ito deservedly received five perfect 6.0s for technical merit from the Belgian, Bulgarian, Hungarian Italian and Swedish judges. Not only was Ito the very first Japanese World Champion in any discipline, but she was the first Japanese skater to receive a 6.0 at the Worlds. The pairs field in Paris was the smallest since 1984, with only eleven couples from seven countries participating. Notably absent were European Champions Larisa Selezneva and Oleg Makarov, who withdrew before the event because Makarov was injured. Ekaterina Gordeeva and Sergei Grinkov showed no signs of the injury that kept them out of the European Championships in the original program. Skating a flawless program with side-by-side double Axels to Rossini's "The Barber of Seville", 'G and G' easily took the lead over Canada's Cindy Landry and Lyndon Johnston and East Germany's Peggy Schwarz and Alexander König. Isabelle Brasseur and Lloyd Eisler got off to a rocky start, finishing only eighth. Brasseur missed the side-by-side double Axel jump and Eisler was suffering from a bout of the flu. Gordeeva had a serious fall in practice, resulting in her having to leave the ice. Ultimately 'G and G' ended up performing flawlessly in the free skate, earning all 5.8s and 5.9s from the judges to win their third World title. Landry and Johnston held on to win the silver medal with an athletic performance featuring a split triple twist, throw triple Salchow and throw double Axel. Landry and Johnston's medal win was altogether remarkable as it was only their fourth competition skating together. A costly fall on a throw by Schwarz and König dropped them down to fourth behind Soviet pair Elena Bechke and Denis Petrov. Brasseur and Eisler did not skate as well as they did at the Canadian Championships, but moved up a spot to seventh. Notably absent from the ice dance event in Paris were Natalia Annenko and Genrikh Sretenski. The Soviets withdrew before the event due to injury. 25 ice dance teams weaved their way through the patterns of the Westminster Waltz and Argentine Tango in the compulsories. Marina Klimova and Sergei Ponomarenko took a strong lead over Maya Usova and Alexandr Zhulin in both dances, earning a perfect 6.0 from Swiss judge Lily Klapp in the Westminster Waltz. Isabelle and Paul Duchesnay finished a surprise third for France, while Canada's Karyn and Rod Garossino and Michelle McDonald and Mark Mitchell settled for eighth and 13th. Injury kept the Duchesnays out of competition all season and there was considerable curiosity and anticipation over the world premiere of their new programs. They pushed buttons in their Charleston OSP by using a feather boa and hat as props, as well as vocals in their music. The majority of the audience loved it but some thought their choices were a bit of a middle finger after being criticized for performing 'show' numbers more suitable for professional competitions. Unfortunately, the duo had a problem with their hat, somewhat marring what was otherwise a delightful program that well captured the free-spirited 1920s prohibition era. The audience didn't care one bit, giving them a long standing ovation. The judges were very divided, awarding them marks ranging from 5.2 to 5.8, which were of course met with boos and whistles. The Duchesnays stance on their props and music was that the hat and feather boa were part of the costume and the vocals were only used before they started skating.

The latter statement wasn't quite true, but they claimed to have 'cleared' the program with ISU Referee Wolfgang Kunz during a training session in Oberstdorf. Their marks put them in fifth in the OSP, well behind Klimova and Ponomarenko who earned perfect 6.0s for presentation from Soviet judge Irina Absaliamova and Czechoslovakian judge Dagmar Řeháková. Klimova and Ponomarenko's "Mack the Knife" free dance earned them no less than six perfect 6.0s - one from the Austrian judge for technical merit and five from American, Soviet, Japanese, French and Italian judges for artistic impression. They were only the second team in history, after Jayne Torvill and Christopher Dean, to earn 6.0s in all three phases in the competition in ice dance at the Worlds. Usova and Zhulin's elegant performance to the music of Holst and Chopin took the silver, but some felt that they should have won the gold. The Duchesnays chose an orchestral version of The Beatles' "Eleanor Rigby" for their thematic program *Eleanor's Dream*. Paul Duchesnay explained the story behind the program in a press conference: "Isabelle is the dream, I'm the reality and through the routine, I'm trying to bring her back to reality from the dream. It's very difficult to do but in the end, reality wins, as it usually does." Their wonderfully imaginative performance earned a 5.5 from American judge Jean Robinson, but it won France's first medal in ice dance at the World Championships in over 25 years. However, *Eleanor's Dream* sparked more controversy, as some claimed that the slide on the ice and shoulder-high lifts they performed were illegal. Klára Engi and Attila Tóth of Hungary and Americans Susie Wynne and Joseph Druar lost the ground they gained on the Duchesnays in the OSP and ended the competition in fourth and fifth. Canadians Karyn and Rod Garossino and Michelle McDonald and Mark Mitchell ended the competition in eighth and 11th place. Italians Stefania Calegari and Pasquale Camerlengo were lucky to finish seventh. Their own country's judge, Vinicio Toncelli, messed up and gave them a 4.4 instead of the 5.4 he had intended. The Duchesnays commitment to pushing the boundaries of the sport had the unintended consequence of alienating some of their peers who followed the rulebook to the letter. The mess played a major role in the Garossinos decision to retire in frustration the month after Worlds. Karyn Garossino pulled no punches at a press conference in Paris, telling reporters, "Bronze medals were awarded for an illegal performance. Somebody is going to have to get the guidelines for this sport straightened out or it's going to be ruined."

*Kurt Browning. Photo courtesy Sarina Stützer.*

*Surya Bonaly. Contributor: Photo 12 / Alamy Stock Photo. Photographer: Jacques Loew.*

# 1989-1990 SEASON

Hit Songs: "If I Could Turn Back Time" by Cher, "Vogue" by Madonna, "Nothing Compares 2 U" by Sinéad O'Connor, "Rhythm Nation" by Janet Jackson, "Step By Step" by New Kids on The Block
Hit Movies: Home Alone, Ghost, Teenage Mutant Ninja Turtles, Kindergarten Cop, Pretty Woman
Hit TV: The Golden Girls, The Kids in the Hall, Unsolved Mysteries, Full House, Murphy Brown
News: South Africa frees Nelson Mandela, The Fall of The Berlin Wall, Romanian uprising overthrows Communist government, École Polytechnique Massacre, Hubble space telescope launched

Natalia Annenko and Genrikh Sretenski joined the cast of Torvill and Dean's World Tour. Claudia Leistner turned professional to tour with *Holiday on Ice*. Elena Kvitchenko and Rashid Kadyrkaev joined Tatiana Tarasova's *Russian All-Stars* troupe. Renée Roca became Jill Trenary's choreographer. Natalie and Wayne Seybold joined the *Ice Capades*, while Jaimee Eggleton took the starring role of Peter Pan in *Walt Disney's World on Ice*. In the spring, Alexandr Fadeev joined the cast of Brian Boitano and Katarina Witt's *Skating* tour and Suzanne Semanick retired to coach at Skating Club of Wilmington in Delaware.

The Duchesnays turned down attractive offers from the *Ice Capades* and *Holiday on Ice*, negotiating a one-year contract with the FFSG that fully covered their living, training, coaching and choreography costs and costumes. In addition, they received a taxable federal training grant and part-time jobs from an unspecified company, with an agreement that they would be offered full-time employment when they retired.

John Curry shocked many by baring it all in a shower scene in an off-Broadway production of Peter Nichols' play *Privates on Parade*, staged by the Roundabout Theatre Company at the Union Square Theatre in New York City. The comedy set in the 1940s, which had strong gay themes, told the story of a group of performers who entertained British troops in Malaysia during the War.

Nicky Slater's father John sadly passed away in September. Slater was a medallist in the ice dance event at the World Championships and the World and British Professional Championships in England in the fifties before emigrating to Canada to coach. Slater was not the only skating pioneer to pass away in September. Adrian Swan, the first man to represent Australia at the Olympics, passed away in Melbourne at the age of 59. Swan had the unusual distinction of being a national senior men's champion of two countries - Australia and the UK. Patricia Jackson, President of South Africa Ice Skating Association for nineteen years, also passed away in September. A teacher and principal for 33 years, Jackson was an important figure in the development of figure skating in South Africa.

An announcement was made that Kristi Yamaguchi and Rudy Galindo were ending their partnership. Balancing two disciplines at an elite level was a daunting workload in itself. However, the decision was largely based on the logistics of travel. Yamaguchi trained in singles in Edmonton and she and Galindo had trained as pair in California. At the time, Yamaguchi reflected, "It was getting harder and harder for me to keep doing both. I will miss pairs. It's like a whole chapter of my life is ending. I realized there was no way I could skate at the level I wanted to by competing in both."

The figure skating community was shocked to learn of the death of Heiko Fischer near Stuttgart in November. Fischer was only 29-years-old when his heart gave out during a squash game. His wife was soon due to give birth to his first child and his death left his family in dire straits financially.

CTV Vice-President of Sports Johnny Esaw announced his retirement in February after 41 years in broadcasting. Esaw, Debbi Wilkes, Brian Pockar and Toller Cranston were 'the voices of figure skating' in Canada in the 80s, drawing in thousands of viewers with their insightful commentary. Esaw worked tirelessly behind the scenes to ensure the sport's television coverage was extensive, entertaining and enlightening. CFSA President Barbara Ryan named Esaw the first director of the Association's new Hall of Fame and announced the establishment of a bursary in his name. Otto Jelinek credited Esaw with bringing figure skating "from the social pages into the forefront of Canadian sport."

In January, Irina Rodnina signed a three-year contract to come to America and coach with Robin Cousins at the Ice Castle International Training Center in Blue Jay, California. Previous to coming to America with her husband and two children, Rodnina was an instructor at the Institute of Physical Culture and Sports and Advanced School of Trainers. She also served as a judge at the Soviet Championships and a consultant to the Moscow Ballet on Ice.

In February, Barbara Ann Scott and Sheldon Galbraith were the first figure skaters to be inducted into the newly formed Olympic Hall of Fame at Canada Olympic Park in Calgary.

Esteemed American judge Katherine Miller Sackett passed away in California in February at the age of 88. Miller Sackett got her start as a judge when it was very much an 'old boys club'. In 1952, she made history as the first American woman to serve as a judge in an officially recognized event at the World Championships.

Scott Hamilton was inducted into the World Figure Skating Hall of Fame. Jayne Torvill and Christopher Dean were honoured as the winners of the coveted *American Skating World* Professional Skater of the Year Award.

Jill Trenary's popularity skyrocketed after she won the World Championships in March. She was chosen as NBC's Sportsperson of the Week and interviewed on *The Today Show*. When she returned home from the Tour of World Figure Skating Champions, she was serenaded by a brass band at a lavish reception at the Broadmoor World Arena where a letter from the Governor of Colorado was read. The Mayor of Colorado Springs declared that April 24 would therefore be known as Jill Trenary Day. Two thirds of *Skating* subscribers voted to award Trenary the Readers' Choice Award for the Amateur Figure Skater of the Year. This award was presented at the USFSA's Governing Council Meeting in Indianapolis in the spring.

U.S. President George H.W. Bush appointed two-time U.S. Champion Gary Visconti to serve on the President's Council on Physical Fitness and Sports. Dorothy Hamill had previously been figure skating's representative on the Council.

In April, Donald Jackson, the first Canadian skater to land a triple jump in competition in 1958, celebrated his fiftieth birthday by landing a beautiful triple Salchow at the Minto Skating Club. The same month, Kurt Browning was inducted into the Canadian Amateur Sports Hall of Fame.

The very first inductees to the CFSA Hall of Fame were announced in June. Figure skating pioneers Louis Rubenstein, Melville Rogers, Montgomery 'Bud' Wilson, Constance Wilson Slatkin and Otto Gold were all inducted posthumously. The Hall of Fame would not have been possible without the important work of Barbara Ryan, who prioritized the preservation and celebration of figure skating history more than any other CFSA or Skate Canada President before or since.

Theresa Weld Blanchard inducted posthumously into Women's Sports Foundation's International Women's Sports Hall of Fame. She was only the fifth figure skater to be so honoured, joining the company of Peggy Fleming, Sonja Henie, Tenley Albright and Irina Rodnina.

Carlo Fassi announced that he had accepted an offer to direct a multi-sport complex in Milan, Italy. The Fassi's had been affiliated with the Broadmoor World Arena for almost 30 years, first hired to replace Edi Scholdan after the Sabena Crash in 1961. PSGA President Kathy Casey was announced as Fassi's replacement.

Janet Lynn Salomon became the first figure skater to be inducted into the National Polish-American Sports Hall of Fame. She was honoured at a banquet at the Polish Century Club in Detroit in June.

## MUSIC

The use of vocal music had long been a contentious issue in amateur figure skating circles. In the 1960s and early 70s, a handful of skaters selected vocal music but it was soon banned in singles and pairs. In 1975, the ISU voted to prohibit the use of vocals in the OSP and free dancing as well but allowed ice dancers the option to skate to "all types of music, including classical ballet, folk and contemporary, provided it is suitable for ice dancing." At the ISU Congress in Christchurch in the spring, the ISU voted to firmly prohibit vocals in all international competitions, as a small handful of skaters had started including music with vocals again even though it was not permitted.

## FUN AND GAMES

Mattel went all in on skating dolls, releasing an *Ice Capades* Barbie and skating rink to celebrate the tour's fiftieth anniversary. There was even an *Ice Capades* Ken, but he wasn't a 10.0. *Ice Capades* Barbie made millions of dollars in retail sales in 1989 alone.

## FASHION

If neon tie-dyed outfits were your thing, the new Elizabeth Manley Signature Line of skating fashions would have been right up your alley. Manley even partnered with Marc Evon Enterprises to release a new line of skate guards, manufactured in partnership with a program that employed individuals living with intellectual disabilities in Tecumseh.

## AROUND THE WORLD

**Canada.** The CFSA's membership grew exponentially over the decade, with all thirteen sections showing an increase in skating clubs. The Quebec Section had the largest membership, with 262 clubs and over 31 000 members, followed by Central and Western Ontario with over 22 000 members each. The smallest section, with only 15 clubs, was Prince Edward Island. The CFSA instituted a new requirement that all national team members participate in a summer competition. Even World Champion Kurt Browning wasn't exempt from the rule, quietly competing under the pseudonym Curtis Brown in an event in Lynnwood, Washington.

**Germany.** Though The Berlin Wall fell in November, the official process of reunification did not happen overnight. The DELV and DEV continued to operate as two separate entities throughout the 1989-1990 season. A joint proposal from both federations was approved at an ISU meeting during the Skate Electric competition in England in the fall of 1990. During the 1990/1991 season, the ISU took the unusual step of permitting four entries from Germany in the women's and pairs disciplines and three in men's and pairs. Real-world events had a significant impact on the skating community in East Germany, with economic conditions forcing rinks around the country to close their doors. Many skaters struggled to afford lessons and the number of skating coaches in East Berlin dwindled from 25 to five. Frau Jutta Müller revealed that some of her fellow coaches had to go to welfare houses.

**Soviet Union.** History was made in December when Candid Productions staged the first professional competition ever held behind the Iron Curtain. Despite being held in a snowstorm, the Challenge of Champions at the Luzhniki Palace of Sports was so popular that people were turned away at the doors because there simply wasn't enough seating. Coincidentally, the long-running Prize of Moscow News international competition was cancelled due to a loss of sponsorship. Moscow News partnered with NutraSweet to sponsor the Challenge of Champions.

## BEHIND THE SCENES

Rumours swirled after it was revealed that the IOC was discussing the possibility of eliminating rhythmic gymnastics from the Olympic Games. Concerned that ice dancing might be in jeopardy as well, the USFSA urged its membership to write letters of support to the Presidents of the USOC and IOC.

History was made in May, when Christchurch, New Zealand played host to the first ISU Congress in the Southern Hemisphere. Speculation had been brewing for about three years as to whether or not the ISU would support professional skaters reinstating in time for the 1992 Winter Olympics. The ISU's members voted 55-6 to uphold the ban on professionals at both the Olympics and ISU Championships. The ISU's position was that amateurs could earn money and remain eligible for the Olympics going forward, but that those who had already turned professional would not be eligible to reinstate. Brian Boitano was vocal in his disappointment with the decision, vowing to continue to push the issue. The PSGA conducted a survey of its own regarding eligibility rules in the spring. Over 70 percent of its members were against professionals being allowed to reinstate and a further 78 percent were against professional skaters competing against amateurs in pro-am competitions.

Precision skating gained recognition when the ISU voted to reinstate "group skating" as a discipline in its Regulations. From 1909 to 1971, group skating had previously been included to accommodate fours skating and by reinstating the discipline, both fours and precision could now be under the ISU umbrella.

Tweaks were made to the elements in both the singles and pairs original programs and a proposal to change back the number of skaters making the final round at the Olympics and ISU Championships to 24, instead of 20, was accepted. Major changes were also made in ice dance, with the OSP being renamed the Original Dance and dancers being permitted to choose whatever music they wanted to for the free dance. Previously, ice dancers were cautioned to choose music "suitable for ice dancing".

In a twist of irony, DELV - infamous for its Staatsplanthema 14.25 doping program - successfully proposed major changes to doping controls at the last ISU Congress the federation attended in the spring. DELV's recommendations included changing the ISU's regulations surrounding which penalties would be attached to different substances. Harsher penalties were imposed for the use of anabolic steroids and stimulants in comparison to ephedrine and similar drugs used as cough suppressants or antihistamines. Another approved proposal allowed the ISU to conduct random doping tests on skaters at any point in the season. Previously to this, the ISU had only done testing at major international competitions. The ISU surveyed its members on doping controls. 26 out of 34 federations that responded said that they were already conducting random testing internally.

The ISU approved a new rule regarding 'country swapping', allowing pairs and ice dance consisting of two members from different countries to skate for the country of either member. The rule further stated that once a decision had been made, teams could not change countries. One of the first teams directly impacted by this decision was Regina Woodward and Csaba Szentpétery. Woodward, an American, opted to represent Hungary with her new partner.

Canada led the way in promoting artistic skating as a discipline by introducing tests and interpretive competitions at Skate Canada. Ellen Burka and Osborne Colson played an instrumental role in this movement. Though competitions that focused solely on "musical interpretation, presentation, timing and costume" were held in England as early as the fifties, never before had the discipline gained much traction. In the interpretive event at Skate Canada in the fall, there were no restrictions on costumes or music. Vocals were allowed but skaters were not permitted to include double Axels or triple jumps in their programs. The whole point of artistic skating was telling a story through musical interpretation.

## ART AND HISTORY

The World Figure Skating Museum and Hall of Fame celebrated its tenth anniversary in Colorado Springs. The Museum's roots traced back to 1965 when a much smaller collection was housed in the USFSA's offices in Boston.

# FILM AND TELEVISION

Barry Samson's *Ice Pawn* was shot in Colorado Springs in the fall, with skating scenes being filmed at the Broadmoor World Arena. The film's plot centered around a champion skater who was being used by his father, coach and sponsors. Christopher Marsh was actor Paul Cross' skating double for the film. Nicole Bobek, Shepherd Clark and Patrick Brault all made appearances.

In November, CBS released the television special *The Ice Stars' Hollywood Revue*, featuring performances by Robin Cousins, John Curry, Tai Babilonia and Randy Gardner and Elizabeth Manley. Based on film themes, the special featured one of Curry's final televised skating performances and a moving performance by Babilonia and Gardner to "Wind Beneath My Wings" from *Beaches*.

In November, WCFE aired the 30-minute documentary *Gustave Lussi: The Man Who Changed Skating*, which traced the legendary coach's career over 60 years.

The popularity of Elizabeth Manley's first television special led to CBC outbidding CTV for her second. *Back to the Beanstalk* aired in December, starring Manley, Robin Cousins and actors Heath Lamberts, Jayne Eastwood and Joe Flaherty. Directed by Emmy Award-nominated M*A*S*H director Burt Metcalfe, the special received rave reviews and Gemini Award nominations for Best Variety Program and Best Costume Design.

Just in time for the U.S. Championships in February, CBS/Fox Video released *Magic Memories on Ice*, an hour-and-a-half video compilation of commentary, performances and interviews spanning almost a century of figure skating history. Narrated by Dick Button and Peggy Fleming, the video featured footage from the archives of ABC, CBS and the World Figure Skating Museum and Hall of Fame.

Marco Entertainment bought the rights to Sonja Henie's story and was "setting up to produce the long-awaited look at skating's most legendary queen." Though the film never ultimately panned out, Elizabeth Manley screen-tested to play Henie in Sun Valley, watching *Sun Valley Serenade* six times a day in preparation. Dorothy Hamill was also reportedly considered to play Henie.

McKeown/McGee Films was busy producing the Duchesnays television special *Pas De Deux with Paul and Isabelle Duchesnay*, which featured footage from their training sessions in Oberstdorf, the World Tour and in their hometown of Aylmer, Quebec. The special was ultimately aired on CBC's *Adrienne Clarkson Presents* in the fall and nominated for a Gemini Award for Best Performing Arts Program or Series or Arts Documentary Program or Series.

*Carmen on Ice* was released in European theaters in February, with its North American debut on HBO in March. Written and directed by Horant H. Hohlfeld and choreographed by Sandra Bezic and Michael Seibert, the stunning on-ice adaptation of *Carmen* was shot in Seville, Spain and studios in East Germany. The production starred Katarina Witt as Carmen, Brian Boitano as Don José and Brian Orser as Escamillo. Anett Pötzsch, Yvonne Gómez, Shaun McGill, Renée Roca, Stephanee Grosscup and Douglas Webster were also among the cast. *Carmen on Ice* earned high praise from critics and Boitano, Witt and Orser all went on to win Emmy Awards for Outstanding Performance in Classical Music/Dance Programming for their starring roles in the film.

# THE FALL OF THE BERLIN WALL

Shae-Lynn Bourne, Marie-Pierre Leray and Mariusz Siudek were among the 51 skaters from 19 countries who witnessed history unfold on the day The Berlin Wall fell in November. The historic event took place the same day the Blue Swords competition kicked off in East Berlin. The news that the East Wall was open broke while skaters were attending a dinner. An East German translator assigned to the American contingent burst into tears, saying "We're free, they're letting us go." She vowed to stay with the group but promptly disappeared. Coach Bob Young went down to see the crowds at the East and West Walls, separated by barbed wire and mines. The East Wall was guarded by soldiers and deathly quiet. From the West Wall, Young could hear singing and cheering and see people attacking the Wall with axes and climbing over. Young learned from a British news crew that at midnight, a hole would be opened for a crossing but the checkpoints couldn't handle the number of people. Young, pairs skater Brian Helgenberg and judge Will Smith watched in shock, in the middle of the night from a side street four blocks from the Brandenberg Gate, as the wall was dismantled by a giant crane. There was a huge celebration at the hotel when they returned. The next morning, Young saw debris from the East Wall fall off a truck and stuffed his shoulder bag full of white rocks. The competition suffered as a result of Real-world events, with many volunteers not showing up, either because they left the country permanently or decided to visit West Berlin. An East German skating official who had travelled the world under strict surveillance brought his 12-year-old son to West Berlin. It was the first time the boy had ever been allowed to leave East Germany. Ten days before the Wall came down, skaters and crew were in East Berlin in rehearsals for *Carmen on Ice*. There had been huge protests in the city and residents of both East and West Berlin both expressed doubt that the Wall would ever come down. Carmen on Ice's team left just ten days before history was made.

# THE AIDS EPIDEMIC

Figure skaters continued to guard their HIV/AIDS diagnoses, as ill-informed immigration and customs regulations didn't allow those infected to cross borders to work.

John Curry's virus progressed into AIDS and he left New York to live with his mother Rita in Birmingham. Rob McCall had to leave Brian Boitano and Katarina Witt's *Skating* tour after being hospitalized in Portland, Maine.

Peter Pender, a former medallist in the novice men's event at the U.S. Championships, made international headlines. The Australian government denied Peter a Visa to attend the World Class Bridge Tournament in Perth because he was HIV-positive. When immigration officials gave him a questionnaire that asked if he'd had "sexual relations with another man since 1980", he told them "it was none of their god-damned business." An outcry by gay rights activists and the World Bridge Federation led the Aussie government to relent and allow him to enter the country to attend. At the time of the incident, Peter told a reporter from the *Bay Area Reporter*, "This is a message that can be sent around the world. People with HIV virus are not going to endanger anybody in their country. I'm going over there to play bridge, not to have sex. On the one hand, I'm very angry. On the other hand, I'm glad there is a story... I want people who have the virus to see that it is possible to lead a full life. You can't get rid of it, but can take medications and lead a full life. I'm healthy and I have my doctor's blessing to go." The six-member U.S. team he was a part of narrowly lost the match.

John Carrell passed away at the age of 42 in September. Carrell got his start in skating at the Seattle Skating Club. After placing third in the Silver Dance event at the 1962 Northwest Pacific Championships with Allana Mittun, he formed a partnership with Lorna Dyer, the bronze medallist at that year's U.S. Championships. Dyer and Carrell won five medals at the U.S. Championships - one of them gold - and the 1965 and 1967 North American titles. They represented America at the World Championships five times, winning two bronze medals and a silver. Though they were sponsored by the Broadmoor Skating Club throughout their career, Dyer and Carrell did much of their training in Canada with World Champion Jean Westwood. Carrell studied political science at the University Of Washington and dabbled in coaching before reinventing himself as a ballet dancer, under the stage name John Aubrey. He danced with a ballet troupe in New York before joining the National Ballet of Canada, where he performed for seven years. Dyer recalled, "John was a funny, wonderful guy. He kept me laughing constantly. He used to sit down on his skates and raise his hands as 'claws' and sneak up behind me and scare me or when 'lurking' (which was a phenomenon in the sixties) he would hide behind a wall or post and lean his hands and head around and wait for me to see him. Just a dislocated head and hands... People were in the closet in those days. You know in skating, maybe a third of men might be gay. It was never an issue with me. I kind of knew but we never talked about it. It was just very quiet in those days. Everybody knew but nobody cared. He was just John. He was like a brother and I loved him very much."

*Peter Pender. Photo courtesy American Contract Bridge League Archives.*

*John Carrell. Photo courtesy James Carrell.*

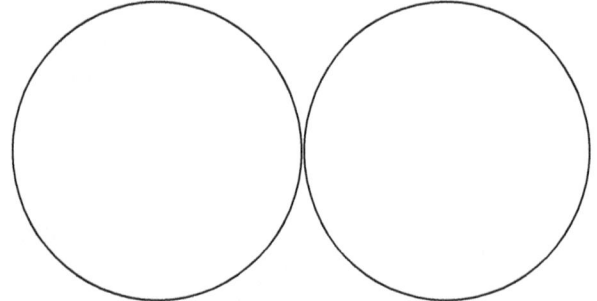

New York City's skating community began rallying together to raise funds for AIDS research, hospice and support programs. John Curry participated in Edwin Cossitt's November 1989 black-tie dinner at the Regimental Armory and *Skating For Life* ice show for DIFFA (Design Industries Foundation for AIDS), alongside a who's who of figure skating including Scott Hamilton, Robin Cousins, Debi Thomas, Tai Babilonia and Randy Gardner, Elizabeth Manley, Denise Biellmann, JoJo Starbuck and Ken Shelley, Ludmila and Oleg Protopopov and Caryn Kadavy. Michael Seibert was unable to perform, so Judy Blumberg skated a duet with John Curry. Peggy Fleming was one of the co-chairs of the event and Dick Button, Liza Minnelli and Mikhail Baryshnikov served on the organizing committee. Sandra Bezic was the show's director.

Tony Panko died in San Francisco at the age of 44 in November. Panko wasn't a skater, but he made a very important contribution to the figure skating world as a costume designer for *Holiday on Ice*. His obituary read, "Tony Panko passed over to the other side on Nov. 11, after a brave four-year struggle with AIDS and KS. His loving friend of seven years, Ted Shuffle, was at his side in their apartment in San Francisco. Despite intense suffering, Tony was cheerful and uncomplaining to the end. He waited for his friend, Ted, to fly back from Europe to say goodbye before passing on. Tony was born in Ottawa, Ill. He served in the army and saw duty in Vietnam. He was a multi-talented artist, florist and decorator. He worked in San Francisco for Podesta-Boldacci, and more recently as a costume designer for *Holiday on Ice* in Bern, Switzerland. He had friends all over the world and he brought joy to every life he touched with his kindness and generosity. He truly loved to give. He was lovingly irreverent, funny and outrageously irresponsible. Completely irreplaceable! A one of a kind. We will all miss you and love you, dear Tony."

In late November, Jim Hulick travelled to Japan to coach his students Kristi Yamaguchi at the NHK Trophy. Upon his return to West Covina, California, he checked into the hospital. He died two weeks later at the age of 38. Hulick got his start in skating at the Valley Figure Skating Club. After winning the bronze medal in the novice pairs event at the 1968 Pacific Coast Championships with Kathleen McKinney, he teamed up with Laurie Brandel. Laurie and Jim won the 1970 Pacific Coast junior pairs title. Jim and his third partner, Cynthia Van Valkenberg, won the U.S. junior pairs title in 1971 and placed in the top ten in senior pairs at both the 1972 and 1973 U.S. Championships. Jim turned professional and toured with the *Ice Follies* for several years before focusing on coaching. Determined to continue working after his diagnosis in August of 1988, Hulick was a great inspiration to his students. Galindo remembered, "It always seemed like he blocked out his sickness for us... I'll never forget him standing there just before we would go out onto the ice and saying, 'Just go out there and have fun.'"

Tommy Miller passed away in Los Angeles in January at the age of 31. Miller got his start in figure skating at the Boulder Figure Skating Club in Colorado. After winning the 1973 Southwestern intermediate men's title, he represented the Colorado Skating Club at the U.S. Championships and won the silver medal in the junior men's event at the 1977 Southwestern Championships.

Miller went on tour as a principal skater with the *Ice Capades*. Kitty DeLio LaForte remembered, "Tommy was an entertainer at heart. He loved the audience and was energized by the crowds. I remember Tommy did not love compulsory school figures. He always was getting off the ice in the Aspen Room, where figures were done at Colorado Ice Arena. He also loved to talk during patch. I remember his smile - it lit up a room - and his laugh. What I remember about him the most is his love for entertaining. He skated many roles in the annual *Showtime on Ice* Production – The Tin Man in *The Wizard of Oz*, The Mad Hatter in *Alice in Wonderland*, Huck Finn in *Tom Sawyer*, just to name a few. He skated each show with energy and commitment. I also remember seeing him at the *Ice Capades* Reunion in November of 1989. He was already very sick then but said to me, 'I made it to the reunion to see everyone.' I think it meant a lot to him to see everyone again, as he knew he was dying. He passed only two months later."

In the spring of 1990, Scott Salzman organized *Blades Against AIDS* at the Wollman Rink. The skating party and series of performances by Patricia Dodd and The Ice Theatre of New York raised much-needed funds for the American Foundation for AIDS Research and God's Love We Deliver.

*Natalia Bestemianova and Andrei Bukin. Photo courtesy Sarina Stützer.*

*Brian Orser. Photo courtesy Sarina Stützer.*

*Denise Biellmann. Photo courtesy Sarina Stützer.*

*Maya Usova and Alexandr Zhulin. Photo courtesy Sarina Stützer.*

# Fall Internationals

**1989 COUPES DES ALPES (Saint Gervais, France and Oberstdorf, West Germany, August 23-26 and August 30-September 3, 1989)**

Grand Prix de St. Gervais Winners:

Colin Vanderveen (USA) - men
Kyoko Ina (USA) - women
Elena Leonova and Gennadi Krasnitski (SOV) - pairs
Irina Romanova and Igor Yaroshenko (SOV) - ice dance

Nebelhorn Trophy (Oberstdorf) Winners:

Shepherd Clark (USA) - men
Kyoko Ina (USA) - women
Elena Leonova and Gennadi Krasnitski (SOV) - pairs
Isabelle Sarech and Xavier Debernis (FRA) - ice dance

**1989 SKATE ELECTRIC UK INTERNATIONAL (London, England, October 2-5, 1989)**

Men:

1. Todd Eldredge (USA)
2. Grzegorz Filipowski (POL)
3. Vladimir Petrenko (SOV)

Women:

1. Tonia Kwiatkowski (USA)
2. Simone Koch (GDR)
3. Patricia Neske (FRG)

Pairs:

1. Isabelle Brasseur and Lloyd Eisler (CAN)
2. Kellie Creel and Bob Pellaton (USA)
3. Radka Kovaříková and René Novotný (CZE)

Ice Dance:

1. Anjelika Krylova and Vladimir Leliukh (SOV)
2. Jeanne Miley and Michael Verlich (USA)
3. Isabelle Sarech and Xavier Debernis (FRA)

**1989 NOVARAT TROPHY (Budapest, Hungary, October 12-15, 1989)**

Men:

1. Viacheslav Zagorodniuk (SOV)
2. Daniel Doran (USA)
3. Ronny Winkler (GDR)

Women:

1. Josée Chouinard (CAN)
2. Tanja Krienke (GDR)
3. Holly Cook (USA)

Ice Dance:

1. Ludmila Berezova and Vladimir Fedorov (SOV)
2. Elizabeth McLean and Ari Leib (AUS)
3. Monika Mandiková and Oliver Pekár (CZE)

**1989 KARL SCHÄFER MEMORIAL (Vienna, Austria, October 16-19, 1989)**

Men:

1. Viacheslav Zagorodniuk (SOV)
2. Elvis Stojko (CAN)
3. Ronny Winkler (GDR)

Women:

1. Josée Chouinard (CAN)
2. Tanja Krienke (GDR)
3. Holly Cook (USA)

Ice Dance:

1. Lyudmila Berezova and Vladimir Fedorov (RUS)
2. Monika Mandiková and Oliver Pekár (CZE)
3. Penny Mann and Richard Perkins (CAN)

**1989 SKATE AMERICA (Indianapolis, IN, October 18-22, 1989)**

Men:

1. Christopher Bowman (USA)
2. Viktor Petrenko (SOV)
3. Kurt Browning (CAN)

Women:

1. Tonya Harding (USA)
2. Jill Trenary (USA)
3. Simone Lang (GDR)

Pairs:

1. Natalia Mishkutenok and Artur Dmitriev (SOV)
2. Kristi Yamaguchi and Rudy Galindo (USA)
3. Peggy Schwarz and Alexander König (GDR)

Ice Dance:

1. Maya Usova and Alexandr Zhulin (SOV)
2. April Sargeant and Russ Witherby (USA)
3. Jo-Anne Borlase and Martin Smith (CAN)

**1989 SKATE CANADA (Cornwall, ON, October 26-28, 1989)**

Men:

1. Petr Barna (CZE)
2. Paul Wylie (USA)
3. Daniel Weiss (FRG)

Women:

1. Kristi Yamaguchi (USA)
2. Simone Lang (GDR)
3. Natalia Lebedeva (SOV)

Pairs:

1. Elena Leonova and Gennadi Krasnitski (SOV)
2. Cindy Landry and Lyndon Johnston (CAN)
3. Michelle Menzies and Kevin Wheeler (CAN)

Ice Dance:

1. Suzanne Semanick and Ron Kravette (USA)
2. Michelle McDonald and Mark Mitchell (CAN)
3. Jacqueline Petr and Mark Janoschak (CAN)

Fours:

1. Christine Hough, Cindy Landry, Doug Ladret and Lyndon Johnston (CAN)
2. Patricia MacNeil, Michelle Menzies, Cory Watson and Kevin Wheeler (CAN)
3. Elaine Asanakis, Calla Urbanski, Joel McKeever and Mark Naylor (USA)

Men's Artistic:

1. Daniel Weiss (FRG)
2. Paul Wylie (USA)
3. Norm Proft (CAN)

Women's Artistic:

1. Yukiko Kashihara (JPN)
2. Dianne Takeuchi (CAN)
3. Jenni Meno (USA)

**1989 PRAGUE SKATE (Prague, Czechoslovakia, November 2-5, 1989)**

Men:

1. Nicolas Pétorin (FRA)
2. Gleb Bokiy (SOV)
3. Mirko Eichhorn (GDR)

Women:

1. Tisha Walker (USA)
2. Simone Koch (GDR)
3. Marcela Kochollová (CZE)

Pairs:

1. Radka Kovaříková and René Novotný (CZE)
2. Ines Müller and Ingo Steuer (GDR)
3. Karina Guchmazova and Sergei Petrovski (SOV)

Ice Dance:

1. Monika Mandiková and Oliver Pekár (CZE)
2. Ivana Střondalová and Milan Brzý (CZE)
3. Maria Orlova and Alexei Kiliako (SOV)

# Fall Internationals

**1989 GOLDEN SPIN OF ZAGREB (Zagreb, Yugoslavia, November 8-12, 1989)**

Men:

1. Sergei Dudakov (SOV)
2. Craig Heath (USA)
3. Peter Johansson (SWE)

Women:

1. Kelly Szmurlo (USA)
2. Dianne Takeuchi (CAN)
3. Lily Lee (KOR)

Ice Dance:

1. Elizaveta Stekolnikova and Oleg Ovsiannikov (SOV)
2. Pascale Vrot and David Quinsac (FRA)
3. Lisa Grove and Scott Myers (USA)

**1989 POKAL DER BLAUEN SCHWERTER (Berlin, East Germany, November 9-12, 1989)**

Men:

1. Mirko Eichhorn (GDR)
2. Sergey Minaev (SOV)
3. Zsolt Kerekes (ROM)

Women:

1. Robyn Petroskey (USA)
2. Tanja Krienke (GDR)
3. Kaisa Kella (FIN)

Pairs:

1. Elena Vlascenko and Sergei Ostriy (SOV)
2. Aimee Offner and Brian Helgenberg (USA)
3. Shae-Lynn Bourne and Andrew Bertleff (CAN)

**1989 TROPHÉE LALIQUE (Paris, France, November 10-12, 1989)**

Men:

1. Viacheslav Zagorodniuk (SOV)
2. Grzegorz Filipowski (POL)
3. Norm Proft (CAN)

Women:

1. Surya Bonaly (FRA)
2. Holly Cook (USA)
3. Laetitia Hubert (FRA)

Pairs:

1. Mandy Wötzel and Axel Rauschenbach (GDR)
2. Isabelle Brasseur and Lloyd Eisler (CAN)
3. Radka Kovaříková and René Novotný (CZE)

Ice Dance:

1. Anjelika Krylova and Vladimir Leliukh (SOV)
2. April Sargent and Russ Witherby (USA)
3. Susanna Rahkamo and Petri Kokko (FIN)

**1989 RWE NATIONS CUP ON ICE (Gelsenkirchen, West Germany, November 16-18, 1989)**

Men:

1. Petr Barna (CZE)
2. Viktor Petrenko (SOV)
3. Paul Wylie (USA)

Women:

1. Tonya Harding (USA)
2. Marina Kielmann (FRG)
3. Patricia Neske (FRG)

Pairs:

1. Elena Bechke and Denis Petrov (SOV)
2. Peggy Schwarz and Alexander König (GDR)
3. Calla Urbanski and Mark Naylor (USA)

Ice Dance:

1. Maya Usova and Alexandr Zhulin (SOV)
2. Suzanne Semanick and Ron Kravette (USA)
3. Andrea Weppelmann and Hendryk Schamberger (FRG)

**1989 GRAND PRIZE SNP (Banská Bystrica, Czechoslovakia, November 16-19, 1989)**

Men:

1. Thomas Dörmer (GDR)
2. Mirko Müller (GDR)
3. Alexandre Orset (FRA)

Women:

1. Cathrin Degler (GDR)
2. Tatiana Rachkova (SOV)
3. Sarah Abitbol (FRA)

Pairs:

1. Oksana Ermakova and Alexei Letov (SOV)
2. Jasmine Schützmeister and Jan Grüske-Weißenbach (FRG)
3. Tracey and Stephen Roberts (AUS)

Ice Dance:

1. Ekaterina Proskurina and Oleg Fediukov (SOV)
2. Zuzana Slobodová and Tomas Morbacher (CZE)
3. Beth Buhl and Neale Smull (USA)

**1989 NHK TROPHY (Kobe, Japan, November 23-26, 1989)**

Men:

1. Viktor Petrenko (SOV)
2. Alexandr Fadeev (SOV)
3. Kurt Browning (CAN)

Women:

1. Midori Ito (JPN)
2. Kristi Yamaguchi (USA)
3. Tonia Kwiatkowski (USA)

Pairs:

1. Ekaterina Gordeeva and Sergei Grinkov (SOV)
2. Larisa Selezneva and Oleg Makarov (SOV)
3. Christine Hough and Doug Ladret (CAN)

Ice Dance:

1. Marina Klimova and Sergei Ponomarenko (SOV)
2. Oksana Grishuk and Evgeni Platov (SOV)
3. Jo-Anne Borlase and Martin Smith (CAN)

**1989 PIRUETTEN (Oslo, Norway, December 1-3, 1989)**

Men:

1. Sergei Dudakov (SOV)
2. Alexandre Orset (FRA)
3. Jan Erik Digernes (NOR)

Women:

1. Stéphanie Ferrer (FRA)
2. Natalia Skrabnevskaya (SOV)
3. Misachi Kashiwagi (JPN)

Junior Men:

1. Lance Vipond (CAN)
2. Fabrizio Garattoni (ITA)
3. Alexandr Abt (SOV)

Junior Women:

1. Marie-Pierre Leray (FRA)
2. Danielle Brunelle (CAN)
3. Yulia Vorobieva (SOV)

# National Championships and Other Competitions

## SENIOR NATIONAL CHAMPIONS BY COUNTRY

### Men

AUS - Cameron Medhurst
AUT - Ralph Burghart
BUL - Alexander Mladenov
CZE - Petr Barna
DEN - Henrik Walentin
FIN - Jari Kauppi
FRA - Éric Millot
FRG - Daniel Weiss
GDR - Ronny Winkler
GRB - Steven Cousins
HOL - Alcuin Schulten
HUN - András Száraz
ITA - Alessandro Riccitelli
JPN - Tatsuya Fuiji
KOR - Sung-il Jung
NOR - Jan Erik Digernes
NZL - Christopher Blong
POL - Marek Sząszor
ROM - Cornel Gheorghe
SAF - Dino Quattrocecere
SOV - Alexandr Fadeev
SUI - Oliver Höner
SWE - Peter Johansson

### Women

AUS - Tamara Heggen
AUT - Yvonne Pokorny
BUL - Milena Marinovich
CHN - Lu Chen
CZE - Lenka Kulovaná
DEN - Anisette Torp-Lind
FIN - Meri Karvosenoja
FRA - Surya Bonaly
FRG - Patricia Neske
GDR - Tanja Krienke
GRB - Emma Murdoch
HOL - Astrid Winkelman
HUN - Tamara Téglássy
ITA - Beatrice Gelmini
JPN - Midori Ito
KOR - Eun-hee Lee
NOR - Anita Thorenfeldt
NZL - Rosanna Blong
POL - Beata Zielińska
SAF - Juanita-Anne Yorke
SOV - Natalia Lebedeva
SUI - Michèle Claret
SWE - Hélène Persson

### Pairs

AUS - Danielle and Stephen Carr
CZE - Radka Kovaříková and René Novotný
FRG - Anuschka Gläser and Stefan Pfrengle
GDR - Mandy Wötzel and Axel Rauschenbach
GRB - Cheryl Peake and Andrew Naylor
POL - Katarzyna Głowacka and Krzysztof Korcarz*
SOV - Larisa Selezneva and Oleg Makarov
SUI - Saskia and Guy Bourgeois

*The Polish pairs title was not awarded as the winning team did not reach the required standard of marks.

### Ice Dance

AUS - Monica MacDonald and Duncan Smart
AUT - Monika Müksch and Bernhard Hatzl
BUL - Petya Gavazova and Nikolay Tonev
CZE - Ivana Střondalová and Milan Brzý
FIN - Susanna Rahkamo and Petri Kokko
FRA - Isabelle and Paul Duchesnay
FRG - Saskia Stahler and Sven Authorsen
GDR - Kati Winkler and René Lohse
GRB - Lynn Burton and Andrew Place
HOL - Joanne and Eerde van Leeuwen
HUN - Klára Engi and Attila Tóth
JPN - Kaoru and Kenji Takino
POL - Małgorzata Grajcar and Andrzej Dostatni
SOV - Marina Klimova and Sergei Ponomarenko
SUI - Diane Gerencser and Bernard Columberg

## 1989 INTERNATIONAL CUP PRECISION CHAMPIONSHIPS (Mölndal, Sweden, December 28-30, 1989)

Team:

1. Whitby Ice Fyre (CAN)
2. Les Pirouettes de Laval (CAN)
3. Burlington Ice Image (CAN)

## 1990 MILK INTERNATIONAL PRECISION COMPETITION (Helsinki, Finland, January 4-6, 1990)

Team:

1. Les Pirouettes de Laval (CAN)
2. Whitby Ice Fyre (CAN)
3. Burlington Ice Image (CAN)

## 1990 NORDISKA MÄSTERSKAPEN (Helsinki, Finland, February 10-11, 1990)

Men:

1. Lars Dresler (DEN)
2. Henrik Walentin (DEN)
3. Oula Jääskeläinen (FIN)

Women:

1. Mari Niskanen (FIN)
2. Ines Klubal (SWE)
3. Mila Kajas (FIN)

## 1990 GILDA MARX U.S. PRECISION CHAMPIONSHIPS (Houston, TX, March 30-31, 1990)

Team:

1. Goldenettes
2. The Haydenettes
3. Fraserettes

Other Winners:

Royalettes (junior)
Ice Mates (novice)
Detroit Royals (adult)

## 1990 MERANO SPRING TROPHY (Merano, Italy, March 29-April 1, 1990)

Women:

1. Claudia Unger (FRG)
2. Charlene von Saher (USA)
3. Rena Inoue (JPN)

## 1990 CHALLENGE LYSIANE LAURET (Grenoble, France, April 5-8, 1990)

Ice Dance:

1. Ilona Melnichenko and Gennadi Kaskov (SOV)
2. Irina Romanova and Igor Yaroshenko (SOV)
3. Anjelika Krylova and Vladimir Leliukh (SOV)

## 1990 CANADIAN PRECISION TEAM CHAMPIONSHIPS (Kitchener, ON, April 6-8, 1990)

Team:

1. Whitby Ice Fyre
2. Les Pirouettes de Laval
3. National Capital Senior Precision Team

Other Winners:

Les Étincelles de Charlesbourg (junior)
Brampton Angelettes (novice)
Edmonton Masters (adult)

## 1990 SKATE ELECTRIC INTERNATIONAL CHALLENGE (Basingstoke, England, April 30-May 1, 1990)

Men:

1. Craig Heath (USA)
2. Daniel Weiss (GDR)
3. Gleb Bokij (SOV)

Women:

1. Surya Bonaly (FRA)
2. Josée Chouinard (CAN)
3. Nancy Kerrigan (USA)

Pairs:

1. Evgenia Shishkova and Vadim Naumov (SOV)
2. Marie-Claude Savard-Gagnon and Luc Bradet (CAN)
3. Calla Urbanski and Mark Naylor (USA)

Ice Dance:

1. Susanna Rahkamo and Petri Kokko (FIN)
2. Jeanne Miley and Michael Verlich (USA)
3. Ludmila Berezova and Vladimir Fedorov (SOV)

# Professional Competitions

**1989 CAMPEONATOS DEL MUNDO DE PATINAJE ARTÍSTICO PROFESSIONAL SOBRE HIELO (Jaca, Spain, December 5-7, 1989)**

Men:

1. Robert Wagenhoffer (USA)
2. Fernand Fédronic (FRA)
3. Mark Cockerell (USA)

Women:

1. Lori Benton (USA)
2. Aimee Kravette (USA)
3. Lisa-Marie Allen (USA)

Pairs:

1. Tracey Solomons and Ian Jenkins (GRB)
2. Anita Hartshorn and Frank Sweiding (USA)
3. Shelley Winters and John Taylor (CAN)

Ice Dance:

1. Kristan Lowery and Chip Rossbach (USA)
2. Karen Quinn and Alan Abretti (GRB)
3. Géraldine Inghelaere and Hervé Casier (FRA)

**1989 CAMPBELL'S WORLD CUP OF FIGURE SKATING II (Ottawa, Ontario, December 10, 1989)**

Men:

1. Robin Cousins (GRB)
2. Charlie Tickner (USA)
3. Robert Wagenhoffer (USA)

Women:

1. Elizabeth Manley (CAN)
2. Tiffany Chin (USA)
3. Linda Fratianne (USA)

Pairs:

1. Barbara Underhill and Paul Martini (CAN)
2. Jill Watson and Peter Oppegard (USA)
3. Natalie and Wayne Seybold (USA)

Ice Dance:

1. Judy Blumberg and Michael Seibert (USA)
2. Lorna Wighton and John Dowding (CAN)

**1989 NUTRASWEET CHALLENGE OF CHAMPIONS (Moscow, Soviet Union, December 14, 1989)**

Men:

1. Brian Boitano (USA)
2. Brian Orser (CAN)
3. Gary Beacom (CAN)
4. Scott Hamilton (USA)

Women:

1. Denise Biellmann (SUI)
2. Debi Thomas (USA)
3. Rosalynn Sumners (USA)
4. Elaine Zayak (USA)

Pairs:

1. Kitty and Peter Carruthers (USA)
2. Elena Valova and Oleg Vassiliev (SOV)
3. Elena Kvitchenko and Rashid Kadyrkaev (SOV)

Ice Dance:

1. Natalia Bestemianova and Andrei Bukin (SOV)
2. Natalia Annenko and Genrikh Sretenski (SOV)
3. Tracy Wilson and Rob McCall (CAN)
4. Judy Blumberg and Michael Seibert (USA)

**1989 U.S. OPEN PROFESSIONAL CHAMPIONSHIPS (Orlando, FL, December 15-17, 1989)**

Men:

1. Robert Wagenhoffer (USA)
2. Jaimee Eggleton (CAN)
3. Paul Guerrero (USA)

Women:

1. Elizabeth Manley (CAN)
2. Kathleen Schmelz (USA)
3. Lori Benton (USA)

Pairs:

1. Barbara Underhill and Paul Martini (CAN)
2. Anita Hartshorn and Frank Sweiding (USA)
3. Natalie and Wayne Seybold (USA)

Ice Dance:

1. Lorna Wighton and John Dowding (CAN)
2. Nina Newby and Bill Aquilino (USA)
3. Kelley Morris and Victor Farrow (USA)

Challenge Cup Winners:

Paul Guerrero (USA) - men
Tracy Prussack Fedourich (USA) - women
Tracy Prussack Fedourich and Garret Petrov (USA) - pairs
Nina Newby and Bill Aquilino (USA) - ice dance

*Natalia Bestemianova and Andrei Bukin. Photo courtesy Sarina Stützer.*

*Midori Ito. Photo courtesy Sarina Stützer.*

*Jill Trenary. Photo courtesy Sarina Stützer.*

# SHOWS AND TOURS

Figure skating shows attracted huge crowds in the summer. A July exhibition in Oakland, California called *Bay Night of International Stars* featured the likes of Brian Boitano, Debi Thomas, Kristi Yamaguchi and Rudy Galindo and Charlie Tickner. Brian Pockar and Lisa-Marie Allen starred in Richard Porter's *Celebration on Ice* at Bally's Grand Hotel on the Boardwalk in Atlantic City. Elizabeth Manley, Tai Babilonia and Randy Gardner, Judy Blumberg and Michael Seibert, Tiffany Chin and Jill Watson and Peter Oppegard joined Pockar and Allen for guest stints.

Willy Bietak Productions was busier than ever. Bietak's show *Hot Ice* at Busch Gardens in Williamsburg was in its fifth year, featuring an ensemble of ten skaters and a non-skating guest star. *Fire and Ice* at Great America in Santa Clarita featured a cast of twelve skaters. At Kings Island in Cincinnati and Sea World of Texas in San Antonio, Bietak ran two shows simultaneously - *Ice Adventure* and *The Legend of Iceskatia*. Randy Gardner directed *Magic on Ice* at Sea World of San Diego, featuring Robert Wagenhoffer and Lori Benton, with Elizabeth Manley, Charlie Tickner, Tiffany Chin and Natalie and Wayne Seybold making guest appearances. Scott Hamilton, Brian Orser, Debi Thomas, Tracy Wilson and Rob McCall and Kitty and Peter Carruthers all made special guest appearances in another Sea World show – *Time Traveler, An Odyssey on Ice*.

Jayne Torvill and Christopher Dean brought their tour back to Canada and the United States in the fall, partnering with the Russian All-Stars, who were coached by Tatiana Tarasova and directed by Yuri Ovchinnikov. Torvill and Dean choreographed the tour along with Tarasova and Andris Toppe. The tour's performers included Ovchinnikov, Natalia Annenko and Genrikh Sretenski, Olga Volozhinskaya and Alexandr Svinin and Elena Garanina and Igor Zavozin. In the spring, the tour came to the UK, performing shows in Northern Ireland, Wales, Scotland and England.

*Benson & Hedges on Ice* gave performances in Los Angeles and Washington D.C. in September, backed by a live symphony orchestra. Performers included Scott Hamilton, Debi Thomas, Brian Orser, Kitty and Peter Carruthers, Toller Cranston and Tracy Wilson and Rob McCall.

The CFSA's *Royal Bank Champions on Ice* tour visited 43 Canadian communities in 90 days in the fall and early winter. Starring Jozef Sabovčík, Tracey Wainman, Gary Beacom and the new partnership of Denise Benning and Mark Rowsom, the tour featured a rotating cast of guests from the national team, including Kurt Browning, Christine Hough and Doug Ladret, Isabelle Brasseur and Lloyd Eisler and Cindy Landry and Lyndon Johnston. Poland's Grzegorz Filipowski, who came to train at the Royal Glenora Club with Michael Jiranek also made an appearance. The tour was choreographed by Gabby Kamino.

In conjunction with National Skating Month, NutraSweet sponsored a new tour called *Skate Across America*. The tour kicked off in Indianapolis in early October, with performances in six U.S. cities in six days. Performers included Dorothy Hamill, Christopher Bowman, Susie Wynne and Joseph Druar and Jessica Mills.

In November, *An Evening With Champions* at Harvard University's Bright Arena celebrated its twentieth anniversary with a star-studded show emceed by Tai Babilonia and Randy Gardner. Performers included Ludmila and Oleg Protopopov, Kristi Yamaguchi and Rudy Galindo and Michael Slipchuk. By the late eighties, the show had raised over 1 000 000 dollars for Eliot House's Jimmy Fund, which contributed to children's cancer research at the Dana Farber Cancer Institute in Boston.

T.J. Maxx sponsored a new *Nutcracker on Ice* tour, produced by Scott Walker. The tour starred Jozef Sabovčík and Tracey Wainman. Only two hundred people attended the Sault Ste. Marie show in December.

Dick Foster produced *Festival on Ice*, a Christmas ice show at Knott's Berry Farm in California, featuring Irina Korina and Viktor Yelchin, Douglas Webster, Cindy Stuart and a skating Snoopy. The show was directed by David Gravatt and choreographed by Randy Gardner and performed three times a day during the holiday season.

*Dorothy Hamill's Nutcracker on Ice* played to packed crowds at the Orpheum Theatre in Minneapolis over the holidays. Starring Hamill, the show also featured performances by Nathan Birch, Shaun McGill, J. Scott Driscoll, Patricia Dodd and Gia Guddat. The show was staged and directed by Dee Dee Wood and choreographed by Birch.

*Ice Capades* celebrated its fiftieth anniversary with a glitzy television special and a reunion gala at Leow's Santa Monica Beach Hotel in California. In June, the tour travelled to Kuwait and Saudi Arabia, where it presented a pared-down show called *Festival on Ice*. Although *Ice Capades* was popular with audiences, the company regularly faced criticism for fining skaters for "infractions" based on its height and weight chart. When *Walt Disney's World on Ice* questioned whether or not the Ice Capades policies were causing skaters to develop eating disorders, performance director Debbie Hummel responded, "It's very unusual. They [Disney on Ice] tend to have heavier girls in their line."

*Walt Disney's Magic Kingdom on Ice* celebrated the fiftieth anniversary of the 1940 Disney animated adaptation of Carlo Collodi's *Pinnochio* by staging *Pinocchio on Ice* at Radio City Music Hall in New York. Choreographed by Olympic Medallist Bob Paul, the show featured Kristiina Wegelius, J. Scott Driscoll, Shannon Sowers and Grant Noroyan.

Orange you glad the Florida Citrus Festival presented a half-hour ice show 44 times in 11 days in February? *Citrus on Ice* was staged on a 33 by 34 foot stage. The show's stars were U.S. Open Professional Champions Anita Hartshorn and Frank Sweiding and Australian *Ice Capades* star David Sadleir.

The 1989-1990 *Discover Card Stars on Ice* tour was Scott Hamilton's first as both a skater and co-producer. Joining Hamilton in the cast were Brian Orser, Debi Thomas, Toller Cranston, Tracy Wilson and Rob McCall, Rosalynn Sumners, Lea Ann Miller and Bill Fauver, Kitty and Peter Carruthers and Kathleen Schmelz. The tour gave its first two Canadian performances in Kingston and Calgary in March.

Willy Bietak Productions presented *Broadway on Ice*, which toured fifteen American cities performing on theater stages. The tour starred Dorothy Hamill, Judy Blumberg and Michael Seibert, Lori Benton and Tracey Solomons and Ian Jenkins.

Tom Collins' *1990 Tour of World Figure Skating Champions* had its opening night in Halifax just after the World Championships ended in March. From Nova Scotia, the tour visited 23 American cities. Performers included Kurt Browning, Jill Trenary, Ekaterina Gordeeva and Sergei Grinkov, Marina Klimova and Sergei Ponomarenko, the Duchesnays, Midori Ito and Christopher Bowman.

Brian Boitano and Katarina Witt's *Skating* tour kicked off in Portland, Maine in April, touring 30 U.S. and Canadian cities in the spring. Sandra Bezic served as the tour's director, collaborating with pop star Paula Abdul on choreography. The cast consisted of Witt, Boitano, Elena Valova and Oleg Vasiliev, Rosalynn Sumners, Barbara Underhill and Paul Martini, Alexandr Fadeev, Caryn Kadavy, Vladimir Kotin, Gary Beacom and Yvonne Gómez. Judy Blumberg and Michael Seibert joined the tour when Tracy Wilson and Rob McCall had to pull out due to McCall's health.

*Petr Barna. Photo courtesy Sarina Stützer.*   *Natalia Mishkutenok and Artur Dmitriev. Photo courtesy Sarina Stützer.*

## Major Competitions

**World Junior Championships.** In late November and early December, talented young skaters from 25 countries competed at the World Junior Championships in Colorado Springs. It was the second time in the eighties that the Broadmoor Skating Club hosted the event. In the pairs event, Svetlana Pristav and Viacheslav Tkachenko and Natalia Krestianinova and Alexei Tikhonov took the top two spots in the original program, followed by Canada's Sherry Ball and Sean Rice and America's Jennifer Heurlin and John Frederiksen. Pristav and Tkachenko's original program win was controversial, because Tkachenko popped the side-by-side double Axel into a single, but it was missed by most of the judges because of the angle at which they were seated. Krestianinova and Torchinski's ragtime program narrowly defeated Pristav and Tkachenko in the free skate, earning them the gold medal. Side-by-side double Axels helped Heurlin and Frederiksen move up to take the bronze. Ball and Rice ended the competition in fifth. Marina Anissina and Gwendal Peizerat squared off in the ice dance event. After the compulsories, Anissina and Ilya Averbukh led the way for the Soviet Union, followed by Peizerat and his partner Marina Morel, skating for France. Morel and Peizerat lost ground in the OSP, finishing fourth behind Anissina and Averbukh, Canada's Marie-France Dubreuil and Bruno Yvars and a second Soviet team, Elena Kustarova and Sergei Romashkin. Anissina and Averbukh effortlessly skated to victory in the free dance, their win particularly remarkable as they were fourteen and sixteen and had only been skating together for eighteen months. Kustarova and Romashkin moved ahead of Dubreuil and Yvars to take the silver. Morel and Peizerat remained in fourth, just ahead of Canada's second team Martine Patenaude and Eric Massé. In the women's event, Japan's Yuka Sato was the surprise winner of the figures, ahead of defending Champion Jessica Mills, West Germany's Susanne Mildenberger and France's Sandra Garde. Sato's win was quite surprising to those who remembered her the year before when she placed an unlucky 13th in figures in Sarajevo. Sato won the original program with a clean program featuring two double Axels, one in combination, the rules having been changed in the spring to allow junior women to repeat the double Axel in their combination if they so wished. France's Surya Bonaly moved from 12th in the figures to finished second ahead of Mills. Bonaly won the free skate with a technically demanding program that included attempts at the triple Lutz, triple flip and triple toe-loop/triple toe-loop combination. While the content in Bonaly's program was far harder than most seniors, all but East German judge Ingrid Linke gave her lower marks for artistic impression than technical merit. Sato had a disappointing free skate, finishing only fifth after popping a triple Salchow into a single and falling on a triple toe-loop and double Lutz. Sato's wins in the figures and original program, coupled with Bonaly's low placement in figures, allowed her to hang on and win the gold over Bonaly. East Germany's Tanja Krienke landed three triples in the free skate to move up and take the bronze over Mills. Canada's two entries, Jacquie Taylor and Sherry Ball's sister Stacey, had a rough outing and finished 12th and 15th. Many skaters made drastic movements in the standings from one phase of the men's competition to the next. The leaders after the figures were John Baldwin Jr. and Scott Davis of the United States and West Germany's Patrick-Rene Reinhardt. In the original program, Baldwin finished third behind Soviets Alexei Urmanov and Igor Pashkevich, who had been fourth and seventh in figures. Davis finished seventh; Reinhardt 12th. Pashkevich took a hard fall on a triple Salchow early in his free skating program but stayed upright on five triple jumps, including the triple Lutz and flip, to move up and win the title. Urmanov won the silver with a performance that featured a triple Axel. Baldwin Jr. took an unfortunate fall on a triple flip and finished only seventh, but his top three finishes in the first two phases of the competition were enough for the bronze.

**1990 WORLD JUNIOR CHAMPIONSHIPS**
(Colorado Springs, CO, November 28-December 3, 1989)

Men:

1. Igor Pashkevich (SOV)
2. Alexei Urmanov (SOV)
3. John Baldwin Jr. (USA)
4. Philippe Candeloro (FRA)
5. Scott Davis (USA)
6. Mirko Eichhorn (GDR)
7. Nicolas Pétorin (FRA)
8. Elvis Stojko (CAN)
9. Steven Cousins (GRB)
10. Tomoaki Koyama (JPN)

Women:

1. Yuka Sato (JPN)
2. Surya Bonaly (FRA)
3. Tanja Krienke (GDR)
4. Jessica Mills (USA)
5. Kyoko Ina (USA)
6. Laetitia Hubert (FRA)
7. Tisha Walker (USA)
8. Mari Kobayashi (JPN)
9. Susanne Mildenberger (FRG)
10. Alma Lepina (SOV)

Pairs:

1. Natalia Krestianinova and Alexei Tikhonov (SOV)
2. Svetlana Pristav and Viacheslav Tkachenko (SOV)
3. Jennifer Heurlin and John Frederiksen (USA)
4. Inna Svetacheva and Vladimir Shagov (SOV)
5. Sherry Ball and Sean Rice (CAN)
6. Aimee Offner and Brian Helgenberg (USA)
7. Rena Inoue and Tomoaki Koyama (JPN)
8. Catherine Barker and Michael Aldred (GRB)
9. Leslie and Cédric Monod (SUI)
10. Tracey and Stephen Roberts (AUS)

Ice Dance:

1. Marina Anissina and Ilya Averbukh (SOV)
2. Elena Kustarova and Sergei Romashkin (SOV)
3. Marie-France Dubreuil and Bruno Yvars (CAN)
4. Marina Morel and Gwendal Peizerat (FRA)
5. Martine Patenaude and Eric Massé (CAN)
6. Virginie and Remi Jacquemard (FRA)
7. Beth Buhl and Neale Smull (USA)
8. Stephanie Egea and Alexandre Piton (FRA)
9. Kinga Zielińska and Marcin Głowacki (POL)
10. Katherine and Ben Williamson (USA)

France's Philippe Candeloro finished second in the free skate with but a 12th place finish in the figures and fifth in the original program kept him off the podium in fourth. Canada's two entries, Elvis Stojko and Stacy-Paul Healy, finished eighth and 14th. Stojko was an unlucky 13th in figures, 11th after the original program and sixth in the free.

**World Professional Championships.** The pot was increased to 320 000 dollars at the World Professional Championships in December, with winners in each of the four disciplines taking home 40 000 dollars. When Dick Button staged a predecessor to the event in Japan in 1973, the Protopopovs were permitted to leave the Soviet Union to compete but after their defection, Soviet officials had been wary about granting permission to its skaters to compete abroad in professionals. History was made in 1989 when skaters from the Soviet Union participated in the Landover event for the first time. Natalia Bestemianova and Andrei Bukin and Elena Valova and Oleg Vasiliev were delighted to participate. Valova told reporters, "We are so excited. We are very happy. It was such a long wait. There were many problems to work out, but now we are here. It is like a dream come true, to be here with old friends... Now we can sign contracts with other countries, without our government being involved. For years we heard our government talking of change. We all hoped, but we all had a wait-and-see outlook... We are finally seeing and feeling the political change." For the second year in a row, ice dancers skated compulsory dances instead of a technical program. As all four teams shared the ice in the compulsories, they had to work together ahead of time to get the timing of each dance down pat. The compulsories were worth 20 percent of the total score and the artistic program worth 80. 'B and B' and Judy Blumberg and Michael Seibert tied for first place in the compulsories, with Tracy Wilson and Rob McCall and Carol Fox and Richard Dalley in third and fourth, separated by three-tenths of a point. In the artistic program, Blumberg and Seibert went a traditional route, skating to a medley of waltzes from Rodgers and Hammerstein musicals. Their program fell somewhat flat with the judges, who awarded them two 9.7's, three 9.8's and two 9.9's. 'B and B' had a nine-month break from skating together. They started practicing and putting together a re-imagined version of their Olympic free dance to Borodin's "Polovtsian Dances" three months before the competition. Bukin told reporters, "Making the new dance has been fun for us. As an amateur, there are so many rules. You just try to find some movement that is possible. Nothing is possible. Now, as professionals... it is possible just to be." Wearing extremely theatrical costumes, 'B and B' brought the drama and technical difficulty but the judges were divided, awarding them one perfect 10.0, four 9.9's and two 9.7's. Wilson and McCall had felt their program the previous year was too similar to the style they used in their amateur days. They went outside of their comfort zone and came up with an ingeniously choreographed roaring twenties program to the Charleston from Paul Gemignani's Broadway production of "Billion Dollar Baby". They received one perfect 10.0, four 9.9's and two 9.8's for their effort. Wilson and McCall and 'B and B' ended up finishing in an exact tie, but Wilson and McCall won the title because they won the artistic program. In the pairs technical program, 'V and V' reworked their "Zorba the Greek" program from the Olympics, taking an unfortunate fall on their throw triple toe-loop. They were no match for Barbara Underhill and Paul Martini, who executed a split triple twist and throw triple Salchow in their program to Rachmaninoff's "Rhapsody on a Theme of Paganini". After the technical program, Underhill and Martini sat in first, followed by 'V and V', Kitty and Peter Carruthers and Lea Ann Miller and Bill Fauver. In the artistic program, Miller and Fauver were crowd favourites, skating to Harry Belafonte's "Day-O" and "Jump in the Line", which were hugely popular after being featured in the hit film *Beetlejuice*.

**1989 NUTRASWEET WORLD PROFESSIONAL CHAMPIONSHIPS** (Landover, MD, December 8, 1989)

Men:
1. Brian Boitano (USA)
2. Scott Hamilton (USA)
3. Gary Beacom (CAN)
4. Brian Orser (CAN)

Women:
1. Debi Thomas (USA)
2. Denise Biellmann (SUI)
3. Rosalynn Sumners (USA)
4. Elaine Zayak (USA)

Pairs:
1. Barbara Underhill and Paul Martini (CAN)
2. Elena Valova and Oleg Vasiliev (SOV)
3. Kitty and Peter Carruthers (USA)
4. Lea Ann Miller and Bill Fauver (USA)

Ice Dance:
1. Tracy Wilson and Rob McCall (CAN)
2. Natalia Bestemianova and Andrei Bukin (SOV)
3. Judy Blumberg and Michael Seibert (USA)
4. Carol Fox and Richard Dalley (USA)

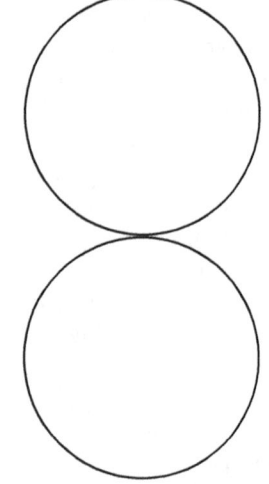

The Carruthers started their program dressed as an elderly couple, then shed their costumes to perform part of their Olympic program from 1984. 'V and V' performed a classical piece with a red scarf as a prop, with Vasiliev taking an unfortunate fall on a single Axel. Underhill and Martini walked away with the title, delivering a sultry and flawless performance to Luba's cover of "When A Man Loves A Woman" and earning perfect 10.0's from all but one of the judges. In the men's technical program, Brian Orser went for the crowd, skating a sultry program to Ken Thorne's "Happy Ending" from *Lassiter* and Sam Taylor's version of "Harlem Nocturne". Though he erred slightly on the landing of his triple Lutz, Orser executed a strong program featuring three triple jumps and a backflip but only received 9.7's and 9.8's from the judges. Gary Beacom made a fantastic first impression at the Landover event with a greatly inventive program to Beethoven's Fifth Symphony. His program included a triple Lutz, a four-jump combination, jumps in both directions and an excellent crossfoot spin. Brian Boitano skated an elegant and difficult program to David Foster's "Just Out of Reach", featuring a triple Axel/double toe-loop combination and his signature 'Tano triple Lutz and spread eagle. He received perfect 10.0's from four of the seven judges and told John 'Misha' Petkevich it was the best he had skated as a professional. Scott Hamilton went for the audience, showing off his fancy footwork in a program to Buster Poindexter's "Screwy Music" that featured a triple Lutz, triple Salchow and triple toe-loop. He ended with a bang, dropping his pants before performing his backflip to finish in his underwear. Hamilton got one 10.0, but when the marks were tallied he finished second to Boitano and ahead of Orser and Beacom. Beacom brought down the house in the artistic program, skating to Soprano Summit's "Song of Songs". Completely different in every possible way to the rest of the field, Beacom's maverick choreography and slicked-back hair drew comparisons to Jack Nicholson but divided the judges. Two judges awarded him perfect 10.0's; two others gave 9.8's. Though he did not win, Beacom's career greatly benefited from the validation and television exposure he received in Landover. Orser skated to Frank Sinatra's "The Girl from Ipanema" and "Cheek to Cheek", but luck was not a lady that night. Though he landed a triple toe-loop, he played it safe and did a double Lutz instead of a triple and a single Axel instead of a double. Scott Hamilton paired fantastic choreography by Sarah Kawahara with famous music from Sammy Davis Jr. in his program to "Mr. Bojangles", earning a standing ovation and a perfect 10.0. Brian Boitano performed to Michael Crawford's "The Music of the Night" for the very first time in competition, delivering a spellbinding performance featuring a 'Tano triple Lutz and two other triple jumps. He earned a prolonged standing ovation and perfect 10.0's from every single judge to win his second World Professional title, ahead of Hamilton, Beacom and Orser. "The Music of The Night" was a breakthrough program for Boitano as a professional and it became such a signature piece that few skaters dared touch it without drawing comparisons to the gold standard he set thanks to Sandra Bezic's choreography. In the women's technical program, Elaine Zayak struggled on the landings of both her triple toe-loop and double Axel. Rosalynn Sumners skated a clean program, but the most difficult jump in her program was a double Axel. Debi Thomas landed a gorgeous triple toe-loop/double toe-loop combination and double Axel in her elegant performance to Gershwin's "Rhapsody in Blue", but she erred on the landing of another double Axel and a triple Salchow. None of the women were able to match the scores of Denise Biellmann, who showed off her sensational triple jumps and superb spins in a program to "Big Spender" from *Sweet Charity*. After the results were tallied, Biellmann was first, followed by Thomas, Sumners and Zayak. In the artistic program, Sumners weaved created a little holiday magic in a nostalgic performance to Arthur Fiedler and the Boston Pops Orchestra's rendition of "White Christmas". Biellmann skated an unorthodox program, combining Europop beats with Strauss' iconic "Blue Danube" waltz. Marks ranging from 9.7 to 9.9 ultimately were not enough to hold on to lead. Thomas' high-energy performance to Paula Abdul's "Cold Hearted Snake" featured a triple toe-loop, double Axel and the Moonwalk. The judges awarded Thomas four 9.8's and three 9.9's - marks just high enough to take the title by three-tenths of a point.

**European Championships.** In late January and early February, the European Championships provided a welcome distraction from the long Russian winters for some 15 000 spectators. Without a doubt, it was a historic competition. The event marked the final time in history that compulsory figures would be skated at Europeans and the first time in 20 years that the event would be held in Leningrad. It was also the final time in history that the event would ever be held in the Soviet Union. The official opening draws were held at the Pulkovskaya Hotel, men's and women's figures were contested at the Yubileiny Sports Palace and all other events were held at The Lenin Sport and Concert Complex. The ISU's representative at the event was Josef Dědič and the chairman of the local organizing committee was Vasily Rogovtsev. Thirteen teams competed in the pairs event. Many thought the event would be a cakewalk for reigning World Champions Ekaterina Gordeeva and Sergei Grinkov. However, Gordeeva was going through a growth spurt at the time and Grinkov was suffering from a shoulder injury. In the original program, 'G and G' made several key errors - a missed double Axel from Gordeeva, unison problems on the side-by-side spins and a slip on the death spiral. These mistakes left them in third, behind their teammates Natalia Mishkutenok and Artur Dmitriev and Larisa Selezneva and Oleg Makarov. The next morning on Soviet television, they were lambasted. They responded with one of their finest performances of their free skate set to "Romeo And Juliet", choreographed by Marina Zoueva. 'G and G' earned a spate of 5.8's and 5.9's and perfect mark of 6.0 from the Yugoslavian judge for artistic impression. They moved up to claim the gold medal ahead of Selezneva and Makarov and Mishkutenok and Dmitriev. East Germans Peggy Schwarz and Alexander König and West Germans Anuschka Gläser and Stefan Pfrengle rounded out the top five. West Germany's Richard Zander earned the distinction of being the final men's figure skater in history to win the figures at the European Championships. However, a disastrous original program ultimately plummeted him out of medal contention. The original program was won brilliantly by Czechoslovakia's Petr Barna, whose masterful performance, which included a triple Lutz/triple toe-loop, triple loop and double Axel, was rewarded with marks ranging from 5.5 to 5.9. Barna held an ever so slight lead over Soviets Viktor Petrenko and Viacheslav Zagorodniuk and Poland's Grzegorz Filipowski entering the final phase of the competition. When Barna faltered on a quadruple toe-loop attempt in the free skate, Petrenko responded with an outstanding free skate that featured six triple jumps (including a solid triple Axel/triple toe-loop combination) to move up and win his first European title in his home country. Barna took the silver, followed by Zagorodniuk, Filipowski, Zander and Switzerland's Oliver Höner. Although he finished eighth after placing 14th in the figures, a young Frenchman named Philippe Candeloro turned many heads by coming out of nowhere and landing two triple Axels in the original program in his European debut and placing eleven spots above the winner of the French senior men's title Éric Millot. After winning the women's figures and original program, the competition appeared to be Natalia Lebedeva's to lose. Unfortunately that's precisely what happened in the free skate. The Soviet skater settled for silver behind 18-year-old Evelyn Großmann of Karl Marx-Stadt, a student of Jutta Müller, who didn't fare much better. West Germany's Marina Kielmann took the bronze ahead of a 16-year-old dynamo from France named Surya Bonaly. Coached by Didier Gailhaguet, Bonaly wasn't even in the top ten in the school figures but she grittily attempted two different quads - the Salchow and the toe-loop - in the free skate. It was the first time a woman attempted a quad at Europeans, let alone two. West Germany's Patricia Neske, the Soviet Union's Natalia Skrabnevskaya and Yugoslavia's Željka Čižmešija, who had placed second through fourth in figures, all turned in disappointing free skating performances as well to place fifth, seventh and 13th respectively.

**1990 EUROPEAN CHAMPIONSHIPS**
(Leningrad, Soviet Union, January 30-February 4, 1990)

Men:

1. Viktor Petrenko (SOV)
2. Petr Barna (CZE)
3. Viacheslav Zagorodniuk (SOV)
4. Grzegorz Filipowski (POL)
5. Richard Zander (FRG)
6. Oliver Höner (SUI)
7. Daniel Weiss (FRG)
8. Philippe Candeloro (FRA)
9. Ralph Burghart (AUT)
10. Peter Johansson (SWE)

Women:

1. Evelyn Großmann (GDR)
2. Natalia Lebedeva (SOV)
3. Marina Kielmann (FRG)
4. Surya Bonaly (FRA)
5. Patricia Neske (FRG)
6. Tanja Krienke (GDR)
7. Natalia Skrabnevskaya (SOV)
8. Tamara Téglássy (HUN)
9. Carola Wolff (FRG)
10. Larisa Zamotina (SOV)

Pairs:

1. Ekaterina Gordeeva and Sergei Grinkov (SOV)
2. Larisa Selezneva and Oleg Makarov (SOV)
3. Natalia Mishkutenok and Artur Dmitriev (SOV)
4. Peggy Schwarz and Alexander König (GDR)
5. Anuschka Gläser and Stefan Pfrengle (FRG)
6. Radka Kovaříková and René Novotný (CZE)
7. Ines Müller and Ingo Steuer (GDR)
8. Cheryl Peake and Andrew Naylor (GRB)
9. Catherine Barker and Michael Aldred (GRB)
10. Henriette Worner and Andreas Sigurdsson (FRG)

Ice Dance:

1. Marina Klimova and Sergei Ponomarenko (SOV)
2. Maya Usova and Alexandr Zhulin (SOV)
3. Isabelle and Paul Duchesnay (FRA)
4. Klára Engi and Attila Tóth (HUN)
5. Oksana Grishuk and Evgeni Platov (SOV)
6. Dominique Yvon and Frédéric Palluel (FRA)
7. Susanna Rahkamo and Petri Kokko (FIN)
8. Anna Croci and Luca Mantovani (ITA)
9. Ivana Střondalová and Milan Brzý (CZE)
10. Małgorzata Grajcar and Andrzej Dostatni (POL)

In contrast with the outstanding skating in the pairs and men's events, the women's event in Leningrad is unfortunately remembered as one of the most lackluster in the history of the European Championships. While commentating for CBS, Scott Hamilton described the women's competition as "one of the worst events I've ever seen". Isabelle and Paul Duchesnay worked with Christopher Dean to develop their new programs for the 1989-1990 season, which both had a South American flavour. Their Samba OSP was set to Paul Simon's "Late In The Evening". Their new free dance was set to "Dolencias" and "Sikuriadas", from Incantation's "Panpipes of the Andes" album. The Duchesnays titled their free dance *Missing*. The program's story aimed to shine a light on the Caravan of Death and 'forced disappearances' that occurred in Argentina's Dirty War. *Missing* drew inspiration from Christopher Bruce's *Ghost Dances* and a piece to the same music that Dean and Jayne Torvill had skated to as professionals. Less than two months before the competition, Paul Duchesnay told reporter Herb Zurowsky, "We try to come up with something new, with innovative programs. This sport can be so much more attractive if a certain degree of freedom is allowed. There are so many rules that are not flexible, that take away the possibilities of what can be achieved on the ice. It's a shame because the sport isn't progressing. Watching the same routines is like watching reruns on television." The Duchesnays didn't get off to a good start in Leningrad, finishing fourth in the compulsories behind Marina Klimova and Sergei Ponomarenko, Maya Usova and Alexander Zhulin and Klára Engi and Attila Tóth. A third-place finish in the OSP all but dashed any hopes of challenging the top two Soviet teams for the gold. However, in the free dance, something surprising happened. The Soviet audience applauded more wildly for the Duchesnays than the two Soviet teams. The judges were mostly lukewarm in their response to the program, though the French judge awarded them a perfect 6.0 for artistic impression. The irony that an audience in Leningrad, of all places, gave a standing ovation to a program about political dictatorship was not lost. Despite the audience's response to The Duchesnays performance, Klimova and Ponomarenko's comparatively safe and elegant free dance to "My Fair Lady" won the gold. Usova and Zhulin's "Tango Argentina" free dance earned the silver. After the event, Isabelle Duchesnay remarked, "We wanted to prove we could compete against the Russians in Russia. Everybody was thinking that the Duchesnays didn't have the guts to come and everything was against them. We had to prove that not only we would come, but also were able to do a good job." Paul added, "Death, the rain and the judges, we found, are three things you can't control. We are quite happy with the way we skated." Former World Champion Andrei Minenkov was so moved by the Duchesnays performance that he declared, "It was like a painting that moves you to ecstasy without even distinguishing the colours. Just stunning."

**U.S. Championships.** In February, over 200 skaters competed at the U.S. Championships in Salt Lake City, Utah. The organizers were originally asked to host the 1989 Nationals but declined to give themselves more time to ensure they were able to pull off a successful competition. Hosted by the Utah Figure Skating Club and the Junior League of Salt Lake City, the competition marked the final time that school figures were included in the senior events. Figures were contested at the Bountiful Recreation Center (about a half-hour drive from the main venue) and free skating events at the Salt Palace. Six skaters participating (Kristi Yamaguchi, Rudy Galindo, Troy Goldstein, Natasha Kuchiki, John Frederiksen and Brad Cox) took on double duty, competing in both singles and pairs, making the drive time between two rinks extremely tight at times. Unfortunately, attendance was not the best, to say the least. The senior women's free skate fell well short of a sellout with just over 5000 tickets sold. Less than 4000 spectators watched the senior men's free skate. Event co-chairperson Nita Sniteman claimed a rumor that tickets were sold out when they in fact were not contributed to the empty seats. Others cited the fact decent television coverage was available and the fact it was a non-Olympic year as reasons that people chose to stay away. Kristi Yamaguchi and Rudy Galindo had a rough road to Salt Lake City. In December, both their longtime coach Jim Hulick and Yamaguchi's grandfather passed away. In the lead-up to Nationals, they trained alone in Canada and crammed in two weeks of practice with John Nicks. They managed to pull off two outstanding performances, easily besting the new partnership of Natasha Kuchiki and Todd Sand, Sharon Carz and Doug Williams and Calla Urbanski and Mark Naylor for the top spot. In their tenth trip to the U.S. Championships, Susie Wynne and Joseph Druar were the class of the ice dance field, expanding upon their lead in the compulsories with a fine Samba OSP and a sensational free dance to "Hit The Road, Jack" and "Singin' In The Rain" choreographed by Phillip Mills, replete with intricate tap dance sequences. Silver medallists April Sargent and Russ Witherby wisely scrapped a Rachmaninoff free dance that hadn't gone over well with the judges at Skate America and returned to the more traditional, ballroom piece that they had used the year previously. Skating an unconventional free dance to "Fire and Ice" and "Remembering A Heartbeat", Suzy Semanick and Ron Kravette settled for bronze ahead of Jeanne Miley and Michael Verlich.

The name on everybody's lips in Salt Lake City was Christopher Bowman. The defending U.S. Champion and World Silver Medallist arrived in Utah with a purported back injury. As a result, he missed five weeks of training. Many felt that there was much more to the story. Despite rumors that were swirling about his life off of the ice, Bowman opted to compete. After losing in the school figures to Todd Eldredge, Daniel Doran and Paul Wylie, he missed two of his three jumping passes in his original program. He placed fourth and opted to withdraw. Backstage, rumors persisted that the USFSA told him to pull out and offered him a bye to the World Championships because he was the one who earned the spots. Allusions were made to the effect that Bowman might have been told to withdraw because he would have failed drug tests. In a 2008 interview, Bowman claimed, "I never competed while under the influence. I was terrified of that. I was very conscientious of the time frame I would most likely be tested. I knew exactly how long a drug would be in my system before I needed to stop for testing. I never failed a test." Both Eldredge and Wylie gave outstanding performances in the original program, Wylie earning two 6.0's for composition and style for his effort, winning that phase of the event. However, Eldredge held the overall lead entering the free skate. With one of his finest competitive performances, Wylie won the free skate, earning another four 6.0's for composition and style but Eldredge's second-place finish in the free skate was enough to secure him his first U.S. title. Hamden, Connecticut's Mark Mitchell claimed the bronze, ahead of Erik Larson and Daniel Doran. Wylie later recalled, "Eight percent of the competition I won. I was third in the figures and it was a factor system. It was the closest I ever came to winning Nationals. Because of the way the factor system was structured, Chris' points (even though he withdrew) didn't disappear. But it's all water under the bridge! What I remember about those Nationals is that it was kind of do or die for me because the year before I had taken a full load at Harvard and didn't have my best skate at Nationals. I was third and didn't make the World team so I was kind of fighting my way back on the World team again. I felt like 'man, I don't even know if I want to continue skating.' At the end of the day, it was a shame that I didn't win. I skated the last figure - I did the loop - and that was the last figure at the Nationals. They all say 'there was senior competition afterwards for figures' but they were the last sort of real, qualifying figures." Doug Mattis, who placed fifth in the figures in 1990 and eighth overall, recalled it differently, claiming it was he and not Paul who skated that final figure. Jill Trenary was a heavy favourite to win her third national title in Salt Lake City. In the women's compulsory figures, Holly Cook won the final figure, a loop, but Trenary's earlier lead was enough to win the first phase of the competition, with Tonya Harding finishing third, Kristi Yamaguchi fifth and Nancy Kerrigan sixth. In the original program, Trenary fell on a double Axel and was defeated by Yamaguchi and Harding but managed to hold on to her overall lead. The free skate was a different story altogether. Trenary delivered an outstanding performance, earning six 5.9's for technical merit and eight 5.9's and one 6.0 for artistic impression, winning her third and final U.S. title with first-place ordinals from all nine judges. She told reporters, "I've never felt better about myself. This is the best I've ever skated - by far." Though she botched multiple jumps in her free skate, Yamaguchi delivered a technically demanding free skate to hold on to the silver medal, narrowly placing ahead of Kerrigan in the free skate in a five-four split. Held back by her result in the figures, Kerrigan lost out on the bronze medal to Cook. Jeri Campbell placed fifth, Tonia Kwiatkowski sixth and Tonya Harding imploded with a disastrous free skate that featured only one clean triple jump and plummeted to seventh. Harding was very sick all week and was later diagnosed with pneumonia. Before the free skate, she allegedly had a fever of 103 degrees and her doctors told her to withdraw. She elected to compete anyway. She told reporters, "I would have to be dying not to skate. I've worked too hard this year to let it stop right here."

**1990 U.S. CHAMPIONSHIPS (Salt Lake City, UT, February 6-11, 1990)**

Men:

1. Todd Eldredge
2. Paul Wylie
3. Mark Mitchell
4. Erik Larson
5. Daniel Doran
6. Craig Heath
7. Shepherd Clark
8. Doug Mattis
9. Aren Nielsen
10. Larry Holliday

Women:

1. Jill Trenary
2. Kristi Yamaguchi
3. Holly Cook
4. Nancy Kerrigan
5. Jeri Campbell
6. Tonia Kwiatkowski
7. Tonya Harding
8. Dena Galech
9. Tisha Walker
10. Kyoko Ina

Pairs:

1. Kristi Yamaguchi and Rudy Galindo
2. Natasha Kuchiki and Todd Sand
3. Sharon Carz and Doug Williams
4. Calla Urbanski and Mark Naylor
5. Angela Deneweth and John Denton
6. Elaine Asanakis and Joel McKeever
7. Maria Lako and Rocky Marval
8. Paula Visingardi and Jason Dungjen
9. Karen Courtland and David Goodman
10. Jennifer Heurlin and John Frederiksen

Ice Dance:

1. Susie Wynne and Joseph Druar
2. April Sargent and Russ Witherby
3. Suzanne Semanick and Ron Kravette
4. Jeanne Miley and Michael Verlich
5. Elizabeth Punsalan and Jerod Swallow
6. Elizabeth McLean and Ari Lieb
7. Lisa Grove and Scott Myers
8. Amy Webster and Leif Erickson
9. Wendy Millette and James Curtis
10. Ann-Morton Neale and Laurence Shaffer

Junior Winners:

Scott Davis (men)
Alice Sue Claeys (women)
Tristen Vega and Richard Alexander (pairs)
Beth Buhl and Neale Smull (ice dance)

Novice Winners:

Michael Weiss (men's figures)
Ryan Hunka (men's free skating)
Natalie Thomas (women's figures)
Lisa Ervin (women's free skating)

**Canadian Championships.** In February, the Walden and Sudbury Arenas in Sudbury, Ontario played host to the Canadian Championships. 246 skaters skaters competed in the event, including a record 65 from the province of Quebec. The competition was sponsored by the Royal Bank and media coverage was more than ample. Debbi Wilkes, Johnny Esaw and Dan Matheson commentated for CTV, newspapers from Vancouver to Halifax covered the action on their sports pages and even TSN, a fledgling network that didn't know a Lutz from a layback spin, recapped the competition as best as they could on their evening sports recap programs. The event marked the last time that school figures were included in the senior events at the Canadian Championships and with the World Championships being held shortly thereafter in Halifax, the pressure was considerable on all the athletes vying for opportunities to compete on the World stage in their home country. Eight teams battled it out in the senior pairs competition. Defending World Silver Medallists Cindy Landry and Lyndon Johnston won the original program in a five-two split with Isabelle Brasseur and Lloyd Eisler. In their "Darktown Strutters Ball" program, Brasseur and Eisler executed more difficult side-by-side jumps than Landry and Johnston - double Axels in fact - and Eisler expressed frustration that they were ranked below Landry and Johnston. Christine Hough and her partner Doug Ladret sat in third after the pairs original program, also turning in a clean performance. The competition was shaping up to be a potential three-way race. That's not exactly how it played out. Hough fell once; Brasseur twice. With a clean performance, 5.8's across the board for technical merit and three 5.9's and four 5.8's for artistic impression, Cindy Landry celebrated her 18th birthday with a Canadian title win with partner Lyndon Johnston. It would prove to be the first and only senior Canadian title either Landry or Johnston would ever win and it was Johnston's ninth try with his sixth partner. Hough and Ladret took the silver and in a five-four split, Brasseur and Eisler won the bronze over Michelle Menzies and Kevin Wheeler. Only two teams vied for the fours title. The winners, coached by Kerry Leitch, were Hough, Landry, Ladret and Johnston. The retirement of the Garossino's left the ice dance field wide open and the nine teams competing in Sudbury were pulling out all the stops to establish themselves as the next 'it' team. After the compulsory dances, Jo-Anne Borlase and Martin Smith held the lead over Penny Mann and Richard Perkins, Michelle McDonald and Mark Mitchell and Jacqueline Petr and Mark Janoschak. McDonald and Mitchell won the Samba OSP and moved up to second overall. Mann and Perkins dropped to third; Petr and Janoschak remained fourth. Borlase and Smith won the free dance and gold medal with their much-praised program to "Bacchanale" from "Samson and Delilah". With a program to "The Last Emperor" developed with Ellen Burka and Toller Cranston, Petr and Janoschak were second in the free dance and third overall behind McDonald and Mitchell. Mann and Perkins dropped to fourth, ahead of Pamela Watson and Michael Farrington and Jennifer Nocito and Brad Hopkins. Although they placed eighth, Allison McLean and Konrad Schaub turned in one of the most talked about free dances of the event. Coached by Lynn Koper at the Ice Palace Figure Skating Club, they made their senior debut with an edgy, post-apocalyptic program set to music from "Back To The Future", "Antarctica" and "Golden Child". The judges didn't warm up to the survivalist theme or the fact they were skating in tattered and torn rags. By dishing out less than favourable marks to McLean and Schaub, the Canadian judges sent a clear message: what the Duchesnays were doing and what the Canadian judges wanted to see were two different things altogether. In the women's compulsory figures, Margot Bion took the win ahead of Lisa Sargeant, Charlene Wong, Susan MacKay, Diane Takeuchi and Josée Chouinard. Karen Preston sat in a disappointing eighth, still feeling the effects of an ankle injury she had suffered in practice in the fall.

1990 CANADIAN CHAMPIONSHIPS (Sudbury, ON, February 6-11, 1990)

Men:

1. Kurt Browning
2. Elvis Stojko
3. Michael Slipchuk
4. Norm Proft
5. Matthew Hall
6. Jeff Partrick
7. Pierre Gignac
8. Stéphane Yvars
9. Kris Wirtz
10. Patrick Brault

Women:

1. Lisa Sargeant
2. Charlene Wong
3. Josée Chouinard
4. Karen Preston
5. Dianne Takeuchi
6. Margot Bion
7. Annie St. Hilaire
8. Susan MacKay
9. Tanya Bingert
10. Josée Arsenault

Pairs:

1. Cindy Landry and Lyndon Johnston
2. Christine Hough and Doug Ladret
3. Isabelle Brasseur and Lloyd Eisler
4. Michelle Menzies and Kevin Wheeler
5. Stacey Ball and Jean-Michel Bombardier
6. Patricia MacNeil and Cory Watson
7. Melanie Gaylor and Lee Barkell
8. Jodi Barnes and Rob Williams

Ice Dance:

1. Jo-Anne Borlase and Martin Smith
2. Michelle McDonald and Mark Mitchell
3. Jacqueline Petr and Mark Janoschak
4. Penny Mann and Richard Perkins
5. Pamela Watson and Michael Farrington
6. Jennifer Nocito and Brad Hopkins
7. Chantal Loyer and Rock Lemay
8. Allison MacLean and Konrad Schaub
9. Karrie Watchorn and Kent Smyth

Fours:

1. Christine Hough, Cindy Landry, Doug Ladret and Lyndon Johnston
2. Patricia MacNeil, Michelle Menzies, Cory Watson and Kevin Wheeler

Junior Winners:

Sébastien Britten (men)
Jacquie Taylor (women)
Marie-Claude Savard-Gagnon and Luc Bradet (pairs)
Isabelle Labossiere and Mitchell Gould (ice dance)

Novice Winners:

Matthew Knight (men)
Jennifer Prowse (women)
Penny Papaionnou and Raoul LeBlanc (pairs)
Masha Soucy and Louis-Philippe Poirier (ice dance)

Asked about the significance of being the last woman to win the figures at the Canadian Championships, Bion told reporters, "It was quite exciting because it was the last time figures are going to be skated. I've always liked figures, so it's a nice thing to go out doing my best. On the last tracing of my rocker I thought 'last time'. It was kind of sad, actually." Karen Preston's struggles continued in the original program, when she fell on her triple flip combination and touched a hand down on another jump attempt. When she placed sixth in that segment of the event and remained in eighth overall, any chance of reclaiming her National title was over. In a four-three split, Chouinard defeated Sargeant and Diane Takeuchi in the original program and heading into the free skate, Sargeant sat in first overall, followed by Chouinard and Wong. Lisa Sargeant planned an ambitious free skate, including a triple/triple combination and a triple loop. She was also working on the triple Axel in practice at the time. Ultimately, Sargeant managed three triples and two double Axels, her only real mistake being a missed double Salchow. Her marks ranged from 5.4 to 5.7 for both technical merit and artistic impression. The rest of the field unraveled Wong fell on one triple, overrotated another and popped a third into a single. Chouinard had a rough performance, falling three times and leaving the ice in tears. Try as she might, Karen Preston wasn't able to move up to the podium. Sargeant took the gold, Wong the silver and Chouinard the bronze. Sargeant credited her younger sister Kristy for helping instill her with the confidence she needed to achieve her Sudbury victory. Fourteen men competed in Sudbury for three 'golden tickets' to the World Championships in Halifax and the drama leading up to the competition was almost as exciting as the event itself. Norm Proft got a bye through Western Divisionals while nursing a blood infection in his foot. Kurt Browning peaked at the event, throwing in a clean quad late in his program after tripling his first attempt. Then he started breaking in new boots and blades. At the Royal Glenora Club, Michael Slipchuk landed his first quad in practice, witnessed by Kevin Cottam and Mark Schmitke. At the Eastern Divisionals, Elvis Stojko of Richmond trounced the competition with a daring free skating program chock full of triples. David Dore firmly believed there were up to six men who would contend for the three spots on the World team. Jeff Partrick defeated Browning, Matthew Hall, Slipchuk and Proft in the final senior men's school figures competition at Canadians. Although Browning's coach Michael Jiranek expressed great regret at the abolition of figures, in an interview with TSN Browning intimated that he couldn't have been happier to see them go. He did, however, express his intent to continue to practice them as a training tool. Norm Proft stole the show in the original program, skating cleanly to music from *Cabaret*. He won this phase of the competition with marks of 5.4 to 5.6 for technical merit and 5.5 to 5.7 for artistic impression, ahead of Stojko, Slipchuk, Browning and Partrick. Browning, who struggled on both parts of his combination and singled the required double Axel, earned marks ranging from 4.6 to 5.3 for technical merit and four 5.8's and two 5.9's for artistic impression. He held on to the overall lead, but Proft's come-from-behind win only added to the suspense of the final. In the free skate, Stojko landed eight triples, earned five 5.8's, a 5.9 and a 5.7 for technical merit and a standing ovation from the boisterous Sudbury crowd. Browning landed two triple Axels in combination but fell on his quadruple toe-loop attempt, missed two triple toe-loops and singled a triple flip. Browning later referred to the program as "an absolute horror show". The judges were generous, giving him a 5.5, two 5.7's and a 5.8 for technical merit and four 5.8's, two 5.7's and a 5.6 for artistic impression. In a five-two decision, Browning retained his national title on the strength of his second mark and Stojko's poor finish in figures. In a post-skate interview on television with Debbi Wilkes, Browning said, "If anything's going to make me skate good in Halifax or make me hungry to train at home, it will be today." Slipchuk fell on his triple Axel but landed seven other triples to finish third ahead of Norm Proft and Matthew Hall. Kurt Browning and Lisa Sargeant's wins marked the first time since 1966 in Peterborough when Ellen Burka coached champions Donald Knight and Petra Burka, that one coach's students won both the senior men's and women's singles at the Canadian Championships. Following the Championships, a bizarre news story emerged. In Toronto, two teenage sisters watching the CTV broadcast of the competition got into a fight over which skater they thought should win. The younger sister, only fourteen, went to the family's garage, loaded a rifle and fired seven shots into the walls and doors of the house. No one was injured but the girl was charged with mischief endangering life, possession of a dangerous weapon and pointing a firearm.

**World Championships.** In March, Halifax played host to the very first (and to date only) World Championships ever held in Atlantic Canada. Ottawa had also put in a bid to host the event but the CFSA decided to support the Nova Scotia section's bid in 1986. More than 1000 volunteers were recruited and 55 local committees were organized to ensure the event went off without a hitch. Atlantic Canadians were given first dibs on tickets before sales were opened to the rest of the world. All-event packages went for 125 dollars and were completely sold out by May of 1989. The cost of putting on the event was an estimated 2 000 000 dollars, but with 85 000 tickets sold and more than 700 000 dollars of corporate support, a 1 000 000 dollar profit was reported before the event even started. Much of that money stayed in Atlantic Canada, supporting local skating clubs and programs. The main event venue was the 9500-seat Halifax Metro Centre in the city's downtown core but practices and the men's and women's school figures were held across the harbour at the Dartmouth Sportsplex. Over 160 athletes from 26 countries participated, along with 450 media representatives including 22 worldwide broadcasters including the CBC, CBS, BBC, Eurovision, Intervision and NHK. The event's logo was designed by Kathy Kaulbach, which could be seen on a giant billboard by the MacDonald Bridge that read, "Their Feet Will Bring You To Yours!" Rob McCall's mother Evelyn penned wonderful columns on the event for the *Chronicle Herald*. David Dore gave a lecture at the Spring Garden Road Library on how figure skating competitions are judged and what to look for when watching a figure skating competition. More than 3000 square metres of carpet was used at both venues and 672 hours of ice time was booked. 700 corsages were made for special events and 175 000 photocopies of media information were made. The official skate sharpener of the event was an aerospace engineer from Colorado. Stanfield's underwear factory in Truro designed everything from t-shirts to long underwear with the World Championships logo on the flap. Seagull Pewter made souvenir spoons and key chains. The backroom at Irises Flowers Ltd. was bustling with activity from midnight until seven in the morning throughout the event, putting together thousands of bouquets of daffodils, tulips, crocuses, hyacinths and forsythia. Yet, that didn't stop people from complaining. Cranky coaches were annoyed at being housed in different hotels than their skaters. There were passive-aggressive articles from reporters who arrived at their hotels only to find out telephones hadn't yet been hooked up in their rooms or complained about their seating area being too far from the ice. Mayor Ronald Wallace's reception for the international media at the Halifax Sheraton was so poorly attended due to back-to-back Canadian and American team press conferences that all the food ended up being sent to a local soup kitchen. There were empty seats in practices because only all-event ticket holders were permitted to attend practices... and then there was a behind-the-scenes debacle that made front-page news. The CFSA's marketing coordinator Debbie Cameron, in explaining that in the future the CFSA planned to only support bids in cities with larger rinks, made the mistake of telling a *Daily News* reporter that "The event won't be coming back to Halifax." Local reporters took that quote and ran with it and there was some bad blood between the CFSA and LOC organizers as a result. CFSA President Barbara Ryan clarified, "Debbie Cameron does not make that kind of decision - that decision is made by the executive committee... Halifax would be in the running for any competition it bid on... I'm just so sorry there has been a perception left that we are less than appreciative." The Canadian media toted Cindy Landry and Lyndon Johnston as medal contenders but a miss from Johnston on a side-by-side double Lutz late in the pairs original program placed the defending World Silver Medallists completely out of contention in tenth place. Soviet pairs Ekaterina Gordeeva and Sergei Grinkov, Natalia Mishkutenok and Artur Dmitriev and Larisa Selezneva and Oleg Makarov occupied the top three spots after the original program. Although 'G and G' skated a clean and confident program and earned unanimous first-place marks, the Halifax audience deferred its two standing ovations of the pairs original program to the second and third place Soviet teams.

**1990 WORLD CHAMPIONSHIPS (Halifax, NS, March 6-11, 1990)**

Men:

1. Kurt Browning (CAN)
2. Viktor Petrenko (SOV)
3. Christopher Bowman (USA)
4. Grzegorz Filipowski (POL)
5. Todd Eldredge (USA)
6. Petr Barna (CZE)
7. Richard Zander (FRG)
8. Viacheslav Zagorodniuk (SOV)
9. Elvis Stojko (CAN)
10. Paul Wylie (USA)

Women:

1. Jill Trenary (USA)
2. Midori Ito (JPN)
3. Holly Cook (USA)
4. Kristi Yamaguchi (USA)
5. Natalia Lebedeva (SOV)
6. Lisa Sargeant (CAN)
7. Patricia Neske (FRG)
8. Evelyn Großmann (GDR)
9. Surya Bonaly (FRA)
10. Marina Kielmann (FRG)

Pairs:

1. Ekaterina Gordeeva and Sergei Grinkov (SOV)
2. Isabelle Brasseur and Lloyd Eisler (CAN)
3. Natalia Mishkutenok and Artur Dmitriev (SOV)
4. Larisa Selezneva and Oleg Makarov (SOV)
5. Kristi Yamaguchi and Rudy Galindo (USA)
6. Christine Hough and Doug Ladret (CAN)
7. Mandy Wötzel and Axel Rauschenbach (GDR)
8. Radka Kovaříková and René Novotný (CZE)
9. Cindy Landry and Lyndon Johnston (CAN)
10. Peggy Schwarz and Alexander König (GDR)

Ice Dance:

1. Marina Klimova and Sergei Ponomarenko (SOV)
2. Isabelle and Paul Duchesnay (FRA)
3. Maya Usova and Alexandr Zhulin (SOV)
4. Susie Wynne and Joseph Druar (USA)
5. Oksana Grishuk and Evgeni Platov (SOV)
6. Susanna Rahkamo and Petri Kokko (FIN)
7. Jo-Anne Borlase and Martin Smith (CAN)
8. April Sargent and Russ Witherby (USA)
9. Michelle McDonald and Mark Mitchell (CAN)
10. Stefania Calegari and Pasquale Camerlengo (ITA)

*Judge's pin from the 1990 World Championships. Author photograph.*

It was no wonder, as Selezneva and Makarov chose to skate to "Thriller" and "Billie Jean" by Michael Jackson. At the Canadian Championships, Lloyd Eisler was quite vocal in his frustration of placing behind Landry and Johnston in the original program after landing more difficult double Axels. Brasseur and Eisler skated their program perfectly once more, placing a strong fourth and validating Eisler's point that double Axels would be the difference at the Worlds. Christine Hough and Doug Ladret finished seventh after Hough put a hand down on the landing of the side-by-side double Lutz jump. Brasseur and Eisler stole the show in the free skate, bringing down the house with their athletic performance and earning a standing ovation that started before their music even ended. They moved up to take the silver behind Gordeeva and Grinkov, who skated beautifully but had problems on both the side-by-side triple toe-loop and double Axel. Many felt that on that day the Canadians should have won the free skate. Mishkutenok and Dmitriev landed side-by-side triple toe-loops and a throw triple toe-loop, but dropped to third ahead of Selezneva and Makarov and U.S. Champions Kristi Yamaguchi and Rudy Galindo. Canadians Hough and Doug and Landry and Johnston both moved up one spot, to sixth and ninth. Natasha Kuchiki and Todd Sand of the United States finished 11th but stood out as the only pair to choose vocal music, the aria from Puccini's "Madama Butterfly". Two relative unknowns in the men's event, each with their own compelling stories, captured the attention of the Halifax media and audiences. The first was Japan's Tatsuya Fujii, a 24-year-old from Tokyo who had trained for fourteen years to have his shot on the world stage only to graduate from university and accept a job as a trainee at a Japanese television network the same year he finally made the World team. Fujii trained at the Citizen Skating Rink under Shigeo Moriyama, a former competitive swimmer, and received zero funding from the Japanese government for his training costs. His parents couldn't make it to watch his big moment - his father had to work and his mother was in the hospital - and sadly, the Japanese Champion didn't make it out of the original program in what proved to be his first and last shot at stardom. The second skater to garner considerable media attention was Romania's Cornel Gheorghe. The 18-year-old trained in Bucharest in one of only four covered rinks in his country. In December, Gheorghe and coach Gabriela Munteanu were forced to live in horrific conditions at the very rink they trained during the Romanian Revolution which toppled dictator Nicolae Ceaușescu. Munteanu told reporters, "We were scared, very scared. The securitate were killing everyone without thinking. They would have killed us inside the rink as well if they could have told from the lights that we were in there." Gheorghe arrived in Halifax with skates that were falling apart. He had applied to the Romanian government the previous three years for new skates and laces and was turned down every time. The government did spring for flights, food and hotel but Gheorghe and his coach only had 60 dollars apiece in pocket money to see them through their entire two-week trip abroad. Not understanding what pay TV was, Gheorghe blew nine dollars of his money on the first night watching *Batman* in his hotel room. Shocked by his story, both the skating community and the people of Halifax opened their hearts and wallets to help. Paul Wylie's mother took Gheorghe's foot measurements and promised to ship him a badly needed pair of skates. Fran Driscoll, the owner of a local skate shop, supplied him with costumes and material. Montreal skating costume designer Rhona Cantor presented him with skate guards, kit bags and skating outfits. Coaches from 27 countries, led by the Canadian contingent, took up their own collection to assist the talented young skater. The offices of the *Daily News* were inundated with phone calls from locals wondering where they could make donations. Munteanu told reporter Neil Hodge, "We never expected anything like this to happen when we came to Canada. The people in Canada, they helped us so much that I don't know quite what to say. Paul Wylie's mother has done us a great service. It is meaningful to us. My skater has needed new skates for a long time. The way the Canadian people helped us... I can't thank them enough. We will always have beautiful memories of our experience in Halifax. We will never forget all the gifts we received here. Right now, Romania is a poor country, but maybe someday we can have the Worlds and help someone out." Like Fujii, Gheorghe failed to make it out of the original program, but his story resonated with the skating world long after the competition in Halifax ended. Kurt Browning also garnered considerable media attention. The defending World Champion had just won his second Canadian title in Sudbury, but had not skated up to his usual high standard. During a practice in Halifax, he fell and cut his thumb on a triple flip attempt. Predictably, the media went to town with a "Browning Falls" storyline. While Browning aimed to avoid the media whirlwind and focus on training, Christopher Bowman, who had taken five days off after the U.S. Championships to reportedly undergo physiotherapy, was talking to any reporter who would listen. "I'm very ready for the competition but I don't know if I'm ready for Kurt Browning," he told one reporter. "People talk about me being wild and crazy. But I've kind of fallen into the shadow of the Marlboro man." Another top contender dealing with an injury, the Soviet Union's Alexandr Fadeev, withdrew before the event. At the Dartmouth Sportsplex, the men etched out school figures for the final time at the World Championships. Representing the Chinese Taipei, David Liu placed 27th but held the distinction of being the final man to perform a figure at the World Championships.

Grzegorz Filipowski, Petr Barna, Bowman, Todd Eldredge and Paul Wylie. Browning's second-place finish was the highest in figures by a Canadian man at the Worlds since Donald Jackson in 1962. After winning the figures, Zander told reporters, "I'm really happy to be the last world champion in figures, but it's a sad day for me to watch it disappear. It's sad because I can never do this competition again. Nobody likes to see things disappear when they're the champion at it." The men's original program was incredibly well-skated, with seven of the eight top contenders executing at least one triple Axel. Philippe Candeloro and Viacheslav Zagorodniuk both landed a triple Axel/triple toe-loop combination and a solo triple Axel. Browning, skating to the music of Joe Jackson, executed a triple Axel/double toe-loop then turned his second triple Axel into a shaky double. Late in his program, he turned a planned triple toe-loop into a triple Axel. Browning's gutsy move paid off. He earned a standing ovation and technical marks ranging from 5.7 to 5.9 and a perfect 6.0 from Hungarian judge Martha Leces for artistic impression. However, Petrenko's program to "See You Later, Alligator" included a triple Axel/triple toe-loop, triple Axel and double Axel and earned 6.0's for artistic impression from both the Australian and Austrian judges. Browning beat Petrenko in figures; Petrenko beat Browning in the original program and it all came down to the free skate. Petrenko skated first, landing a triple Axel/triple toe-loop combination but popping two triples into doubles and two-footing a triple loop attempt. Eldredge, who had moved up to third after the original program with an outstanding program that featured a clean triple Axel/triple toe-loop combination and a solo triple Axel, took a bad fall on his opening triple Axel but pulled off five other triples. When Browning took the ice for his turn, he was on fire. Though he opted not to attempt a quad, he completed seven triples and had the crowd on its feet before his program was even over. A slew of 5.8's and 5.9's later, he successfully managed to defend his World title in his home country. It was the first time in history that a Canadian man had ever won back-to-back World titles. Petrenko settled for silver ahead of Bowman, who went for broke and won over the crowd but left his coach Frank Carroll less than enthused when he improvised part of his program. Many were impressed with Elvis Stojko, whose athletic free skate brought down the house and helped him leap from a 17th place finish in figures to ninth overall. Zander ended the event in seventh and Canada's third man, Michael Slipchuk, placed 11th. Though he finished only tenth because of a disappointing original program, Wylie landed a triple Axel in his performance and earned a standing ovation from the crowd.

*Kurt Browning. Photo courtesy Sarina Stützer.*

*Viktor Petrenko. Photo courtesy Sarina Stützer.*

*Petr Barna. Photo courtesy Sarina Stützer.*

There were two women the media had their eye on in Halifax and both had an incredible gift for jumping. While half of the media were enthralled with the triple Axels from the reigning World Champion Midori Ito, the other half were eyeing a 16-year-old newcomer on the World stage, Surya Bonaly of France, who reportedly landed several quads in practice. 700 spectators showed up to watch the women's compulsory figures at the Dartmouth Sportsplex. One of the highlights of the entire competition came when Željka Čižmešija of Yugoslavia skated the final figure ever performed at the World Championships. The ice was littered with flowers after her paragraph loop and more than one tear welled up in the eyes of skaters and judges alike when the realization that this was the end of an era dawned upon them. The judges presented Čižmešija with flowers and a box of chocolates and one jovial judge jokingly held up a 6.0 placard. America's Jill Trenary won the figures by a wide margin, followed by Natalia Lebedeva of the Soviet Union, West Germany's Patricia Neske. Midori Ito placed a dismal tenth, all but ruining her chances of defending the World title she had won a year prior in Paris. America's Holly Cook skated the best figures of her life to finish fourth. British judge Vanessa Riley placed her first. The result was a huge shock as her goal was to place in the top ten. Showing a great fight, Ito stole the show and won both the original program and free skate with spectacular performances. Performing a triple Axel that was even better than the one she executed at the Worlds in Paris in 1989, Ito earned a standing ovation in the free skate and perfect 6.0's for technical merit from the Hungarian, Italian and Swiss judges. Unfortunately, Ito's efforts proved to be in vain. Although she placed fifth in the original program and second in the free, the lead Jill Trenary amassed in the figures was more than enough to win the gold. Ito would have needed to place ninth and not tenth in figures and Trenary third or lower in both the short and free for her to win the gold. Kristi Yamaguchi finished ahead of Cook in both the original program and free skate, landing triple Lutzes in both programs. However, Cook's lead in the figures and third-place finish in the original program was enough to win the bronze medal. To Cook's credit, the clean original program she performed to Santa Esmeralda's "Another Cha Cha" was a big crowd-pleaser. Though Natalia Lebedeva won the figures and skated a clean original program, her narrow lead over Trenary and the rest of the field after the original program evaporated in the free skate and she dropped to fifth overall, behind Yamaguchi. Canada's Lisa Sargeant placed a strong sixth; Surya Bonaly ninth with a failed quadruple toe-loop attempt. Future World Champion Yuka Sato ended up 14th in her debut at the senior Worlds. After the event concluded, Jill Trenary told reporters, "It's tough to find the right words to describe how I feel right now... I've wondered for a long time what it would feel like to stand on the medal podium and listen to the anthem. I wasn't sobbing, but a couple of tears started rolling down my cheeks at the end of the anthem." Through a translator, Ito explained, "I tried to make [the comeback] but I just couldn't do it. When I started out in tenth place I never expected to win a silver medal so in that sense I'm happy with finishing in second place. A silver isn't too bad considering the way I began."

*Jill Trenary. Photo courtesy Sarina Stützer.*     *Midori Ito. Photo courtesy Sarina Stützer.*

*Viktor Petrenko. Photo courtesy Sarina Stützer.*

*Kurt Browning. Photo courtesy Sarina Stützer.*

*Viktor Petrenko, Kurt Browning and Christopher Bowman. Photo courtesy Sarina Stützer.*

*Ekaterina Gordeeva and Sergei Grinkov. Photo by A. Raclare Kanal, courtesy Jaya Kanal.*

*The Halifax Metro Centre. Photo courtesy Sarina Stützer.*

*Maya Usova and Alexandr Zhulin. Photo courtesy Sarina Stützer.*

*Marina Klimova and Sergei Ponomarenko. Photo courtesy Sarina Stützer.*

*Isabelle Brasseur and Lloyd Eisler. Photo courtesy Sarina Stützer.*

*Natalia Mishkutenok and Artur Dmitriev. Photo courtesy Sarina Stützer.*

Due to a scheduling mishap, spectators made it to their seats at two in the afternoon to watch the compulsory dances only to find out that the event had started half-hour prior. Once everyone watched the 27 teams weave their way through the Paso Doble and Tango Romantica, the chatter in the stands shifted to speculation as to how long the compulsory dances would stick around after the elimination of the compulsory figures. A rumor was swirling that the ISU planned to cut down the number of compulsory dances to one and force dance teams to skate their compulsory dance and OSP on the same day. Soviets Marina Klimova and Sergei Ponomarenko received rave reviews for their Paso, while the U.S. and Czechoslovakian judges gave Isabelle and Paul Duchesnay marks as low as 5.3. However, in the Tango Romantica the only judge to award the Duchesnays less-than-stellar marks was America's Ron Pfenning. After the marks were tabulated following both dances, Klimova and Ponomarenko were first, their teammates Maya Usova and Alexander Zhulin second and the Duchesnays third. The fourth team to skate in the OSP narrowly averted being disqualified. Fifteen seconds into Monica MacDonald and Duncan Smart of Australia's program, one of MacDonald's blades came loose. The referee allowed them two minutes to repair the skate, but when the clock ran down they still weren't on the ice. The ISU rulebook was consulted and they were allotted additional time to fix the problem. About a minute later they appeared on the ice and skated a strong program, but the judges placed them 24th. Pushing the boundaries once more by skating large sections of the dance separately, the Duchesnays were the only team to earn a standing ovation and the Polish and French judges both awarded them perfect 6.0's for presentation. The audience booed Canadian judge Jane Garden, who gave the Duchesnays their lowest mark, a 5.6. The fact that the 5.6 came from a Canadian judge only fueled the media narrative that the Duchesnays were justified in their decision to leave Canada to represent France, yet Garden had a long reputation for being a conservative marker. Klimova and Ponomarenko received a 6.0 of their own for presentation from Japanese judge Mieko Fujimora. When the marks were tallied, Klimova and Ponomarenko defeated the Duchesnays in the OSP six judges to three and Usova and Zhulin dropped to third. Hungarians Klára Engi and Attila Tóth were just behind the leaders but withdrew before the free dance because Engi twisted her ankle in a fall during the OSP. Many of the earlier teams to skate the free dances in Halifax left strong impressions on the audience. Italians Stefania Calegari and Pasquale Camerlengo injected comedy into the mix, while Canadians Michelle McDonald and Mark Mitchell brought sizzle with their sultry interpretation of "Fever". Oksana Grishuk and Evgeni Platov's "Zorba The Greek" was a big crowd-pleaser. Jo-Anne Borlase and Martin Smith's "Samson and Delilah" was smooth and impressive. As had so often been the case throughout the Duchesnays career, the judges didn't quite know what to do with their training mates, the innovative Finnish team of Susanna Rahkamo and Petri Kokko. Their theatrical Apache tango earned marks ranging from sixth place to 11th from British judge Mary Parry. The first to skate in the final group were Usova and Zhulin. Also skating a Piazzolla tango, they received a spate of 5.7 and 5.8's for an exceptional performance that perhaps on another day would have been good enough for more than bronze. However, it was the next performance - the Duchesnays *Missing* - that mesmerized the Halifax audience, bringing them to their feet with tears in their eyes, their hands sore from clapping and throats raw from cheering. Their standing ovation was the longest of the competition, lasting a full two minutes. The judges responded with 5.8's and 5.9's for technical merit and 6.0's for artistic impression from the American, Bulgarian, Czechoslovakian, French and Polish judges. Klimova and Ponomarenko followed the Duchesnays, skating to "My Fair Lady". They gave an outstanding performance and earned a standing ovation as well. Klimova and Ponomarenko received rows of 5.9's and one perfect 6.0 for artistic impression from Czechoslovakian judge Olga Žáková to finish second in the free dance and first overall ahead of the Duchesnays and Usova and Zhulin. Susie Wynne and Joseph Druar's tap dance number to "Singin' In The Rain" and "42nd Street" was hugely popular with the crowd but only good enough for fourth place marks from the judges. Borlase and Smith moved up to seventh; McDonald and Mitchell to ninth. To this day, people in Halifax who don't even follow skating still get a twinkle in their eye when the 1990 World Championships are brought up. The first words out of their mouth are always... "The Duchesnays". A decade of *Sequins, Scandals and Scandals* came to an end in Halifax. The triumphs and triple Axels continued but the tragedy no one wanted to talk about lingered on.

# A DECADE FOR THE RECORD BOOKS

*MOST PERFECT 6.0s AT THE WINTER OLYMPICS (1980-1990)*

Torvill and Dean – 19
Bestemianova and Bukin – 3
Robin Cousins – 1
Brian Orser – 1
Rosalynn Sumners – 1

*MOST PERFECT 6.0s AT THE WORLD CHAMPIONSHIPS (1980-1990)*

Torvill and Dean - 56
Klimova and Ponomarenko – 15
Bestemianova and Bukin – 14
Midori Ito – 10
The Duchesnays – 7
Katarina Witt - 5
Robin Cousins – 3
Brian Orser – 3
Viktor Petrenko – 2
Kurt Browning - 1
Moiseeva and Minenkov – 1

*MOST PERFECT 6.0s AT THE CANADIAN CHAMPIONSHIPS (1980-1990)*

Brian Orser - 26
Wilson and McCall - 9
Elizabeth Manley - 1

*MOST PERFECT 6.0s AT THE U.S. CHAMPIONSHIPS (1980-1990)*

Brian Boitano – 9
Paul Wylie – 7
Scott Hamilton – 6
Blumberg and Seibert – 5
Jill Trenary - 1

*A WORLD WITHOUT FIGURES (1980-1990)*

A question that often pops up is, "Who would have won the Winter Olympics and World Championships if there were no figures?" The protocols reveal some interesting results.

Winter Olympics:

1980 - Robin Cousins, Denise Biellmann
1984 - Brian Orser, Katarina Witt
1988 - Brian Boitano, Elizabeth Manley

World Championships:

1980 - Robin Cousins, Linda Fratianne
1981 - Scott Hamilton, Denise Biellmann
1982 - Scott Hamilton, Katarina Witt
1983 - Scott Hamilton, Katarina Witt
1984 - Brian Orser, Katarina Witt
1985 - Alexandr Fadeev, Katarina Witt
1986 - Brian Orser, Debi Thomas
1987 - Brian Orser, Katarina Witt
1988 - Brian Orser, Katarina Witt
1989 - Kurt Browning, Midori Ito
1990 - Kurt Browning, Midori Ito

There are some very compelling data points here. Brian Orser would have won four World titles and the Olympic gold medal in 1984. Canada would have had its first Olympic Gold Medallist in women's figure skating since Barbara Ann Scott. Katarina Witt would have won six World titles, not four. Elaine Zayak, who climbed all the way from 7th after the short program to win in 1982, would not have won because of her 10th place short program result. Zayak's figures helped her win the title, as did her free skating.

*Kurt Browning. Photos courtesy Sarina Stützer.*

*Isabelle and Paul Duchesnay. Photo courtesy Sarina Stützer.*

# EPILOGUE

*"People just ignored it because they entitled it at that time 'the gay cancer' and they didn't know what caused it. They thought only homosexuals got it, which was a ridiculous thing. And the press was kind of stifled on it. It wasn't until the mid-80s that the realization hit people that this thing is spreading like wildfire... Thousands and thousands of people could have been saved." - Robert Wagenhoffer, ASW*

AIDS painfully and slowly rocked the figure skating world to its very core in the nineties. Many professional skaters continued to keep their HIV diagnoses a closely guarded secret, as ill-informed immigration and customs regulations didn't allow those affected to cross borders to work.

In February of 1988, Calgary journalist Christie Blatchford was the first mainstream reporter to breach the subject, in a thought-provoking article on homophobia in figure skating, which attributed Dennis Coi's death to an AIDS-related illness. In November of 1991, Halifax reporter Shane Ross penned a candid article about Rob McCall's death. By the following autumn, Brian Pockar's death and John Curry's diagnosis made headlines. Skate The Dream, a star-studded fundraiser in McCall's memory, was organized. The production struggled to find support from the CFSA in the beginning, because officials claimed: "The current publicity about AIDS and skaters [reinforced] the perception that many male skaters are homosexuals, a perception which has hampered recruiting efforts in the past." To ultimately gain the CFSA's nod of approval, Brian Orser and Tracy Wilson had to change the messaging surrounding the event, stressing that AIDS wasn't "a skating problem" but instead "a problem for everyone. As skaters, we can help find a solution."

Skate The Dream ultimately raised over 500 000 dollars. "It's Rob's dream, and he wanted to have a cure for AIDS," Rob's mother Evelyn said. "It's too late for him, but we can do a lot of good with this and we can help a lot of people... I tell everybody, because I think the more we talk about this the more you don't hide it and the more that can be done about it. If you push AIDS into a corner and pretend it'll go away, it won't help. It's no longer a lifestyle disease, you just have to look at it because it can just happen to anybody." Evelyn went on to serve with CARAS, a predecessor to the AIDS Coalition of Nova Scotia, which set up a residence/hospice for people living with HIV/AIDS in North End Halifax.

New York City journalist Filip Bondy's bombshell article on the impact of HIV/AIDS on the skating world broke in mid-November of 1992 and was picked up by The New York Times, The Globe And Mail, The Chronicle Herald, The Ottawa Citizen, The Vancouver Sun and The Montreal Gazette. The following year, Susan Reed penned another highly-read article about the issue for People magazine. In a 1993 interview, American skater Mark Mitchell announced, "AIDS is a skating issue because it's an issue in all walks of life. Everyone should address AIDS. Has it hurt the movie industry? Has it hurt the fashion industry? No. And I don't think it will hurt skating, either. It's a serious problem, and we can't ignore it anymore."

Young men in their prime were dying one after another from a virus few understood and many didn't wish to discuss publicly, and skating associations couldn't turn a blind eye indefinitely. The CFSA quietly began educating skaters about HIV/AIDS in 1991. The USFSA's Sports Medicine Committee published an educational article on AIDS in Skating "as a direct response to the request of the World Team parents" the same year.

As the days and years passed, Skating's obituary columns were perpetually filled with obituaries of young men who died "after a long illness".

As friends, families and partners mourned, they had to endure a parade of newspaper articles extolling the sport's athleticism and masculinity. At best, the campaigns were tone-deaf. At worst, they were a slap in the face to dozens of gay men connected to figure skating who were dying after contracting a virus that few people understood and even less wanted to talk about.

Two Pride flags on display for the first time at the World Championships in Edmonton in 1996 were perhaps a case of too little, too late. In the most tactless way, straight people in positions of power downplayed the issue of HIV/AIDS in skating. CFSA President Doug Steele went so far as to call it "historical non-fiction", at the same time praising straight skaters for being "the farthest from gay you could get." There was also a big push of the narrative that AIDS was a societal issue that wasn't affecting the skating world disproportionately as hard as compared to other sports. These stances, unhelpful at best, did little to celebrate the legacies of a generation of men whose lives ended far too soon.

More than twice as many members of the skating community passed away as a result of AIDS-related illnesses than the Sabena Crash that killed the entire U.S. figure skating team in Belgium in 1961. Nearly every male skater in John Curry's Theatre Of Skating. Olympic Medallists, World Champions, Ice Capades stars, coaches, choreographers, judges, costume designers, writers, builders, brothers, sons, partners and dear friends.

Phil. Douglas. Alastair. Brian. Guy. Michael. Yusuke. Peter. Richard. Paul. John. Todd. Tom. Ian. Greg. Dennis. Larry. Gene. André. Ondrej. Ron. Don. Bobby. René. Tim. John. Tony. Jim. Tommy. Michael. Yusuke. Peter. Rick. Paul. John. Todd. Charlie. David. Rob. Chris. Shaun. Louis. Rubin. Frank. Brian. Tod. Paul. Glenn. John. Bob. Val. Anthony. Robert. Tom. Barry. Jack. Patrick. Frank. Ron. John. Larry. Tony. Daniel. Richard. John. Bob. Ricky. Doug. Billy. Troy. William. Kevin. Bill. Lars. Eddie. Michael. Garry. Ted. Robert. Ronald. Tom. Muri. Bob. Brian. Chris. David. Rolf. Christian. Remember them.

*Rob and Evelyn McCall. Photo courtesy Steve McCall.*

# SOURCES

Every effort has been made to cite all source material in this book. In an effort to make the book as reader-friendly as possible, I refrained from including inline footnotes. Sources are listed below and organized by season. A glossary of abbreviations used can be found at the beginning of the book.

**1979-1980 SEASON**

PEOPLE: Rodnina and Zaitsev: Soviet Life, Vladimir Vatutin, Feb 1980. SK, Anatoli Shelukhin, Nov 1979. Thompson and Maxwell: Interview with Warren Maxwell, August 2017. Figure Skating History: The Evolution of Dance on Ice, Lynn Copley-Graves, 1992. Julie Lynn Holmes: SK, Oct 1979. Ice Capades West Co. Show Roster, Nov 1974.The Protopopovs: NYT, The Associated Press, Sep Sep 1979. SK, Mary Ann Purpura, Nov 1979. SK, Nigel Brown, Dec 1980. BG, Steve Marantz, Jan 6, 1980. SK, May 1980. Moiseeva and Minenkov: Soviet Life, Vladimir Vatutin, Feb 1980. Arnold Gerschwiler: CS, John Hennessy, Dec/Jan 1980/81. Freddy Mésot: HR. The Sault Daily Star, Feb 18, 1942. Cemetery records, Floral Hills Memory Gardens, Tucker, GA. Morris D. Chalfen: SK, Dec 1979. The Skating Scene: The Fact Book of Skating, Arthur R. Goodfellow, 1981. Stanislav Zhuk: Soviet Life, Andrei Batashov, Nov 1979. Fritz Greiger: SK, Jul 1980. Dorothy Glazier Dodson and Stephen Tanner: SK, Jun 1980. Kurt Browning: SK, Jun 1980. Cecilia Colledge and Barbara Wagner and Bob Paul: HR, World Figure Skating Museum and Hall of Fame. AROUND THE WORLD:Australia: SK, Gayna Grant, Jul 1980. Japan: SK, Junko Hiramatsu, Jan 1980.North Korea: HR. Historical Dictionary of Pyongyang, Justin Corfield, 2014. Skating Around The World 1892-1992: The One Hundredth Anniversary History of the International Skating Union, Benjamin T. Wright, 1992. Soviet Union: Soviet Life, Anatoli Shelukhin, Feb 1983. United States: SK, Nov 1979. SK, Ruth L. Jackson, Jul 1980. SK, Brooks Stewart, Oct 1980. BEHIND THE SCENES: Flea and Gorilla Pairs: HR. DS, Feb 17, 1980. International Skating Union, Communication No. 536, 1979.Candid Productions: Skating Around The World 1892-1992: The One Hundredth Anniversary History of the International Skating Union, Benjamin T. Wright, 1992. Figures: CS, June/Jul 1980. Mail-Order Businesses: SK, Nov 1979. SK, Apr 1980. Tours: SK, various 1979-1990. ISU Spring Congress: Skating Around The World 1892-1992: The One Hundredth Anniversary History of the International Skating Union, Benjamin T. Wright, 1992. SHOWS AND TOURS:Ice Capades: San Bernardino Sun, Associated Press, Apr 4, 1980. NYT, John Corry, Jan 24, 1980. Ice Capades Continental Show Roster, 1979. Ice Follies/Holiday on Ice: The Skating Scene: The Fact Book of Skating, Arthur R. Goodfellow, 1981. The Vickie: GM, Oct 26, 1979. Zena Cherry, Apr 3, 1981. Superskates: NYT, Oct 17, 1979. NYT, Nov 13, 1979. Refugee Benefit Show: SK, Jun 1980. Tom Collins Tour: WP, Apr 19, 1980. SK, Mar 1980. Queen's Gala: Fulham Chronicle, Jun 6, 1980. BOOKS AND MAGAZINES: Our Skating Heritage: Our Skating Heritage: A Centenary History of the National Skating Association of Great Britain, 1879-1979, Dennis L. Bird, 1979. The Ice Skating Book: The Ice Skating Book, Robert Sheffield and Richard Woodward, 1980. Choreography & Style for Ice Skaters: Choreography & Style for Ice Skaters", Ricky Harris. SK, Feb 1980. Origins of Ice Dance Music: Origins of Ice Music, Muriel Wald, 1979. SK, Oct 1979. Figure Skating with Carlo Fassi: Figure Skating with Carlo Fassi, Carlo Fassi and Gregory R. Smith, 1980. Ice Dancing Illustrated: Ice Dancing Illustrated, Lorna Dyer, 1979. Interview with Lorna Dyer, Jun 10, 2019. FILMS AND TELEVISION: Dream Weaver: GM, Donn Downey, Nov 20, 1979. GM, May 12, 1980. Joni Mitchell: Shadows and Light, Karen O'Brien, 2001. BBC Christmas Special: Birmingham Daily Post, Dec 24, 1979. Peanuts and ABC Specials: The Art and Making of Peanuts Animation: Celebrating Fifty Years of Television Specials, Charles Solomon, 2012. The Leader-Post, Feb 5, 1982. Audiovisual Materials, Library of Congress, 1981. 5,336 Entertainment Programs, 1936-2012, Vincent Terrace, 2013. The Watcher in The Woods: SK, May 1980. The Big Show: SK, Jul 1980. The Complete Directory to Prime Time Network and Cable TV Shows 1946-Present, Tim Brooks and Earle Marsh, 1999. Bob Hope Special: The Daily Herald, May 26, 1980. SK, Jul 1980. FASHIONS: USFSA Fashion Show: SK, Jerry McGaha, May 1980. MUSIC: Cassettes: CS, Fall 1979. High Bias: The Distorted History of the Cassette Tape, Marc Masters, 2023. ART AND HISTORY: Sky Rink Exhibit: SK, Gisela Roessiger, Jun 1980. COMPETITIONS: World Junior Championships: VF. HR. SK, Mar 1980. SK, Debbie Stoery, May 1980. U.S. Championships: VF. HR. SK, Donna Stone, Feb 1980. Ebony, Lynn Norment, May 1986. Canadian Championships: VF. HR. CS, MG, Nov 10, 1979. GM, Deborah King, Jun 17, 1980. GM, Deborah King, Jun 21, 1980. OC, Jan 25, 1980. GM, Canadian Press, Jan 26, 1980. Anne Keohane Mason and Frank Nowosad, Spring 1980. European Championships: VF. HR. GM, Reuters, Jan 23, 1980. Daily Mirror, Graham Baker, Jan 25, 1980. Daily Mirror, Frank Taylor, Jan 31, 1980. SK, Howard Bass, Mar 1980. DS, Mar 16, 1980. Olympic Games: VF. HR. SK, Oct 1979. Politics Today, Cary Goodman, May/June 1979. Red Deer Advocate, Feb 16, 1980. WP, Thomas Boswell, Feb 16, 1980. GM, Feb 21, 1980. SK, Mar 1980. SK, Mary-Lucile Ager and Howard Bass, Apr 1980. Figure Skating History: The Evolution of Dance on Ice, Lynn Copley-Graves, 1992. World Championships: VF. HR. GM, Mar 10, 1980. GM, Norman Webster, Mar 15, 1980. GM, Norman Webster, Mar 17, 1980. SK, Apr 1980. SK, Howard Bass, May 1980. Figure Skating History: The Evolution of Dance on Ice, Lynn Copley-Graves, 1992.

**1980-1981 SEASON**

PEOPLE: New Professionals/Retirements: HR. Birmingham Mail, February 4, 1980. TP, Nov 7, 1980. The Stage, May 1, 1980. SP, Ice Follies/Holiday on Ice, 1980. ASW, May 1990. Skating Around The World 1892-1992: The One Hundredth Anniversary History of the International Skating Union, Benjamin T. Wright, 1992. Robin Cousins: BBC Archives. Richard Dwyer: Interview with Richard Dwyer, May 2015. Anett Pötzsch/Linichuk and Karponosov: GM, Feb 24, 1981. The Guardian, Sandra Stevenson, Mar 3, 1981. International Jewish Sports Hall of Fame. Carlo Fassi/ Carol Heiss: SK, Apr 1981. Doreen Denny: SK, Apr 1982. Lisa-Marie Allen: SK, Dec 1980. Norris Bowden: Professional Engineers Awards, Past Honorees. TS, Peter Small, Apr 10, 1991. Hall of Fame Inductees: HR. SK, Ruth L. Jackson, Jul 1981. Our Skating Heritage: A Centenary History of the National Skating Association of Great Britain, 1879-1979, Dennis L. Bird, 1979. SK, Feb 1982. Skating in America: The 75th Anniversary History of the United States Figure Skating Association, Benjamin T. Wright, 1996. SK, Benjamin T. Wright, Jan 1982. AROUND THE WORLD: Canada: GM, Oct 1, 1981. A Pocket Guide to Figure Skating in Canada, CFSA Public Relations Department, 1978. GM, Oct 31, 1980. GM, Jun 4, 1981. Reflections on the CFSA, 1887-1990: A History of the Canadian Figure Skating Association, Teresa Moore, 1993. China: CS, Carole Stafford, Oct/Nov 1981. SK, Peter Edwards, Mar 1981. SK, Ian A. Anderson, Jul 81. SK, Gretchen S. Brainerd, Nov 1985. Sport Under Communism: The USSR, Czechoslovakia, The GDR, China, Cuba, James Riordan, 1981. The Second Mark: Courage, Corruption and the Battle for Olympic Gold, Joy Goodwin, 2007. South Africa: SK, Howard Bass, May 1975. The Outside Edge, Rev. Kevin Reynolds, Sep 1989. South Africa 1980/81: Official Yearbook of the Republic of South Africa, South Africa Department of Foreign Affairs and Information, 1981. SK, Jun 1983. ISSA Skating News, Irvine Green. First Fifty Years 1937-1987, Rev. Kevin Reynolds, 1987. United States: SK, Ruth L. Jackson, Dec 1980. SK, Feb 1981. SK, Paul Wylie, Jul 1980. The Skating Scene: The Fact Book of Skating, Arthur R. Goodfellow, 1981. BEHIND THE SCENES: New ISU President: Skating Around The World 1892-1992: The One Hundredth Anniversary History of the International Skating Union, Benjamin T. Wright, 1992. New ISU President: HR. GM, Dick Beddoes, Jan 19, 1980. GM, Oct 31, 1980. New Judging System: SK, Howard Bass, Jan 1981. Amateurism: Skating Around The World 1892-1992: The One Hundredth Anniversary History of the International Skating Union, Benjamin T. Wright, 1992. SHOWS AND TOURS: War of the Worlds: Bay Area Reporter, Jul 3, 1980. Superskates: SK, Nov 1980. SK, Jun 1981. China Shows: CS, Carole Stafford, Oct/Nov 1981. Atami Show: Salt Lake Tribune, Carolyn Monson, May 11, 1990. Tom Collins Tour: SP. GM, Beverley Smith, Mar 10, 1981. SK, Feb 1981. British and European Shows: The Stage, Jan 31, 1980 and Oct 15, 1981. Hull Daily Mail, Pru Clark, May 26, 1981. BOOKS AND MAGAZINES: American Skating World: A Decade of Excellence, 1981-1991, ASW. In Time To Be A Champion: SK, Jan 1979. SK, Mar 1981. FILMS AND TELEVISION: The World of Figure Skating: VF and brochure, courtesy Barb and Donald Jackson. Showtime on Ice: Bennington Banner, Feb 23, 1981. Fantasy Island/Osmond Special: VF. WP, Carla Hall, Dec 23, 1980. To Tell The Truth: VF. FASHION: Le Suit: Hartford Courant, Mar 5, 1981.MUSIC: Skatetape: SK, Jan 1981. ART AND HISTORY: Champions of American Sport: SK, Oct 1981. SK, Dec 1981. COMPETITIONS: World Junior Championships: HR. VF. CS, Michael Cosgrove and Sandra Stevenson, Feb 1981. SK, Peter Edwards, Mar 1981. EJ, Dec 10, 1980. MG, Dec 15, 1980. MacLean's, Bill Glaister, Dec 22, 1980. World Professional Championships: HR. VF. The Press Democrat, Dec 16, 1980. WP, Bart Barnes, Dec 18, 1981. Push Dick's Button: A Conversation on Skating... Dick Button, 2013. The Evening Sun, Dec 13, 1980. The Press Democrat, Dec 16, 1980. Canadian Championships: HR. VF. CS, Michael Cosgrove, Mar/Apr 1981. CHMS, Feb 2, 1981. Press Clippings from CHMS on Microfiche, Halifax Public Library. SK, Frank Nowosad, Jun 1981. GM, Beverley Smith, Jan 27-29 and Feb 2, 1981. 1980 Canadian Figure Skating Team (Media Guide), CFSA, 1980. U.S. Championships: VF. HR. CS, Gloria Williams, May/June 1981. SK, Gloria Williams, Apr 1981. Figure Skating History: The Evolution of Dance on Ice, Lynn Copley-Graves, 1992. Spokane Daily Chronicle, Feb 6, 1981. Lodi News-Sentinel, Feb 6, 1981. Landing It: My Life On and Off The Ice, Scott Hamilton, 1999. Little Winners: Inside The World Of The Child Sports Star, Emily Greenspan, 1983. European Championships: HR. VF. CS, Gertraud Mayer, Apr 1981. SK, Howard Bass and Mary Ann Purpura, May 1981. Torvill & Dean, Facing The Music, Jayne Torvill and Christopher Dean, 1995. World Championships: HR. VF. CS, Frank Nowosad, May/June 1981. SK, Howard Bass, May 1981. GM, Beverley Smith, Mar 2-10, 1981. CH, Mar 5, 1981. Hartford Courant, Feb 27 and Mar 3, 1981. The Record, Mar 6, 1981. The Guardian, Sandra Stevenson, Mar 3, 1981. The Guardian Book of Sport 1981/82, Sandra Stevenson.

## 1981-1982 SEASON

PEOPLE: New Professionals/Retirements: HR. Denise Biellmann: Die Biografie, Denise Biellmann, 2022. NYT, Neil Amdur, Dec 25, 1982. Ogoniok, Ekaterina Makarova, 2005. CS, Dec/Jan 1983. VF courtesy Nova Scotia Sport Hall of Fame. NTV, Aug 8, 2019. Stuttgarter Zeitung, Frank Buchmeier, Feb 2, 2013. Barry Hagan: SK, Barry Hagan, Dec 1981. San Bernardino County Sun, Jul 15 and 17, 1981. UPI Archives, Jul 18, 1981. Herber and Baier: Jan 1982. Peggy Fleming: NYT, George Vecsey, Sep 6, 1981. Women's Sports Foundation Hall of Fame Inductees, Nov 4, 2019. John Curry: The Stage, Oct 22, 1981. Derby Daily Telegraph, Aug 28, 1981. Screen Actors Guild Awards, Nominees and Recipients. Norman Mackie Scott: HR, MG, Oct 6, 1981. Canadian Expeditionary Force (CEF) First World War personnel records, Government of Canada Archives. Torvill and Dean: Liverpool Daily Post, Nov 24, 1981. SI, Bob Ottum, Nov 7, 1983. Donald B. Cruikshank: HR, CS, July/Aug 1982. Linda Fratianne: Des Moines Register, Dec 16, 1982. CT, Dec 22, 1983. Sonja Currie Jacobson: HR, CH, Nov 23, 1981. Scott Hamilton: HR, WP, Angus Phillips, Jan 29, 1982. Pierre Baugniet: HR, Bulletin des Assurances, May/Jun 1968. Blog, Matthias Milders, 2022. Mitsuru Matsumura: SK, Junko Hiramatsu, Mar 1982. Tracey Wainman: GM, Dec 15, 1981. Tenley Albright/Dorothy Hamill: BG, Dec 3, 1981. NYT, Leslie Bennetts and Dorothy J. Gaiter, Dec 31, 1981. Peter Dunfield: OC, May 28, 2014. PSA Coaches Hall of Fame, Professional Skaters Association. Anne Ewan: Orphan obituary clipping, author's files. Irina Rodnina: Skating Around The World 1892-1992: The One Hundredth Anniversary History of the International Skating Union, Benjamin T. Wright, 1992. Edwin Mosler: Bridgeport Post, Oct 3, 1975. NYT, Dorothy J. Gaiter, Mar 21, 1982. SK, May 1982. Dorothy Hamill: On and Off The Ice, Dorothy Hamill and Elva Oglanby Clairmont, 1983. Black Ice: The Life and Death of John Curry, Elva Oglanby, 1995. Clarence Hislop: SK, Jul 1982. Legends of Australian Ice, Ross Carpenter. Brian Pockar: GM, Zena Cherry, May 3, 1982. Skate Canada Hall of Fame. Everett McGowan: The Skating Scene: The Fact Book of Skating, Arthur R. Goodfellow, 1981. SK, Jul 1982. Herma Szabo: HR. SI, Dec 26, 1983. SK, Benjamin T. Wright, 1983. Dr. James Koch/Armand Perren: Skating Around The World 1892-1992: The One Hundredth Anniversary History of the International Skating Union, Benjamin T. Wright, 1992. SK, Oct 1982. The Independent, Dennis L. Bird, Jul 6, 1993. The Queen: A Decade of Excellence, 1981-1991, ASW. The London Gazette, Jun 11, 1982. The Independent, Dennis L. Bird, Dec 24, 2004. Zhenhua Bao and Xu Zhaoxiao: SK, Ian A. Anderson, Jul 1981. AROUND THE WORLD: Canada: Reflections on the CFSA, 1887-1990: A History of the Canadian Figure Skating Association, Teresa Moore, 1993. Japan: SK, Junko Hiramatsu, Mar 1982. LAT, Gary Klein, Feb 22, 2002. SK, Theresa Weld Blanchard, Apr 1936. SK, Betty Ann Bagley, Apr 1982. Prince Ice World History, Seibu Holdings. United States: SK, Ruth L. Jackson, Jul 1981. Skating in America: The 75th Anniversary History of the United States Figure Skating Association, Benjamin T. Wright, 1996. BEHIND THE SCENES: Anniversaries: HR. VF. Skating Around The World 1892-1992: The One Hundredth Anniversary History of the International Skating Union, Benjamin T. Wright, 1992. Pacific Championship/'B' Rounds and Country-Swapping: Skating Around The World 1892-1992: The One Hundredth Anniversary History of the International Skating Union, Benjamin T. Wright, 1992. New Logo for Worlds: SK, Jan 1982. Ban on Triple Jumps/New Precision Guidelines: SK, Ruth L. Jackson, Dec 1981. Skating in America: The 75th Anniversary History of the United States Figure Skating Association, Benjamin T. Wright, 1996. Pro-Skate tour: HR. VP. CS, Nov/Dec 1982. Jump Tender: SK, Nov 1981. THE AIDS EPIDEMIC: AIDS Epidemic: A Timeline of HIV and AIDS, U.S. Department of Health & Human Services. MMWR Weekly, June 5, 1981. NYT, Lawrence K. Altman, May 11, 1982. SHOWS AND TOURS: Walt Disney's World on Ice: The Skating Scene: The Fact Book of Skating, Arthur R. Goodfellow, 1981. Streatham Gala: Aberdeen Press and Journal, Nov 14, 1981. Superskates: NYT, Judy Klemesrud, Nov 20, 1981. United Press International, Glenne Currie, Sep 18, 1981. The Nutcracker: SP. San Francisco Examiner, Dec 17, 1981. Harrah's Show: Oakland Tribune, Feb 28, 1982. ISU European Tour: The Guardian Book of Sport 1982/83, Sandra Stevenson. Birmingham Mail, Mar 15, 1982. The Stage, Jun 17, 1982. Huddersfield Daily Examiner, May 13, 1982. Leicester Daily Mercury, Mar 18, 1982. FILMS AND TELEVISION: Stars on Ice: VF. Orphan newspaper articles by Evan Leibovitch and Jack Miller, courtesy Diana Flynn. EJ, Aug 9, 1980. GM, Maya Gallus, Apr 16, 1983. Piratensender Powerplay: Schweizer Illustrierten, Nadine Bauer and Denise Biellmann, Nov 7, 2011. Perry Como's Canadian Christmas: VF. John Curry Skates Peter and The Wolf and Other Dances: VF. From Concept to Curtain Call: SK, Feb 1982. Strawberry Ice: VF. GM, Hester Riches, Mar 15, 1982. GM, Rick Groen, Apr 18, 1983. Mister Rogers' Neighborhood: VF. MUSIC: Stephenson Cassette Music Library: SK, Nov 1981. ART AND HISTORY: New Exhibits at Museum: SK, Pat Cataldi, Dec 1981. Gillis Grafström Collection: SK, May 1982. COMPETITIONS: World Junior Championships: HR. VF. CS, Barbara Graham and Elizabeth Manley, Feb 1982. SK, Feb 1982. SK, Debbie Stoery, Mar 1982. GM, Dec 19 and 21, 1981. World Professional Championships: HR. VF. The Evening Sun, Dec 17, 1981. Arizona Republic, Dec 18, 1981. Ticket Stub, Smithsonian Institute. U.S. Championships: HR. VF. SK, Feb 1982. SK, Ian A. Anderson, Feb 1982. Landing It: My Life On And Off The Ice, Scott Hamilton, 1999. SK, Mrs. R. Sanders Miller, May 1952. Canadian Championships: HR. VF. CS, Donald Jackson, Frank Nowosad, Barbara Graham and Greg Young, Apr 1982. GM, Beverley Smith, Jan 28-Feb 1, 1982. Orser: A Skater's Life, Brian Orser and Steve Milton, 1988. Thumbs Up!: The Elizabeth Manley Story, Elizabeth Manley and Elva Oglanby, 1989. European Championships: HR. VF. CS, Howard Bass, Mar/Apr 1982. SK, Howard Bass, Mar 1982. GM, Feb 6, 1982. Jumpin' Joe: The Jozef Sabovčík Story, Jozef Sabovčík and Lynda D. Prouse, 1998. Nottingham Recorder, Feb 11, 1982. World Championships: HR. VF. CP. CS, Jim Proudfoot, Barbara Graham, Howard Bass, John Hennessy and Sandra Stevenson, May/June 1982. SK, Apr 1982. SK, Howard Bass, May 1982. GM, Jeffrey Simpson, Mar 10-15, 1982. Daily Mirror, Mar 11, 13 and 19, 1982. TS, Mar 5, 1982. The Guardian, Sandra Stevenson, Mar 10, 1982.

## 1982-1983 SEASON

PEOPLE: New Professionals/Retirements: HR. The Manleywoman SkateCast, Dec 18, 2007. The Pantagraph, Oct 19, 1982. Der Standard, Birgit Riezinger, Jan 7, 2015. Sandwell Evening Mail, Oct 6, 1982. GM, Beverley Smith, Mar 4, 1985. Бизнес-журнáл, Marina Badina, Jan 18, 2005. Peggy Fleming/Dick Button: Ashbury Park Press, Jan 21, 1983. André Calame: HR. IRS, Dennis L. Bird, Feb 1983. Bestemianova, Bukin and Bobrin: The Ice Trio, Natalia Bestemianova, Andrei Bukin and Igor Bobrin. Kira Ivanova: Одиночное катание. Смерть фигуристки, 2003. B. Valiev, Dec 23, 2006. Elaine Zayak: SK, Mar 1983. Paul Feigay: NYT, Mar 2, 1983. SK, Jun 1983. George H. Browne and Eugene Turner: SK, Dec 1983. SK, Libby Slate, Jun 1983. Harry N. Keighley: CT, May 8, 1983. Skating in America: The 75th Anniversary History of the United States Figure Skating Association, Benjamin T. Wright, 1996. John Nicks/Yvonne Littlefield: SK, Jul 1983. George T. Yonekura: SK, John R. Shoemaker, Oct 1983. National Archives, Records About Japanese Americans Relocated During World War II, created 1988-1989, documenting the period 1942 – 1946. AROUND THE WORLD: Canada: SK, Jul 1983. Reflections on the CFSA, 1887-1990: A History of the Canadian Figure Skating Association, Teresa Moore, 1993. Soviet Union: Soviet Life, Anatoli Shelushin, Feb 1983. Sweden: History, Stockholms Allmänna skridskoklubb (SASK). Correspondence with Lennart Månsson, Dec 4, 2022. United Kingdom: IRS, February 1983. United States: SK, Dec 1982. SK, Jul 1983. Skating in America: The 75th Anniversary History of the United States Figure Skating Association, Benjamin T. Wright, 1996. BEHIND THE SCENES: New ISU Members: Skating Around The World 1892-1992: The One Hundredth Anniversary History of the International Skating Union, Benjamin T. Wright, 1992. Rock 'N Roll OSP: SK, Lawrence Demmy and ISU Ice Dance Committee, Jul 1982. Smoking: A Decade of Excellence, 1981-1991, ASW. THE AIDS EPIDEMIC: AIDS Epidemic: A Timeline of HIV and AIDS, U.S. Department of Health & Human Services. MMWR Weekly, Mar 4, 1983. NYT, Robert Pear, May 25, 1983. Phil Romayne: Genealogical Research. Correspondence from Jim Hendricks. National Ice Skating Guide, 1946, 1948, 1961, 1965, 1966. Daily News (NY), Jan 11, 1970. Interview With Cathy Steele. February 16, 2016. SHOWS AND TOURS: Superskates: NYT, Malcolm Moran, Nov 11, 1982. NYT, Nov 15, 1982. SK, Jun 1986. Torvill and Dean Shows: IRS, Enid G. Lowe, Feb 1983. The Stage, Dec 2, 1982. Paradise on Ice: Daily News (NY), Mar 15, 1983. Salt Lake Tribune, Carolyn Monson, May 11, 1990. Ice at Radio City Music Hall: SP, Feb 10, 1983. Tom Collins Tour: SP. SK, Jan 1983. FILMS AND TELEVISION: Television Specials: VF. TS, Sid Adilman, Oct 30, 1985. Indianapolis Star, Jan 8, 1983. The Courier-Journal, Jul 9, 1983. Daily News, Dec 7, 1982. Kentish Express, Jan 22, 1982. Six Weeks: A Decade of Excellence, 1981-1991, ASW. Curtains: VF. A Cut Below: A Celebration of B Horror Movies, 1950s-1980s, Scott Drebit, 2024. The Terror Trap, Peter Simpson, Aug 2004. Skating Now and Then: SK, Jun 1983. FASHION: Trends: VF. SK, Dec 1983. Robin Cousins' Costume: SK, Pat Cataldi, Jan 1983. ART AND HISTORY: Blumberg and Seibert Skate Art: SK, Jan 1983. Beauty, Fantasy, and Fun on Ice: SK, Oct 1983. COMPETITIONS: World Junior Championships: HR. VF. CS, Barbara Graham and Marc Ferland, Feb/Mar 1983. IRS, Alexandra Stevenson, Feb 1982. SK, Keith Lichtman, Mar 1983. SK, Ian A. Anderson, Jul 1983. GM, Beverley Smith, Nov 12, 2001. Skating Around The World 1892-1992: The One Hundredth Anniversary History of the International Skating Union, Benjamin T. Wright, 1992. World Professional Championships: HR. VF. A Decade of Excellence, 1981-1991, ASW. The Evening Sun (Baltimore), Dec 16, 1982. The York Dispatch, Dec 18, 1982. Canadian Championships: HR. VF. A Decade of Excellence, 1981-1991, ASW. CS, Anne Mason, Beverley Smith, Michael Cosgrove and Barbara Graham, Feb/Mar 1983. SK, Frank Nowosad, Apr 1983. GM, Beverley Smith, Feb 3-8, 1983. OC, Martin Cleary, Feb 5 and 7, 1983. PJ Kwong and Elizabeth Manley, Open Kwong Dore podcast, Dec 2013. Reflections on the CFSA, 1887-1990: A History of the Canadian Figure Skating Association, Teresa Moore, 1993. Orser: A Skater's Life, Brian Orser and Steve Milton, 1988. U.S. Championships: HR. VF. A Decade of Excellence, 1981-1991, ASW. CS, Vicki Fassinger, Feb/Mar 1983. SK, Mar 1983. SK, Susan Johnson, Apr 1983. GM, Feb 7, 1983. Interview with Judy Sladky, Apr 15, 2020. CT, Feb 2, 1983. Landing It: My Life On And Off The Ice, Scott Hamilton, 1999. SI, E.M. Swift, Feb 14, 1983. European Championships: HR. VF. CS, Howard Bass, Feb/Mar 1983. SK, Mar 1983. SK, Howard Bass, Mar 1983. Katarina-Witt.de, Katarina Witt, 2017. Figure Skating History: The Evolution of Dance on Ice, Lynn Copley-Graves, 1992. Jumpin' Joe: The Jozef Sabovčík Story, Jozef Sabovčík and Lynda D. Prouse, 1998. GM, Feb 4, 1983. World Championships: HR. VF. SK, Apr 1983. SK, Howard Bass and Ralph Routon, May 1983. SK, Frank Nowosad, Jul 1983. GM, Zena Cherry, Feb 26, 1983. GM, Michael Cosgrove, Mar 8- 11, 1983. GM, Beverley Smith, Mar 17, 1983. Time, Alana Abramson, Feb 20, 2018. NYT, Mar 9, 1983. SI, Bob Ottum, Mar 21, 1983. Who's Who in International Sports, David Emery, 1983.

**1983-1984 SEASON**

PEOPLE: New Professionals/Retirements: HR. VF. The Ice Trio, Natalia Bestemianova, Andrei Bukin and Igor Bobrin. Team, Wheaton Ice Skating Academy. My Sergei: A Love Story, Ekaterina Gordeeva and E.M. Swift, 1996. The Millville Daily, Dec 20, 1985. Nottingham Evening Post, Dec 28, 1983. The Stage, Jan 12, 1984. Gustave Lussi Dinner: SK, Jun 1984. Alexia Bryn: Correspondence with Hans Martin Farstad, Skøytemuseet, August 21, 2016. Weddings: SK, Nov 1983. Mary Rose Thacker: HR. Skate Canada Hall of Fame. Canada's Ice Dance Theatre, Ron Vincent. John Curry: Burton Daily Mail, May 6, 1983. M. Bland Jameson: The Long Day 1883-1983, M. Bland Jameson, 1983. Our Skating Heritage: A Centenary History of the National Skating Association of Great Britain, 1879-1979, Dennis L. Bird, 1979. SK, Nov 1983. Scott Hamilton: The Millville Daily, Mar 29, 1984. Eva Pawlik: Interview with Dr. Roman Seeliger, July 15, 2015. Bobby Beauchamp/Debi Thomas: HR. SK, Ryan Stevens, Feb 2022. SK, Libby Slate, Jul 1984. Lawrence Demmy: The London Gazette, Dec 30, 1983. WS, Pete McMartin, Feb 25, 1988. OC, Martin Cleary, Feb 14, 1992. Torvill & Dean, John Hennessy, 1984. Len Seagrave: Orphan obituary clipping, author's files. Harrow Observer, Jan 5, 1973. Our Skating Heritage: A Centenary History of the National Skating Association of Great Britain, 1879-1979, Dennis L. Bird, 1979. Ollie Haupt Jr.: SK, Apr 1984. Betty Callaway: The London Gazette, Jun 16, 1984. The Independent, Sandra Stevenson, Jul 9, 2011. Hall of Fame Inductees: SK, Oct 1985. AROUND THE WORLD: Canada. CS, Winter 1984. GM, Philip King, Jan 26, 1985. 1983. Reflections on the CFSA, 1887-1990: A History of the Canadian Figure Skating Association, Teresa Moore, 1993. Mexico: SK, Nov 1983. Romania: History of Federatia Romana de Patinaj, 1999. BEHIND THE SCENES: Soviet Entries At Fall Internationals: TR, Sandra Stevenson, Fall 1983. GM, Apr 12, 1980. ISU Congress: Skating Around The World 1892-1992: The One Hundredth Anniversary History of the International Skating Union, Benjamin T. Wright, 1992. SK, Jul 1984. Zayak Rule: Dec 1983. Retirement Age: Skating Around The World 1892-1992: The One Hundredth Anniversary History of the International Skating Union, Benjamin T. Wright, 1992.THE AIDS EPIDEMIC: AIDS Epidemic: A Timeline of HIV and AIDS, U.S. Department of Health & Human Services. MMWR Weekly, American Journal of Public Health, Oct 2013. Orphan obituary clipping, Brian Jones. NYT, Philip Shenon, Oct 1, 1983. KQED, Amanda Stupi, Jun 3, 2022. All Things Considered (NPR), Joe Wright, May 8, 2006. SHOWS AND TOURS: Symphony on Skates: SK, Mar 1985. Precision Meets Hockey: CS, Winter 1984. Superskates: SK, Mar 1984. NYT, Oct 23, 1983. Electric Ice: Robin Cousins: SP, Electric Ice. The Authorized Biography, Martha Lowder Kimball, 1998. The Stage, May 3, 1984. Fulham Chronicle, Aug 26, 1983. Home News, Philip Key and Carolyn Fleming, Jun 14, 1984. The Stage, Oct 18, 1984. Symphony on Ice: VF. Royal Albert Hall Archives. CH, Oct 14, 1983. The Best of Torvill and Dean/Tour: VF. Sunday Mirror, Apr 15, 1984. Nottingham Evening Post, May 2, 1984. Aberdeen Evening Express, May 14, 1984. The Canberra Times, Apr 13, 1984. GM, May 11, 1984. Tom Collins Tour: SP. SK, Feb 1984. BOOKS AND MAGAZINES: Dorothy Hamill Book: Albany Democratic-Herald, Oct 28, 1983. NYT, Bestsellers, Nov 20, 1983. BBC Book of Skating/The Skater's Handbook: Reading Evening Post, Jan 20, 1984. SK, Mar 1984. Death Spiral: Death Spiral: Oakland Tribune, May 20, 1984. A Decade of Excellence, 1981-1991, ASW. LAT, Jan 14, 1994. Muppet Magazine: Muppet Magazine, Winter 1984. Canadian Skater: CS, Winter 1979. Reflections on the CFSA, 1887-1990: A History of the Canadian Figure Skating Association, Teresa Moore, 1993. FASHION: Fashions: CS, Winter 1984. Around the Ice in Eighty Years: An Irreverent Memoir by an Accidental Champion, Courtney Jones and Helen Cox, 2021. NYT, Neil Amdur, Feb 5, 1984. Figure Skating History: The Evolution of Dance on Ice, Lynn Copley-Graves, 1992. FILMS AND TELEVISION: Guinness World Records Show: Aberdeen Evening Express, Nov 16, 1983. Romeo and Juliet on Ice: VF. GM, Beverly Bowen, May 10, 1983. GM, Sharon Clark, Dec 17, 1983. The Lakeland Ledger, Nov 25, 1983. Hart to Hart/Other TV Shows: VF. A Decade of Excellence, 1981-1991, ASW. The Golden Age of Canadian Skating: VF. GM, Donald Martin, Mar 10, 1984. COMPETITIONS: World Junior Championships: HR. VF. SK, Jan 1984. SK, Lois Huffman, Feb 1984. World Professional Championships: HR. VF. A Decade of Excellence, 1981-1991, ASW. The Evening Sun, Dec 8, 1983. ASW, Dec 1993. Lansing State Journal, Dec 18, 1983. U.S. Championships: HR. VF. A Decade of Excellence, 1981-1991, ASW. SK, Feb 1984. SK, Mar 1984. TR, Sandra Stevens, New Englands Issue 1983/84. NYT, Neil Amdur, Jan 18, 22 and Feb 5, 1984. U.S. Figure Skating, Ryan Stevens, May 16, 2022. Landing It: My Life On And Off The Ice, Scott Hamilton, 1999. Canadian Championships: HR. VF. GM, Beverley Smith, Jan 7, 10-16 and Feb 3, 1984. SK, Frank Nowosad, Feb 1984. CS, Winter 1984. European Championships: HR, VF. SK, Howard Bass, Feb 1984. GM, Jan 11-14, 1984. Belfast News-Letter, Jan 14, 1984. Figure Skating History: The Evolution of Dance on Ice, Lynn Copley-Graves, 1992. Olympic Games: HR. VF. SK, Mar 1984. SK, Apr 1984. GM, Feb 10-19, 1984. MacLean's, Feb 6, 1984. SI, Bob Ottum, Mar 1983. SI, Feb 20, 1984. The Gettysburg Times, Feb 16, 1984. Interview with Gary Beacom, Oct 12, 2013. MG, Jack Todd, Jan 27, 1988. The Manleywoman SkateCast, Allison Manley and Norbert Schramm, Nov 23, 2012. U.S. Figure Skating, Ryan Stevens, May 16, 2022. Landing It: My Life On And Off The Ice, Scott Hamilton, 1999. World Championships: HR. VF. A Decade of Excellence, 1981-1991, ASW. SK, Apr 1984. SK, Howard Bass, May 1984. GM, Beverley Smith and Nora McCabe, Mar 7-8 and 17-27, 1984. OC, Mar 19 and 22, 1984. The Independent Record, Mar 21, 1984. Cracked Ice - Figure Skating's Inner World, Sonia Bianchetti Garbato, 2004. Figure Skating History: The Evolution of Dance on Ice, Lynn Copley-Graves, 1992. Reflections on the CFSA, 1887-1990: A History of the Canadian Figure Skating Association, Teresa Moore, 1993. The Manleywoman SkateCast, Allison Manley and Norbert Schramm, Nov 23, 2012.

**1984-1985 SEASON**

PEOPLE: New Professionals/Retirements: VF. HR. Deseret News, Ivan M. Lincoln, Dec 2, 1988. The Leader-Post, Jan 24, 1985. MG, Oct 26, 1984. Press and Sun-Bulletin, Oct 15, 1984. Еженедельник "Аргументы и Факты, May 21, 2008. Birmingham Daily Post, May 15, 1984. Sandwell Evening Mail, Sep 10, 1985. HR. SP, Torvill & Dean Tour. Vivi-Anne Hultén: SK, Vivi-Anne Hultén, Oct 1984. Valova and Vasiliev/Klimova and Ponomarenko: Soviet Life, Jun 1985. NYT, Michael Janofsky, Mar 13, 1991. Michael McGean: HR. Dartmouth Alumni Magazine, Jun/Jul 1984. Charlotte: SK, Richard Stephenson and Benjamin T. Wright, Jul 1985. Ice-Skating: A History, Nigel Brown, 1959. The Skating Scene: The Fact Book of Skating, Arthur R. Goodfellow, 1981. Torvill and Dean: Burton Daily Mail, Nov 20, 1984. Born and Schönborn: SK, Frank Nowosad, Feb 1985. Figure Skating History: The Evolution of Dance on Ice, Lynn Copley-Graves, 1992. Jeanne Chevalier: HR. Au Fil Du Temps, Henri Rousseau, January 2013. Georg Häsler/Howard Craker: ISU Communication No. 625, 1985. SK, Mar 1985. Skating Around The World 1892-1992: The One Hundredth Anniversary History of the International Skating Union, Benjamin T. Wright, 1992. Georges Gautschi: HR. Letter from Dr. Georges Gautschi to USFSA, January 4, 1931. Neue Zürcher Zeitung, Feb 19, 1985. Linichuk and Karponosov: Philadelphia Inquirer, Frank Fitzpatrick, Feb 9, 2010. Marcus Nikkanen/Norman A. Falkner/Svea Norén/Roger Wickson: HR. Yle Uutiset, Arto Teronen, Sep 20, 2013. Star-Phoenix, Sep 3, 2005. The Golden Age of Canadian Figure Skating, David Young, 1984. Svenskt kvinnobiografiskt lexikon, Lennart K. Persson and Alexia Grosjean, Mar 8, 2018. Province of British Columbia Department of Health, Division of Vital Statistics, Certificate of Death of Roger Wickson, 1985. Starbuck and Shelley: SK, Libby Slate, Oct 1984. Underhill and Martini: GM, Apr 25, 1985. Kenneth Zeller: GM, Jun 26, 1985. TS, Jan 26, 1986. GM, Alanna Mitchell, May 29, 2004. AROUND THE WORLD: Canada: Reflections on the CFSA, 1887-1990: A History of the Canadian Figure Skating Association, Teresa Moore, 1993. East Germany: Das Bundesarchiv, Stasi-Unterlagen Archiv - Geheimakte Doping. The East German Sports System: Image and Reality, Barbara Carol Cole, 2000. Barbara Carol Cole interview with Anett Pötzsch-Rauschenbach, June 26, 1997. CS, Anne Keohane, Dec/Jan 1978. The Guardian, Katrin Kanitz, Sep 9, 2016. CNN, Matt Majendie and Laura Goehler, Nov 13, 2015. PBS, Secrets of The Dead - Doping For Gold, June 13, 2011. DS, Nov 22, 1992. The Guardian, Nov 4, 2001. DS, Alexander Osang, April 28, 29, 2002. United States: Skating in America: The 75th Anniversary History of the United States Figure Skating Association, Benjamin T. Wright, 1996. SK, Jul 1985. BEHIND THE SCENES: Quickstep OSP: SK, May 1984. THE AIDS EPIDEMIC: AIDS Epidemic: AIDS Epidemic: A Timeline of HIV and AIDS, U.S. Department of Health & Human Services. NYT, Frank Rich, Mar 11 and Apr 22, 1985. Frank Tyler: Bay Area Reporter, Jun 11, 1992. SK, Nov 1962. Douglas J. Norwick: Theatre World, 1984-1985 Season, John Willis, 1986. SK, Apr 1958. SK, Mar and Apr 1961. SK, Mar 1962. SK, Feb 1979. NYT, Jennifer Dunning, Dec 23, 1977. SP, Ice Dancing, 1978. Robert John Quinn's Memorial Books, The History Project (Boston and Massachusetts LGBTQ+ Archive). Charlie Copehaver: SK, Jun 1991. Colorado Springs Gazette Telegraph, Apr 3, 1991. Interview with Mark Motiff, Apr 11, 2021. SK, Lois C. Miller, Feb 1976. SK, Jan 1979. SK, Feb 1979. HOMOPHOBIA: Homophobia: CT, Jan 21, 1984. Kansas City Times, Feb 6, 1984. A Decade of Excellence, 1981-1991, ASW. SHOWS AND TOURS: The Met/Kennedy Center: SP. UPI Archive, Frederick M. Winship, Jul 24, 1984. NYT, Jennifer Dunning, Jul 27, 1984. NYT, Anna Kisselgoff, Jul 28, 1984. WP, Pamela Kessler, Aug 17, 1984. Superskates: NYT, George Vecsey, Nov 18, 1984. Torvill and Dean Tour: National Library of New Zealand. Press, March 18 and June 14, 1985. Ice Theatre of New York: Interview with Moira North, April 14, 2021. NYT, Anna Kisselgoff, May 22, 1988. Special Olympics Performances: SK, Jun 1985. BOOKS AND MAGAZINES: Queen Of Ice, Queen of Shadows: Daily News (NY), Apr 14, 1985. BG, Fanny Howe, May 30, 1985. TR, Fall 1985. FILMS AND TELEVISION: A Christmas Dream: Historical Dictionary of African American Television, Kathleen Fearn-Banks, Anne Burford-Johnson, 2014. ISU Film/Music: SK, Nov 1984. SK, Feb 1985. ART AND HISTORY: Flood at Museum: SK, Oct 1984. COMPETITIONS: World Junior Championships: HR. VF. SK, Jan and Feb 1985. GM, Dec 12-15, 1984. World Professional Championships: HR. VF. A Decade of Excellence, 1981-1991, ASW. The Evening Sun, Dec 13 and 14, 1984. ASW, Dec 1993. European Championships: HR. VF. SK, Mar 1985. SK, Howard Bass, Apr 1985. Huddersfield Daily Examiner, Feb 8, 1985. Liverpool Echo, Feb 9, 1985. U.S. Championships: HR. VF. Kansas City Times, Mike McKenzie, January 28 and Feb 1, 1985. Kansas City Star, Jo-Ann Barnas and Gib Twyman, January 28 and 31, Feb 1, 1985. SK, Mar 1985. NYT, Feb 2, 1985. GM, Feb 4, 1985. The Sunday Observer-Dispatch, Feb 3, 1985. Figure Skating History: The Evolution Of Dance On Ice, Lynn Copley-Graves, 1992. Canadian Championships: HR. VF. GM, Beverley Smith, Feb 4-13, 1985. MG, Steve Milton, Feb 7, 9 and 11, 1985. GM, Matthew Fisher, Feb 23, 1985. SK, Frank Nowosad, May 1985. World Championships: HR. VF. SK, Apr and May 1985. TR, Frank Nowosad, Mar 1985. MG, Randy Starkman and Mary Hynes, Mar 5-9, 1985. GM, Michael Cosgrove and Allen Abel, Mar 5-11, 1985. Figure Skating History: The Evolution Of Dance On Ice, Lynn Copley-Graves, 1992. The Scotsman, Mar 9, 1985. Huddersfield Daily Examiner, Mar 6, 1985. Figure Skating: A Celebration, Beverley Smith, 1994. Fort Worth Star-Telegram, Mar 7, 1985. A Decade of Excellence, 1981-1991, ASW.

**1985-1986 SEASON**

PEOPLE: New Professionals/Retirements: IRS Skate Yearbook, 1986. SP, Torvill and Dean Tour. Citizen's Voice, Sep 26, 1985. Show Roster, Ice Capades East Division, Aug 1985. VS, Susan Mertens, Jan 8, 1987. NYT, Richard F. Shepard, Jan 17, 1987. Christopher Dean: Nottingham Evening Post, Oct 8, 1985. IRS Skate Yearbook, Sandra Stevenson, 1986. Debi Thomas/Alex McGowan: VF. TR, Fall 1985. Helene Engelmann: HR. Records, Friedhof Hernals Cemetery, Vienna. Tiffany Chin: TR, Fall Issue. SI, E.M. Swift, Feb 17, 1986. The Duchesnays: MG, Oct 25, 1985. GM, Beverley Smith, Oct 25, 1985. OC, Martin Cleary, Oct 26, 1986. GM, Oct 28, 1985. GM, Beverley Smith, Nov 1, 1985. OC, Martin Cleary, Mar 15, 1986. Gladys Hogg: SK, Feb 1986. Interview with Warren Maxwell, Aug 21, 2017. Scott Ethan Allen: SK, Mar 1986. Herma Szabo/Lyudmila Pakhomova: SK, May 1986. Harenberg, Das Buch der 1000 Frauen, Christine Laue-Bothen, Ulrike Issel, 2004. Kandi Amelon and Alec Binnie: SK, Apr 1986. Peter Mumford: Reflections on the CFSA, 1887-1990: A History of the Canadian Figure Skating Association, Teresa Moore, 1993.OC, Dec 28, 1973. OC, Jun 10, 1986. OC, Nov 18, 1994. Hall of Fame Inductees: IRS Skate Yearbook, 1986. SK, Apr 1986. AROUND THE WORLD: Canada: Reflections on the CFSA, 1887-1990: A History of the Canadian Figure Skating Association, Teresa Moore, 1993. SK, May 1986. China: SK, Gretchen S. Brainerd, Nov 1985. SI, Robert Sullivan, Jan 27, 1988. Greece: Η ΚΑΘΗΜΕΡΙΝΗ, Spyridoulas Spanea, Dec 31, 2008. When Hell Freezes Over, Should I Bring My Skates? Toller Cranston, 2000. Robin Cousins: The Authorized Biography, 1999. South Africa: IRS Skate Yearbook, 1986. Zero Tollerance: An Intimate Memoir by the Man who Revolutionized Figure Skating, Toller Cranston, 1997. United States: HR. SK, May 1986. UD Messenger, Vol.8. No. 2, 1999. BEHIND THE SCENES: USA/USSR Agreement: SK, Nov 1985. Flutz Rule/Age Changes: Figure Skating History: The Evolution of Dance on Ice, Lynn Copley-Graves, 1992. Rule Changes: Skating Around The World 1892-1992: The One Hundredth Anniversary History of the International Skating Union, Benjamin T. Wright, 1992. THE AIDS EPIDEMIC: AIDS Epidemic: AIDS Epidemic: A Timeline of HIV and AIDS, U.S. Department of Health & Human Services. NYT, Maurice Carroll, Oct 26, 1985. LAT, John Balzar, Dec 19, 1985. MMWR, Jan 17, 1986. Daily News (NY), Oct 3, 1985. Alastair Munro: HR. OC, Sep 10, 1983. OC, Aug 1, 1985. Alumni News (Carleton University), Vol. 5, No. 6, Nov/Dec 1985. Brian Grant: National AIDS Memorial, The Names Project Memorial Quilt. Interview with Darlene Parent, May 3, 2021. Interview with Mary Gaillard, Apr 20, 2021. Interview with Moira North, Apr 14, 2021. NYT, Anna Kisselgoff, Nov 30, 1978. SP, John Curry's Ice Dancing, 1978. Guy Nick: BC Gay and Lesbian Archives. HR. SK, Nellie Jensen, Apr 1951. SK, Apr 1952. SK, Mrs. R. Sanders Miller, May 1952. SK, Sandy Thomas, May 1953. SK, Sevy Von Sonn, May 1954. SK, Apr 1959. SK, Nov 1961. CH, Michael Clarkson, Dec 13, 1992. SHOWS AND TOURS: Torvill and Dean Tour: SP, Torvill and Dean World Tour. IRS Skate Yearbook, Sandra Stevenson, 1986. Sun Valley: IRS Skate Yearbook, Sandra Stevenson, 1986. The Times-News, Jul 4, 1980. The Times-News, Aug 13, 1984. The Times-News, Aug 4, 1985. The Times-News, Aug 17, 1986. The Times-News, Jul 26, 1987. The Times-News, Jun 11, 1989. Superskates: The Daily Times, Nov 10, 1985. Ice Majesty: IRS Skate Yearbook, Sandra Stevenson, 1986. Liverpool Daily Post, Aug 13, 1985. The Stage, Aug 15, 1985. Nottingham Evening Post, Aug 29, 1985. John Curry at The Kennedy Center: TR, Fall 1985. Alone: The Triumph And Tragedy Of John Curry, 2014. CT, Jul 28, 1985. NYT, Barbara Gamarekian, Aug 23, 1985. WP, Alexandra Tamalonis, Aug 19, 1985. Blackpool/Viva! Ice World: The Stage, Aug 15, 1985. The Stage, Jul 24, 1986. Deep Dive from The Japan Times, 2016. Evening With Champions: TR, Nov 1985. Southern Ice: VF. Orlando Sentinel, Jan 12, 1986. Festival on Ice/City Lites: VF. The Central, David Spatz, Dec 6, 1985. ISU Asian Tour: SK, Gretchen S. Brainerd, Nov 1985. Bobrin Ice Theatre: Soviet Ballet, Nina Ershova, 1987. The Ice Trio, Natalia Bestemianova, Andrei Bukin and Igor Bobrin. Ice Classics: SK, Mary Little, Jun 1986. BBC Sport AID Gala: IRS Skate Yearbook, Sandra Stevenson, 1986. A Decade of Excellence, 1981-1991, ASW. SK, May 1986. Waterloo Record, Jul 26, 1986. BOOKS AND MAGAZINES: Spice on Ice: TR, Nov 1985. IRS Skate Yearbook, Dennis L. Bird, 1986. Playgirl: A Decade of Excellence, 1981-1991, ASW. Playgirl, Mar 1986. FILMS AND TELEVISION: Jeopardy: J! Archive. The True Gift of Christmas: VF. GM, Rick Groen, Dec 7, 1985. FUN AND GAMES: Winter Games: EPYX Winter Games Instruction Manual for the Commodore 64, 1985. EPYX Product Catalogue, 1987. ART AND HISTORY: Queen Victoria's Skates: A Decade of Excellence, 1981-1991, ASW. Museum Expansion: SK, Jul 1986. Sabena Crash Anniversary: Indelible Tracings: The Story of the 1961 U.S. World Figure Skating Team, Patricia Shelley Bushman, 2010. SK, Apr 1986. COMPETITIONS: World Professional Championships: HR. VF. A Decade of Excellence, 1981-1991, ASW. The Evening Sun, Phil Jackman, Dec 12, 1985. The Record Sun, Dec 15, 1985. ASW, Dec 1993. World Junior Championships: HR. VF. IRS Skate Yearbook, Sandra Stevenson, 1986. OC, Dec 16, 1985. TS, Dec 18, 1985. European Championships: HR. VF. SK, Howard Bass, Mar 1986. IRS Skate Yearbook, Sandra Stevenson, 1986. Figure Skating History: The Evolution of Dance on Ice, Lynn Copley-Graves, 1992. MG, Jan 29, 1986. OC, Jan 31 and Feb 3, 1986. Canadian Championships: HR. VF. SK, Frank Nowosad, Mar 1986. IRS Skate Yearbook, 1986. GM, Beverley Smith, Feb 6, 7, 8 and 10, 1986. Figure Skating History: The Evolution of Dance on Ice, Lynn Copley-Graves, 1992. OC, Martin Cleary, Feb 6, 8 and 10, 11 and March 5, 1986. MG, Feb 7, 8 and 10, 1986. TR, Spring 1986. Orser: A Skater's Life, Brian Orser and Steve Milton, 1988. Thumbs Up!: The Elizabeth Manley Story, Elizabeth Manley and Elva Oglanby, 1989. CH, Feb 9, 1986. Red Deer Advocate, Feb 6, 1986. TP, Feb 6, 1986. WS, Feb 6, 8 and 10, 1986. Times Colonist, Feb 9, 1986. TS, Mary Ormsby, Feb 5, 1986. U.S. Championships: HR. VF. Uniondale Public Library. SK, Feb 1986. SK, Lorna Simmons Nolt, Mar 1986. IRS Skate Yearbook, Sandra Stevenson, 1986. Figure Skating History: The Evolution of Dance on Ice, Lynn Copley-Graves, 1992. SI, E.M. Swift, Feb 17, 1986. Newsday, Helene Elliott, Feb 6-10, 1986.World Championships: HR. VF. IRS Skate Yearbook, Sandra Stevenson, 1986. SK, Mar and Apr 1986. Figure Skating History: The Evolution of Dance on Ice, Lynn Copley-Graves, 1992. SI, E.M. Swift, Mar 17, 1986. Ebony, Lynn Norment, May 1986. TS, Steve Milton, Mar 16, 1986. MG, Steve Milton, Mar 17-19, 1986. GM, Doug Harrison, Mar 20-24, 1986.

**1986-1987 SEASON**

PEOPLE: New Professionals/Retirements: VF. HR. SP, Torvill and Dean Tour. Jumpin' Joe: The Jozef Sabovčík Story. Jozef Sabovčík, 1998. SK, Oct 1986. SK, Jan 1987. Cynthia Coull: MG, Kate Smith, Nov 12, 1986. Debi Thomas: SK, Nov 1986. The Times Herald, Feb 2, 1986. SK, Apr 1987. Juli McKinstry: SK, Oct 1986. SK, Feb 1987. Donald Jackson/Robin Cousins: OC, Lynn McAuley, Oct 4 and 9, 1986. SK, Marilyn Frampton-Beard, Oct 1986. Ria Baran Falk: SK, Jul 1993. Historical Dictionary of Figure Skating, James R. Hines, 2011. Tiffany Chin: SK, Mar 1987. Dénes Pataky: Interview with Anna Pataky, Dec 11, 2019. Krönika, Jul/Aug 1987, Dr. László Pokoly. Tracy Wilson: VS, Wendy Long, Nov 5, 1987. VS, Archie McDonald, Jan 25, 1988. Susan Garland/Mildred Richardson: Western Daily Press, Apr 11, 1987. SK, Feb 17, 1952. SK, Oct 1987. AROUND THE WORLD: WEV: VF. Canada: SK, Oct 1986. MG, Kate Smith, Nov 12, 1986. Hong Kong: GM, Allen Abel, Mar 5, 1985. Ottawa Citizen, Martin Cleary, Mar 10, 1987. IRS Yearbook, 1986. United States: SK, Apr 1987. SK, Oct 1986. BEHIND THE SCENES: Olympic Tickets: OC, GM, Kevin Cox, Jan 9, 1987. OC, Wayne Scanlan, Jun 3, 1987. TS, Nov 13, 1987. SK, Jun 1987. 1992 Olympic Bids: SK, Dec 1986. MG, Oct 16, 1986. Yankee Polka/Golden Waltz: HR. Figure Skating History: The Evolution of Dance on Ice, Lynn Copley-Graves, 1992. Figures/Original Program: SK, Jul 1987. Skating Around The World 1892-1992: The One Hundredth Anniversary History of the International Skating Union, Benjamin T. Wright, 1992. THE AIDS EPIDEMIC: AIDS Epidemic: AIDS Epidemic: A Timeline of HIV and AIDS, U.S. Department of Health & Human Services. UPI Archives, Apr 9, 1987. PBS Frontline: The Age of AIDS, 2006. Tom Steinruck: National AIDS Memorial, The Names Project Memorial Quilt. Bay Area Reporter, Oct 16, 1986. SK, Jun 1966. SK, Feb, Mar and Apr 1969. Ian Knight: HR. Oakland Public Library. On Edge: Backroom Dealing, Cocktail Scheming, Triple Axels, and How Top Skaters Get Screwed, Jon Jackson, 2005. Oakland Tribune, Jan 13, 1987. Liberace/Brian Pockar: NYT, Feb 5, 1987. WP, Feb 10, 1987. UPI Archives, Oct 25, 1986. Greg Welch: SK, Apr and May 1972. SK, Feb, Mar, May and Jun, 1974. Interview with Laurie Welch, Apr 13, 2021. National AIDS Memorial, The Names Project Memorial Quilt. SHOWS AND TOURS: Goodwill Games: VF. SK, Tiffany Chin, Nov 1986. Sun Sentinel, Jul 21, 1986. America on Ice: VF. SK, Susan Dresel Caudill, Dec 1986. Soviet Stars on Ice: OC, Oct 11, 1986. Scott Hamilton America Tour/Stars on Ice: Stars on Ice: An Intimate Look at Skating's Greatest Tour, Barry Wilner, 1998. Tour History, Stars on Ice, IMG. Daily News (NY), Oct 23, 1986. A Decade of Excellence, 1981-1991, ASW. Torvill and Dean Tour: NYT, Dec 5, 1986. SK, Gary Beacom, Mar 1987. Wollman Rink Show: SK, Nov 1986. A Decade of Excellence, 1981-1991, ASW. Indianapolis Star, Nov 24, 1986. Disney on Ice: Disney on Ice Company Profile, Feld Entertainment. Minto Show: Minto: Skating Through Time, History of the Minto Skating Club 1904-2004, Janet B. Uren, 2004. Skate Festival China '87: SK, Jun 1987. A Decade of Excellence, 1981-1991, ASW. BOOKS AND MAGAZINES: Moskvina/Moskvin Book: Pair Skating as Sport and Art, Tamara Moskvina and Igor Moskvin, 1987. SK, Jul 1987. Patinage: Patinage, Dec/Jan 1987. FILMS AND TELEVISION: Game Shows: VF. SK, Apr and Nov 1988. Fire and Ice: VF. Coleshill Chronicle, Dec 26, 1986. Nottingham, Mar 26, 1988. How To Ice Skate: VF. SK, Jan 1987. 25 Years of Champions/Tom Collins tour video: SK, Apr 1987. SK, Nov 1987. Today Show: SK, Jun 1987. ART AND HISTORY. Taft Museum Exhibition: Skating in the Arts of 17th Century Holland: An Exhibition Honoring the 1987 World Figure Skating Championships, Laurinda S. Dixon, 1987. FUN AND GAMES: Ice Skating Trivia: SK, Oct 1986. Rules, Ice Skating Trivia game, Typographics. World Junior Championships: HR. VF. GM, Beverley Smith, Dec 6 and 8, 1986. OC, Dec 5, 1986. TS, Dec 7, 1986. SK, Harland L. Burge, Joan Burns and Dr. Morton Rosenstein, Feb 1987. Figure Skating History: The Evolution of Dance on Ice, Lynn Copley-Graves, 1992. World Professional Championships: HR. VF. Baltimore Sun, Dec 11 and 12, 1987. The York Dispatch, Dec 12, 1987. ASW, Dec 1993. U.S. Championships: HR. VF. SK, Jan, Mar, Apr and May 1987. SI, E.M. Swift, Feb 16, 1987. Figure Skating History: The Evolution of Dance on Ice, Lynn Copley-Graves, 1992. OC, Feb 9, 1987. WS, Feb 9, 1987. European Championships: HR. VF. SK, Howard Bass, Apr 1987. Skating Around The World 1892-1992: The One Hundredth Anniversary History of the International Skating Union, Benjamin T. Wright, 1992. Figure Skating History: The Evolution of Dance on Ice, Lynn Copley-Graves, 1992. MG, Feb 4, 1987. OC, Feb 4 and 6, 1987. OC, Feb 5 and 9, 1987. TS, Feb 5, 1987. VS, Feb 9, 1987. My Sergei: A Love Story, Ekaterina Gordeeva and E.M. Swift, 2009. The Cincinnati Enquirer, Feb 9, 1987. Canadian Championships: HR. VF. SK, Gary Beacom, Apr 1987. CH, Feb 4, 1987. MG, Feb 6, 1987. Ottawa Citizen, Jan 31 and Feb 9, 1987. TP, Feb 8, 1987. VS, Feb 5, 1987. Orser: A Skater's Life, Brian Orser and Steve Milton, 1988. Thumbs Up!: The Elizabeth Manley Story, Elizabeth Manley and Elva Oglanby, 1989. GM, Beverley Smith, Feb 4-9, 1987. OC, Martin Cleary and Lynn McAuley, Feb 3-9, 1987. WS, Steve Milton, Feb 4, 1987. MG, Feb 5, 6, 1987. TS, Paul Hunter, Feb 5-6, 1987. VS, Feb 7, 1987. World Championships: HR. VF. SK, Apr and May 1987. The Cincinnati Enquirer, Mar 7 and 9, 1987. Orser: A Skater's Life, Brian Orser and Steve Milton, 1988. Thumbs Up!: The Elizabeth Manley Story, Elizabeth Manley and Elva Oglanby, 1989. Figure Skating History: The Evolution of Dance on Ice, Lynn Copley-Graves, 1992. GM, Beverley Smith, Mar 10-16, 1987. TS, Jim Proudfoot and Frank Orr, Mar 5-16, 1987. OC, Martin Cleary, Mar 7-16, 1987. VS, Denny Boyd, Mar 9-14, 1987. MG, Neil Stevens and Kristin Huckshorn, Mar 10-16, 1987. WS, Al Halbertadt, Mar 11-16, 1987.

**1987-1988 SEASON**

PEOPLE: Retirements/New Professionals: HR. SK, Nov 1987. VS, Aug 12, 1987. OC, Martin Cleary, Dec 2, 1987. Weddings: Jumpin' Joe: The Jozef Sabovčík Story. Jozef Sabovčík, 1998. SK, Nov 1991. The Cincinnati Enquirer, Feb 26, 1987. SK, Apr 1988. SK, Jun 1988. Rory and Roberta Flack: SK, Oct 1987. Tracey Damigella: HR. SK, Oct 1987. Torvill and Dean: TS, Chris Welner, Nov 11, 1987. Times (Victor Harbor, SA), Feb 26, 1988. Terry Kubicka/Scott Cramer: SK, Oct 1987. SK, Jul 1988. Pakhomova and Gorshkov/Babilonia and Gardner/Scott Hamilton: SK, Jul and Nov 1987. ASW, Dec 1993. Brian Orser/Suzanne Morrow-Francis: VS, Apr 19, 1988. Citius, Altius, Fortius, Karel Wendl, 1995. More New Professionals: OC, Martin Cleary, Mar 28 and Dec 1, 1988. VS, Mar 28 and Apr 27, 1988. SK, May 1988. Edith and John Shoemaker: SK, Jun and Jul 1988. Tenley Albright: SK, Jul 1988. AROUND THE WORLD: New Zealand: NZISA 50th Jubilee 1937-1987, Rhona Whitehouse, 1987. EJ, Jessica Leeder, May 13, 2004. United States: SK, Nov 1987. A Decade of Excellence, 1981-1991, ASW. WP, Herbert H. Denton, Feb 28, 1988. SK, Jul 1988. BEHIND THE SCENES: New ISU Members: Skating Around The World 1892-1992: The One Hundredth Anniversary History of the International Skating Union, Benjamin T. Wright, 1992. ISU Appointments and Awards: HR. Skating Around The World 1892-1992: The One Hundredth Anniversary History of the International Skating Union, Benjamin T. Wright, 1992. SK, Jul 1988. ISU Rule Changes: Skating Around The World 1892-1992: The One Hundredth Anniversary History of the International Skating Union, Benjamin T. Wright, 1992. SK, Dec 1987 and Jul 1988. MG, Jun 8, 1988. TS, Frank Orr, Mar 24, 1988. The Baltimore Sun, Susan Reimer, Dec 11, 1987. IOC Rules: GM, James Christie, Mar 2, 1985. MG, Feb 13, 1986 and Sep 18, 1987. The Baltimore Sun, Susan Reimer, Dec 11, 1987. THE AIDS EPIDEMIC: AIDS Epidemic: AIDS Epidemic: A Timeline of HIV and AIDS, U.S. Department of Health & Human Services. National Library of Medicine, The C. Everett Koop Papers. Popul Today, R. Yared, Feb 17, 1989. Dennis Coi: HR. The Canadian AIDS Memorial Quilt. Interview with Laurie Welch, Apr 13, 2021. Calgary Sun, Christie Blatchford, Feb 20, 1988. GM, Feb 3, 1978, Feb 1 and Sep 30, 1982. CS, Michael Cosgrove, Fall 1979. CH, Michael Clarkson, Dec 13, 1992. CFSA: Calgary Sun, Christie Blatchford, Feb 20, 1988. Larry Rost: Houston Arch, The Houston Area Rainbow Collective History. Montrose Voice, Jun 3, 1988. SK, Mar 1952. SK, Apr 1955. SK, Jun 1956. SK, Apr 1957. SK, Apr 1959. John Curry: Alone: The Triumph and Tragedy of John Curry, Bill Jones, 2014. Black Ice: The Life and Death of John Curry, Elva Oglanby, 1995. Interview with Lorna Brown, Jun 10, 2019. SHOWS AND TOURS: Broadway on Ice/America on Ice: ASW, Aug 1989 and May 1990. Stars on Ice: SK, Oct 1987. Stars on Ice: An Intimate Look at Skating's Greatest Tour, Barry Wilner, 1998. Hard Edge: OC, Mar 16, 1988. VS, Lloyd Dykk, Mar 22, 1988. NYT, Anna Kisselgoff, May 22, 1988. Dance Magazine, David Gesmer, Mar 1, 1995. ISU European Tour/Tom Collins tour: VF. SK, Mar, Apr and Jun 1988. Bristol Evening Post, Apr 2, 1988. Show for King and Queen of Sweden: SK, May 1988. FILMS AND TELEVISION: GM, Rick Groen, Dec 20, 1986. Blades of Courage: VF. VS, Oct 2, 1987. OC, Tony Atherton, Oct 3, 1987. TS, Rita Zekas, Jim Bawden and Roy Shields, Oct 3, 1987. SK, Oct 1988. VS, Dec 1, 1988. The Sleeping Beauty: VF. NYT, Anna Kisselgoff, Nov 29, 1987. Skating Beautifully: SK, Nov 1987. The Elephant Show: MG, Janice Kennedy, Dec 24, 1987. Dorothy Hamill Special: VF. Daily News (NY), Jan 20, 1988. FUN AND GAMES: Stuffed Animals: SK, Dec 1987. FASHION: Skating Around The World 1892-1992: The One Hundredth Anniversary History of the International Skating Union, Benjamin T. Wright, 1992. SK, Jul 1988. GM, Mary Hynes, Jun 11, 1988. Lauren MacDonald Sheehan: OC, Jill Gerston, Feb 25, 1988. Frances Dafoe: SK, Martin Cleary, Jan 28, 1988. GM, David Livingstone and Cathryn Motherwell, Feb 9 and 29, 1988. Figure Skating and the Arts: Eight Centuries of Sport and Inspiration, Frances Dafoe, 2011. Skating Through Time, Frances Dafoe, Feb 1998. ART AND HISTORY: HR. COMPETITIONS: World Junior Championships: HR. VF. The Canberra Times, Nov 1, 1987. SK, Jan 1988. VS, Dec 12, 1987. TS, Dec 12, 1987. The Whig-Standard, Dec 15, 1987. Figure Skating History: The Evolution of Dance on Ice, Lynn Copley-Graves, 1992. World Professional Championships: HR. VF. The Baltimore Sun, Dec 9, 10 and 12, 1988. U.S. Championships: HR. VF. A Decade of Excellence, 1981-1991, ASW. SK, Jan and Feb 1988. Correspondence with Debi Thomas, Feb 12, 2024. VS, Jan 7, 1988. OC, Jan 11, 1988. WS, Jan 11, 1988. GM, Jan 7 and 11, 1988. Figure Skating History: The Evolution of Dance on Ice, Lynn Copley-Graves, 1992. SI, E.M. Swift, Jan 18 and 27, 1988. WP, Sally Jenkins, Feb 12, 1988. CH, Mar 18, 1995. European Championships: HR. VF. SK, Howard Bass, Feb 1988. VS, Jan 15 and 16, 1988. MG, Jan 15, 1988, OC, Jan 15-16, 1988. GM, Jan 16, 1988. GM, Beverley Smith, Feb 18, 1988. My Sergei: A Love Story, Ekaterina Gordeeva and E.M. Swift, 1996. Figure Skating History: The Evolution of Dance on Ice, Lynn Copley-Graves, 1992. CT, Phil Hersh, Feb 24, 1988. TS, Bob Koep, Jan 18, 1988. Canadian Championships: HR. VF. SK, Peter K. Robertson, Mar 1988. CH, Jan 23-24, 1988. GM, Beverley Smith, Jan 18-25, 1988. OC, Martin Cleary and Grant Kerr, Jan 19-23, 1988. VS, Archie McDonald, Jan 21-25, 1988. TS, Jan 20, Jan 19-24, 1988. WS, Jan 20-23, 1988. MG, Jack Todd, Jan 22, 23 and 30, 1988. TP, Jan 24, 1988. Orser: A Skater's Life, Brian Orser and Steve Milton, 1988. Thumbs Up!: The Elizabeth Manley Story, Elizabeth Manley and Elva Oglanby, 1989. Figure Skating History: The Evolution of Dance on Ice, Lynn Copley-Graves, 1992. Olympic Games: HR. VF. SK, Staff and Christopher Bowman, Mar and Apr 1988. City of Calgary Archives, Olympic Winter Games Fonds, Sports Group - Protocols, Start Orders, Official Reports, Statistics. Champion, David Stubbs, Spring 1988. GM, Beverley Smith, Jan 2 and Feb 25, 1988. MacLean's, Jane O'Hara and John Howse, Nov 9, 1987. CT, Phil Hersh, Feb 26, 1988. The Philadelphia Inquirer, Feb 28, 1988. My Sergei: A Love Story, Ekaterina Gordeeva and E.M. Swift, 1996. Orser: A Skater's Life, Brian Orser and Steve Milton, 1988. Thumbs Up!: The Elizabeth Manley Story, Elizabeth Manley and Elva Oglanby, 1989. Figure Skating History: The Evolution of Dance on Ice, Lynn Copley-Graves, 1992. OC, Bruce Ward, Feb 11, 24 and 29, 1988. VS, Feb 29, 1988. OC, Martin Cleary, Feb 23, 1988. Aha!, Monika Brabcová, 1996. NYT, Michael Janofsky, Feb 17, 1988. CH, Mil Dunnell and Ekaterina Gordeeva, Feb 29, 1988 and Jan 13, 1998. TS, Frank Orr, Feb 25, 1988. World Championships: HR. VF. SK, Apr and May 1988. MacLean's, Hal Quinn, undated clipping. My Sergei: A Love Story, Ekaterina Gordeeva and E.M. Swift, 1996. Orser: A Skater's Life, Brian Orser and Steve Milton, 1988. Thumbs Up!: The Elizabeth Manley Story, Elizabeth Manley and Elva Oglanby, 1989. Figure Skating History: The Evolution of Dance on Ice, Lynn Copley-Graves, 1992. WS, Mar 23, 1988. Southam News, Martin Cleary, Mar 23, 1988. OC, Jan 16, 1988. TS, Jim Proudfoot and Frank Orr, Mar 11, 24, 26 and 29, 1988. GM, Mary Hynes, Mar 26, 1988. OC, Martin Cleary, Mar 25 and 26, 1988. VS, Mar 26, 1988. EJ, May 21, 1989. Kurt Browning: Forcing The Edge, Kurt Browning and Neil Stevens, 1991.

**1988-1989 SEASON**

PEOPLE: New Professionals/Retirements: HR. OC, Martin Cleary, Dec 1, 1988. The Ice Trio, Natalia Bestemianova, Andrei Bukin and Igor Bobrin. SP, Ice Capades. Weddings/Births: SK, Nov 1988. SK, Feb, Jun, Jul and Oct 1989. SK, Mar 1990. Frank Zamboni: SK, Nov 1988. Zamboni: The Coolest Machines on Ice, Eric Dregni, 2006. Press Release from Zamboni, Feb 24, 2006. Bestemianova and Bukin/Tatiana Tarasova: The Ice Trio, Natalia Bestemianova, Andrei Bukin and Igor Bobrin. The Ice Trio, Natalia Bestemianova, Andrei Bukin and Igor Bobrin. Pierre Béchu: SK, Feb 1989. Figure Skating History: The Evolution of Dance on Ice, Lynn Copley-Graves, 1992. Katarina Witt: GM, Jul 26, 1988. Unicef Annual Report, 1990. Underhill and Martini: GM, Tom Hawthorn, Oct 20, 1988. Marina Kielmann: HR from National Museum of Rollerskating. Brian Boitano: HR, Oct 1988. Midori Ito: SK, Dec 1988. TS, Nov 27, 1988. Elizabeth Manley: Chatelaine, Katie Underwood, Nov 3, 2017. Arthur Bourque: SK, May 1989. President George H.W. Bush: SK, Apr 1989. Kristi Yamaguchi: SK, Jul 1989. Toller Cranston: ASW, Dec 1993. EJ, Mar 30, 1989. Ilene Misheloff: SK, Mar 1989. Richard Dwyer: Coaches Hall of Fame, Professional Skaters Association. Lois Waring McGean: HR. SK, Apr 1989. Elizabeth Manley/Wilson and McCall: WS, Apr 13, 1989. MG, Apr 16, 1989. Pierre Brunet: HR. SK, Jun 1989. Irina Rodnina/Torvill and Dean: HR. SK, Jul 1989. Alex Fulton: Skate Canada BC/YT Section Hall of Fame. Courtney Jones: The London Gazette, Jun 16, 1989. Around the Ice in Eighty Years: An Irreverent Memoir by an Accidental Champion, Courtney Jones and Helen Cox, 2021. Katarina Witt: Daily Mirror, Jun 27, 1989. NYT, Jun 28, 1989. EJ, Jun 29, 1989. LAT, Jun 26 and Jul 15, 1989. AROUND THE WORLD: Canada: Reflections on the CFSA, 1887-1990: A History of the Canadian Figure Skating Association, Teresa Moore, 1993. OC, Martin Cleary, Dec 22, 1988. SK, Dec 1988. Singapore: Orphan newspaper clipping, 1976. SK, Jun 1977. The Straits Times, Apr 13, Jun 26 and Jul 1, 1989. The New Paper, Harinder Gill, May 23, 1989. United States: SK, Jul 1989. Skating in America: The 75th Anniversary History of the United States Figure Skating Association, Benjamin T. Wright, 1996. BEHIND THE SCENES: Cancelled Urgent Meeting/Fours/Precision: GM, Beverley Smith, May 11, 1989. OC, Martin Cleary, May 4, 1989. VS, Lyndon Little, Nov 4, 1989. War on Flowers: VF. SK, Feb 1989. The Baltimore Sun, Feb 5, 1989. Cha Cha Congelado: Figure Skating History: The Evolution of Dance on Ice, Lynn Copley-Graves, 1992. Sports Monitor: SK, Oct 1988. THE AIDS EPIDEMIC: AIDS Epidemic: A Timeline of HIV and AIDS, U.S. Department of Health & Human Services. WP, Paul Duggan, Oct 12, 1988. LAT, Lori Silver, Oct 20, 1988. Gene Gant: National AIDS Memorial, The Names Project Memorial Quilt. Las Vegas Review-Journal, Jul 12, 1988. Courier, Sep 10, 1975. Amsterdam News (NY), Ali Stanton, Feb 9, 1980. André Denis: CH, Michael Clarkson, Dec 13, 1992. Interview with Lorna Wighton Aldridge Gosvenor, Mar 23, 2021. Interview with Jean Pierre Boulais, Apr 7, 2021. Ondrej Nepela: HR. National AIDS Memorial, The Names Project Memorial Quilt. SK, Mar 1989. Denník N daily, Peter Kováč, Nov 22, 2021. MG, Pat Hickey, Dec 19, 1992. Ondrej Nepela, Juraj Jakubisko, 1973. Ron Alexander: AIDS Vancouver. VS, Denise Ryan, Nov 21, 2013. Alone: The Triumph And Tragedy Of John Curry, Bill Jones, 2014. SP, John Curry's Ice Dancing. SK, Dec 1958. Donald Bonacci: HR. SK, May 1964. SK, Apr 1970. SP, Ice Follies. Icebreaker: the autobiography of Rudy Galindo, Rudy Galindo and Eric Marcus, 1997. Interview with Barbara Brown, Jun 14, 2021. Bobby Black: BG, Jun 28, 1989. National AIDS Memorial, The Names Project Memorial Quilt. When Hell Freezes Over, Should I Bring My Skates?, Toller Cranston, Martha Lowder Kimball, 2000. The Skating Club of Boston. René Vancampen: Interview with Edward Vancampen, Apr 2, 2021. HOMOPHOBIA: SK, May 1986. SK, May 1989. VS, Archie McDonald, Mar 25, 1988. Spokane Chronicle, Feb 25, 1988. Daily News (NY), Feb 26, 1988. Calgary Sun, Christie Blatchford, Feb 20, 1988. SHOWS AND TOURS: Torvill and Dean Tour: The Canberra Times, Nov 3 and Dec 15, 1988 and Mar 12, 1989. Sunday Sun, Mar 12, 1989. Daily Mirror, Jun 12, 1989. Broadmoor Anniversary Show: SK, Oct 1988. CFSA Champions on Ice: Reflections on the CFSA, 1887-1990: A History of the Canadian Figure Skating Association, Teresa Moore, 1993. OC, Martin Cleary and Barbara Crook, Aug 12 and Oct 13, 1988. The Whig-Standard, Oct 3, 1988. Holiday on Ice: SK, Oct 1988. Celebration on Ice: SK, Jun, Aug and Dec 1989. Symphony on Ice: GM, Beverley Smith, Aug 23, 1988. The Record, Oct 9, 1988. SK, Nov 1988. Nudes on Ice: LAT, May 14 and 15, 1988. Stars on Ice: Stars on Ice: An Intimate Look at Skating's Greatest Tour, Barry Wilner, 1998. SK, Oct 1988. The Oklahoman, Nicole LeWand, Mar 1, 1989. Skate Electric Gala: VF. Huddersfield Daily Examiner, Mar 31, 1988. Tom Collins tour: SK, Mar 1989. SK, Dale Mitch, Jul 1989. Symphony of Sports: UPI Archives, Ira Kaufman, May 31, 1989. SK, May 1989. ASW, Aug 1989. Books and Magazines: Skating/Blades on Ice: SK, Dec 1988. Correspondence with Yvonne Butorac, winter 2023. The Fine Art of Figure Skating: The Fine Art of Figure Skating: An Illustrated History and Portfolio of Stars, Julia Whedon, 1988. Orser: A Skater's Life: Orser: A Skater's Life, Brian Orser and Steve Milton, 1988. GM, Nov 12, 1988. TS, Dec 13, 1988. CM, Bessie Egan, Vol. 17 No. 4, 1989. Phone Book Fiasco: OC, Mar 23, 1989. FILMS AND TELEVISION: Various: UPI Archives, Michele Digirolamo, Sep 9, 1988. VF. SK, Nov 1988 and Jan, Feb and May 1989. GM, Hugh Fraser, Dec 10, 1988. Breaking the Ice: SK, Feb 1989. Canvas of Ice: The Passion to Skate: An Intimate View of Figure Skating, Sandra Bezic, 1996. SK, Dec 1988 and Jan 1989. Skating Free: VF. CH, Bob Blakey, Jan 14, 1989. OC, Stephen Nicholls, Dec 2, 1989. Ice Capades TV Special: VF. LAT, Nov 13, 1988. Happy New Year U.S.A.: VF, SK, Dec 1988. The Next Ice Age. From The Heart: VF. TS, Feb 3, 1989. Dear Elizabeth: VF. OC, Tony Atherton, Dec 7, 1988. TS, Greg Quill, Apr 29, 1989. Nora McCabe, GM, Dec 8, 1990. Precision Documentary: Whitby Free Press, Feb 8, 1989. OC, Martin Cleary, May 4, 1989. FUN AND GAMES: Dolls: SK, Jun and Oct 1989. A Decade of Excellence, 1981-1991, ASW. MUSIC: Torvill and Dean album: Our Life on Ice: The Autobiography, Jayne Torvill and Christopher Dean, 2014.

FASHION: Toller Cranston: TS, Jane Mussett, Oct 27, 1988. ART AND HISTORY: Blessed Spirit Statue: SK, Nov 1988. COMPETITIONS: World Junior Championships: HR. VF. SK, Feb 1989. Figure Skating History: The Evolution of Dance on Ice, Lynn Copley-Graves, 1992. MG, Patrick Gelinas, Nov 24, 1988. GM, Dec 2, 1988. VS, Dec 2, 1988. World Professional Championships: HR. VF. The Evening Sun, Dec 9, 1988. The Baltimore Sun, Dec 9, 10 and 12, 1988. European Championships: HR. VF. CP, 1989 European Championships. SK,Mar 1989. The Manleywoman SkateCast, Allison Manley and Alexandr Fadeev, Mar 31, 2009. Figure Skating History: The Evolution of Dance on Ice, Lynn Copley-Graves, 1992. Aberdeen Evening Express, Jan 17 and 18, 1989. Liverpool Echo, Jan 17, 1989. Bristol Evening Post, Jan 21, 1989. Sandwell Evening Mail, Jan 16, 20 and 21, 1989. GM, Jan 4, 19-23, 1989. GM, Jan 16 and 17, 1989. VS, Jan 17 and 23, 1989. MG, Jan 18 and 23, 1989. OC, Jan 23, 1989. U.S. Championships: HR. VF. A Decade of Excellence, 1981-1991, ASW. SK, Mar and Apr 1989. WP, Sally Jenkins, Feb 7, 1989. Figure Skating History: The Evolution of Dance on Ice, Lynn Copley-Graves, 1992. OC, Feb 9, 1989. MG, Feb 11 and 12, 1989. SI, E.M. Swift, Feb 20, 1989. Canadian Championships: HR. VF. SK, Michael Graham, Mar 1989. CH, Feb 11, 1989. EJ, Feb 9 and 10, 1989. MG, Feb 11, 1989. OC, Jan 19, 1989. TP, Feb 12, 1989. VS, Feb 10, 1989. WS, Feb 9, 1989. Times-Colonist, Feb 11, 1989. Figure Skating History: The Evolution of Dance on Ice, Lynn Copley-Graves, 1992. GM, Beverley Smith, Feb 9-13, 1989. OC, Neil Stevens, Feb 8-12, 1989. TS, Frank Orr, Feb 9-12, 1989. MG, Feb 9-12, 1989. VS, Feb 9-12, 1989. WS, Ted Shaw, Feb 9-12, 1989. World Championships: HR. VF. SK, Mary-Lucile Ager, Apr and May 1989. MacLean's, Anne Steacey and Brigid Janssen, Mar 27, 1989. Figure Skating History: The Evolution of Dance on Ice, Lynn Copley-Graves, 1992. GM, Beverley Smith and John Gray, Mar 8-23, 1989. OC, Neil Stevens, Mar 14-22, 1989. TS, Mike Beggs and Frank Orr, Mar 14-22, 1989. VS, Mar 14-22, 1989. WS, Mary Caton, Mar 14-22, 1989. EJ, Bill Glauber, Cam Cole and Marty Knack, Mar 15-22, 1989. MG, Mike Boone, Pat Hickey, and Red Fisher, Mar 15-22, 1989.

**1989-1990 SEASON**

PEOPLE: New Professionals/Retirements: SP, Torvill and Dean Tour. SP, Holiday on Ice. Deseret News, Marianne Funk, Dec 1, 1989. MG, Dec 26, 1991. CH, Kate Zimmerman, May 8, 1990. Figure Skating History: The Evolution of Dance on Ice, Lynn Copley-Graves, 1992. SK, Dec 1991. The Duchesnays: OC, Martin Cleary, Jun 21, 1989. John Curry: A Decade of Excellence, 1981-1991, ASW. National Post, Oct 9, 1989. Lortel Archives. John Slater/Adrian Swan/Patricia Jackson: HR. Figure Skating History: The Evolution of Dance on Ice, Lynn Copley-Graves, 1992. SK, Nov 1989 and May 1990. Legends of Australian ice, Ross Carpenter. Scott Gregory: SK, Nov 1989. Yamaguchi and Galindo: SK, May 1990. Heiko Fischer: DS, Nov 27, 1989. Munzinger Archive, Jan 8, 1990. Johnny Esaw: VF. TS, Ken McKee, Feb 19, 1990. Irina Rodnina: SK, Jan 1990. ASW, May 1990. Barbara Ann Scott/Sheldon Galbraith: CH, Helen Dolik, Feb 24, 1990. Katherine Miller Sackett: HR. SK, Mar 1990. Scott Hamilton/Torvill and Dean: ASW, Dec 1993. U.S. Figure Skating Hall of Fame. Jill Trenary: SK, Apr, Mar and Jun 1990. Gary Visconti: SK, Mar 1990. Press Release from President Jimmy Carter, Nov 15, 1978. Donald Jackson/Kurt Browning: Technical Merit: A History of Figure Skating Jumps, Ryan Stevens, 2023. EJ, Marty Knack, Apr 11, 1990. CFSA Hall of Fame: Reflections on the CFSA, 1887-1990: A History of the Canadian Figure Skating Association, Teresa Moore, 1993. OC, Jun 12, 1990. MG, Jun 12, 1990. Theresa Weld Blanchard: Women's Sports and Fitness, Kathryn Reith, Mar 1990. Carlo Fassi: SK, Jul and Sep 1990. Janet Lynn: Jun 1990. Inductees, National Polish-American Sports Hall of Fame. AROUND THE WORLD: Canada: Skating... An Inside Look, CFSA, 1990. CFSA, Keeping In Touch, Feb 1974. A Decade of Excellence, 1981-1991, ASW. Reflections on the CFSA, 1887-1990: A History of the Canadian Figure Skating Association, Teresa Moore, 1993. SK, Oct 1989. Germany: Today's Skater, CFSA, 1991. Skating Around The World 1892-1992: The One Hundredth Anniversary History of the International Skating Union, Benjamin T. Wright, 1992. Soviet Union: EJ, Nov 15, 1989. SK, Nov 1989. BEHIND THE SCENES: Berlin Wall: HR. Salt Lake Tribune, Carolyn Monson, May 11, 1990. SK, Jan 1990. IOC: SK, Jan 1990. ISU Congress: Skating Around The World 1892-1992: The One Hundredth Anniversary History of the International Skating Union, Benjamin T. Wright, 1992. ASW, May 1990. TS, May 3, 1990. Precision Skating: Skating Around The World 1892-1992: The One Hundredth Anniversary History of the International Skating Union, Benjamin T. Wright, 1992. OP/OSP: Skating Around The World 1892-1992: The One Hundredth Anniversary History of the International Skating Union, Benjamin T. Wright, 1992. Doping: Skating Around The World 1892-1992: The One Hundredth Anniversary History of the International Skating Union, Benjamin T. Wright, 1992. Country Swapping: Skating Around The World 1892-1992: The One Hundredth Anniversary History of the International Skating Union, Benjamin T. Wright, 1992. Artistic/Interpretive Skating: SK, Peter K. Robertson, Dec 1989. Skating World, T.D. Richardson, Jan and Jun 1958. OC, Mar 3, 1990. A Skating Life: My Story, Dorothy Hamill, 2007. Interview with Doug Haw, Apr 3, 2020. THE AIDS EPIDEMIC: John Curry/Rob McCall: Alone: The Triumph and Tragedy of John Curry, Bill Jones, 2014. Daily News (Halifax, NS), EJ, Marty Knack, Jun 19, 1990. Pat Connolly, Nov 17, 1991. Peter Pender: American Contract Bridge League Archives. VS, Sep 9, 1989. Bay Area Reporter, Sep 1989. Tim Brown: HR. Letters from Jeffrey Brown, Dec 28, 2021 and Feb 21, 2023. CH, Michael Clarkson, Dec 13, 1992. Indelible Tracings: The Story of the 1961 U.S. World Figure Skating Team, Patricia Shelley Bushman, 2010. Oregon Statesman, Feb 16, 1961. Canada Ice Dance Theatre, Ron Vincent. John Carrell: HR. SK, Nov 1989. CH, Michael Clarkson, Dec 13, 1992. Interview with Lorna Dyer, Jun 10, 2019. Skating For Life: ASW, Aug 1989. A Decade of Excellence, 1981-1991, ASW. Sun Sentinel, Dec 2, 1992. Tony Panko: Bay Area Reporter, Nov 23, 1989. Jim Hulick: HR. Icebreaker: the autobiography of Rudy Galindo, Rudy Galindo and Eric Marcus, 1997. SK, Jan 1990. LAT, Randy Harvey, Dec 19, 1989. Tommy Miller: HR. SP, Ice Capades. Interview with Kitty DeLio Laforte, April 2021. Blades Against AIDS: ASW, Jun 1990. SHOWS AND TOURS: Bay Night of International Stars/Celebration on Ice: SK, May 1989. ASW, Aug 1989 and May 1990. Willy Bietak Shows: ASW, May 1990. A Decade of Excellence, 1981-1991, ASW. Torvill and Dean Tour: SP, Torvill and Dean Tour. Birmingham Mail, Jan 30, 1990. Daily Record, Apr 12, 1990. Belfast News-Letter, Jun 28, 1990. Lurgan Mail, Aug 23, 1990. Benson and Hedges on Ice: A Decade of Excellence, 1981-1991, ASW. SK, Jul 1989 and Mar 1990. Royal Bank Champions on Ice: SP. OC, Martin Cleary, Aug 12, 1988. The Sault Star, Sep 22, 1989. The Morning Star, Oct 29, 1989. WS, Nov 28, 1989. GM, James Christie, Dec 8, 1989. Skate Across America: SK, Nov 1989. Evening with Champions: ASW, Aug 1989. Harvard Crimson, Lan N. Nguyen, Nov 4, 1989. Nutcracker on Ice: A Decade of Excellence, 1981-1991, ASW. The Sault Star, Dec 7, 1989. Festival on Ice: LAT, Libby Slate, Dec 22, 1989. Nutcracker on Ice: VF. SP, Nutcracker on Ice. CT, Dec 17, 1989. Ice Capades: SK, Dec 1989 and Jul 1990. A Decade of Excellence, 1981-1991, ASW. Pinocchio on Ice: NYT, Feb 20, 1990. Roanoke Times, Tracie Fellers, April 2, 1990. Citrus on Ice: Orlando Sentinel, Feb 12, 1990. Stars on Ice: SP, Stars on Ice. The Whig-Standard, Michael Woloschuk, Feb 15, 1990. CH, Kate Zimmerman, Mar 23, 1990. Broadway on Ice: SK, Jul 1989. The Pantagraph, Jan 28, 1990. Tom Collins tour: SK, May 1990. Skating: SP, Skating. VS, Terry Bell, Apr 11, 1990. FILMS AND TELEVISION: Ice Pawn: SK, Oct 1989. The Ice Stars' Hollywood Ice Revue: VF. Gustave Lussi Documentary: SK, Mary-Lucile Ager, Nov 1989. Back to the Beanstalk: VF. TS, Greg Quill, Dec 14, 1990. GM, Christopher Harris, Jan 23, 1992. Magic Memories on Ice: VF. SK, Jan 1990. Sonja Henie film: TS, Rita Zekas, Mar 4, 1989. ASW, May 1990. Pas De Deux: MG, Mike Boone, Jun 20, 1990. TS, Antonia Zerbisias, Jun 22, 1990. TS, Jim Bawden, Mar 7, 1992. Carmen on Ice: VF. SK, Dec 1989 and Jan, Feb, Mar, Apr and Nov 1990. MG, Paul DeLean, Apr 22, 1990. EJ, Sep 17, 1990. MUSIC: VF. SK, Nov 1975. GM, Beverley Smith, Apr 29, 2008. Skating Around The World 1892-1992: The One Hundredth Anniversary History of the International Skating Union, Benjamin T. Wright, 1992. FUN AND GAMES: Barbie: ASW, Aug 1989. FASHION: Elizabeth Manley Signature Line: WS, David Morelli, Aug 22, 1990. ART AND HISTORY: SK, Oct 1989. COMPETITIONS: World Professional Championships: HR. VF. The Baltimore Sun, Dec 7, 1989. The Evening Sun, Dec 7-9, 1989. World Junior Championships: HR. VF. SK, Jan 1990. MG, Nov 29-30, 1989. TS, Dec 1, 1989. OC, Dec 2, 1989. Figure Skating History: The Evolution of Dance on Ice, Lynn Copley-Graves, 1992. European Championships: HR. SK, Feb 1990. VF. SP, 1990 European Championships. Figure Skating History: The Evolution of Dance on Ice, Lynn Copley-Graves, 1992. U.S. Championships: HR. VF. SK, Feb and Mar 1990. Salt Lake Tribune, Lex Hemphill, Feb 12, 1990. Figure Skating History: The Evolution of Dance on Ice, Lynn Copley-Graves, 1992. SI, E.M. Swift, Feb 12, 1990. MG, Feb 4, 1990. The Baltimore Sun, Bill Glauber, Jan 10, 1990. Canadian Championships: HR. VF. SK, Peter K. Robertson, Mar 1990. Figure Skating History: The Evolution of Dance on Ice, Lynn Copley-Graves, 1992. EJ, Marty Knack, Jan 9-12, 1990. GM, Mary Jollimore, Feb 3 and 8-12, 1990. TS, Catherine Dunphy and Frank Orr, Feb 3-12, 1990. MG, Feb 7-12, 1990. OC, Martin Cleary, Feb 7-12, 1990. VS, Neil Stevens, Feb 8-13, 1990. World Championships: HR. VF. SK, Apr 1990. SP, 1990 World Championships. Event Protocol, Nova Scotia Sport Hall of Fame. Large file of undated newspaper clippings from CHMS and Daily News (Halifax, NS), Halifax Public Library. CHMS, Greg Guy, Mar 1 and 8, 1990. CHMS, Rob Mills, Mar 14, 1990. Daily News (Halifax, NS), Neil Hodge, Mar 12, 1990. ASW, May 1990. MacLean's, Glen Allen, 1990. Figure Skating History: The Evolution of Dance on Ice, Lynn Copley-Graves, 1992. SI, E.M. Swift, Mar 19, 1990. OC, Martin Cleary, Mar 5-12, 1990. EJ, Marty Knack and Cam Cole, Mar 5-12, 1990. MG, Paul DeLean, Mar 5-12, 1990. TP, Laurie Nealin, Mar 5-12, 1990. TS, Frank Orr, Mar 5-12, 1990. VS, Lyndon Little, Mar 5-11, 1990. GM, James Christie, Mar 5-12, 1990.

**EPILOGUE**

Spokane Chronicle, Feb 25, 1988. Daily News (NY), Feb 26, 1988. ASW, Martha Lowder Kimball, Nov 1993. Indelible Tracings: The Story of the 1961 U.S. World Figure Skating Team, Patricia Shelley Bushman, 2010. The Victorian City: Everyday Life in Dickens' London, Judith Flanders, 2012. United States HIV Immigration and Travel Policy", ACT UP AIDS Coalition To Unleash Power. ASW, Aug 1989. ASW, Lois Elfman, May 1990. Daily News (Halifax, NS), Shane Ross, Nov 16, 1991. EJ, Michael Clarkson, Dec 14, 1992. Daily News (Halifax, NS), Sheryl Ubelacker, Sep 11, 1992. MG, Pat Hickey, Dec 19, 1992. TS, Nov 22, 1992. Mail Star (Halifax, NS), Greg Guy, Nov 18, 1992. Nova Scotia LGBT Seniors Archive, Father Louis Caissie fonds. NYT, Filip Bondy, Nov 19, 1992. People, Susan Reed, Fanny Weinstein and Lorenzo Benet, Jan 25, 1993. Detroit Free Press, Jan 21, 1993. GM, Nov 9, 1991. SK, Dr. Thomas R. Kosten, Jul 1991.VS, Lyndon Little, Nov 29, 1996. Bay Area Reporter, Wayne Friday, Mar 28, 1996. OC, Susan Riley, Nov 17, 1992. And The Band Played On: Politics, People and the AIDS Epidemic, Randy Shilts, 1987. National AIDS Memorial, The Names Project Memorial Quilt. The Canadian AIDS Memorial Quilt. Robert John Quinn's Memorial Books, The History Project (Boston and Massachusetts LGBTQ+ Archive). Toronto AIDS Memorial (Church Street). UK AIDS Memorial Quilt. Interview with Doug Mattis, November 2014. CH, Michael Clarkson, Dec 13, 1992. Bay Area Reporter, Nov 23, 1989. LAT, Apr 17, 1993. CH, Allan Maki and Mario Toneguzzi, Apr 30, 1992. SK, Oct 2003. Interview with Mark Motiff, April 2021 Beverley Smith, Bev Smith Writes, Dec 27, 2016. Houston Arch, The Houston Area Rainbow Collective History. LAT, Sep 2, 1994. The Daily Star, Sep 28, 2011. News & Record, Mar 8, 1993. SK, Jan 1993. Bay Area Reporter, Nov 23, 1989. Bay Area Reporter, Jun 11, 1992. Times-Colonist, Nov 6, 1993. Interview with Diana Flynn, April 2021. Bay Area Reporter, Apr 15, 1993. Icebreaker: the autobiography of Rudy Galindo, Rudy Galindo and Eric Marcus, 1997. Interview with David Hicks, April 2021. Tampa Bay Times, Jan 28, 1993. GM, Filip Bondy, Nov 18, 1992. The Acton Tanner, Oct 11, 1995. Interview with Lorna Brown, Apr 2014. NYT, Mar 27, 1993. First Comes Love, Marion Winik, 1996. Santa Fe New Mexican, Apr 21, 1996. Interview with Doug Haw, Mar 2021. When Hell Freezes Over, Should I Bring My Skates?, Toller Cranston and Martha Lowder Kimball, 2000. NYT, Nov 21, 1990. BG, Sep 13, 1994. LAT, Dec 17, 1999. Daily News (Halifax, NS), Shane Ross, Nov 16, 1991. Rolf Bernard Juario Memorial Fund. Advocate, Jacob Ogles, Feb 2, 2018. Orphan newspaper clipping, Vanessa Ho, Apr 10, 1994. Alone: The Triumph And Tragedy Of John Curry, Bill Jones, 2014. VS, Mar 24, 1993. Interview with Mardi McKerrow, Apr 2021. Interview with Kitty DeLio Laforte, Apr 2021. On Edge : Backroom Dealing, Cocktail Scheming, Triple Axels, And How Top Skaters Get Screwed, Jon Jackson, 2006. Feather River Bulletin, Apr 5, 1995. LAT, Mar 25, 1995. A Skating Life: My Story, Dorothy Hamill, 2007.

# ACKNOWLEDGMENTS

I would like to acknowledge the extraordinary debt I owe to the many journalists and television commentators who chronicled the sport in the 1980s. Without their insightful commentary, a project of this scale simply would not have been possible. I would particularly like to acknowledge the work of Dick Button, Peggy Fleming, Martin Cleary, Michael Cosgrove, Toller Cranston, Steve Milton, Beverley Smith, Debbi Wilkes and the late Howard Bass, Johnny Esaw, Frank Loeser Nowosad, Brian Pockar and Sandra Stevenson.

I must express my gratitude to Lynn Copley-Graves and her book "Figure Skating: The Evolution of Dance on Ice" for inspiring the format of this book. Lynn Copley-Graves has truly set the bar high, and I hope that this book can, in its own unique way, continue in the footsteps of that remarkable work.

This project could not have been accomplished without the many wonderful people in the skating world who were interviewed for this project and/or stepped up and answered my (many) questions: Lisa-Marie Allen, Petr Barna, Gary Beacom, Denise Biellmann, Jean-Pierre Boulais, Barbara Brown, Lorna Brown, Kitty DeLio Laforte, Lorna Dyer, Diana Flynn, Mary Gaillard, Karyn Garossino, Douglas Haw, David Hicks, Donald Jackson, Warren Maxwell, Mardi McKerrow, Mark Motiff, Moira North, Darlene Parent, Anna Pataky, Jirina Ribbens, David Santee, Norbert Schramm, Suzanne Semanick Schurman, Judy Sladky, Cathy Steele, Debi Thomas, Edward Vancampen, Tracey Wainman, Laurie Welch, Lorna Wighton Aldridge Gosvenor and the late Doug Mattis and Benjamin T. Wright, who are so very missed!

A very special thanks to Yvonne Butorac, whose very generous donations of printed materials provided many of the key sources for this book. I couldn't not thank Frazer Ormondroyd, whose private video collection remains an absolute treasure trove.

The sourcing of photos for the book was a challenging process. I'm indebted to Elaine Hooper, Paul Dean, Sarina Stützer, Steve McCall, Library and Archives Canada, Canada's Sports Hall of Fame, James Carrell, Edward Vancampen, Jaya Kanal, the Danmarks Idrætsforbunds Museum, Laurie Welch, Jane Piercy and The Skating Club of Boston, the American Contract Bridge League Archives, the B.C. Gay and Lesbian Archives and the Dalhousie University Archives for contributing many of the wonderful photographs found in this book. The remainder of the photographs featured were fully licensed through Alamy.

I am all about archives and libraries! A special thank-you to the wonderful reference teams at the the following libraries, archives and organizations for their assistance in tracking down hard-to-find primary sources: The 519 (Church Street Community Centre), Lambda Archives of San Diego, B.C. Gay and Lesbian Archives, Houston Arch/Rainbow Collective History, Salem State University Archives, Carleton University Alumni Association, Eagle Rock Valley Historical Society, Greensboro Public Library, Kansas City Public Library, LA County Library, Las Vegas-Clark County Library District, Louis Round Wilson Special Collections Library at The University of North Carolina, Oakland Public Library, Pikes Peak Library District, Rush University Medical Center Archives, San Antonio Public Library, Schwules Museum, Tufts University Archives, Vancouver Public Library and Miami University Libraries.

People absolutely do judge a book by its cover and I cannot thank Stefan Prodanovic enough for his wonderful design. I wanted something inspired by the cover art from skating programs in the 1980s and you nailed it!

A huge thank you to everyone on my ARC team for stepping up and providing much needed feedback and constructive criticism. You are so appreciated.

Writing is a joy but it is also a very solitary pursuit. I couldn't do what I love without the most incredible support system. Mom, Dad, Jenna, Lee and Michel, Craig, Alex, Bruce... thank you for being my biggest cheerleaders and letting me vent!

Lastly, I would like to sincerely thank the people who get this book and understand why it's important. I really wouldn't do this if I didn't care about the sport's history. For every nine skating fans who don't know or care what happened before 2002, there's one gem that does... and those are the people I write for. Thank you for your support and interest! It means so much.

# AUTHOR'S NOTE

I genuinely hope that you have enjoyed reading *Sequins, Scandals and Salchows: Figure Skating in the 1980s* as much as I enjoyed researching and writing it.

Reviews play a pivotal role in the success of all books, but they hold even greater importance for independently published ones.

I sincerely ask for a small favour – could you please spare a few minutes to write a brief review on the retailer's website and popular book review platforms?

I would also be extremely appreciative if you could visit your local library's website and fill out a short 'Suggest a Purchase' form.

I am grateful for your kind support in helping this important history reach the hands of more people!

# BOOKS BY THIS AUTHOR

Jackson Haines: The Skating King
Technical Merit: A History of Figure Skating Jumps
A Bibliography of Figure Skating
The Almanac of Canadian Figure Skating

www.ingramcontent.com/pod-product-compliance
Lightning Source LLC
Chambersburg PA
CBHW080607170426
43209CB00007B/1365